אִיּוֹב

וְלֹא נִמְצָא נָשִׁים יָפוֹת, כִּבְנוֹת אִיּוֹב--בְּכָל-הָאָרֶץ
velo nimtza nashim yafot kivnot iyov bechol-ha'aretz
And in all the land were no women found so fair as the daughters of Job;

וַיִּתֵּן לָהֶם אֲבִיהֶם נַחֲלָה, בְּתוֹךְ אֲחֵיהֶם
vayitten lahem avihem nachalah betoch acheihem
and their father gave them inheritance among their brethren.

וַיְחִי אִיּוֹב אַחֲרֵי-זֹאת, מֵאָה וְאַרְבָּעִים שָׁנָה; וַיִּרְאֶה, אֶת-בָּנָיו וְאֶת-בְּנֵי בָנָיו--אַרְבָּעָה, דֹּרוֹת
vaychi iyov acharei-zot, me'ah ve'arba'im shanah; vayir'eh, et-banav ve'et-benei vanav, arba'ah dorot
And after this Job lived a hundred and forty years, and saw his sons, and his sons' sons, even four generations.

וַיָּמָת אִיּוֹב, זָקֵן וּשְׂבַע יָמִים
vayamot iyov, zaken useva yamim
So Job died, being old and full of days.

אִיּוֹב

vahashem, shav et-shevut iyov, behitpalelo be'ad re'ehu
And the LORD changed the fortune of Job, when he prayed for his friends;

וַיֹּסֶף יְהוָה אֶת-כָּל-אֲשֶׁר לְאִיּוֹב, לְמִשְׁנֶה
vayosef hashem et-kol-'asher le'iyov lemishneh
and the LORD gave Job twice as much as he had before.

וַיָּבֹאוּ אֵלָיו כָּל-אֶחָיו וְכָל-אַחְיֹתָיו
vayavo'u elav kol-'echav vechol-'achyotav vechol-'achyotav
Then came there unto him all his brethren, and all his sisters,

וְכָל-יֹדְעָיו לְפָנִים
vechol-yode'av lefanim
and all they that had been of his acquaintance before,

וַיֹּאכְלוּ עִמּוֹ לֶחֶם בְּבֵיתוֹ, וַיָּנֻדוּ לוֹ
vayochelu immo lechem beveito vayanudu lo
and did eat bread with him in his house; and they bemoaned him,

וַיְנַחֲמוּ אֹתוֹ, עַל כָּל-הָרָעָה אֲשֶׁר-הֵבִיא יְהוָה עָלָיו
vaynachamu oto, al kol-hara'ah, asher-hevi hashem alav
and comforted him concerning all the evil that the LORD had brought upon him;

וַיִּתְּנוּ-לוֹ, אִישׁ קְשִׂיטָה אֶחָת, וְאִישׁ, נֶזֶם זָהָב אֶחָד
vayittenu-lo, ish kesitah echat, ve'ish nezem zahav echad
every man also gave him a piece of money, and every one a ring of gold.

וַיהוָה, בֵּרַךְ אֶת-אַחֲרִית אִיּוֹב--מֵרֵאשִׁתוֹ; וַיְהִי-לוֹ אַרְבָּעָה עָשָׂר אֶלֶף צֹאן
vahashem, berach et-'acharit iyov mereshito; vayhi-lo arba'ah asar elef tzon
So the LORD blessed the latter end of Job more than his beginning; and he had fourteen thousand sheep,

וְשֵׁשֶׁת אֲלָפִים גְּמַלִּים, וְאֶלֶף-צֶמֶד בָּקָר, וְאֶלֶף אֲתוֹנוֹת
vesheshet alafim gemallim, ve'elef-tzemed bakar ve'elef atonot
and six thousand camels, and a thousand yoke of oxen, and a thousand she-asses.

וַיְהִי-לוֹ שִׁבְעָנָה בָנִים, וְשָׁלוֹשׁ בָּנוֹת
vayhi-lo shiv'anah vanim veshalosh banot
He had also seven sons and three daughters.

וַיִּקְרָא שֵׁם-הָאַחַת יְמִימָה, וְשֵׁם הַשֵּׁנִית קְצִיעָה
vayikra shem-ha'achat yemimah, veshem hashenit ketzi'ah
And he called the name of the first, Jemimah; and the name of the second, Keziah;

וְשֵׁם הַשְּׁלִישִׁית, קֶרֶן הַפּוּךְ
veshem hashelishit keren happuch
and the name of the third, Keren-happuch.

איוב

לָכֵן הִגַּדְתִּי, וְלֹא אָבִין; נִפְלָאוֹת מִמֶּנִּי, וְלֹא אֵדָע
lachen higgadti velo avin; nifla'ot mimmenni, velo eda
Therefore have I uttered that which I understood not, things too wonderful for me, which I knew not.

שְׁמַע-נָא, וְאָנֹכִי אֲדַבֵּר; אֶשְׁאָלְךָ, וְהוֹדִיעֵנִי
shema'-na ve'anochi adabber; esh'alecha, vehodi'eni
Hear, I beseech Thee, and I will speak; I will demand of Thee, and declare Thou unto me.

לְשֵׁמַע-אֹזֶן שְׁמַעְתִּיךָ; וְעַתָּה, עֵינִי רָאָתְךָ
leshema'-'ozen shema'ticha; ve'attah, eini ra'atcha
I had heard of Thee by the hearing of the ear; but now mine eye seeth Thee;

עַל-כֵּן, אֶמְאַס וְנִחַמְתִּי--עַל-עָפָר וָאֵפֶר
'al-ken em'as venichamti; al-'afar va'efer
Wherefore I abhor my words, and repent, seeing I am dust and ashes.

וַיְהִי, אַחַר דִּבֶּר יְהוָה אֶת-הַדְּבָרִים הָאֵלֶּה--אֶל-אִיּוֹב; וַיֹּאמֶר יְהוָה אֶל-אֱלִיפַז הַתֵּימָנִי
vayhi, achar dibber hashem et-haddevarim ha'elleh el-'iyov; vayomer hashem el-'elifaz hatteimani
And it was so, that after the LORD had spoken these words unto Job, the LORD said to Eliphaz the Temanite:

חָרָה אַפִּי בְךָ וּבִשְׁנֵי רֵעֶיךָ
charah appi vecha uvishnei re'eicha
'My wrath is kindled against thee, and against thy two friends;

כִּי לֹא דִבַּרְתֶּם אֵלַי נְכוֹנָה, כְּעַבְדִּי אִיּוֹב
ki lo dibbartem elai nechonah ke'avdi iyov
for ye have not spoken of Me the thing that is right, as My servant Job hath.

וְעַתָּה קְחוּ-לָכֶם שִׁבְעָה-פָרִים וְשִׁבְעָה אֵילִים וּלְכוּ אֶל-עַבְדִּי אִיּוֹב
ve'attah kechu-lachem shiv'ah-farim veshiv'ah eilim ulechu el-'avdi iyov
Now therefore, take unto you seven bullocks and seven rams, and go to My servant Job,

וְהַעֲלִיתֶם עוֹלָה בַּעַדְכֶם, וְאִיּוֹב עַבְדִּי, יִתְפַּלֵּל עֲלֵיכֶם: כִּי אִם-פָּנָיו אֶשָּׂא
veha'alitem olah ba'adchem, ve'iyov avdi, yitpallel aleichem; ki im-panav essa
and offer up for yourselves a burnt-offering; and My servant Job shall pray for you; for him will I accept,

לְבִלְתִּי עֲשׂוֹת עִמָּכֶם נְבָלָה--כִּי לֹא דִבַּרְתֶּם אֵלַי נְכוֹנָה, כְּעַבְדִּי אִיּוֹב
levilti asot immachem nevalah, ki lo dibbartem elai nechonah ke'avdi iyov
that I do not unto you aught unseemly; for ye have not spoken of Me the thing that is right, as my servant Job hath.'

וַיֵּלְכוּ אֱלִיפַז הַתֵּימָנִי וּבִלְדַּד הַשּׁוּחִי, צֹפַר הַנַּעֲמָתִי
vayelechu elifaz hatteimani uvildad hashuchi, tzofar hanna'amati
So Eliphaz the Temanite and Bildad the Shuhite and Zophar the Naamathite went,

וַיַּעֲשׂוּ, כַּאֲשֶׁר דִּבֶּר אֲלֵיהֶם יְהוָה; וַיִּשָּׂא יְהוָה, אֶת-פְּנֵי אִיּוֹב
vaya'asu, ka'asher dibber aleihem hashem vayissa hashem et-penei iyov
and did according as the LORD commanded them; and the LORD accepted Job.

וַיהוָה, שָׁב אֶת-שְׁבוּת אִיּוֹב, בְּהִתְפַּלְלוֹ, בְּעַד רֵעֵהוּ

איוב

יַחְשֹׁב לְתֶבֶן בַּרְזֶל; לְעֵץ רִקָּבוֹן נְחוּשָׁה

yachshov leteven barzel; le'etz rikkavon nechushah
He esteemeth iron as straw, and brass as rotten wood.

לֹא-יַבְרִיחֶנּוּ בֶן-קָשֶׁת; לְקַשׁ, נֶהְפְּכוּ-לוֹ אַבְנֵי-קָלַע

lo-yavrichennu ven-kashet; lekash, nehpechu-lo avnei-kala
The arrow cannot make him flee; slingstones are turned with him into stubble.

כְּקַשׁ, נֶחְשְׁבוּ תוֹתָח; וְיִשְׂחַק, לְרַעַשׁ כִּידוֹן

kekash nechshevu totach; veyischak, lera'ash kidon
Clubs are accounted as stubble; he laugheth at the rattling of the javelin.

תַּחְתָּיו, חַדּוּדֵי חָרֶשׂ; יִרְפַּד חָרוּץ עֲלֵי-טִיט

tachtav chaddudei chares; yirpad charutz alei-tit
Sharpest potsherds are under him; he spreadeth a threshing-sledge upon the mire.

יַרְתִּיחַ כַּסִּיר מְצוּלָה; יָם, יָשִׂים כַּמֶּרְקָחָה

yartiach kassir metzulah; yam, yasim kammerkachah
He maketh the deep to boil like a pot; he maketh the sea like a seething mixture.

אַחֲרָיו, יָאִיר נָתִיב; יַחְשֹׁב תְּהוֹם לְשֵׂיבָה

'acharav ya'ir nativ; yachshov tehom leseivah
He maketh a path to shine after him; one would think the deep to be hoary.

אֵין-עַל-עָפָר מָשְׁלוֹ; הֶעָשׂוּ, לִבְלִי-חָת

'ein-'al-'afar moshelo; he'asu, livli-chat
Upon earth there is not his like, who is made to be fearless.

אֵת-כָּל-גָּבֹהַּ יִרְאֶה; הוּא, מֶלֶךְ עַל-כָּל-בְּנֵי-שָׁחַץ

'et-kol-gavoah yir'eh; hu, melech al-kol-benei-shachatz
He looketh at all high things; he is king over all the proud beasts.

מב

וַיַּעַן אִיּוֹב אֶת-יְהוָה; וַיֹּאמַר

Vaya'an iyov et-hashem vayomar
Then Job answered the LORD, and said:

יָדַעְתִּי, כִּי-כֹל תּוּכָל; וְלֹא-יִבָּצֵר מִמְּךָ מְזִמָּה

yada'ti ki-chol tuchal; velo-yibbatzer mimmecha mezimmah
I know that Thou canst do every thing, and that no purpose can be withholden from Thee.

מִי זֶה, מַעְלִים עֵצָה--בְּלִי-דָעַת

mi zeh ma'lim etzah, beli da'at
Who is this that hideth counsel without knowledge?

אִיּוֹב

גַּאֲוָה, אֲפִיקֵי מָגִנִּים; סָגוּר, חוֹתָם צָר

ga'avah afikei maginnim; sagur, chotam tzar

His scales are his pride, shut up together as with a close seal.

אֶחָד בְּאֶחָד יִגַּשׁוּ; וְרוּחַ, לֹא-יָבֹא בֵינֵיהֶם

'echad be'echad yiggashu; veruach, lo-yavo veineihem

One is so near to another, that no air can come between them.

אִישׁ-בְּאָחִיהוּ יְדֻבָּקוּ; יִתְלַכְּדוּ, וְלֹא יִתְפָּרָדוּ

'ish-be'achihu yedubbaku; yitlakkedu, velo yitparadu

They are joined one to another; they stick together, that they cannot be sundered.

עֲטִישֹׁתָיו, תָּהֶל אוֹר; וְעֵינָיו, כְּעַפְעַפֵּי-שָׁחַר

'atishotav tahel or; ve'einav, ke'af'appei-shachar

His sneezings flash forth light, and his eyes are like the eyelids of the morning.

מִפִּיו, לַפִּידִים יַהֲלֹכוּ; כִּידוֹדֵי אֵשׁ, יִתְמַלָּטוּ

mippiv lappidim yahalochu; kidodei esh, yitmallatu

Out of his mouth go burning torches, and sparks of fire leap forth.

מִנְּחִירָיו, יֵצֵא עָשָׁן--כְּדוּד נָפוּחַ וְאַגְמֹן

minnechirav yetzei ashan; kedud nafuach ve'agmon

Out of his nostrils goeth smoke, as out of a seething pot and burning rushes.

נַפְשׁוֹ, גֶּחָלִים תְּלַהֵט; וְלַהַב, מִפִּיו יֵצֵא

nafsho gechalim telahet; velahav, mippiv yetze

His breath kindleth coals, and a flame goeth out of his mouth.

בְּצַוָּארוֹ, יָלִין עֹז; וּלְפָנָיו, תָּדוּץ דְּאָבָה

betzavvaro yalin oz; ulefanav, tadutz de'avah

In his neck abideth strength, and dismay danceth before him.

מַפְּלֵי בְשָׂרוֹ דָבֵקוּ; יָצוּק עָלָיו, בַּל-יִמּוֹט

mappelei vesaro daveku; yatzuk alav, bal-yimmot

The flakes of his flesh are joined together; they are firm upon him; they cannot be moved.

לִבּוֹ, יָצוּק כְּמוֹ-אָבֶן; וְיָצוּק, כְּפֶלַח תַּחְתִּית

libbo yatzuk kemo-'aven; veyatzuk, kefelach tachtit

His heart is as firm as a stone; yea, firm as the nether millstone.

מִשֵּׂתוֹ, יָגוּרוּ אֵלִים; מִשְּׁבָרִים, יִתְחַטָּאוּ

misseto yaguru elim; mishevarim, yitchatta'u

When he raiseth himself up, the mighty are afraid; by reason of despair they are beside themselves.

מַשִּׂיגֵהוּ חֶרֶב, בְּלִי תָקוּם; חֲנִית מַסָּע וְשִׁרְיָה

massigehu cherev beli takum; chanit massa veshiryah

If one lay at him with the sword, it will not hold; nor the spear, the dart, nor the pointed shaft.

אִיּוֹב

הֲיִכְרֹת בְּרִית עִמָּךְ; תִּקָּחֶנּוּ, לְעֶבֶד עוֹלָם
hayichrot berit immach; tikkachennu, le'eved olam
Will he make a covenant with thee, that thou shouldest take him for a servant for ever?

הַתְשַׂחֶק-בּוֹ, כַּצִּפּוֹר; וְתִקְשְׁרֶנּוּ, לְנַעֲרוֹתֶיךָ
hatsachek-bo katzippor; vetiksherennu, lena'aroteicha
Wilt thou play with him as with a bird? Or wilt thou bind him for thy maidens?

יִכְרוּ עָלָיו, חַבָּרִים; יֶחֱצוּהוּ, בֵּין כְּנַעֲנִים
yichru alav chabbarim; yechetzuhu, bein kena'anim
Will the bands of fishermen make a banquet of him? Will they part him among the merchants?

הַתְמַלֵּא בְשֻׂכּוֹת עוֹרוֹ; וּבְצִלְצַל דָּגִים רֹאשׁוֹ
hatmallei vesukkot oro; uvetziltzal dagim rosho
Canst thou fill his skin with barbed irons? Or his head with fish-spears?

שִׂים-עָלָיו כַּפֶּךָ; זְכֹר מִלְחָמָה, אַל-תּוֹסַף
sim-'alav kappecha; zechor milchamah, al-tosaf
Lay thy hand upon him; think upon the battle, thou wilt do so no more.

מא

הֵן-תֹּחַלְתּוֹ נִכְזָבָה; הֲגַם אֶל-מַרְאָיו יֻטָל
Hen-tochalto nichzavah; hagam el-mar'av yutal
Behold, the hope of him is in vain; shall not one be cast down even at the sight of him?

לֹא-אַכְזָר, כִּי יְעוּרֶנּוּ; וּמִי הוּא, לְפָנַי יִתְיַצָּב
lo-'achzor ki ye'urennu; umi hu, lefanai yityatzav
None is so fierce that dare stir him up; who then is able to stand before Me?

מִי הִקְדִּימַנִי, וַאֲשַׁלֵּם; תַּחַת כָּל-הַשָּׁמַיִם לִי-הוּא
mi hikdimani va'ashallem; tachat kol-hashamayim li-hu
Who hath given Me anything beforehand, that I should repay him? Whatsoever is under the whole heaven is Mine.

לֹא-אַחֲרִישׁ בַּדָּיו; וּדְבַר-גְּבוּרוֹת, וְחִין עֶרְכּוֹ
lo-'acharish baddav; udevar-gevurot, vechin erko
Would I keep silence concerning his boastings, or his proud talk, or his fair array of words?

מִי-גִלָּה, פְּנֵי לְבוּשׁוֹ; בְּכֶפֶל רִסְנוֹ, מִי יָבוֹא
mi-gillah penei levusho; bechefel risno, mi yavo
Who can uncover the face of his garment? Who shall come within his double bridle?

דַּלְתֵי פָנָיו, מִי פִתֵּחַ; סְבִיבוֹת שִׁנָּיו אֵימָה
daltei fanav mi fitteach; sevivot shinnav eimah
Who can open the doors of his face? Round about his teeth is terror.

אִיּוֹב

הִנֵּה-נָא כֹחוֹ בְמָתְנָיו; וְאֹנוֹ, בִּשְׁרִירֵי בִטְנוֹ
hinneh-na chocho vemotenav; ve'ono, bishrirei vitno
Lo now, his strength is in his loins, and his force is in the stays of his body.

יַחְפֹּץ זְנָבוֹ כְמוֹ-אָרֶז; גִּידֵי פַחֲדָו יְשֹׂרָגוּ
yachpotz zenavo chemo-'arez; gidei fachadav fachadav yesoragu
He straineth his tail like a cedar; the sinews of his thighs are knit together.

עֲצָמָיו, אֲפִיקֵי נְחוּשָׁה; גְּרָמָיו, כִּמְטִיל בַּרְזֶל
'atzamav afikei nechushah; geramav, kimtil barzel
His bones are as pipes of brass; his gristles are like bars of iron.

הוּא, רֵאשִׁית דַּרְכֵי-אֵל; הָעֹשׂוֹ, יַגֵּשׁ חַרְבּוֹ
hu reshit darchei-'el; ha'oso yaggesh charbo
He is the beginning of the ways of God; He only that made him can make His sword to approach unto him.

כִּי-בוּל, הָרִים יִשְׂאוּ-לוֹ; וְכָל-חַיַּת הַשָּׂדֶה, יְשַׂחֲקוּ-שָׁם
ki-vul harim yis'u-lo; vechol-chayat hassadeh, yesachaku-sham
Surely the mountains bring him forth food, and all the beasts of the field play there.

תַּחַת-צֶאֱלִים יִשְׁכָּב--בְּסֵתֶר קָנֶה וּבִצָּה
tachat-tze'elim yishkav; beseter kaneh uvitzah
He lieth under the lotus-trees, in the covert of the reed, and fens.

יְסֻכֻּהוּ צֶאֱלִים צִלְלוֹ; יְסֻבּוּהוּ, עַרְבֵי-נָחַל
yesukkuhu tze'elim tzilalo; yesubbuhu, arvei-nachal
The lotus-trees cover him with their shadow; the willows of the brook compass him about.

הֵן יַעֲשֹׁק נָהָר, לֹא יַחְפּוֹז; יִבְטַח, כִּי-יָגִיחַ יַרְדֵּן אֶל-פִּיהוּ
hen ya'ashok nahar lo yachpoz; yivtach ki-yagiach yarden el-pihu
Behold, if a river overflow, he trembleth not; he is confident, though the Jordan rush forth to his mouth.

בְּעֵינָיו יִקָּחֶנּוּ; בְּמוֹקְשִׁים, יִנְקָב-אָף
be'einav yikkachennu; bemokeshim, yinkav-'af
Shall any take him by his eyes, or pierce through his nose with a snare?

תִּמְשֹׁךְ לִוְיָתָן בְּחַכָּה; וּבְחֶבֶל, תַּשְׁקִיעַ לְשֹׁנוֹ
timshoch livyatan bechakkah; uvechevel, tashkia leshono
Canst thou draw out leviathan with a fish-hook? Or press down his tongue with a cord?

הֲתָשִׂים אַגְמוֹן בְּאַפּוֹ; וּבְחוֹחַ, תִּקֹּב לֶחֱיוֹ
hatasim agmon be'appo; uvechoach, tikkov lecheyo
Canst thou put a ring into his nose? Or bore his jaw through with a hook?

הֲיַרְבֶּה אֵלֶיךָ, תַּחֲנוּנִים; אִם-יְדַבֵּר אֵלֶיךָ רַכּוֹת
hayarbeh eleicha tachanunim; im-yedabber eleicha rakkot
Will he make many supplications unto thee? Or will he speak soft words unto thee?

אִיּוֹב

הֵן קַלֹּתִי, מָה אֲשִׁיבֶךָּ; יָדִי, שַׂמְתִּי לְמוֹ-פִי
hen kalloti mah ashiveka; yadi, samti lemo-fi
Behold, I am of small account; what shall I answer Thee? I lay my hand upon my mouth.

אַחַת דִּבַּרְתִּי, וְלֹא אֶעֱנֶה; וּשְׁתַּיִם, וְלֹא אוֹסִיף
'achat dibbarti velo e'eneh; ushtayim, velo osif
Once have I spoken, but I will not answer again; yea, twice, but I will proceed no further.

וַיַּעַן-יְהוָה אֶת-אִיּוֹב, מִן סְעָרָה; וַיֹּאמַר
vaya'an-hashem et-'iyov min se'arah, vayomar
Then the LORD answered Job out of the whirlwind, and said:

אֱזָר-נָא כְגֶבֶר חֲלָצֶיךָ; אֶשְׁאָלְךָ, וְהוֹדִיעֵנִי
'ezor-na chegever chalatzeicha; esh'alecha, vehodi'eni
Gird up thy loins now like a man; I will demand of thee, and declare thou unto Me.

הַאַף, תָּפֵר מִשְׁפָּטִי; תַּרְשִׁיעֵנִי, לְמַעַן תִּצְדָּק
ha'af tafer mishpati; tarshi'eni, lema'an titzdak
Wilt thou even make void My judgment? Wilt thou condemn Me, that thou mayest be justified?

וְאִם-זְרוֹעַ כָּאֵל לָךְ; וּבְקוֹל, כָּמֹהוּ תַרְעֵם
ve'im-zeroa ka'el lach; uvekol, kamohu tar'em
Or hast thou an arm like God? And canst thou thunder with a voice like Him?

עֲדֵה נָא גָאוֹן וָגֹבַהּ; וְהוֹד וְהָדָר תִּלְבָּשׁ
'adeh na ga'on vagovah; vehod vehadar tilbash
Deck thyself now with majesty and excellency, and array thyself with glory and beauty.

הָפֵץ, עֶבְרוֹת אַפֶּךָ; וּרְאֵה כָל-גֵּאֶה, וְהַשְׁפִּילֵהוּ
hafetz evrot appecha; ure'eh chol-ge'eh, vehashpilehu
Cast abroad the rage of thy wrath; and look upon every one that is proud, and abase him.

רְאֵה כָל-גֵּאֶה, הַכְנִיעֵהוּ; וַהֲדֹךְ רְשָׁעִים תַּחְתָּם
re'eh chol-ge'eh hachni'ehu; vahadoch resha'im tachtam
Look on every one that is proud, and bring him low; and tread down the wicked in their place.

טָמְנֵם בֶּעָפָר יָחַד; פְּנֵיהֶם, חֲבֹשׁ בַּטָּמוּן
tomnem be'afar yachad; peneihem, chavosh battamun
Hide them in the dust together; bind their faces in the hidden place.

וְגַם-אֲנִי אוֹדֶךָּ: כִּי-תוֹשִׁעַ לְךָ יְמִינֶךָ
vegam-'ani odeka; ki-toshia lecha yeminecha
Then will I also confess unto thee that thine own right hand can save thee.

הִנֵּה-נָא בְהֵמוֹת, אֲשֶׁר-עָשִׂיתִי עִמָּךְ; חָצִיר, כַּבָּקָר יֹאכֵל
hinneh-na vehemot asher-'asiti immach; chatzir, kabbakar yochel
Behold now behemoth, which I made with thee; he eateth grass as an ox.

איוב

בְּרַעַשׁ וְרֹגֶז, יְגַמֵּא-אָרֶץ; וְלֹא-יַאֲמִין, כִּי-קוֹל שׁוֹפָר
bera'ash verogez yegamme-'aretz; velo-ya'amin, ki-kol shofar
He swalloweth the ground with storm and rage; neither believeth he that it is the voice of the horn.

בְּדֵי שֹׁפָר, יֹאמַר הֶאָח
bedei shofar yomar he'ach
As oft as he heareth the horn he saith: 'Ha, ha!'

וּמֵרָחוֹק, יָרִיחַ מִלְחָמָה; רַעַם שָׂרִים, וּתְרוּעָה
umerachok yariach milchamah; ra'am sarim uteru'ah
and he smelleth the battle afar off, the thunder of the captains, and the shouting.

הֲמִבִּינָתְךָ, יַאֲבֶר-נֵץ; יִפְרֹשׂ כְּנָפָו לְתֵימָן
hamibbinatecha ya'aver-netz; yifros kenafav kenafav leteiman
Doth the hawk soar by thy wisdom, and stretch her wings toward the south?

אִם-עַל-פִּיךָ, יַגְבִּיהַּ נָשֶׁר; וְכִי, יָרִים קִנּוֹ
'im-'al-picha yagbiah nasher; vechi, yarim kinno
Doth the vulture mount up at thy command, and make her nest on high?

סֶלַע יִשְׁכֹּן, וְיִתְלֹנָן--עַל שֶׁן-סֶלַע, וּמְצוּדָה
sela yishkon veyitlonan; al-shen-sela', umetzudah
She dwelleth and abideth on the rock, upon the crag of the rock, and the stronghold.

מִשָּׁם חָפַר-אֹכֶל; לְמֵרָחוֹק, עֵינָיו יַבִּיטוּ
misham chafar-'ochel; lemerachok, einav yabbitu
From thence she spieth out the prey; her eyes behold it afar off.

וְאֶפְרֹחָו יְעַלְעוּ-דָם; וּבַאֲשֶׁר חֲלָלִים, שָׁם הוּא
ve'efrochav ve'efrochav ye'al'u-dam; uva'asher chalalim, sham hu
Her young ones also suck up blood; and where the slain are, there is she.

מ

וַיַּעַן יְהוָה אֶת-אִיּוֹב; וַיֹּאמַר
Vaya'an hashem et-'iyov, vayomar
Moreover the LORD answered Job, and said:

הֲרֹב, עִם-שַׁדַּי יִסּוֹר; מוֹכִיחַ אֱלוֹהַּ יַעֲנֶנָּה
harov im-shaddai yissor; mochiach eloah ya'anennah
Shall he that reproveth contend with the Almighty? He that argueth with God, let him answer it.

וַיַּעַן אִיּוֹב אֶת-יְהוָה; וַיֹּאמַר
vaya'an iyov et-hashem vayomar
Then Job answered the LORD, and said:

אִיּוֹב

הַתַאֲמִין בּוֹ, כִּי-יָשִׁיב זַרְעֶךָ; וְגׇרְנְךָ יֶאֱסֹף
hata'amin bo ki-yashiv zar'echa; vegornecha ye'esof
Wilt thou rely on him, that he will bring home thy seed, and gather the corn of thy threshing-floor?

כְּנַף-רְנָנִים נֶעֱלָסָה; אִם-אֶבְרָה, חֲסִידָה וְנֹצָה
kenaf-renanim ne'elasah; im-'evrah, chasidah venotzah
The wing of the ostrich beateth joyously; but are her pinions and feathers the kindly stork's?

כִּי-תַעֲזֹב לָאָרֶץ בֵּצֶיהָ; וְעַל-עָפָר תְּחַמֵּם
ki-ta'azov la'aretz betzeiha; ve'al-'afar techammem
For she leaveth her eggs on the earth, and warmeth them in dust,

וַתִּשְׁכַּח, כִּי-רֶגֶל תְּזוּרֶהָ; וְחַיַּת הַשָּׂדֶה תְדוּשֶׁהָ
vattishkach ki-regel tezureha; vechayat hassadeh tedusheha
And forgetteth that the foot may crush them, or that the wild beast may trample them.

הִקְשִׁיחַ בָּנֶיהָ לְּלֹא-לָהּ; לְרִיק יְגִיעָהּ בְּלִי-פָחַד
hikshiach baneiha lelo-lah; lerik yegi'ah beli-fachad
She is hardened against her young ones, as if they were not hers; though her labour be in vain, she is without fear;

כִּי-הִשָּׁהּ אֱלוֹהַּ חָכְמָה; וְלֹא-חָלַק לָהּ, בַּבִּינָה
ki-hishah eloah chochmah velo-chalak lah, babbinah
Because God hath deprived her of wisdom, neither hath He imparted to her understanding.

כָּעֵת, בַּמָּרוֹם תַּמְרִיא; תִּשְׂחַק לַסּוּס, וּלְרֹכְבוֹ
ka'et bammarom tamri; tischak lassus, ulerochevo
When the time cometh, she raiseth her wings on high, and scorneth the horse and his rider.

הֲתִתֵּן לַסּוּס גְּבוּרָה; הֲתַלְבִּישׁ צַוָּארוֹ רַעְמָה
hatitten lassus gevurah; hatalbish tzavvaro ra'mah
Hast thou given the horse his strength? Hast thou clothed his neck with fierceness?

הֲתַרְעִישֶׁנּוּ, כָּאַרְבֶּה; הוֹד נַחְרוֹ אֵימָה
hetar'ishennu ka'arbeh; hod nachro eimah
Hast thou made him to leap as a locust? The glory of his snorting is terrible.

יַחְפְּרוּ בָעֵמֶק, וְיָשִׂישׂ בְּכֹחַ; יֵצֵא, לִקְרַאת-נָשֶׁק
yachperu va'emek veyasis bechoach; yetze, likrat-nashek
He paweth in the valley, and rejoiceth in his strength; he goeth out to meet the clash of arms.

יִשְׂחַק לְפַחַד, וְלֹא יֵחָת; וְלֹא-יָשׁוּב, מִפְּנֵי-חָרֶב
yischak lefachad velo yechat; velo-yashuv, mippenei-charev
He mocketh at fear, and is not affrighted; neither turneth he back from the sword.

עָלָיו, תִּרְנֶה אַשְׁפָּה; לַהַב חֲנִית וְכִידוֹן
'alav tirneh ashpah; lahav chanit vechidon
The quiver rattleth upon him, the glittering spear and the javelin.

אִיּוֹב

לט

הֲיָדַעְתָּ--עֵת, לֶדֶת יַעֲלֵי-סָלַע; חֹלֵל אַיָּלוֹת תִּשְׁמֹר
Hayada'ta, et ledet ya'alei-sala'; cholel ayalot tishmor
Knowest thou the time when the wild goats of the rock bring forth? Or canst thou mark when the hinds do calve?

תִּסְפֹּר יְרָחִים תְּמַלֶּאנָה; וְיָדַעְתָּ, עֵת לִדְתָּנָה
tispor yerachim temallenah; veyada'ta, et lidtanah
Canst thou number the months that they fulfil? Or knowest thou the time when they bring forth?

תִּכְרַעְנָה, יַלְדֵיהֶן תְּפַלַּחְנָה; חֶבְלֵיהֶם תְּשַׁלַּחְנָה
tichra'nah yaldeihen tefallachnah; chevleihem teshallachnah
They bow themselves, they bring forth their young, they cast out their fruit.

יַחְלְמוּ בְנֵיהֶם, יִרְבּוּ בַבָּר; יָצְאוּ, וְלֹא-שָׁבוּ לָמוֹ
yachlemu veneihem yirbu vabbar; yatze'u, velo-shavu lamo
Their young ones wax strong, they grow up in the open field; they go forth, and return not again.

מִי-שִׁלַּח פֶּרֶא חָפְשִׁי; וּמֹסְרוֹת עָרוֹד, מִי פִתֵּחַ
mi-shillach perei chofeshi; umoserot arod, mi fitteach
Who hath sent out the wild ass free? Or who hath loosed the bands of the wild ass?

אֲשֶׁר-שַׂמְתִּי עֲרָבָה בֵיתוֹ; וּמִשְׁכְּנוֹתָיו מְלֵחָה
'asher-samti aravah veito; umishkenotav melechah
Whose house I have made the wilderness, and the salt land his dwelling-place.

יִשְׂחַק, לַהֲמוֹן קִרְיָה; תְּשֻׁאוֹת נוֹגֵשׂ, לֹא יִשְׁמָע
yischak lahamon kiryah; teshu'ot noges, lo yishma
He scorneth the tumult of the city, neither heareth he the shoutings of the driver.

יְתוּר הָרִים מִרְעֵהוּ; וְאַחַר כָּל-יָרוֹק יִדְרוֹשׁ
yetur harim mir'ehu; ve'achar kol-yarok yidrosh
The range of the mountains is his pasture, and he searcheth after every green thing.

הֲיֹאבֶה רֵּים עָבְדֶךָ; אִם-יָלִין, עַל-אֲבוּסֶךָ
hayoveh reim avedecha; im-yalin, al-'avusecha
Will the wild-ox be willing to serve thee? Or will he abide by thy crib?

הֲתִקְשָׁר-רֵים, בְּתֶלֶם עֲבֹתוֹ; אִם-יְשַׂדֵּד עֲמָקִים אַחֲרֶיךָ
hatikshor-reim betelem avoto; im-yesadded amakim achareicha
Canst thou bind the wild-ox with his band in the furrow? Or will he harrow the valleys after thee?

הֲתִבְטַח-בּוֹ, כִּי-רַב כֹּחוֹ; וְתַעֲזֹב אֵלָיו יְגִיעֶךָ
hativtach-bo ki-rav kocho; veta'azov elav yegi'echa
Wilt thou trust him, because his strength is great? Or wilt thou leave thy labour to him?

איוב

כְּאֶבֶן, מַיִם יִתְחַבָּאוּ; וּפְנֵי תְהוֹם, יִתְלַכָּדוּ
ka'even mayim yitchabba'u; ufenei tehom, yitlakkadu
The waters are congealed like stone, and the face of the deep is frozen.

הַתְקַשֵּׁר, מַעֲדַנּוֹת כִּימָה; אוֹ-מֹשְׁכוֹת כְּסִיל תְּפַתֵּחַ
hatekasher ma'adannot kimah; o-moshechot kesil tefatteach
Canst thou bind the chains of the Pleiades, or loose the bands of Orion?

הֲתֹצִיא מַזָּרוֹת בְּעִתּוֹ; וְעַיִשׁ, עַל-בָּנֶיהָ תַנְחֵם
hatotzi mazzarot be'itto; ve'ayish, al-baneiha tanchem
Canst thou lead forth the Mazzaroth in their season? Or canst thou guide the Bear with her sons?

הֲיָדַעְתָּ, חֻקּוֹת שָׁמָיִם; אִם-תָּשִׂים מִשְׁטָרוֹ בָאָרֶץ
hayada'ta chukkot shamayim; im-tasim mishtaro va'aretz
Knowest thou the ordinances of the heavens? Canst thou establish the dominion thereof in the earth?

הֲתָרִים לָעָב קוֹלֶךָ; וְשִׁפְעַת-מַיִם תְּכַסֶּךָּ
hatarim la'av kolecha; veshif'at-mayim techasseka
Canst thou lift up thy voice to the clouds, that abundance of waters may cover thee?

הַתְשַׁלַּח בְּרָקִים וְיֵלֵכוּ; וְיֹאמְרוּ לְךָ הִנֵּנוּ
hateshallach berakim veyelechu; veyomeru lecha hinnenu
Canst thou send forth lightnings, that they may go, and say unto thee: 'Here we are'?

מִי-שָׁת, בַּטֻּחוֹת חָכְמָה; אוֹ מִי-נָתַן לַשֶּׂכְוִי בִינָה
mi-shat battuchot chochmah o mi-natan lassechvi vinah
Who hath put wisdom in the inward parts? Or who hath given understanding to the mind?

מִי-יְסַפֵּר שְׁחָקִים בְּחָכְמָה; וְנִבְלֵי שָׁמַיִם, מִי יַשְׁכִּיב
mi-yesapper shechakim bechochmah venivlei shamayim, mi yashkiv
Who can number the clouds by wisdom? Or who can pour out the bottles of heaven,

בְּצֶקֶת עָפָר, לַמּוּצָק; וּרְגָבִים יְדֻבָּקוּ
betzeket afor lammutzak; uregavim yedubbaku
When the dust runneth into a mass, and the clods cleave fast together?

הֲתָצוּד לְלָבִיא טָרֶף; וְחַיַּת כְּפִירִים תְּמַלֵּא
hatatzud lelavi taref; vechayat kefirim temalle
Wilt thou hunt the prey for the lioness? Or satisfy the appetite of the young lions,

כִּי-יָשֹׁחוּ בַמְּעוֹנוֹת; יֵשְׁבוּ בַסֻּכָּה לְמוֹ-אָרֶב
ki-yashochu vamme'onot; yeshevu vassukkah lemo-'arev
When they couch in their dens, and abide in the covert to lie in wait?

מִי יָכִין לָעֹרֵב, צֵידוֹ: כִּי-יְלָדָו, אֶל-אֵל יְשַׁוֵּעוּ; יִתְעוּ, לִבְלִי-אֹכֶל
mi yachin la'orev, tzeido ki-yeladav el-'el yeshavve'u; yit'u, livli-'ochel
Who provideth for the raven his prey, when his young ones cry unto God, and wander for lack of food?

אִיּוֹב

הִתְבֹּנַנְתָּ, עַד-רַחֲבֵי-אָרֶץ; הַגֵּד, אִם-יָדַעְתָּ כֻלָּהּ
hitbonanta ad-rachavei-'aretz; hagged, im-yada'ta chullah
Hast thou surveyed unto the breadths of the earth? Declare, if thou knowest it all.

אֵי-זֶה הַדֶּרֶךְ, יִשְׁכָּן-אוֹר; וְחֹשֶׁךְ, אֵי-זֶה מְקֹמוֹ
'ei-zeh hadderech yishkon-'or; vechoshech, ei-zeh mekomo
Where is the way to the dwelling of light, and as for darkness, where is the place thereof;

כִּי תִקָּחֶנּוּ אֶל-גְּבוּלוֹ; וְכִי-תָבִין, נְתִיבוֹת בֵּיתוֹ
ki tikkachennu el-gevulo; vechi-tavin, netivot beito
That thou shouldest take it to the bound thereof, and that thou shouldest know the paths to the house thereof?

יָדַעְתָּ, כִּי-אָז תִּוָּלֵד; וּמִסְפַּר יָמֶיךָ רַבִּים
yada'ta ki-'az tivvaled; umispar yameicha rabbim
Thou knowest it, for thou wast then born, and the number of thy days is great!

הֲבָאתָ, אֶל-אֹצְרוֹת שָׁלֶג; וְאֹצְרוֹת בָּרָד תִּרְאֶה
havata el-'otzerot shaleg; ve'otzerot barad tir'eh
Hast thou entered the treasuries of the snow, or hast thou seen the treasuries of the hail,

אֲשֶׁר-חָשַׂכְתִּי לְעֶת-צָר; לְיוֹם קְרָב, וּמִלְחָמָה
'asher-chasachti le'et-tzar; leyom kerav, umilchamah
Which I have reserved against the time of trouble, against the day of battle and war?

אֵי-זֶה הַדֶּרֶךְ, יֵחָלֶק אוֹר; יָפֵץ קָדִים עֲלֵי-אָרֶץ
'ei-zeh hadderech yechalek or; yafetz kadim alei-'aretz
By what way is the light parted, or the east wind scattered upon the earth?

מִי-פִלַּג לַשֶּׁטֶף תְּעָלָה; וְדֶרֶךְ, לַחֲזִיז קֹלוֹת
mi-fillag lashetef te'alah; vederech, lachaziz kolot
Who hath cleft a channel for the waterflood, or a way for the lightning of the thunder;

לְהַמְטִיר, עַל-אֶרֶץ לֹא-אִישׁ--מִדְבָּר, לֹא-אָדָם בּוֹ
lehamtir al-'eretz lo-'ish; midbar, lo-'adam bo
To cause it to rain on a land where no man is, on the wilderness, wherein there is no man;

לְהַשְׂבִּיעַ שֹׁאָה, וּמְשֹׁאָה; וּלְהַצְמִיחַ, מֹצָא דֶשֶׁא
lehasbia sho'ah umesho'ah; ulehatzmiach, motza deshe
To satisfy the desolate and waste ground, and to cause the bud of the tender herb to spring forth?

הֲיֶשׁ-לַמָּטָר אָב; אוֹ מִי-הוֹלִיד, אֶגְלֵי-טָל
hayesh-lammatar av; o mi-holid, eglei-tal
Hath the rain a father? Or who hath begotten the drops of dew?

מִבֶּטֶן מִי, יָצָא הַקָּרַח; וּכְפֹר שָׁמַיִם, מִי יְלָדוֹ
mibbeten mi yatza hakkarach; uchefor shamayim mi yelado
Out of whose womb came the ice? And the hoar-frost of heaven, who hath gendered it?

אִיּוֹב

עַל-מָה, אֲדָנֶיהָ הָטְבָּעוּ; אוֹ מִי-יָרָה, אֶבֶן פִּנָּתָהּ
'al-mah adaneiha hotba'u; o mi-yarah, even pinnatah
Whereupon were the foundations thereof fastened? Or who laid the corner-stone thereof,

בְּרָן-יַחַד, כּוֹכְבֵי בֹקֶר; וַיָּרִיעוּ, כָּל-בְּנֵי אֱלֹהִים
beran-yachad kochevei voker; vayari'u, kol-benei elohim
When the morning stars sang together, and all the sons of God shouted for joy?

וַיָּסֶךְ בִּדְלָתַיִם יָם; בְּגִיחוֹ, מֵרֶחֶם יֵצֵא
vayasech bidlatayim yam; begicho, merechem yetze
Or who shut up the sea with doors, when it broke forth, and issued out of the womb;

בְּשׂוּמִי עָנָן לְבֻשׁוֹ; וַעֲרָפֶל, חֲתֻלָּתוֹ
besumi anan levusho; va'arafel, chatullato
When I made the cloud the garment thereof, and thick darkness a swaddlingband for it,

וָאֶשְׁבֹּר עָלָיו חֻקִּי; וָאָשִׂים, בְּרִיחַ וּדְלָתָיִם
va'eshbor alav chukki; va'asim, beriach udelatayim
And prescribed for it My decree, and set bars and doors,

וָאֹמַר--עַד-פֹּה תָבוֹא, וְלֹא תֹסִיף; וּפֹא-יָשִׁית, בִּגְאוֹן גַּלֶּיךָ
va'omar, ad-poh tavo velo tosif; ufo-yashit, big'on galleicha
And said: 'Thus far shalt thou come, but no further; and here shall thy proud waves be stayed'?

הְמִיָּמֶיךָ, צִוִּיתָ בֹּקֶר; יִדַּעְתָּה הַשַּׁחַר מְקֹמוֹ
hemiyameicha tzivvita boker; yidda'ta hashachar mekomo
Hast thou commanded the morning since thy days began, and caused the dayspring to know its place;

לֶאֱחֹז, בְּכַנְפוֹת הָאָרֶץ; וְיִנָּעֲרוּ רְשָׁעִים מִמֶּנָּה
le'echoz bechanfot ha'aretz; veyinna'aru resha'im mimmennah
That it might take hold of the ends of the earth, and the wicked be shaken out of it?

תִּתְהַפֵּךְ, כְּחֹמֶר חוֹתָם; וְיִתְיַצְּבוּ, כְּמוֹ לְבוּשׁ
tit'happech kechomer chotam; veyityatzevu, kemo levush
It is changed as clay under the seal; and they stand as a garment.

וְיִמָּנַע מֵרְשָׁעִים אוֹרָם; וּזְרוֹעַ רָמָה, תִּשָּׁבֵר
veyimmana meresha'im oram; uzroa ramah, tishaver
But from the wicked their light is withholden, and the high arm is broken.

הֲבָאתָ, עַד-נִבְכֵי-יָם; וּבְחֵקֶר תְּהוֹם, הִתְהַלָּכְתָּ
havata ad-nivchei-yam; uvecheker tehom, hit'hallachta
Hast thou entered into the springs of the sea? Or hast thou walked in the recesses of the deep?

הֲנִגְלוּ לְךָ, שַׁעֲרֵי-מָוֶת; וְשַׁעֲרֵי צַלְמָוֶת תִּרְאֶה
haniglu lecha sha'arei-mavet; vesha'arei tzalmavet tir'eh
Have the gates of death been revealed unto thee? Or hast thou seen the gates of the shadow of death?

איוֹב

הַיְסֻפַּר-לוֹ, כִּי אֲדַבֵּר; אִם-אָמַר אִישׁ, כִּי יְבֻלָּע
haysuppar-lo ki adabber; im-'amar ish, ki yevulla
Shall it be told Him that I would speak? Or should a man wish that he were swallowed up?

וְעַתָּה, לֹא רָאוּ אוֹר--בָּהִיר הוּא, בַּשְּׁחָקִים; וְרוּחַ עָבְרָה, וַתְּטַהֲרֵם
ve'attah lo ra'u or, bahir hu bashechakim; veruach averah, vattetaharem
And now men see not the light which is bright in the skies; but the wind passeth, and cleanseth them.

מִצָּפוֹן, זָהָב יֶאֱתֶה; עַל-אֱלוֹהַּ, נוֹרָא הוֹד
mitzafon zahav ye'eteh; al-'eloah, nora hod
Out of the north cometh golden splendour, about God is terrible majesty.

שַׁדַּי לֹא-מְצָאנֻהוּ, שַׂגִּיא-כֹחַ
shaddai lo-metzanuhu saggi-choach
The Almighty, whom we cannot find out, is excellent in power,

וּמִשְׁפָּט וְרֹב-צְדָקָה, לֹא יְעַנֶּה
umishpat verov-tzedakah, lo ye'anneh
yet to judgment and plenteous justice He doeth no violence.

לָכֵן, יְרֵאוּהוּ אֲנָשִׁים; לֹא-יִרְאֶה, כָּל-חַכְמֵי-לֵב
lachen yere'uhu anashim; lo-yir'eh, kol-chachmei-lev
Men do therefore fear Him; He regardeth not any that are wise of heart.

לח

וַיַּעַן-יְהוָה אֶת-אִיּוֹב, מִן הַסְּעָרָה; וַיֹּאמַר
Vaya'an-hashem et-'iyov min hasse'arah, vayomar
Then the LORD answered Job out of the whirlwind, and said:

מִי זֶה, מַחְשִׁיךְ עֵצָה בְמִלִּין--בְּלִי-דָעַת
mi zeh machshich etzah vemillin, beli-da'at
Who is this that darkeneth counsel by words without knowledge?

אֱזָר-נָא כְגֶבֶר חֲלָצֶיךָ; וְאֶשְׁאָלְךָ, וְהוֹדִיעֵנִי
'ezar-na chegever chalatzeicha; ve'esh'alecha, vehodi'eni
Gird up now thy loins like a man; for I will demand of thee, and declare thou unto Me.

אֵיפֹה הָיִיתָ, בְּיָסְדִי-אָרֶץ; הַגֵּד, אִם-יָדַעְתָּ בִינָה
'eifoh hayita beyosdi-'aretz; hagged, im-yada'ta vinah
Where wast thou when I laid the foundations of the earth? Declare, if thou hast the understanding.

מִי-שָׂם מְמַדֶּיהָ, כִּי תֵדָע; אוֹ מִי-נָטָה עָלֶיהָ קָּו
mi-sam memaddeiha ki teda'; o mi-natah aleiha kav
Who determined the measures thereof, if thou knowest? Or who stretched the line upon it?

איוב

מִן־הַחֶדֶר, תָּבוֹא סוּפָה; וּמִמְּזָרִים קָרָה
min-hacheder tavo sufah; umimmezarim karah
Out of the Chamber cometh the storm; and cold out of the north.

מִנִּשְׁמַת־אֵל יִתֶּן־קָרַח; וְרֹחַב מַיִם בְּמוּצָק
minnishmat-'el yitten-karach; verochav mayim bemutzak
By the breath of God ice is given, and the breadth of the waters is straitened.

אַף־בְּרִי, יַטְרִיחַ עָב; יָפִיץ, עֲנַן אוֹרוֹ
'af-beri yatriach av; yafitz, anan oro
Yea, He ladeth the thick cloud with moisture, He spreadeth abroad the cloud of His lightning;

וְהוּא מְסִבּוֹת, מִתְהַפֵּךְ בְּתַחְבּוּלֹתָו
vehu mesibbot mit'happech betachbulotav
And they are turned round about by His guidance,

לְפָעֳלָם: כֹּל אֲשֶׁר יְצַוֵּם, עַל־פְּנֵי תֵבֵל אָרְצָה
lefo'olam; kol asher yetzavvem al-penei tevel artzah
that they may do whatsoever He commandeth them upon the face of the habitable world:

אִם־לְשֵׁבֶט אִם־לְאַרְצוֹ-- אִם־לְחֶסֶד, יַמְצִאֵהוּ
'im-leshevet im-le'artzo; im-lechesed, yamtzi'ehu
Whether it be for correction, or for His earth, or for mercy, that He cause it to come.

הַאֲזִינָה זֹּאת אִיּוֹב; עֲמֹד, וְהִתְבּוֹנֵן נִפְלְאוֹת אֵל
ha'azinah zot iyov; amod, vehitbonen nifle'ot el
Hearken unto this, O Job; stand still, and consider the wondrous works of God.

הֲתֵדַע, בְּשׂוּם־אֱלוֹהַּ עֲלֵיהֶם; וְהוֹפִיעַ, אוֹר עֲנָנוֹ
hateda besum-'eloah aleihem; vehofia', or anano
Dost thou know how God enjoineth them, and causeth the lightning of His cloud to shine?

הֲתֵדַע, עַל־מִפְלְשֵׂי־עָב; מִפְלְאוֹת, תְּמִים דֵּעִים
hateda al-miflesei-'av; mifle'ot, temim de'im
Dost thou know the balancings of the clouds, the wondrous works of Him who is perfect in knowledge?

אֲשֶׁר־בְּגָדֶיךָ חַמִּים-- בְּהַשְׁקִט אֶרֶץ, מִדָּרוֹם
'asher-begadeicha chammim; behashkit eretz, middarom
Thou whose garments are warm, when the earth is still by reason of the south wind;

תַּרְקִיעַ עִמּוֹ, לִשְׁחָקִים; חֲזָקִים, כִּרְאִי מוּצָק
tarkia immo lishchakim; chazakim, kir'i mutzak
Canst thou with Him spread out the sky, which is strong as a molten mirror?

הוֹדִיעֵנוּ, מַה־נֹּאמַר לוֹ; לֹא־נַעֲרֹךְ, מִפְּנֵי־חֹשֶׁךְ
hodi'enu mah-nomar lo; lo-na'aroch, mippenei-choshech
Teach us what we shall say unto Him; for we cannot order our speech by reason of darkness.

אִיּוֹב

עַל-כַּפַּיִם כִּסָּה-אוֹר; וַיְצַו עָלֶיהָ בְמַפְגִּיעַ
'al-kappayim kissah-'or; vayetzav aleiha vemafgia
He covereth His hands with the lightning, and giveth it a charge that it strike the mark.

יַגִּיד עָלָיו רֵעוֹ; מִקְנֶה, אַף עַל-עוֹלֶה
yaggid alav re'o; mikneh, af al-'oleh
The noise thereof telleth concerning it, the cattle also concerning the storm that cometh up.

לז

אַף-לְזֹאת, יֶחֱרַד לִבִּי; וְיִתַּר, מִמְּקוֹמוֹ
Af-lezot yecherad libbi; veyittar, mimmekomo
At this also my heart trembleth, and is moved out of its place.

שִׁמְעוּ שָׁמוֹעַ בְּרֹגֶז קֹלוֹ; וְהֶגֶה, מִפִּיו יֵצֵא
shim'u shamoa berogez kolo; vehegeh, mippiv yetze
Hear attentively the noise of His voice, and the sound that goeth out of His mouth.

תַּחַת-כָּל-הַשָּׁמַיִם יִשְׁרֵהוּ; וְאוֹרוֹ, עַל-כַּנְפוֹת הָאָרֶץ
tachat-kol-hashamayim yishrehu; ve'oro, al-kanfot ha'aretz
He sendeth it forth under the whole heaven, and His lightning unto the ends of the earth.

אַחֲרָיו, יִשְׁאַג-קוֹל--יַרְעֵם, בְּקוֹל גְּאוֹנוֹ
'acharav yish'ag-kol, yar'em bekol ge'ono
After it a voice roareth; He thundereth with the voice of His majesty;

וְלֹא יְעַקְּבֵם, כִּי-יִשָּׁמַע קוֹלוֹ
velo ye'akkevem, ki-yishama kolo
and He stayeth them not when His voice is heard.

יַרְעֵם אֵל בְּקוֹלוֹ, נִפְלָאוֹת; עֹשֶׂה גְדֹלוֹת, וְלֹא נֵדָע
yar'em el bekolo nifla'ot; oseh gedolot, velo neda
God thundereth marvellously with His voice; great things doeth He, which we cannot comprehend.

כִּי לַשֶּׁלֶג, יֹאמַר-- הֱוֵא-אָרֶץ; וְגֶשֶׁם מָטָר, וְגֶשֶׁם, מִטְרוֹת עֻזּוֹ
ki lashelag yomar, hevei aretz vegeshem matar; vegeshem, mitrot uzzo
For He saith to the snow: 'Fall thou on the earth'; likewise to the shower of rain, and to the showers of His mighty rain.

בְּיַד-כָּל-אָדָם יַחְתּוֹם--לָדַעַת, כָּל-אַנְשֵׁי מַעֲשֵׂהוּ
beyad-kol-'adam yachtom; lada'at, kol-'anshei ma'asehu
He sealeth up the hand of every man, that all men whom He hath made may know it.

וַתָּבוֹא חַיָּה בְמוֹ-אָרֶב; וּבִמְעוֹנֹתֶיהָ תִשְׁכֹּן
vattavo chayah vemo-'arev; uvim'onoteiha tishkon
Then the beasts go into coverts, and remain in their dens.

אִיּוֹב

אַל-תִּשְׁאַף הַלָּיְלָה--לַעֲלוֹת עַמִּים תַּחְתָּם
'al-tish'af hallayelah; la'alot ammim tachtam
Desire not the night, when peoples are cut off in their place.

הִשָּׁמֶר, אַל-תֵּפֶן אֶל-אָוֶן: כִּי-עַל-זֶה, בָּחַרְתָּ מֵעֹנִי
hishamer al-tefen el-'aven; ki-'al-zeh, bacharta me'oni
Take heed, regard not iniquity; for this hast thou chosen rather than affliction.

הֶן-אֵל, יַשְׂגִּיב בְּכֹחוֹ; מִי כָמֹהוּ מוֹרֶה
hen-'el yasgiv bechocho; mi chamohu moreh
Behold, God doeth loftily in His power; who is a teacher like Him?

מִי-פָקַד עָלָיו דַּרְכּוֹ; וּמִי-אָמַר, פָּעַלְתָּ עַוְלָה
mi-fakad alav darko; umi-'amar, pa'alta avlah
Who hath enjoined Him His way? Or who hath said: 'Thou hast wrought unrighteousness'?

זְכֹר, כִּי-תַשְׂגִּיא פָעֳלוֹ--אֲשֶׁר שֹׁרְרוּ אֲנָשִׁים
zechor ki-tasgi fo'olo; asher shoreru anashim
Remember that thou magnify His work, whereof men have sung.

כָּל-אָדָם חָזוּ-בוֹ; אֱנוֹשׁ, יַבִּיט מֵרָחוֹק
kol-'adam chazu-vo; enosh, yabbit merachok
All men have looked thereon; man beholdeth it afar off.

הֶן-אֵל שַׂגִּיא, וְלֹא נֵדָע; מִסְפַּר שָׁנָיו וְלֹא-חֵקֶר
hen-'el saggi velo neda'; mispar shanav velo-cheker
Behold, God is great, beyond our knowledge; the number of His years is unsearchable.

כִּי, יְגָרַע נִטְפֵי-מָיִם; יָזֹקּוּ מָטָר לְאֵדוֹ
ki yegara nitfei-mayim; yazokku matar le'edo
For He draweth away the drops of water, which distil rain from His vapour;

אֲשֶׁר-יִזְּלוּ שְׁחָקִים; יִרְעֲפוּ, עֲלֵי אָדָם רָב
'asher-yizzelu shechakim; yir'afu, alei adam rav
Which the skies pour down and drop upon the multitudes of men.

אַף אִם-יָבִין, מִפְרְשֵׂי-עָב; תְּשֻׁאוֹת, סֻכָּתוֹ
'af im-yavin mifresei-'av; teshu'ot, sukkato
Yea, can any understand the spreadings of the clouds, the crashings of His pavilion?

הֵן-פָּרַשׂ עָלָיו אוֹרוֹ; וְשָׁרְשֵׁי הַיָּם כִּסָּה
hen-paras alav oro; veshoreshei hayam kissah
Behold, He spreadeth His light upon it; and He covereth the depths of the sea.

כִּי-בָם, יָדִין עַמִּים; יִתֶּן-אֹכֶל לְמַכְבִּיר
ki-vam yadin ammim; yitten-'ochel lemachbir
For by these He judgeth the peoples; He giveth food in abundance.

אִיּוֹב

וַיַּגֵּד לָהֶם פָּעֳלָם; וּפִשְׁעֵיהֶם, כִּי יִתְגַּבָּרוּ
vayagged lahem po'olam; ufish'eihem, ki yitgabbaru
Then He declareth unto them their work, and their transgressions, that they have behaved themselves proudly.

וַיִּגֶל אָזְנָם, לַמּוּסָר; וַיֹּאמֶר, כִּי-יְשֻׁבוּן מֵאָוֶן
vayigel azenom lammusar; vayomer, ki-yeshuvun me'aven
He openeth also their ear to discipline, and commandeth that they return from iniquity.

אִם-יִשְׁמְעוּ, וְיַעֲבֹדוּ: יְכַלּוּ יְמֵיהֶם בַּטּוֹב; וּשְׁנֵיהֶם, בַּנְּעִימִים
'im-yishme'u, veya'avodu yechallu yemeihem battov; usheneihem, banne'imim
If they hearken and serve Him, they shall spend their days in prosperity, and their years in pleasures.

וְאִם-לֹא יִשְׁמְעוּ, בְּשֶׁלַח יַעֲבֹרוּ; וְיִגְוְעוּ, בִּבְלִי-דָעַת
ve'im-lo yishme'u beshelach ya'avoru; veyigve'u, kivli-da'at
But if they hearken not, they shall perish by the sword, and they shall die without knowledge.

וְחַנְפֵי-לֵב, יָשִׂימוּ אָף; לֹא יְשַׁוְּעוּ, כִּי אֲסָרָם
vechanfei-lev yasimu af; lo yeshavve'u, ki asaram
But they that are godless in heart lay up anger; they cry not for help when He bindeth them.

תָּמֹת בַּנֹּעַר נַפְשָׁם; וְחַיָּתָם, בַּקְּדֵשִׁים
tamot banno'ar nafsham; vechayatam, bakkedeshim
Their soul perisheth in youth, and their life as that of the depraved.

יְחַלֵּץ עָנִי בְעָנְיוֹ; וְיִגֶל בַּלַּחַץ אָזְנָם
yechalletz ani ve'aneyo; veyigel ballachatz oznam
He delivereth the afflicted by His affliction, and openeth their ear by tribulation.

וְאַף הֲסִיתְךָ, מִפִּי-צָר-- רַחַב
ve'af hasitecha mippi-tzar, rachav
Yea, He hath allured thee out of distress into a broad place,

לֹא-מוּצָק תַּחְתֶּיהָ; וְנַחַת שֻׁלְחָנְךָ, מָלֵא דָשֶׁן
lo-mutzak tachteiha; venachat shulchanecha, malei dashen
where there is no straitness; and that which is set on thy table is full of fatness;

וְדִין-רָשָׁע מָלֵאתָ; דִּין וּמִשְׁפָּט יִתְמֹכוּ
vedin-rasha maleta; din umishpat yitmochu
And thou art full of the judgment of the wicked; judgment and justice take hold on them.

כִּי-חֵמָה, פֶּן-יְסִיתְךָ בְסָפֶק; וְרָב-כֹּפֶר, אַל-יַטֶּךָּ
ki-chemah pen-yesitecha vesafek; verav-kofer, al-yatteka
For beware of wrath, lest thou be led away by thy sufficiency; neither let the greatness of the ransom turn thee aside.

הֲיַעֲרֹךְ שׁוּעֲךָ, לֹא בְצָר; וְכֹל, מַאֲמַצֵּי-כֹחַ
haya'aroch shu'acha lo vetzar; vechol ma'amatzei-choach
Will thy riches avail, that are without stint, or all the forces of thy strength?

אִיּוֹב

וְעַתָּה--כִּי-אַיִן, פָּקַד אַפּוֹ; וְלֹא-יָדַע בַּפַּשׁ מְאֹד
ve'attah, ki-'ayin pakad appo; velo-yada bappash me'od
And now, is it for nought that He punished in His anger? And hath He not full knowledge of arrogance?

וְאִיּוֹב, הֶבֶל יִפְצֶה-פִּיהוּ; בִּבְלִי-דַעַת, מִלִּין יַכְבִּר
ve'iyov hevel yiftzeh-pihu; bivli-da'at, millin yachbir
But Job doth open his mouth in vanity; he multiplieth words without knowledge.

לו

וַיֹּסֶף אֱלִיהוּא, וַיֹּאמַר
Vayosef elihu, vayomar
Elihu also proceeded, and said:

כַּתַּר-לִי זְעֵיר, וַאֲחַוֶּךָּ: כִּי עוֹד לֶאֱלוֹהַּ מִלִּים
kattar-li ze'eir va'achavveka; ki od le'eloah millim
Suffer me a little, and I will tell thee; for there are yet words on God's behalf.

אֶשָּׂא דֵעִי, לְמֵרָחוֹק; וּלְפֹעֲלִי, אֶתֵּן-צֶדֶק
'essa de'i lemerachok; ulefo'ali, etten-tzedek
I will fetch my knowledge from afar, and will ascribe righteousness to my Maker.

כִּי-אָמְנָם, לֹא-שֶׁקֶר מִלָּי; תְּמִים דֵּעוֹת עִמָּךְ
ki-'omenam lo-sheker millai; temim de'ot immach
For truly my words are not false; one that is upright in mind is with thee.

הֶן-אֵל כַּבִּיר, וְלֹא יִמְאָס: כַּבִּיר, כֹּחַ לֵב
hen-'el kabbir velo yim'as; kabbir, koach lev
Behold, God is mighty, yet He despiseth not any; He is mighty in strength of understanding.

לֹא-יְחַיֶּה רָשָׁע; וּמִשְׁפַּט עֲנִיִּים יִתֵּן
lo-yechayeh rasha'; umishpat aniyim yitten
He preserveth not the life of the wicked; but giveth to the poor their right.

לֹא-יִגְרַע מִצַּדִּיק, עֵינָיו
lo-yigra mitzaddik, einav
He withdraweth not His eyes from the righteous;

וְאֶת-מְלָכִים לַכִּסֵּא; וַיֹּשִׁיבֵם לָנֶצַח, וַיִּגְבָּהוּ
ve'et-melachim lakkisse; vayoshivem lanetzach, vayigbahu
but with kings upon the throne He setteth them for ever, and they are exalted.

וְאִם-אֲסוּרִים בַּזִּקִּים; יִלָּכְדוּן, בְּחַבְלֵי-עֹנִי
ve'im-'asurim bazzikkim; yillachedun, bechavlei-'oni
And if they be bound in fetters, and be holden in cords of affliction;

איוב

אֲנִי, אֲשִׁיבְךָ מִלִּין--וְאֶת-רֵעֶיךָ עִמָּךְ
'ani ashivecha millin; ve'et-re'eicha immach
I will give thee answer, and thy companions with thee.

הַבֵּט שָׁמַיִם וּרְאֵה; וְשׁוּר שְׁחָקִים, גָּבְהוּ מִמֶּךָּ
habbet shamayim ure'eh; veshur shechakim, gavehu mimmeka
Look unto the heavens, and see; and behold the skies, which are higher than thou.

אִם-חָטָאתָ, מַה-תִּפְעָל-בּוֹ
'im-chatata mah-tif'al-bo
If thou hast sinned, what doest thou against Him?

וְרַבּוּ פְשָׁעֶיךָ, מַה-תַּעֲשֶׂה-לּוֹ
verabbu fesha'eicha, mah-ta'aseh-lo
And if thy transgressions be multiplied, what doest thou unto Him?

אִם-צָדַקְתָּ, מַה-תִּתֶּן-לוֹ; אוֹ מַה-מִיָּדְךָ יִקָּח
'im-tzadakta mah-titten-lo; o mah-miyadecha yikkach
If thou be righteous, what givest thou Him? Or what receiveth He of thy hand?

לְאִישׁ-כָּמוֹךָ רִשְׁעֶךָ; וּלְבֶן-אָדָם, צִדְקָתֶךָ
le'ish-kamocha rish'echa; uleven-'adam, tzidkatecha
Thy wickedness concerneth a man as thou art; and thy righteousness a son of man.

מֵרֹב, עֲשׁוּקִים יַזְעִיקוּ; יְשַׁוְּעוּ מִזְּרוֹעַ רַבִּים
merov ashukim yaz'iku; yeshavve'u mizzeroa rabbim
By reason of the multitude of oppressions they cry out; they cry for help by reason of the arm of the mighty.

וְלֹא-אָמַר, אַיֵּה--אֱלוֹהַּ עֹשָׂי: נֹתֵן זְמִרוֹת בַּלָּיְלָה
velo-'amar, ayeh eloah osai; noten zemirot ballayelah
But none saith: 'Where is God my Maker, who giveth songs in the night;

מַלְּפֵנוּ, מִבַּהֲמוֹת אָרֶץ; וּמֵעוֹף הַשָּׁמַיִם יְחַכְּמֵנוּ
mallefenu mibbahamot aretz; ume'of hashamayim yechakkemenu
Who teacheth us more than the beasts of the earth, and maketh us wiser than the fowls of heaven?'

שָׁם יִצְעֲקוּ, וְלֹא יַעֲנֶה-- מִפְּנֵי, גְּאוֹן רָעִים
sham yitz'aku velo ya'aneh; mippenei, ge'on ra'im
There they cry, but none giveth answer, because of the pride of evil men.

אַךְ-שָׁוְא, לֹא-יִשְׁמַע אֵל; וְשַׁדַּי, לֹא יְשׁוּרֶנָּה
'ach-shav lo-yishma el; veshaddai, lo yeshurennah
Surely God will not hear vanity, neither will the Almighty regard it.

אַף כִּי-תֹאמַר, לֹא תְשׁוּרֶנּוּ; דִּין לְפָנָיו, וּתְחוֹלֵל לוֹ
'af ki-tomar lo teshurennu; din lefanav, utecholel lo
Yea, when thou sayest thou canst not see Him--the cause is before Him; therefore wait thou for Him.

איוב

כִּי-אֶל-אֵל, הֶאָמַר נָשָׂאתִי--לֹא אֶחְבֹּל
ki-'el-'el he'amar nasati, lo echbol
For hath any said unto God: 'I have borne chastisement, though I offend not;

בִּלְעֲדֵי אֶחֱזֶה, אַתָּה הֹרֵנִי; אִם-עָוֶל פָּעַלְתִּי, לֹא אֹסִיף
bil'adei echezeh attah horeni; im-'avel pa'alti, lo osif
That which I see not teach Thou me; if I have done iniquity, I will do it no more'?

הַמֵעִמְּךָ יְשַׁלְמֶנָּה, כִּי-מָאַסְתָּ--כִּי-אַתָּה תִבְחַר
hame'immecha yeshalmennah ki-ma'asta, ki-'attah tivchar
Shall His recompense be as thou wilt? For thou loathest it,

וְלֹא-אָנִי; וּמַה-יָדַעְתָּ דַבֵּר
velo-'ani; umah-yada'ta dabber
so that thou must choose, and not I; therefore speak what thou knowest.

אַנְשֵׁי לֵבָב, יֹאמְרוּ לִי; וְגֶבֶר חָכָם, שֹׁמֵעַ לִי
'anshei levov yomeru li; vegever chacham, shomea li
Men of understanding will say unto me, yea, every wise man that heareth me:

אִיּוֹב, לֹא-בְדַעַת יְדַבֵּר; וּדְבָרָיו, לֹא בְהַשְׂכֵּיל
'iyov lo-veda'at yedabber; udevarav, lo vehaskeil
'Job speaketh without knowledge, and his words are without discernment.'

אָבִי--יִבָּחֵן אִיּוֹב עַד-נֶצַח: עַל-תְּשֻׁבֹת, בְּאַנְשֵׁי-אָוֶן
'avi, yibbachen iyov ad-netzach; al-teshuvot, be'anshei-'aven
Would that Job were tried unto the end, because of his answering like wicked men.

כִּי יֹסִיף עַל-חַטָּאתוֹ פֶשַׁע, בֵּינֵינוּ יִשְׂפּוֹק; וְיֶרֶב אֲמָרָיו לָאֵל
ki yosif al-chattato fesha beineinu yispok; veyerev amarav la'el
For he addeth rebellion unto his sin, he clappeth his hands among us, and multiplieth his words against God.

לה

וַיַּעַן אֱלִיהוּ, וַיֹּאמַר
Vaya'an elihu, vayomar
Moreover Elihu answered and said:

הֲזֹאת, חָשַׁבְתָּ לְמִשְׁפָּט; אָמַרְתָּ, צִדְקִי מֵאֵל
hazot chashavta lemishpat; amarta, tzidki me'el
Thinkest thou this to be thy right, or sayest thou: 'I am righteousness before God',

כִּי-תֹאמַר, מַה-יִּסְכָּן-לָךְ; מָה-אֹעִיל, מֵחַטָּאתִי
ki-tomar mah-yiskan-lach; mah-'o'il, mechattati
That thou inquirest: 'What advantage will it be unto Thee?' And: 'What profit shall I have, more than if I had sinned?'

אִיּוֹב

וְיָסִירוּ אַבִּיר, לֹא בְיָד
veyasiru abbir, lo veyad
and the mighty are taken away without hand.

כִּי-עֵינָיו, עַל-דַּרְכֵי-אִישׁ; וְכָל-צְעָדָיו יִרְאֶה
ki-'einav al-darchei-'ish; vechol-tze'adav yir'eh
For His eyes are upon the ways of a man, and He seeth all his goings.

אֵין-חֹשֶׁךְ, וְאֵין צַלְמָוֶת--לְהִסָּתֶר שָׁם, פֹּעֲלֵי אָוֶן
'ein-choshech ve'ein tzalmavet; lehissater sham, po'alei aven
There is no darkness, nor shadow of death, where the workers of iniquity may hide themselves.

כִּי לֹא עַל-אִישׁ, יָשִׂים עוֹד--לַהֲלֹךְ אֶל-אֵל, בַּמִּשְׁפָּט
ki lo al-'ish yasim od; lahaloch el-'el, bammishpat
For He doth not appoint a time unto any man, when he should go before God in judgment.

יָרֹעַ כַּבִּירִים לֹא-חֵקֶר; וַיַּעֲמֵד אֲחֵרִים תַּחְתָּם
yaroa kabbirim lo-cheker; vaya'amed acherim tachtam
He breaketh in pieces mighty men without inquisition, and setteth others in their stead.

לָכֵן--יַכִּיר, מַעְבָּדֵיהֶם; וְהָפַךְ לַיְלָה, וְיִדַּכָּאוּ
lachen, yakkir ma'badeihem; vehafach laylah, veyiddakka'u
Therefore He taketh knowledge of their works; and He overturneth them in the night, so that they are crushed.

תַּחַת-רְשָׁעִים סְפָקָם--בִּמְקוֹם רֹאִים
tachat-resha'im sefakam, bimkom ro'im
He striketh them as wicked men in the open sight of others;

אֲשֶׁר עַל-כֵּן, סָרוּ מֵאַחֲרָיו; וְכָל-דְּרָכָיו, לֹא הִשְׂכִּילוּ
'asher al-ken saru me'acharav; vechol-derachav, lo hiskilu
Because they turned aside from following Him, and would not have regard to any of His ways;

לְהָבִיא עָלָיו, צַעֲקַת-דָּל; וְצַעֲקַת עֲנִיִּים יִשְׁמָע
lehavi alav tza'akat-dal; vetza'akat aniyim yishma
So that they cause the cry of the poor to come unto Him, and He heareth the cry of the afflicted.

וְהוּא יַשְׁקִט, וּמִי יַרְשִׁעַ--וְיַסְתֵּר פָּנִים, וּמִי יְשׁוּרֶנּוּ
vehu yashkit umi yarshia', veyaster panim
When He giveth quietness, who then can condemn? And when He hideth His face,

וְעַל-גּוֹי וְעַל-אָדָם יָחַד
umi yeshurennu; ve'al-goy ve'al-'adam yachad
who then can behold Him? whether it be done unto a nation, or unto a man, alike;

מִמְּלֹךְ, אָדָם חָנֵף--מִמֹּקְשֵׁי עָם
mimmeloch adam chanef, mimmokeshei am
That the godless man reign not, that there be none to ensnare the people.

אִיּוֹב

וְשַׁדַּי מֵעָוֶל
veshaddai me'avel
and from the Almighty, that He should commit iniquity.

כִּי פֹעַל אָדָם, יְשַׁלֶּם-לוֹ; וּכְאֹרַח אִישׁ, יַמְצִאֶנּוּ
ki fo'al adom yeshallem-lo; uche'orach ish, yamtzi'ennu
For the work of a man will He requite unto him, and cause every man to find according to his ways.

אַף-אָמְנָם, אֵל לֹא-יַרְשִׁיעַ; וְשַׁדַּי, לֹא-יְעַוֵּת מִשְׁפָּט
'af-'amenam, el lo-yarshia'; veshaddai, lo-ye'avvet mishpat
Yea, of a surety, God will not do wickedly, neither will the Almighty pervert justice.

מִי-פָקַד עָלָיו אָרְצָה; וּמִי שָׂם, תֵּבֵל כֻּלָּהּ
mi-fakad alav aretzah; umi sam, tevel kullah
Who gave Him a charge over the earth? Or who hath disposed the whole world?

אִם-יָשִׂים אֵלָיו לִבּוֹ; רוּחוֹ וְנִשְׁמָתוֹ, אֵלָיו יֶאֱסֹף
'im-yasim elav libbo; rucho venishmato, elav ye'esof
If He set His heart upon man, if He gather unto Himself his spirit and his breath;

יִגְוַע כָּל-בָּשָׂר יָחַד; וְאָדָם, עַל-עָפָר יָשׁוּב
yigva kol-basar yachad; ve'adam, al-'afar yashuv
All flesh shall perish together, and man shall return unto dust.

וְאִם-בִּינָה, שִׁמְעָה-זֹּאת; הַאֲזִינָה, לְקוֹל מִלָּי
ve'im-binah shim'ah-zot; ha'azinah, lekol millai
If now thou hast understanding, hear this; hearken to the voice of my words.

הַאַף שׂוֹנֵא מִשְׁפָּט יַחֲבוֹשׁ; וְאִם-צַדִּיק כַּבִּיר תַּרְשִׁיעַ
ha'af sonei mishpat yachavosh; ve'im-tzaddik kabbir tarshia
Shall even one that hateth right govern? And wilt thou condemn Him that is just and mighty--

הַאֲמֹר לְמֶלֶךְ בְּלִיָּעַל-- רָשָׁע, אֶל-נְדִיבִים
ha'amor lemelech beliya'al; rasha', el-nedivim
Is it fit to say to a king: 'Thou art base'? Or to nobles: 'Ye are wicked'?--

אֲשֶׁר לֹא-נָשָׂא, פְּנֵי שָׂרִים, וְלֹא נִכַּר-שׁוֹעַ, לִפְנֵי-דָל
'asher lo-nasa penei sarim, velo nikkar-shoa lifnei-dal
That respecteth not the persons of princes, nor regardeth the rich more than the poor?

כִּי-מַעֲשֵׂה יָדָיו כֻּלָּם
ki-ma'aseh yadav kullam
For they all are the work of His hands.

רֶגַע, יָמֻתוּ-- וַחֲצוֹת לָיְלָה: יְגֹעֲשׁוּ עָם וְיַעֲבֹרוּ
rega yamutu vachatzot laylah yego'ashu am veya'avoru
In a moment they die, even at midnight; the people are shaken and pass away,

איוב

אִם-אַיִן אַתָּה שְׁמַע-לִי; הַחֲרֵשׁ, וַאֲאַלֶּפְךָ חָכְמָה
'im-'ayin attah shema'-li; hacharesh, va'a'allefcha chochmah
If not, hearken thou unto me; hold thy peace, and I will teach thee wisdom.

לד

וַיַּעַן אֱלִיהוּא, וַיֹּאמַר
Vaya'an elihu, vayomar
Moreover Elihu answered and said:

שִׁמְעוּ חֲכָמִים מִלָּי; וְיֹדְעִים, הַאֲזִינוּ לִי
shim'u chachamim millai; veyode'im, ha'azinu li
Hear my words, ye wise men; and give ear unto me, ye that have knowledge.

כִּי-אֹזֶן, מִלִּין תִּבְחָן; וְחֵךְ, יִטְעַם לֶאֱכֹל
ki-'ozen millin tivchan; vechech, yit'am le'echol
For the ear trieth words, as the palate tasteth food.

מִשְׁפָּט נִבְחֲרָה-לָּנוּ; נֵדְעָה בֵינֵינוּ מַה-טּוֹב
mishpat nivcharah-lanu; nede'ah veineinu mah-tov
Let us choose for us that which is right; let us know among ourselves what is good.

כִּי-אָמַר אִיּוֹב צָדַקְתִּי; וְאֵל, הֵסִיר מִשְׁפָּטִי
ki-'amar iyov tzadakti; ve'el, hesir mishpati
For Job hath said: 'I am righteous, and God hath taken away my right;

עַל-מִשְׁפָּטִי אֲכַזֵּב; אָנוּשׁ חִצִּי בְלִי-פָשַׁע
'al-mishpati achazzev; anush chitzi veli-fasha
Notwithstanding my right I am accounted a liar; my wound is incurable, though I am without transgression.'

מִי-גֶבֶר כְּאִיּוֹב; יִשְׁתֶּה-לַּעַג כַּמָּיִם
mi-gever ke'iyov; yishteh-la'ag kammayim
What man is like Job, who drinketh up scorning like water?

וְאָרַח לְחֶבְרָה, עִם-פֹּעֲלֵי אָוֶן; וְלָלֶכֶת, עִם-אַנְשֵׁי-רֶשַׁע
ve'arach lechevrah im-po'alei aven; velalechet, im-'anshei-resha
Who goeth in company with the workers of iniquity, and walketh with wicked men.

כִּי-אָמַר, לֹא יִסְכָּן-גָּבֶר--בִּרְצֹתוֹ, עִם-אֱלֹהִים
ki-'amar lo yiskon-gaver; birtzoto, im-'elohim
For he hath said: 'It profiteth a man nothing that he should be in accord with God.'

לָכֵן, אַנְשֵׁי לֵבָב--שִׁמְעוּ-לִי: חָלִלָה לָאֵל מֵרֶשַׁע
lachen anashei levav, shim'u li chalilah la'el meresha'
Therefore hearken unto me, ye men of understanding: Far be it from God, that He should do wickedness;

אִיּוֹב

וַתִּקְרַב לַשַּׁחַת נַפְשׁוֹ; וְחַיָּתוֹ, לַמְמִתִים
vattikrav lashachat nafsho; vechayato, lamemitim
Yea, his soul draweth near unto the pit, and his life to the destroyers.

אִם-יֵשׁ עָלָיו, מַלְאָךְ--מֵלִיץ, אֶחָד מִנִּי-אָלֶף: לְהַגִּיד לְאָדָם יָשְׁרוֹ
'im-yesh alav mal'ach, melitz, echad minni-'alef; lehaggid le'adam yoshero
If there be for him an angel, an intercessor, one among a thousand, to vouch for a man's uprightness;

וַיְחֻנֶּנּוּ--וַיֹּאמֶר, פְּדָעֵהוּ מֵרֶדֶת שָׁחַת; מָצָאתִי כֹפֶר
vaychunnennu, vayomer, peda'ehu meredet shachat, matzati chofer
Then He is gracious unto him, and saith: 'Deliver him from going down to the pit, I have found a ransom.'

רֻטֲפַשׁ בְּשָׂרוֹ מִנֹּעַר; יָשׁוּב, לִימֵי עֲלוּמָיו
rutafash besaro minno'ar; yashuv, liymei alumav
His flesh is tenderer than a child's; he returneth to the days of his youth;

יֶעְתַּר אֶל-אֱלוֹהַּ, וַיִּרְצֵהוּ, וַיַּרְא פָּנָיו, בִּתְרוּעָה
ye'tar el-'eloah vayirtzehu, vayar panav bitru'ah
He prayeth unto God, and He is favourable unto him; so that he seeth His face with joy;

וַיָּשֶׁב לֶאֱנוֹשׁ, צִדְקָתוֹ
vayashev le'enosh, tzidkato
and He restoreth unto man his righteousness.

יָשֹׁר, עַל-אֲנָשִׁים, וַיֹּאמֶר, חָטָאתִי וְיָשָׁר הֶעֱוֵיתִי; וְלֹא-שָׁוָה לִי
yashor al-'anashim, vayomer, chatati veyashar he'eveiti, velo-shavah li
He cometh before men, and saith: 'I have sinned, and perverted that which was right, and it profited me not.'

פָּדָה נַפְשׁוֹ, מֵעֲבֹר בַּשָּׁחַת; וְחַיָּתוֹ, בָּאוֹר תִּרְאֶה
padah nafsho me'avor bashachat; vechayato ba'or tir'eh
So He redeemeth his soul from going into the pit, and his life beholdeth the light.

הֶן-כָּל-אֵלֶּה, יִפְעַל-אֵל-- פַּעֲמַיִם שָׁלוֹשׁ עִם-גָּבֶר
hen-kol-'elleh yif'al-'el; pa'amayim shalosh im-gaver
Lo, all these things doth God work, twice, yea thrice, with a man,

לְהָשִׁיב נַפְשׁוֹ, מִנִּי-שָׁחַת--לֵאוֹר, בְּאוֹר הַחַיִּים
lehashiv nafsho minni-shachat; le'or, be'or hachayim
To bring back his soul from the pit, that he may be enlightened with the light of the living.

הַקְשֵׁב אִיּוֹב שְׁמַע-לִי; הַחֲרֵשׁ, וְאָנֹכִי אֲדַבֵּר
hakshev iyov shema'-li; hacharesh, ve'anochi adabber
Mark well, O Job, hearken unto me; hold thy peace, and I will speak.

אִם-יֵשׁ-מִלִּין הֲשִׁיבֵנִי; דַּבֵּר, כִּי-חָפַצְתִּי צַדְּקֶךָּ
'im-yesh-millin hashiveni; dabber, ki-chafatzti tzaddekeka
If thou hast any thing to say, answer me; speak, for I desire to justify thee.

אִיּוֹב

הֵן תְּנוּאוֹת, עָלַי יִמְצָא; יַחְשְׁבֵנִי לְאוֹיֵב לוֹ
hen tenu'ot alai yimtza; yachsheveni le'oyev lo
Behold, He findeth occasions against me, He counteth me for His enemy;

יָשֵׂם בַּסַּד רַגְלָי; יִשְׁמֹר, כָּל-אָרְחֹתָי
yasem bassad raglai; yishmor, kol-'orchotai
He putteth my feet in the stocks, He marketh all my paths.'

הֶן-זֹאת לֹא-צָדַקְתָּ אֱעֱנֶךָּ: כִּי-יִרְבֶּה אֱלוֹהַּ, מֵאֱנוֹשׁ
hen-zot lo-tzadakta e'eneka; ki-yirbeh eloha, me'enosh
Behold, I answer thee: In this thou art not right, that God is too great for man;

מַדּוּעַ, אֵלָיו רִיבוֹתָ: כִּי כָל-דְּבָרָיו, לֹא יַעֲנֶה
maddua elav rivota; ki chol-devarav, lo-ya'aneh
Why hast thou striven against Him? seeing that He will not answer any of his words.

כִּי-בְאַחַת יְדַבֶּר-אֵל; וּבִשְׁתַּיִם, לֹא יְשׁוּרֶנָּה
ki-ve'achat yedabber-'el; uvishtayim, lo yeshurennah
For God speaketh in one way, yea in two, though man perceiveth it not.

בַּחֲלוֹם, חֶזְיוֹן לַיְלָה--בִּנְפֹל תַּרְדֵּמָה, עַל-אֲנָשִׁים; בִּתְנוּמוֹת, עֲלֵי מִשְׁכָּב
bachalom chezyon laylah, binfol tardemah al-'anashim; bitnumot, alei mishkav
In a dream, in a vision of the night, when deep sleep falleth upon men, in slumberings upon the bed;

אָז יִגְלֶה, אֹזֶן אֲנָשִׁים; וּבְמֹסָרָם יַחְתֹּם
'az yigleh ozen anashim; uvemosaram yachtom
Then He openeth the ears of men, and by their chastisement sealeth the decree,

לְהָסִיר, אָדָם מַעֲשֶׂה; וְגֵוָה מִגֶּבֶר יְכַסֶּה
lehasir adam ma'aseh; vegevah miggever yechasseh
That men may put away their purpose, and that He may hide pride from man;

יַחְשֹׂךְ נַפְשׁוֹ, מִנִּי-שָׁחַת; וְחַיָּתוֹ, מֵעֲבֹר בַּשָּׁלַח
yachsoch nafsho minni-shachat; vechayato, me'avor bashalach
That He may keep back his soul from the pit, and his life from perishing by the sword.

וְהוּכַח בְּמַכְאוֹב, עַל-מִשְׁכָּבוֹ; וְרֹב עֲצָמָיו אֵתָן
vehuchach bemach'ov al-mishkavo; verov atzamav etan
He is chastened also with pain upon his bed, and all his bones grow stiff;

וְזִהֲמַתּוּ חַיָּתוֹ לָחֶם; וְנַפְשׁוֹ, מַאֲכַל תַּאֲוָה
vezihamattu chayato lachem; venafsho, ma'achal ta'avah
So that his life maketh him to abhor bread, and his soul dainty food.

יִכֶל בְּשָׂרוֹ מֵרֹאִי; וְשֻׁפּוּ עַצְמֹתָיו, לֹא רֻאּוּ
yichel besaro mero'i; veshuppu atzmotav, lo ru'u
His flesh is consumed away, that it cannot be seen; and his bones corrode to unsightliness.

אִיּוֹב

אַל-נָא, אֶשָּׂא פְנֵי-אִישׁ; וְאֶל-אָדָם, לֹא אֲכַנֶּה
'al-na essa fenei-'ish; ve'el-'adam, lo achanneh
Let me not, I pray you, respect any man's person; neither will I give flattering titles unto any man.

כִּי לֹא יָדַעְתִּי אֲכַנֶּה; כִּמְעַט, יִשָּׂאֵנִי עֹשֵׂנִי
ki lo yada'ti achanneh; kim'at, yissa'eni oseni
For I know not to give flattering titles; else would my Maker soon take me away.

לג

וְאוּלָם--שְׁמַע-נָא אִיּוֹב מִלָּי; וְכָל-דְּבָרַי הַאֲזִינָה
Ve'olam--shema'-na iyov millai; vechol-devarai ha'azinah
Howbeit, Job, I pray thee, hear my speech, and hearken to all my words.

הִנֵּה-נָא, פָּתַחְתִּי פִי; דִּבְּרָה לְשׁוֹנִי בְחִכִּי
hinneh-na patachti fi; dibberah leshoni vechikki
Behold now, I have opened my mouth, my tongue hath spoken in my mouth.

יֹשֶׁר-לִבִּי אֲמָרָי; וְדַעַת שְׂפָתַי, בָּרוּר מִלֵּלוּ
yosher-libbi amarai; veda'at sefatai, barur millelu
My words shall utter the uprightness of my heart; and that which my lips know they shall speak sincerely.

רוּחַ-אֵל עָשָׂתְנִי; וְנִשְׁמַת שַׁדַּי תְּחַיֵּנִי
ruach-'el asateni; venishmat shaddai techayeni
The spirit of God hath made me, and the breath of the Almighty given me life.

אִם-תּוּכַל הֲשִׁיבֵנִי; עֶרְכָה לְפָנַי, הִתְיַצָּבָה
'im-tuchal hashiveni; erchah lefanai, hityatzavah
If thou canst, answer thou me, set thy words in order before me, stand forth.

הֵן-אֲנִי כְפִיךָ לָאֵל; מֵחֹמֶר, קֹרַצְתִּי גַם-אָנִי
hen-'ani cheficha la'el; mechomer, koratzti gam-'ani
Behold, I am toward God even as thou art; I also am formed out of the clay.

הִנֵּה אֵמָתִי, לֹא תְבַעֲתֶךָּ; וְאַכְפִּי, עָלֶיךָ לֹא-יִכְבָּד
hinneh emati lo teva'ateka; ve'achpi, aleicha lo-yichbad
Behold, my terror shall not make thee afraid, neither shall my pressure be heavy upon thee.

אַךְ, אָמַרְתָּ בְאָזְנָי; וְקוֹל מִלִּין אֶשְׁמָע
'ach amarta ve'ozenai; vekol millin eshma
Surely thou hast spoken in my hearing, and I have heard the voice of thy words;

זַךְ אֲנִי, בְּלִי-פָשַׁע: חַף אָנֹכִי; וְלֹא עָוֺן לִי
zach ani, beli fasha chaf anochi; velo avon li
'I am clean, without transgression, I am innocent, neither is there iniquity in me;

אִיּוֹב

לֹא-רַבִּים יֶחְכָּמוּ; וּזְקֵנִים, יָבִינוּ מִשְׁפָּט
lo-rabbim yechkamu; uzekenim, yavinu mishpat
It is not the great that are wise, nor the aged that discern judgment.

לָכֵן אָמַרְתִּי, שִׁמְעָה-לִּי; אֲחַוֶּה דֵעִי אַף-אָנִי
lachen amarti shim'ah-li; achavveh de'i af-'ani
Therefore I say: 'Hearken to me; I also will declare mine opinion.'

הֵן הוֹחַלְתִּי, לְדִבְרֵיכֶם--אָזִין, עַד-תְּבוּנֹתֵיכֶם: עַד-תַּחְקְרוּן מִלִּין
hen hochalti ledivreichem, azin ad-tevunoteichem; ad-tachkerun millin
Behold, I waited for your words, I listened for your reasons, whilst ye searched out what to say.

וְעָדֵיכֶם, אֶתְבּוֹנָן; וְהִנֵּה אֵין לְאִיּוֹב מוֹכִיחַ--עוֹנֶה אֲמָרָיו מִכֶּם
ve'adeichem, etbonan vehinneh ein le'iyov mochiach; oneh amarav mikkem
Yea, I attended unto you, and, behold, there was none that convinced Job, or that answered his words, among you.

פֶּן-תֹּאמְרוּ, מָצָאנוּ חָכְמָה; אֵל יִדְּפֶנּוּ לֹא-אִישׁ
pen-tomeru matzanu chochmah el yiddefennu lo-'ish
Beware lest ye say: 'We have found wisdom; God may vanquish him, not man!'

וְלֹא-עָרַךְ אֵלַי מִלִּין; וּבְאִמְרֵיכֶם, לֹא אֲשִׁיבֶנּוּ
velo-'arach elai millin; uve'imreichem, lo ashivennu
For he hath not directed his words against me; neither will I answer him with your speeches.

חַתּוּ, לֹא-עָנוּ עוֹד; הֶעְתִּיקוּ מֵהֶם מִלִּים
chattu lo-'anu od; he'tiku mehem millim
They are amazed, they answer no more; words are departed from them.

וְהוֹחַלְתִּי, כִּי-לֹא יְדַבֵּרוּ: כִּי עָמְדוּ, לֹא-עָנוּ עוֹד
vehochalti ki-lo yedabberu; ki amedu, lo-'anu od
And shall I wait, because they speak not, because they stand still, and answer no more?

אַעֲנֶה אַף-אֲנִי חֶלְקִי; אֲחַוֶּה דֵעִי אַף-אָנִי
'a'aneh af-'ani chelki; achavveh de'i af-'ani
I also will answer my part, I also will declare mine opinion.

כִּי, מָלֵתִי מִלִּים; הֱצִיקַתְנִי, רוּחַ בִּטְנִי
ki maleti millim; hetzikatni, ruach bitni
For I am full of words; the spirit within me constraineth me.

הִנֵּה-בִטְנִי--כְּיַיִן לֹא-יִפָּתֵחַ; כְּאֹבוֹת חֲדָשִׁים, יִבָּקֵעַ
hinneh-vitni, keyayin lo-yippateach; ke'ovot chadashim, yibbakea
Behold, mine inwards are as wine which hath no vent; like new wine-skins which are ready to burst.

אֲדַבְּרָה וְיִרְוַח-לִי; אֶפְתַּח שְׂפָתַי וְאֶעֱנֶה
'adabberah veyirvach-li; eftach sefatai ve'e'eneh
I will speak, that I may find relief; I will open my lips and answer.

אִיּוֹב

תַּחַת חִטָּה, יֵצֵא חוֹחַ--וְתַחַת-שְׂעֹרָה בָאְשָׁה: תַּמּוּ, דִּבְרֵי אִיּוֹב
tachat chittah yetzei choach, vetachat-se'orah vo'eshah; tammu, divrei iyov
Let thistles grow instead of wheat, and noisome weeds instead of barley. The words of Job are ended.

לב

וַיִּשְׁבְּתוּ, שְׁלֹשֶׁת הָאֲנָשִׁים הָאֵלֶּה--מֵעֲנוֹת אֶת-אִיּוֹב: כִּי הוּא צַדִּיק בְּעֵינָיו
Vayishbetu sheloshet ha'anashim ha'elleh me'anot et-'iyov; ki hu tzaddik be'einav
So these three men ceased to answer Job, because he was righteous in his own eyes.

וַיִּחַר אַף, אֱלִיהוּא בֶן-בַּרַכְאֵל הַבּוּזִי מִמִּשְׁפַּחַת-רָם
vayichar af elihu ven-barach'el habbuzi mimmishpachat ram
Then was kindled the wrath of Elihu the son of Barachel the Buzite, of the family of Ram;

בְּאִיּוֹב, חָרָה אַפּוֹ--עַל-צַדְּקוֹ נַפְשׁוֹ, מֵאֱלֹהִים
be'iyov charah appo; al-tzaddeko nafsho, me'elohim
against Job was his wrath kindled, because he justified himself rather than God.

וּבִשְׁלֹשֶׁת רֵעָיו, חָרָה אַפּוֹ: עַל אֲשֶׁר לֹא-מָצְאוּ מַעֲנֶה-- וַיַּרְשִׁיעוּ, אֶת-אִיּוֹב
uvishloshet re'av charah appo al asher lo-matze'u ma'aneh; vayarshi'u, et-'iyov
Also against his three friends was his wrath kindled, because they had found no answer, and yet had condemned Job.

וֶאֱלִיהוּ--חִכָּה אֶת-אִיּוֹב, בִּדְבָרִים: כִּי זְקֵנִים-הֵמָּה מִמֶּנּוּ לְיָמִים
ve'elihu, chikkah et-'iyov bidvarim; ki zekenim-hemmah mimmennu leyamim
Now Elihu had waited to speak unto Job, because they were older than he.

וַיַּרְא אֱלִיהוּא--כִּי אֵין מַעֲנֶה, בְּפִי שְׁלֹשֶׁת הָאֲנָשִׁים; וַיִּחַר אַפּוֹ
vayar elihu, ki ein ma'aneh, befi sheloshet ha'anashim, vayichar appo
And when Elihu saw that there was no answer in the mouth of these three men, his wrath was kindled.

וַיַּעַן, אֱלִיהוּא בֶן-בַּרַכְאֵל הַבּוּזִי--וַיֹּאמַר: צָעִיר אֲנִי לְיָמִים, וְאַתֶּם יְשִׁישִׁים
vaya'an elihu ven-barach'el habbuzi, vayomar tza'ir ani leyamim ve'attem yeshishim
And Elihu the son of Barachel the Buzite answered and said: I am young, and ye are very old;

עַל-כֵּן זָחַלְתִּי וָאִירָא, מֵחַוֺּת דֵּעִי אֶתְכֶם
al-ken zachalti va'ira mechavot de'i etchem
wherefore I held back, and durst not declare you mine opinion.

אָמַרְתִּי, יָמִים יְדַבֵּרוּ; וְרֹב שָׁנִים, יֹדִיעוּ חָכְמָה
'amarti yamim yedabberu; verov shanim, yodi'u chochmah
I said: 'Days should speak, and multitude of years should teach wisdom.'

אָכֵן, רוּחַ-הִיא בֶאֱנוֹשׁ; וְנִשְׁמַת שַׁדַּי תְּבִינֵם
'achen ruach-hi ve'enosh; venishmat shaddai tevinem
But it is a spirit in man, and the breath of the Almighty, that giveth them understanding.

אִיּוֹב

וְלֹא-נָתַתִּי לַחֲטֹא חִכִּי--לִשְׁאֹל בְּאָלָה נַפְשׁוֹ
velo-natatti lachato chikki; lish'ol be'alah nafsho
Yea, I suffered not my mouth to sin by asking his life with a curse.

אִם-לֹא אָמְרוּ, מְתֵי אָהֳלִי; מִי-יִתֵּן מִבְּשָׂרוֹ, לֹא נִשְׂבָּע
'im-lo ameru metei oholi; mi-yitten mibbesaro, lo nisba
If the men of my tent said not: 'Who can find one that hath not been satisfied with his meat?'

בַּחוּץ, לֹא-יָלִין גֵּר; דְּלָתַי, לָאֹרַח אֶפְתָּח
bachutz lo-yalin ger; delatai, la'orach eftach
The stranger did not lodge in the street; my doors I opened to the roadside.

אִם-כִּסִּיתִי כְאָדָם פְּשָׁעָי--לִטְמוֹן בְּחֻבִּי עֲוֹנִי
'im-kissiti che'adam pesha'ai; litmon bechubbi avoni
If after the manner of men I covered my transgressions, by hiding mine iniquity in my bosom--

כִּי אֶעֱרוֹץ, הָמוֹן רַבָּה--וּבוּז-מִשְׁפָּחוֹת יְחִתֵּנִי
ki e'erotz hamon rabbah, uvuz-mishpachot yechitteni
Because I feared the great multitude, and the most contemptible among families terrified me,

וָאֶדֹּם, לֹא-אֵצֵא פָתַח
va'eddom, lo-'etzei fatach
so that I kept silence, and went not out of the door.

מִי יִתֶּן-לִי, שֹׁמֵעַ לִי--הֶן-תָּוִי, שַׁדַּי יַעֲנֵנִי
mi yitten-li shomea li, hen-tavi shaddai ya'aneni
Oh that I had one to hear me!--Lo, here is my signature, let the Almighty answer me--

וְסֵפֶר כָּתַב, אִישׁ רִיבִי
vesefer katav, ish rivi
and that I had the indictment which mine adversary hath written!

אִם-לֹא עַל-שִׁכְמִי, אֶשָּׂאֶנּוּ; אֶעֶנְדֶנּוּ עֲטָרוֹת לִי
'im-lo al-shichmi essa'ennu; e'endennu atarot li
Surely I would carry it upon my shoulder; I would bind it unto me as a crown.

מִסְפַּר צְעָדַי, אַגִּידֶנּוּ; כְּמוֹ-נָגִיד, אֲקָרְבֶנּוּ
mispar tze'adai aggidennu; kemo-nagid, akaravennu
I would declare unto him the number of my steps; as a prince would I go near unto him.

אִם-עָלַי, אַדְמָתִי תִזְעָק; וְיַחַד, תְּלָמֶיהָ יִבְכָּיוּן
'im-'alai admati tiz'ak; veyachad, telameiha yivkayun
If my land cry out against me, and the furrows thereof weep together;

אִם-כֹּחָהּ, אָכַלְתִּי בְלִי-כָסֶף; וְנֶפֶשׁ בְּעָלֶיהָ הִפָּחְתִּי
'im-kochah achalti veli-chasef; venefesh be'aleiha hippachti
If I have eaten the fruits thereof without money, or have caused the tillers thereof to be disappointed--

אִיּוֹב

כִּי מִנְּעוּרַי, גְּדֵלַנִי כְאָב; וּמִבֶּטֶן אִמִּי אַנְחֶנָּה
ki minne'urai gedelani che'av; umibbeten immi anchennah
Nay, from my youth he grew up with me as with a father, and I have been her guide from my mother's womb.

אִם-אֶרְאֶה אוֹבֵד, מִבְּלִי לְבוּשׁ; וְאֵין כְּסוּת, לָאֶבְיוֹן
'im-'er'eh oved mibbeli levush; ve'ein kesut, la'evyon
If I have seen any wanderer in want of clothing, or that the needy had no covering;

אִם-לֹא בֵרְכוּנִי חֲלָצָו; וּמִגֵּז כְּבָשַׂי, יִתְחַמָּם
'im-lo verachuni chalatzav chalatzav; umiggez kevasai yitchammam
If his loins have not blessed me, and if he were not warmed with the fleece of my sheep;

אִם-הֲנִיפוֹתִי עַל-יָתוֹם יָדִי: כִּי-אֶרְאֶה בַשַּׁעַר, עֶזְרָתִי
'im-hanifoti al-yatom yadi; ki-'er'eh vasha'ar, ezrati
If I have lifted up my hand against the fatherless, because I saw my help in the gate;

כְּתֵפִי, מִשִּׁכְמָה תִפּוֹל; וְאֶזְרֹעִי, מִקָּנֶה תִשָּׁבֵר
ketefi mishichmah tippol; ve'ezro'i, mikkanah tishaver
Then let my shoulder fall from the shoulder-blade, and mine arm be broken from the bone.

כִּי פַחַד אֵלַי, אֵיד אֵל; וּמִשְּׂאֵתוֹ, לֹא אוּכָל
ki fachad elai eid el; umisse'eto, lo uchal
For calamity from God was a terror to me, and by reason of His majesty I could do nothing.

אִם-שַׂמְתִּי זָהָב כִּסְלִי; וְלַכֶּתֶם, אָמַרְתִּי מִבְטַחִי
'im-samti zahav kisli; velakketem, amarti mivtachi
If I have made gold my hope, and have said to the fine gold: 'Thou art my confidence';

אִם-אֶשְׂמַח, כִּי-רַב חֵילִי; וְכִי-כַבִּיר, מָצְאָה יָדִי
'im-'esmach ki-rav cheili; vechi-chabbir, matze'ah yadi
If I rejoiced because my wealth was great, and because my hand had gotten much;

אִם-אֶרְאֶה אוֹר, כִּי יָהֵל; וְיָרֵחַ, יָקָר הֹלֵךְ
'im-'er'eh or ki yahel; veyareach, yakar holech
If I beheld the sun when it shined, or the moon walking in brightness;

וַיִּפְתְּ בַּסֵּתֶר לִבִּי; וַתִּשַּׁק יָדִי לְפִי
vayift basseter libbi; vattishak yadi lefi
And my heart hath been secretly enticed, and my mouth hath kissed my hand;

גַּם-הוּא, עָו‍ֹן פְּלִילִי: כִּי-כִחַשְׁתִּי לָאֵל מִמָּעַל
gam-hu avon pelili; ki-chichashti la'el mimma'al
This also were an iniquity to be punished by the judges; for I should have lied to God that is above.

אִם-אֶשְׂמַח, בְּפִיד מְשַׂנְאִי; וְהִתְעֹרַרְתִּי, כִּי-מְצָאוֹ רָע
'im-'esmach befid mesan'i; vehit'orarti, ki-metza'o ra
If I rejoiced at the destruction of him that hated me, or exulted when evil found him—

אִיּוֹב

אִם תִּטֶּה אֲשֻׁרִי, מִנִּי הַדָּרֶךְ: וְאַחַר עֵינַי, הָלַךְ לִבִּי
'im titteh ashuri minni haddarech ve'achar einai halach libbi
If my step hath turned out of the way, and my heart walked after mine eyes,

וּבְכַפַּי, דָּבַק מאוּם
uvechappai, davak mu'um
and if any spot hath cleaved to my hands;

אֶזְרְעָה, וְאַחֵר יֹאכֵל; וְצֶאֱצָאַי יְשֹׁרָשׁוּ
'ezre'ah ve'acher yochel; vetze'etza'ai yeshorashu
Then let me sow, and let another eat; yea, let the produce of my field be rooted out.

אִם-נִפְתָּה לִבִּי, עַל-אִשָּׁה; וְעַל-פֶּתַח רֵעִי אָרָבְתִּי
'im-niftah libbi al-'ishah; ve'al-petach re'i araveti
If my heart have been enticed unto a woman, and I have lain in wait at my neighbour's door;

תִּטְחַן לְאַחֵר אִשְׁתִּי; וְעָלֶיהָ, יִכְרְעוּן אֲחֵרִין
titchan le'acher ishti; ve'aleiha, yichre'un acherin
Then let my wife grind unto another, and let others bow down upon her.

כִּי-הִיא זִמָּה; וְהוּא, עָוֺן פְּלִילִים
ki-hi zimmah; vehu, avon pelilim
For that were a heinous crime; yea, it were an iniquity to be punished by the judges.

כִּי אֵשׁ הִיא, עַד-אֲבַדּוֹן תֹּאכֵל; וּבְכָל-תְּבוּאָתִי תְשָׁרֵשׁ
ki esh hi ad-'avaddon tochel; uvechol-tevu'ati tesharesh
For it is a fire that consumeth unto destruction, and would root out all mine increase.

אִם-אֶמְאַס--מִשְׁפַּט עַבְדִּי, וַאֲמָתִי: בְּרִבָם, עִמָּדִי
'im-'em'as, mishpat avdi va'amati; berivam, immadi
If I did despise the cause of my man-servant, or of my maid-servant, when they contended with me--

וּמָה אֶעֱשֶׂה, כִּי-יָקוּם אֵל; וְכִי-יִפְקֹד, מָה אֲשִׁיבֶנּוּ
umah e'eseh ki-yakum el; vechi-yifkod, mah ashivennu
What then shall I do when God riseth up? And when He remembereth, what shall I answer Him?

הֲלֹא-בַבֶּטֶן, עֹשֵׂנִי עָשָׂהוּ; וַיְכֻנֶנּוּ, בָּרֶחֶם אֶחָד
halo-vabbeten oseni asahu; vayechunennu, barechem echad
Did not He that made me in the womb make him? And did not One fashion us in the womb?

אִם-אֶמְנַע, מֵחֵפֶץ דַּלִּים; וְעֵינֵי אַלְמָנָה אֲכַלֶּה
'im-'emna mechefetz dallim; ve'einei almanah achalleh
If I have withheld aught that the poor desired, or have caused the eyes of the widow to fail;

וְאֹכַל פִּתִּי לְבַדִּי; וְלֹא-אָכַל יָתוֹם מִמֶּנָּה
ve'ochal pitti levaddi; velo-'achal yatom mimmennah
Or have eaten my morsel myself alone, and the fatherless hath not eaten thereof--

אִיּוֹב

מֵעַי רֻתְּחוּ וְלֹא-דָמּוּ; קִדְּמֻנִי יְמֵי-עֹנִי
me'ai ruttechu velo-dammu, kiddemuni yemei-'oni
Mine inwards boil, and rest not; days of affliction are come upon me.

קֹדֵר הִלַּכְתִּי, בְּלֹא חַמָּה; קַמְתִּי בַקָּהָל אֲשַׁוֵּעַ
koder hillachti belo chammah; kamti vakkahal ashavvea
I go mourning without the sun; I stand up in the assembly, and cry for help.

אָח, הָיִיתִי לְתַנִּים; וְרֵעַ, לִבְנוֹת יַעֲנָה
'ach hayiti letannim; verea', livnot ya'anah
I am become a brother to jackals, and a companion to ostriches.

עוֹרִי, שָׁחַר מֵעָלָי; וְעַצְמִי-חָרָה, מִנִּי-חֹרֶב
'ori shachar me'alai; ve'atzmi-charah, minni-chorev
My skin is black, and falleth from me, and my bones are burned with heat.

וַיְהִי לְאֵבֶל, כִּנֹּרִי; וְעֻגָבִי, לְקוֹל בֹּכִים
vayhi le'evel kinnori; ve'ugavi, lekol bochim
Therefore is my harp turned to mourning, and my pipe into the voice of them that weep.

לא

בְּרִית, כָּרַתִּי לְעֵינָי; וּמָה אֶתְבּוֹנֵן, עַל-בְּתוּלָה
Berit karatti le'einai; umah etbonen, al-betulah
I made a covenant with mine eyes; how then should I look upon a maid?

וּמֶה, חֵלֶק אֱלוֹהַּ מִמָּעַל; וְנַחֲלַת שַׁדַּי, מִמְּרֹמִים
umeh chelek eloah mimma'al; venachalat shaddai, mimmeromim
For what would be the portion of God from above, and the heritage of the Almighty from on high?

הֲלֹא-אֵיד לְעַוָּל; וְנֵכֶר, לְפֹעֲלֵי אָוֶן
halo-'eid le'avval; venecher, lefo'alei aven
Is it not calamity to the unrighteous, and disaster to the workers of iniquity?

הֲלֹא-הוּא, יִרְאֶה דְרָכָי; וְכָל-צְעָדַי יִסְפּוֹר
halo-hu yir'eh derachai; vechol-tze'adai yispor
Doth not He see my ways, and count all my steps?

אִם-הָלַכְתִּי עִם-שָׁוְא; וַתַּחַשׁ עַל-מִרְמָה רַגְלִי
'im-halachti im-shav; vattachash al-mirmah ragli
If I have walked with vanity, and my foot hath hasted to deceit--

יִשְׁקְלֵנִי בְמֹאזְנֵי-צֶדֶק; וְיֵדַע אֱלוֹהַּ, תֻּמָּתִי
yishkeleni vemozenei-tzedek; veyeda eloah, tummati
Let me be weighed in a just balance, that God may know mine integrity--

אִיּוֹב

הָהְפַּךְ עָלַי, בַּלָּהוֹת: תִּרְדֹּף כָּרוּחַ, נְדִבָתִי; וּכְעָב, עָבְרָה יְשֻׁעָתִי
hahepach alai, ballahot tirdof karuach nedivati; uche'av, averah yeshu'ati
Terrors are turned upon me, they chase mine honour as the wind; and my welfare is passed away as a cloud.

וְעַתָּה--עָלַי, תִּשְׁתַּפֵּךְ נַפְשִׁי; יֹאחֲזוּנִי יְמֵי-עֹנִי
ve'attah, alai tishtappech nafshi; yochazuni yemei-'oni
And now my soul is poured out within me; days of affliction have taken hold upon me.

לַיְלָה--עֲצָמַי, נִקַּר מֵעָלָי; וְעֹרְקַי, לֹא יִשְׁכָּבוּן
laylah, atzamai nikkar me'alai; ve'orekai, lo yishkavun
In the night my bones are pierced, and fall from me, and my sinews take no rest.

בְּרָב-כֹּחַ, יִתְחַפֵּשׂ לְבוּשִׁי; כְּפִי כֻתָּנְתִּי יַאַזְרֵנִי
berav-koach yitchappes levushi; kefi chuttonti ya'azreni
By the great force [of my disease] is my garment disfigured; it bindeth me about as the collar of my coat.

הֹרָנִי לַחֹמֶר; וָאֶתְמַשֵּׁל, כֶּעָפָר וָאֵפֶר
horani lachomer; va'etmashel, ke'afar va'efer
He hath cast me into the mire, and I am become like dust and ashes.

אֲשַׁוַּע אֵלֶיךָ, וְלֹא תַעֲנֵנִי; עָמַדְתִּי, וַתִּתְבֹּנֶן בִּי
'ashavva eleicha velo ta'aneni; amadti, vattitbonen bi
I cry unto Thee, and Thou dost not answer me; I stand up, and Thou lookest at me.

תֵּהָפֵךְ לְאַכְזָר לִי; בְּעֹצֶם יָדְךָ תִשְׂטְמֵנִי
tehafech le'achzar li; be'otzem yadecha tistemeni
Thou art turned to be cruel to me; with the might of Thy hand Thou hatest me.

תִּשָּׂאֵנִי אֶל-רוּחַ תַּרְכִּיבֵנִי; וּתְמֹגְגֵנִי, תֻּשִׁיָּה
tissa'eni el-ruach tarkiveni; utemogegeni, tushiyah
Thou liftest me up to the wind, Thou causest me to ride upon it; and Thou dissolvest my substance.

כִּי-יָדַעְתִּי, מָוֶת תְּשִׁיבֵנִי; וּבֵית מוֹעֵד לְכָל-חָי
ki-yada'ti mavet teshiveni; uveit mo'ed lechol-chai
For I know that Thou wilt bring me to death, and to the house appointed for all living.

אַךְ לֹא-בְעִי, יִשְׁלַח-יָד; אִם-בְּפִידוֹ, לָהֶן שׁוּעַ
'ach lo-ve'i yishlach-yad; im-befido, lahen shua
Surely none shall put forth his hand to a ruinous heap, neither because of these things shall help come in one's calamity,

אִם-לֹא בָכִיתִי, לִקְשֵׁה-יוֹם; עָגְמָה נַפְשִׁי, לָאֶבְיוֹן
'im-lo vachiti liksheh-yom; agemah nafshi, la'evyon
If I have not wept for him that was in trouble, and if my soul grieved not for the needy.

כִּי טוֹב קִוִּיתִי, וַיָּבֹא רָע; וַאֲיַחֲלָה לְאוֹר, וַיָּבֹא אֹפֶל
ki tov kivviti vayavo ra'; va'ayachalah le'or, vayavo ofel
Yet, when I looked for good, there came evil; and when I waited for light, there came darkness.

אִיּוֹב

בְּחֶסֶר וּבְכָפָן, גַּלְמוּד: הַעֹרְקִים צִיָּה--אֶמֶשׁ, שׁוֹאָה וּמְשֹׁאָה
becheser uvechafan, galmud ha'orekim tziyah; emesh, sho'ah umesho'ah
They are gaunt with want and famine; they gnaw the dry ground, in the gloom of wasteness and desolation.

הַקֹּטְפִים מַלּוּחַ עֲלֵי-שִׂיחַ; וְשֹׁרֶשׁ רְתָמִים לַחְמָם
hakkotefim malluach alei-siach; veshoresh retamim lachmam
They pluck salt-wort with wormwood; and the roots of the broom are their food.

מִן-גֵּו יְגֹרָשׁוּ; יָרִיעוּ עָלֵימוֹ, כַּגַּנָּב
min-gev yegorashu; yari'u aleimo, kaggannav
They are driven forth from the midst of men; they cry after them as after a thief.

בַּעֲרוּץ נְחָלִים לִשְׁכֹּן; חֹרֵי עָפָר וְכֵפִים
ba'arutz nechalim lishkon; chorei afar vechefim
In the clefts of the valleys must they dwell, in holes of the earth and of the rocks.

בֵּין-שִׂיחִים יִנְהָקוּ; תַּחַת חָרוּל יְסֻפָּחוּ
bein-sichim yinhaku; tachat charul yesuppachu
Among the bushes they bray; under the nettles they are gathered together.

בְּנֵי-נָבָל, גַּם-בְּנֵי בְלִי-שֵׁם--נִכְּאוּ, מִן-הָאָרֶץ
benei-naval gam-benei veli-shem; nikke'u, min-ha'aretz
They are children of churls, yea, children of ignoble men; they were scourged out of the land.

וְעַתָּה, נְגִינָתָם הָיִיתִי; וָאֱהִי לָהֶם לְמִלָּה
ve'attah neginatam hayiti; va'ehi lahem lemillah
And now I am become their song, yea, I am a byword unto them.

תִּעֲבוּנִי, רָחֲקוּ מֶנִּי; וּמִפָּנַי, לֹא-חָשְׂכוּ רֹק
ti'avuni rachaku menni; umippanai, lo-chasechu rok
They abhor me, they flee far from me, and spare not to spit in my face.

כִּי-יִתְרִי פִתַּח, וַיְעַנֵּנִי; וְרֶסֶן, מִפָּנַי שִׁלֵּחוּ
ki-yitri fittach vay'anneni; veresen, mippanai shillechu
For He hath loosed my cord, and afflicted me, and they have cast off the bridle before me.

עַל-יָמִין, פִּרְחַח יָקוּמוּ: רַגְלַי שִׁלֵּחוּ; וַיָּסֹלּוּ עָלַי, אָרְחוֹת אֵידָם
'al-yamin pirchach yakumu raglai shillechu; vayasollu alai, orechot eidam
Upon my right hand rise the brood; they entangle my feet, and they cast up against me their ways of destruction.

נָתְסוּ, נְתִיבָתִי: לְהַוָּתִי יֹעִילוּ; לֹא עֹזֵר לָמוֹ
natesu, netivati lehavvati yo'ilu; lo ozer lamo
They break up my path, they further my calamity, even men that have no helper.

כְּפֶרֶץ רָחָב יֶאֱתָיוּ; תַּחַת שֹׁאָה, הִתְגַּלְגָּלוּ
keferetz rachav ye'etayu; tachat sho'ah, hitgalgalu
As through a wide breach they come; in the midst of the ruin they roll themselves upon me.

אִיּוֹב

וָאֲשַׁבְּרָה, מְתַלְּעוֹת עַוָּל; וּמִשִּׁנָּיו, אַשְׁלִיךְ טָרֶף
va'ashabberah metalle'ot avval; umishinnav, ashlich taref
And I broke the jaws of the unrighteous, and plucked the prey out of his teeth.

וָאֹמַר, עִם-קִנִּי אֶגְוָע; וְכַחוֹל, אַרְבֶּה יָמִים
va'omar im-kinni egva'; vechachol, arbeh yamim
Then I said: 'I shall die with my nest, and I shall multiply my days as the phoenix;

שָׁרְשִׁי פָתוּחַ אֱלֵי-מָיִם; וְטַל, יָלִין בִּקְצִירִי
shoreshi fatuach elei-mayim; vetal, yalin biktziri
My root shall be spread out to the waters, and the dew shall lie all night upon my branch;

כְּבוֹדִי, חָדָשׁ עִמָּדִי; וְקַשְׁתִּי, בְּיָדִי תַחֲלִיף
kevodi chadash immadi; vekashti, beyadi tachalif
My glory shall be fresh in me, and my bow shall be renewed in my hand.'

לִי-שָׁמְעוּ וְיִחֵלּוּ; וְיִדְּמוּ, לְמוֹ עֲצָתִי
li-shame'u veyichellu; veyiddemu, lemo atzati
Unto me men gave ear, and waited, and kept silence for my counsel.

אַחֲרֵי דְבָרִי, לֹא יִשְׁנוּ; וְעָלֵימוֹ, תִּטֹּף מִלָּתִי
'acharei devari lo yishnu; ve'aleimo, tittof millati
After my words they spoke not again; and my speech dropped upon them.

וְיִחֲלוּ כַמָּטָר לִי; וּפִיהֶם, פָּעֲרוּ לְמַלְקוֹשׁ
veyichalu chammatar li; ufihem, pa'aru lemalkosh
And they waited for me as for the rain; and they opened their mouth wide as for the latter rain.

אֶשְׂחַק אֲלֵהֶם, לֹא יַאֲמִינוּ; וְאוֹר פָּנַי, לֹא יַפִּילוּן
'eschak alehem lo ya'aminu; ve'or panai, lo yappilun
If I laughed on them, they believed it not; and the light of my countenance they cast not down.

אֶבְחַר דַּרְכָּם, וְאֵשֵׁב רֹאשׁ: וְאֶשְׁכּוֹן, כְּמֶלֶךְ בַּגְּדוּד; כַּאֲשֶׁר אֲבֵלִים יְנַחֵם
'evchar darkam ve'eshev rosh ve'eshkon kemelech baggedud; ka'asher avelim yenachem
I chose out their way, and sat as chief, and dwelt as a king in the army, as one that comforteth the mourners.

ל

וְעַתָּה, שָׂחֲקוּ עָלַי--צְעִירִים מִמֶּנִּי, לְיָמִים: אֲשֶׁר-מָאַסְתִּי אֲבוֹתָם--לָשִׁית, עִם-כַּלְבֵי צֹאנִי
Ve'attah sachaku alai tze'irim mimmenni, leyamim asher-ma'asti avotam; lashit, im-kalvei tzoni
But now they that are younger than I have me in derision, whose fathers I disdained to set with the dogs of my flock.

גַּם-כֹּחַ יְדֵיהֶם, לָמָּה לִּי; עָלֵימוֹ, אָבַד כָּלַח
gam-koach yedeihem lammah li; aleimo, avad kalach
Yea, the strength of their hands, whereto should it profit me? Men in whom ripe age is perished.

איוֹב

בְּעוֹד שַׁדַּי, עִמָּדִי; סְבִיבוֹתַי נְעָרָי
be'od shaddai immadi; sevivotai ne'arai
When the Almighty was yet with me, and my children were about me;

בִּרְחֹץ הֲלִיכַי בְּחֵמָה; וְצוּר יָצוּק עִמָּדִי, פַּלְגֵי-שָׁמֶן
birchotz halichai bechemah; vetzur yatzuk immadi, palgei-shamen
When my steps were washed with butter, and the rock poured me out rivers of oil!

בְּצֵאתִי שַׁעַר עֲלֵי-קָרֶת; בָּרְחוֹב, אָכִין מוֹשָׁבִי
betzeti sha'ar alei-karet; barechov, achin moshavi
When I went forth to the gate unto the city, when I prepared my seat in the broad place,

רָאוּנִי נְעָרִים וְנֶחְבָּאוּ; וִישִׁישִׁים, קָמוּ עָמָדוּ
ra'uni ne'arim venechba'u; vishishim kamu amadu
The young men saw me and hid themselves, and the aged rose up and stood;

שָׂרִים, עָצְרוּ בְמִלִּים; וְכַף, יָשִׂימוּ לְפִיהֶם
sarim atzeru vemillim; vechaf, yasimu lefihem
The princes refrained talking, and laid their hand on their mouth;

קוֹל-נְגִידִים נֶחְבָּאוּ; וּלְשׁוֹנָם, לְחִכָּם דָּבֵקָה
kol-negidim nechba'u; uleshonam, lechikkam davekah
The voice of the nobles was hushed, and their tongue cleaved to the roof of their mouth.

כִּי אֹזֶן שָׁמְעָה, וַתְּאַשְּׁרֵנִי; וְעַיִן רָאֲתָה, וַתְּעִידֵנִי
ki ozen shame'ah vatte'ashreni; ve'ayin ra'atah, vatte'ideni
For when the ear heard me, then it blessed me, and when the eye saw me, it gave witness unto me;

כִּי-אֲמַלֵּט, עָנִי מְשַׁוֵּעַ; וְיָתוֹם, וְלֹא-עֹזֵר לוֹ
ki-'amallet ani meshavvea'; veyatom, velo-'ozer lo
Because I delivered the poor that cried, the fatherless also, that had none to help him.

בִּרְכַּת אֹבֵד, עָלַי תָּבֹא; וְלֵב אַלְמָנָה אַרְנִן
birkat oved alai tavo; velev almanah arnin
The blessing of him that was ready to perish came upon me; and I caused the widow's heart to sing for joy.

צֶדֶק לָבַשְׁתִּי, וַיִּלְבָּשֵׁנִי; כִּמְעִיל וְצָנִיף, מִשְׁפָּטִי
tzedek lavashti vayilbasheni; kim'il vetzanif, mishpati
I put on righteousness, and it clothed itself with me; my justice was as a robe and a diadem.

עֵינַיִם הָיִיתִי, לַעִוֵּר; וְרַגְלַיִם לַפִּסֵּחַ אָנִי
'einayim hayiti la'ivver; veraglayim lappisseach ani
I was eyes to the blind, and feet was I to the lame.

אָב אָנֹכִי, לָאֶבְיוֹנִים; וְרִב לֹא-יָדַעְתִּי אֶחְקְרֵהוּ
'av anochi la'evyonim; veriv lo-yada'ti echkerehu
I was a father to the needy; and the cause of him that I knew not I searched out.

איוב

אֲבַדּוֹן וָמָוֶת, אָמְרוּ; בְּאָזְנֵינוּ, שָׁמַעְנוּ שִׁמְעָהּ
'avaddon vamavet ameru; be'azeneinu, shama'nu shim'ah
Destruction and Death say: 'We have heard a rumor thereof with our ears.'

אֱלֹהִים, הֵבִין דַּרְכָּהּ; וְהוּא, יָדַע אֶת-מְקוֹמָהּ
'elohim hevin darkah; vehu, yada et-mekomah
God understandeth the way thereof, and He knoweth the place thereof.

כִּי-הוּא, לִקְצוֹת-הָאָרֶץ יַבִּיט; תַּחַת כָּל-הַשָּׁמַיִם יִרְאֶה
ki-hu liktzot-ha'aretz yabbit; tachat kol-hashamayim yir'eh
For He looketh to the ends of the earth, and seeth under the whole heaven;

לַעֲשׂוֹת לָרוּחַ מִשְׁקָל; וּמַיִם, תִּכֵּן בְּמִדָּה
la'asot laruach mishkal; umayim, tikken bemiddah
When He maketh a weight for the wind, and meteth out the waters by measure.

בַּעֲשֹׂתוֹ לַמָּטָר חֹק; וְדֶרֶךְ, לַחֲזִיז קֹלוֹת
ba'asoto lammatar chok; vederech, lachaziz kolot
When He made a decree for the rain, and a way for the storm of thunders;

אָז רָאָהּ, וַיְסַפְּרָהּ; הֱכִינָהּ, וְגַם-חֲקָרָהּ
'az ra'ah vaysapperah; hechinah, vegam-chakarah
Then did He see it, and declare it; He established it, yea, and searched it out.

וַיֹּאמֶר, לָאָדָם--הֵן יִרְאַת אֲדֹנָי, הִיא חָכְמָה; וְסוּר מֵרָע בִּינָה
vayomer la'adam, hen yir'at adonai hi chochmah vesur mera binah
And unto man He said: 'Behold, the fear of the Lord, that is wisdom; and to depart from evil is understanding.'

כט

וַיֹּסֶף אִיּוֹב, שְׂאֵת מְשָׁלוֹ; וַיֹּאמַר
Vayosef iyov se'et meshalo, vayomar
And Job again took up his parable, and said:

מִי-יִתְּנֵנִי כְיַרְחֵי-קֶדֶם; כִּימֵי, אֱלוֹהַּ יִשְׁמְרֵנִי
mi-yitteneni cheyarchei-kedem; kimei, eloah yishmereni
Oh that I were as in the months of old, as in the days when God watched over me;

בְּהִלּוֹ נֵרוֹ, עֲלֵי רֹאשִׁי; לְאוֹרוֹ, אֵלֶךְ חֹשֶׁךְ
behillo nero alei roshi; le'oro elech choshech
When His lamp shined above my head, and by His light I walked through darkness;

כַּאֲשֶׁר הָיִיתִי, בִּימֵי חָרְפִּי; בְּסוֹד אֱלוֹהַּ, עֲלֵי אָהֳלִי
ka'asher hayiti bimei chorpi; besod eloah, alei oholi
As I was in the days of my youth, when the converse of God was upon my tent;

אִיּוֹב

בַּצּוּרוֹת, יְאֹרִים בִּקֵּעַ; וְכָל-יְקָר, רָאֲתָה עֵינוֹ
batzurot ye'orim bikkea'; vechol-yekar, ra'atah eino
He cutteth out channels among the rocks; and his eye seeth every precious thing.

מִבְּכִי, נְהָרוֹת חִבֵּשׁ; וְתַעֲלֻמָהּ, יֹצִא אוֹר
mibbechi neharot chibbesh; veta'alumah, yotzi or
He bindeth the streams that they trickle not; and the thing that is hid bringeth he forth to light.

וְהַחָכְמָה, מֵאַיִן תִּמָּצֵא; וְאֵי זֶה, מְקוֹם בִּינָה
vehachochemah me'ayin timmatze; ve'ei zeh mekom binah
But wisdom, where shall it be found? And where is the place of understanding?

לֹא-יָדַע אֱנוֹשׁ עֶרְכָּהּ; וְלֹא תִמָּצֵא, בְּאֶרֶץ הַחַיִּים
lo-yada enosh erkah; velo timmatze, be'eretz hachayim
Man knoweth not the price thereof; neither is it found in the land of the living.

תְּהוֹם אָמַר, לֹא בִי-הִיא; וְיָם אָמַר, אֵין עִמָּדִי
tehom amar lo vi-hi; veyam amar, ein immadi
The deep saith: 'It is not in me'; and the sea saith: 'It is not with me.'

לֹא-יֻתַּן סְגוֹר תַּחְתֶּיהָ; וְלֹא יִשָּׁקֵל, כֶּסֶף מְחִירָהּ
lo-yuttan segor tachteiha; velo yishakel, kesef mechirah
It cannot be gotten for gold, neither shall silver be weighed for the price thereof.

לֹא-תְסֻלֶּה, בְּכֶתֶם אוֹפִיר; בְּשֹׁהַם יָקָר וְסַפִּיר
lo-tesulleh bechetem ofir; beshoham yakar vesappir
It cannot be valued with the gold of Ophir, with the precious onyx, or the sapphire.

לֹא-יַעַרְכֶנָּה זָהָב, וּזְכוֹכִית; וּתְמוּרָתָהּ כְּלִי-פָז
lo-ya'archennah zahav uzechochit; utemuratah keli-faz
Gold and glass cannot equal it; neither shall the exchange thereof be vessels of fine gold.

רָאמוֹת וְגָבִישׁ, לֹא יִזָּכֵר; וּמֶשֶׁךְ חָכְמָה, מִפְּנִינִים
ramot vegavish lo yizzacher; umeshech chochmah mippeninim
No mention shall be made of coral or of crystal; yea, the price of wisdom is above rubies.

לֹא-יַעַרְכֶנָּה, פִּטְדַת-כּוּשׁ; בְּכֶתֶם טָהוֹר, לֹא תְסֻלֶּה
lo-ya'archennah pitdat-kush; bechetem tahor, lo tesulleh
The topaz of Ethiopia shall not equal it, neither shall it be valued with pure gold.

וְהַחָכְמָה, מֵאַיִן תָּבוֹא; וְאֵי זֶה, מְקוֹם בִּינָה
vehachochemah me'ayin tavo; ve'ei zeh, mekom binah
Whence then cometh wisdom? And where is the place of understanding?

וְנֶעֶלְמָה, מֵעֵינֵי כָל-חָי; וּמֵעוֹף הַשָּׁמַיִם נִסְתָּרָה
vene'elmah me'einei chol-chai; ume'of hashamayim nistarah
Seeing it is hid from the eyes of all living, and kept close from the fowls of the air.

איוב

כח

כִּי יֵשׁ לַכֶּסֶף מוֹצָא; וּמָקוֹם, לַזָּהָב יָזֹקּוּ
Ki yesh lakkesef motza; umakom, lazzahav yazokku
For there is a mine for silver, and a place for gold which they refine.

בַּרְזֶל, מֵעָפָר יֻקָּח; וְאֶבֶן, יָצוּק נְחוּשָׁה
barzel me'afar yukkach; ve'even, yatzuk nechushah
Iron is taken out of the dust, and brass is molten out of the stone.

קֵץ, שָׂם לַחֹשֶׁךְ, וּלְכָל-תַּכְלִית, הוּא חוֹקֵר
ketz sam lachoshech, ulechol-tachlit hu choker
Man setteth an end to darkness, and searcheth out to the furthest bound

אֶבֶן אֹפֶל וְצַלְמָוֶת
even ofel vetzalmavet
the stones of thick darkness and of the shadow of death.

פָּרַץ נַחַל, מֵעִם-גָּר--הַנִּשְׁכָּחִים מִנִּי-רָגֶל
paratz nachal me'im-gar, hannishkachim minni-ragel
He breaketh open a shaft away from where men sojourn; they are forgotten of the foot that passeth by;

דַּלּוּ מֵאֱנוֹשׁ נָעוּ
dallu me'enosh na'u
they hang afar from men, they swing to and fro.

אֶרֶץ--מִמֶּנָּה יֵצֵא-לָחֶם; וְתַחְתֶּיהָ, נֶהְפַּךְ כְּמוֹ-אֵשׁ
'eretz, mimmennah yetze-lachem; vetachteiha, nehpach kemo-'esh
As for the earth, out of it cometh bread, and underneath it is turned up as it were by fire.

מְקוֹם-סַפִּיר אֲבָנֶיהָ; וְעַפְרֹת זָהָב לוֹ
mekom-sappir avaneiha; ve'afrot zahav lo
The stones thereof are the place of sapphires, and it hath dust of gold.

נָתִיב, לֹא-יְדָעוֹ עָיִט; וְלֹא שְׁזָפַתּוּ, עֵין אַיָּה
nativ lo-yeda'o ayit; velo shezafattu, ein ayah
That path no bird of prey knoweth, neither hath the falcon's eye seen it;

לֹא-הִדְרִיכוּהוּ בְנֵי-שָׁחַץ; לֹא-עָדָה עָלָיו שָׁחַל
lo-hidrichuhu venei-shachatz; lo-'adah alav shachal
The proud beasts have not trodden it, nor hath the lion passed thereby.

בַּחַלָּמִישׁ, שָׁלַח יָדוֹ; הָפַךְ מִשֹּׁרֶשׁ הָרִים
bachallamish shalach yado; hafach mishoresh harim
He putteth forth his hand upon the flinty rock; He overturneth the mountains by the roots.

אִיּוֹב

הֵן-אַתֶּם כֻּלְּכֶם חֲזִיתֶם; וְלָמָּה-זֶּה, הֶבֶל תֶּהְבָּלוּ
hen-'attem kullechem chazitem; velammah-zeh, hevel tehbalu
Behold, all ye yourselves have seen it; why then are ye become altogether vain?

זֶה, חֵלֶק-אָדָם רָשָׁע עִם-אֵל; וְנַחֲלַת עָרִיצִים, מִשַּׁדַּי יִקָּחוּ
zeh chelek-'adam rasha im-'el; venachalat aritzim, mishaddai yikkachu
This is the portion of a wicked man with God, and the heritage of oppressors, which they receive from the Almighty.

אִם-יִרְבּוּ בָנָיו לְמוֹ-חָרֶב; וְצֶאֱצָאָיו, לֹא יִשְׂבְּעוּ-לָחֶם
'im-yirbu vanav lemo-charev; vetze'etza'av, lo yisbe'u-lachem
If his children be multiplied, it is for the sword; and his offspring shall not have bread enough.

שְׂרִידָו, בַּמָּוֶת יִקָּבֵרוּ; וְאַלְמְנֹתָיו, לֹא תִבְכֶּינָה
seridav bammavet yikkaveru; ve'almenotav, lo tivkeinah
Those that remain of him shall be buried by pestilence, and his widows shall make no lamentation.

אִם-יִצְבֹּר כֶּעָפָר כָּסֶף; וְכַחֹמֶר, יָכִין מַלְבּוּשׁ
'im-yitzbor ke'afar kasef; vechachomer, yachin malbush
Though he heap up silver as the dust, and prepare raiment as the clay;

יָכִין, וְצַדִּיק יִלְבָּשׁ; וְכֶסֶף, נָקִי יַחֲלֹק
yachin vetzaddik yilbash; vechesef, naki yachalok
He may prepare it, but the just shall put it on, and the innocent shall divide the silver.

בָּנָה כָעָשׁ בֵּיתוֹ; וּכְסֻכָּה, עָשָׂה נֹצֵר
banah cha'ash beito; uchesukkah, asah notzer
He buildeth his house as a moth, and as a booth which the keeper maketh.

עָשִׁיר יִשְׁכַּב, וְלֹא יֵאָסֵף; עֵינָיו פָּקַח וְאֵינֶנּוּ
'ashir yishkav velo ye'asef; einav pakach ve'einennu
He lieth down rich, but there shall be nought to gather; he openeth his eyes, and his wealth is not.

תַּשִּׂיגֵהוּ כַמַּיִם, בַּלָּהוֹת; לַיְלָה, גְּנָבַתּוּ סוּפָה
tassigehu chammayim ballahot; laylah, genavattu sufah
Terrors overtake him like waters; a tempest stealeth him away in the night.

יִשָּׂאֵהוּ קָדִים וְיֵלַךְ; וִישָׂעֲרֵהוּ, מִמְּקֹמוֹ
yissa'ehu kadim veyelach; visa'arehu, mimmekomo
The east wind carrieth him away, and he departeth; and it sweepeth him out of his place.

וְיַשְׁלֵךְ עָלָיו, וְלֹא יַחְמֹל; מִיָּדוֹ, בָּרוֹחַ יִבְרָח
veyashlech alav velo yachmol; miyado, baroach yivrach
Yea, it hurleth at him, and spareth not; he would fain flee from its power.

יִשְׂפֹּק עָלֵימוֹ כַפֵּימוֹ; וְיִשְׁרֹק עָלָיו, מִמְּקֹמוֹ
yispok aleimo chappeimo; veyishrok alav, mimmekomo
Men shall clap their hands at him, and shall hiss him out of his place.

איוב

כז

וַיֹּסֶף אִיּוֹב, שְׂאֵת מְשָׁלוֹ; וַיֹּאמַר
Vayosef iyov se'et meshalo, vayomar
And Job again took up his parable, and said:

חַי-אֵל, הֵסִיר מִשְׁפָּטִי; וְשַׁדַּי, הֵמַר נַפְשִׁי
chai-'el hesir mishpati; veshaddai, hemar nafshi
As God liveth, who hath taken away my right; and the Almighty, who hath dealt bitterly with me;

כִּי-כָל-עוֹד נִשְׁמָתִי בִי; וְרוּחַ אֱלוֹהַּ בְּאַפִּי
ki-chol-'od nishmati vi; veruach eloah be'appi
All the while my breath is in me, and the spirit of God is in my nostrils,

אִם-תְּדַבֵּרְנָה שְׂפָתַי עַוְלָה; וּלְשׁוֹנִי, אִם-יֶהְגֶּה רְמִיָּה
'im-tedabbernah sefatai avlah; uleshoni, im-yehgeh remiyah
Surely my lips shall not speak unrighteousness, neither shall my tongue utter deceit;

חָלִילָה לִּי, אִם-אַצְדִּיק אֶתְכֶם: עַד-אֶגְוָע--לֹא-אָסִיר תֻּמָּתִי מִמֶּנִּי.
chalilah li im-'atzdik etchem ad-'egva'; lo-'asir tummati mimmenni
Far be it from me that I should justify you; till I die I will not put away mine integrity from me.

בְּצִדְקָתִי הֶחֱזַקְתִּי, וְלֹא אַרְפֶּהָ; לֹא-יֶחֱרַף לְבָבִי, מִיָּמָי
betzidkati hechezakti velo arpeha; lo-yecheraf levavi, miyamai
My righteousness I hold fast, and will not let it go; my heart shall not reproach me so long as I live.

יְהִי כְרָשָׁע, אֹיְבִי; וּמִתְקוֹמְמִי כְעַוָּל
yehi cherasha oyevi; umitkomemi che'avval
Let mine enemy be as the wicked, and let him that riseth up against me be as the unrighteous.

כִּי מַה-תִּקְוַת חָנֵף, כִּי יִבְצָע; כִּי יֵשֶׁל אֱלוֹהַּ נַפְשׁוֹ
ki mah-tikvat chanef ki yivtza'; ki yeshel eloah nafsho
For what is the hope of the godless, though he get him gain, when God taketh away his soul?

הַצַעֲקָתוֹ, יִשְׁמַע אֵל--כִּי-תָבוֹא עָלָיו צָרָה
hatza'akato yishma el; ki-tavo alav tzarah
Will God hear his cry, when trouble cometh upon him?

אִם-עַל-שַׁדַּי יִתְעַנָּג; יִקְרָא אֱלוֹהַּ בְּכָל-עֵת
'im-'al-shaddai yit'annag; yikra eloah bechol-'et
Will he have his delight in the Almighty, and call upon God at all times?

אוֹרֶה אֶתְכֶם בְּיַד-אֵל; אֲשֶׁר עִם-שַׁדַּי, לֹא אֲכַחֵד
'oreh etchem beyad-'el; asher im-shaddai, lo achached
I will teach you concerning the hand of God; that which is with the Almighty will I not conceal.

אִיּוֹב

אֶת-מִי, הִגַּדְתָּ מִלִּין; וְנִשְׁמַת-מִי, יָצְאָה מִמֶּךָּ
'et-mi higgadta millin; venishmat-mi yatze'ah mimmeka
With whose help hast thou uttered words? And whose spirit came forth from thee?

הָרְפָאִים יְחוֹלָלוּ--מִתַּחַת מַיִם, וְשֹׁכְנֵיהֶם
harefa'im yecholalu; mittachat mayim, veshocheneihem
The shades tremble beneath the waters and the inhabitants thereof.

עָרוֹם שְׁאוֹל נֶגְדּוֹ; וְאֵין כְּסוּת, לָאֲבַדּוֹן
'arom she'ol negdo; ve'ein kesut, la'avaddon
The nether-world is naked before Him, and Destruction hath no covering.

נֹטֶה צָפוֹן עַל-תֹּהוּ; תֹּלֶה אֶרֶץ, עַל-בְּלִי-מָה
noteh tzafon al-tohu; toleh eretz, al-beli-mah
He stretcheth out the north over the empty space, and hangeth the earth over nothing.

צֹרֵר-מַיִם בְּעָבָיו; וְלֹא-נִבְקַע עָנָן תַּחְתָּם
tzorer-mayim be'avav; velo-nivka anan tachtam
He bindeth up the waters in His thick clouds; and the cloud is not rent under them.

מְאַחֵז פְּנֵי-כִסֵּה; פַּרְשֵׁז עָלָיו עֲנָנוֹ
me'achez penei-chisseh; parshez alav anano
He closeth in the face of His throne, and spreadeth His cloud upon it.

חֹק-חָג, עַל-פְּנֵי-מָיִם--עַד-תַּכְלִית אוֹר עִם-חֹשֶׁךְ
chok-chag al-penei-mayim; ad-tachlit or im-choshech
He hath described a boundary upon the face of the waters, unto the confines of light and darkness.

עַמּוּדֵי שָׁמַיִם יְרוֹפָפוּ; וְיִתְמְהוּ, מִגַּעֲרָתוֹ
'ammudei shamayim yerofafu; veyitmehu, migga'arato
The pillars of heaven tremble and are astonished at His rebuke.

בְּכֹחוֹ, רָגַע הַיָּם; וּבִתְבוּנָתוֹ, מָחַץ רָהַב
bechocho raga hayam; uvitvunato, machatz rahav
He stirreth up the sea with His power, and by His understanding He smiteth through Rahab.

בְּרוּחוֹ, שָׁמַיִם שִׁפְרָה; חֹלְלָה יָדוֹ, נָחָשׁ בָּרִחַ
berucho shamayim shifrah; cholalah yado, nachash bariach
By His breath the heavens are serene; His hand hath pierced the slant serpent.

הֶן-אֵלֶּה, קְצוֹת דְּרָכָו--וּמַה-שֵּׁמֶץ דָּבָר, נִשְׁמַע-בּוֹ
hen-'elleh ketzot derachav, umah-shemetz davor nishma'-bo
Lo, these are but the outskirts of His ways; and how small a whisper is heard of Him!

וְרַעַם גְּבוּרֹתָו, מִי יִתְבּוֹנָן
vera'am gevurotav, mi yitbonan
But the thunder of His mighty deeds who can understand?

איוב

וְאִם-לֹא אֵפוֹ, מִי יַכְזִיבֵנִי; וְיָשֵׂם לְאַל, מִלָּתִי
ve'im-lo efo mi yachziveni; veyasem le'al, millati
And if it be not so now, who will prove me a liar, and make my speech nothing worth?

כה

וַיַּעַן, בִּלְדַּד הַשֻּׁחִי; וַיֹּאמַר
Vaya'an bildad hashuchi, vayomar
Then answered Bildad the Shuhite, and said:

הַמְשֵׁל וָפַחַד עִמּוֹ; עֹשֶׂה שָׁלוֹם, בִּמְרוֹמָיו
hamshel vafachad immo; oseh shalom, bimromav
Dominion and fear are with Him; He maketh peace in His high places.

הֲיֵשׁ מִסְפָּר, לִגְדוּדָיו; וְעַל-מִי, לֹא-יָקוּם אוֹרֵהוּ
hayesh mispar ligdudav; ve'al-mi, lo-yakum orehu
Is there any number of His armies? And upon whom doth not His light arise?

וּמַה-יִּצְדַּק אֱנוֹשׁ עִם-אֵל; וּמַה-יִּזְכֶּה, יְלוּד אִשָּׁה
umah-yitzdak enosh im-'el; umah-yizkeh, yelud ishah
How then can man be just with God? Or how can he be clean that is born of a woman?

הֵן עַד-יָרֵחַ, וְלֹא יַאֲהִיל; וְכוֹכָבִים, לֹא-זַכּוּ בְעֵינָיו
hen ad-yareach velo ya'ahil; vechochavim, lo-zakku ve'einav
Behold, even the moon hath no brightness, and the stars are not pure in His sight;

אַף, כִּי-אֱנוֹשׁ רִמָּה; וּבֶן-אָדָם, תּוֹלֵעָה
'af ki-'enosh rimmah; uven-'adam, tole'ah
How much less man, that is a worm! and the son of man, that is a maggot!

כו

וַיַּעַן אִיּוֹב, וַיֹּאמַר
Vaya'an iyov, vayomar
Then Job answered and said:

מֶה-עָזַרְתָּ לְלֹא-כֹחַ; הוֹשַׁעְתָּ, זְרוֹעַ לֹא-עֹז
meh-'azarta lelo-choach; hosha'ta, zeroa lo-'oz
How hast thou helped him that is without power! How hast thou saved the arm that hath no strength!

מַה-יָּעַצְתָּ, לְלֹא חָכְמָה; וְתוּשִׁיָּה, לָרֹב הוֹדָעְתָּ
mah-ya'atzta lelo chochmah vetushiyah, larov hoda'eta
How hast thou counselled him that hath no wisdom, and plentifully declared sound knowledge!

אִיּוֹב

לֹא-תְשׁוּרֵנִי עָיִן; וְסֵתֶר פָּנִים יָשִׂים
lo-teshureni ayin; veseter panim yasim
'No eye shall see me'; and he putteth a covering on his face.

חָתַר בַּחֹשֶׁךְ, בָּתִּים: יוֹמָם חִתְּמוּ-לָמוֹ; לֹא-יָדְעוּ אוֹר
chatar bachoshech, battim yomam chittemu-lamo, lo-yade'u or
In the dark they dig through houses; they shut themselves up in the day-time; they know not the light.

כִּי יַחְדָּו, בֹּקֶר לָמוֹ צַלְמָוֶת; כִּי-יַכִּיר, בַּלְהוֹת צַלְמָוֶת
ki yachdav boker lamo tzalmavet; ki-yakkir, balhot tzalmavet
For the shadow of death is to all of them as the morning; for they know the terrors of the shadow of death.

קַל-הוּא, עַל-פְּנֵי-מַיִם--תְּקֻלַּל חֶלְקָתָם בָּאָרֶץ; לֹא-יִפְנֶה, דֶּרֶךְ כְּרָמִים
kal-hu al-penei-mayim, tekullal chelkatam ba'aretz; lo-yifneh derech keramim
He is swift upon the face of the waters; their portion is cursed in the earth; he turneth not by the way of the vineyards.

צִיָּה גַם-חֹם, יִגְזְלוּ מֵימֵי-שֶׁלֶג; שְׁאוֹל חָטָאוּ
tziyah gam-chom, yigzelu meimei-sheleg, she'ol chata'u
Drought and heat consume the snow waters; so doth the nether-world those that have sinned.

יִשְׁכָּחֵהוּ רֶחֶם, מְתָקוֹ רִמָּה--עוֹד לֹא-יִזָּכֵר
yishkachehu rechem metako rimmah, od lo-yizzacher
The womb forgetteth him; the worm feedeth sweetly on him; he shall be no more remembered;

וַתִּשָּׁבֵר כָּעֵץ עַוְלָה
vattishaver ka'etz avlah
and unrighteousness is broken as a tree.

רֹעֶה עֲקָרָה, לֹא תֵלֵד; וְאַלְמָנָה, לֹא יְיֵטִיב
ro'eh akarah lo teled; ve'almanah, lo yeyetiv
He devoureth the barren that beareth not; and doeth not good to the widow.

וּמָשַׁךְ אַבִּירִים בְּכֹחוֹ; יָקוּם, וְלֹא-יַאֲמִין בַּחַיִּין
umashach abbirim bechocho; yakum, velo-ya'amin bachayin
He draweth away the mighty also by his power; he riseth up, and he trusteth not his own life.

יִתֶּן-לוֹ לָבֶטַח, וְיִשָּׁעֵן; וְעֵינֵיהוּ, עַל-דַּרְכֵיהֶם
yitten-lo lavetach veyisha'en; ve'eineihu, al-darcheihem
Though it be given him to be in safety, whereon he resteth, yet His eyes are upon their ways.

רוֹמּוּ מְּעַט, וְאֵינֶנּוּ, וְהֻמְּכוּ
rommu me'at ve'einennu, vehummechu
They are exalted for a little while, and they are gone; yea, they are brought low,

כַּכֹּל יִקָּפְצוּן; וּכְרֹאשׁ שִׁבֹּלֶת יִמָּלוּ
kakkol yikkafetzun; ucherosh shibbolet yimmalu
they are gathered in as all others, and wither as the tops of the ears of corn.

אִיּוֹב

מְשַׁחֲרֵי לַטָּרֶף; עֲרָבָה לוֹ לֶחֶם, לַנְּעָרִים
meshacharei lattaref; aravah lo lechem, lanne'arim
seeking diligently for food; the desert yieldeth them bread for their children.

בַּשָּׂדֶה, בְּלִילוֹ יִקְצוֹרוּ; וְכֶרֶם רָשָׁע יְלַקֵּשׁוּ
bassadeh belilo yiktzoru; vecherem rasha yelakkeshu
They cut his provender in the field; and they despoil the vineyard of the wicked.

עָרוֹם יָלִינוּ, מִבְּלִי לְבוּשׁ; וְאֵין כְּסוּת, בַּקָּרָה
'arom yalinu mibbeli levush; ve'ein kesut, bakkarah
They lie all night naked without clothing, and have no covering in the cold.

מִזֶּרֶם הָרִים יִרְטָבוּ; וּמִבְּלִי מַחְסֶה, חִבְּקוּ-צוּר
mizzerem harim yirtavu; umibbeli machseh, chibbeku-tzur
They are wet with the showers of the mountains, and embrace the rock for want of a shelter.

יִגְזְלוּ, מִשֹּׁד יָתוֹם; וְעַל-עָנִי יַחְבֹּלוּ
yigzelu mishod yatom; ve'al-'ani yachbolu
There are that pluck the fatherless from the breast, and take a pledge of the poor;

עָרוֹם הִלְּכוּ, בְּלִי לְבוּשׁ; וּרְעֵבִים, נָשְׂאוּ עֹמֶר
'arom hillechu beli levush; ure'evim, nase'u omer
So that they go about naked without clothing, and being hungry they carry the sheaves;

בֵּין-שׁוּרֹתָם יַצְהִירוּ; יְקָבִים דָּרְכוּ, וַיִּצְמָאוּ
bein-shurotam yatzhiru; yekavim darechu, vayitzma'u
They make oil within the rows of these men; they tread their winepresses, and suffer thirst.

מֵעִיר מְתִים, יִנְאָקוּ--וְנֶפֶשׁ-חֲלָלִים תְּשַׁוֵּעַ:
me'ir metim yin'aku, venefesh-chalalim teshavvea'
From out of the populous city men groan, and the soul of the wounded crieth out;

וֶאֱלוֹהַּ, לֹא-יָשִׂים תִּפְלָה
ve'eloah, lo-yasim tiflah
yet God imputeth it not for unseemliness.

הֵמָּה, הָיוּ--בְּמֹרְדֵי-אוֹר: לֹא-הִכִּירוּ דְרָכָיו; וְלֹא יָשְׁבוּ, בִּנְתִיבֹתָיו
hemmah hayu bemoredei-'or lo-hikkiru derachav; velo yashevu, bintivotav
These are of them that rebel against the light; they know not the ways thereof, nor abide in the paths thereof.

לָאוֹר, יָקוּם רוֹצֵחַ--יִקְטָל-עָנִי וְאֶבְיוֹן; וּבַלַּיְלָה, יְהִי כַגַּנָּב
la'or yakum rotzeach, yiktol-'ani ve'evyon; uvallaylah, yehi chaggannav
The murderer riseth with the light, to kill the poor and needy; and in the night he is as a thief.

וְעֵין נֹאֵף, שָׁמְרָה נֶשֶׁף לֵאמֹר
ve'ein no'ef shamerah neshef lemor
The eye also of the adulterer waiteth for the twilight, saying:

איוב

מֵחֻקִּי, צָפַנְתִּי אִמְרֵי-פִיו
mechukki, tzafanti imrei-fiv
I have treasured up the words of His mouth more than my necessary food.

וְהוּא בְאֶחָד, וּמִי יְשִׁיבֶנּוּ; וְנַפְשׁוֹ אִוְּתָה וַיָּעַשׂ
vehu ve'echad umi yeshivennu; venafsho ivvetah vaya'as
But He is at one with Himself, and who can turn Him? And what His soul desireth, even that He doeth.

כִּי, יַשְׁלִים חֻקִּי; וְכָהֵנָּה רַבּוֹת עִמּוֹ
ki yashlim chukki; vechahennah rabbot immo
For He will perform that which is appointed for me; and many such things are with Him.

עַל-כֵּן, מִפָּנָיו אֶבָּהֵל; אֶתְבּוֹנֵן, וְאֶפְחַד מִמֶּנּוּ
'al-ken mippanav ebbahel; etbonen, ve'efchad mimmennu
Therefore am I affrighted at His presence; when I consider, I am afraid of Him.

וְאֵל, הֵרַךְ לִבִּי; וְשַׁדַּי, הִבְהִילָנִי
ve'el herach libbi; veshaddai, hivhilani
Yea, God hath made my heart faint, and the Almighty hath affrighted me;

כִּי-לֹא נִצְמַתִּי, מִפְּנֵי-חֹשֶׁךְ; וּמִפָּנַי, כִּסָּה-אֹפֶל
ki-lo nitzmatti mippenei-choshech; umippanai, kissah-'ofel
Because I was not cut off before the darkness, neither did He cover the thick darkness from my face.

כד

מַדּוּעַ--מִשַּׁדַּי, לֹא-נִצְפְּנוּ עִתִּים; וְיֹדְעָו, לֹא-חָזוּ יָמָיו
Maddua', mishaddai lo-nitzpenu ittim; veyode'av, lo-chazu yamav
Why are times not laid up by the Almighty? And why do not they that know Him see His days?

גְּבֻלוֹת יַשִּׂיגוּ; עֵדֶר גָּזְלוּ, וַיִּרְעוּ
gevulot yassigu; eder gazelu, vayir'u
There are that remove the landmarks; they violently take away flocks, and feed them.

חֲמוֹר יְתוֹמִים יִנְהָגוּ; יַחְבְּלוּ, שׁוֹר אַלְמָנָה
chamor yetomim yinhagu; yachbelu, shor almanah
They drive away the ass of the fatherless, they take the widow's ox for a pledge.

יַטּוּ אֶבְיוֹנִים מִדָּרֶךְ; יַחַד חֻבְּאוּ, עֲנִיֵּי-אָרֶץ
yattu evyonim middarech; yachad chubbe'u, aniyei-'aretz
They turn the needy out of the way; the poor of the earth hide themselves together.

הֵן פְּרָאִים, בַּמִּדְבָּר-- יָצְאוּ בְּפָעֳלָם
hen pera'im bammidbar, yatze'u befo'olam
Behold, as wild asses in the wilderness they go forth to their work,

איוב

גַּם־הַיּוֹם, מְרִי שִׂחִי; יָדִי, כָּבְדָה עַל־אַנְחָתִי
gam-hayom meri sichi; yadi, kavedah al-'anchati
Even to-day is my complaint bitter; my hand is become heavy because of my groaning.

מִי־יִתֵּן יָדַעְתִּי, וְאֶמְצָאֵהוּ; אָבוֹא, עַד־תְּכוּנָתוֹ
mi-yitten yada'ti ve'emtza'ehu; avo, ad-techunato
Oh that I knew where I might find Him, that I might come even to His seat!

אֶעֶרְכָה לְפָנָיו מִשְׁפָּט; וּפִי, אֲמַלֵּא תוֹכָחוֹת
'e'erchah lefanav mishpat; ufi, amallei tochachot
I would order my cause before Him, and fill my mouth with arguments.

אֵדְעָה, מִלִּים יַעֲנֵנִי; וְאָבִינָה, מַה־יֹּאמַר לִי
'ede'ah millim ya'aneni; ve'avinah, mah-yomar li
I would know the words which He would answer me, and understand what He would say unto me.

הַבְּרָב־כֹּחַ, יָרִיב עִמָּדִי; לֹא אַךְ־הוּא, יָשִׂם בִּי
habberov-koach yariv immadi; lo ach-hu, yasim bi
Would He contend with me in His great power? Nay; but He would give heed unto me.

שָׁם--יָשָׁר, נוֹכָח עִמּוֹ; וַאֲפַלְּטָה לָנֶצַח, מִשֹּׁפְטִי
sham, yashor nochach immo; va'afalletah lanetzach, mishofeti
There the upright might reason with Him; so should I be delivered for ever from my Judge.

הֵן קֶדֶם אֶהֱלֹךְ וְאֵינֶנּוּ; וְאָחוֹר, וְלֹא־אָבִין לוֹ
hen kedem eheloch ve'einennu; ve'achor, velo-'avin lo
Behold, I go forward, but He is not there, and backward, but I cannot perceive Him;

שְׂמֹאול בַּעֲשֹׂתוֹ, וְלֹא־אָחַז
semol ba'asoto velo-'achaz
On the left hand, when He doth work, but I cannot behold Him,

יַעְטֹף יָמִין, וְלֹא אֶרְאֶה
ya'tof yamin, velo er'eh
He turneth Himself to the right hand, but I cannot see Him.

כִּי־יָדַע, דֶּרֶךְ עִמָּדִי; בְּחָנַנִי, כַּזָּהָב אֵצֵא
ki-yada derech immadi; bechanani, kazzahav etze
For He knoweth the way that I take; when He hath tried me, I shall come forth as gold.

בַּאֲשֻׁרוֹ, אָחֲזָה רַגְלִי; דַּרְכּוֹ שָׁמַרְתִּי וְלֹא־אָט
ba'ashuro achazah ragli; darko shamarti velo-'at
My foot hath held fast to His steps, His way have I kept, and turned not aside.

מִצְוַת שְׂפָתָיו, וְלֹא אָמִישׁ
mitzvat sefatav velo amish
I have not gone back from the commandment of His lips;

אִיּוֹב

הַסְכֶּן-נָא עִמּוֹ וּשְׁלָם; בָּהֶם, תְּבוֹאַתְךָ טוֹבָה
hasken-na immo; ushlam bahem, tevo'atcha tovah
Acquaint now thyself with Him, and be at peace; thereby shall thine increase be good.

קַח-נָא מִפִּיו תּוֹרָה; וְשִׂים אֲמָרָיו, בִּלְבָבֶךָ
kach-na mippiv torah; vesim amarav, bilvavecha
Receive, I pray thee, instruction from His mouth, and lay up His words in thy heart.

אִם-תָּשׁוּב עַד-שַׁדַּי, תִּבָּנֶה; תַּרְחִיק עַוְלָה, מֵאֹהָלֶךָ
'im-tashuv ad-shaddai tibbaneh; tarchik avlah, me'oholecha
If thou return to the Almighty, thou shalt be built up--if thou put away unrighteousness far from thy tents,

וְשִׁית-עַל-עָפָר בָּצֶר; וּכְצוּר נְחָלִים אוֹפִיר
veshit-'al-'afar batzer; uvetzur nechalim ofir
And lay thy treasure in the dust, and the gold of Ophir among the stones of the brooks;

וְהָיָה שַׁדַּי בְּצָרֶיךָ; וְכֶסֶף תּוֹעָפוֹת לָךְ
vehayah shaddai betzareicha; vechesef to'afot lach
And the Almighty be thy treasure, and precious silver unto thee;

כִּי-אָז, עַל-שַׁדַּי תִּתְעַנָּג; וְתִשָּׂא אֶל-אֱלוֹהַּ פָּנֶיךָ
ki-'az al-shaddai tit'annag; vetissa el-'eloah paneicha
Then surely shalt thou have thy delight in the Almighty, and shalt lift up thy face unto God.

תַּעְתִּיר אֵלָיו, וְיִשְׁמָעֶךָּ; וּנְדָרֶיךָ תְשַׁלֵּם
ta'tir elav veyishma'eka; unedareicha teshallem
Thou shalt make thy prayer unto Him, and He will hear thee, and thou shalt pay thy vows;

וְתִגְזַר-אֹמֶר, וְיָקָם לָךְ; וְעַל-דְּרָכֶיךָ, נָגַהּ אוֹר
vetigzar-'omer veyakom lach; ve'al-deracheicha, nagah or
Thou shalt also decree a thing, and it shall be established unto thee, and light shall shine upon thy ways.

כִּי-הִשְׁפִּילוּ, וַתֹּאמֶר גֵּוָה; וְשַׁח עֵינַיִם יוֹשִׁעַ
ki-hishpilu vattomer gevah; veshach einayim yoshia
When they cast thee down, thou shalt say: 'There is lifting up'; for the humble person He saveth.

יְמַלֵּט אִי-נָקִי; וְנִמְלַט, בְּבֹר כַּפֶּיךָ
yemallet i-naki; venimlat, bevor kappeicha
He delivereth him that is innocent, yea, thou shalt be delivered through the cleanness of thy hands.

כג

וַיַּעַן אִיּוֹב, וַיֹּאמַר
Vaya'an iyov, vayomar
Then Job answered and said:

אִיּוֹב

אַלְמָנוֹת, שִׁלַּחְתָּ רֵיקָם; וּזְרֹעוֹת יְתֹמִים יְדֻכָּא
'almanot shillachta reikam; uzero'ot yetomim yedukka
Thou hast sent widows away empty, and the arms of the fatherless have been broken.

עַל-כֵּן, סְבִיבוֹתֶיךָ פַחִים; וִיבַהֶלְךָ, פַּחַד פִּתְאֹם
'al-ken sevivoteicha fachim; vivahelcha pachad pit'om
Therefore snares are round about thee, and sudden dread affrighted thee,

אוֹ-חֹשֶׁךְ לֹא-תִרְאֶה; וְשִׁפְעַת-מַיִם תְּכַסֶּךָּ
'o-choshech lo-tir'eh; veshif'at-mayim techasseka
Or darkness, that thou canst not see, and abundance of waters cover thee.

הֲלֹא-אֱלוֹהַּ, גֹּבַהּ שָׁמָיִם; וּרְאֵה רֹאשׁ כּוֹכָבִים כִּי-רָמּוּ
halo-'eloah govah shamayim; ure'eh rosh kochavim ki-rammu
Is not God in the height of heaven? And behold the topmost of the stars, how high they are!

וְאָמַרְתָּ, מַה-יָּדַע אֵל; הַבְעַד עֲרָפֶל יִשְׁפּוֹט
ve'amarta mah-yada el; hav'ad arafel yishpot
And thou sayest: 'What doth God know? Can He judge through the dark cloud?

עָבִים סֵתֶר-לוֹ, וְלֹא יִרְאֶה; וְחוּג שָׁמַיִם, יִתְהַלָּךְ
'avim seter-lo velo yir'eh; vechug shamayim, yit'hallach
Thick clouds are a covering to Him, that He seeth not; and He walketh in the circuit of heaven.'

הַאֹרַח עוֹלָם תִּשְׁמֹר--אֲשֶׁר דָּרְכוּ מְתֵי-אָוֶן
ha'orach olam tishmor; asher darechu metei-'aven
Wilt thou keep the old way which wicked men have trodden?

אֲשֶׁר-קֻמְּטוּ וְלֹא-עֵת; נָהָר, יוּצַק יְסוֹדָם
'asher-kummetu velo-'et; nahar, yutzak yesodam
Who were snatched away before their time, whose foundation was poured out as a stream;

הָאֹמְרִים לָאֵל, סוּר מִמֶּנּוּ; וּמַה-יִּפְעַל שַׁדַּי לָמוֹ
ha'omerim la'el sur mimmennu; umah-yif'al shaddai lamo
Who said unto God: 'Depart from us'; and what could the Almighty do unto them?

וְהוּא מִלֵּא בָתֵּיהֶם טוֹב; וַעֲצַת רְשָׁעִים, רָחֲקָה מֶנִּי
vehu millei vatteihem tov; va'atzat resha'im, rachakah menni
Yet He filled their houses with good things--but the counsel of the wicked is far from me.

יִרְאוּ צַדִּיקִים וְיִשְׂמָחוּ; וְנָקִי, יִלְעַג-לָמוֹ
yir'u tzaddikim veyismachu; venaki, yil'ag-lamo
The righteous saw it, and were glad, and the innocent laugh them to scorn:

אִם-לֹא נִכְחַד קִימָנוּ; וְיִתְרָם, אָכְלָה אֵשׁ
'im-lo nichchad kimanu; veyitram, achelah esh
'Surely their substance is cut off, and their abundance the fire hath consumed.'

אִיּוֹב

וְהוּא, לִקְבָרוֹת יוּבָל; וְעַל-גָּדִישׁ יִשְׁקוֹד
vehu likvarot yuval; ve'al-gadish yishkod
For he is borne to the grave, and watch is kept over his tomb.

מָתְקוּ-לוֹ, רִגְבֵי-נָחַל: וְאַחֲרָיו, כָּל-אָדָם יִמְשׁוֹךְ; וּלְפָנָיו, אֵין מִסְפָּר
mateku-lo, rigvei nachal ve'acharav kol-'adam yimshoch; ulefanav, ein mispar
The clods of the valley are sweet unto him, and all men draw after him, as there were innumerable before him.

וְאֵיךְ, תְּנַחֲמוּנִי הָבֶל; וּתְשׁוּבֹתֵיכֶם, נִשְׁאַר-מָעַל
ve'eich tenachamuni havel; uteshuvoteichem, nish'ar-ma'al
How then comfort ye me in vain? And as for your answers, there remaineth only faithlessness?

כב

וַיַּעַן, אֱלִיפַז הַתֵּימָנִי; וַיֹּאמַר
Vaya'an elifaz hattemani, vayomar
Then answered Eliphaz the Temanite, and said:

הַלְאֵל יִסְכָּן-גָּבֶר--כִּי-יִסְכֹּן עָלֵימוֹ מַשְׂכִּיל
hal'el yiskan-gaver; ki-yiskon aleimo maskil
Can a man be profitable unto God? Or can he that is wise be profitable unto Him?

הַחֵפֶץ לְשַׁדַּי, כִּי תִצְדָּק; וְאִם-בֶּצַע, כִּי-תַתֵּם דְּרָכֶיךָ
hachefetz leshaddai ki titzdak; ve'im-betza', ki-tattem deracheicha
Is it any advantage to the Almighty, that thou art righteous? Or is it gain to Him, that thou makest thy ways blameless?

הֲמִיִּרְאָתְךָ יֹכִיחֶךָ; יָבוֹא עִמְּךָ, בַּמִּשְׁפָּט
hamiyir'atecha yochichecha; yavo immecha, bammishpat
Is it for thy fear of Him that He reproveth thee, that He entereth with thee into judgment?

הֲלֹא רָעָתְךָ רַבָּה; וְאֵין-קֵץ, לַעֲוֹנֹתֶיךָ
halo ra'atecha rabbah; ve'ein-ketz, la'avonoteicha
Is not thy wickedness great? And are not thine iniquities without end?

כִּי-תַחְבֹּל אַחֶיךָ חִנָּם; וּבִגְדֵי עֲרוּמִּים תַּפְשִׁיט
ki-tachbol acheicha chinnam; uvigdei arummim tafshit
For thou hast taken pledges of thy brother for nought, and stripped the naked of their clothing.

לֹא-מַיִם, עָיֵף תַּשְׁקֶה; וּמֵרָעֵב, תִּמְנַע-לָחֶם
lo-mayim ayef tashkeh; umera'ev, timna'-lachem
Thou hast not given water to the weary to drink, and thou hast withholden bread from the hungry.

וְאִישׁ זְרוֹעַ, לוֹ הָאָרֶץ; וּנְשׂוּא פָנִים, יֵשֶׁב בָּהּ
ve'ish zeroa lo ha'aretz; unesu fanim, yeshev bah
And as a mighty man, who hath the earth, and as a man of rank, who dwelleth in it,

אִיּוֹב

יִרְאוּ עֵינָו כִּידוֹ; וּמֵחֲמַת שַׁדַּי יִשְׁתֶּה
yir'u einav kido; umechamat shaddai yishteh
Let his own eyes see his destruction, and let him drink of the wrath of the Almighty.

כִּי מַה-חֶפְצוֹ בְּבֵיתוֹ אַחֲרָיו; וּמִסְפַּר חֳדָשָׁיו חֻצָּצוּ
ki mah-cheftzo beveito acharav; umispar chodashav chutzatzu
For what pleasure hath he in his house after him? seeing the number of his months is determined.

הַלְאֵל יְלַמֶּד-דָּעַת; וְהוּא, רָמִים יִשְׁפּוֹט
hal'el yelammed-da'at; vehu, ramim yishpot
Shall any teach God knowledge? seeing it is He that judgeth those that are high.

זֶה--יָמוּת, בְּעֶצֶם תֻּמּוֹ; כֻּלּוֹ, שַׁלְאֲנַן וְשָׁלֵיו
zeh, yamut be'etzem tummo; kullo, shal'anan veshaleiv
One dieth in his full strength, being wholly at ease and quiet;

עֲטִינָיו, מָלְאוּ חָלָב; וּמֹחַ עַצְמוֹתָיו יְשֻׁקֶּה
'atinav male'u chalav; umoach atzmotav yeshukkeh
His pails are full of milk, and the marrow of his bones is moistened.

וְזֶה--יָמוּת, בְּנֶפֶשׁ מָרָה; וְלֹא-אָכַל, בַּטּוֹבָה
vezeh, yamut benefesh marah; velo-'achal, battovah
And another dieth in bitterness of soul, and hath never tasted of good.

יַחַד, עַל-עָפָר יִשְׁכָּבוּ; וְרִמָּה, תְּכַסֶּה עֲלֵיהֶם
yachad al-'afar yishkavu; verimmah, techasseh aleihem
They lie down alike in the dust, and the worm covereth them.

הֵן יָדַעְתִּי, מַחְשְׁבוֹתֵיכֶם; וּמְזִמּוֹת, עָלַי תַּחְמֹסוּ
hen yada'ti machshevoteichem; umezimmot, alai tachmosu
Behold, I know your thoughts, and the devices which ye wrongfully imagine against me.

כִּי תֹאמְרוּ, אַיֵּה בֵית-נָדִיב; וְאַיֵּה, אֹהֶל מִשְׁכְּנוֹת רְשָׁעִים
ki tomeru, ayeh veit-nadiv; ve'ayeh, ohel mishkenot resha'im
For ye say: 'Where is the house of the prince? And where is the tent wherein the wicked dwelt?'

הֲלֹא שְׁאֶלְתֶּם, עוֹבְרֵי דָרֶךְ; וְאֹתֹתָם, לֹא תְנַכֵּרוּ
halo she'eltem overei darech; ve'ototam, lo tenakkeru
Have ye not asked them that go by the way; and will ye misdeem their tokens,

כִּי לְיוֹם אֵיד, יֵחָשֶׂךְ רָע; לְיוֹם עֲבָרוֹת יוּבָלוּ
ki leyom eid yechasech ra'; leyom avarot yuvalu
That the evil man is reserved to the day of calamity, that they are led forth to the day of wrath?

מִי-יַגִּיד עַל-פָּנָיו דַּרְכּוֹ; וְהוּא-עָשָׂה, מִי יְשַׁלֶּם-לוֹ
mi-yaggid al-panav darko; vehu-'asah, mi yeshallem-lo
But who shall declare his way to his face? And who shall repay him what he hath done?

אִיּוֹב

בָּתֵּיהֶם שָׁלוֹם מִפָּחַד; וְלֹא שֵׁבֶט אֱלוֹהַּ עֲלֵיהֶם
batteihem shalom mippachad; velo shevet eloah aleihem
Their houses are safe, without fear, neither is the rod of God upon them.

שׁוֹרוֹ עִבַּר, וְלֹא יַגְעִל; תְּפַלֵּט פָּרָתוֹ, וְלֹא תְשַׁכֵּל
shoro ibbar velo yag'il; tefallet parato, velo teshakkel
Their bull gendereth, and faileth not; their cow calveth, and casteth not her calf.

יְשַׁלְּחוּ כַצֹּאן, עֲוִילֵיהֶם; וְיַלְדֵיהֶם, יְרַקֵּדוּן
yeshallechu chatzon avileihem; veyaldeihem, yerakkedun
They send forth their little ones like a flock, and their children dance.

יִשְׂאוּ, כְּתֹף וְכִנּוֹר; וְיִשְׂמְחוּ, לְקוֹל עוּגָב
yis'u ketof vechinnor; veyismechu, lekol ugav
They sing to the timbrel and harp, and rejoice at the sound of the pipe.

יְכַלּוּ בַטּוֹב יְמֵיהֶם; וּבְרֶגַע, שְׁאוֹל יֵחָתּוּ
yechallu vattov yemeihem; uverega', she'ol yechattu
They spend their days in prosperity, and peacefully they go down to the grave.

וַיֹּאמְרוּ לָאֵל, סוּר מִמֶּנּוּ; וְדַעַת דְּרָכֶיךָ, לֹא חָפָצְנוּ
vayomeru la'el sur mimmennu; veda'at deracheicha, lo chafatzenu
Yet they said unto God: 'Depart from us; for we desire not the knowledge of Thy ways.

מַה-שַּׁדַּי כִּי-נַעַבְדֶנּוּ; וּמַה-נּוֹעִיל, כִּי נִפְגַּע-בּוֹ
mah-shaddai ki-na'avdennu; umah-no'il, ki nifga'-bo
What is the Almighty, that we should serve Him? And what profit should we have, if we pray unto Him?'--

הֵן לֹא בְיָדָם טוּבָם; עֲצַת רְשָׁעִים, רָחֲקָה מֶנִּי
hen lo veyadam tuvam; atzat resha'im, rachakah menni
Lo, their prosperity is not in their hand; the counsel of the wicked is far from me.

כַּמָּה, נֵר-רְשָׁעִים יִדְעָךְ--וְיָבֹא עָלֵימוֹ אֵידָם
kammah ner-resha'im yid'ach, veyavo aleimo eidam
How oft is it that the lamp of the wicked is put out? that their calamity cometh upon them?

חֲבָלִים, יְחַלֵּק בְּאַפּוֹ
chavalim, yechallek be'appo
that He distributeth pains in His anger?

יִהְיוּ, כְּתֶבֶן לִפְנֵי-רוּחַ; וּכְמֹץ, גְּנָבַתּוּ סוּפָה
yihyu, keteven lifnei-ruach; uchemotz, genavattu sufah
That they are as stubble before the wind, and as chaff that the storm stealeth away?

אֱלוֹהַּ, יִצְפֹּן-לְבָנָיו אוֹנוֹ; יְשַׁלֵּם אֵלָיו וְיֵדָע
'eloah, yitzpon-levanav ono; yeshallem elav veyeda
'God layeth up his iniquity for his children!'--let Him recompense it unto himself, that he may know it.

אִיּוֹב

יְגַלּוּ שָׁמַיִם עֲוֹנוֹ; וְאֶרֶץ, מִתְקוֹמָמָה לוֹ
yegallu shamayim avono; ve'eretz, mitkomamah lo
The heavens shall reveal his iniquity, and the earth shall rise up against him.

יִגֶל, יְבוּל בֵּיתוֹ; נִגָּרוֹת, בְּיוֹם אַפּוֹ
yigel yevul beito; niggarot, beyom appo
The increase of his house shall depart, his goods shall flow away in the day of his wrath.

זֶה, חֵלֶק-אָדָם רָשָׁע--מֵאֱלֹהִים; וְנַחֲלַת אִמְרוֹ מֵאֵל
zeh chelek-'adam rasha me'elohim; venachalat imro me'el
This is the portion of a wicked man from God, and the heritage appointed unto him by God.

כא

וַיַּעַן אִיּוֹב, וַיֹּאמַר
Vaya'an iyov, vayomar
Then Job answered and said:

שִׁמְעוּ שָׁמוֹעַ, מִלָּתִי; וּתְהִי-זֹאת, תַּנְחוּמֹתֵיכֶם
shim'u shamoa millati; utehi-zot, tanchumoteichem
Hear diligently my speech; and let this be your consolations.

שָׂאוּנִי, וְאָנֹכִי אֲדַבֵּר; וְאַחַר דַּבְּרִי תַלְעִיג
sa'uni ve'anochi adabber; ve'achar dabberi tal'ig
Suffer me, that I may speak; and after that I have spoken, mock on.

הֶאָנֹכִי, לְאָדָם שִׂיחִי; וְאִם-מַדּוּעַ, לֹא-תִקְצַר רוּחִי
he'anochi le'adam sichi; ve'im-maddua', lo-tiktzar ruchi
As for me, is my complaint to man? Or why should I not be impatient?

פְּנוּ-אֵלַי וְהָשַׁמּוּ; וְשִׂימוּ יָד עַל-פֶּה
penu-'elai vehashammu; vesimu yad al-peh
Turn unto me, and be astonished, and lay your hand upon your mouth.

וְאִם-זָכַרְתִּי וְנִבְהָלְתִּי; וְאָחַז בְּשָׂרִי, פַּלָּצוּת
ve'im-zacharti venivhaleti; ve'achaz besari, pallatzut
Even when I remember I am affrighted, and horror hath taketh hold on my flesh.

מַדּוּעַ, רְשָׁעִים יִחְיוּ; עָתְקוּ, גַּם-גָּבְרוּ חָיִל
maddua resha'im yichyu; ateku, gam-gaveru chayil
Wherefore do the wicked live, become old, yea, wax mighty in power?

זַרְעָם נָכוֹן לִפְנֵיהֶם עִמָּם; וְצֶאֱצָאֵיהֶם, לְעֵינֵיהֶם
zar'am nachon lifneihem immam; vetze'etza'eihem, le'eineihem
Their seed is established in their sight with them, and their offspring before their eyes.

אִיּוֹב

מֵשִׁיב יָגָע, וְלֹא יִבְלָע
meshiv yago velo yivla'
That which he laboured for shall he give back, and shall not swallow it down;

כְּחֵיל תְּמוּרָתוֹ, וְלֹא יַעֲלֹס
kecheil temurato, velo ya'alos
according to the substance that he hath gotten, he shall not rejoice.

כִּי-רִצַּץ, עָזַב דַּלִּים; בַּיִת גָּזַל, וְלֹא יִבְנֵהוּ
ki-ritzatz azav dallim; bayit gazal, velo yivenehu
For he hath oppressed and forsaken the poor; he hath violently taken away a house, and he shall not build it up.

כִּי, לֹא-יָדַע שָׁלֵו בְּבִטְנוֹ; בַּחֲמוּדוֹ, לֹא יְמַלֵּט
ki lo-yada shalev bevitno; bachamudo, lo yemallet
Because he knew no quietness within him, in his greed he suffered nought to escape,

אֵין-שָׂרִיד לְאָכְלוֹ; עַל-כֵּן, לֹא-יָחִיל טוּבוֹ
'ein-sarid le'achelo; al-ken, lo-yachil tuvo
There was nothing left that he devoured not--therefore his prosperity shall not endure.

בִּמְלֹאות שִׂפְקוֹ, יֵצֶר לוֹ; כָּל-יַד עָמֵל תְּבֹאֶנּוּ
bimlot sifko yetzer lo; kol-yad amel tevo'ennu
In the fulness of his sufficiency he shall be in straits; the hand of every one that is in misery shall come upon him.

יְהִי, לְמַלֵּא בִטְנוֹ
yehi lemallei vitno
It shall be for the filling of his belly;

יְשַׁלַּח-בּוֹ, חֲרוֹן אַפּוֹ; וְיַמְטֵר עָלֵימוֹ, בִּלְחוּמוֹ
yeshallach-bo charon appo; veyamter aleimo, bilchumo
He shall cast the fierceness of His wrath upon him, and shall cause it to rain upon him into his flesh.

יִבְרַח, מִנֵּשֶׁק בַּרְזֶל; תַּחְלְפֵהוּ, קֶשֶׁת נְחוּשָׁה
yivrach minneshek barzel; tachlefehu, keshet nechushah
If he flee from the iron weapon, the bow of brass shall strike him through.

שָׁלַף, וַיֵּצֵא מִגֵּוָה: וּבָרָק, מִמְּרֹרָתוֹ יַהֲלֹךְ; עָלָיו אֵמִים
shalaf vayetzei miggevah uvarak mimmerorato yahaloch, alav emim
He draweth it forth, and it cometh out of his body; yea, the glittering point cometh out of his gall; terrors are upon him.

כָּל-חֹשֶׁךְ, טָמוּן לִצְפּוּנָיו: תְּאָכְלֵהוּ, אֵשׁ לֹא-נֻפָּח
kol-choshech tamun litzpunav te'ochlehu esh lo-nuppach
All darkness is laid up for his treasures; a fire not blown by man shall consume him;

יֵרַע שָׂרִיד בְּאָהֳלוֹ
yera sarid be'oholo
it shall go ill with him that is left in his tent.

אִיּוֹב

אִם-יַעֲלֶה לַשָּׁמַיִם שִׂיאוֹ; וְרֹאשׁוֹ, לָעָב יַגִּיעַ
'im-ya'aleh lashamayim si'o; verosho, la'av yaggia
Though his excellency mount up to the heavens, and his head reach unto the clouds;

כְּגֶלְלוֹ, לָנֶצַח יֹאבֵד; רֹאָיו, יֹאמְרוּ אַיּוֹ
kegelalo lanetzach yoved; ro'av, yomeru ayo
Yet he shall perish for ever like his own dung; they that have seen him shall say: 'Where is he?'

כַּחֲלוֹם יָעוּף, וְלֹא יִמְצָאוּהוּ; וְיֻדַּד, כְּחֶזְיוֹן לָיְלָה
kachalom ya'uf velo yimtza'uhu; veyuddad, kechezyon laylah
He shall fly away as a dream, and shall not be found; yea, he shall be chased away as a vision of the night.

עַיִן שְׁזָפַתּוּ, וְלֹא תוֹסִיף; וְלֹא-עוֹד, תְּשׁוּרֶנּוּ מְקוֹמוֹ
'ayin shezafattu velo tosif; velo-'od, teshurennu mekomo
The eye which saw him shall see him no more; neither shall his place any more behold him.

בָּנָיו, יְרַצּוּ דַלִּים; וְיָדָיו, תָּשֵׁבְנָה אוֹנוֹ
banav yeratzu dallim; veyadav, tashevnah ono
His children shall appease the poor, and his hands shall restore his wealth.

עַצְמוֹתָיו, מָלְאוּ עֲלוּמָו; וְעִמּוֹ, עַל-עָפָר תִּשְׁכָּב
'atzmotav male'u alumav; ve'immo, al-'afar tishkav
His bones are full of his youth, but it shall lie down with him in the dust.

אִם-תַּמְתִּיק בְּפִיו רָעָה--יַכְחִידֶנָּה, תַּחַת לְשֹׁנוֹ
'im-tamtik befiv ra'ah; yachchidennah, tachat leshono
Though wickedness be sweet in his mouth, though he hide it under his tongue;

יַחְמֹל עָלֶיהָ, וְלֹא יַעַזְבֶנָּה; וְיִמְנָעֶנָּה, בְּתוֹךְ חִכּוֹ
yachmol aleiha velo ya'azvennah; veyimna'ennah, betoch chikko
Though he spare it, and will not let it go, but keep it still within his mouth;

לַחְמוֹ, בְּמֵעָיו נֶהְפָּךְ; מְרוֹרַת פְּתָנִים בְּקִרְבּוֹ
lachmo beme'av nehpach; merorat petanim bekirbo
Yet his food in his bowels is turned, it is the gall of asps within him.

חַיִל בָּלַע, וַיְקִאֶנּוּ; מִבִּטְנוֹ, יוֹרִשֶׁנּוּ אֵל
chayil bala vayki'ennu; mibbitno, yorishennu el
He hath swallowed down riches, and he shall vomit them up again; God shall cast them out of his belly.

רֹאשׁ-פְּתָנִים יִינָק; תַּהַרְגֵהוּ, לְשׁוֹן אֶפְעֶה
rosh-petanim yinak; tahargehu, leshon ef'eh
He shall suck the poison of asps; the viper's tongue shall slay him.

אַל-יֵרֶא בִפְלַגּוֹת--נַהֲרֵי נַחֲלֵי, דְּבַשׁ וְחֶמְאָה
'al-yerei viflaggot; naharei nachalei, devash vechem'ah
He shall not look upon the rivers, the flowing streams of honey and curd.

אִיּוֹב

בְּעֵט-בַּרְזֶל וְעֹפָרֶת--לָעַד, בַּצּוּר יֵחָצְבוּן
be'et-barzel ve'ofaret; la'ad, batzur yechatzevun
That with an iron pen and lead they were graven in the rock for ever!

וַאֲנִי יָדַעְתִּי, גֹּאֲלִי חָי; וְאַחֲרוֹן, עַל-עָפָר יָקוּם
va'ani yada'ti go'ali chai; ve'acharon, al-'afar yakum
But as for me, I know that my Redeemer liveth, and that He will witness at the last upon the dust;

וְאַחַר עוֹרִי, נִקְּפוּ-זֹאת; וּמִבְּשָׂרִי, אֶחֱזֶה אֱלוֹהַּ
ve'achar ori nikkefu-zot; umibbesari, echezeh eloah
And when after my skin this is destroyed, then without my flesh shall I see God;

אֲשֶׁר אֲנִי, אֶחֱזֶה-לִּי--וְעֵינַי רָאוּ וְלֹא-זָר: כָּלוּ כִלְיֹתַי בְּחֵקִי
'asher ani echezeh-li, ve'einai ra'u velo-zar; kalu chilyotai becheki
Whom I, even I, shall see for myself, and mine eyes shall behold, and not another's. My reins are consumed within me.

כִּי תֹאמְרוּ, מַה-נִּרְדָּף-לוֹ; וְשֹׁרֶשׁ דָּבָר, נִמְצָא-בִי
ki tomeru mah-nirdaf-lo; veshoresh davar, nimtza-vi
If ye say: 'How we will persecute him!' seeing that the root of the matter is found in me;

גּוּרוּ לָכֶם, מִפְּנֵי-חֶרֶב--כִּי-חֵמָה, עֲוֺנוֹת חָרֶב: לְמַעַן תֵּדְעוּן שדיּן
guru lachem mippenei-cherev, ki-chemah avonot charev; lema'an tede'un shaddun
Be ye afraid of the sword; for wrath bringeth the punishments of the sword, that ye may know there is a judgment.

כ

וַיַּעַן, צֹפַר הַנַּעֲמָתִי; וַיֹּאמַר
Vaya'an tzofar hanna'amati, vayomar
Then answered Zophar the Naamathite, and said:

לָכֵן, שְׂעִפַּי יְשִׁיבוּנִי; וּבַעֲבוּר, חוּשִׁי בִי
lachen se'ippai yeshivuni; uva'avur, chushi vi
Therefore do my thoughts give answer to me, even by reason of mine agitation that is in me.

מוּסַר כְּלִמָּתִי אֶשְׁמָע; וְרוּחַ, מִבִּינָתִי יַעֲנֵנִי
musar kelimmati eshma'; veruach, mibbinati ya'aneni
I have heard the reproof which putteth me to shame, but out of my understanding my spirit answereth me.

הֲזֹאת יָדַעְתָּ, מִנִּי-עַד; מִנִּי שִׂים אָדָם עֲלֵי-אָרֶץ
hazot yada'ta minni-'ad; minni sim adam alei-'aretz
Knowest thou not this of old time, since man was placed upon earth,

כִּי רִנְנַת רְשָׁעִים, מִקָּרוֹב; וְשִׂמְחַת חָנֵף עֲדֵי-רָגַע
ki rinenat resha'im mikkarov; vesimchat chanef adei-raga
That the triumphing of the wicked is short, and the joy of the godless but for a moment?

אִיּוֹב

יַחַד, יָבֹאוּ גְדוּדָיו--וַיָּסֹלּוּ עָלַי דַּרְכָּם; וַיַּחֲנוּ סָבִיב לְאָהֳלִי
yachad yavo'u gedudav, vayasollu alai darkam; vayachanu saviv le'oholi
His troops come on together, and cast up their way against me, and encamp round about my tent.

אַחַי, מֵעָלַי הִרְחִיק; וְיֹדְעַי, אַךְ-זָרוּ מִמֶּנִּי
'achai me'alai hirchik; veyode'ai, ach-zaru mimmenni
He hath put my brethren far from me, and mine acquaintance are wholly estranged from me.

חָדְלוּ קְרוֹבָי; וּמְיֻדָּעַי שְׁכֵחוּנִי
chadelu kerovai; umeyudda'ai shechechuni
My kinsfolk have failed, and my familiar friends have forgotten me.

גָּרֵי בֵיתִי וְאַמְהֹתַי, לְזָר תַּחְשְׁבֻנִי; נָכְרִי, הָיִיתִי בְעֵינֵיהֶם
garei veiti ve'amhotai lezar tachshevuni; nochri, hayiti ve'eineihem
They that dwell in my house, and my maids, count me for a stranger; I am become an alien in their sight.

לְעַבְדִּי קָרָאתִי, וְלֹא יַעֲנֶה; בְּמוֹ-פִי, אֶתְחַנֶּן-לוֹ
le'avdi karati velo ya'aneh; bemo-fi, etchannen-lo
I call unto my servant, and he giveth me no answer, though I entreat him with my mouth.

רוּחִי, זָרָה לְאִשְׁתִּי; וְחַנֹּתִי, לִבְנֵי בִטְנִי
ruchi zarah le'ishti; vechannoti, livnei vitni
My breath is abhorred of my wife, and I am loathsome to the children of my tribe.

גַּם-עֲוִילִים, מָאֲסוּ בִי; אָקוּמָה, וַיְדַבְּרוּ-בִי
gam-'avilim ma'asu vi; akumah, vaydabberu-vi
Even urchins despised me; if I arise, they speak against me.

תִּעֲבוּנִי, כָּל-מְתֵי סוֹדִי; וְזֶה-אָהַבְתִּי, נֶהְפְּכוּ-בִי
ti'avuni kol-metei sodi; vezeh-'ahavti, nehpechu-vi
All my intimate friends abhor me; and they whom I loved are turned against me.

בְּעוֹרִי וּבִבְשָׂרִי, דָּבְקָה עַצְמִי; וָאֶתְמַלְּטָה, בְּעוֹר שִׁנָּי
be'ori uvivsari davekah atzmi; va'etmalletah, be'or shinnai
My bone cleaveth to my skin and to my flesh, and I am escaped with the skin of my teeth.

חָנֻּנִי חָנֻּנִי אַתֶּם רֵעָי: כִּי יַד-אֱלוֹהַּ, נָגְעָה בִּי
chonnuni chonnuni attem re'ai; ki yad-'eloah, nage'ah bi
Have pity upon me, have pity upon me, O ye my friends; for the hand of God hath touched me.

לָמָּה, תִּרְדְּפֻנִי כְמוֹ-אֵל; וּמִבְּשָׂרִי, לֹא תִשְׂבָּעוּ
lammah tirdefuni chemo-'el; umibbesari, lo tisba'u
Why do ye persecute me as God, and are not satisfied with my flesh?

מִי-יִתֵּן אֵפוֹ, וְיִכָּתְבוּן מִלָּי: מִי-יִתֵּן בַּסֵּפֶר וְיֻחָקוּ
mi-yitten efo veyikkatevun millai; mi-yitten bassefer veyuchaku
Oh that my words were now written! Oh that they were inscribed in a book!

איוֹב

יט

וַיַּעַן אִיּוֹב, וַיֹּאמַר
Vaya'an iyov, vayomar
Then Job answered and said:

עַד-אָנָה, תּוֹגְיוּן נַפְשִׁי; וּתְדַכְּאוּנַנִי בְמִלִּים
'ad-'anah togeyun nafshi; utedakke'unani vemillim
How long will ye vex my soul, and crush me with words?

זֶה עֶשֶׂר פְּעָמִים, תַּכְלִימוּנִי; לֹא-תֵבֹשׁוּ, תַּהְכְּרוּ-לִי
zeh eser pe'amim tachlimuni; lo-tevoshu, tahkeru-li
These ten times have ye reproached me; ye are not ashamed that ye deal harshly with me.

וְאַף-אָמְנָם שָׁגִיתִי; אִתִּי, תָּלִין מְשׁוּגָתִי
ve'af-'omenam shagiti; itti, talin meshugati
And be it indeed that I have erred, mine error remaineth with myself.

אִם-אָמְנָם, עָלַי תַּגְדִּילוּ; וְתוֹכִיחוּ עָלַי, חֶרְפָּתִי
'im-'omenam alai tagdilu; vetochichu alai, cherpatti
If indeed ye will magnify yourselves against me, and plead against me my reproach;

דְּעוּ-אֵפוֹ, כִּי-אֱלוֹהַּ עִוְּתָנִי; וּמְצוּדוֹ, עָלַי הִקִּיף
de'u-'efo ki-'eloah ivvetani; umetzudo, alai hikkif
Know now that God hath subverted my cause, and hath compassed me with His net.

הֵן אֶצְעַק חָמָס, וְלֹא אֵעָנֶה; אֲשַׁוַּע, וְאֵין מִשְׁפָּט
hen etz'ak chamas velo e'aneh; ashavva', ve'ein mishpat
Behold, I cry out: 'Violence!' but I am not heard; I cry aloud, but there is no justice.

אָרְחִי גָדַר, וְלֹא אֶעֱבוֹר; וְעַל נְתִיבוֹתַי, חֹשֶׁךְ יָשִׂים
'orechi gadar velo e'evor; ve'al netivotai, choshech yasim
He hath fenced up my way that I cannot pass, and hath set darkness in my paths.

כְּבוֹדִי, מֵעָלַי הִפְשִׁיט; וַיָּסַר, עֲטֶרֶת רֹאשִׁי
kevodi me'alai hifshit; vayasar, ateret roshi
He hath stripped me of my glory, and taken the crown from my head.

יִתְּצֵנִי סָבִיב, וָאֵלַךְ; וַיַּסַּע כָּעֵץ, תִּקְוָתִי
yittetzeni saviv va'elach; vayassa ka'etz, tikvati
He hath broken me down on every side, and I am gone; and my hope hath He plucked up like a tree.

וַיַּחַר עָלַי אַפּוֹ; וַיַּחְשְׁבֵנִי לוֹ כְצָרָיו
vayachar alai appo; vayachsheveni lo chetzarav
He hath also kindled His wrath against me, and He counteth me unto Him as one of His adversaries.

אִיּוֹב

טָמוּן בָּאָרֶץ חַבְלוֹ; וּמַלְכֻּדְתּוֹ, עֲלֵי נָתִיב
tamun ba'aretz chavlo; umalkudto, alei nativ
A noose is hid for him in the ground, and a trap for him in the way.

סָבִיב, בִּעֲתֻהוּ בַלָּהוֹת; וֶהֱפִיצֻהוּ לְרַגְלָיו
saviv bi'atuhu vallahot; vehefitzuhu leraglav
Terrors shall overwhelm him on every side, and shall entrap him at his feet.

יְהִי-רָעֵב אֹנוֹ; וְאֵיד, נָכוֹן לְצַלְעוֹ
yehi-ra'ev ono; ve'eid, nachon letzal'o
His trouble shall be ravenous, and calamity shall be ready for his fall.

יֹאכַל, בַּדֵּי עוֹרוֹ; יֹאכַל בַּדָּיו, בְּכוֹר מָוֶת
yochal baddei oro; yochal baddav, bechor mavet
It shall devour the members of his body, yea, the first-born of death shall devour his members.

יִנָּתֵק מֵאָהֳלוֹ, מִבְטַחוֹ; וְתַצְעִדֵהוּ, לְמֶלֶךְ בַּלָּהוֹת
yinnatek me'oholo mivtacho; vetatz'idehu, lemelech ballahot
That wherein he trusteth shall be plucked out of his tent; and he shall be brought to the king of terrors.

תִּשְׁכּוֹן בְּאָהֳלוֹ, מִבְּלִי-לוֹ; יְזֹרֶה עַל-נָוֵהוּ גָפְרִית
tishkon be'oholo mibbeli-lo; yezoreh al-navehu goferit
There shall dwell in his tent that which is none of his; brimstone shall be scattered upon his habitation.

מִתַּחַת, שָׁרָשָׁיו יִבָשׁוּ; וּמִמַּעַל, יִמַּל קְצִירוֹ
mittachat sharashav yivashu; umimma'al, yimmal ketziro
His roots shall dry up beneath, and above shall his branch wither.

זִכְרוֹ-אָבַד, מִנִּי-אָרֶץ; וְלֹא-שֵׁם לוֹ, עַל-פְּנֵי-חוּץ
zichro-'avad minni-'aretz; velo-shem lo, al-penei-chutz
His remembrance shall perish from the earth, and he shall have no name abroad.

יֶהְדְּפֻהוּ, מֵאוֹר אֶל-חֹשֶׁךְ; וּמִתֵּבֵל יְנִדֻּהוּ
yehdefuhu me'or el-choshech; umittevel yenidduhu
He shall be driven from light into darkness, and chased out of the world.

לֹא נִין לוֹ וְלֹא-נֶכֶד בְּעַמּוֹ; וְאֵין שָׂרִיד, בִּמְגוּרָיו
lo nin lo velo-neched be'ammo; ve'ein sarid, bimgurav
He shall have neither son nor son's son among his people, nor any remaining in his dwellings.

עַל-יוֹמוֹ, נָשַׁמּוּ אַחֲרֹנִים; וְקַדְמֹנִים, אָחֲזוּ שָׂעַר
'al-yomo nashammu acharonim; vekadmonim, achazu sa'ar
They that come after shall be astonished at his day, as they that went before are affrighted.

אַךְ-אֵלֶּה, מִשְׁכְּנוֹת עַוָּל; וְזֶה, מְקוֹם לֹא-יָדַע-אֵל
'ach-'elleh mishkenot avval; vezeh, mekom lo-yada'-'el
Surely such are the dwellings of the wicked, and this is the place of him that knoweth not God.

אִיּוֹב

בַּדֵּי שְׁאֹל תֵּרַדְנָה; אִם-יַחַד עַל-עָפָר נָחַת
baddei she'ol teradnah; im-yachad al-'afar nachat
They shall go down to the bars of the nether-world, when we are at rest together in the dust.

חי

וַיַּעַן, בִּלְדַּד הַשֻּׁחִי; וַיֹּאמַר
Vaya'an bildad hashuchi, vayomar
Then answered Bildad the Shuhite, and said:

עַד-אָנָה, תְּשִׂימוּן קִנְצֵי לְמִלִּין; תָּבִינוּ, וְאַחַר נְדַבֵּר
'ad-'anah tesimun kintzei lemillin; tavinu, ve'achar nedabber
How long will ye lay snares for words? Consider, and afterwards we will speak.

מַדּוּעַ, נֶחְשַׁבְנוּ כַבְּהֵמָה; נִטְמִינוּ, בְּעֵינֵיכֶם
maddua nechshavnu chabbehemah; nitminu, be'eineichem
Wherefore are we counted as beasts, and reputed dull in your sight?

טֹרֵף נַפְשׁוֹ, בְּאַפּוֹ: הַלְמַעַנְךָ, תֵּעָזַב אָרֶץ
toref nafsho, be'appo halma'ancha te'azav aretz
Thou that tearest thyself in thine anger, shall the earth be forsaken for thee?

וְיֶעְתַּק-צוּר, מִמְּקֹמוֹ
veye'tak-tzur, mimmekomo
Or shall the rock be removed out of its place?

גַּם אוֹר רְשָׁעִים יִדְעָךְ; וְלֹא-יִגַּהּ, שְׁבִיב אִשּׁוֹ
gam or resha'im yid'ach; velo-yiggah, sheviv isho
Yea, the light of the wicked shall be put out, and the spark of his fire shall not shine.

אוֹר, חָשַׁךְ בְּאָהֳלוֹ; וְנֵרוֹ, עָלָיו יִדְעָךְ
'or chashach be'oholo; venero, alav yid'ach
The light shall be dark in his tent, and his lamp over him shall be put out.

יֵצְרוּ, צַעֲדֵי אוֹנוֹ; וְתַשְׁלִיכֵהוּ עֲצָתוֹ
yetzru tza'adei ono; vetashlichehu atzato
The steps of his strength shall be straitened, and his own counsel shall cast him down.

כִּי-שֻׁלַּח בְּרֶשֶׁת בְּרַגְלָיו; וְעַל-שְׂבָכָה, יִתְהַלָּךְ
ki-shullach bereshet beraglav; ve'al-sevachah, yit'hallach
For he is cast into a net by his own feet, and he walketh upon the toils.

יֹאחֵז בְּעָקֵב פָּח; יַחֲזֵק עָלָיו צַמִּים
yochez be'akev pach; yachazek alav tzammim
A gin shall take him by the heel, and a snare shall lay hold on him.

איוב

כִּי-לִבָּם, צָפַנְתָּ מִשָּׂכֶל; עַל-כֵּן, לֹא תְרֹמֵם
ki-libbam tzafanta missachel; al-ken, lo teromem
For Thou hast hid their heart from understanding; therefore shalt Thou not exalt them.

לְחֵלֶק, יַגִּיד רֵעִים; וְעֵינֵי בָנָיו תִּכְלֶנָה
lechelek yaggid re'im; ve'einei vanav tichlenah
He that denounceth his friends for the sake of flattery, even the eyes of his children shall fail.

וְהִצִּיגַנִי, לִמְשֹׁל עַמִּים; וְתֹפֶת לְפָנִים אֶהְיֶה
vehitzigani limshol ammim; vetofet lefanim ehyeh
He hath made me also a byword of the people; and I am become one in whose face they spit.

וַתֵּכַהּ מִכַּעַשׂ עֵינִי; וִיצֻרַי כַּצֵּל כֻּלָּם
vattechah mikka'as eini; viytzurai katzel kullam
Mine eye also is dimmed by reason of vexation, and all my members are as a shadow.

יָשֹׁמּוּ יְשָׁרִים עַל-זֹאת; וְנָקִי, עַל-חָנֵף יִתְעֹרָר
yashommu yesharim al-zot; venaki, al-chanef yit'orar
Upright men are astonished at this, and the innocent stirreth up himself against the godless.

וְיֹאחֵז צַדִּיק דַּרְכּוֹ; וּטְהָר-יָדַיִם, יֹסִיף אֹמֶץ
veyochez tzaddik darko; utohor-yadayim, yosif ometz
Yet the righteous holdeth on his way, and he that hath clean hands waxeth stronger and stronger.

וְאוּלָם--כֻּלָּם תָּשֻׁבוּ, וּבֹאוּ נָא; וְלֹא-אֶמְצָא בָכֶם חָכָם
ve'ulam, kullam tashuvu uvo'u na; velo-'emtza vachem chacham
But as for you all, do ye return, and come now; and I shall not find a wise man among you.

יָמַי עָבְרוּ, זִמֹּתַי נִתְּקוּ--מוֹרָשֵׁי לְבָבִי
yamai averu zimmotai nitteku; morashei levavi
My days are past, my purposes are broken off, even the thoughts of my heart.

לַיְלָה, לְיוֹם יָשִׂימוּ; אוֹר, קָרוֹב מִפְּנֵי-חֹשֶׁךְ
laylah leyom yasimu; or, karov mippenei-choshech
They change the night into day; the light is short because of darkness.

אִם-אֲקַוֶּה, שְׁאוֹל בֵּיתִי; בַּחֹשֶׁךְ, רִפַּדְתִּי יְצוּעָי
'im-'akavveh she'ol beiti; bachoshech, rippadti yetzu'ai
If I look for the nether-world as my house; if I have spread my couch in the darkness;

לַשַּׁחַת קָרָאתִי, אָבִי אָתָּה; אִמִּי וַאֲחֹתִי, לָרִמָּה
lashachat karati avi attah; immi va'achoti, larimmah
If I have said to corruption: 'Thou art my father', to the worm: 'Thou art my mother, and my sister';

וְאַיֵּה, אֵפוֹ תִקְוָתִי; וְתִקְוָתִי, מִי יְשׁוּרֶנָּה
ve'ayeh efo tikvati; vetikvati, mi yeshurennah
Where then is my hope? And as for my hope, who shall see it?

אִיּוֹב

שַׂק תָּפַרְתִּי, עֲלֵי גִלְדִּי; וְעֹלַלְתִּי בֶעָפָר קַרְנִי
sak tafarti alei gildi; ve'olalti ve'afar karni
I have sewed sackcloth upon my skin, and have laid my horn in the dust.

פָּנַי חֳמַרְמְרוּ, מִנִּי-בֶכִי; וְעַל עַפְעַפַּי צַלְמָוֶת
panai chomarmeru minni-vechi; ve'al af'appai tzalmavet
My face is reddened with weeping, and on my eyelids is the shadow of death;

עַל, לֹא-חָמָס בְּכַפָּי; וּתְפִלָּתִי זַכָּה
'al lo-chamas bechappai; utefillati zakkah
Although there is no violence in my hands, and my prayer is pure.

אֶרֶץ, אַל-תְּכַסִּי דָמִי; וְאַל-יְהִי מָקוֹם, לְזַעֲקָתִי
'eretz al-techassi dami; ve'al-yehi makom, leza'akati
O earth, cover not thou my blood, and let my cry have no resting-place.

גַּם-עַתָּה, הִנֵּה-בַשָּׁמַיִם עֵדִי; וְשָׂהֲדִי, בַּמְּרֹמִים
gam-'attah hinneh-vashamayim edi; vesahadi, bammeromim
Even now, behold, my Witness is in heaven, and He that testifieth of me is on high.

מְלִיצַי רֵעָי; אֶל-אֱלוֹהַּ, דָּלְפָה עֵינִי
melitzai re'ai; el-'eloah, dalefah eini
Mine inward thoughts are my intercessors, mine eye poureth out tears unto God;

וְיוֹכַח לְגֶבֶר עִם-אֱלוֹהַּ; וּבֶן-אָדָם לְרֵעֵהוּ
veyochach legever im-'eloah; uven-'adam lere'ehu
That He would set aright a man contending with God, as a son of man setteth aright his neighbour!

כִּי-שְׁנוֹת מִסְפָּר יֶאֱתָיוּ; וְאֹרַח לֹא-אָשׁוּב אֶהֱלֹךְ
ki-shenot mispar ye'etayu; ve'orach lo-'ashuv eheloch
For the years that are few are coming on, and I shall go the way whence I shall not return.

יז

רוּחִי חֻבָּלָה, יָמַי נִזְעָכוּ; קְבָרִים לִי
Ruchi chubbalah yamai niz'achu, kevarim li
My spirit is consumed, my days are extinct, the grave is ready for me.

אִם-לֹא הֲתֻלִים, עִמָּדִי; וּבְהַמְּרוֹתָם, תָּלַן עֵינִי
'im-lo hatulim immadi; uvehammerotam, talan eini
Surely there are mockers with me, and mine eye abideth in their provocation.

שִׂימָה-נָּא, עָרְבֵנִי עִמָּךְ; מִי הוּא, לְיָדִי יִתָּקֵעַ
simah-na areveni immach; mi hu, leyadi yittakea
Give now a pledge, be surety for me with Thyself; who else is there that will strike hands with me?

אִיּוֹב

וַתִּקְמְטֵנִי, לְעֵד הָיָה
vattikmeteni le'ed hayah
And Thou hast shrivelled me up, which is a witness against me;

וַיָּקָם בִּי כַחֲשִׁי, בְּפָנַי יַעֲנֶה
vayakom bi chachashi, befanai ya'aneh
and my leanness riseth up against me, it testifieth to my face.

אַפּוֹ טָרַף, וַיִּשְׂטְמֵנִי--חָרַק עָלַי בְּשִׁנָּיו
'appo taraf vayistemeni, charak alai beshinnav
He hath torn me in His wrath, and hated me; He hath gnashed upon me with His teeth;

צָרִי, יִלְטוֹשׁ עֵינָיו לִי
tzari yiltosh einav li
mine adversary sharpeneth his eyes upon me.

פָּעֲרוּ עָלַי, בְּפִיהֶם--בְּחֶרְפָּה, הִכּוּ לְחָיָי
pa'aru alai befihem, becherpah hikku lechayai
They have gaped upon me with their mouth; they have smitten me upon the cheek scornfully;

יַחַד, עָלַי יִתְמַלָּאוּן
yachad, alai yitmalla'un
they gather themselves together against me.

יַסְגִּירֵנִי אֵל, אֶל עֲוִיל; וְעַל-יְדֵי רְשָׁעִים יִרְטֵנִי
yasgireni el el avil; ve'al-yedei resha'im yirteni
God delivereth me to the ungodly, and casteth me into the hands of the wicked.

שָׁלֵו הָיִיתִי, וַיְפַרְפְּרֵנִי--וְאָחַז בְּעָרְפִּי
shalev hayiti vayfarpereni, ve'achaz be'orpi
I was at ease, and He broke me asunder; yea, He hath taken me by the neck,

וַיְפַצְפְּצֵנִי; וַיְקִימֵנִי לוֹ, לְמַטָּרָה
vayfatzpetzeni; vaykimeni lo, lemattarah
and dashed me to pieces; He hath also set me up for His mark.

יָסֹבּוּ עָלַי, רַבָּיו--יְפַלַּח כִּלְיוֹתַי, וְלֹא יַחְמֹל
yasobbu alai rabbav, yefallach kilyotai velo yachmol
His archers compass me round about, He cleaveth my reins asunder, and doth not spare;

יִשְׁפֹּךְ לָאָרֶץ, מְרֵרָתִי
yishpoch la'aretz, mererati
He poureth out my gall upon the ground.

יִפְרְצֵנִי פֶרֶץ, עַל-פְּנֵי-פָרֶץ; יָרֻץ עָלַי כְּגִבּוֹר
yifretzeni feretz al-penei-faretz; yarutz alai kegibbor
He breaketh me with breach upon breach; He runneth upon me like a giant.

איוב

יַחְמֹס כַּגֶּפֶן בִּסְרוֹ; וְיַשְׁלֵךְ כַּזַּיִת, נִצָּתוֹ
yachmos kaggefen bisro; veyashlech kazzayit, nitzato
He shall shake off his unripe grape as the vine, and shall cast off his flower as the olive.

כִּי-עֲדַת חָנֵף גַּלְמוּד; וְאֵשׁ, אָכְלָה אָהֳלֵי-שֹׁחַד
ki-'adat chanef galmud; ve'esh, achelah oholei-shochad
For the company of the godless shall be desolate, and fire shall consume the tents of bribery.

הָרֹה עָמָל, וְיָלֹד אָוֶן; וּבִטְנָם, תָּכִין מִרְמָה
haroh amol veyalod aven; uvitnam, tachin mirmah
They conceive mischief, and bring forth iniquity, and their belly prepareth deceit.

טז

וַיַּעַן אִיּוֹב, וַיֹּאמַר
Vaya'an iyov, vayomar
Then Job answered and said:

שָׁמַעְתִּי כְאֵלֶּה רַבּוֹת; מְנַחֲמֵי עָמָל כֻּלְּכֶם
shama'ti che'elleh rabbot; menachamei amal kullechem
I have heard many such things; sorry comforters are ye all.

הֲקֵץ לְדִבְרֵי-רוּחַ; אוֹ מַה-יַּמְרִיצְךָ, כִּי תַעֲנֶה
haketz ledivrei-ruach; o mah-yamritzecha, ki ta'aneh
Shall windy words have an end? Or what provoketh thee that thou answerest?

גַּם, אָנֹכִי--כָּכֶם אֲדַבֵּרָה: לוּ-יֵשׁ נַפְשְׁכֶם, תַּחַת נַפְשִׁי
gam anochi kachem adabberah lu-yesh nafshechem tachat nafshi
I also could speak as ye do; if your soul were in my soul's stead,

אַחְבִּירָה עֲלֵיכֶם בְּמִלִּים; וְאָנִיעָה עֲלֵיכֶם, בְּמוֹ רֹאשִׁי
achbirah aleichem bemillim; ve'ani'ah aleichem, bemo roshi
I could join words together against you, and shake my head at you.

אֲאַמִּצְכֶם בְּמוֹ-פִי; וְנִיד שְׂפָתַי יַחְשֹׂךְ
'a'ammitzchem bemo-fi; venid sefatai yachsoch
I would strengthen you with my mouth, and the moving of my lips would assuage your grief.

אִם-אֲדַבְּרָה, לֹא-יֵחָשֵׂךְ כְּאֵבִי; וְאַחְדְּלָה, מַה-מִּנִּי יַהֲלֹךְ
'im-'adabberah lo-yechasech ke'evi; ve'achdelah, mah-minni yahaloch
Though I speak, my pain is not assuaged; and though I forbear, what am I eased?

אַךְ-עַתָּה הֶלְאָנִי; הֲשִׁמּוֹתָ, כָּל-עֲדָתִי
'ach-'attah hel'ani; hashimmota, kol-'adati
But now He hath made me weary; Thou hast made desolate all my company.

איוב

קוֹל-פְּחָדִים בְּאָזְנָיו; בַּשָּׁלוֹם, שׁוֹדֵד יְבוֹאֶנּוּ
kol-pechadim be'ozenav; bashalom, shoded yevo'ennu
A sound of terrors is in his ears: in prosperity the destroyer shall come upon him.

לֹא-יַאֲמִין שׁוּב, מִנִּי-חֹשֶׁךְ; וְצָפוּי הוּא אֱלֵי-חָרֶב
lo-ya'amin shuv minni-choshech; vetzafui hu elei-charev
He believeth not that he shall return out of darkness, and he is waited for of the sword.

נֹדֵד הוּא לַלֶּחֶם אַיֵּה; יָדַע, כִּי-נָכוֹן בְּיָדוֹ יוֹם-חֹשֶׁךְ
noded hu lallechem ayeh; yada ki-nachon beyado yom-choshech
He wandereth abroad for bread: 'Where is it?' He knoweth that the day of darkness is ready at his hand.

יְבַעֲתֻהוּ, צַר וּמְצוּקָה; תִּתְקְפֵהוּ, כְּמֶלֶךְ עָתִיד לַכִּידוֹר
yeva'atuhu tzar umetzukah; titkefehu, kemelech atid lakkidor
Distress and anguish overwhelm him; they prevail against him, as a king ready to the battle.

כִּי-נָטָה אֶל-אֵל יָדוֹ; וְאֶל-שַׁדַּי, יִתְגַּבָּר
ki-natah el-'el yado; ve'el-shaddai, yitgabbar
Because he hath stretched out his hand against God, and behaveth himself proudly against the Almighty;

יָרוּץ אֵלָיו בְּצַוָּאר; בַּעֲבִי, גַּבֵּי מָגִנָּיו
yarutz elav betzavvar; ba'avi, gabbei maginnav
He runneth upon him with a stiff neck, with the thick bosses of his bucklers.

כִּי-כִסָּה פָנָיו בְּחֶלְבּוֹ; וַיַּעַשׂ פִּימָה עֲלֵי-כָסֶל
ki-chissah fanav bechelbo; vaya'as pimah alei-chasel
Because he hath covered his face with his fatness, and made collops of fat on his loins;

וַיִּשְׁכּוֹן, עָרִים נִכְחָדוֹת--בָּתִּים, לֹא-יֵשְׁבוּ לָמוֹ: אֲשֶׁר הִתְעַתְּדוּ לְגַלִּים
vayishkon arim nichchadot, battim lo-yeshevu lamo; asher hit'attedu legallim
And he hath dwelt in desolate cities, in houses which no man would inhabit, which were ready to become heaps.

לֹא-יֶעְשַׁר, וְלֹא-יָקוּם חֵילוֹ; וְלֹא-יִטֶּה לָאָרֶץ מִנְלָם
lo-ye'shar velo-yakum cheilo; velo-yitteh la'aretz minlam
He shall not be rich, neither shall his substance continue, neither shall their produce bend to the earth.

לֹא-יָסוּר, מִנִּי-חֹשֶׁךְ--יֹנַקְתּוֹ, תְּיַבֵּשׁ שַׁלְהָבֶת; וְיָסוּר, בְּרוּחַ פִּיו
lo-yasur minni-choshech, yonakto teyabbesh shalhavet; veyasur, beruach piv
He shall not depart out of darkness; the flame shall dry up his branches, and by the breath of His mouth shall he go away.

אַל-יַאֲמֵן בַּשָּׁו נִתְעָה: כִּי-שָׁוְא, תִּהְיֶה תְמוּרָתוֹ
'al-ya'amen bashav bashav nit'ah; ki-shav, tihyeh temurato
Let him not trust in vanity, deceiving himself; for vanity shall be his recompense.

בְּלֹא-יוֹמוֹ, תִּמָּלֵא; וְכִפָּתוֹ, לֹא רַעֲנָנָה
belo-yomo timmale; vechippato, lo ra'ananah
It shall be accomplished before his time, and his branch shall not be leafy.

אִיּוֹב

מַה-יָּדַעְתָּ, וְלֹא נֵדָע; תָּבִין, וְלֹא-עִמָּנוּ הוּא
mah-yada'ta velo neda'; tavin, velo-'immanu hu
What knowest thou, that we know not? What understandest thou, which is not in us?

גַּם-שָׂב גַּם-יָשִׁישׁ בָּנוּ--כַּבִּיר מֵאָבִיךָ יָמִים
gam-sav gam-yashish banu; kabbir me'avicha yamim
With us are both the gray-headed and the very aged men, much older than thy father.

הַמְעַט מִמְּךָ, תַּנְחֻמוֹת אֵל; וְדָבָר, לָאַט עִמָּךְ
ham'at mimmecha tanchumot el; vedavar, la'at immach
Are the consolations of God too small for thee, and the word that dealeth gently with thee?

מַה-יִּקָּחֲךָ לִבֶּךָ; וּמַה-יִּרְזְמוּן עֵינֶיךָ
mah-yikkachacha libbecha; umah-yirzemun eineicha
Why doth thy heart carry thee away? And why do thine eyes wink?

כִּי-תָשִׁיב אֶל-אֵל רוּחֶךָ; וְהֹצֵאתָ מִפִּיךָ מִלִּין
ki-tashiv el-'el ruchecha; vehotzeta mippicha millin
That thou turnest thy spirit against God, and lettest such words go out of thy mouth.

מָה-אֱנוֹשׁ כִּי-יִזְכֶּה; וְכִי-יִצְדַּק, יְלוּד אִשָּׁה
mah-'enosh ki-yizkeh; vechi-yitzdak, yelud ishah
What is man, that he should be clean? And he that is born of a woman, that he should be righteous?

הֵן בִּקְדֹשָׁו, לֹא יַאֲמִין; וְשָׁמַיִם, לֹא-זַכּוּ בְעֵינָיו
hen bikdoshav bikdoshav lo ya'amin; veshamayim, lo-zakku ve'einav
Behold, He putteth no trust in His holy ones; yea, the heavens are not clean in His sight.

אַף, כִּי-נִתְעָב וְנֶאֱלָח; אִישׁ-שֹׁתֶה כַמַּיִם עַוְלָה
'af ki-nit'av vene'elach; ish-shoteh chammayim avlah
How much less one that is abominable and impure, man who drinketh iniquity like water!

אֲחַוְךָ שְׁמַע-לִי; וְזֶה-חָזִיתִי, וַאֲסַפֵּרָה
'achavcha shema'-li; vezeh-chaziti, va'asapperah
I will tell thee, hear thou me; and that which I have seen I will declare--

אֲשֶׁר-חֲכָמִים יַגִּידוּ; וְלֹא כִחֲדוּ, מֵאֲבוֹתָם
'asher-chachamim yaggidu; velo chichadu, me'avotam
Which wise men have told from their fathers, and have not hid it;

לָהֶם לְבַדָּם, נִתְּנָה הָאָרֶץ; וְלֹא-עָבַר זָר בְּתוֹכָם
lahem levaddam nittenah ha'aretz; velo-'avar zar betocham
Unto whom alone the land was given, and no stranger passed among them.

כָּל-יְמֵי רָשָׁע, הוּא מִתְחוֹלֵל; וּמִסְפַּר שָׁנִים, נִצְפְּנוּ לֶעָרִיץ
kol-yemei rasho hu mitcholel; umispar shanim, nitzpenu le'aritz
The wicked man travaileth with pain all his days, even the number of years that are laid up for the oppressor.

אִיּוֹב

תִּתְקְפֵהוּ לָנֶצַח, וַיַּהֲלֹךְ; מְשַׁנֶּה פָנָיו, וַתְּשַׁלְּחֵהוּ
titkefehu lanetzach vayahaloch; meshanneh fanav, vatteshallechehu
Thou prevailest for ever against him, and he passeth; Thou changest his countenance, and sendest him away.

יִכְבְּדוּ בָנָיו, וְלֹא יֵדָע; וְיִצְעֲרוּ, וְלֹא-יָבִין לָמוֹ
yichbedu vanav velo yeda'; veyitz'aru, velo-yavin lamo
His sons come to honour, and he knoweth it not; and they are brought low, but he regardeth them not.

אַךְ-בְּשָׂרוֹ, עָלָיו יִכְאָב; וְנַפְשׁוֹ, עָלָיו תֶּאֱבָל
'ach-besaro alav yich'av; venafsho, alav te'eval
But his flesh grieveth for him, and his soul mourneth over him.

טו

וַיַּעַן, אֱלִיפַז הַתֵּימָנִי; וַיֹּאמַר
Vaya'an elifaz hatteimani, vayomar
Then answered Eliphaz the Temanite, and said:

הֶחָכָם, יַעֲנֶה דַעַת-רוּחַ; וִימַלֵּא קָדִים בִּטְנוֹ
hechacham, ya'aneh da'at-ruach; viymallei kadim bitno
Should a wise man make answer with windy knowledge, and fill his belly with the east wind?

הוֹכֵחַ בְּדָבָר, לֹא יִסְכּוֹן; וּמִלִּים, לֹא-יוֹעִיל בָּם
hocheach bedavor lo yiskon; umillim, lo-yo'il bam
Should he reason with unprofitable talk, or with speeches wherewith he can do no good?

אַף-אַתָּה, תָּפֵר יִרְאָה; וְתִגְרַע שִׂיחָה, לִפְנֵי-אֵל
'af-'attah tafer yir'ah; vetigra sichah, lifnei-'el
Yea, thou doest away with fear, and impairest devotion before God.

כִּי יְאַלֵּף עֲוֺנְךָ פִיךָ; וְתִבְחַר, לְשׁוֹן עֲרוּמִים
ki ye'allef avonecha ficha; vetivchar, leshon arumim
For thine iniquity teacheth thy mouth, and thou choosest the tongue of the crafty.

יַרְשִׁיעֲךָ פִיךָ וְלֹא-אָנִי; וּשְׂפָתֶיךָ, יַעֲנוּ-בָךְ
yarshi'acha ficha velo-'ani; usefateicha, ya'anu-vach
Thine own mouth condemneth thee, and not I; yea, thine own lips testify against thee.

הֲרִאישׁוֹן אָדָם, תִּוָּלֵד; וְלִפְנֵי גְבָעוֹת חוֹלָלְתָּ
hariyoshon adam tivvaled; velifnei geva'ot cholaleta
Art thou the first man that was born? Or wast thou brought forth before the hills?

הַבְסוֹד אֱלוֹהַּ תִּשְׁמָע; וְתִגְרַע אֵלֶיךָ חָכְמָה
havesod eloha tishma'; vetigra eleicha chochmah
Dost thou hearken in the council of God? And dost thou restrain wisdom to thyself?

אִיּוֹב

וְגֶבֶר יָמוּת, וַיֶּחֱלָשׁ; וַיִּגְוַע אָדָם וְאַיּוֹ
vegever yamut vayechelash; vayigva adam ve'ayo
But man dieth, and lieth low; yea, man perisheth, and where is he?

אָזְלוּ-מַיִם, מִנִּי-יָם; וְנָהָר, יֶחֱרַב וְיָבֵשׁ
'azelu-mayim minni-yam; venahar, yecherav veyavesh
As the waters fail from the sea, and the river is drained dry;

וְאִישׁ שָׁכַב, וְלֹא-יָקוּם: עַד-בִּלְתִּי שָׁמַיִם, לֹא יָקִיצוּ; וְלֹא-יֵעֹרוּ, מִשְּׁנָתָם
ve'ish shachav, velo-yakum ad-bilti shamayim lo yakitzu; velo-ye'oru, mishenatam
So man lieth down and riseth not; till the heavens be no more, they shall not awake, nor be roused out of their sleep.

מִי יִתֵּן, בִּשְׁאוֹל תַּצְפִּנֵנִי--תַּסְתִּירֵנִי
mi yitten bish'ol tatzpineni, tastireni
Oh that Thou wouldest hide me in the nether-world, that Thou wouldest keep me secret,

עַד-שׁוּב אַפֶּךָ; תָּשִׁית לִי חֹק וְתִזְכְּרֵנִי
ad-shuv appecha; tashit li chok vetizkereni
until Thy wrath be past, that Thou wouldest appoint me a set time, and remember me!--

אִם-יָמוּת גֶּבֶר, הֲיִחְיֶה: כָּל-יְמֵי צְבָאִי אֲיַחֵל--עַד-בּוֹא, חֲלִיפָתִי
'im-yamut gever, hayichyeh kol-yemei tzeva'i ayachel; ad-bo, chalifati
If a man die, may he live again? All the days of my service would I wait, till my relief should come--

תִּקְרָא, וְאָנֹכִי אֶעֱנֶךָּ; לְמַעֲשֵׂה יָדֶיךָ תִכְסֹף
tikra ve'anochi e'eneka; lema'aseh yadeicha tichsof
Thou wouldest call, and I would answer Thee; Thou wouldest have a desire to the work of Thy hands.

כִּי-עַתָּה, צְעָדַי תִּסְפּוֹר; לֹא-תִשְׁמֹר, עַל-חַטָּאתִי
ki-'attah tze'adai tispor; lo-tishmor, al-chattati
But now Thou numberest my steps, Thou dost not even wait for my sin;

חָתֻם בִּצְרוֹר פִּשְׁעִי; וַתִּטְפֹּל, עַל-עֲוֹנִי
chatum bitzror pish'i; vattitpol, al-'avoni
My transgression is sealed up in a bag, and Thou heapest up mine iniquity.

וְאוּלָם, הַר-נוֹפֵל יִבּוֹל; וְצוּר, יֶעְתַּק מִמְּקֹמוֹ
ve'ulom har-nofel yibbol; vetzur, ye'tak mimmekomo
And surely the mountain falling crumbleth away, and the rock is removed out of its place;

אֲבָנִים, שָׁחֲקוּ מַיִם-- תִּשְׁטֹף-סְפִיחֶיהָ עֲפַר-אָרֶץ
'avanim shachaku mayim, tishtof-seficheiha afar-'aretz
The waters wear the stones; the overflowings thereof wash away the dust of the earth;

וְתִקְוַת אֱנוֹשׁ הֶאֱבַדְתָּ
vetikvat enosh he'evadta
so Thou destroyest the hope of man.

אִיּוֹב

וְהוּא, כְּרָקָב יִבְלֶה; כְּבֶגֶד, אֲכָלוֹ עָשׁ

vehu kerakav yivleh; keveged, achalo ash

Though I am like a wine-skin that consumeth, like a garment that is moth-eaten.

יד

אָדָם, יְלוּד אִשָּׁה--קְצַר יָמִים, וּשְׂבַע-רֹגֶז

Adom yelud ishah; ketzar yamim, useva'-rogez

Man that is born of a woman is of few days, and full of trouble.

כְּצִיץ יָצָא, וַיִּמָּל; וַיִּבְרַח כַּצֵּל, וְלֹא יַעֲמוֹד

ketzitz yatza vayimmal; vayivrach katzel, velo ya'amod

He cometh forth like a flower, and withereth; he fleeth also as a shadow, and continueth not.

אַף-עַל-זֶה, פָּקַחְתָּ עֵינֶךָ; וְאֹתִי תָבִיא בְמִשְׁפָּט עִמָּךְ

'af-'al-zeh pakachta einecha; ve'oti tavi vemishpat immach

And dost Thou open Thine eyes upon such a one, and bringest me into judgment with Thee?

מִי-יִתֵּן טָהוֹר, מִטָּמֵא--לֹא אֶחָד

mi-yitten tahor mittame, lo echad

Who can bring a clean thing out of an unclean? not one.

אִם חֲרוּצִים, יָמָיו--מִסְפַּר-חֳדָשָׁיו אִתָּךְ

'im charutzim yamav, mispar-chodashav ittach

Seeing his days are determined, the number of his months is with Thee,

חֻקָּו עָשִׂיתָ, וְלֹא יַעֲבוֹר

chukkav asita, velo ya'avor

and Thou hast appointed his bounds that he cannot pass;

שְׁעֵה מֵעָלָיו וְיֶחְדָּל-- עַד-יִרְצֶה, כְּשָׂכִיר יוֹמוֹ

she'eh me'alav veyechdal; ad-yirtzeh, kesachir yomo

Look away from him, that he may rest, till he shall accomplish, as a hireling, his day.

כִּי יֵשׁ לָעֵץ, תִּקְוָה: אִם-יִכָּרֵת, וְעוֹד יַחֲלִיף; וְיוֹנַקְתּוֹ, לֹא תֶחְדָּל

ki yesh la'etz, tikvah im-yikkaret ve'od yachalif; veyonakto, lo techdal

For there is hope of a tree, if it be cut down, that it will sprout again, and that the tender branch thereof will not cease.

אִם-יַזְקִין בָּאָרֶץ שָׁרְשׁוֹ; וּבֶעָפָר, יָמוּת גִּזְעוֹ

'im-yazkin ba'aretz shoresho; uve'afar, yamut giz'o

Though the root thereof wax old in the earth, and the stock thereof die in the ground;

מֵרֵיחַ מַיִם יַפְרִחַ; וְעָשָׂה קָצִיר כְּמוֹ-נָטַע

mereiach mayim yafriach; ve'asah katzir kemo-nata

Yet through the scent of water it will bud, and put forth boughs like a plant.

אִיּוֹב

שִׁמְעוּ שָׁמוֹעַ, מִלָּתִי; וְאַחֲוָתִי, בְּאָזְנֵיכֶם
shim'u shamoa millati; ve'achavati, be'ozneichem
Hear diligently my speech, and let my declaration be in your ears.

הִנֵּה-נָא, עָרַכְתִּי מִשְׁפָּט; יָדַעְתִּי, כִּי-אֲנִי אֶצְדָּק
hinneh-na arachti mishpat; yada'ti, ki-'ani etzdak
Behold now, I have ordered my cause; I know that I shall be justified.

מִי-הוּא, יָרִיב עִמָּדִי: כִּי-עַתָּה אַחֲרִישׁ וְאֶגְוָע
mi-hu yariv immadi; ki-'attah acharish ve'egva
Who is he that will contend with me? For then would I hold my peace and die.

אַךְ-שְׁתַּיִם, אַל-תַּעַשׂ עִמָּדִי; אָז מִפָּנֶיךָ, לֹא אֶסָּתֵר
'ach-shetayim al-ta'as immadi; az mippaneicha, lo essater
Only do not two things unto me, then will I not hide myself from Thee:

כַּפְּךָ, מֵעָלַי הַרְחַק; וְאֵמָתְךָ, אַל-תְּבַעֲתַנִּי
kappecha me'alai harchak; ve'ematecha, al-teva'atanni
Withdraw Thy hand far from me; and let not Thy terror make me afraid.

וּקְרָא, וְאָנֹכִי אֶעֱנֶה; אוֹ-אֲדַבֵּר, וַהֲשִׁיבֵנִי
ukra ve'anochi e'eneh; o-'adabber, vahashiveni
Then call Thou, and I will answer; or let me speak, and answer Thou me.

כַּמָּה לִי, עֲוֹנוֹת וְחַטָּאוֹת-- פִּשְׁעִי וְחַטָּאתִי, הֹדִיעֵנִי
kammah li avonot vechatta'ot; pish'i vechattati, hodi'eni
How many are mine iniquities and sins? Make me to know my transgression and my sin.

לָמָּה-פָנֶיךָ תַסְתִּיר; וְתַחְשְׁבֵנִי לְאוֹיֵב לָךְ
lammah-faneicha tastir; vetachsheveni le'oyev lach
Wherefore hidest Thou Thy face, and holdest me for Thine enemy?

הֶעָלֶה נִדָּף תַּעֲרוֹץ; וְאֶת-קַשׁ יָבֵשׁ תִּרְדֹּף
he'aleh niddaf ta'arotz; ve'et-kash yavesh tirdof
Wilt Thou harass a driven leaf? And wilt Thou pursue the dry stubble?

כִּי-תִכְתֹּב עָלַי מְרֹרוֹת; וְתוֹרִישֵׁנִי, עֲוֹנוֹת נְעוּרָי
ki-tichtov alai merorot; vetorisheni, avonot ne'urai
That Thou shouldest write bitter things against me, and make me to inherit the iniquities of my youth.

וְתָשֵׂם בַּסַּד, רַגְלַי--וְתִשְׁמוֹר כָּל-אָרְחוֹתָי
vetasem bassad raglai, vetishmor kol-orchotai
Thou puttest my feet also in the stocks, and lookest narrowly unto all my paths;

עַל-שָׁרְשֵׁי רַגְלַי, תִּתְחַקֶּה
al-shareshei raglai, titchakkeh
Thou drawest Thee a line about the soles of my feet;

איוב

מִי-יִתֵּן, הַחֲרֵשׁ תַּחֲרִישׁוּן; וּתְהִי לָכֶם לְחָכְמָה
mi-yitten hacharesh tacharishun; utehi lachem lechochemah
Oh that ye would altogether hold your peace! and it would be your wisdom.

שִׁמְעוּ-נָא תוֹכַחְתִּי; וְרִבוֹת שְׂפָתַי הַקְשִׁיבוּ
shim'u-na tochachti; verivot sefatai hakshivu
Hear now my reasoning, and hearken to the pleadings of my lips.

הַלְאֵל, תְּדַבְּרוּ עַוְלָה; וְלוֹ, תְּדַבְּרוּ רְמִיָּה
hal'el tedabberu avlah; velo, tedabberu remiyah
Will ye speak unrighteously for God, and talk deceitfully for Him?

הֲפָנָיו תִּשָּׂאוּן; אִם-לָאֵל תְּרִיבוּן
hafanav tissa'un; im-la'el terivun
Will ye show Him favour? Will ye contend for God?

הֲטוֹב, כִּי-יַחְקֹר אֶתְכֶם; אִם-כְּהָתֵל בֶּאֱנוֹשׁ, תְּהָתֵלּוּ בוֹ
hatov ki-yachkor etchem; im-kehatel be'enosh, tehatellu vo
Would it be good that He should search you out? Or as one mocketh a man, will ye mock Him?

הוֹכֵחַ יוֹכִיחַ אֶתְכֶם--אִם-בַּסֵּתֶר, פָּנִים תִּשָּׂאוּן
hocheach yochiach etchem; im-basseter, panim tissa'un
He will surely reprove you, if ye do secretly show favour.

הֲלֹא שְׂאֵתוֹ, תְּבַעֵת אֶתְכֶם; וּפַחְדּוֹ, יִפֹּל עֲלֵיכֶם
halo se'eto teva'et etchem; ufachdo, yippol aleichem
Shall not His majesty terrify you, and His dread fall upon you?

זִכְרֹנֵיכֶם, מִשְׁלֵי-אֵפֶר; לְגַבֵּי-חֹמֶר, גַּבֵּיכֶם
zichroneichem mishlei-'efer; legabbei-chomer, gabbeichem
Your memorials shall be like unto ashes, your eminences to eminences of clay.

הַחֲרִישׁוּ מִמֶּנִּי, וַאֲדַבְּרָה-אָנִי; וְיַעֲבֹר עָלַי מָה
hacharishu mimmenni va'adabberah-'ani; veya'avor alai mah
Hold your peace, let me alone, that I may speak, and let come on me what will.

עַל-מָה, אֶשָּׂא בְשָׂרִי בְשִׁנָּי; וְנַפְשִׁי, אָשִׂים בְּכַפִּי
'al-mah essa vesari veshinnai; venafshi, asim bechappi
Wherefore? I will take my flesh in my teeth, and put my life in my hand.

הֵן יִקְטְלֵנִי, לוֹ אֲיַחֵל; אַךְ-דְּרָכַי, אֶל-פָּנָיו אוֹכִיחַ
hen yikteleni lo ayachel; ach-derachai, el-panav ochiach
Though He slay me, yet will I trust in Him; but I will argue my ways before Him.

גַּם-הוּא-לִי לִישׁוּעָה: כִּי-לֹא לְפָנָיו, חָנֵף יָבוֹא
gam-hu-li lishu'ah; ki-lo lefanav, chanef yavo
This also shall be my salvation, that a hypocrite cannot come before Him.

אִיּוֹב

מֵסִיר שָׂפָה, לְנֶאֱמָנִים; וְטַעַם זְקֵנִים יִקָּח

mesir safah lene'emanim; veta'am zekenim yikkach
He removeth the speech of men of trust, and taketh away the sense of the elders.

שׁוֹפֵךְ בּוּז, עַל-נְדִיבִים; וּמְזִיחַ אֲפִיקִים רִפָּה

shofech buz al-nedivim; umeziach afikim rippah
He poureth contempt upon princes, and looseth the belt of the strong.

מְגַלֶּה עֲמֻקוֹת, מִנִּי-חֹשֶׁךְ; וַיֹּצֵא לָאוֹר צַלְמָוֶת

megalleh amukot minni-choshech; vayotzei la'or tzalmavet
He uncovereth deep things out of darkness, and bringeth out to light the shadow of death.

מַשְׂגִּיא לַגּוֹיִם, וַיְאַבְּדֵם; שֹׁטֵחַ לַגּוֹיִם, וַיַּנְחֵם

masgi laggoyim vay'abbedem; shoteach laggoyim, vayanchem
He increaseth the nations, and destroyeth them; He enlargeth the nations, and leadeth them away.

מֵסִיר--לֵב, רָאשֵׁי עַם-הָאָרֶץ

mesir, lev rashei am-ha'aretz
He taketh away the heart of the chiefs of the people of the land,

וַיַּתְעֵם, בְּתֹהוּ לֹא-דָרֶךְ

vayat'em, betohu lo-darech
and causeth them to wander in a wilderness where there is no way.

יְמַשְׁשׁוּ-חֹשֶׁךְ וְלֹא-אוֹר; וַיַּתְעֵם, כַּשִּׁכּוֹר

yemasheshu-choshech velo-'or; vayat'em, kashikkor
They grope in the dark without light, and He maketh them to stagger like a drunken man.

יג

הֶן-כֹּל, רָאֲתָה עֵינִי; שָׁמְעָה אָזְנִי, וַתָּבֶן לָהּ

Hen-kol ra'atah eini; shame'ah ozeni, vattaven lah
Lo, mine eye hath seen all this, mine ear hath heard and understood it.

כְּדַעְתְּכֶם, יָדַעְתִּי גַם-אָנִי: לֹא-נֹפֵל אָנֹכִי מִכֶּם

keda'techem yada'ti gam-'ani; lo-nofel anochi mikkem
What ye know, do I know also; I am not inferior unto you.

אוּלָם--אֲנִי, אֶל-שַׁדַּי אֲדַבֵּר; וְהוֹכֵחַ אֶל-אֵל אֶחְפָּץ

'ulam, ani el-shaddai adabber; vehocheach el-'el echpatz
Notwithstanding I would speak to the Almighty, and I desire to reason with God.

וְאוּלָם, אַתֶּם טֹפְלֵי-שָׁקֶר; רֹפְאֵי אֱלִל כֻּלְּכֶם

ve'ulam, attem tofelei-shaker; rofe'ei elil kullechem
But ye are plasterers of lies, ye are all physicians of no value.

אִיּוֹב

אוֹ שִׂיחַ לָאָרֶץ וְתֹרֶךָּ; וִיסַפְּרוּ לְךָ, דְּגֵי הַיָּם
'o siach la'aretz vetoreka; visapperu lecha, degei hayam
Or speak to the earth, and it shall teach thee; and the fishes of the sea shall declare unto thee;

מִי, לֹא-יָדַע בְּכָל-אֵלֶּה: כִּי יַד-יְהוָה, עָשְׂתָה זֹּאת
mi lo-yada bechol-'elleh; ki yad-hashem asetah zot
Who knoweth not among all these, that the hand of the LORD hath wrought this?

אֲשֶׁר בְּיָדוֹ, נֶפֶשׁ כָּל-חָי; וְרוּחַ, כָּל-בְּשַׂר-אִישׁ
'asher beyado nefesh kol-chai; veruach, kol-besar-'ish
In whose hand is the soul of every living thing, and the breath of all mankind.--

הֲלֹא-אֹזֶן, מִלִּין תִּבְחָן; וְחֵךְ, אֹכֶל יִטְעַם-לוֹ
halo-'ozen millin tivchan; vechech, ochel yit'am-lo
Doth not the ear try words, even as the palate tasteth its food?

בִּישִׁישִׁים חָכְמָה; וְאֹרֶךְ יָמִים תְּבוּנָה
bishishim chochmah ve'orech yamim tevunah
Is wisdom with aged men, and understanding in length of days?--

עִמּוֹ, חָכְמָה וּגְבוּרָה; לוֹ, עֵצָה וּתְבוּנָה
'immo chochmah ugevurah; lo, etzah utevunah
With Him is wisdom and might; He hath counsel and understanding.

הֵן יַהֲרוֹס, וְלֹא יִבָּנֶה; יִסְגֹּר עַל-אִישׁ, וְלֹא יִפָּתֵחַ
hen yaharos velo yibbaneh; yisgor al-'ish, velo yippateach
Behold, He breaketh down, and it cannot be built again; He shutteth up a man, and there can be no opening.

הֵן יַעְצֹר בַּמַּיִם וְיִבָשׁוּ; וִישַׁלְּחֵם, וְיַהַפְכוּ אָרֶץ
hen ya'tzor bammayim veyivashu; vishallechem, veyahafchu aretz
Behold, He withholdeth the waters, and they dry up; also He sendeth them out, and they overturn the earth.

עִמּוֹ, עֹז וְתוּשִׁיָּה; לוֹ, שֹׁגֵג וּמַשְׁגֶּה
'immo oz vetushiyah; lo, shogeg umashgeh
With Him is strength and sound wisdom; the deceived and the deceiver are His.

מוֹלִיךְ יוֹעֲצִים שׁוֹלָל; וְשֹׁפְטִים יְהוֹלֵל
molich yo'atzim sholal; veshofetim yeholel
He leadeth counsellors away stripped, and judges maketh He fools.

מוּסַר מְלָכִים פִּתֵּחַ; וַיֶּאְסֹר אֵזוֹר, בְּמָתְנֵיהֶם
musar melachim pitteach; vaye'sor ezor, bemoteneihem
He looseth the bond of kings, and bindeth their loins with a girdle.

מוֹלִיךְ כֹּהֲנִים שׁוֹלָל; וְאֵתָנִים יְסַלֵּף
molich kohanim sholal; ve'etanim yesallef
He leadeth priests away stripped, and overthroweth the mighty.

אִיּוֹב

וּבָטַחְתָּ, כִּי-יֵשׁ תִּקְוָה; וְחָפַרְתָּ, לָבֶטַח תִּשְׁכָּב
uvatachta ki-yesh tikvah; vechafarta, lavetach tishkav
And thou shalt be secure, because there is hope; yea, thou shalt look about thee, and shalt take thy rest in safety.

וְרָבַצְתָּ, וְאֵין מַחֲרִיד; וְחִלּוּ פָנֶיךָ רַבִּים
veravatzta ve'ein macharid; vechillu faneicha rabbim
Also thou shalt lie down, and none shall make thee afraid; yea, many shall make suit unto thee.

וְעֵינֵי רְשָׁעִים, תִּכְלֶינָה: וּמָנוֹס, אָבַד מִנְהֶם; וְתִקְוָתָם, מַפַּח-נָפֶשׁ
ve'einei resha'im, tichleinah umanos avad minhem; vetikvatam, mappach-nafesh
But the eyes of the wicked shall fail, and they shall have no way to flee, and their hope shall be the drooping of the soul.

יב

וַיַּעַן אִיּוֹב, וַיֹּאמַר
Vaya'an iyov, vayomar
Then Job answered and said:

אָמְנָם, כִּי אַתֶּם-עָם; וְעִמָּכֶם, תָּמוּת חָכְמָה
'amenom ki attem-'am; ve'immachem, tamut chochmah
No doubt but ye are the people, and wisdom shall die with you.

גַּם-לִי לֵבָב, כְּמוֹכֶם--לֹא-נֹפֵל אָנֹכִי מִכֶּם; וְאֶת-מִי-אֵין כְּמוֹ-אֵלֶּה
gam-li levav kemochem, lo-nofel anochi mikkem; ve'et-mi-'ein kemo-'elleh
But I have understanding as well as you; I am not inferior to you; yea, who knoweth not such things as these?

שְׂחֹק לְרֵעֵהוּ, אֶהְיֶה--קֹרֵא לֶאֱלוֹהַּ
sechok lere'ehu ehyeh, korei le'eloah
I am as one that is a laughing-stock to his neighbour, a man that called upon God,

וַיַּעֲנֵהוּ; שְׂחוֹק, צַדִּיק תָּמִים
vaya'anehu; sechok, tzaddik tamim
and He answered him; the just, the innocent man is a laughing-stock,

לַפִּיד בּוּז, לְעַשְׁתּוּת שַׁאֲנָן--נָכוֹן, לְמוֹעֲדֵי רָגֶל
lappid buz le'ashtut sha'anan; nachon, lemo'adei ragel
A contemptible brand in the thought of him that is at ease, a thing ready for them whose foot slippeth.

יִשְׁלָיוּ אֹהָלִים, לְשֹׁדְדִים, וּבַטֻּחוֹת, לְמַרְגִּיזֵי אֵל--לַאֲשֶׁר הֵבִיא אֱלוֹהַּ בְּיָדוֹ
yishlayu ohalim leshodedim, uvattuchot lemargizei el; la'asher hevi eloah beyado
The tents of robbers prosper, and they that provoke God are secure, in whatsoever God bringeth into their hand.

וְאוּלָם--שְׁאַל-נָא בְהֵמוֹת וְתֹרֶךָּ; וְעוֹף הַשָּׁמַיִם, וְיַגֶּד-לָךְ
ve'ulam, she'al-na vehemot vetoreka; ve'of hashamayim, veyagged-lach
But ask now the beasts, and they shall teach thee; and the fowls of the air, and they shall tell thee;

איוב

וְדַע-- כִּי-יַשֶּׁה לְךָ אֱלוֹהַּ, מֵעֲוֺנֶךָ
veda ki-yasheh lecha eloah, me'avonecha
Know therefore that God exacteth of thee less than thine iniquity deserveth.

הַחֵקֶר אֱלוֹהַּ תִּמְצָא; אִם עַד-תַּכְלִית שַׁדַּי תִּמְצָא
hacheker eloah timtza; im ad-tachlit shaddai timtza
Canst thou find out the deep things of God? Canst thou attain unto the purpose of the Almighty?

גָּבְהֵי שָׁמַיִם, מַה-תִּפְעָל; עֲמֻקָּה מִשְּׁאוֹל, מַה-תֵּדָע
gavehei shamayim mah-tif'al; amukkah mishe'ol, mah-teda
It is high as heaven; what canst thou do? Deeper than the nether-world; what canst thou know?

אֲרֻכָּה מֵאֶרֶץ מִדָּהּ; וּרְחָבָה, מִנִּי-יָם
'arukkah me'eretz middah; urechavah, minni-yam
The measure thereof is longer than the earth, and broader than the sea.

אִם-יַחֲלֹף וְיַסְגִּיר; וְיַקְהִיל, וּמִי יְשִׁיבֶנּוּ
'im-yachalof veyasgir; veyak'hil, umi yeshivennu
If He pass by, and shut up, or gather in, then who can hinder Him?

כִּי-הוּא, יָדַע מְתֵי-שָׁוְא; וַיַּרְא-אָוֶן, וְלֹא יִתְבּוֹנָן
ki-hu yada metei-shav; vayar-'aven, velo yitbonan
For He knoweth base men; and when He seeth iniquity, will He not then consider it?

וְאִישׁ נָבוּב, יִלָּבֵב; וְעַיִר פֶּרֶא, אָדָם יִוָּלֵד
ve'ish navuv yillavev; ve'ayir pere, adam yivvaled
But an empty man will get understanding, when a wild ass's colt is born a man.

אִם-אַתָּה, הֲכִינוֹתָ לִבֶּךָ; וּפָרַשְׂתָּ אֵלָיו כַּפֶּךָ
'im-'attah, hachinota libbecha; ufarasta elav kappecha
If thou set thy heart aright, and stretch out thy hands toward Him--

אִם-אָוֶן בְּיָדְךָ, הַרְחִיקֵהוּ; וְאַל-תַּשְׁכֵּן בְּאֹהָלֶיךָ עַוְלָה
'im-'aven beyadecha harchikehu; ve'al-tashken be'ohaleicha avlah
If iniquity be in thy hand, put it far away, and let not unrighteousness dwell in thy tents--

כִּי-אָז, תִּשָּׂא פָנֶיךָ מִמּוּם; וְהָיִיתָ מֻצָק, וְלֹא תִירָא
ki-'az tissa faneicha mimmum; vehayita mutzak, velo tira
Surely then shalt thou lift up thy face without spot; yea, thou shalt be stedfast, and shalt not fear;

כִּי-אַתָּה, עָמָל תִּשְׁכָּח; כְּמַיִם עָבְרוּ תִזְכֹּר
ki-'attah amal tishkach; kemayim averu tizkor
For thou shalt forget thy misery; thou shalt remember it as waters that are passed away;

וּמִצָּהֳרַיִם, יָקוּם חָלֶד; תָּעֻפָה, כַּבֹּקֶר תִּהְיֶה
umitzohorayim yakum chaled; ta'ufah, kabboker tihyeh
And thy life shall be clearer than the noonday; though there be darkness, it shall be as the morning.

אִיּוֹב

כַּאֲשֶׁר לֹא-הָיִיתִי אֶהְיֶה; מִבֶּטֶן, לַקֶּבֶר אוּבָל
ka'asher lo-hayiti ehyeh; mibbeten, lakkever uval
I should have been as though I had not been; I should have been carried from the womb to the grave.

הֲלֹא-מְעַט יָמַי וַחֲדָל; וְשִׁית מִמֶּנִּי, וְאַבְלִיגָה מְּעָט
halo-me'at yamai vachadal; veshit mimmenni, ve'avligah me'at
Are not my days few? Cease then, and let me alone, that I may take comfort a little,

בְּטֶרֶם אֵלֵךְ, וְלֹא אָשׁוּב--אֶל-אֶרֶץ חֹשֶׁךְ וְצַלְמָוֶת
beterem elech velo ashuv; el-'eretz choshech vetzalmavet
Before I go whence I shall not return, even to the land of darkness and of the shadow of death;

אֶרֶץ עֵיפָתָה, כְּמוֹ אֹפֶל--צַלְמָוֶת
'eretz eifatah kemo ofel, tzalmavet
A land of thick darkness, as darkness itself; a land of the shadow of death,

וְלֹא סְדָרִים; וַתֹּפַע כְּמוֹ-אֹפֶל
velo sedarim, vattofa kemo-'ofel
without any order, and where the light is as darkness.

יא

וַיַּעַן, צֹפַר הַנַּעֲמָתִי; וַיֹּאמַר
Vaya'an tzofar hanna'amati, vayomar
Then answered Zophar the Naamathite, and said:

הֲרֹב דְּבָרִים, לֹא יֵעָנֶה; וְאִם-אִישׁ שְׂפָתַיִם יִצְדָּק
harov devarim lo ye'aneh; ve'im-'ish sefatayim yitzdak
Should not the multitude of words be answered? And should a man full of talk be accounted right?

בַּדֶּיךָ, מְתִים יַחֲרִישׁוּ; וַתִּלְעַג, וְאֵין מַכְלִם
baddeicha metim yacharishv; vattil'ag, ve'ein machlim
Thy boastings have made men hold their peace, and thou hast mocked, with none to make thee ashamed;

וַתֹּאמֶר, זַךְ לִקְחִי; וּבַר, הָיִיתִי בְעֵינֶיךָ
vattomer zach likchi; uvar, hayiti ve'eineicha
And thou hast said: 'My doctrine is pure, and I am clean in Thine eyes.'

וְאוּלָם--מִי-יִתֵּן אֱלוֹהַּ דַּבֵּר; וְיִפְתַּח שְׂפָתָיו עִמָּךְ
ve'ulam, mi-yitten eloah dabber; veyiftach sefatav immach
But oh that God would speak, and open His lips against thee;

וְיַגֶּד-לְךָ, תַּעֲלֻמוֹת חָכְמָה--כִּי-כִפְלַיִם לְתוּשִׁיָּה
veyagged-lecha ta'alumot chochmah ki-chiflayim letushiyah
And that He would tell thee the secrets of wisdom, that sound wisdom is manifold!

אִיּוֹב

זְכָר-נָא, כִּי-כַחֹמֶר עֲשִׂיתָנִי; וְאֶל-עָפָר תְּשִׁיבֵנִי
zechor-na ki-chachomer asitani; ve'el-'afar teshiveni
Remember, I beseech Thee, that Thou hast fashioned me as clay; and wilt Thou bring me into dust again?

הֲלֹא כֶחָלָב, תַּתִּיכֵנִי; וְכַגְּבִנָּה, תַּקְפִּיאֵנִי
halo chechalav tatticheni; vechaggevinnah, takpi'eni
Hast Thou not poured me out as milk, and curdled me like cheese?

עוֹר וּבָשָׂר, תַּלְבִּישֵׁנִי; וּבַעֲצָמוֹת וְגִידִים, תְּסֹכְכֵנִי
'or uvasor talbisheni; uva'atzamot vegidim, tesochecheni
Thou hast clothed me with skin and flesh, and knit me together with bones and sinews.

חַיִּים וָחֶסֶד, עָשִׂיתָ עִמָּדִי; וּפְקֻדָּתְךָ, שָׁמְרָה רוּחִי
chayim vachesed asita immadi; ufkuddatecha, shamerah ruchi
Thou hast granted me life and favour, and Thy providence hath preserved my spirit.

וְאֵלֶּה, צָפַנְתָּ בִלְבָבֶךָ; יָדַעְתִּי, כִּי-זֹאת עִמָּךְ
ve'elleh tzafanta vilvavecha; yada'ti, ki-zot immach
Yet these things Thou didst hide in Thy heart; I know that this is with Thee;

אִם-חָטָאתִי וּשְׁמַרְתָּנִי; וּמֵעֲוֹנִי, לֹא תְנַקֵּנִי
'im-chatati ushmartani; ume'avoni, lo tenakkeni
If I sin, then Thou markest me, and Thou wilt not acquit me from mine iniquity.

אִם-רָשַׁעְתִּי, אַלְלַי לִי--וְצָדַקְתִּי, לֹא-אֶשָּׂא רֹאשִׁי
'im-rasha'ti alelai li, vetzadakti lo-'essa roshi
If I be wicked, woe unto me; and if I be righteous, yet shall I not lift up my head--

שְׂבַע קָלוֹן, וּרְאֵה עָנְיִי
seva kalon, ure'eh oneyi
being filled with ignominy and looking upon mine affliction.

וְיִגְאֶה, כַּשַּׁחַל תְּצוּדֵנִי; וְתָשֹׁב, תִּתְפַּלָּא-בִי
veyig'eh kashachal tetzudeni; vetashov, titpalla-vi
And if it exalt itself, Thou huntest me as a lion; and again Thou showest Thyself marvellous upon me.

תְּחַדֵּשׁ עֵדֶיךָ, נֶגְדִּי, וְתֶרֶב כַּעַשְׂךָ, עִמָּדִי
techaddesh edeicha negdi, veterev ka'ascha immadi
Thou renewest Thy witnesses against me, and increasest Thine indignation upon me;

חֲלִיפוֹת וְצָבָא עִמִּי
chalifot vetzava immi
host succeeding host against me.

וְלָמָּה מֵרֶחֶם, הֹצֵאתָנִי; אֶגְוַע, וְעַיִן לֹא-תִרְאֵנִי
velammah merechem hotzetani; egva', ve'ayin lo-tir'eni
Wherefore then hast Thou brought me forth out of the womb? Would that I had perished, and no eye had seen me!

אִיּוֹב

יָסֵר מֵעָלַי שִׁבְטוֹ; וְאֵמָתוֹ, אַל-תְּבַעֲתַנִּי

yaser me'alai shivto; ve'emato, al-teva'atanni

Let Him take His rod away from me, and let not His terror make me afraid;

אֲדַבְּרָה, וְלֹא אִירָאֶנּוּ: כִּי לֹא-כֵן אָנֹכִי, עִמָּדִי.

'adabberah velo ira'ennu; ki lo-chen anochi, immadi

Then would I speak, and not fear Him; for I am not so with myself.

▌

נָקְטָה נַפְשִׁי, בְּחַיָּי: אֶעֶזְבָה עָלַי שִׂיחִי; אֲדַבְּרָה, בְּמַר נַפְשִׁי

Naketah nafshi, bechayai e'ezvah alai sichi; adabberah, bemar nafshi

My soul is weary of my life; I will give free course to my complaint; I will speak in the bitterness of my soul.

אֹמַר אֶל-אֱלוֹהַּ, אַל-תַּרְשִׁיעֵנִי; הוֹדִיעֵנִי, עַל מַה-תְּרִיבֵנִי

'omar el-'eloah al-tarshi'eni; hodi'eni, al mah-teriveni

I will say unto God: Do not condemn me; make me know wherefore Thou contendest with me.

הֲטוֹב לְךָ, כִּי-תַעֲשֹׁק

hatov lecha ki-ta'ashok

Is it good unto Thee that Thou shouldest oppress,

כִּי-תִמְאַס, יְגִיעַ כַּפֶּיךָ; וְעַל-עֲצַת רְשָׁעִים הוֹפָעְתָּ

ki-tim'as yegia kappeicha; ve'al-'atzat resha'im hofa'eta

that Thou shouldest despise the work of Thy hands, and shine upon the counsel of the wicked?

הַעֵינֵי בָשָׂר לָךְ: אִם-כִּרְאוֹת אֱנוֹשׁ תִּרְאֶה

ha'einei vasar lach; im-kir'ot enosh tir'eh

Hast Thou eyes of flesh? Or seest Thou as man seeth?

הֲכִימֵי אֱנוֹשׁ יָמֶיךָ: אִם-שְׁנוֹתֶיךָ, כִּימֵי גָבֶר

hachimei enosh yameicha; im-shenoteicha, kiymei gaver

Are Thy days as the days of man, or Thy years as a man's days,

כִּי-תְבַקֵּשׁ לַעֲוֹנִי; וּלְחַטָּאתִי תִדְרוֹשׁ

ki-tevakkesh la'avoni; ulechattati tidrosh

That Thou inquirest after mine iniquity, and searchest after my sin,

עַל-דַּעְתְּךָ, כִּי-לֹא אֶרְשָׁע; וְאֵין מִיָּדְךָ מַצִּיל

'al-da'techa ki-lo ersha'; ve'ein miyadecha matzil

Although Thou knowest that I shall not be condemned; and there is none that can deliver out of Thy hand?

יָדֶיךָ עִצְּבוּנִי, וַיַּעֲשׂוּנִי; יַחַד סָבִיב, וַתְּבַלְּעֵנִי

yadeicha itzevuni vaya'asuni; yachad saviv, vattevalle'eni

Thy hands have framed me and fashioned me together round about; yet Thou dost destroy me!

אִיּוֹב

אַחַת, הִיא: עַל-כֵּן אָמַרְתִּי--תָּם וְרָשָׁע, הוּא מְכַלֶּה
'achat, hi al-ken amarti; tam verasha', hu mechalleh
It is all one--therefore I say: He destroyeth the innocent and the wicked.

אִם-שׁוֹט, יָמִית פִּתְאֹם--לְמַסַּת נְקִיִּם יִלְעָג
'im-shot yamit pit'om; lemassat nekiyim yil'ag
If the scourge slay suddenly, He will mock at the calamity of the guiltless.

אֶרֶץ, נִתְּנָה בְיַד-רָשָׁע--פְּנֵי-שֹׁפְטֶיהָ יְכַסֶּה; אִם-לֹא אֵפוֹא מִי-הוּא
'eretz nittenah veyad-rasha', penei-shofeteiha yechasseh; im-lo efo mi-hu
The earth is given into the hand of the wicked; he covereth the faces of the judges thereof; if it be not He, who then is it?

וְיָמַי קַלּוּ, מִנִּי-רָץ; בָּרְחוּ, לֹא-רָאוּ טוֹבָה
veyamai kallu minni-ratz; barechu, lo-ra'u tovah
Now my days are swifter than a runner; they flee away, they see no good.

חָלְפוּ, עִם-אֳנִיּוֹת אֵבֶה; כְּנֶשֶׁר, יָטוּשׂ עֲלֵי-אֹכֶל
chalefu im-'oniyot eveh; kenesher, yatus alei-'ochel
They are passed away as the swift ships; as the vulture that swoopeth on the prey.

אִם-אָמְרִי, אֶשְׁכְּחָה שִׂיחִי; אֶעֶזְבָה פָנַי וְאַבְלִיגָה
'im-'omeri eshkechah sichi; e'ezvah fanai ve'avligah
If I say: 'I will forget my complaint, I will put off my sad countenance, and be of good cheer',

יָגֹרְתִּי כָל-עַצְּבֹתָי; יָדַעְתִּי, כִּי-לֹא תְנַקֵּנִי
yagorti chol-'atzevotai; yada'ti, ki-lo tenakkeni
I am afraid of all my pains, I know that Thou wilt not hold me guiltless.

אָנֹכִי אֶרְשָׁע; לָמָּה-זֶּה, הֶבֶל אִיגָע
'anochi ersha'; lammah-zeh, hevel iga
I shall be condemned; why then do I labour in vain?

אִם-הִתְרָחַצְתִּי בְמֵי-שָׁלֶג; וַהֲזִכּוֹתִי, בְּבֹר כַּפָּי
'im-hitrachatzti vemei-shaleg; vahazikkoti, bevor kappai
If I wash myself with snow water, and make my hands never so clean;

אָז, בַּשַּׁחַת תִּטְבְּלֵנִי; וְתִעֲבוּנִי, שַׂלְמוֹתָי
'az bashachat titbeleni; veti'avuni, salmotai
Yet wilt Thou plunge me in the ditch, and mine own clothes shall abhor me.

כִּי-לֹא-אִישׁ כָּמוֹנִי אֶעֱנֶנּוּ; נָבוֹא יַחְדָּו, בַּמִּשְׁפָּט
ki-lo-'ish kamoni e'enennu; navo yachdav, bammishpat
For He is not a man, as I am, that I should answer Him, that we should come together in judgment.

לֹא יֵשׁ-בֵּינֵינוּ מוֹכִיחַ--יָשֵׁת יָדוֹ עַל-שְׁנֵינוּ
lo yesh-beineinu mochiach; yashet yado al-sheneinu
There is no arbiter betwixt us, that might lay his hand upon us both.

אִיּוֹב

עֹשֶׂה גְדֹלוֹת, עַד-אֵין חֵקֶר; וְנִפְלָאוֹת, עַד-אֵין מִסְפָּר
'oseh gedolot ad-'ein cheker; venifla'ot, ad-'ein mispar
Who doeth great things past finding out; yea, marvellous things without number.

הֵן יַעֲבֹר עָלַי, וְלֹא אֶרְאֶה; וְיַחֲלֹף, וְלֹא-אָבִין לוֹ
hen ya'avor alai velo er'eh; veyachalof, velo-'avin lo
Lo, He goeth by me, and I see Him not. He passeth on also, but I perceive Him not.

הֵן יַחְתֹּף, מִי יְשִׁיבֶנּוּ; מִי-יֹאמַר אֵלָיו, מַה-תַּעֲשֶׂה
hen yachtof mi yeshivennu; mi-yomar elav, mah-ta'aseh
Behold, He snatcheth away, who can hinder Him? Who will say unto Him: 'What doest Thou?'

אֱלוֹהַּ, לֹא-יָשִׁיב אַפּוֹ; תַּחְתָּו שָׁחֲחוּ, עֹזְרֵי רָהַב
'eloah lo-yashiv appo; tachtav shachachu, ozerei rahav
God will not withdraw His anger; the helpers of Rahab did stoop under Him.

אַף, כִּי-אָנֹכִי אֶעֱנֶנּוּ; אֶבְחֲרָה דְבָרַי עִמּוֹ
'af ki-'anochi e'enennu; evcharah devarai immo
How much less shall I answer Him, and choose out my arguments with Him?

אֲשֶׁר אִם-צָדַקְתִּי, לֹא אֶעֱנֶה; לִמְשֹׁפְטִי, אֶתְחַנָּן
'asher im-tzadakti lo e'eneh; limshofti, etchannan
Whom, though I were righteous, yet would I not answer; I would make supplication to Him that contendeth with me.

אִם-קָרָאתִי וַיַּעֲנֵנִי--לֹא-אַאֲמִין, כִּי-יַאֲזִין קוֹלִי
'im-karati vaya'aneni; lo-'a'amin, ki-ya'azin koli
If I had called, and He had answered me; yet would I not believe that He would hearken unto my voice--

אֲשֶׁר-בִּשְׂעָרָה יְשׁוּפֵנִי; וְהִרְבָּה פְצָעַי חִנָּם
'asher-bis'arah yeshufeni; vehirbah fetza'ai chinnam
He that would break me with a tempest, and multiply my wounds without cause;

לֹא-יִתְּנֵנִי, הָשֵׁב רוּחִי: כִּי יַשְׂבִּעַנִי, מַמְּרֹרִים
lo-yittenneni hashev ruchi; ki yasbi'ani, mammerorim
That would not suffer me to take my breath, but fill me with bitterness.

אִם-לְכֹחַ אַמִּיץ הִנֵּה; וְאִם-לְמִשְׁפָּט, מִי יוֹעִידֵנִי
'im-lechoach ammitz hinneh; ve'im-lemishpat, mi yo'ideni
If it be a matter of strength, lo, He is mighty! and if of justice, who will appoint me a time?

אִם-אֶצְדָּק, פִּי יַרְשִׁיעֵנִי; תָּם-אָנִי, וַיַּעְקְשֵׁנִי
'im-'etzdok pi yarshi'eni; tam-'ani, vaya'ksheni
Though I be righteous, mine own mouth shall condemn me; though I be innocent, He shall prove me perverse.

תָּם-אָנִי, לֹא-אֵדַע נַפְשִׁי; אֶמְאַס חַיָּי
tam-'ani lo-'eda nafshi, em'as chayai
I am innocent--I regard not myself, I despise my life.

אִיּוֹב

עַד-יְמַלֵּה שְׂחוֹק פִּיךָ; וּשְׂפָתֶיךָ תְרוּעָה
'ad-yemalleh sechok picha; usefateicha teru'ah
Till He fill thy mouth with laughter, and thy lips with shouting.

שֹׂנְאֶיךָ יִלְבְּשׁוּ-בֹשֶׁת; וְאֹהֶל רְשָׁעִים אֵינֶנּוּ
sone'eicha yilbeshu-voshet; ve'ohel resha'im einennu
They that hate thee shall be clothed with shame; and the tent of the wicked shall be no more.

ט

וַיַּעַן אִיּוֹב, וַיֹּאמַר
Vaya'an iyov, vayomar
Then Job answered and said:

אָמְנָם, יָדַעְתִּי כִי-כֵן; וּמַה-יִּצְדַּק אֱנוֹשׁ עִם-אֵל
'amenom yada'ti chi-chen; umah-yitzdak enosh im-'el
Of a truth I know that it is so; and how can man be just with God?

אִם-יַחְפֹּץ, לָרִיב עִמּוֹ--לֹא-יַעֲנֶנּוּ, אַחַת מִנִּי-אָלֶף
'im-yachpotz lariv immo; lo-ya'anennu, achat minni-'alef
If one should desire to contend with Him, he could not answer Him one of a thousand.

חֲכַם לֵבָב, וְאַמִּיץ כֹּחַ--מִי-הִקְשָׁה אֵלָיו, וַיִּשְׁלָם
chacham levov ve'ammitz koach; mi-hikshah elav, vayishlam
He is wise in heart, and mighty in strength; who hath hardened himself against Him, and prospered?

הַמַּעְתִּיק הָרִים, וְלֹא יָדָעוּ--אֲשֶׁר הֲפָכָם בְּאַפּוֹ
hamma'tik harim velo yada'u; asher hafacham be'appo
Who removeth the mountains, and they know it not, when He overturneth them in His anger.

הַמַּרְגִּיז אֶרֶץ, מִמְּקוֹמָהּ; וְעַמּוּדֶיהָ, יִתְפַלָּצוּן
hammargiz eretz mimmekomah; ve'ammudeiha, yitfallatzun
Who shaketh the earth out of her place, and the pillars thereof tremble.

הָאֹמֵר לַחֶרֶס, וְלֹא יִזְרָח; וּבְעַד כּוֹכָבִים יַחְתֹּם
ha'omer lacheres velo yizrach; uve'ad kochavim yachtom
Who commandeth the sun, and it riseth not; and sealeth up the stars.

נֹטֶה שָׁמַיִם לְבַדּוֹ; וְדוֹרֵךְ, עַל-בָּמֳתֵי יָם
noteh shamayim levaddo; vedorech, al-bomotei yam
Who alone stretcheth out the heavens, and treadeth upon the waves of the sea.

עֹשֶׂה-עָשׁ, כְּסִיל וְכִימָה; וְחַדְרֵי תֵמָן
'oseh-'ash kesil vechimah, vechadrei teman
Who maketh the Bear, Orion, and the Pleiades, and the chambers of the south.

איוֹב

כִּי-תְמוֹל אֲנַחְנוּ, וְלֹא נֵדָע: כִּי צֵל יָמֵינוּ עֲלֵי-אָרֶץ
ki-temol anachnu velo neda'; ki tzel yameinu alei-'aretz
For we are but of yesterday, and know nothing, because our days upon earth are a shadow--

הֲלֹא-הֵם יוֹרוּךָ, יֹאמְרוּ לָךְ; וּמִלִּבָּם, יוֹצִאוּ מִלִּים
halo-hem yorucha yomeru lach; umillibbam, yotzi'u millim
Shall not they teach thee, and tell thee, and utter words out of their heart?

הֲיִגְאֶה-גֹּמֶא, בְּלֹא בִצָּה; יִשְׂגֶּה-אָחוּ בְלִי-מָיִם
hayig'eh-gomei belo vitzah; yisgeh-'achu veli-mayim
Can the rush shoot up without mire? Can the reed-grass grow without water?

עֹדֶנּוּ בְאִבּוֹ, לֹא יִקָּטֵף; וְלִפְנֵי כָל-חָצִיר יִיבָשׁ
'odennu ve'ibbo lo yikkatef; velifnei chol-chatzir yivash
Whilst it is yet in its greenness, and not cut down, it withereth before any other herb.

כֵּן--אָרְחוֹת, כָּל-שֹׁכְחֵי אֵל; וְתִקְוַת חָנֵף תֹּאבֵד
ken, orechot kol-shochechei el; vetikvat chanef toved
So are the paths of all that forget God; and the hope of the godless man shall perish;

אֲשֶׁר-יָקוֹט כִּסְלוֹ; וּבֵית עַכָּבִישׁ, מִבְטַחוֹ
'asher-yakot kislo; uveit akkavish, mivtacho
Whose confidence is gossamer, and whose trust is a spider's web.

יִשָּׁעֵן עַל-בֵּיתוֹ, וְלֹא יַעֲמֹד; יַחֲזִיק בּוֹ, וְלֹא יָקוּם
yisha'en al-beito velo ya'amod; yachazik bo, velo yakum
He shall lean upon his house, but it shall not stand; he shall hold fast thereby, but it shall not endure.

רָטֹב הוּא, לִפְנֵי-שָׁמֶשׁ; וְעַל גַּנָּתוֹ, יֹנַקְתּוֹ תֵצֵא
ratov hu lifnei-shamesh; ve'al gannato, yonakto tetze
He is green before the sun, and his shoots go forth over his garden.

עַל-גַּל, שָׁרָשָׁיו יְסֻבָּכוּ; בֵּית אֲבָנִים יֶחֱזֶה
'al-gal sharashav yesubbachu; beit avanim yechezeh
His roots are wrapped about the heap, he beholdeth the place of stones.

אִם-יְבַלְּעֶנּוּ מִמְּקוֹמוֹ; וְכִחֶשׁ בּוֹ, לֹא רְאִיתִיךָ
'im-yevalle'ennu mimmekomo; vechichesh bo, lo re'iticha
If he be destroyed from his place, then it shall deny him: 'I have not seen thee.'

הֶן-הוּא, מְשׂוֹשׂ דַּרְכּוֹ; וּמֵעָפָר, אַחֵר יִצְמָחוּ
hen-hu mesos darko; ume'afar, acher yitzmachu
Behold, this is the joy of his way, and out of the earth shall others spring.

הֶן-אֵל, לֹא יִמְאַס-תָּם; וְלֹא-יַחֲזִיק, בְּיַד-מְרֵעִים
hen-'el lo yim'as-tam; velo-yachazik, beyad-mere'im
Behold, God will not cast away an innocent man, neither will He uphold the evil-doers;

אִיּוֹב

וּמֶה, לֹא-תִשָּׂא פִשְׁעִי--וְתַעֲבִיר אֶת-עֲוֺנִי
umeh lo-tissa fish'i veta'avir et-'avoni
And why dost Thou not pardon my transgression, and take away mine iniquity?

כִּי-עַתָּה, לֶעָפָר אֶשְׁכָּב; וְשִׁחַרְתַּנִי וְאֵינֶנִּי
ki-'attah le'afar eshkav; veshichartani ve'einenni
For now shall I lie down in the dust; and Thou wilt seek me, but I shall not be.

ח

וַיַּעַן, בִּלְדַּד הַשֻּׁחִי; וַיֹּאמַר
Vaya'an bildad hashuchi, vayomar
Then answered Bildad the Shuhite, and said:

עַד-אָן, תְּמַלֶּל-אֵלֶּה; וְרוּחַ כַּבִּיר, אִמְרֵי-פִיךָ
'ad-'an temallel-'elleh; veruach kabbir imrei-ficha
How long wilt thou speak these things, seeing that the words of thy mouth are as a mighty wind?

הַאֵל, יְעַוֵּת מִשְׁפָּט; וְאִם-שַׁדַּי, יְעַוֵּת-צֶדֶק
ha'el ye'avvet mishpat; ve'im-shaddai, ye'avvet-tzedek
Doth God pervert judgment? Or doth the Almighty pervert justice?

אִם-בָּנֶיךָ חָטְאוּ-לוֹ; וַיְשַׁלְּחֵם, בְּיַד-פִּשְׁעָם
'im-baneicha chate'u-lo; vayshallechem, beyad-pish'am
If thy children sinned against Him, He delivered them into the hand of their transgression.

אִם-אַתָּה, תְּשַׁחֵר אֶל-אֵל; וְאֶל-שַׁדַּי, תִּתְחַנָּן
'im-'attah teshacher el-'el; ve'el-shaddai, titchannan
If thou wouldest seek earnestly unto God, and make thy supplication to the Almighty;

אִם-זַךְ וְיָשָׁר, אָתָּה: כִּי-עַתָּה, יָעִיר עָלֶיךָ
'im-zach veyashar, attah ki-'attah ya'ir aleicha
If thou wert pure and upright; surely now He would awake for thee,

וְשִׁלַּם, נְוַת צִדְקֶךָ
veshillam, nevat tzidkecha
and make the habitation of thy righteousness prosperous.

וְהָיָה רֵאשִׁיתְךָ מִצְעָר; וְאַחֲרִיתְךָ, יִשְׂגֶּה מְאֹד
vehayah reshitecha mitz'ar; ve'acharitecha, yisgeh me'od
And though thy beginning was small, yet thy end should greatly increase.

כִּי-שְׁאַל-נָא, לְדֹר רִישׁוֹן; וְכוֹנֵן, לְחֵקֶר אֲבוֹתָם
ki-she'al-na ledor rishon; vechonen, lecheker avotam
For inquire, I pray thee, of the former generation, and apply thyself to that which their fathers have searched out--

אִיּוֹב

גַּם-אֲנִי, לֹא אֶחֱשָׂךְ-פִּי: אֲדַבְּרָה, בְּצַר רוּחִי
gam-'ani lo echesach pi adabberah betzar ruchi
Therefore I will not refrain my mouth; I will speak in the anguish of my spirit;

אָשִׂיחָה, בְּמַר נַפְשִׁי
asichah, bemar nafshi
I will complain in the bitterness of my soul.

הֲיָם-אָנִי, אִם-תַּנִּין: כִּי-תָשִׂים עָלַי מִשְׁמָר
hayam-'ani im-tannin; ki-tasim alai mishmar
Am I a sea, or a sea-monster, that Thou settest a watch over me?

כִּי-אָמַרְתִּי, תְּנַחֲמֵנִי עַרְשִׂי; יִשָּׂא בְשִׂיחִי, מִשְׁכָּבִי
ki-'amarti tenachameni arsi; yissa vesichi, mishkavi
When I say: 'My bed shall comfort me, my couch shall ease my complaint';

וְחִתַּתַּנִי בַחֲלֹמוֹת; וּמֵחֶזְיֹנוֹת תְּבַעֲתַנִּי
vechittattani vachalomot; umechezyonot teva'atanni
Then Thou scarest me with dreams, and terrifiest me through visions;

וַתִּבְחַר מַחֲנָק נַפְשִׁי; מָוֶת, מֵעַצְמוֹתָי
vattivchar machanak nafshi; mavet, me'atzmotai
So that my soul chooseth strangling, and death rather than these my bones.

מָאַסְתִּי, לֹא-לְעֹלָם אֶחְיֶה; חֲדַל מִמֶּנִּי, כִּי-הֶבֶל יָמָי
ma'asti lo-le'olam echyeh; chadal mimmenni, ki-hevel yamai
I loathe it; I shall not live always; let me alone; for my days are vanity.

מָה-אֱנוֹשׁ, כִּי תְגַדְּלֶנּוּ; וְכִי-תָשִׁית אֵלָיו לִבֶּךָ
mah-'enosh ki tegaddelennu; vechi-tashit elav libbecha
What is man, that Thou shouldest magnify him, and that Thou shouldest set Thy heart upon him,

וַתִּפְקְדֶנּוּ לִבְקָרִים; לִרְגָעִים, תִּבְחָנֶנּוּ
vattifkedennu livkarim; lirga'im, tivchanennu
And that Thou shouldest remember him every morning, and try him every moment?

כַּמָּה, לֹא-תִשְׁעֶה מִמֶּנִּי; לֹא-תַרְפֵּנִי, עַד-בִּלְעִי רֻקִּי
kammah lo-tish'eh mimmenni; lo-tarpeni, ad-bil'i rukki
How long wilt Thou not look away from me, nor let me alone till I swallow down my spittle?

חָטָאתִי, מָה אֶפְעַל לָךְ--נֹצֵר הָאָדָם
chatati mah ef'al lach notzer ha'adam
If I have sinned, what do I unto Thee, O Thou watcher of men?

לָמָה שַׂמְתַּנִי לְמִפְגָּע לָךְ; וָאֶהְיֶה עָלַי לְמַשָּׂא
lamah samtani lemifga lach; va'ehyeh alai lemassa
Why hast Thou set me as a mark for Thee, so that I am a burden to myself?

איוב

ז

הֲלֹא-צָבָא לֶאֱנוֹשׁ עֲלֵי-אָרֶץ; וְכִימֵי שָׂכִיר יָמָיו
Halo-tzava le'enosh 'alei-'aretz; vechimei sachir yamav
Is there not a time of service to man upon earth? And are not his days like the days of a hireling?

כְּעֶבֶד יִשְׁאַף-צֵל; וּכְשָׂכִיר, יְקַוֶּה פָעֳלוֹ
ke'eved yish'af-tzel; uchesachir, yekavveh fo'olo
As a servant that eagerly longeth for the shadow, and as a hireling that looketh for his wages;

כֵּן הָנְחַלְתִּי לִי, יַרְחֵי-שָׁוְא; וְלֵילוֹת עָמָל, מִנּוּ-לִי
ken hanechalti li yarchei-shav; veleilot amal, minnu-li
So am I made to possess--months of vanity, and wearisome nights are appointed to me.

אִם-שָׁכַבְתִּי--וְאָמַרְתִּי, מָתַי אָקוּם וּמִדַּד-עָרֶב
'im-shachavti, ve'amarti, matai akum umiddad-'arev
When I lie down, I say: 'When shall I arise?' But the night is long,

וְשָׂבַעְתִּי נְדֻדִים עֲדֵי-נָשֶׁף
vesava'ti nedudim adei-nashef
and I am full of tossings to and fro unto the dawning of the day.

לָבַשׁ בְּשָׂרִי רִמָּה, וְגוּשׁ עָפָר; עוֹרִי רָגַע, וַיִּמָּאֵס
lavash besari rimmah vegush afar; ori raga', vayimma'es
My flesh is clothed with worms and clods of dust; my skin closeth up and breaketh out afresh.

יָמַי קַלּוּ, מִנִּי-אָרֶג; וַיִּכְלוּ, בְּאֶפֶס תִּקְוָה
yamai kallu minni-'areg; vayichlu, be'efes tikvah
My days are swifter than a weaver's shuttle, and are spent without hope.

זְכֹר, כִּי-רוּחַ חַיָּי; לֹא-תָשׁוּב עֵינִי, לִרְאוֹת טוֹב
zechor ki-ruach chayai; lo-tashuv eini, lir'ot tov
O remember that my life is a breath; mine eye shall no more see good.

לֹא-תְשׁוּרֵנִי, עֵין רֹאִי; עֵינֶיךָ בִּי וְאֵינֶנִּי
lo-teshureni ein ro'i; eineicha bi ve'einenni
The eye of him that seeth me shall behold me no more; while Thine eyes are upon me, I am gone.

כָּלָה עָנָן, וַיֵּלַךְ; כֵּן יוֹרֵד שְׁאוֹל, לֹא יַעֲלֶה
kalah anan vayelach; ken yored she'ol, lo ya'aleh
As the cloud is consumed and vanisheth away, so he that goeth down to the grave shall come up no more.

לֹא-יָשׁוּב עוֹד לְבֵיתוֹ; וְלֹא-יַכִּירֶנּוּ עוֹד מְקֹמוֹ
lo-yashuv od leveito; velo-yakkirennu od mekomo
He shall return no more to his house, neither shall his place know him any more.

אִיּוֹב

בֹּשׁוּ כִּי-בָטָח; בָּאוּ עָדֶיהָ, וַיֶּחְפָּרוּ
boshu ki-vatach; ba'u adeiha, vayechparu
They were ashamed because they had hoped; they came thither, and were confounded.

כִּי-עַתָּה, הֱיִיתֶם לֹא; תִּרְאוּ חֲתַת, וַתִּירָאוּ
ki-'attah heyitem lo lo; tir'u chatat, vattira'u
For now ye are become His; ye see a terror, and are afraid.

הֲכִי-אָמַרְתִּי, הָבוּ לִי; וּמִכֹּחֲכֶם, שִׁחֲדוּ בַעֲדִי
hachi-'amarti havu li; umikkochachem, shichadu va'adi
Did I say: 'Give unto me'? or: 'Offer a present for me of your substance'?

וּמַלְּטוּנִי מִיַּד-צָר; וּמִיַּד עָרִיצִים תִּפְדּוּנִי
umalletuni miyad-tzar; umiyad aritzim tifduni
or: 'Deliver me from the adversary's hand'? or: 'Redeem me from the hand of the oppressors'?

הוֹרוּנִי, וַאֲנִי אַחֲרִישׁ; וּמַה-שָּׁגִיתִי, הָבִינוּ לִי
horuni va'ani acharish; umah-shagiti, havinu li
Teach me, and I will hold my peace; and cause me to understand wherein I have erred.

מַה-נִּמְרְצוּ אִמְרֵי-יֹשֶׁר; וּמַה-יּוֹכִיחַ הוֹכֵחַ מִכֶּם
mah-nimretzu imrei-yosher; umah-yochiach hocheach mikkem
How forcible are words of uprightness! But what doth your arguing argue?

הַלְהוֹכַח מִלִּים תַּחְשֹׁבוּ; וּלְרוּחַ, אִמְרֵי נֹאָשׁ
halhochach millim tachshovu; uleruach, imrei no'ash
Do ye hold words to be an argument, but the speeches of one that is desperate to be wind?

אַף-עַל-יָתוֹם תַּפִּילוּ; וְתִכְרוּ, עַל-רֵיעֲכֶם
'af-'al-yatom tappilu; vetichru, al-rei'achem
Yea, ye would cast lots upon the fatherless, and dig a pit for your friend.

וְעַתָּה, הוֹאִילוּ פְנוּ-בִי; וְעַל-פְּנֵיכֶם, אִם-אֲכַזֵּב
ve'attah ho'ilu fenu-vi; ve'al peneichem, im-'achazzev
Now therefore be pleased to look upon me; for surely I shall not lie to your face.

שֻׁבוּ-נָא, אַל-תְּהִי עַוְלָה; וְשֻׁבוּ עוֹד, צִדְקִי-בָהּ
shuvu-na al-tehi avlah; veshuvu od tzidki-vah
Return, I pray you, let there be no injustice; yea, return again, my cause is righteous.

הֲיֵשׁ-בִּלְשׁוֹנִי עַוְלָה; אִם-חִכִּי, לֹא-יָבִין הַוּוֹת
hayesh-bilshoni avlah; im-chikki, lo-yavin havvot
Is there injustice on my tongue? Cannot my taste discern crafty devices?

איוב

וְיֹאֵל אֱלוֹהַּ, וִידַכְּאֵנִי; יַתֵּר יָדוֹ, וִיבַצְּעֵנִי
veyo'el eloah vidakke'eni; yatter yado, vivatze'eni
Even that it would please God to crush me; that He would let loose His hand, and cut me off!

וּתְהִי-עוֹד, נֶחָמָתִי--וַאֲסַלְּדָה בְחִילָה, לֹא יַחְמוֹל
utehi od nechamati, va'asalledah vechilah lo yachmol
Then should I yet have comfort; yea, I would exult in pain, though He spare not;

כִּי-לֹא כִחַדְתִּי, אִמְרֵי קָדוֹשׁ
ki-lo chichadti, imrei kadosh
for I have not denied the words of the Holy One.

מַה-כֹּחִי כִי-אֲיַחֵל; וּמַה-קִּצִּי, כִּי-אַאֲרִיךְ נַפְשִׁי
mah-kochi chi-'ayachel; umah-kitzi, ki-'a'arich nafshi
What is my strength, that I should wait? and what is mine end, that I should be patient?

אִם-כֹּחַ אֲבָנִים כֹּחִי; אִם-בְּשָׂרִי נָחוּשׁ
'im-koach avanim kochi; im-besari nachush
Is my strength the strength of stones? Or is my flesh of brass?

הַאִם אֵין עֶזְרָתִי בִי; וְתֻשִׁיָּה, נִדְּחָה מִמֶּנִּי
ha'im ein ezrati vi; vetushiyah, niddechah mimmenni
Is it that I have no help in me, and that sound wisdom is driven quite from me?

לַמָּס מֵרֵעֵהוּ חָסֶד; וְיִרְאַת שַׁדַּי יַעֲזוֹב
lammas mere'ehu chased; veyir'at shaddai ya'azov
To him that is ready to faint kindness is due from his friend, even to him that forsaketh the fear of the Almighty.

אַחַי, בָּגְדוּ כְמוֹ-נָחַל; כַּאֲפִיק נְחָלִים יַעֲבֹרוּ
'achai bagedu chemo-nachal; ka'afik nechalim ya'avoru
My brethren have dealt deceitfully as a brook, as the channel of brooks that overflow,

הַקֹּדְרִים מִנִּי-קָרַח; עָלֵימוֹ, יִתְעַלֶּם-שָׁלֶג
hakkoderim minni-karach; aleimo, yit'allem-shaleg
Which are black by reason of the ice, and wherein the snow hideth itself;

בְּעֵת יְזֹרְבוּ נִצְמָתוּ; בְּחֻמּוֹ, נִדְעֲכוּ מִמְּקוֹמָם
be'et yezorevu nitzmatu; bechummo, nid'achu mimmekomam
What time they wax warm, they vanish, when it is hot, they are consumed out of their place.

יִלָּפְתוּ, אָרְחוֹת דַּרְכָּם; יַעֲלוּ בַתֹּהוּ וְיֹאבֵדוּ
yillafetu orechot darkam; ya'alu vattohu veyovedu
The paths of their way do wind, they go up into the waste, and are lost.

הִבִּיטוּ, אָרְחוֹת תֵּמָא; הֲלִיכֹת שְׁבָא, קִוּוּ-לָמוֹ
hibbitu orechot tema; halichot sheva, kivvu-lamo
The caravans of Tema looked, the companies of Sheba waited for them--

איוֹב

תָּבוֹא בְכֶלַח אֱלֵי-קָבֶר; כַּעֲלוֹת גָּדִישׁ בְּעִתּוֹ
tavo vechelach elei-kaver; ka'alot gadish be'itto
Thou shalt come to thy grave in a ripe age, like as a shock of corn cometh in in its season.

הִנֵּה-זֹאת חֲקַרְנוּהָ כֶּן-הִיא; שְׁמָעֶנָּה, וְאַתָּה דַע-לָךְ
hinneh-zot chakarnuha ken-hi; shema'ennah, ve'attah da'-lach
Lo this, we have searched it, so it is; hear it, and know thou it for thy good.

I

וַיַּעַן אִיּוֹב, וַיֹּאמַר
Vaya'an iyov, vayomar
Then Job answered and said:

לוּ--שָׁקוֹל יִשָּׁקֵל כַּעְשִׂי; וְהַוָּתִי, בְּמֹאזְנַיִם יִשְׂאוּ-יָחַד
lu, shakol yishakel ka'si; vehavvati, bemozenayim yis'u-yachad
Oh that my vexation were but weighed, and my calamity laid in the balances altogether!

כִּי-עַתָּה--מֵחוֹל יַמִּים יִכְבָּד; עַל-כֵּן, דְּבָרַי לָעוּ
ki-'attah, mechol yammim yichbad; al-ken, devarai la'u
For now it would be heavier than the sand of the seas; therefore are my words broken.

כִּי חִצֵּי שַׁדַּי, עִמָּדִי--אֲשֶׁר חֲמָתָם, שֹׁתָה רוּחִי
ki chitzei shaddai immadi, asher chamatom shotah ruchi;
For the arrows of the Almighty are within me, the poison whereof my spirit drinketh up;

בִּעוּתֵי אֱלוֹהַּ יַעַרְכוּנִי
bi'utei eloah ya'archuni
the terrors of God do set themselves in array against me.

הֲיִנְהַק-פֶּרֶא עֲלֵי-דֶשֶׁא; אִם יִגְעֶה-שּׁוֹר, עַל-בְּלִילוֹ
hayinhak-perei alei-deshe; im yig'eh-shor, al-belilo
Doth the wild ass bray when he hath grass? Or loweth the ox over his fodder?

הֲיֵאָכֵל תָּפֵל, מִבְּלִי-מֶלַח; אִם-יֶשׁ-טַעַם, בְּרִיר חַלָּמוּת
haye'achel tafel mibbeli-melach; im-yesh-ta'am, berir challamut
Can that which hath no savour be eaten without salt? or is there any taste in the juice of mallows?

מֵאֲנָה לִנְגּוֹעַ נַפְשִׁי; הֵמָּה, כִּדְוֵי לַחְמִי
me'anah lingoa nafshi; hemmah, kidvei lachmi
My soul refuseth to touch them; they are as the sickness of my flesh.

מִי-יִתֵּן, תָּבוֹא שֶׁאֱלָתִי; וְתִקְוָתִי, יִתֵּן אֱלוֹהַּ
mi-yitten tavo she'elati; vetikvati, yitten eloah
Oh that I might have my request, and that God would grant me the thing that I long for!

איוב

יוֹמָם יְפַגְּשׁוּ-חֹשֶׁךְ; וְכַלַּיְלָה, יְמַשְׁשׁוּ בַצָּהֳרָיִם
yomam yefaggeshu-choshech; vechallaylah, yemasheshu vatzohorayim
They meet with darkness in the day-time, and grope at noonday as in the night.

וַיֹּשַׁע מֵחֶרֶב, מִפִּיהֶם; וּמִיַּד חָזָק אֶבְיוֹן
vayosha mecherev mippihem; umiyad chazak evyon
But He saveth from the sword of their mouth, even the needy from the hand of the mighty.

וַתְּהִי לַדַּל תִּקְוָה; וְעֹלָתָה, קָפְצָה פִּיהָ
vattehi laddal tikvah; ve'olatah, kafetzah piha
So the poor hath hope, and iniquity stoppeth her mouth.

הִנֵּה אַשְׁרֵי אֱנוֹשׁ, יוֹכִחֶנּוּ אֱלוֹהַּ; וּמוּסַר שַׁדַּי, אַל-תִּמְאָס
hinneh ashrei enosh yochichennu eloah; umusar shaddai, al-tim'as
Behold, happy is the man whom God correcteth; therefore despise not thou the chastening of the Almighty.

כִּי הוּא יַכְאִיב וְיֶחְבָּשׁ; יִמְחַץ, וְיָדָו תִּרְפֶּינָה
ki hu yach'iv veyechbash; yimchatz, veyado veyadav tirpeinah
For He maketh sore, and bindeth up; He woundeth, and His hands make whole.

בְּשֵׁשׁ צָרוֹת, יַצִּילֶךָּ; וּבְשֶׁבַע, לֹא-יִגַּע בְּךָ רָע
beshesh tzarot yatzileka; uvesheva lo-yigga becha ra
He will deliver thee in six troubles; yea, in seven there shall no evil touch thee.

בְּרָעָב, פָּדְךָ מִמָּוֶת; וּבְמִלְחָמָה, מִידֵי חָרֶב
bera'ov padecha mimmavet; uvemilchamah, midei charev
In famine He will redeem thee from death; and in war from the power of the sword.

בְּשׁוֹט לָשׁוֹן, תֵּחָבֵא; וְלֹא-תִירָא מִשֹּׁד, כִּי יָבוֹא
beshot lashon techave; velo-tira mishod, ki yavo
Thou shalt be hid from the scourge of the tongue; neither shalt thou be afraid of destruction when it cometh.

לְשֹׁד וּלְכָפָן תִּשְׂחָק; וּמֵחַיַּת הָאָרֶץ, אַל-תִּירָא
leshod ulechafan tischak; umechayat ha'aretz, al-tira
At destruction and famine thou shalt laugh; neither shalt thou be afraid of the beasts of the earth.

כִּי עִם-אַבְנֵי הַשָּׂדֶה בְרִיתֶךָ; וְחַיַּת הַשָּׂדֶה, הָשְׁלְמָה-לָךְ
ki im-'avnei hassadeh veritecha; vechayat hassadeh, hoshlemah-lach
For thou shalt be in league with the stones of the field; and the beasts of the field shall be at peace with thee.

וְיָדַעְתָּ, כִּי-שָׁלוֹם אָהֳלֶךָ; וּפָקַדְתָּ נָוְךָ, וְלֹא תֶחֱטָא
veyada'ta ki-shalom oholecha; ufakadta navecha velo techeta
And thou shalt know that thy tent is in peace; and thou shalt visit thy habitation, and shalt miss nothing.

וְיָדַעְתָּ, כִּי-רַב זַרְעֶךָ; וְצֶאֱצָאֶיךָ, כְּעֵשֶׂב הָאָרֶץ
veyada'ta ki-rav zar'echa; vetze'etza'eicha, ke'esev ha'aretz
Thou shalt know also that thy seed shall be great, and thine offspring as the grass of the earth.

אִיּוֹב

כִּי-לֶאֱוִיל, יַהֲרָג-כָּעַשׂ; וּפֹתֶה, תָּמִית קִנְאָה
ki-le'evil yaharag-ka'as; ufoteh, tamit kin'ah
For anger killeth the foolish man, and envy slayeth the silly one.

אֲנִי-רָאִיתִי, אֱוִיל מַשְׁרִישׁ; וָאֶקּוֹב נָוֵהוּ פִתְאֹם
'ani-ra'iti evil mashrish; va'ekkov navehu fit'om
I have seen the foolish taking root; but suddenly I beheld his habitation cursed.

יִרְחֲקוּ בָנָיו מִיֶּשַׁע; וְיִדַּכְּאוּ בַשַּׁעַר, וְאֵין מַצִּיל
yirchaku vanav miyesha'; veyiddakke'u vasha'ar, ve'ein matzil
His children are far from safety, and are crushed in the gate, with none to deliver them.

אֲשֶׁר קְצִירוֹ, רָעֵב יֹאכֵל--וְאֶל-מִצִּנִּים יִקָּחֵהוּ; וְשָׁאַף צַמִּים חֵילָם
'asher ketziro ra'ev yochel, ve'el-mitzinnim yikkachehu; vesha'af tzammim cheilam
Whose harvest the hungry eateth up, and taketh it even out of the thorns, and the snare gapeth for their substance.

כִּי, לֹא-יֵצֵא מֵעָפָר אָוֶן; וּמֵאֲדָמָה, לֹא-יִצְמַח עָמָל
ki lo-yetzei me'afar aven; ume'adamah, lo-yitzmach amal
For affliction cometh not forth from the dust, neither doth trouble spring out of the ground;

כִּי-אָדָם, לְעָמָל יוּלָּד; וּבְנֵי-רֶשֶׁף, יַגְבִּיהוּ עוּף
ki-'adom le'amal yullad; uvenei-reshef, yagbihu uf
But man is born unto trouble, as the sparks fly upward.

אוּלָם--אֲנִי, אֶדְרֹשׁ אֶל-אֵל; וְאֶל-אֱלֹהִים, אָשִׂים דִּבְרָתִי
'ulam, ani edrosh el-'el; ve'el-'elohim, asim divrati
But as for me, I would seek unto God, and unto God would I commit my cause;

עֹשֶׂה גְדֹלוֹת, וְאֵין חֵקֶר; נִפְלָאוֹת, עַד-אֵין מִסְפָּר
'oseh gedolot ve'ein cheker; nifla'ot, ad-'ein mispar
Who doeth great things and unsearchable, marvellous things without number;

הַנֹּתֵן מָטָר, עַל-פְּנֵי-אָרֶץ; וְשֹׁלֵחַ מַיִם, עַל-פְּנֵי חוּצוֹת
hannoten matar al-penei-'aretz; vesholeach mayim al-penei chutzot
Who giveth rain upon the earth, and sendeth waters upon the fields;

לָשׂוּם שְׁפָלִים לְמָרוֹם; וְקֹדְרִים, שָׂגְבוּ יֶשַׁע
lasum shefalim lemarom; vekoderim, sagevu yesha
So that He setteth up on high those that are low, and those that mourn are exalted to safety.

מֵפֵר, מַחְשְׁבוֹת עֲרוּמִים; וְלֹא-תַעֲשֶׂינָה יְדֵיהֶם, תּוּשִׁיָּה
mefer machshevot arumim; velo-ta'aseinah yedeihem, tushiyah
He frustrateth the devices of the crafty, so that their hands can perform nothing substantial.

לֹכֵד חֲכָמִים בְּעָרְמָם; וַעֲצַת נִפְתָּלִים נִמְהָרָה
loched chachamim be'oremam; va'atzat niftalim nimharah
He taketh the wise in their own craftiness; and the counsel of the wily is carried headlong.

איוב

וְאֵלַי, דָּבָר יְגֻנָּב; וַתִּקַּח אָזְנִי, שֵׁמֶץ מֶנְהוּ
ve'elai davar yegunnav; vattikkach ozeni, shemetz menhu
Now a word was secretly brought to me, and mine ear received a whisper thereof.

בִּשְׂעִפִּים, מֵחֶזְיֹנוֹת לָיְלָה; בִּנְפֹל תַּרְדֵּמָה, עַל-אֲנָשִׁים
bis'ippim mechezyonot layelah; binfol tardemah, al-'anashim
In thoughts from the visions of the night, when deep sleep falleth on men,

פַּחַד קְרָאַנִי, וּרְעָדָה; וְרֹב עַצְמוֹתַי הִפְחִיד
pachad kera'ani ure'adah; verov atzmotai hifchid
Fear came upon me, and trembling, and all my bones were made to shake.

וְרוּחַ, עַל-פָּנַי יַחֲלֹף; תְּסַמֵּר, שַׂעֲרַת בְּשָׂרִי
veruach al-panai yachalof; tesammer, sa'arat besari
Then a spirit passed before my face, that made the hair of my flesh to stand up.

יַעֲמֹד, וְלֹא-אַכִּיר מַרְאֵהוּ--תְּמוּנָה, לְנֶגֶד עֵינָי; דְּמָמָה וָקוֹל אֶשְׁמָע
ya'amod velo-'akkir mar'ehu, temunah leneged einai; demamah vakol eshma
It stood still, but I could not discern the appearance thereof; a form was before mine eyes; I heard a still voice:

הַאֱנוֹשׁ, מֵאֱלוֹהַּ יִצְדָּק; אִם מֵעֹשֵׂהוּ, יִטְהַר-גָּבֶר
ha'enosh me'eloha yitzdak; im me'osehu, yit'har-gaver
'Shall mortal man be just before God? Shall a man be pure before his Maker?

הֵן בַּעֲבָדָיו, לֹא יַאֲמִין; וּבְמַלְאָכָיו, יָשִׂים תָּהֳלָה
hen ba'avadav lo ya'amin; uvemal'achav, yasim toholah
Behold, He putteth no trust in His servants, and His angels He chargeth with folly;

אַף, שֹׁכְנֵי בָתֵּי-חֹמֶר--אֲשֶׁר-בֶּעָפָר יְסוֹדָם: יְדַכְּאוּם, לִפְנֵי-עָשׁ
'af shochenei vattei-chomer, asher-be'afar yesodam; yedakke'um, lifnei-'ash
How much more them that dwell in houses of clay, whose foundation is in the dust, who are crushed before the moth!

מִבֹּקֶר לָעֶרֶב יֻכַּתּוּ; מִבְּלִי מֵשִׂים, לָנֶצַח יֹאבֵדוּ
mibboker la'erev yukkattu; mibbeli mesim, lanetzach yovedu
Betwixt morning and evening they are shattered; they perish for ever without any regarding it.

הֲלֹא-נִסַּע יִתְרָם בָּם; יָמוּתוּ, וְלֹא בְחָכְמָה
halo-nissa yitram bam; yamutu, velo vechochemah
Is not their tent-cord plucked up within them? They die, and that without wisdom.'

ה

קְרָא-נָא, הֲיֵשׁ עוֹנֶךָּ; וְאֶל-מִי מִקְּדֹשִׁים תִּפְנֶה
Kera-na hayesh oneka; ve'el-mi mikkedoshim tifneh
Call now; is there any that will answer thee? And to which of the holy ones wilt thou turn?

אִיוֹב

ד

וַיַּעַן, אֱלִיפַז הַתֵּימָנִי; וַיֹּאמַר
Vaya'an elifaz hatteimani, vayomar
Then answered Eliphaz the Temanite, and said:

הֲנִסָּה דָבָר אֵלֶיךָ תִּלְאֶה; וַעְצֹר בְּמִלִּין, מִי יוּכָל
hanissah davar eleicha til'eh; va'tzor bemillin, mi yuchal
If one venture a word unto thee, wilt thou be weary? But who can withhold himself from speaking?

הִנֵּה, יִסַּרְתָּ רַבִּים; וְיָדַיִם רָפוֹת תְּחַזֵּק
hinneh yissarta rabbim; veyadayim rafot techazzek
Behold, thou hast instructed many, and thou hast strengthened the weak hands.

כּוֹשֵׁל, יְקִימוּן מִלֶּיךָ; וּבִרְכַּיִם כֹּרְעוֹת תְּאַמֵּץ
koshel yekimun milleicha; uvirkayim kore'ot te'ammetz
Thy words have upholden him that was falling, and thou hast strengthened the feeble knees.

כִּי עַתָּה, תָּבוֹא אֵלֶיךָ וַתֵּלֶא; תִּגַּע עָדֶיךָ, וַתִּבָּהֵל
ki attah tavo eleicha vattele; tigga adeicha, vattibbahel
But now it is come upon thee, and thou art weary; it toucheth thee, and thou art affrighted.

הֲלֹא יִרְאָתְךָ, כִּסְלָתֶךָ; תִּקְוָתְךָ, וְתֹם דְּרָכֶיךָ
halo yir'atecha kislatecha; tikvatecha, vetom deracheicha
Is not thy fear of God thy confidence, and thy hope the integrity of thy ways?

זְכָר-נָא--מִי הוּא נָקִי אָבָד; וְאֵיפֹה, יְשָׁרִים נִכְחָדוּ
zechar-na, mi hu naki avad; ve'eifoh, yesharim nichchadu
Remember, I pray thee, who ever perished, being innocent? Or where were the upright cut off?

כַּאֲשֶׁר רָאִיתִי, חֹרְשֵׁי אָוֶן; וְזֹרְעֵי עָמָל יִקְצְרֻהוּ
ka'asher ra'iti choreshei aven; vezore'ei amal yiktzeruhu
According as I have seen, they that plow iniquity, and sow mischief, reap the same.

מִנִּשְׁמַת אֱלוֹהַּ יֹאבֵדוּ; וּמֵרוּחַ אַפּוֹ יִכְלוּ
minnishmat eloah yovedu; umeruach appo yichlu
By the breath of God they perish, and by the blast of His anger are they consumed.

שַׁאֲגַת אַרְיֵה, וְקוֹל שָׁחַל; וְשִׁנֵּי כְפִירִים נִתָּעוּ
sha'agat aryeh vekol shachal; veshinnei chefirim nitta'u
The lion roareth, and the fierce lion howleth--yet the teeth of the young lions are broken.

לַיִשׁ, אֹבֵד מִבְּלִי-טָרֶף; וּבְנֵי לָבִיא, יִתְפָּרָדוּ
layish oved mibbeli-taref; uvenei lavi, yitparadu
The old lion perisheth for lack of prey, and the whelps of the lioness are scattered abroad.

אִיּוֹב

אוֹ כְנֵפֶל טָמוּן, לֹא אֶהְיֶה; כְּעֹלְלִים, לֹא-רָאוּ אוֹר
'o chenefel tamun lo ehyeh; ke'olelim, lo-ra'u or
Or as a hidden untimely birth I had not been; as infants that never saw light.

שָׁם רְשָׁעִים, חָדְלוּ רֹגֶז; וְשָׁם יָנוּחוּ, יְגִיעֵי כֹחַ
sham resha'im chadelu rogez; vesham yanuchu, yegi'ei choach
There the wicked cease from troubling; and there the weary are at rest.

יַחַד, אֲסִירִים שַׁאֲנָנוּ; לֹא שָׁמְעוּ, קוֹל נֹגֵשׂ
yachad asirim sha'ananu; lo shame'u, kol noges
There the prisoners are at ease together; they hear not the voice of the taskmaster.

קָטֹן וְגָדוֹל, שָׁם הוּא; וְעֶבֶד, חָפְשִׁי מֵאֲדֹנָיו
katon vegadol sham hu; ve'eved, chofshi me'adonav
The small and great are there alike; and the servant is free from his master.

לָמָּה יִתֵּן לְעָמֵל אוֹר; וְחַיִּים, לְמָרֵי נָפֶשׁ
lammah yitten le'amel or; vechayim, lemarei nafesh
Wherewith is light given to him that is in misery, and life unto the bitter in soul--

הַמְחַכִּים לַמָּוֶת וְאֵינֶנּוּ; וַיַּחְפְּרֻהוּ, מִמַּטְמוֹנִים
hamchakkim lammavet ve'einennu; vayachperuhu, mimmatmonim
Who long for death, but it cometh not; and dig for it more than for hid treasures;

הַשְּׂמֵחִים אֱלֵי-גִיל--יָשִׂישׂוּ, כִּי יִמְצְאוּ-קָבֶר
hassemechim elei-gil; yasisu, ki yimtze'u-kaver
Who rejoice unto exultation, and are glad, when they can find the grave?--

לְגֶבֶר, אֲשֶׁר-דַּרְכּוֹ נִסְתָּרָה; וַיָּסֶךְ אֱלוֹהַּ בַּעֲדוֹ
legever asher-darko nistarah; vayasech eloah ba'ado
To a man whose way is hid, and whom God hath hedged in?

כִּי-לִפְנֵי לַחְמִי, אַנְחָתִי תָבֹא; וַיִּתְּכוּ כַמַּיִם, שַׁאֲגֹתָי
ki-lifnei lachmi anchati tavo; vayittechu chammayim, sha'agotai
For my sighing cometh instead of my food, and my roarings are poured out like water.

כִּי פַחַד פָּחַדְתִּי, וַיֶּאֱתָיֵנִי; וַאֲשֶׁר יָגֹרְתִּי, יָבֹא לִי
ki fachad pachadti vaye'etayeni; va'asher yagoreti, yavo li
For the thing which I did fear is come upon me, and that which I was afraid of hath overtaken me.

לֹא שָׁלַוְתִּי, וְלֹא שָׁקַטְתִּי וְלֹא-נָחְתִּי; וַיָּבֹא רֹגֶז
lo shalavti velo shakatti velo-nachti, vayavo rogez
I was not at ease, neither was I quiet, neither had I rest; but trouble came.

אִיּוֹב

הַלַּיְלָה הַהוּא, יִקָּחֵהוּ-אֹפֶל: אַל-יִחַדְּ, בִּימֵי שָׁנָה
hallaylah hahu yikkachehu ofel al-yichad biymei shanah
As for that night, let thick darkness seize upon it; let it not rejoice among the days of the year;

בְּמִסְפַּר יְרָחִים, אַל-יָבֹא
bemispar yerachim, al-yavo
let it not come into the number of the months.

הִנֵּה הַלַּיְלָה הַהוּא, יְהִי גַלְמוּד; אַל-תָּבוֹא רְנָנָה בוֹ
hinneh hallaylah hahu yehi galmud; al-tavo renanah vo
Lo, let that night be desolate; let no joyful voice come therein.

יִקְּבֻהוּ אֹרְרֵי-יוֹם; הָעֲתִידִים, עֹרֵר לִוְיָתָן
yikkevuhu orerei-yom; ha'atidim, orer livyatan
Let them curse it that curse the day, who are ready to rouse up leviathan.

יֶחְשְׁכוּ, כּוֹכְבֵי נִשְׁפּוֹ: יְקַו-לְאוֹר וָאַיִן
yechshechu kochevei nishpo yekav-le'or va'ayin
Let the stars of the twilight thereof be dark; let it look for light, but have none;

וְאַל-יִרְאֶה, בְּעַפְעַפֵּי-שָׁחַר
ve'al-yir'eh, be'af'appei-shachar
neither let it behold the eyelids of the morning;

כִּי לֹא סָגַר, דַּלְתֵי בִטְנִי; וַיַּסְתֵּר עָמָל, מֵעֵינָי
ki lo sagar daltei vitni; vayaster amal, me'einai
Because it shut not up the doors of my [mother's] womb, nor hid trouble from mine eyes.

לָמָּה לֹא מֵרֶחֶם אָמוּת; מִבֶּטֶן יָצָאתִי וְאֶגְוָע
lammah lo merechem amut; mibbeten yatzati ve'egva
Why died I not from the womb? Why did I not perish at birth?

מַדּוּעַ, קִדְּמוּנִי בִרְכָּיִם; וּמַה-שָּׁדַיִם, כִּי אִינָק
maddua kiddemuni virkayim; umah-shadayim, ki inak
Why did the knees receive me? And wherefore the breasts, that I should suck?

כִּי-עַתָּה, שָׁכַבְתִּי וְאֶשְׁקוֹט; יָשַׁנְתִּי, אָז יָנוּחַ לִי
ki-'attah shachavti ve'eshkot; yashanti, az yanuach li
For now should I have lain still and been quiet; I should have slept; then had I been at rest--

עִם-מְלָכִים, וְיֹעֲצֵי אָרֶץ; הַבֹּנִים חֳרָבוֹת לָמוֹ
'im-melachim veyo'atzei aretz; habbonim choravot lamo
With kings and counsellors of the earth, who built up waste places for themselves;

אוֹ עִם-שָׂרִים, זָהָב לָהֶם; הַמְמַלְאִים בָּתֵּיהֶם כָּסֶף
'o im-sarim zahav lahem; hamemal'im batteihem kasef
Or with princes that had gold, who filled their houses with silver;

איוב

וַיִּוָּעֲדוּ יַחְדָּו, לָבוֹא לָנוּד-לוֹ וּלְנַחֲמוֹ
vayivva'adu yachdav, lavo lanud-lo ulenachamo
and they made an appointment together to come to bemoan him and to comfort him.

וַיִּשְׂאוּ אֶת-עֵינֵיהֶם מֵרָחוֹק וְלֹא הִכִּירֻהוּ, וַיִּשְׂאוּ קוֹלָם וַיִּבְכּוּ
vayis'u et-'eineihem merachok velo hikkiruhu, vayis'u kolam vayivku
And when they lifted up their eyes afar off, and knew him not, they lifted up their voice, and wept;

וַיִּקְרְעוּ אִישׁ מְעִלוֹ, וַיִּזְרְקוּ עָפָר עַל-רָאשֵׁיהֶם הַשָּׁמָיְמָה
vayikre'u ish me'ilo, vayizreku afar al-rasheihem hashamaymah
and they rent every one his mantle, and threw dust upon their heads toward heaven.

וַיֵּשְׁבוּ אִתּוֹ לָאָרֶץ, שִׁבְעַת יָמִים וְשִׁבְעַת לֵילוֹת
vayeshevu itto la'aretz, shiv'at yamim veshiv'at leilot
So they sat down with him upon the ground seven days and seven nights,

וְאֵין-דֹּבֵר אֵלָיו, דָּבָר--כִּי רָאוּ, כִּי-גָדַל הַכְּאֵב מְאֹד
ve'ein-dover elav davar, ki ra'u, ki-gadal hakke'ev me'od
and none spoke a word unto him; for they saw that his grief was very great.

ג

אַחֲרֵי-כֵן, פָּתַח אִיּוֹב אֶת-פִּיהוּ, וַיְקַלֵּל, אֶת-יוֹמוֹ
Acharei-chen, patach iyov et-pihu, vaykallel et-yomo
After this opened Job his mouth, and cursed his day.

וַיַּעַן אִיּוֹב, וַיֹּאמַר
vaya'an iyov, vayomar
And Job spoke, and said:

יֹאבַד יוֹם, אִוָּלֶד בּוֹ; וְהַלַּיְלָה אָמַר, הֹרָה גָבֶר
yovad yom ivvaled bo; vehallaylah amar, horah gaver
Let the day perish wherein I was born, and the night wherein it was said: 'A man-child is brought forth.'

הַיּוֹם הַהוּא, יְהִי-חֹשֶׁךְ: אַל-יִדְרְשֵׁהוּ אֱלוֹהַּ מִמָּעַל; וְאַל-תּוֹפַע עָלָיו נְהָרָה
hayom hahu, yehi choshech al-yidreshehu eloah mimma'al; ve'al-tofa alav neharah
Let that day be darkness; let not God inquire after it from above, neither let the light shine upon it.

יִגְאָלֻהוּ, חֹשֶׁךְ וְצַלְמָוֶת--תִּשְׁכָּן-עָלָיו עֲנָנָה
yig'aluhu choshech vetzalmavet tishkan-'alav ananah
Let darkness and the shadow of death claim it for their own; let a cloud dwell upon it;

יְבַעֲתֻהוּ, כִּמְרִירֵי יוֹם
yeva'atuhu, kimrirei yom
let all that maketh black the day terrify it.

אִיּוֹב

וְעֹדֶנּוּ מַחֲזִיק בְּתֻמָּתוֹ, וַתְּסִיתֵנִי בוֹ לְבַלְּעוֹ חִנָּם
ve'odennu machazik betummato, vattesiteni vo levalle'o chinnam
and he still holdeth fast his integrity, although thou didst move Me against him, to destroy him without cause.'

וַיַּעַן הַשָּׂטָן אֶת-יְהוָה, וַיֹּאמַר: עוֹר בְּעַד-עוֹר, וְכֹל אֲשֶׁר לָאִישׁ--יִתֵּן, בְּעַד נַפְשׁוֹ
vaya'an hassatan et-hashem vayomar; or be'ad-'or, vechol asher la'ish, yitten be'ad nafsho
And Satan answered the LORD, and said: 'Skin for skin, yea, all that a man hath will he give for his life.

אוּלָם שְׁלַח-נָא יָדְךָ, וְגַע אֶל-עַצְמוֹ וְאֶל-בְּשָׂרוֹ--אִם-לֹא אֶל-פָּנֶיךָ, יְבָרְכֶךָּ
'ulam shelach-na yadecha, vega el-'atzmo ve'el-besaro; im-lo el-paneicha yevarecheka
But put forth Thy hand now, and touch his bone and his flesh, surely he will blaspheme Thee to Thy face.'

וַיֹּאמֶר יְהוָה אֶל-הַשָּׂטָן, הִנּוֹ בְיָדֶךָ: אַךְ, אֶת-נַפְשׁוֹ שְׁמֹר
vayomer hashem el-hassatan hinno veyadecha; ach et-nafsho shemor
And the LORD said unto Satan: 'Behold, he is in thy hand; only spare his life.'

וַיֵּצֵא, הַשָּׂטָן, מֵאֵת, פְּנֵי יְהוָה
vayetzei hassatan, me'et penei hashem
So Satan went forth from the presence of the LORD,

וַיַּךְ אֶת-אִיּוֹב בִּשְׁחִין רָע, מִכַּף רַגְלוֹ וְעַד קָדְקֳדוֹ
vayach et-'iyov bishchin ra', mikkaf raglo ve'ad kadekodo
and smote Job with sore boils from the sole of his foot even unto his crown.

וַיִּקַּח-לוֹ חֶרֶשׂ, לְהִתְגָּרֵד בּוֹ; וְהוּא, יֹשֵׁב בְּתוֹךְ-הָאֵפֶר
vayikkach-lo cheres, lehitgared bo; vehu yoshev betoch-ha'efer
And he took him a potsherd to scrape himself therewith; and he sat among the ashes.

וַתֹּאמֶר לוֹ אִשְׁתּוֹ, עֹדְךָ מַחֲזִיק בְּתֻמָּתֶךָ; בָּרֵךְ אֱלֹהִים, וָמֻת
vattomer lo ishto, odecha machazik betummatecha; barech elohim vamut
Then said his wife unto him: 'Dost thou still hold fast thine integrity? Blaspheme God, and die.'

וַיֹּאמֶר אֵלֶיהָ, כְּדַבֵּר אַחַת הַנְּבָלוֹת תְּדַבֵּרִי
vayomer eleiha, kedabber achat hannevalot tedabberi
But he said unto her: 'Thou speakest as one of the impious women speaketh.

גַּם אֶת-הַטּוֹב נְקַבֵּל מֵאֵת הָאֱלֹהִים, וְאֶת-הָרָע לֹא נְקַבֵּל; בְּכָל-זֹאת לֹא-חָטָא אִיּוֹב, בִּשְׂפָתָיו
gam et-hattov, nekabbel me'et ha'elohim, ve'et-hara lo nekabbel; bechol-zot lo-chata iyov bisfatav
What? shall we receive good at the hand of God, and shall we not receive evil?' For all this did not Job sin with his lips.

וַיִּשְׁמְעוּ שְׁלֹשֶׁת רֵעֵי אִיּוֹב, אֵת כָּל-הָרָעָה הַזֹּאת הַבָּאָה עָלָיו, וַיָּבֹאוּ אִישׁ מִמְּקֹמוֹ
vayishme'u sheloshet re'ei iyov, et kol-hara'ah hazzot habba'ah alav vayavo'u ish mimmekomo
Now when Job's three friends heard of all this evil that was come upon him, they came every one from his own place,

אֱלִיפַז הַתֵּימָנִי וּבִלְדַּד הַשּׁוּחִי וְצוֹפַר הַנַּעֲמָתִי
elifaz hatteimani uvildad hashuchi, vetzofar hanna'amati
Eliphaz the Temanite, and Bildad the Shuhite, and Zophar the Naamathite;

אִיּוֹב

וַיִּפֹּל עַל-הַנְּעָרִים, וַיָּמוּתוּ; וָאִמָּלְטָה רַק-אֲנִי לְבַדִּי, לְהַגִּיד לָךְ
vayippol al-hanne'arim vayamutu; va'immaletah rak-'ani levaddi lehaggid lach
and it fell upon the young people, and they are dead; and I only am escaped alone to tell thee.'

וַיָּקָם אִיּוֹב וַיִּקְרַע אֶת-מְעִלוֹ, וַיָּגָז אֶת-רֹאשׁוֹ; וַיִּפֹּל אַרְצָה, וַיִּשְׁתָּחוּ
vayakom iyov vayikra et-me'ilo, vayagoz et-rosho; vayippol artzah vayishtachu
Then Job arose, and rent his mantle, and shaved his head, and fell down upon the ground, and worshipped;

וַיֹּאמֶר עָרֹם יָצָתִי מִבֶּטֶן אִמִּי, וְעָרֹם אָשׁוּב שָׁמָּה
vayomer arom yatzati mibbeten immi, ve'arom ashuv shamah
And he said; naked came I out of my mother's womb, and naked shall I return thither;

יְהוָה נָתַן, וַיהוָה לָקָח; יְהִי שֵׁם יְהוָה, מְבֹרָךְ
hashem natan, vahashem lakach; yehi shem hashem mevorach
the LORD gave, and the LORD hath taken away; blessed be the name of the LORD.

בְּכָל-זֹאת, לֹא-חָטָא אִיּוֹב; וְלֹא-נָתַן תִּפְלָה, לֵאלֹהִים
bechol-zot lo-chata iyov; velo-natan tiflah le'elohim
For all this Job sinned not, nor ascribed aught unseemly to God.

ב

וַיְהִי הַיּוֹם--וַיָּבֹאוּ בְּנֵי הָאֱלֹהִים, לְהִתְיַצֵּב עַל-יְהוָה
Vayhi hayom, vayavo'u benei ha'elohim, lehityatzev al-hashem
Again it fell upon a day, that the sons of God came to present themselves before the LORD,

וַיָּבוֹא גַם-הַשָּׂטָן בְּתֹכָם, לְהִתְיַצֵּב עַל-יְהוָה
vayavo gam-hassatan betocham, lehityatzev al-hashem
and Satan came also among them to present himself before the LORD.

וַיֹּאמֶר יְהוָה אֶל-הַשָּׂטָן, אֵי מִזֶּה תָּבֹא; וַיַּעַן הַשָּׂטָן אֶת-יְהוָה, וַיֹּאמַר
vayomer hashem el-hassatan, ei mizzeh tavo; vaya'an hassatan et-hashem vayomar
And the LORD said unto Satan: 'From whence comest thou?' And Satan answered the LORD, and said:

מִשּׁוּט בָּאָרֶץ, וּמֵהִתְהַלֵּךְ בָּהּ
mishut ba'aretz, umehit'hallech bah
'From going to and fro in the earth, and from walking up and down in it.'

וַיֹּאמֶר יְהוָה אֶל-הַשָּׂטָן, הֲשַׂמְתָּ לִבְּךָ אֶל-עַבְדִּי אִיּוֹב--כִּי אֵין כָּמֹהוּ בָּאָרֶץ
vayomer hashem el-hassatan, hasamta libbecha el-'avdi iyov ki ein kamohu ba'aretz
And the LORD said unto Satan: 'Hast thou considered my servant Job, that there is none like him in the earth,

אִישׁ תָּם וְיָשָׁר יְרֵא אֱלֹהִים, וְסָר מֵרָע
ish tam veyashar yerei elohim vesar mera'
a whole-hearted and an upright man, one that feareth God, and shunneth evil?

אִיּוֹב

וַיְהִי, הַיּוֹם; וּבָנָיו וּבְנֹתָיו אֹכְלִים וְשֹׁתִים יַיִן, בְּבֵית אֲחִיהֶם הַבְּכוֹר
vayhi hayom; uvanav uvenotav ochelim veshotim yayin, beveit achihem habbechor
And it fell on a day when his sons and his daughters were eating and drinking wine in their eldest brother's house,

וּמַלְאָךְ בָּא אֶל-אִיּוֹב, וַיֹּאמַר: הַבָּקָר הָיוּ חֹרְשׁוֹת, וְהָאֲתֹנוֹת רֹעוֹת עַל-יְדֵיהֶם
umal'ach ba el-'iyov vayomar; habbakar hayu choreshot, veha'atonot ro'ot al-yedeihem
that there came a messenger unto Job, and said: 'The oxen were plowing, and the asses feeding beside them;

וַתִּפֹּל שְׁבָא וַתִּקָּחֵם
vattippol sheva vattikkachem
and the Sabeans made a raid, and took them away;

וְאֶת-הַנְּעָרִים הִכּוּ לְפִי-חָרֶב; וָאִמָּלְטָה רַק-אֲנִי לְבַדִּי, לְהַגִּיד לָךְ
ve'et-hanne'arim hikku lefi-charev; va'immaletah rak-'ani levaddi lehaggid lach
yea, they have slain the servants with the edge of the sword; and I only am escaped alone to tell thee.'

עוֹד זֶה מְדַבֵּר, וְזֶה בָּא וַיֹּאמַר, אֵשׁ אֱלֹהִים, נָפְלָה מִן-הַשָּׁמַיִם
'od zeh medabber, vezeh ba vayomar esh elohim, nafelah min-hashamayim
While he was yet speaking, there came also another, and said: 'A fire of God is fallen from heaven,

וַתִּבְעַר בַּצֹּאן וּבַנְּעָרִים וַתֹּאכְלֵם; וָאִמָּלְטָה רַק-אֲנִי לְבַדִּי, לְהַגִּיד לָךְ
vattiv'ar batzon uvanne'arim vattochelem; va'immaletah rak-'ani levaddi lehaggid lach
and hath burned up the sheep, and the servants, and consumed them; and I only am escaped alone to tell thee.'

עוֹד זֶה מְדַבֵּר, וְזֶה בָּא וַיֹּאמַר
'od zeh medabber, vezeh ba vayomar
While he was yet speaking, there came also another, and said:

כַּשְׂדִּים שָׂמוּ שְׁלֹשָׁה רָאשִׁים וַיִּפְשְׁטוּ עַל-הַגְּמַלִּים וַיִּקָּחוּם
kasdim samu sheloshah rashim, vayifshetu al-haggemallim vayikkachum
'The Chaldeans set themselves in three bands, and fell upon the camels, and have taken them away,

וְאֶת-הַנְּעָרִים הִכּוּ לְפִי-חָרֶב; וָאִמָּלְטָה רַק-אֲנִי לְבַדִּי, לְהַגִּיד לָךְ
ve'et-hanne'arim hikku lefi-charev; va'immaletah rak-'ani levaddi lehaggid lach
yea, and slain the servants with the edge of the sword; and I only am escaped alone to tell thee.'

עַד זֶה מְדַבֵּר, וְזֶה בָּא וַיֹּאמַר
'ad zeh medabber, vezeh ba vayomar
While he was yet speaking, there came also another, and said:

בָּנֶיךָ וּבְנוֹתֶיךָ אֹכְלִים וְשֹׁתִים יַיִן, בְּבֵית אֲחִיהֶם הַבְּכוֹר
baneicha uvenoteicha ochelim veshotim yayin, beveit achihem habbechor
'Thy sons and thy daughters were eating and drinking wine in their eldest brother's house;

וְהִנֵּה רוּחַ גְּדוֹלָה בָּאָה מֵעֵבֶר הַמִּדְבָּר, וַיִּגַּע בְּאַרְבַּע פִּנּוֹת הַבַּיִת
vehinneh ruach gedolah ba'ah me'ever hammidbar, vayigga be'arba pinnot habbayit
And, behold, there came a great wind from across the wilderness, and smote the four corners of the house,

אִיּוֹב

וַיְהִי הַיּוֹם--וַיָּבֹאוּ בְּנֵי הָאֱלֹהִים, לְהִתְיַצֵּב עַל-יְהוָה

vayhi hayom, vayavo'u benei ha'elohim, lehityatzev al-hashem

Now it fell upon a day, that the sons of God came to present themselves before the LORD,

וַיָּבוֹא גַם-הַשָּׂטָן, בְּתוֹכָם

vayavo gam-hassatan betocham

and Satan came also among them.

וַיֹּאמֶר יְהוָה אֶל-הַשָּׂטָן, מֵאַיִן תָּבֹא; וַיַּעַן הַשָּׂטָן אֶת-יְהוָה, וַיֹּאמַר

vayomer hashem el-hassatan me'ayin tavo; vaya'an hassatan et-hashem vayomar

And the LORD said unto Satan: 'Whence comest thou?' Then Satan answered the LORD, and said:

מִשּׁוּט בָּאָרֶץ, וּמֵהִתְהַלֵּךְ בָּהּ

mishut ba'aretz, umehit'hallech bah

'From going to and fro in the earth, and from walking up and down in it.'

וַיֹּאמֶר יְהוָה אֶל-הַשָּׂטָן, הֲשַׂמְתָּ לִבְּךָ עַל-עַבְדִּי אִיּוֹב: כִּי אֵין כָּמֹהוּ בָּאָרֶץ

vayomer hashem el-hassatan, hasamta libbecha al-'avdi iyov; ki ein kamohu ba'aretz

And the LORD said unto Satan: 'Hast thou considered My servant Job, that there is none like him in the earth,

אִישׁ תָּם וְיָשָׁר יְרֵא אֱלֹהִים וְסָר מֵרָע

ish tam veyashar yerei elohim vesar mera

a whole-hearted and an upright man, one that feareth God, and shunneth evil?'

וַיַּעַן הַשָּׂטָן אֶת-יְהוָה, וַיֹּאמַר: הַחִנָּם, יָרֵא אִיּוֹב אֱלֹהִים

vaya'an hassatan et-hashem vayomar; hachinnam, yarei iyov elohim

Then Satan answered the LORD, and said: 'Doth Job fear God for nought?

הֲלֹא-אַתָּה שַׂכְתָּ בַעֲדוֹ וּבְעַד-בֵּיתוֹ, וּבְעַד כָּל-אֲשֶׁר-לוֹ--מִסָּבִיב

halo-'attah sachta va'ado uve'ad-beito uve'ad kol-'asher-lo missaviv

Hast not Thou made a hedge about him, and about his house, and about all that he hath, on every side?

מַעֲשֵׂה יָדָיו בֵּרַכְתָּ, וּמִקְנֵהוּ פָּרַץ בָּאָרֶץ

ma'aseh yadav berachta, umiknehu paratz ba'aretz

Thou hast blessed the work of his hands, and his possessions are increased in the land.

וְאוּלָם שְׁלַח-נָא יָדְךָ, וְגַע בְּכָל-אֲשֶׁר-לוֹ--אִם-לֹא עַל-פָּנֶיךָ, יְבָרְכֶךָּ

ve'ulam shelach-na yadecha, vega bechol-'asher-lo; im-lo al-paneicha yevarecheka

But put forth Thy hand now, and touch all that he hath, surely he will blaspheme Thee to Thy face.'

וַיֹּאמֶר יְהוָה אֶל-הַשָּׂטָן, הִנֵּה כָל-אֲשֶׁר-לוֹ בְּיָדֶךָ

vayomer hashem el-hassatan, hinneh chol-'asher-lo beyadecha

And the LORD said unto Satan: 'Behold, all that he hath is in thy power;

רַק אֵלָיו, אַל-תִּשְׁלַח יָדֶךָ; וַיֵּצֵא, הַשָּׂטָן, מֵעִם, פְּנֵי יְהוָה

rak elav, al-tishlach yadecha; vayetzei hassatan, me'im penei hashem

only upon himself put not forth thy hand.' So Satan went forth from the presence of the LORD.

אִיּוֹב

אִיּוֹב א

אִישׁ הָיָה בְאֶרֶץ-עוּץ, אִיּוֹב שְׁמוֹ
Ish hayah ve'eretz-'utz iyov shemo
There was a man in the land of Uz, whose name was Job;

וְהָיָה הָאִישׁ הַהוּא, תָּם וְיָשָׁר וִירֵא אֱלֹהִים--וְסָר מֵרָע
vehayah ha'ish hahu, tam veyashar viyrei elohim vesar mera
and that man was whole-hearted and upright, and one that feared God, and shunned evil.

וַיִּוָּלְדוּ לוֹ שִׁבְעָה בָנִים, וְשָׁלוֹשׁ בָּנוֹת
vayivvaledu lo shiv'ah vanim veshalosh banot
And there were born unto him seven sons and three daughters.

וַיְהִי מִקְנֵהוּ שִׁבְעַת אַלְפֵי-צֹאן וּשְׁלֹשֶׁת אַלְפֵי גְמַלִּים, וַחֲמֵשׁ מֵאוֹת צֶמֶד-בָּקָר
vayhi miknehu shiv'at alfei-tzon usheloshet alfei gemallim, vachamesh me'ot tzemed-bakar
His possessions also were seven thousand sheep, and three thousand camels, and five hundred yoke of oxen,

וַחֲמֵשׁ מֵאוֹת אֲתוֹנוֹת, וַעֲבֻדָּה, רַבָּה מְאֹד
vachamesh me'ot atonot, va'avuddah rabbah me'od
and five hundred she-asses, and a very great household;

וַיְהִי הָאִישׁ הַהוּא, גָּדוֹל מִכָּל-בְּנֵי-קֶדֶם
vayhi ha'ish hahu, gadol mikkol-benei-kedem
so that this man was the greatest of all the children of the east.

וְהָלְכוּ בָנָיו וְעָשׂוּ מִשְׁתֶּה, בֵּית אִישׁ יוֹמוֹ
vehalechu vanav ve'asu mishteh, beit ish yomo
And his sons used to go and hold a feast in the house of each one upon his day;

וְשָׁלְחוּ וְקָרְאוּ לִשְׁלֹשֶׁת אַחְיֹתֵיהֶם, לֶאֱכֹל וְלִשְׁתּוֹת, עִמָּהֶם
veshalechu vekare'u lishloshet achyoteihem achyoteihem, le'echol velishtot immahem
and they would send and invite their three sisters to eat and to drink with them.

וַיְהִי כִּי הִקִּיפוּ יְמֵי הַמִּשְׁתֶּה וַיִּשְׁלַח אִיּוֹב וַיְקַדְּשֵׁם
vayhi ki hikkifu yemei hammishteh vayishlach iyov vaykaddeshem
And it was so, when the days of their feasting were gone about, that Job sent and sanctified them,

וְהִשְׁכִּים בַּבֹּקֶר וְהֶעֱלָה עֹלוֹת מִסְפַּר כֻּלָּם--כִּי אָמַר אִיּוֹב
vehishkim babboker vehe'elah olot mispar kullam ki amar iyov
and rose up early in the morning, and offered burnt-offerings according to the number of them all; for Job said:

אוּלַי חָטְאוּ בָנַי, וּבֵרְכוּ אֱלֹהִים בִּלְבָבָם: כָּכָה יַעֲשֶׂה אִיּוֹב, כָּל-הַיָּמִים
ulai chate'u vanai, uverechu elohim bilvavam; kachah ya'aseh iyov kol-hayamim
'It may be that my sons have sinned, and blasphemed God in their hearts.' Thus did Job continually.

מִשְׁלֵי

שֶׁקֶר הַחֵן, וְהֶבֶל הַיֹּפִי: אִשָּׁה יִרְאַת-יְהוָה, הִיא תִתְהַלָּל
sheker hachen vehevel hayofi; ishah yir'at-hashem hi tit'hallal
Grace is deceitful, and beauty is vain; but a woman that feareth the LORD, she shall be praised.

תְּנוּ-לָהּ, מִפְּרִי יָדֶיהָ; וִיהַלְלוּהָ בַשְּׁעָרִים מַעֲשֶׂיהָ
tenu-lah mipperi yadeiha; viyhaleluha vashe'arim ma'aseiha
Give her of the fruit of her hands; and let her works praise her in the gates.

מִשְׁלֵי

טָעֲמָה, כִּי-טוֹב סַחְרָהּ; לֹא-יִכְבֶּה בַלַּיְלָה נֵרָהּ
ta'amah ki-tov sachrah; lo-yichbeh vallaylah nerah
She perceiveth that her merchandise is good; her lamp goeth not out by night.

יָדֶיהָ, שִׁלְּחָה בַכִּישׁוֹר; וְכַפֶּיהָ, תָּמְכוּ פָלֶךְ
yadeiha shillechah vakkishor; vechappeiha, tamechu falech
She layeth her hands to the distaff, and her hands hold the spindle.

כַּפָּהּ, פָּרְשָׂה לֶעָנִי; וְיָדֶיהָ, שִׁלְּחָה לָאֶבְיוֹן
kappah paresah le'ani; veyadeiha, shillechah la'evyon
She stretcheth out her hand to the poor; yea, she reacheth forth her hands to the needy.

לֹא-תִירָא לְבֵיתָהּ מִשָּׁלֶג: כִּי כָל-בֵּיתָהּ, לָבֻשׁ שָׁנִים
lo-tira leveitah mishaleg; ki chol-beitah, lavush shanim
She is not afraid of the snow for her household; for all her household are clothed with scarlet.

מַרְבַדִּים עָשְׂתָה-לָּהּ; שֵׁשׁ וְאַרְגָּמָן לְבוּשָׁהּ
marvaddim asetah-lah; shesh ve'argaman levushah
She maketh for herself coverlets; her clothing is fine linen and purple.

נוֹדָע בַּשְּׁעָרִים בַּעְלָהּ; בְּשִׁבְתּוֹ, עִם-זִקְנֵי-אָרֶץ
noda bashe'arim ba'lah; beshivto, im-ziknei-'aretz
Her husband is known in the gates, when he sitteth among the elders of the land.

סָדִין עָשְׂתָה, וַתִּמְכֹּר; וַחֲגוֹר, נָתְנָה לַכְּנַעֲנִי
sadin asetah vattimkor; vachagor, natenah lakkena'ani
She maketh linen garments and selleth them; and delivereth girdles unto the merchant.

עֹז-וְהָדָר לְבוּשָׁהּ; וַתִּשְׂחַק, לְיוֹם אַחֲרוֹן
'oz-vehadar levushah; vattischak, leyom acharon
Strength and dignity are her clothing; and she laugheth at the time to come.

פִּיהָ, פָּתְחָה בְחָכְמָה; וְתוֹרַת חֶסֶד, עַל-לְשׁוֹנָהּ
piha patechah vechochmah; vetorat-chesed, al-leshonah
She openeth her mouth with wisdom; and the law of kindness is on her tongue.

צוֹפִיָּה, הֲלִיכוֹת בֵּיתָהּ; וְלֶחֶם עַצְלוּת, לֹא תֹאכֵל
tzofiyah halichot beitah; velechem atzlut, lo tochel
She looketh well to the ways of her household, and eateth not the bread of idleness.

קָמוּ בָנֶיהָ, וַיְאַשְּׁרוּהָ; בַּעְלָהּ, וַיְהַלְלָהּ
kamu vaneiha vay'asheruha; ba'lah, vayhalelah
Her children rise up, and call her blessed; her husband also, and he praiseth her:

רַבּוֹת בָּנוֹת, עָשׂוּ חָיִל; וְאַתְּ, עָלִית עַל-כֻּלָּנָה
rabbot banot asu chayil; ve'at, alit al-kullanah
'Many daughters have done valiantly, but thou excellest them all.'

מִשְׁלֵי

תְּנוּ-שֵׁכָר לְאוֹבֵד; וְיַיִן, לְמָרֵי נָפֶשׁ
tenu-shechar le'oved; veyayin lemarei nafesh
Give strong drink unto him that is ready to perish, and wine unto the bitter in soul;

יִשְׁתֶּה, וְיִשְׁכַּח רִישׁוֹ; וַעֲמָלוֹ, לֹא יִזְכָּר-עוֹד
yishteh veyishkach risho; va'amalo, lo yizkor-'od
Let him drink, and forget his poverty, and remember his misery no more

פְּתַח-פִּיךָ לְאִלֵּם; אֶל-דִּין, כָּל-בְּנֵי חֲלוֹף
petach-picha le'illem; el-din, kol-benei chalof
Open thy mouth for the dumb, in the cause of all such as are appointed to destruction.

פְּתַח-פִּיךָ שְׁפָט-צֶדֶק; וְדִין, עָנִי וְאֶבְיוֹן
petach-picha shefat-tzedek; vedin, ani ve'evyon
Open thy mouth, judge righteously, and plead the cause of the poor and needy.

אֵשֶׁת-חַיִל, מִי יִמְצָא; וְרָחֹק מִפְּנִינִים מִכְרָהּ
'eshet-chayil mi yimtza; verachok mippeninim michrah
A woman of valour who can find? for her price is far above rubies.

בָּטַח בָּהּ, לֵב בַּעְלָהּ; וְשָׁלָל, לֹא יֶחְסָר
batach bah lev ba'lah; veshalal, lo yechsar
The heart of her husband doth safely trust in her, and he hath no lack of gain.

גְּמָלַתְהוּ טוֹב וְלֹא-רָע--כֹּל, יְמֵי חַיֶּיהָ
gemalat'hu tov velo-ra'; kol yemei chayeih
She doeth him good and not evil all the days of her life.

דָּרְשָׁה, צֶמֶר וּפִשְׁתִּים; וַתַּעַשׂ, בְּחֵפֶץ כַּפֶּיהָ
dareshah tzemer ufishtim; vatta'as, bechefetz kappeiha
She seeketh wool and flax, and worketh willingly with her hands.

הָיְתָה, כָּאֳנִיּוֹת סוֹחֵר; מִמֶּרְחָק, תָּבִיא לַחְמָהּ
hayetah ko'oniyot socher; mimmerchak, tavi lachmah
She is like the merchant-ships; she bringeth her food from afar.

וַתָּקָם, בְּעוֹד לַיְלָה--וַתִּתֵּן טֶרֶף לְבֵיתָהּ; וְחֹק, לְנַעֲרֹתֶיהָ
vattakom be'od laylah, vattitten teref leveitah; vechok, lena'aroteiha
She riseth also while it is yet night, and giveth food to her household, and a portion to her maidens.

זָמְמָה שָׂדֶה, וַתִּקָּחֵהוּ; מִפְּרִי כַפֶּיהָ, נָטְעָה כָּרֶם
zamemah sadeh vattikkachehu; mipperi chappeiha, nate'ah karem
She considereth a field, and buyeth it; with the fruit of her hands she planteth a vineyard.

חָגְרָה בְעוֹז מָתְנֶיהָ; וַתְּאַמֵּץ, זְרוֹעֹתֶיהָ
chagerah ve'oz moteneiha; vatte'ammetz, zero'oteiha
She girdeth her loins with strength, and maketh strong her arms.

מִשְׁלֵי

שְׁלֹשָׁה הֵמָּה, מֵיטִיבֵי צָעַד; וְאַרְבָּעָה, מֵיטִבֵי לָכֶת
sheloshah hemmah meitivei tza'ad; ve'arba'ah, meitivei lachet
There are three things which are stately in their march, yea, four which are stately in going:

לַיִשׁ, גִּבּוֹר בַּבְּהֵמָה; וְלֹא-יָשׁוּב, מִפְּנֵי-כֹל.
layish gibbor babbehemah; velo-yashuv, mippenei-chol
The lion, which is mightiest among beasts, and turneth not away for any;

זַרְזִיר מָתְנַיִם אוֹ-תָיִשׁ; וּמֶלֶךְ, אַלְקוּם עִמּוֹ
zarzir motenayim o-tayish; umelech, alkum immo
The greyhound; the he-goat also; and the king, against whom there is no rising up.

אִם-נָבַלְתָּ בְהִתְנַשֵּׂא; וְאִם-זַמּוֹתָ, יָד לְפֶה
'im-navalta vehitnasse; ve'im-zammota, yad lefeh
If thou hast done foolishly in lifting up thyself, or if thou hast planned devices, lay thy hand upon thy mouth.

כִּי מִיץ חָלָב, יוֹצִיא חֶמְאָה--וּמִיץ-אַף, יוֹצִיא דָם
ki mitz chalav yotzi chem'ah, umitz-'af yotzi dam
For the churning of milk bringeth forth curd, and the wringing of the nose bringeth forth blood;

וּמִיץ אַפַּיִם, יוֹצִיא רִיב
umitz appayim, yotzi riv
so the forcing of wrath bringeth forth strife.

לא

דִּבְרֵי, לְמוּאֵל מֶלֶךְ--מַשָּׂא, אֲשֶׁר-יִסְּרַתּוּ אִמּוֹ
Divrei lemu'el melech; massa, asher-yisserattu immo
The words of king Lemuel; the burden wherewith his mother corrected him.

מַה-בְּרִי, וּמַה-בַּר-בִּטְנִי; וּמֶה, בַּר-נְדָרָי
mah-beri umah-bar-bitni; umeh bar-nedarai
What, my son? and what, O son of my womb? and what, O son of my vows?

אַל-תִּתֵּן לַנָּשִׁים חֵילֶךָ; וּדְרָכֶיךָ, לַמְחוֹת מְלָכִין
'al-titten lannashim cheilecha; uderacheicha, lamchot melachin
Give not thy strength unto women, nor thy ways to that which destroyeth kings.

אַל לַמְלָכִים, לְמוֹאֵל--אַל לַמְלָכִים שְׁתוֹ-יָיִן; וּלְרוֹזְנִים, אֵי שֵׁכָר
'al lamlachim lemo'el, al lamlachim sheto-yayin; ulerozenim, ei shechar
It is not for kings, O Lemuel, it is not for kings to drink wine: nor for princes to say: 'Where is strong drink?'

פֶּן-יִשְׁתֶּה, וְיִשְׁכַּח מְחֻקָּק; וִישַׁנֶּה, דִּין כָּל-בְּנֵי-עֹנִי
pen-yishteh veyishkach mechukkak; vishanneh din kol-benei-'oni
Lest they drink, and forget that which is decreed, and pervert the justice due to any that is afflicted.

מִשְׁלֵי

שְׁלֹשָׁה הֵמָּה, נִפְלְאוּ מִמֶּנִּי; וְאַרְבָּעָה, לֹא יְדַעְתִּים
sheloshah hemmah nifle'u mimmenni; ve'arba'ah, lo yeda'tim
There are three things which are too wonderful for me, yea, four which I know not:

דֶּרֶךְ הַנֶּשֶׁר, בַּשָּׁמַיִם--דֶּרֶךְ נָחָשׁ, עֲלֵי-צוּר
derech hannesher bashamayim derech nachash, alei tzur
The way of an eagle in the air; the way of a serpent upon a rock;

דֶּרֶךְ-אֳנִיָּה בְלֶב-יָם-וְדֶרֶךְ גֶּבֶר בְּעַלְמָה
derech-'oniyah velev-yam; vederech gever be'almah
the way of a ship in the midst of the sea; and the way of a man with a young woman.

כֵּן, דֶּרֶךְ אִשָּׁה--מְנָאָפֶת: אָכְלָה, וּמָחֲתָה פִיהָ; וְאָמְרָה, לֹא-פָעַלְתִּי אָוֶן
ken derech ishah, mena'afet achelah umachatah fiha; ve'amerah, lo-fa'alti aven
So is the way of an adulterous woman; she eateth, and wipeth her mouth, and saith: 'I have done no wickedness.'

תַּחַת שָׁלוֹשׁ, רָגְזָה אֶרֶץ; וְתַחַת אַרְבַּע, לֹא-תוּכַל שְׂאֵת
tachat shalosh ragezah eretz; vetachat arba', lo-tuchal se'et
For three things the earth doth quake, and for four it cannot endure:

תַּחַת-עֶבֶד, כִּי יִמְלוֹךְ; וְנָבָל, כִּי יִשְׂבַּע-לָחֶם
tachat-'eved ki yimloch; venaval, ki yisba'-lachem
For a servant when he reigneth; and a churl when he is filled with food;

תַּחַת שְׂנוּאָה, כִּי תִבָּעֵל; וְשִׁפְחָה, כִּי-תִירַשׁ גְּבִרְתָּהּ
tachat senu'ah ki tibba'el; veshifchah, ki-tirash gevirtah
For an odious woman when she is married; and a handmaid that is heir to her mistress.

אַרְבָּעָה הֵם, קְטַנֵּי-אָרֶץ; וְהֵמָּה, חֲכָמִים מְחֻכָּמִים
'arba'ah hem ketannei-'aretz; vehemmah, chachamim mechukkamim
There are four things which are little upon the earth, but they are exceeding wise:

הַנְּמָלִים, עַם לֹא-עָז; וַיָּכִינוּ בַקַּיִץ לַחְמָם
hannemalim am lo-'az; vayachinu vakkayitz lachmam
The ants are a people not strong, yet they provide their food in the summer;

שְׁפַנִּים, עַם לֹא-עָצוּם; וַיָּשִׂימוּ בַסֶּלַע בֵּיתָם
shefannim, am lo-'atzum; vayasimu vassela beitam
The rock-badgers are but a feeble folk, yet make they their houses in the crags;

מֶלֶךְ, אֵין לָאַרְבֶּה; וַיֵּצֵא חֹצֵץ כֻּלּוֹ
melech ein la'arbeh; vayetzei chotzetz kullo
The locusts have no king, yet go they forth all of them by bands;

שְׂמָמִית, בְּיָדַיִם תְּתַפֵּשׂ; וְהִיא, בְּהֵיכְלֵי מֶלֶךְ
semamit beyadayim tetappes; vehi, beheichelei melech
The spider thou canst take with the hands, yet is she in kings' palaces.

מִשְׁלֵי

פֶּן-אִוָּרֵשׁ וְגָנַבְתִּי; וְתָפַשְׂתִּי, שֵׁם אֱלֹהָי
ufen-'ivvaresh veganavti; vetafasti, shem elohai
Or lest I be poor, and steal, and profane the name of my God.

אַל-תַּלְשֵׁן עֶבֶד, אֶל-אֲדֹנָו: פֶּן-יְקַלֶּלְךָ וְאָשָׁמְתָּ.
'al-talshen eved el-'adonav; pen-yekallelcha ve'ashameta
Slander not a servant unto his master, lest he curse thee, and thou be found guilty.

דּוֹר, אָבִיו יְקַלֵּל; וְאֶת-אִמּוֹ, לֹא יְבָרֵךְ
dor aviv yekallel; ve'et-'immo, lo yevarech
There is a generation that curse their father, and do not bless their mother.

דּוֹר, טָהוֹר בְּעֵינָיו; וּמִצֹּאָתוֹ, לֹא רֻחָץ
dor tahor be'einav; umitzo'ato, lo ruchatz
There is a generation that are pure in their own eyes, and yet are not washed from their filthiness.

דּוֹר, מָה-רָמוּ עֵינָיו; וְעַפְעַפָּיו, יִנָּשֵׂאוּ
dor mah-ramu einav; ve'af'appav, yinnase'u
There is a generation, Oh how lofty are their eyes! and their eyelids are lifted up.

דּוֹר, חֲרָבוֹת שִׁנָּיו--וּמַאֲכָלוֹת מְתַלְּעֹתָיו
dor charavot shinnav uma'achalot metalle'otav
There is a generation whose teeth are as swords, and their great teeth as knives,

לֶאֱכֹל עֲנִיִּים מֵאֶרֶץ; וְאֶבְיוֹנִים, מֵאָדָם
le'echol aniyim me'eretz; ve'evyonim, me'adam
to devour the poor from off the earth, and the needy from among men.

לַעֲלוּקָה, שְׁתֵּי בָנוֹת--הַב הַב
la'alukah shetei vanot hav hav
The horseleech hath two daughters: 'Give, give.'

שָׁלוֹשׁ הֵנָּה, לֹא תִשְׂבַּעְנָה; אַרְבַּע, לֹא-אָמְרוּ הוֹן
shalosh hennah lo tisba'nah; arba', lo-'ameru hon
There are three things that are never satisfied, yea, four that say not: 'Enough':

שְׁאוֹל, וְעֹצֶר-רָחַם: אֶרֶץ, לֹא-שָׂבְעָה מַּיִם; וְאֵשׁ, לֹא-אָמְרָה הוֹן
she'ol ve'otzer racham eretz lo-save'ah mayim; ve'esh, lo-'amerah hon
The grave; and the barren womb; the earth that is not satisfied with water; and the fire that saith not: 'Enough.'

עַיִן, תִּלְעַג לְאָב--וְתָבֻז לִיקֲּהַת-אֵם
'ayin til'ag le'av vetavuz likkahat-'em
The eye that mocketh at his father, and despiseth to obey his mother,

יִקְּרוּהָ, עֹרְבֵי-נַחַל; וְיֹאכְלוּהָ בְנֵי-נָשֶׁר
yikkeruha orevei-nachal; veyocheluha venei-nasher
the ravens of the valley shall pick it out, and the young vultures shall eat it.

מִשְׁלֵי

ל

דִּבְרֵי, אָגוּר בִּן-יָקֶה--הַמַּשָּׂא: נְאֻם הַגֶּבֶר, לְאִיתִיאֵל; לְאִיתִיאֵל וְאֻכָל
Divrei agur bin-yakeh, hammassa ne'um haggever le'iti'el; le'iti'el ve'uchal
The words of Agur the son of Jakeh; the burden. The man saith unto Ithiel, unto Ithiel and Ucal:

כִּי בַעַר אָנֹכִי מֵאִישׁ; וְלֹא-בִינַת אָדָם לִי
ki va'ar anochi me'ish; velo-vinat adam li
Surely I am brutish, unlike a man, and have not the understanding of a man;

וְלֹא-לָמַדְתִּי חָכְמָה; וְדַעַת קְדֹשִׁים אֵדָע.
velo-lamadti chochmah veda'at kedoshim eda
And I have not learned wisdom, that I should have the knowledge of the Holy One.

מִי עָלָה-שָׁמַיִם וַיֵּרַד, מִי אָסַף-רוּחַ בְּחָפְנָיו
mi alah-shamayim vayerad mi asaf-ruach bechofnav
Who hath ascended up into heaven, and descended? Who hath gathered the wind in his fists?

מִי צָרַר-מַיִם בַּשִּׂמְלָה--מִי, הֵקִים כָּל-אַפְסֵי-אָרֶץ
mi tzarar-mayim bassimlah, mi hekim kol-'afsei-'aretz
Who hath bound the waters in his garment? Who hath established all the ends of the earth?

מַה-שְּׁמוֹ וּמַה-שֶּׁם-בְּנוֹ, כִּי תֵדָע
mah-shemo umah-shem-beno, ki teda
What is his name, and what is his son's name, if thou knowest?

כָּל-אִמְרַת אֱלוֹהַּ צְרוּפָה; מָגֵן הוּא, לַחֹסִים בּוֹ
kol-'imrat eloah tzerufah; magen hu, lachosim bo
Every word of God is tried; He is a shield unto them that take refuge in Him.

אַל-תּוֹסְףְּ עַל-דְּבָרָיו: פֶּן-יוֹכִיחַ בְּךָ וְנִכְזָבְתָּ
'al-tosef al-devarav; pen-yochiach becha venichzaveta
Add thou not unto His words, lest He reprove thee, and thou be found a liar.

שְׁתַּיִם, שָׁאַלְתִּי מֵאִתָּךְ; אַל-תִּמְנַע מִמֶּנִּי, בְּטֶרֶם אָמוּת
shetayim sha'alti me'ittach; al-timna mimmenni, beterem amut
Two things have I asked of Thee; deny me them not before I die:

שָׁוְא וּדְבַר-כָּזָב, הַרְחֵק מִמֶּנִּי--רֵאשׁ וָעֹשֶׁר אַל-תִּתֶּן-לִי; הַטְרִיפֵנִי, לֶחֶם חֻקִּי.
shav udevar-kazav harchek mimmenni, resh va'osher al-titten-li; hatrifeni, lechem chukki
Remove far from me falsehood and lies; give me neither poverty nor riches; feed me with mine allotted bread;

פֶּן אֶשְׂבַּע, וְכִחַשְׁתִּי--וְאָמַרְתִּי, מִי יְהוָה
pen esba vechichashti ve'amarti, mi hashem
Lest I be full, and deny, and say: 'Who is the LORD?'

מִשְׁלֵי

בִּרְבוֹת רְשָׁעִים, יִרְבֶּה-פָּשַׁע; וְצַדִּיקִים, בְּמַפַּלְתָּם יִרְאוּ
birvot resha'im yirbeh-pasha'; vetzaddikim, bemappaltam yir'u
When the wicked are increased, transgression increaseth; but the righteous shall gaze upon their fall.

יַסֵּר בִּנְךָ, וִינִיחֶךָ; וְיִתֵּן מַעֲדַנִּים לְנַפְשֶׁךָ
yasser bincha viynichecha; veyitten ma'adannim lenafshecha
Correct thy son, and he will give thee rest; yea, he will give delight unto thy soul.

בְּאֵין חָזוֹן, יִפָּרַע עָם; וְשֹׁמֵר תּוֹרָה אַשְׁרֵהוּ
be'ein chazon yippara am; veshomer torah ashrehu
Where there is no vision, the people cast off restraint; but he that keepeth the law, happy is he.

בִּדְבָרִים, לֹא-יִוָּסֶר עָבֶד: כִּי-יָבִין, וְאֵין מַעֲנֶה
bidvarim lo-yivvaser aved; ki-yavin, ve'ein ma'aneh
A servant will not be corrected by words; for though he understand, there will be no response.

חָזִיתָ--אִישׁ, אָץ בִּדְבָרָיו: תִּקְוָה לִכְסִיל מִמֶּנּוּ
chazita, ish atz bidvarav; tikvah lichsil mimmennu
Seest thou a man that is hasty in his words? there is more hope for a fool than for him.

מְפַנֵּק מִנֹּעַר עַבְדּוֹ; וְאַחֲרִיתוֹ, יִהְיֶה מָנוֹן
mefannek minno'ar avdo; ve'acharito, yihyeh manon
He that delicately bringeth up his servant from a child shall have him become master at the last.

אִישׁ-אַף, יְגָרֶה מָדוֹן; וּבַעַל חֵמָה רַב-פָּשַׁע
'ish-'af yegareh madon; uva'al chemah rav-pasha
An angry man stirreth up strife, and a wrathful man aboundeth in transgression.

גַּאֲוַת אָדָם, תַּשְׁפִּילֶנּוּ; וּשְׁפַל-רוּחַ, יִתְמֹךְ כָּבוֹד
ga'avat adom tashpilennu; ushefal-ruach, yitmoch kavod
A man's pride shall bring him low; but he that is of a lowly spirit shall attain to honour.

חוֹלֵק עִם-גַּנָּב, שׂוֹנֵא נַפְשׁוֹ; אָלָה יִשְׁמַע, וְלֹא יַגִּיד
cholek im-gannav sonei nafsho; alah yishma', velo yaggid
Whoso is partner with a thief hateth his own soul: he heareth the adjuration and uttereth nothing.

חֶרְדַּת אָדָם, יִתֵּן מוֹקֵשׁ; וּבוֹטֵחַ בַּיהוָה יְשֻׂגָּב
cherdat adom yitten mokesh; uvoteach bahashem yesuggav
The fear of man bringeth a snare; but whoso putteth his trust in the LORD shall be set up on high.

רַבִּים, מְבַקְשִׁים פְּנֵי-מוֹשֵׁל; וּמֵיְהוָה, מִשְׁפַּט-אִישׁ
rabbim mevakshim penei-moshel; umehashem, mishpat-'ish
Many seek the ruler's favour; but a man's judgment cometh from the LORD.

תּוֹעֲבַת צַדִּיקִים, אִישׁ עָוֶל; וְתוֹעֲבַת רָשָׁע יְשַׁר-דָּרֶךְ
to'avat tzaddikim ish avel; veto'avat rasha yeshar-darech
An unjust man is an abomination to the righteous; and he that is upright in the way is an abomination to the wicked.

מִשְׁלֵי

מֶלֶךְ--בְּמִשְׁפָּט, יַעֲמִיד אָרֶץ; וְאִישׁ תְּרוּמוֹת יֶהֶרְסֶנָּה
melech, bemishpot ya'amid aretz; ve'ish terumot yehersennah
The king by justice establisheth the land; but he that exacteth gifts overthroweth it.

גֶּבֶר, מַחֲלִיק עַל-רֵעֵהוּ; רֶשֶׁת, פּוֹרֵשׂ עַל-פְּעָמָיו
gever machalik al-re'ehu; reshet, pores al-pe'amav
A man that flattereth his neighbour spreadeth a net for his steps.

בְּפֶשַׁע אִישׁ רָע מוֹקֵשׁ; וְצַדִּיק, יָרוּן וְשָׂמֵחַ
befesha ish ra mokesh; vetzaddik, yarun vesameach
In the transgression of an evil man there is a snare; but the righteous doth sing and rejoice.

יֹדֵעַ צַדִּיק, דִּין דַּלִּים; רָשָׁע, לֹא-יָבִין דָּעַת
yodea tzaddik din dallim; rasha', lo-yavin da'at
The righteous taketh knowledge of the cause of the poor; the wicked understandeth not knowledge.

אַנְשֵׁי לָצוֹן, יָפִיחוּ קִרְיָה; וַחֲכָמִים, יָשִׁיבוּ אָף
'anshei latzon yafichu kiryah; vachachamim, yashivu af
Scornful men set a city in a blaze; but wise men turn away wrath.

אִישׁ-חָכָם--נִשְׁפָּט, אֶת-אִישׁ אֱוִיל: וְרָגַז וְשָׂחַק, וְאֵין נָחַת
'ish-chacham, nishpot et-'ish evil; veragaz vesachak, ve'ein nachat
If a wise man contendeth with a foolish man, whether he be angry or laugh, there will be no rest.

אַנְשֵׁי דָמִים, יִשְׂנְאוּ-תָם; וִישָׁרִים, יְבַקְשׁוּ נַפְשׁוֹ
'anshei damim yisne'u-tam; viysharim, yevakshu nafsho
The men of blood hate him that is sincere; and as for the upright, they seek his life.

כָּל-רוּחוֹ, יוֹצִיא כְסִיל; וְחָכָם, בְּאָחוֹר יְשַׁבְּחֶנָּה
kol-rucho yotzi chesil; vechacham, be'achor yeshabbechennah
A fool spendeth all his spirit; but a wise man stilleth it within him.

מֹשֵׁל, מַקְשִׁיב עַל-דְּבַר-שָׁקֶר--כָּל-מְשָׁרְתָיו רְשָׁעִים
moshel makshiv al-devar-shaker; kol-mesharetav resha'im
If a ruler hearkeneth to falsehood, all his servants are wicked.

רָשׁ וְאִישׁ תְּכָכִים נִפְגָּשׁוּ--מֵאִיר-עֵינֵי שְׁנֵיהֶם יְהוָה
rash ve'ish techachim nifgashu; me'ir-'einei sheneihem hashem
The poor man and the oppressor meet together; the LORD giveth light to the eyes of them both.

מֶלֶךְ שׁוֹפֵט בֶּאֱמֶת דַּלִּים--כִּסְאוֹ, לָעַד יִכּוֹן
melech shofet be'emet dallim; kis'o, la'ad yikkon
The king that faithfully judgeth the poor, his throne shall be established for ever.

שֵׁבֶט וְתוֹכַחַת, יִתֵּן חָכְמָה; וְנַעַר מְשֻׁלָּח, מֵבִישׁ אִמּוֹ
shevet vetochachat yitten chochmah vena'ar meshullach, mevish immo
The rod and reproof give wisdom; but a child left to himself causeth shame to his mother.

מִשְׁלֵי

נִבְהָל לַהוֹן--אִישׁ, רַע עָיִן; וְלֹא-יֵדַע, כִּי-חֶסֶר יְבֹאֶנּוּ
nivhal lahon, ish ra ayin; velo-yeda ki-cheser yevo'ennu
He that hath an evil eye hasteneth after riches, and knoweth not that want shall come upon him.

מוֹכִיחַ אָדָם אַחֲרַי, חֵן יִמְצָא--מִמַּחֲלִיק לָשׁוֹן
mochiach adam acharai chen yimtza; mimmachalik lashon
He that rebuketh a man shall in the end find more favour than he that flattereth with the tongue.

גּוֹזֵל, אָבִיו וְאִמּוֹ--וְאֹמֵר
gozel aviv ve'immo, ve'omer
Whoso robbeth his father or his mother, and saith:

אֵין-פָּשַׁע: חָבֵר הוּא, לְאִישׁ מַשְׁחִית
ein-pasha'; chaver hu, le'ish mashchit
'It is no transgression', the same is the companion of a destroyer.

רְחַב-נֶפֶשׁ, יְגָרֶה מָדוֹן; וּבֹטֵחַ עַל-יְהוָה יְדֻשָּׁן
rechav-nefesh yegareh madon; uvoteach al-hashem yedushan
He that is of a greedy spirit stirreth up strife; but he that putteth his trust in the LORD shall be abundantly gratified.

בּוֹטֵחַ בְּלִבּוֹ, הוּא כְסִיל; וְהוֹלֵךְ בְּחָכְמָה, הוּא יִמָּלֵט
boteach belibbo hu chesil; veholech bechochmah hu yimmalet
He that trusteth in his own heart is a fool; but whoso walketh wisely, he shall escape.

נוֹתֵן לָרָשׁ, אֵין מַחְסוֹר; וּמַעְלִים עֵינָיו, רַב-מְאֵרוֹת
noten larash ein machsor; uma'lim einav, rav-me'erot
He that giveth unto the poor shall not lack; but he that hideth his eyes shall have many a curse.

בְּקוּם רְשָׁעִים, יִסָּתֵר אָדָם; וּבְאָבְדָם, יִרְבּוּ צַדִּיקִים
bekum resha'im yissater adam; uve'avedam, yirbu tzaddikim
When the wicked rise, men hide themselves; but when they perish, the righteous increase.

כט

אִישׁ תּוֹכָחוֹת, מַקְשֶׁה-עֹרֶף--פֶּתַע יִשָּׁבֵר, וְאֵין מַרְפֵּא
Ish tochachot maksheh-'oref; peta yishaver, ve'ein marpe
He that being often reproved hardeneth his neck shall suddenly be broken, and that without remedy.

בִּרְבוֹת צַדִּיקִים, יִשְׂמַח הָעָם; וּבִמְשֹׁל רָשָׁע, יֵאָנַח עָם
birvot tzaddikim yismach ha'am; uvimshol rasha', ye'anach am
When the righteous are increased, the people rejoice; but when the wicked beareth rule, the people sigh.

אִישׁ-אֹהֵב חָכְמָה, יְשַׂמַּח אָבִיו; וְרֹעֶה זוֹנוֹת, יְאַבֶּד-הוֹן
'ish-'ohev chochmah yesammach aviv; vero'eh zonot, ye'abbed-hon
Whoso loveth wisdom rejoiceth his father; but he that keepeth company with harlots wasteth his substance.

מִשְׁלֵי

בַּעֲלֹץ צַדִּיקִים, רַבָּה תִפְאָרֶת; וּבְקוּם רְשָׁעִים, יְחֻפַּשׂ אָדָם

ba'alotz tzaddikim rabbah tif'aret; uvekum resha'im, yechuppas adam
When the righteous exult, there is great glory; but when the wicked rise, men must be sought for.

מְכַסֶּה פְשָׁעָיו, לֹא יַצְלִיחַ; וּמוֹדֶה וְעֹזֵב יְרֻחָם

mechasseh fesha'av lo yatzliach; umodeh ve'ozev yerucham
He that covereth his transgressions shall not prosper; but whoso confesseth and forsaketh them shall obtain mercy.

אַשְׁרֵי אָדָם, מְפַחֵד תָּמִיד; וּמַקְשֶׁה לִבּוֹ, יִפּוֹל בְּרָעָה

'ashrei adam mefached tamid; umaksheh libbo, yippol bera'ah
Happy is the man that feareth alway; but he that hardeneth his heart shall fall into evil.

אֲרִי-נֹהֵם, וְדֹב שׁוֹקֵק--מוֹשֵׁל רָשָׁע, עַל עַם-דָּל

'ari-nohem vedov shokek; moshel rasha', al am-dal
As a roaring lion, and a ravenous bear; so is a wicked ruler over a poor people.

נָגִיד--חֲסַר תְּבוּנוֹת, וְרַב מַעֲשַׁקּוֹת

nagid, chasar tevunot verav ma'ashakkot
The prince that lacketh understanding is also a great oppressor;

שֹׂנֵא בֶצַע, יַאֲרִיךְ יָמִים

sonei vetza', ya'arich yamim
but he that hateth covetousness shall prolong his days.

אָדָם, עָשֻׁק בְּדַם-נָפֶשׁ--עַד-בּוֹר יָנוּס, אַל-יִתְמְכוּ-בוֹ

'adom ashuk bedam-nafesh; ad-bor yanus, al-yitmechu-vo
A man that is laden with the blood of any person shall hasten his steps unto the pit; none will support him.

הוֹלֵךְ תָּמִים, יִוָּשֵׁעַ; וְנֶעְקַשׁ דְּרָכַיִם, יִפּוֹל בְּאֶחָת

holech tamim yivvashea'; vene'kash derachayim, yippol be'echat
Whoso walketh uprightly shall be saved; but he that is perverse in his ways shall fall at once.

עֹבֵד אַדְמָתוֹ, יִשְׂבַּע-לָחֶם

'oved admato yisba'-lachem
He that tilleth his ground shall have plenty of bread;

וּמְרַדֵּף רֵיקִים, יִשְׂבַּע-רִישׁ

umeraddef rekim, yisba'-rish
but he that followeth after vain things shall have poverty enough.

אִישׁ אֱמוּנוֹת, רַב-בְּרָכוֹת; וְאָץ לְהַעֲשִׁיר, לֹא יִנָּקֶה

'ish emunot rav-berachot; ve'atz leha'ashir, lo yinnakeh
A faithful man shall abound with blessings; but he that maketh haste to be rich shall not be unpunished.

הַכֵּר-פָּנִים לֹא-טוֹב; וְעַל-פַּת-לֶחֶם, יִפְשַׁע-גָּבֶר

hakker-panim lo-tov; ve'al-pat-lechem, yifsha'-gaver
To have respect of persons is not good; for a man will transgress for a piece of bread.

מִשְׁלֵי

בְּפֶשַׁע אֶרֶץ, רַבִּים שָׂרֶיהָ
befesha eretz rabbim sareiha
For the transgression of a land many are the princes thereof;

וּבְאָדָם מֵבִין יֹדֵעַ, כֵּן יַאֲרִיךְ
uve'adam mevin yodea', ken ya'arich
but by a man of understanding and knowledge established order shall long continue.

גֶּבֶר-רָשׁ, וְעֹשֵׁק דַּלִּים--מָטָר סֹחֵף, וְאֵין לָחֶם
gever rash ve'oshek dallim; matar sochef, ve'ein lachem
A poor man that oppresseth the weak is like a sweeping rain which leaveth no food.

עֹזְבֵי תוֹרָה, יְהַלְלוּ רָשָׁע; וְשֹׁמְרֵי תוֹרָה, יִתְגָּרוּ בָם
'ozevei torah yehalelu rasha'; veshomerei torah, yitgaru vam
They that forsake the law praise the wicked; but such as keep the law contend with them.

אַנְשֵׁי-רָע, לֹא-יָבִינוּ מִשְׁפָּט; וּמְבַקְשֵׁי יְהוָה, יָבִינוּ כֹל
'anshei-ra lo-yavinu mishpat; umevakshei hashem yavinu chol
Evil men understand not justice; but they that seek the LORD understand all things.

טוֹב-רָשׁ, הוֹלֵךְ בְּתֻמּוֹ--מֵעִקֵּשׁ דְּרָכַיִם, וְהוּא עָשִׁיר
tov-rash holech betummo; me'ikkesh derachayim, vehu ashir
Better is the poor that walketh in his integrity, than he that is perverse in his ways, though he be rich.

נוֹצֵר תּוֹרָה, בֵּן מֵבִין; וְרֹעֶה זוֹלְלִים, יַכְלִים אָבִיו
notzer torah ben mevin; vero'eh zolelim, yachlim aviv
A wise son observeth the teaching; but he that is a companion of gluttonous men shameth his father.

מַרְבֶּה הוֹנוֹ, בְּנֶשֶׁךְ וְתַרְבִּית--לְחוֹנֵן דַּלִּים יִקְבְּצֶנּוּ
marbeh hono beneshech vetarbit; lechonen dallim yikbetzennu
He that augmenteth his substance by interest and increase, gathereth it for him that is gracious to the poor.

מֵסִיר אָזְנוֹ, מִשְּׁמֹעַ תּוֹרָה--גַּם תְּפִלָּתוֹ, תּוֹעֵבָה
mesir ozeno mishemoa torah; gam-tefillato, to'evah
He that turneth away his ear from hearing the law, even his prayer is an abomination.

מַשְׁגֶּה יְשָׁרִים, בְּדֶרֶךְ רָע
mashgeh yesharim bederech ra'
Whoso causeth the upright to go astray in an evil way,

בִּשְׁחוּתוֹ הוּא-יִפּוֹל; וּתְמִימִים, יִנְחֲלוּ-טוֹב
bishchuto hu-yippol; utemimim, yinchalu-tov
he shall fall himself into his own pit; but the whole-hearted shall inherit good.

חָכָם בְּעֵינָיו, אִישׁ עָשִׁיר; וְדַל מֵבִין יַחְקְרֶנּוּ
chacham be'einav ish ashir; vedal mevin yachkerennu
The rich man is wise in his own eyes; but the poor that hath understanding searcheth him through.

מִשְׁלֵי

נֹצֵר תְּאֵנָה, יֹאכַל פִּרְיָהּ; וְשֹׁמֵר אֲדֹנָיו יְכֻבָּד
notzer te'enah yochal piryah; veshomer adonav yechubbad
Whoso keepeth the fig-tree shall eat the fruit thereof; and he that waiteth on his master shall be honoured.

כַּמַּיִם, הַפָּנִים לַפָּנִים--כֵּן לֵב־הָאָדָם, לָאָדָם
kammayim happanim lappanim; ken lev-ha'adam, la'adam
As in water face answereth to face, so the heart of man to man.

שְׁאוֹל וַאֲבַדֹּה, לֹא תִשְׂבַּעְנָה; וְעֵינֵי הָאָדָם, לֹא תִשְׂבַּעְנָה
she'ol va'avaddo lo tisba'nah; ve'einei ha'adam, lo tisba'nah
The nether-world and Destruction are never satiated; so the eyes of man are never satiated.

מַצְרֵף לַכֶּסֶף, וְכוּר לַזָּהָב; וְאִישׁ, לְפִי מַהֲלָלוֹ
matzref lakkesef vechur lazzahav; ve'ish, lefi mahalalo
The refining pot is for silver, and the furnace for gold, and a man is tried by his praise.

אִם תִּכְתּוֹשׁ־אֶת־הָאֱוִיל, בַּמַּכְתֵּשׁ בְּתוֹךְ הָרִיפוֹת--בַּעֱלִי: לֹא־תָסוּר מֵעָלָיו, אִוַּלְתּוֹ
'im tichtosh-'et-ha'evil bammachtesh betoch harifot ba'eli; lo-tasur me'alav, ivvalto
Though thou shouldest bray a fool in a mortar with a pestle among groats, yet will not his foolishness depart from him.

יָדֹעַ תֵּדַע, פְּנֵי צֹאנֶךָ; שִׁית לִבְּךָ, לַעֲדָרִים
yadoa teda penei tzonecha; shit libbecha, la'adarim
Be thou diligent to know the state of thy flocks, and look well to thy herds;

כִּי לֹא לְעוֹלָם חֹסֶן; וְאִם־נֵזֶר, לְדוֹר וָדוֹר
ki lo le'olam chosen; ve'im-nezer, ledor vador
For riches are not for ever; and doth the crown endure unto all generations?

גָּלָה חָצִיר, וְנִרְאָה־דֶשֶׁא; וְנֶאֶסְפוּ, עִשְּׂבוֹת הָרִים
galah chatzir venir'ah-deshe; vene'esfu, issevot harim
When the hay is mown, and the tender grass showeth itself, and the herbs of the mountains are gathered in;

כְּבָשִׂים לִלְבוּשֶׁךָ; וּמְחִיר שָׂדֶה, עַתּוּדִים
kevasim lilvushecha; umechir sadeh, attudim
The lambs will be for thy clothing, and the goats the price for a field.

וְדֵי, חֲלֵב עִזִּים--לְלַחְמְךָ, לְלֶחֶם בֵּיתֶךָ; וְחַיִּים, לְנַעֲרוֹתֶיךָ
vedei chalev izzim, lelachmecha lelechem beitecha; vechayim, lena'aroteicha
And there will be goats' milk enough for thy food, for the food of thy household; and maintenance for thy maidens.

כח

נָסוּ וְאֵין־רֹדֵף רָשָׁע; וְצַדִּיקִים, כִּכְפִיר יִבְטָח
Nasu ve'ein-rodef rasha'; vetzaddikim, kichfir yivtach
The wicked flee when no man pursueth; but the righteous are secure as a young lion.

מִשְׁלֵי

נֶפֶשׁ שְׂבֵעָה, תָּבוּס נֹפֶת; וְנֶפֶשׁ רְעֵבָה, כָּל-מַר מָתוֹק
nefesh seve'ah tavus nofet; venefesh re'evah, kol-mar matok
The full soul loatheth a honeycomb; but to the hungry soul every bitter thing is sweet.

כְּצִפּוֹר, נוֹדֶדֶת מִן-קִנָּהּ--כֵּן-אִישׁ, נוֹדֵד מִמְּקוֹמוֹ
ketzippor nodedet min-kinnah; ken-'ish, noded mimmekomo
As a bird that wandereth from her nest, so is a man that wandereth from his place.

שֶׁמֶן וּקְטֹרֶת, יְשַׂמַּח-לֵב; וּמֶתֶק רֵעֵהוּ, מֵעֲצַת-נָפֶשׁ
shemen uketoret yesammach-lev; umetek re'ehu, me'atzat-nafesh
Ointment and perfume rejoice the heart; so doth the sweetness of a man's friend by hearty counsel.

רֵעֲךָ וְרֵעַ אָבִיךָ, אַל-תַּעֲזֹב--וּבֵית אָחִיךָ, אַל-תָּבוֹא בְּיוֹם אֵידֶךָ
re'acha verea avicha al-ta'azov, uveit achicha, al-tavo beyom eidecha
Thine own friend, and thy father's friend, forsake not; neither go into thy brother's house in the day of thy calamity;

טוֹב שָׁכֵן קָרוֹב, מֵאָח רָחוֹק
tov shachen karov, me'ach rachok
better is a neighbour that is near than a brother far off.

חֲכַם בְּנִי, וְשַׂמַּח לִבִּי; וְאָשִׁיבָה חֹרְפִי דָבָר
chacham beni vesammach libbi; ve'ashivah chorefi davar
My son, be wise, and make my heart glad, that I may answer him that taunteth me.

עָרוּם, רָאָה רָעָה נִסְתָּר; פְּתָאיִם, עָבְרוּ נֶעֱנָשׁוּ
'arum ra'ah ra'ah nistar; petayim, averu ne'enashu
A prudent man seeth the evil, and hideth himself; but the thoughtless pass on, and are punished.

קַח-בִּגְדוֹ, כִּי-עָרַב זָר; וּבְעַד נָכְרִיָּה חַבְלֵהוּ
kach-bigdo ki-'arav zar; uve'ad nacheriyah chavlehu
Take his garment that is surety for a stranger; and hold him in pledge that is surety for an alien woman.

מְבָרֵךְ רֵעֵהוּ, בְּקוֹל גָּדוֹל--בַּבֹּקֶר הַשְׁכֵּים: קְלָלָה, תֵּחָשֶׁב לוֹ
mevarech re'ehu bekol gadol babboker hashkeim; kelalah, techashev lo
He that blesseth his friend with a loud voice, rising early in the morning, it shall be counted a curse to him.

דֶּלֶף טוֹרֵד, בְּיוֹם סַגְרִיר; וְאֵשֶׁת מִדְיָנִים, נִשְׁתָּוָה
delef tored beyom sagrir; ve'eshet midyanim, nishtavah
A continual dropping in a very rainy day and a contentious woman are alike;

צֹפְנֶיהָ צָפַן-רוּחַ; וְשֶׁמֶן יְמִינוֹ יִקְרָא
tzofeneiha tzafan-ruach; veshemen yemino yikra
He that would hide her hideth the wind, and the ointment of his right hand betrayeth itself.

בַּרְזֶל בְּבַרְזֶל יָחַד; וְאִישׁ, יַחַד פְּנֵי-רֵעֵהוּ
barzel bevarzel yachad; ve'ish, yachad penei-re'ehu
Iron sharpeneth iron; so a man sharpeneth the countenance of his friend.

מִשְׁלֵי

בִּשְׂפָתָו, יִנָּכֵר שׂוֹנֵא; וּבְקִרְבּוֹ, יָשִׁית מִרְמָה
bisfatav yinnacher sone; uvekirbo, yashit mirmah
He that hateth dissembleth with his lips, but he layeth up deceit within him.

כִּי-יְחַנֵּן קוֹלוֹ, אַל-תַּאֲמֶן-בּוֹ: כִּי שֶׁבַע תּוֹעֵבוֹת בְּלִבּוֹ
ki-yechannen kolo al-ta'amen-bo; ki sheva to'evot belibbo
When he speaketh fair, believe him not; for there are seven abominations in his heart.

תִּכַּסֶּה שִׂנְאָה, בְּמַשָּׁאוֹן; תִּגָּלֶה רָעָתוֹ בְקָהָל
tikkasseh sin'ah bemasha'on; tiggaleh ra'ato vekahal
Though his hatred be concealed with deceit, his wickedness shall be revealed before the congregation.

כֹּרֶה-שַּׁחַת, בָּהּ יִפּוֹל; וְגוֹלֵל אֶבֶן, אֵלָיו תָּשׁוּב
koreh-shachat bah yippol; vegolel even elav tashuv
Whoso diggeth a pit shall fall therein; and he that rolleth a stone, it shall return upon him.

לְשׁוֹן-שֶׁקֶר, יִשְׂנָא דַכָּיו; וּפֶה חָלָק, יַעֲשֶׂה מִדְחֶה
leshon-sheker yisna dakkav; ufeh chalak, ya'aseh midcheh
A lying tongue hateth those that are crushed by it; and a flattering mouth worketh ruin.

כז

אַל-תִּתְהַלֵּל, בְּיוֹם מָחָר: כִּי לֹא-תֵדַע, מַה-יֵּלֶד יוֹם
Al-tit'hallel beyom machar; ki lo-teda', mah-yeled yom
Boast not thyself of to-morrow; for thou knowest not what a day may bring forth.

יְהַלֶּלְךָ זָר וְלֹא-פִיךָ; נָכְרִי, וְאַל-שְׂפָתֶיךָ
yehallelcha zar velo-ficha; nocheri, ve'al-sefateicha
Let another man praise thee, and not thine own mouth; a stranger, and not thine own lips.

כֹּבֶד-אֶבֶן, וְנֵטֶל הַחוֹל; וְכַעַס אֱוִיל, כָּבֵד מִשְּׁנֵיהֶם
koved-'even venetel hachol; vecha'as evil, kaved misheneihem
A stone is heavy, and the sand weighty; but a fool's vexation is heavier than they both.

אַכְזְרִיּוּת חֵמָה, וְשֶׁטֶף אָף; וּמִי יַעֲמֹד, לִפְנֵי קִנְאָה
'achzeriyut chemah veshetef af; umi ya'amod lifnei kin'ah
Wrath is cruel, and anger is overwhelming; but who is able to stand before jealousy?

טוֹבָה, תּוֹכַחַת מְגֻלָּה--מֵאַהֲבָה מְסֻתָּרֶת
tovah tochachat megullah; me'ahavah mesuttaret
Better is open rebuke than love that is hidden.

נֶאֱמָנִים, פִּצְעֵי אוֹהֵב; וְנַעְתָּרוֹת, נְשִׁיקוֹת שׂוֹנֵא
ne'emanim pitz'ei ohev; vena'tarot, neshikot sone
Faithful are the wounds of a friend; but the kisses of an enemy are importunate.

מִשְׁלֵי

רָאִיתָ--אִישׁ, חָכָם בְּעֵינָיו: תִּקְוָה לִכְסִיל מִמֶּנּוּ
ra'ita, ish chacham be'einav; tikvah lichsil mimmennu
Seest thou a man wise in his own eyes? there is more hope of a fool than of him.

אָמַר עָצֵל, שַׁחַל בַּדָּרֶךְ;   אֲרִי, בֵּין הָרְחֹבוֹת
'amar atzel shachal baddarech; ari, bein harechovot
The sluggard saith: 'There is a lion in the way; yea, a lion is in the streets.'

הַדֶּלֶת, תִּסּוֹב עַל-צִירָהּ;   וְעָצֵל, עַל-מִטָּתוֹ
haddelet tissov al-tzirah; ve'atzel, al-mittato
The door is turning upon its hinges, and the sluggard is still upon his bed.

טָמַן עָצֵל יָדוֹ, בַּצַּלָּחַת;   נִלְאָה, לַהֲשִׁיבָהּ אֶל-פִּיו
taman atzel yado batzallachat; nil'ah, lahashivah el-piv
The sluggard burieth his hand in the dish; it wearieth him to bring it back to his mouth.

חָכָם עָצֵל בְּעֵינָיו--   מִשִּׁבְעָה, מְשִׁיבֵי טָעַם
chacham atzel be'einav; mishiv'ah, meshivei ta'am
The sluggard is wiser in his own eyes than seven men that give wise answer.

מַחֲזִיק בְּאָזְנֵי-כָלֶב--   עֹבֵר מִתְעַבֵּר, עַל-רִיב לֹּא-לוֹ
machazik be'ozenei-chalev; over mit'abber, al-riv lo-lo
He that passeth by, and meddleth with strife not his own, is like one that taketh a dog by the ears.

כְּמִתְלַהְלֵהַּ, הַיֹּרֶה זִקִּים--   חִצִּים וָמָוֶת
kemitlahleah hayoreh zikkim, chitzim vamavet
As a madman who casteth firebrands, arrows, and death;

כֵּן-אִישׁ, רִמָּה אֶת-רֵעֵהוּ;   וְאָמַר, הֲלֹא-מְשַׂחֵק אָנִי
ken-'ish rimmah et-re'ehu; ve'amar, halo-mesachek ani
So is the man that deceiveth his neighbour, and saith: 'Am not I in sport?'

בְּאֶפֶס עֵצִים, תִּכְבֶּה-אֵשׁ;   וּבְאֵין נִרְגָּן, יִשְׁתֹּק מָדוֹן
be'efes etzim tichbeh-'esh; uve'ein nirgan, yishtok madon
Where no wood is, the fire goeth out; and where there is no whisperer, contention ceaseth.

פֶּחָם לְגֶחָלִים, וְעֵצִים לְאֵשׁ;   וְאִישׁ מדונים (מִדְיָנִים), לְחַרְחַר-רִיב
pecham legechalim ve'etzim le'esh; ve'ish midyanim, lecharchar-riv
As coals are to burning coals, and wood to fire; so is a contentious man to kindle strife.

דִּבְרֵי נִרְגָּן, כְּמִתְלַהֲמִים;   וְהֵם, יָרְדוּ חַדְרֵי-בָטֶן
divrei nirgan kemitlahamim; vehem, yaredu chadrei-vaten
The words of a whisperer are as dainty morsels, and they go down into the innermost parts of the body.

כֶּסֶף סִיגִים, מְצֻפֶּה עַל-חָרֶשׂ--   שְׂפָתַיִם דֹּלְקִים וְלֶב-רָע
kesef sigim metzuppeh al-chares; sefatayim dolekim velev-ra
Burning lips and a wicked heart are like an earthen vessel overlaid with silver dross.

מִשְׁלֵי

כו

כַּשֶּׁלֶג, בַּקַּיִץ--וְכַמָּטָר בַּקָּצִיר: כֵּן לֹא-נָאוֶה לִכְסִיל כָּבוֹד
Kasheleg bakkayitz, vechammatar bakkatzir; ken lo-naveh lichsil kavod
As snow in summer, and as rain in harvest, so honour is not seemly for a fool.

כַּצִּפּוֹר לָנוּד, כַּדְּרוֹר לָעוּף--כֵּן קִלְלַת חִנָּם, לֹא תָבֹא
katzippor lanud kadderor la'uf; ken kilelat chinnam, lo tavo
As the wandering sparrow, as the flying swallow, so the curse that is causeless shall come home.

שׁוֹט לַסּוּס, מֶתֶג לַחֲמוֹר; וְשֵׁבֶט, לְגֵו כְּסִילִים
shot lassus meteg lachamor; veshevet, legev kesilim
A whip for the horse, a bridle for the ass, and a rod for the back of fools.

אַל-תַּעַן כְּסִיל, כְּאִוַּלְתּוֹ: פֶּן-תִּשְׁוֶה-לּוֹ גַם-אָתָּה
'al-ta'an kesil ke'ivvalto; pen-tishveh-lo gam-'attah
Answer not a fool according to his folly, lest thou also be like unto him.

עֲנֵה כְסִיל, כְּאִוַּלְתּוֹ: פֶּן-יִהְיֶה חָכָם בְּעֵינָיו
'aneh chesil ke'ivvalto; pen-yihyeh chacham be'einav
Answer a fool according to his folly, lest he be wise in his own eyes.

מְקַצֶּה רַגְלַיִם, חָמָס שֹׁתֶה--שֹׁלֵחַ דְּבָרִים בְּיַד-כְּסִיל
mekatzeh raglayim chamas shoteh; sholeach devarim beyad-kesil
He that sendeth a message by the hand of a fool cutteth off his own feet, and drinketh damage.

דַּלְיוּ שֹׁקַיִם, מִפִּסֵּחַ; וּמָשָׁל, בְּפִי כְסִילִים
dalyu shokayim mippisseach; umashal, befi chesilim
The legs hang limp from the lame; so is a parable in the mouth of fools.

כִּצְרוֹר אֶבֶן, בְּמַרְגֵּמָה--כֵּן-נוֹתֵן לִכְסִיל כָּבוֹד
kitzror even bemargemah; ken-noten lichsil kavod
As a small stone in a heap of stones, so is he that giveth honour to a fool.

חוֹחַ, עָלָה בְיַד-שִׁכּוֹר; וּמָשָׁל, בְּפִי כְסִילִים
choach alah veyad-shikkor; umashal, befi chesilim
As a thorn that cometh into the hand of a drunkard, so is a parable in the mouth of fools.

רַב מְחוֹלֵל-כֹּל; וְשֹׂכֵר כְּסִיל, וְשֹׂכֵר עֹבְרִים
rav mecholel-kol vesocher kesil, vesocher overim
A master performeth all things; but he that stoppeth a fool is as one that stoppeth a flood.

כְּכֶלֶב, שָׁב עַל-קֵאוֹ--כְּסִיל, שׁוֹנֶה בְאִוַּלְתּוֹ
kechelev shav al-ke'o; kesil, shoneh ve'ivvalto
As a dog that returneth to his vomit, so is a fool that repeateth his folly.

מִשְׁלֵי

הֹקַר רַגְלְךָ, מִבֵּית רֵעֶךָ: פֶּן-יִשְׂבָּעֲךָ, וּשְׂנֵאֶךָ
hokar raglecha mibbeit re'echa; pen-yisba'acha, usene'echa
Let thy foot be seldom in thy neighbour's house; lest he be sated with thee, and hate thee.

מֵפִיץ וְחֶרֶב, וְחֵץ שָׁנוּן--אִישׁ עֹנֶה בְרֵעֵהוּ, עֵד שָׁקֶר
mefitz vecherev vechetz shanun; ish oneh vere'ehu, ed shaker
As a maul, and a sword, and a sharp arrow, so is a man that beareth false witness against his neighbour.

שֵׁן רֹעָה, וְרֶגֶל מוּעָדֶת--מִבְטָח בּוֹגֵד, בְּיוֹם צָרָה
shen ro'ah veregel mu'adet; mivtach boged, beyom tzarah
Confidence in an unfaithful man in time of trouble is like a broken tooth, and a foot out of joint.

מַעֲדֶה-בֶּגֶד, בְּיוֹם קָרָה--חֹמֶץ עַל-נָתֶר; וְשָׁר בַּשִּׁרִים, עַל לֶב-רָע
ma'adeh beged beyom karah chometz al-nater; veshar bashirim, al lev-ra
As one that taketh off a garment in cold weather, and as vinegar upon nitre, so is he that singeth songs to a heavy heart.

אִם-רָעֵב שֹׂנַאֲךָ, הַאֲכִלֵהוּ לָחֶם; וְאִם-צָמֵא, הַשְׁקֵהוּ מָיִם
'im-ra'ev sona'acha ha'achilehu lachem; ve'im-tzame, hashkehu mayim
If thine enemy be hungry, give him bread to eat, and if he be thirsty, give him water to drink;

כִּי גֶחָלִים--אַתָּה, חֹתֶה עַל-רֹאשׁוֹ; וַיהוָה, יְשַׁלֶּם-לָךְ
ki gechalim, attah choteh al-rosho; vahashem, yeshallem-lach
For thou wilt heap coals of fire upon his head, and the LORD will reward thee.

רוּחַ צָפוֹן, תְּחוֹלֵל גָּשֶׁם; וּפָנִים נִזְעָמִים, לְשׁוֹן סָתֶר
ruach tzafon techolel gashem; ufanim niz'amim, leshon sater
The north wind bringeth forth rain, and a backbiting tongue an angry countenance.

טוֹב, שֶׁבֶת עַל-פִּנַּת-גָּג--מֵאֵשֶׁת מִדְיָנִים, וּבֵית חָבֶר
tov, shevet al-pinnat-gag; me'eshet midyanim, uveit chaver
It is better to dwell in a corner of the housetop, than in a house in common with a contentious woman.

מַיִם קָרִים, עַל-נֶפֶשׁ עֲיֵפָה; וּשְׁמוּעָה טוֹבָה, מֵאֶרֶץ מֶרְחָק
mayim karim al-nefesh ayefah; ushemu'ah tovah, me'eretz merchak
As cold waters to a faint soul, so is good news from a far country.

מַעְיָן נִרְפָּשׂ, וּמָקוֹר מָשְׁחָת--צַדִּיק, מָט לִפְנֵי-רָשָׁע
ma'yan nirpas umakor mashechat; tzaddik, mat lifnei-rasha
As a troubled fountain, and a corrupted spring, so is a righteous man that giveth way before the wicked.

אָכֹל דְּבַשׁ הַרְבּוֹת לֹא-טוֹב; וְחֵקֶר כְּבֹדָם כָּבוֹד
'achol devash harbot lo-tov; vecheker kevodam kavod
It is not good to eat much honey; so for men to search out their own glory is not glory.

עִיר פְּרוּצָה, אֵין חוֹמָה--אִישׁ, אֲשֶׁר אֵין מַעְצָר לְרוּחוֹ
'ir perutzah ein chomah; ish, asher ein ma'tzar lerucho
Like a city broken down and without a wall, so is he whose spirit is without restraint.

מִשְׁלֵי

מֵהַשְׁפִּילְךָ, לִפְנֵי נָדִיב--אֲשֶׁר רָאוּ עֵינֶיךָ
mehashpilecha lifnei nadiv; asher ra'u eineicha
than that thou shouldest be put lower in the presence of the prince, whom thine eyes have seen.

אַל-תֵּצֵא לָרִב, מַהֵר: פֶּן מַה-תַּעֲשֶׂה, בְּאַחֲרִיתָהּ
'al-tetzei lariv, maher pen mah-ta'aseh be'acharitah
Go not forth hastily to strive, lest thou know not what to do in the end thereof,

בְּהַכְלִים אֹתְךָ רֵעֶךָ
behachlim otecha re'echa
when thy neighbour hath put thee to shame.

רִיבְךָ, רִיב אֶת-רֵעֶךָ; וְסוֹד אַחֵר אַל-תְּגָל
rivecha riv et-re'echa; vesod acher al-tegal
Debate thy cause with thy neighbour, but reveal not the secret of another;

פֶּן-יְחַסֶּדְךָ שֹׁמֵעַ; וְדִבָּתְךָ, לֹא תָשׁוּב
pen-yechassedcha shomea'; vedibbatecha, lo tashuv
Lest he that heareth it revile thee, and thine infamy turn not away.

תַּפּוּחֵי זָהָב, בְּמַשְׂכִּיּוֹת כָּסֶף--דָּבָר, דָּבֻר עַל-אָפְנָיו
tappuchei zahov bemaskiyot kasef; davar, davur al-'afenav
A word fitly spoken is like apples of gold in settings of silver.

נֶזֶם זָהָב, וַחֲלִי-כָתֶם--מוֹכִיחַ חָכָם, עַל-אֹזֶן שֹׁמָעַת
nezem zahov vachali-chatem; mochiach chacham, al-'ozen shoma'at
As an ear-ring of gold, and an ornament of fine gold, so is a wise reprover upon an obedient ear.

כְּצִנַּת שֶׁלֶג, בְּיוֹם קָצִיר--צִיר נֶאֱמָן, לְשֹׁלְחָיו
ketzinnat-sheleg beyom katzir, tzir ne'emon lesholechav
As the cold of snow in the time of harvest, so is a faithful messenger to him that sendeth him;

וְנֶפֶשׁ אֲדֹנָיו יָשִׁיב
venefesh adonav yashiv
for he refresheth the soul of his master.

נְשִׂיאִים וְרוּחַ, וְגֶשֶׁם אָיִן--אִישׁ מִתְהַלֵּל, בְּמַתַּת-שָׁקֶר
nesi'im veruach vegeshem ayin; ish mit'hallel, bemattat-shaker
As vapours and wind without rain, so is he that boasteth himself of a false gift.

בְּאֹרֶךְ אַפַּיִם, יְפֻתֶּה קָצִין; וְלָשׁוֹן רַכָּה, תִּשְׁבָּר-גָּרֶם
be'orech appayim yefutteh katzin; velashon rakkah, tishbor-garem
By long forbearing is a ruler persuaded, and a soft tongue breaketh the bone.

דְּבַשׁ מָצָאתָ, אֱכֹל דַּיֶּךָ: פֶּן-תִּשְׂבָּעֶנּוּ, וַהֲקֵאתוֹ
devash matzata echol dayeka; pen-tisba'ennu, vahaketo
Hast thou found honey? eat so much as is sufficient for thee, lest thou be filled therewith, and vomit it.

מִשְׁלֵי

כָּסּוּ פָנָיו חֲרֻלִּים; וְגֶדֶר אֲבָנָיו נֶהֱרָסָה
kassu fanav charullim; vegeder avanav neherasah
the face thereof was covered with nettles, and the stone wall thereof was broken down.

וָאֶחֱזֶה אָנֹכִי, אָשִׁית לִבִּי; רָאִיתִי, לָקַחְתִּי מוּסָר
va'echezeh anochi ashit libbi; ra'iti, lakachti musar
Then I beheld, and considered well; I saw, and received instruction.

מְעַט שֵׁנוֹת, מְעַט תְּנוּמוֹת; מְעַט, חִבֻּק יָדַיִם לִשְׁכָּב
me'at shenot me'at tenumot; me'at chibbuk yadayim lishkav
'Yet a little sleep, a little slumber, a little folding of the hands to sleep'--

וּבָא-מִתְהַלֵּךְ רֵישֶׁךָ; וּמַחְסֹרֶיךָ, כְּאִישׁ מָגֵן
uva-mit'hallech reishecha; umachsoreicha, ke'ish magen
So shall thy poverty come as a runner, and thy want as an armed man.

כה

גַּם-אֵלֶּה, מִשְׁלֵי שְׁלֹמֹה--אֲשֶׁר הֶעְתִּיקוּ, אַנְשֵׁי חִזְקִיָּה מֶלֶךְ-יְהוּדָה
Gam-'elleh mishlei shelomoh; asher he'tiku, anshei chizkiyah melech-yehudah
These also are proverbs of Solomon, which the men of Hezekiah king of Judah copied out.

כְּבֹד אֱלֹהִים, הַסְתֵּר דָּבָר; וּכְבֹד מְלָכִים, חֲקֹר דָּבָר
kevod elohim haster davar; uchevod melachim, chakor davar
It is the glory of God to conceal a thing; but the glory of kings is to search out a matter.

שָׁמַיִם לָרוּם, וָאָרֶץ לָעֹמֶק; וְלֵב מְלָכִים, אֵין חֵקֶר
shamayim larum va'aretz la'omek; velev melachim, ein cheker
The heaven for height, and the earth for depth, and the heart of kings is unsearchable.

הָגוֹ סִיגִים מִכָּסֶף; וַיֵּצֵא לַצֹּרֵף כֶּלִי
hago sigim mikkasef; vayetzei latzoref keli
Take away the dross from the silver, and there cometh forth a vessel for the refiner;

הָגוֹ רָשָׁע, לִפְנֵי-מֶלֶךְ; וְיִכּוֹן בַּצֶּדֶק כִּסְאוֹ
hago rasho lifnei-melech; veyikkon batzedek kis'o
Take away the wicked from before the king, and his throne shall be established in righteousness.

אַל-תִּתְהַדַּר לִפְנֵי-מֶלֶךְ; וּבִמְקוֹם גְּדֹלִים, אַל-תַּעֲמֹד
'al-tit'haddar lifnei-melech; uvimkom gedolim, al-ta'amod
Glorify not thyself in the presence of the king, and stand not in the place of great men;

כִּי טוֹב אֲמָר-לְךָ, עֲלֵה-הֵנָּה
ki tov amar-lecha, aleh hennah
For better is it that it be said unto thee: 'Come up hither',

מִשְׁלֵי

כִּי, לֹא-תִהְיֶה אַחֲרִית לָרָע; נֵר רְשָׁעִים יִדְעָךְ

ki lo-tihyeh acharit lara'; ner resha'im yid'ach

For there will be no future to the evil man, the lamp of the wicked shall be put out.

יְרָא-אֶת-יְהוָה בְּנִי וָמֶלֶךְ; עִם-שׁוֹנִים, אַל-תִּתְעָרָב

yera-'et-hashem beni vamelech; im-shonim, al-tit'arav

My son, fear thou the LORD and the king, and meddle not with them that are given to change;

כִּי-פִתְאֹם, יָקוּם אֵידָם; וּפִיד שְׁנֵיהֶם, מִי יוֹדֵעַ

ki-fit'om yakum eidam; ufid sheneihem, mi yodea

For their calamity shall rise suddenly; and who knoweth the ruin from them both?

גַּם-אֵלֶּה לַחֲכָמִים: הַכֵּר-פָּנִים בְּמִשְׁפָּט בַּל-טוֹב

gam-'elleh lachachamim; hakker-panim bemishpat bal-tov

These also are sayings of the wise. To have respect of persons in judgment is not good.

אֹמֵר, לְרָשָׁע--צַדִּיק אָתָּה: יִקְּבֻהוּ עַמִּים; יִזְעָמוּהוּ לְאֻמִּים

'omer lerasha tzaddik attah yikkevuhu ammim; yiz'amuhu le'ummim

He that saith unto the wicked: 'Thou art righteous', peoples shall curse him, nations shall execrate him;

וְלַמּוֹכִיחִים יִנְעָם; וַעֲלֵיהֶם, תָּבוֹא בִרְכַּת-טוֹב

velammochichim yin'am; va'aleihem, tavo virkat-tov

But to them that decide justly shall be delight, and a good blessing shall come upon them.

שְׂפָתַיִם יִשָּׁק; מֵשִׁיב, דְּבָרִים נְכֹחִים

sefatayim yishak; meshiv, devarim nechochim

He kisseth the lips that giveth a right answer.

הָכֵן בַּחוּץ, מְלַאכְתֶּךָ--וְעַתְּדָהּ בַּשָּׂדֶה לָךְ; אַחַר, וּבָנִיתָ בֵיתֶךָ

hachen bachutz melachtecha, ve'attedah bassadeh lach; achar, uvanita veitecha

Prepare thy work without, and make it fit for thyself in the field; and afterwards build thy house.

אַל-תְּהִי עֵד-חִנָּם בְּרֵעֶךָ; וַהֲפִתִּיתָ, בִּשְׂפָתֶיךָ

'al-tehi ed-chinnam bere'echa; vahafittita, bisfateicha

Be not a witness against thy neighbour without cause; and deceive not with thy lips.

אַל-תֹּאמַר--כַּאֲשֶׁר עָשָׂה-לִי, כֵּן אֶעֱשֶׂה-לּוֹ; אָשִׁיב לָאִישׁ כְּפָעֳלוֹ

'al-tomar, ka'asher asah-li ken e'eseh-lo; ashiv la'ish kefo'olo

Say not: 'I will do so to him as he hath done to me; I will render to the man according to his work.'

עַל-שְׂדֵה אִישׁ-עָצֵל עָבַרְתִּי; וְעַל-כֶּרֶם, אָדָם חֲסַר-לֵב

'al-sedeh ish-'atzel avarti; ve'al-kerem, adam chasar-lev

I went by the field of the slothful, and by the vineyard of the man void of understanding;

וְהִנֵּה עָלָה כֻלּוֹ, קִמְּשֹׂנִים

vehinneh alah chullo kimmesonim

And, lo, it was all grown over with thistles,

מִשְׁלֵי

הִתְרַפִּיתָ, בְּיוֹם צָרָה--צַר כֹּחֶכָה
hitrappita beyom tzarah, tzar kochechah
If thou faint in the day of adversity, thy strength is small indeed.

הַצֵּל, לְקֻחִים לַמָּוֶת; וּמָטִים לַהֶרֶג, אִם-תַּחְשׂוֹךְ
hatzel lekuchim lammavet; umatim lahereg, im-tachsoch
Deliver them that are drawn unto death; and those that are ready to be slain wilt thou forbear to rescue?

כִּי-תֹאמַר--הֵן, לֹא-יָדַעְנוּ-זֶה: הֲלֹא-תֹכֵן לִבּוֹת, הוּא-יָבִין
ki-tomar, hen lo-yada'nu zeh halo-tochen libbot hu-yavin
If thou sayest: 'Behold, we knew not this', doth not He that weigheth the hearts consider it?

וְנֹצֵר נַפְשְׁךָ, הוּא יֵדָע; וְהֵשִׁיב לְאָדָם כְּפָעֳלוֹ
venotzer nafshecha hu yeda'; veheshiv le'adam kefo'olo
And He that keepeth thy soul, doth not He know it? And shall not He render to every man according to his works?

אֱכָל-בְּנִי דְבַשׁ כִּי-טוֹב; וְנֹפֶת מָתוֹק, עַל-חִכֶּךָ
'echal-beni devash ki-tov; venofet matok, al-chikkecha
My son, eat thou honey, for it is good, and the honeycomb is sweet to thy taste;

כֵּן, דְּעֶה חָכְמָה--לְנַפְשֶׁךָ: אִם-מָצָאתָ, וְיֵשׁ אַחֲרִית
ken de'eh chochmah lenafshecha im-matzata veyesh acharit;
So know thou wisdom to be unto thy soul; if thou hast found it, then shall there be a future,

וְתִקְוָתְךָ, לֹא תִכָּרֵת
vetikvatecha, lo tikkaret
and thy hope shall not be cut off.

אַל-תֶּאֱרֹב רָשָׁע, לִנְוֵה צַדִּיק; אַל-תְּשַׁדֵּד רִבְצוֹ
'al-te'erov rasha linveh tzaddik; al-teshadded rivtzo
Lie not in wait, O wicked man, against the dwelling of the righteous, spoil not his resting-place;

כִּי שֶׁבַע, יִפּוֹל צַדִּיק וָקָם; וּרְשָׁעִים, יִכָּשְׁלוּ בְרָעָה
ki sheva yippol tzaddik vakam; uresha'im, yikkashelu vera'ah
For a righteous man falleth seven times, and riseth up again, but the wicked stumble under adversity.

בִּנְפֹל אוֹיִבְךָ, אַל-תִּשְׂמָח; וּבִכָּשְׁלוֹ, אַל-יָגֵל לִבֶּךָ
binfol oyivcha al-tismach; uvikkashelo, al-yagel libbecha
Rejoice not when thine enemy falleth, and let not thy heart be glad when he stumbleth;

פֶּן-יִרְאֶה יְהוָה, וְרַע בְּעֵינָיו; וְהֵשִׁיב מֵעָלָיו אַפּוֹ
pen-yir'eh hashem vera be'einav; veheshiv me'alav appo
Lest the LORD see it, and it displease Him, and He turn away His wrath from him.

אַל-תִּתְחַר בַּמְּרֵעִים; אַל-תְּקַנֵּא, בָּרְשָׁעִים
'al-titchar bammere'im; al-tekanne, baresha'im
Fret not thyself because of evildoers, neither be thou envious at the wicked;

מִשְׁלֵי

הִכּוּנִי בַל-חָלִיתִי--הֲלָמוּנִי, בַּל-יָדָעְתִּי
hikkuni val-chaliti halamuni, bal-yada'eti
'They have struck me, and I felt it not, they have beaten me, and I knew it not;

מָתַי אָקִיץ; אוֹסִיף, אֲבַקְשֶׁנּוּ עוֹד
matai akitz; osif, avakshennu od
when shall I awake? I will seek it yet again.'

כד

אַל-תְּקַנֵּא, בְּאַנְשֵׁי רָעָה; וְאַל-תִּתְאָו, לִהְיוֹת אִתָּם
Al-tekannei be'anshei ra'ah; ve'al-tit'av ve'al-tit'av, lihyot ittam
Be not thou envious of evil men, neither desire to be with them.

כִּי-שֹׁד, יֶהְגֶּה לִבָּם; וְעָמָל, שִׂפְתֵיהֶם תְּדַבֵּרְנָה
ki-shod yehgeh libbam; ve'amal, sifteihem tedabbernah
For their heart studieth destruction, and their lips talk of mischief.

בְּחָכְמָה, יִבָּנֶה בָּיִת; וּבִתְבוּנָה, יִתְכּוֹנָן
bechochmah yibbaneh bayit; uvitvunah, yitkonan
Through wisdom is a house builded; and by understanding it is established;

וּבְדַעַת, חֲדָרִים יִמָּלְאוּ--כָּל-הוֹן יָקָר וְנָעִים
uveda'at chadarim yimmale'u; kol-hon yakar vena'im
And by knowledge are the chambers filled with all precious and pleasant riches.

גֶּבֶר-חָכָם בַּעוֹז; וְאִישׁ-דַּעַת, מְאַמֶּץ-כֹּחַ
gever-chacham ba'oz; ve'ish-da'at, me'ammetz-koach
A wise man is strong; yea, a man of knowledge increaseth strength.

כִּי בְתַחְבֻּלוֹת, תַּעֲשֶׂה-לְּךָ מִלְחָמָה; וּתְשׁוּעָה, בְּרֹב יוֹעֵץ
ki vetachbulot ta'aseh-lecha milchamah; uteshu'ah, berov yo'etz
For with wise advice thou shalt make thy war; and in the multitude of counsellors there is safety.

רָאמוֹת לֶאֱוִיל חָכְמוֹת; בַּשַּׁעַר, לֹא יִפְתַּח-פִּיהוּ
ramot le'evil chochemot; basha'ar, lo yiftach-pihu
Wisdom is as unattainable to a fool as corals; he openeth not his mouth in the gate.

מְחַשֵּׁב לְהָרֵעַ--לוֹ, בַּעַל-מְזִמּוֹת יִקְרָאוּ
mechashev leharea'; lo, ba'al-mezimmot yikra'u
He that deviseth to do evil, men shall call him a mischievous person.

זִמַּת אִוֶּלֶת חַטָּאת; וְתוֹעֲבַת לְאָדָם לֵץ
zimmat ivvelet chattat; veto'avat le'adam letz
The thought of foolishness is sin; and the scorner is an abomination to men.

מִשְׁלֵי

גִּיל יָגִיל, אֲבִי צַדִּיק; וְיוֹלֵד חָכָם, יִשְׂמַח-בּוֹ
gil yagol yagil avi tzaddik; veyoled chacham, yismach-bo
The father of the righteous will greatly rejoice; and he that begetteth a wise child will have joy of him.

יִשְׂמַח-אָבִיךָ וְאִמֶּךָ; וְתָגֵל, יוֹלַדְתֶּךָ
yismach-'avicha ve'immecha; vetagel, yoladtecha
Let thy father and thy mother be glad, and let her that bore thee rejoice.

תְּנָה-בְנִי לִבְּךָ לִי; וְעֵינֶיךָ, דְּרָכַי תִּצֹּרְנָה
tenah-veni libbecha li; ve'eineicha, derachai titzorenah
My son, give me thy heart, and let thine eyes observe my ways.

כִּי-שׁוּחָה עֲמֻקָּה זוֹנָה; וּבְאֵר צָרָה, נָכְרִיָּה
ki-shuchah amukkah zonah; uve'er tzarah, nocheriyah
For a harlot is a deep ditch; and an alien woman is a narrow pit.

אַף-הִיא, כְּחֶתֶף תֶּאֱרֹב; וּבוֹגְדִים, בְּאָדָם תּוֹסִף
'af-hi kechetef te'erov; uvogedim, be'adam tosif
She also lieth in wait as a robber, and increaseth the faithless among men.

לְמִי אוֹי לְמִי אֲבוֹי, לְמִי מִדְיָנִים לְמִי שִׂיחַ
lemi oy lemi avoy lemi midyanim lemi siach
Who crieth: 'Woe'? who: 'Alas'? who hath contentions? who hath raving?

לְמִי, פְּצָעִים חִנָּם; לְמִי, חַכְלִלוּת עֵינָיִם
lemi petza'im chinnam; lemi, chachlilut einayim
Who hath wounds without cause? Who hath redness of eyes?

לַמְאַחֲרִים עַל-הַיָּיִן--לַבָּאִים, לַחְקֹר מִמְסָךְ
lam'acharim al-hayayin; labba'im, lachkor mimsach
They that tarry long at the wine; they that go to try mixed wine.

אַל-תֵּרֶא יַיִן, כִּי יִתְאַדָּם: כִּי-יִתֵּן בַּכּוֹס עֵינוֹ; יִתְהַלֵּךְ, בְּמֵישָׁרִים
'al-terei yayin ki yit'addam ki-yitten bakkos eino; yit'hallech, bemeisharim
Look not thou upon the wine when it is red, when it giveth its colour in the cup, when it glideth down smoothly;

אַחֲרִיתוֹ, כְּנָחָשׁ יִשָּׁךְ; וּכְצִפְעֹנִי יַפְרִשׁ
'acharito kenachash yishach; uchetzif'oni yafrish
At the last it biteth like a serpent, and stingeth like a basilisk.

עֵינֶיךָ, יִרְאוּ זָרוֹת; וְלִבְּךָ, יְדַבֵּר תַּהְפֻּכוֹת
'eineicha yir'u zarot; velibbecha, yedabber tahpuchot
Thine eyes shall behold strange things, and thy heart shall utter confused things.

וְהָיִיתָ, כְּשֹׁכֵב בְּלֶב-יָם; וּכְשֹׁכֵב, בְּרֹאשׁ חִבֵּל
vehayita kheshochev belev-yam; ucheshochev, berosh chibbel
Yea, thou shalt be as he that lieth down in the midst of the sea, or as he that lieth upon the top of a mast.

מִשְׁלֵי

הָבִיאָה לַמּוּסָר לִבֶּךָ; וְאָזְנֶךָ, לְאִמְרֵי-דָעַת
havi'ah lammusar libbecha; ve'azenecha, le'imrei-da'at
Apply thy heart unto instruction, and thine ears to the words of knowledge.

אַל-תִּמְנַע מִנַּעַר מוּסָר: כִּי-תַכֶּנּוּ בַשֵּׁבֶט, לֹא יָמוּת
'al-timna minna'ar musar; ki-takkennu vashevet, lo yamut
Withhold not correction from the child; for though thou beat him with the rod, he will not die.

אַתָּה, בַּשֵּׁבֶט תַּכֶּנּוּ; וְנַפְשׁוֹ, מִשְּׁאוֹל תַּצִּיל
'attah bashevet takkennu; venafsho, mishe'ol tatzil
Thou beatest him with the rod, and wilt deliver his soul from the nether-world.

בְּנִי, אִם-חָכַם לִבֶּךָ--יִשְׂמַח לִבִּי גַם-אָנִי
beni im-chacham libbecha; yismach libbi gam-'ani
My son, if thy heart be wise, my heart will be glad, even mine;

וְתַעְלֹזְנָה כִלְיוֹתָי--בְּדַבֵּר שְׂפָתֶיךָ, מֵישָׁרִים
veta'lozenah chilyotai; bedabber sefateicha, meisharim
Yea, my reins will rejoice, when thy lips speak right things.

אַל-יְקַנֵּא לִבְּךָ, בַּחַטָּאִים: כִּי אִם-בְּיִרְאַת-יְהוָה, כָּל-הַיּוֹם
'al-yekannei libbecha bachatta'im; ki im-beyir'at-hashem kol-hayom
Let not thy heart envy sinners, but be in the fear of the LORD all the day;

כִּי, אִם-יֵשׁ אַחֲרִית; וְתִקְוָתְךָ, לֹא תִכָּרֵת
ki im-yesh acharit; vetikvatecha, lo tikkaret
For surely there is a future; and thy hope shall not be cut off.

שְׁמַע-אַתָּה בְנִי וַחֲכָם; וְאַשֵּׁר בַּדֶּרֶךְ לִבֶּךָ
shema'-'attah veni vachacham; ve'asher badderech libbecha
Hear thou, my son, and be wise, and guide thy heart in the way.

אַל-תְּהִי בְסֹבְאֵי-יָיִן--בְּזֹלְלֵי בָשָׂר לָמוֹ
'al-tehi vesove'ei-yayin; bezolalei vasar lamo
Be not among winebibbers; among gluttonous eaters of flesh;

כִּי-סֹבֵא וְזוֹלֵל, יִוָּרֵשׁ; וּקְרָעִים, תַּלְבִּישׁ נוּמָה
ki-sovei vezolel yivvaresh; ukera'im, talbish numah
For the drunkard and the glutton shall come to poverty; and drowsiness shall clothe a man with rags.

שְׁמַע לְאָבִיךָ, זֶה יְלָדֶךָ; וְאַל-תָּבוּז, כִּי-זָקְנָה אִמֶּךָ
shema le'avicha zeh yeladecha; ve'al-tavuz, ki-zakenah immecha
Hearken unto thy father that begot thee, and despise not thy mother when she is old.

אֱמֶת קְנֵה, וְאַל-תִּמְכֹּר; חָכְמָה וּמוּסָר וּבִינָה
'emet keneh ve'al-timkor; chochmah umusar uvinah
Buy the truth, and sell it not; also wisdom, and instruction, and understanding.

מִשְׁלֵי

כג

כִּי-תֵשֵׁב, לִלְחוֹם אֶת-מוֹשֵׁל; בִּין תָּבִין, אֶת-אֲשֶׁר לְפָנֶיךָ
Ki-teshev lilchom et-moshel; bin tavin, et-'asher lefaneicha
When thou sittest to eat with a ruler, consider well him that is before thee;

וְשַׂמְתָּ שַׂכִּין בְּלֹעֶךָ-- אִם-בַּעַל נֶפֶשׁ אָתָּה
vesamta sakkin belo'echa; im-ba'al nefesh attah
And put a knife to thy throat, if thou be a man given to appetite.

אַל-תִּתְאָו, לְמַטְעַמּוֹתָיו; וְהוּא, לֶחֶם כְּזָבִים
'al-tit'ov lemat'ammotav; vehu, lechem kezavim
Be not desirous of his dainties; seeing they are deceitful food.

אַל-תִּיגַע לְהַעֲשִׁיר; מִבִּינָתְךָ חֲדָל
'al-tiga leha'ashir; mibbinatecha chadal
Weary not thyself to be rich; cease from thine own wisdom.

הֲתָעִיף עֵינֶיךָ בּוֹ, וְאֵינֶנּוּ: כִּי עָשֹׂה יַעֲשֶׂה-לּוֹ כְנָפַיִם; כְּנֶשֶׁר, יָעוּף הַשָּׁמָיִם
hata'if eineicha bo, ve'einennu ki asoh ya'aseh-lo chenafayim; kenesher, ya'uf hashamayim
Wilt thou set thine eyes upon it? it is gone; for riches certainly make themselves wings, like an eagle that flieth toward heaven.

אַל-תִּלְחַם--אֶת-לֶחֶם, רַע עָיִן; וְאַל-תִּתְאָו, לְמַטְעַמֹּתָיו
'al-tilcham, et-lechem ra ayin; ve'al-tit'av, lemat'ammotav
Eat thou not the bread of him that hath an evil eye, neither desire thou his dainties;

כִּי, כְּמוֹ שָׁעַר בְּנַפְשׁוֹ--כֶּן-הוּא: אֱכֹל וּשְׁתֵה, יֹאמַר לָךְ; וְלִבּוֹ, בַּל-עִמָּךְ
ki kemo-sha'ar benafsho, ken-hu echol usheteh yomar lach; velibbo, bal-'immach
For as one that hath reckoned within himself, so is he: 'Eat and drink', saith he to thee; but his heart is not with thee.

פִּתְּךָ-אָכַלְתָּ תְקִיאֶנָּה; וְשִׁחַתָּ, דְּבָרֶיךָ הַנְּעִימִים
pittecha-'achalta teki'ennah; veshichata, devareicha hanne'imim
The morsel which thou hast eaten shalt thou vomit up, and lose thy sweet words.

בְּאָזְנֵי כְסִיל, אַל-תְּדַבֵּר: כִּי-יָבוּז, לְשֵׂכֶל מִלֶּיךָ
be'ozenei chesil al-tedabber; ki-yavuz, lesechel milleicha
Speak not in the ears of a fool; for he will despise the wisdom of thy words.

אַל-תַּסֵּג, גְּבוּל עוֹלָם; וּבִשְׂדֵי יְתוֹמִים, אַל-תָּבֹא
'al-tasseg gevul olam; uvisdei yetomim, al-tavo
Remove not the ancient landmark; and enter not into the fields of the fatherless;

כִּי-גֹאֲלָם חָזָק; הוּא-יָרִיב אֶת-רִיבָם אִתָּךְ
ki-go'alam chazak; hu-yariv et-rivam ittach
For their Redeemer is strong; He will plead their cause with thee.

מִשְׁלֵי

הֲלֹא כָתַבְתִּי לְךָ, שָׁלִשִׁים--בְּמוֹעֵצוֹת וָדָעַת
halo chatavti lecha shalishim; bemo'etzot vada'at
Have not I written unto thee excellent things of counsels and knowledge;

לְהוֹדִיעֲךָ--קֹשְׁטְ, אִמְרֵי אֱמֶת
lehodi'acha, kosht imrei emet;
That I might make thee know the certainty of the words of truth,

לְהָשִׁיב אֲמָרִים אֱמֶת, לְשֹׁלְחֶיךָ
lehashiv amarim emet, lesholecheicha
that thou mightest bring back words of truth to them that send thee?

אַל-תִּגְזָל-דָּל, כִּי דַל-הוּא; וְאַל-תְּדַכֵּא עָנִי בַשָּׁעַר
'al-tigzal-dal ki dal-hu; ve'al-tedakkei ani vasha'ar
Rob not the weak, because he is weak, neither crush the poor in the gate;

כִּי-יְהוָה, יָרִיב רִיבָם; וְקָבַע אֶת-קֹבְעֵיהֶם נָפֶשׁ
ki-hashem yariv rivam; vekava et-kove'eihem nafesh
For the LORD will plead their cause, and despoil of life those that despoil them.

אַל-תִּתְרַע, אֶת-בַּעַל אָף; וְאֶת-אִישׁ חֵמוֹת, לֹא תָבוֹא
'al-titra et-ba'al af; ve'et-'ish chemot lo tavo
Make no friendship with a man that is given to anger; and with a wrathful man thou shalt not go;

פֶּן-תֶּאֱלַף אֹרְחֹתָו; וְלָקַחְתָּ מוֹקֵשׁ לְנַפְשֶׁךָ
pen-te'elaf orechotav; velakachta mokesh lenafshecha
Lest thou learn his ways, and get a snare to thy soul.

אַל-תְּהִי בְתֹקְעֵי-כָף; בַּעֹרְבִים, מַשָּׁאוֹת
'al-tehi vetoke'ei-chaf; ba'orevim, masha'ot
Be thou not of them that strike hands, or of them that are sureties for debts;

אִם-אֵין-לְךָ לְשַׁלֵּם--לָמָּה יִקַּח מִשְׁכָּבְךָ, מִתַּחְתֶּיךָ
'im-'ein-lecha leshallem; lammah yikkach mishkavecha, mittachteicha
If thou hast not wherewith to pay, why should he take away thy bed from under thee?

אַל-תַּסֵּג, גְּבוּל עוֹלָם--אֲשֶׁר עָשׂוּ אֲבוֹתֶיךָ
'al-tasseg gevul olam; asher asu avoteicha
Remove not the ancient landmark, which thy fathers have set.

חָזִיתָ אִישׁ, מָהִיר בִּמְלַאכְתּוֹ--לִפְנֵי-מְלָכִים יִתְיַצָּב; בַּל-יִתְיַצֵּב, לִפְנֵי חֲשֻׁכִּים
chazita ish mahir bimlachto, lifnei-melachim yityatzav; bal-yityatzev lifnei chashukkim
Seest thou a man diligent in his business? he shall stand before kings; he shall not stand before mean men.

מִשְׁלֵי

זוֹרֵעַ עַוְלָה, יִקְצָר-אָוֶן; וְשֵׁבֶט עֶבְרָתוֹ יִכְלֶה
zorea avlah yiktzar-'aven; veshevet evrato yichleh
He that soweth iniquity shall reap vanity; and the rod of his wrath shall fail.

טוֹב-עַיִן, הוּא יְבֹרָךְ: כִּי-נָתַן מִלַּחְמוֹ לַדָּל
tov-'ayin hu yevorach; ki-natan millachmo laddal
He that hath a bountiful eye shall be blessed; for he giveth of his bread to the poor.

גָּרֵשׁ לֵץ, וְיֵצֵא מָדוֹן; וְיִשְׁבֹּת, דִּין וְקָלוֹן.
garesh letz veyetzei madon; veyishbot, din vekalon
Cast out the scorner, and contention will go out; yea, strife and shame will cease.

אֹהֵב טְהָר-לֵב--חֵן שְׂפָתָיו, רֵעֵהוּ מֶלֶךְ
'ohev tehar-lev; chen sefatav, re'ehu melech
He that loveth pureness of heart, that hath grace in his lips, the king shall be his friend.

עֵינֵי יְהוָה, נָצְרוּ דָעַת; וַיְסַלֵּף, דִּבְרֵי בֹגֵד
'einei hashem natzeru da'at; vaysallef, divrei voged
The eyes of the LORD preserve him that hath knowledge, but He overthroweth the words of the faithless man.

אָמַר עָצֵל, אֲרִי בַחוּץ; בְּתוֹךְ רְחֹבוֹת, אֵרָצֵחַ
'amar atzel ari vachutz; betoch rechovot, eratzeach
The sluggard saith: 'There is a lion without; I shall be slain in the streets.'

שׁוּחָה עֲמֻקָּה, פִּי זָרוֹת; זְעוּם יְהוָה, יִפָּל-שָׁם
shuchah amukkah pi zarot; ze'um hashem yippal-sham
The mouth of strange women is a deep pit: he that is abhorred of the LORD shall fall therein.

אִוֶּלֶת, קְשׁוּרָה בְלֶב-נָעַר; שֵׁבֶט מוּסָר, יַרְחִיקֶנָּה מִמֶּנּוּ
'ivvelet keshurah velev-na'ar; shevet musar, yarchikennah mimmennu
Foolishness is bound up in the heart of a child; but the rod of correction shall drive it far from him.

עֹשֵׁק דָּל, לְהַרְבּוֹת לוֹ--נֹתֵן לְעָשִׁיר, אַךְ-לְמַחְסוֹר
'oshek dal leharbot lo; noten le'ashir, ach-lemachsor
One may oppress the poor, yet will their gain increase; one may give to the rich, yet will want come.

הַט אָזְנְךָ--וּשְׁמַע, דִּבְרֵי חֲכָמִים; וְלִבְּךָ, תָּשִׁית לְדַעְתִּי
hat ozenecha, ushema divrei chachamim; velibbecha, tashit leda'ti
Incline thine ear, and hear the words of the wise, and apply thy heart unto my knowledge.

כִּי-נָעִים, כִּי-תִשְׁמְרֵם בְּבִטְנֶךָ; יִכֹּנוּ יַחְדָּו, עַל-שְׂפָתֶיךָ
ki-na'im ki-tishmerem bevitnecha; yikkonu yachdav, al-sefateicha
For it is a pleasant thing if thou keep them within thee; let them be established altogether upon thy lips.

לִהְיוֹת בַּיהוָה, מִבְטַחֶךָ--הוֹדַעְתִּיךָ הַיּוֹם אַף-אָתָּה
lihyot bahashem mivtachecha; hoda'ticha hayom af-'attah
That thy trust may be in the LORD, I have made them known to thee this day, even to thee.

מִשְׁלֵי

עֵד-כְּזָבִים יֹאבֵד; וְאִישׁ שׁוֹמֵעַ, לָנֶצַח יְדַבֵּר
'ed-kezavim yoved; ve'ish shomea', lanetzach yedabber
A false witness shall perish; but the man that obeyeth shall speak unchallenged.

הֵעֵז אִישׁ רָשָׁע בְּפָנָיו; וְיָשָׁר, הוּא יָבִין דַּרְכּוֹ
he'ez ish rasha befanav; veyashar, hu yavin darko
A wicked man hardeneth his face; but as for the upright, he looketh well to his way.

אֵין חָכְמָה, וְאֵין תְּבוּנָה--וְאֵין עֵצָה, לְנֶגֶד יְהוָה
'ein chochmah ve'ein tevunah; ve'ein etzah, leneged hashem
There is no wisdom nor understanding nor counsel against the LORD.

סוּס--מוּכָן, לְיוֹם מִלְחָמָה; וְלַיהוָה, הַתְּשׁוּעָה
sus, muchon leyom milchamah; velahashem, hatteshu'ah
The horse is prepared against the day of battle; but victory is of the LORD.

כב

נִבְחָר שֵׁם, מֵעֹשֶׁר רָב: מִכֶּסֶף וּמִזָּהָב, חֵן טוֹב
Nivchar shem me'osher rav; mikkesef umizzahav, chen tov
A good name is rather to be chosen than great riches, and loving favour rather than silver and gold.

עָשִׁיר וָרָשׁ נִפְגָּשׁוּ; עֹשֵׂה כֻלָּם יְהוָה
'ashir varash nifgashu; oseh chullam hashem
The rich and the poor meet together--the LORD is the maker of them all.

עָרוּם, רָאָה רָעָה וְנִסְתָּר; וּפְתָיִים, עָבְרוּ וְנֶעֱנָשׁוּ
'arum ra'ah ra'ah venistar; ufetayim, averu vene'enashu
A prudent man seeth the evil, and hideth himself; but the thoughtless pass on, and are punished.

עֵקֶב עֲנָוָה, יִרְאַת יְהוָה; עֹשֶׁר וְכָבוֹד וְחַיִּים
'ekev anavah yir'at hashem osher vechavod vechayim
The reward of humility is the fear of the LORD, even riches, and honour, and life.

צִנִּים פַּחִים, בְּדֶרֶךְ עִקֵּשׁ; שׁוֹמֵר נַפְשׁוֹ, יִרְחַק מֵהֶם
tzinnim pachim bederech ikkesh; shomer nafsho, yirchak mehem
Thorns and snares are in the way of the froward; he that keepeth his soul holdeth himself far from them.

חֲנֹךְ לַנַּעַר, עַל-פִּי דַרְכּוֹ--גַּם כִּי-יַזְקִין, לֹא-יָסוּר מִמֶּנָּה
chanoch lanna'ar al-pi darko; gam ki-yazkin, lo-yasur mimmennah
Train up a child in the way he should go, and even when he is old, he will not depart from it.

עָשִׁיר, בְּרָשִׁים יִמְשׁוֹל; וְעֶבֶד לֹוֶה, לְאִישׁ מַלְוֶה
'ashir berashim yimshol; ve'eved loveh, le'ish malveh
The rich ruleth over the poor, and the borrower is servant to the lender.

מִשְׁלֵי

אִישׁ מַחְסוֹר, אֹהֵב שִׂמְחָה; אֹהֵב יַיִן-וָשֶׁמֶן, לֹא יַעֲשִׁיר
'ish machsor ohev simchah; ohev yayin-vashemen, lo ya'ashir
He that loveth pleasure shall be a poor man; he that loveth wine and oil shall not be rich.

כֹּפֶר לַצַּדִּיק רָשָׁע; וְתַחַת יְשָׁרִים בּוֹגֵד
kofer latzaddik rasha'; vetachat yesharim boged
The wicked is a ransom for the righteous; and the faithless cometh in the stead of the upright.

טוֹב, שֶׁבֶת בְּאֶרֶץ-מִדְבָּר--מֵאֵשֶׁת מִדְיָנִים וָכָעַס
tov, shevet be'eretz-midbar; me'eshet midyanim vacha'as
It is better to dwell in a desert land, than with a contentious and fretful woman.

אוֹצָר, נֶחְמָד וָשֶׁמֶן--בִּנְוֵה חָכָם; וּכְסִיל אָדָם יְבַלְּעֶנּוּ
'otzar nechmad vashemen binveh chacham; uchesil adam yevalle'ennu
There is desirable treasure and oil in the dwelling of the wise; but a foolish man swalloweth it up.

רֹדֵף, צְדָקָה וָחָסֶד--יִמְצָא חַיִּים, צְדָקָה וְכָבוֹד
rodef tzedakah vachased; yimtza chayim, tzedakah vechavod
He that followeth after righteousness and mercy findeth life, prosperity, and honour.

עִיר גִּבֹּרִים, עָלָה חָכָם; וַיֹּרֶד, עֹז מִבְטֶחָה
'ir gibborim alah chacham; vayored, oz mivtechah
A wise man scaleth the city of the mighty, and bringeth down the stronghold wherein it trusteth.

שֹׁמֵר פִּיו, וּלְשׁוֹנוֹ--שֹׁמֵר מִצָּרוֹת נַפְשׁוֹ
shomer piv uleshono; shomer mitzarot nafsho
Whoso keepeth his mouth and his tongue keepeth his soul from troubles.

זֵד יָהִיר, לֵץ שְׁמוֹ--עוֹשֶׂה, בְּעֶבְרַת זָדוֹן
zed yahir letz shemo; oseh, be'evrat zadon
A proud and haughty man, scorner is his name, even he that dealeth in overbearing pride.

תַּאֲוַת עָצֵל תְּמִיתֶנּוּ: כִּי-מֵאֲנוּ יָדָיו לַעֲשׂוֹת
ta'avat atzel temitennu; ki-me'anu yadav la'asot
The desire of the slothful killeth him; for his hands refuse to labour.

כָּל-הַיּוֹם, הִתְאַוָּה תַאֲוָה; וְצַדִּיק יִתֵּן, וְלֹא יַחְשֹׂךְ
kol-hayom hit'avvah ta'avah; vetzaddik yitten, velo yachsoch
There is that coveteth greedily all the day long; but the righteous giveth and spareth not.

זֶבַח רְשָׁעִים, תּוֹעֵבָה
zevach resha'im to'evah
The sacrifice of the wicked is an abomination;

אַף, כִּי-בְזִמָּה יְבִיאֶנּוּ
af, ki-vezimmah yevi'ennu
how much more, when he bringeth it with the proceeds of wickedness?

מִשְׁלֵי

מַחְשְׁבוֹת חָרוּץ, אַךְ-לְמוֹתָר; וְכָל-אָץ, אַךְ-לְמַחְסוֹר
machshevot charutz ach-lemotar; vechol-'atz, ach-lemachsor
The thoughts of the diligent tend only to plenteousness; but every one that is hasty hasteth only to want.

פֹּעַל אֹצָרוֹת, בִּלְשׁוֹן שָׁקֶר--הֶבֶל נִדָּף, מְבַקְשֵׁי-מָוֶת
po'al otzarot bilshon shaker; hevel niddaf, mevakshei-mavet
The getting of treasures by a lying tongue is a vapour driven to and fro; they [that seek them] seek death.

שֹׁד-רְשָׁעִים יְגוֹרֵם: כִּי מֵאֲנוּ, לַעֲשׂוֹת מִשְׁפָּט
shod-resha'im yegorem; ki me'anu, la'asot mishpat
The violence of the wicked shall drag them away; because they refuse to do justly.

הֲפַכְפַּךְ דֶּרֶךְ אִישׁ וָזָר; וְזַךְ, יָשָׁר פָּעֳלוֹ
hafachpach derech ish vazar; vezach, yashar po'olo
The way of man is froward and strange; but as for the pure, his work is right.

טוֹב, לָשֶׁבֶת עַל-פִּנַּת-גָּג--מֵאֵשֶׁת מִדְיָנִים, וּבֵית חָבֶר
tov, lashevet al-pinnat-gag; me'eshet midyanim, uveit chaver
It is better to dwell in a corner of the housetop, than in a house in common with a contentious woman.

נֶפֶשׁ רָשָׁע, אִוְּתָה-רָע; לֹא-יֻחַן בְּעֵינָיו רֵעֵהוּ
nefesh rasho ivvetah-ra'; lo-yuchan be'einav re'ehu
The soul of the wicked desireth evil; his neighbour findeth no favour in his eyes.

בַּעְנָשׁ-לֵץ, יֶחְכַּם-פֶּתִי; וּבְהַשְׂכִּיל לְחָכָם, יִקַּח-דָּעַת
ba'nosh-letz yechkam-peti; uvehaskil lechacham, yikkach-da'at
When the scorner is punished, the thoughtless is made wise; and when the wise is instructed, he receiveth knowledge.

מַשְׂכִּיל צַדִּיק, לְבֵית רָשָׁע; מְסַלֵּף רְשָׁעִים לָרָע
maskil tzaddik leveit rasha'; mesallef resha'im lara
The Righteous One considereth the house of the wicked; overthrowing the wicked to their ruin.

אֹטֵם אָזְנוֹ, מִזַּעֲקַת-דָּל--גַּם-הוּא יִקְרָא, וְלֹא יֵעָנֶה
'otem azeno mizza'akat-dal; gam-hu yikra, velo ye'aneh
Whoso stoppeth his ears at the cry of the poor, he also shall cry himself, but shall not be answered.

מַתָּן בַּסֵּתֶר, יִכְפֶּה-אָף; וְשֹׁחַד בַּחֵק, חֵמָה עַזָּה
mattan basseter yichpeh-'af; veshochad bachek, chemah azzah
A gift in secret pacifieth anger, and a present in the bosom strong wrath.

שִׂמְחָה לַצַּדִּיק, עֲשׂוֹת מִשְׁפָּט; וּמְחִתָּה, לְפֹעֲלֵי אָוֶן
simchah latzaddik asot mishpat; umechittah, lefo'alei aven
To do justly is joy to the righteous, but ruin to the workers of iniquity.

אָדָם--תּוֹעֶה, מִדֶּרֶךְ הַשְׂכֵּל: בִּקְהַל רְפָאִים יָנוּחַ
'adam, to'eh midderech haskel; bik'hal refa'im yanuach
The man that strayeth out of the way of understanding shall rest in the congregation of the shades.

מִשְׁלֵי

מֵיְהוָה מִצְעֲדֵי-גָבֶר; וְאָדָם, מַה-יָּבִין דַּרְכּוֹ
mehashem mitz'adei-gaver; ve'adam, mah-yavin darko
A man's goings are of the LORD; how then can man look to his way?

מוֹקֵשׁ אָדָם, יָלַע קֹדֶשׁ; וְאַחַר נְדָרִים לְבַקֵּר
mokesh adom yala kodesh; ve'achar nedarim levakker
It is a snare to a man rashly to say: 'Holy', and after vows to make inquiry.

מְזָרֶה רְשָׁעִים, מֶלֶךְ חָכָם; וַיָּשֶׁב עֲלֵיהֶם אוֹפָן
mezareh resha'im melech chacham; vayashev aleihem ofan
A wise king sifteth the wicked, and turneth the wheel over them.

נֵר יְהוָה, נִשְׁמַת אָדָם; חֹפֵשׂ, כָּל-חַדְרֵי-בָטֶן
ner hashem nishmat adam; chofes, kol-chadrei-vaten
The spirit of man is the lamp of the LORD, searching all the inward parts.

חֶסֶד וֶאֱמֶת, יִצְּרוּ-מֶלֶךְ; וְסָעַד בַּחֶסֶד כִּסְאוֹ
chesed ve'emet yitzeru-melech; vesa'ad bachesed kis'o
Mercy and truth preserve the king; and his throne is upheld by mercy.

תִּפְאֶרֶת בַּחוּרִים כֹּחָם; וַהֲדַר זְקֵנִים שֵׂיבָה
tif'eret bachurim kocham; vahadar zekenim seivah
The glory of young men is their strength; and the beauty of old men is the hoary head.

חַבֻּרוֹת פֶּצַע, תַּמְרוּק בְּרָע; וּמַכּוֹת, חַדְרֵי-בָטֶן
chabburot petza tamruk bera'; umakkot, chadrei-vaten
Sharp wounds cleanse away evil; so do stripes that reach the inward parts.

כא

פַּלְגֵי-מַיִם לֶב-מֶלֶךְ, בְּיַד-יְהוָה; עַל-כָּל-אֲשֶׁר יַחְפֹּץ יַטֶּנּוּ
Palgei-mayim lev-melech beyad-hashem al-kol-'asher yachpotz yattennu
The king's heart is in the hand of the LORD as the watercourses: He turneth it whithersoever He will.

כָּל-דֶּרֶךְ-אִישׁ, יָשָׁר בְּעֵינָיו; וְתֹכֵן לִבּוֹת יְהוָה
kol-derech-'ish yashar be'einav; vetochen libbot hashem
Every way of a man is right in his own eyes; but the LORD weigheth the hearts.

עֲשֹׂה, צְדָקָה וּמִשְׁפָּט--נִבְחָר לַיהוָה מִזָּבַח
'asoh tzedakah umishpat; nivchar lahashem mizzavach
To do righteousness and justice is more acceptable to the LORD than sacrifice.

רוּם-עֵינַיִם, וּרְחַב-לֵב--נִר רְשָׁעִים חַטָּאת
rum-'einayim urechav-lev; nir resha'im chattat
A haughty look, and a proud heart--the tillage of the wicked is sin.

מִשְׁלֵי

אֹזֶן שֹׁמַעַת, וְעַיִן רֹאָה--יְהוָה, עָשָׂה גַם-שְׁנֵיהֶם
'ozen shoma'at ve'ayin ro'ah; hashem asah gam-sheneihem
The hearing ear, and the seeing eye, the LORD hath made even both of them.

אַל-תֶּאֱהַב שֵׁנָה, פֶּן-תִּוָּרֵשׁ; פְּקַח עֵינֶיךָ שְׂבַע-לָחֶם
'al-te'ehav shenah pen-tivvaresh; pekach eineicha seva'-lachem
Love not sleep, lest thou come to poverty; open thine eyes, and thou shalt have bread in plenty.

רַע רַע, יֹאמַר הַקּוֹנֶה; וְאֹזֵל לוֹ, אָז יִתְהַלָּל
ra ra yomar hakkoneh; ve'ozel lo, az yit'hallal
'It is bad, it is bad', saith the buyer; but when he is gone his way, then he boasteth.

יֵשׁ זָהָב, וְרָב-פְּנִינִים; וּכְלִי יְקָר, שִׂפְתֵי-דָעַת
yesh zahav verav-peninim; ucheli yekar, siftei-da'at
There is gold, and a multitude of rubies; but the lips of knowledge are a precious jewel.

לְקַח-בִּגְדוֹ, כִּי-עָרַב זָר; וּבְעַד נָכְרִיָּה חַבְלֵהוּ
lekach-bigdo ki-'arav zar; uve'ad nocheriyah chavlehu
Take his garment that is surety for a stranger; and hold him in pledge that is surety for an alien woman.

עָרֵב לָאִישׁ, לֶחֶם שָׁקֶר; וְאַחַר, יִמָּלֵא-פִיהוּ חָצָץ
'arev la'ish lechem shaker; ve'achar, yimmale-fihu chatzatz
Bread of falsehood is sweet to a man; but afterwards his mouth shall be filled with gravel.

מַחֲשָׁבוֹת, בְּעֵצָה תִכּוֹן; וּבְתַחְבֻּלוֹת, עֲשֵׂה מִלְחָמָה
machashavot be'etzah tikkon; uvetachbulot, aseh milchamah
Every purpose is established by counsel; and with good advice carry on war.

גּוֹלֶה-סּוֹד, הוֹלֵךְ רָכִיל; וּלְפֹתֶה שְׂפָתָיו, לֹא תִתְעָרָב
goleh-sod holech rachil; ulefoteh sefatav, lo tit'arav
He that goeth about as a talebearer revealeth secrets; therefore meddle not with him that openeth wide his lips.

מְקַלֵּל, אָבִיו וְאִמּוֹ--יִדְעַךְ נֵרוֹ, בְּאֶשׁוּן חֹשֶׁךְ
mekallel aviv ve'immo; yid'ach nero, be'eshun choshech
Whoso curseth his father or his mother, his lamp shall be put out in the blackest darkness.

נַחֲלָה, מְבֹהֶלֶת בָּרִאשֹׁנָה; וְאַחֲרִיתָהּ, לֹא תְבֹרָךְ
nachalah mevohelet barishonah; ve'acharitah, lo tevorach
An estate may be gotten hastily at the beginning; but the end thereof shall not be blessed.

אַל-תֹּאמַר אֲשַׁלְּמָה-רָע; קַוֵּה לַיהוָה, וְיֹשַׁע לָךְ
'al-tomar ashallemah-ra'; kavveh lahashem veyosha lach
Say not thou: 'I will requite evil'; wait for the LORD, and He will save thee.

תּוֹעֲבַת יְהוָה, אֶבֶן וָאָבֶן; וּמֹאזְנֵי מִרְמָה לֹא-טוֹב
to'avat hashem even va'aven; umozenei mirmah lo-tov
Divers weights are an abomination to the LORD; and a false balance is not good.

מִשְׁלֵי

כ

לֵץ הַיַּיִן, הֹמֶה שֵׁכָר; וְכָל-שֹׁגֶה בּוֹ, לֹא יֶחְכָּם
Letz hayain homeh shechar; vechol-shogeh bo, lo yechkam
Wine is a mocker, strong drink is riotous; and whosoever reeleth thereby is not wise.

נַהַם כַּכְּפִיר, אֵימַת מֶלֶךְ; מִתְעַבְּרוֹ, חוֹטֵא נַפְשׁוֹ
naham kakkefir eimat melech; mit'abbero, chotei nafsho
The terror of a king is as the roaring of a lion: he that provoketh him to anger forfeiteth his life.

כָּבוֹד לָאִישׁ, שֶׁבֶת מֵרִיב; וְכָל-אֱוִיל, יִתְגַּלָּע
kavod la'ish shevet meriv; vechol-'evil, yitgalla
It is an honour for a man to keep aloof from strife; but every fool will be snarling.

מֵחֹרֶף, עָצֵל לֹא-יַחֲרֹשׁ; וְשָׁאַל בַּקָּצִיר וָאָיִן
mechoref atzel lo-yacharosh; vesha'al bakkatzir va'ayin
The sluggard will not plow when winter setteth in; therefore he shall beg in harvest, and have nothing.

מַיִם עֲמֻקִּים, עֵצָה בְלֶב-אִישׁ; וְאִישׁ תְּבוּנָה יִדְלֶנָּה
mayim amukkim etzah velev-'ish; ve'ish tevunah yidlennah
Counsel in the heart of man is like deep water; but a man of understanding will draw it out.

רָב-אָדָם--יִקְרָא, אִישׁ חַסְדּוֹ; וְאִישׁ אֱמוּנִים, מִי יִמְצָא
rav-'adam, yikra ish chasdo; ve'ish emunim, mi yimtza
Most men will proclaim every one his own goodness; but a faithful man who can find?

מִתְהַלֵּךְ בְּתֻמּוֹ צַדִּיק; אַשְׁרֵי בָנָיו אַחֲרָיו
mit'hallech betummo tzaddik; ashrei vanav acharav
He that walketh in his integrity as a just man, happy are his children after him.

מֶלֶךְ, יוֹשֵׁב עַל-כִּסֵּא-דִין--מְזָרֶה בְעֵינָיו כָּל-רָע
melech, yoshev al-kisse-din; mezareh ve'einav kol-ra
A king that sitteth on the throne of judgment scattereth away all evil with his eyes.

מִי-יֹאמַר, זִכִּיתִי לִבִּי; טָהַרְתִּי, מֵחַטָּאתִי
mi-yomar zikkiti libbi; taharti, mechattati
Who can say: 'I have made my heart clean, I am pure from my sin'?

אֶבֶן וָאֶבֶן, אֵיפָה וְאֵיפָה--תּוֹעֲבַת יְהוָה, גַּם-שְׁנֵיהֶם
'even va'even eifah ve'eifah; to'avat hashem gam-sheneihem
Divers weights, and divers measures, both of them alike are an abomination to the LORD.

גַּם בְּמַעֲלָלָיו, יִתְנַכֶּר-נָעַר--אִם-זַךְ וְאִם-יָשָׁר פָּעֳלוֹ
gam bema'alalav yitnakker-na'ar; im-zach ve'im-yashar po'olo
Even a child is known by his doings, whether his work be pure, and whether it be right.

מִשְׁלֵי

גְּדָל-חֵמָה, נֹשֵׂא עֹנֶשׁ: כִּי אִם-תַּצִּיל, וְעוֹד תּוֹסִף
gedol-chemah nosei onesh; ki im-tatzil, ve'od tosif
A man of great wrath shall suffer punishment; for if thou interpose, thou wilt add thereto.

שְׁמַע עֵצָה, וְקַבֵּל מוּסָר--לְמַעַן, תֶּחְכַּם בְּאַחֲרִיתֶךָ
shema etzah vekabbel musar; lema'an, techkam be'acharitecha
Hear counsel, and receive instruction, that thou mayest be wise in thy latter end.

רַבּוֹת מַחֲשָׁבוֹת בְּלֶב-אִישׁ; וַעֲצַת יְהוָה, הִיא תָקוּם
rabbot machashavot belev-'ish; va'atzat hashem hi takum
There are many devices in a man's heart; but the counsel of the LORD, that shall stand.

תַּאֲוַת אָדָם חַסְדּוֹ; וְטוֹב-רָשׁ, מֵאִישׁ כָּזָב
ta'avat adam chasdo; vetov-rash me'ish kazav
The lust of a man is his shame; and a poor man is better than a liar.

יִרְאַת יְהוָה לְחַיִּים; וְשָׂבֵעַ יָלִין, בַּל-יִפָּקֶד רָע
yir'at hashem lechayim; vesavea yalin, bal-yippaked ra
The fear of the LORD tendeth to life; and he that hath it shall abide satisfied, he shall not be visited with evil.

טָמַן עָצֵל יָדוֹ, בַּצַּלָּחַת; גַּם-אֶל-פִּיהוּ, לֹא יְשִׁיבֶנָּה
taman atzel yado batzallachat; gam-'el-pihu, lo yeshivennah
The sluggard burieth his hand in the dish, and will not so much as bring it back to his mouth.

לֵץ תַּכֶּה, וּפֶתִי יַעְרִם
letz takkeh ufeti ya'rim
When thou smitest a scorner, the simple will become prudent;

וְהוֹכִיחַ לְנָבוֹן, יָבִין דָּעַת
vehochiach lenavon, yavin da'at
and when one that hath understanding is reproved, he will understand knowledge.

מְשַׁדֶּד-אָב, יַבְרִיחַ אֵם--בֵּן, מֵבִישׁ וּמַחְפִּיר
meshadded-'av yavriach em; ben, mevish umachpir
A son that dealeth shamefully and reproachfully will despoil his father, and chase away his mother.

חֲדַל-בְּנִי, לִשְׁמֹעַ מוּסָר; לִשְׁגוֹת, מֵאִמְרֵי-דָעַת
chadal-beni lishmoa musar; lishgot, me'imrei-da'at
Cease, my son, to hear the instruction that causeth to err from the words of knowledge.

עֵד בְּלִיַּעַל, יָלִיץ מִשְׁפָּט; וּפִי רְשָׁעִים, יְבַלַּע-אָוֶן
'ed beliya'al yalitz mishpat; ufi resha'im, yevalla'-'aven
An ungodly witness mocketh at right; and the mouth of the wicked devoureth iniquity.

נָכוֹנוּ לַלֵּצִים שְׁפָטִים; וּמַהֲלֻמוֹת, לְגֵו כְּסִילִים
nachonu lalletzim shefatim; umahalumot, legev kesilim
Judgments are prepared for scorners, and stripes for the back of fools.

מִשְׁלֵי

מְרַדֵּף אֲמָרִים לוֹ-הֵמָּה
meraddef amarim lo-hemmah
He that pursueth words, they turn against him.

קֹנֶה-לֵּב, אֹהֵב נַפְשׁוֹ; שֹׁמֵר תְּבוּנָה, לִמְצֹא-טוֹב
koneh-lev ohev nafsho; shomer tevunah, limtzo-tov
He that getteth wisdom loveth his own soul; he that keepeth understanding shall find good.

עֵד שְׁקָרִים, לֹא יִנָּקֶה; וְיָפִיחַ כְּזָבִים יֹאבֵד
'ed shekarim lo yinnakeh; veyafiach kezavim yoved
A false witness shall not be unpunished; and he that breatheth forth lies shall perish

לֹא-נָאוֶה לִכְסִיל תַּעֲנוּג; אַף, כִּי-לְעֶבֶד מְשֹׁל בְּשָׂרִים
lo-naveh lichsil ta'anug; af, ki-le'eved meshol besarim
Luxury is not seemly for a fool; much less for a servant to have rule over princes.

שֵׂכֶל אָדָם, הֶאֱרִיךְ אַפּוֹ; וְתִפְאַרְתּוֹ, עֲבֹר עַל-פָּשַׁע
sechel adam he'erich appo; vetif'arto, avor al-pasha
It is the discretion of a man to be slow to anger, and it is his glory to pass over a transgression.

נַהַם כַּכְּפִיר, זַעַף מֶלֶךְ; וּכְטַל עַל-עֵשֶׂב רְצוֹנוֹ
naham kakkefir za'af melech; uchetal al-'esev retzono
The king's wrath is as the roaring of a lion; but his favour is as dew upon the grass.

הַוֹּת לְאָבִיו, בֵּן כְּסִיל; וְדֶלֶף טֹרֵד, מִדְיְנֵי אִשָּׁה
havvot le'aviv ben kesil; vedelef tored, midyenei ishah
A foolish son is the calamity of his father; and the contentions of a wife are a continual dropping.

בַּיִת וָהוֹן, נַחֲלַת אָבוֹת; וּמֵיְהוָה, אִשָּׁה מַשְׂכָּלֶת
bayit vahon nachalat avot; umehashem, ishah maskalet
House and riches are the inheritance of fathers; but a prudent wife is from the LORD.

עַצְלָה, תַּפִּיל תַּרְדֵּמָה; וְנֶפֶשׁ רְמִיָּה תִרְעָב
'atzlah tappil tardemah; venefesh remiyah tir'av
Slothfulness casteth into a deep sleep; and the idle soul shall suffer hunger.

שֹׁמֵר מִצְוָה, שֹׁמֵר נַפְשׁוֹ; בּוֹזֵה דְרָכָיו יָמוּת
shomer mitzvah shomer nafsho; bozeh derachav yamut
He that keepeth the commandment keepeth his soul; but he that despiseth His ways shall die.

מַלְוֵה יְהוָה, חוֹנֵן דָּל; וּגְמֻלוֹ, יְשַׁלֶּם-לוֹ
malveh hashem chonen dal; ugemulo, yeshallem-lo
He that is gracious unto the poor lendeth unto the LORD; and his good deed will He repay unto him.

יַסֵּר בִּנְךָ, כִּי-יֵשׁ תִּקְוָה; וְאֶל-הֲמִיתוֹ, אַל-תִּשָּׂא נַפְשֶׁךָ
yasser bincha ki-yesh tikvah; ve'el-hamito, al-tissa nafshecha
Chasten thy son, for there is hope; but set not thy heart on his destruction.

מִשְׁלֵי

מָוֶת וְחַיִּים, בְּיַד-לָשׁוֹן; וְאֹהֲבֶיהָ, יֹאכַל פִּרְיָהּ
mavet vechayim beyad-lashon; ve'ohaveiha, yochal piryah
Death and life are in the power of the tongue; and they that indulge it shall eat the fruit thereof.

מָצָא אִשָּׁה, מָצָא טוֹב; וַיָּפֶק רָצוֹן, מֵיְהוָה
matza ishah matza tov; vayafek ratzon, mehashem
Whoso findeth a wife findeth a great good, and obtaineth favour of the LORD.

תַּחֲנוּנִים יְדַבֶּר-רָשׁ; וְעָשִׁיר, יַעֲנֶה עַזּוֹת
tachanunim yedabber-rash; ve'ashir, ya'aneh azzot
The poor useth entreaties; but the rich answereth impudently.

אִישׁ רֵעִים, לְהִתְרֹעֵעַ; וְיֵשׁ אֹהֵב, דָּבֵק מֵאָח
'ish re'im lehitro'ea'; veyesh ohev, davek me'ach
There are friends that one hath to his own hurt; but there is a friend that sticketh closer than a brother.

יט

טוֹב-רָשׁ, הוֹלֵךְ בְּתֻמּוֹ--מֵעִקֵּשׁ שְׂפָתָיו, וְהוּא כְסִיל
Tov-rash holech betummo; me'ikkesh sefatav, vehu chesil
Better is the poor that walketh in his integrity than he that is perverse in his lips and a fool at the same time.

גַּם בְּלֹא-דַעַת נֶפֶשׁ לֹא-טוֹב; וְאָץ בְּרַגְלַיִם חוֹטֵא
gam belo-da'at nefesh lo-tov; ve'atz beraglayim chote
Also, that the soul be without knowledge is not good; and he that hasteth with his feet sinneth.

אִוֶּלֶת אָדָם, תְּסַלֵּף דַּרְכּוֹ; וְעַל-יְהוָה, יִזְעַף לִבּוֹ
'ivvelet adom tesallef darko; ve'al-hashem yiz'af libbo
The foolishness of man perverteth his way; and his heart fretteth against the LORD.

הוֹן--יֹסִיף, רֵעִים רַבִּים; וְדָל, מֵרֵעֵהוּ יִפָּרֵד
hon, yosif re'im rabbim; vedal, mere'hu yippared
Wealth addeth many friends; but as for the poor, his friend separateth himself from him.

עֵד שְׁקָרִים, לֹא יִנָּקֶה; וְיָפִיחַ כְּזָבִים, לֹא יִמָּלֵט
'ed shekarim lo yinnakeh; veyafiach kezavim, lo yimmalet
A false witness shall not be unpunished; and he that breatheth forth lies shall not escape.

רַבִּים, יְחַלּוּ פְנֵי-נָדִיב; וְכָל-הָרֵעַ, לְאִישׁ מַתָּן
rabbim yechallu fenei-nadiv; vechol-harea', le'ish mattan
Many will entreat the favour of the liberal man; and every man is a friend to him that giveth gifts.

כָּל אֲחֵי-רָשׁ, שְׂנֵאֻהוּ--אַף כִּי מְרֵעֵהוּ, רָחֲקוּ מִמֶּנּוּ
kol achei-rash sene'uhu, af ki mere'ehu rachaku mimmennu
All the brethren of the poor do hate him; how much more do his friends go far from him!

מִשְׁלֵי

גַּם, מִתְרַפֶּה בִמְלַאכְתּוֹ--אָח הוּא, לְבַעַל מַשְׁחִית
gam mitrappeh vimlachto; ach hu, leva'al mashchit
Even one that is slack in his work is brother to him that is a destroyer.

מִגְדַּל-עֹז, שֵׁם יְהוָה; בּוֹ-יָרוּץ צַדִּיק וְנִשְׂגָּב
migdal-'oz shem hashem bo-yarutz tzaddik venisgav
The name of the LORD is a strong tower: the righteous runneth into it, and is set up on high.

הוֹן עָשִׁיר, קִרְיַת עֻזּוֹ; וּכְחוֹמָה נִשְׂגָּבָה, בְּמַשְׂכִּתוֹ
hon ashir kiryat uzzo; uchechomah nisgavah, bemaskito
The rich man's wealth is his strong city, and as a high wall in his own conceit.

לִפְנֵי-שֶׁבֶר, יִגְבַּהּ לֵב-אִישׁ; וְלִפְנֵי כָבוֹד עֲנָוָה
lifnei-shever yigbah lev-'ish; velifnei chavod anavah
Before destruction the heart of a man is haughty, and before honour goeth humility.

מֵשִׁיב דָּבָר, בְּטֶרֶם יִשְׁמָע--אִוֶּלֶת הִיא-לוֹ, וּכְלִמָּה
meshiv davor beterem yishma'; ivvelet hi-lo, uchelimmah
He that giveth answer before he heareth, it is folly and confusion unto him.

רוּחַ-אִישׁ, יְכַלְכֵּל מַחֲלֵהוּ; וְרוּחַ נְכֵאָה, מִי יִשָּׂאֶנָּה
ruach-'ish yechalkel machalehu; veruach neche'ah, mi yissa'ennah
The spirit of a man will sustain his infirmity; but a broken spirit who can bear?

לֵב נָבוֹן, יִקְנֶה-דָּעַת; וְאֹזֶן חֲכָמִים, תְּבַקֶּשׁ-דָּעַת
lev navon yikneh-da'at; ve'ozen chachamim, tevakkesh-da'at
The heart of the prudent getteth knowledge; and the ear of the wise seeketh knowledge.

מַתָּן אָדָם, יַרְחִיב לוֹ; וְלִפְנֵי גְדֹלִים יַנְחֶנּוּ
mattan adam yarchiv lo; velifnei gedolim yanchennu
A man's gift maketh room for him, and bringeth him before great men.

צַדִּיק הָרִאשׁוֹן בְּרִיבוֹ; וּבָא-רֵעֵהוּ, וַחֲקָרוֹ
tzaddik harishon berivo; uva-re'ehu, vachakaro
He that pleadeth his cause first seemeth just; but his neighbour cometh and searcheth him out.

מִדְיָנִים, יַשְׁבִּית הַגּוֹרָל; וּבֵין עֲצוּמִים יַפְרִיד
midyanim yashbit haggoral; uvein atzumim yafrid
The lot causeth strife to cease, and parteth asunder the contentious.

אָח--נִפְשָׁע מִקִּרְיַת-עֹז; וּמִדְיָנִים, כִּבְרִיחַ אַרְמוֹן
'ach, nifsha mikkiryat-'oz; umidyanim, kivriach armon
A brother offended is harder to be won than a strong city; and their contentions are like the bars of a castle.

מִפְּרִי פִי-אִישׁ, תִּשְׂבַּע בִּטְנוֹ; תְּבוּאַת שְׂפָתָיו יִשְׂבָּע
mipperi fi-'ish tisba bitno; tevu'at sefatav yisba
A man's belly shall be filled with the fruit of his mouth; with the increase of his lips shall he be satisfied.

מִשְׁלֵי

חוֹשֵׂךְ אֲמָרָיו, יוֹדֵעַ דָּעַת; יְקַר-רוּחַ, אִישׁ תְּבוּנָה

chosech amarav yodea da'at; yekar-ruach, ish tevunah

He that spareth his words hath knowledge; and he that husbandeth his spirit is a man of discernment.

גַּם אֱוִיל מַחֲרִישׁ, חָכָם יֵחָשֵׁב

gam evil macharish chacham yechashev

Even a fool, when he holdeth his peace, is counted wise;

אֹטֵם שְׂפָתָיו נָבוֹן

otem sefatav navon

and he that shutteth his lips is esteemed as a man of understanding.

ח

לְתַאֲוָה, יְבַקֵּשׁ נִפְרָד; בְּכָל-תּוּשִׁיָּה, יִתְגַּלָּע

Leta'avah yevakkesh nifrad; bechol-tushiyah, yitgalla

He that separateth himself seeketh his own desire, and snarlest against all sound wisdom.

לֹא-יַחְפֹּץ כְּסִיל, בִּתְבוּנָה: כִּי, אִם-בְּהִתְגַּלּוֹת לִבּוֹ

lo-yachpotz kesil bitvunah; ki, im-behitgallot libbo

A fool hath no delight in understanding, but only that his heart may lay itself bare.

בְּבוֹא-רָשָׁע, בָּא גַם-בּוּז; וְעִם-קָלוֹן חֶרְפָּה

bevo-rasha ba gam-buz; ve'im-kalon cherpah

When the wicked cometh, there cometh also contempt, and with ignominy reproach.

מַיִם עֲמֻקִּים, דִּבְרֵי פִי-אִישׁ; נַחַל נֹבֵעַ, מְקוֹר חָכְמָה

mayim amukkim divrei fi-'ish; nachal novea', mekor chochmah

The words of a man's mouth are as deep waters; a flowing brook, a fountain of wisdom.

שְׂאֵת פְּנֵי-רָשָׁע לֹא-טוֹב--לְהַטּוֹת צַדִּיק, בַּמִּשְׁפָּט

se'et penei-rasha lo-tov; lehattot tzaddik, bammishpat

It is not good to respect the person of the wicked, so as to turn aside the righteous in judgment.

שִׂפְתֵי כְסִיל, יָבֹאוּ בְרִיב; וּפִיו, לְמַהֲלֻמוֹת יִקְרָא

siftei chesil yavo'u veriv; ufiv, lemahalumot yikra

A fool's lips enter into contention, and his mouth calleth for strokes.

פִּי-כְסִיל, מְחִתָּה-לוֹ; וּשְׂפָתָיו, מוֹקֵשׁ נַפְשׁוֹ

pi-chesil mechittah-lo; usefatav, mokesh nafsho

A fool's mouth is his ruin, and his lips are the snare of his soul.

דִּבְרֵי נִרְגָּן, כְּמִתְלַהֲמִים; וְהֵם, יָרְדוּ חַדְרֵי-בָטֶן

divrei nirgon kemitlahamim; vehem, yaredu chadrei-vaten

The words of a whisperer are as dainty morsels, and they go down into the innermost parts of the belly.

מִשְׁלֵי

מַצְדִּיק רָשָׁע, וּמַרְשִׁיעַ צַדִּיק--תּוֹעֲבַת יְהוָה, גַּם-שְׁנֵיהֶם
matzdik rasho umarshia tzaddik; to'avat hashem gam-sheneihem
He that justifieth the wicked, and he that condemneth the righteous, even they both are an abomination to the LORD.

לָמָּה-זֶּה מְחִיר בְּיַד-כְּסִיל--לִקְנוֹת חָכְמָה וְלֶב-אָיִן
lammah-zeh mechir beyad-kesil; liknot chochmah velev-'ayin
Wherefore is there a price in the hand of a fool to buy wisdom, seeing he hath no understanding?

בְּכָל-עֵת, אֹהֵב הָרֵעַ; וְאָח לְצָרָה, יִוָּלֵד
bechol-'et ohev harea'; ve'ach letzarah, yivvaled
A friend loveth at all times, and a brother is born for adversity.

אָדָם חֲסַר-לֵב, תּוֹקֵעַ כָּף; עֹרֵב עֲרֻבָּה, לִפְנֵי רֵעֵהוּ
'adam chasar-lev tokea kaf; orev arubbah, lifnei re'ehu
A man void of understanding is he that striketh hands, and becometh surety in the presence of his neighbour.

אֹהֵב פֶּשַׁע, אֹהֵב מַצָּה; מַגְבִּיהַּ פִּתְחוֹ, מְבַקֶּשׁ-שָׁבֶר
'ohev pesha ohev matzah; magbiah pitcho, mevakkesh-shaver
He loveth transgression that loveth strife; he that exalteth his gate seeketh destruction.

עִקֶּשׁ-לֵב, לֹא יִמְצָא-טוֹב; וְנֶהְפָּךְ בִּלְשׁוֹנוֹ, יִפּוֹל בְּרָעָה
'ikkesh-lev lo yimtza-tov; venehpach bilshono, yippol bera'ah
He that hath a froward heart findeth no good; and he that hath a perverse tongue falleth into evil.

יֹלֵד כְּסִיל, לְתוּגָה לוֹ; וְלֹא-יִשְׂמַח, אֲבִי נָבָל
yoled kesil letugah lo; velo-yismach, avi naval
He that begetteth a fool doeth it to his sorrow; and the father of a churl hath no joy.

לֵב שָׂמֵחַ, יֵיטִב גֵּהָה; וְרוּחַ נְכֵאָה, תְּיַבֶּשׁ-גָּרֶם
lev sameach yeitiv gehah; veruach neche'ah, teyabbesh-garem
A merry heart is a good medicine; but a broken spirit drieth the bones.

שֹׁחַד מֵחֵיק, רָשָׁע יִקָּח--לְהַטּוֹת, אָרְחוֹת מִשְׁפָּט
shochad mecheik rasha yikkach; lehattot, orechot mishpat
A wicked man taketh a gift out of the bosom, to pervert the ways of justice.

אֶת-פְּנֵי מֵבִין חָכְמָה; וְעֵינֵי כְסִיל, בִּקְצֵה-אָרֶץ
'et-penei mevin chochmah ve'einei chesil, biktzeh-'aretz
Wisdom is before him that hath understanding; but the eyes of a fool are in the ends of the earth.

כַּעַס לְאָבִיו, בֵּן כְּסִיל; וּמֶמֶר, לְיוֹלַדְתּוֹ
ka'as le'aviv ben kesil; umemer, leyoladto
A foolish son is vexation to his father, and bitterness to her that bore him.

גַּם עֲנוֹשׁ לַצַּדִּיק לֹא-טוֹב--לְהַכּוֹת נְדִיבִים עַל-יֹשֶׁר
gam anosh latzaddik lo-tov; lehakkot nedivim al-yosher
To punish also the righteous is not good, nor to strike the noble for their uprightness.

מִשְׁלֵי

מִצְרֵף לַכֶּסֶף, וְכוּר לַזָּהָב; וּבֹחֵן לִבּוֹת יְהוָה
matzref lakkesef vechur lazzahav; uvochen libbot hashem
The refining pot is for silver, and the furnace for gold; but the LORD trieth the hearts.

מֵרַע, מַקְשִׁיב עַל-שְׂפַת-אָוֶן; שֶׁקֶר מֵזִין, עַל-לְשׁוֹן הַוֹּת
mera makshiv al-sefat-'aven; sheker mezin al-leshon havvot
A evil-doer giveth heed to wicked lips; and a liar giveth ear to a mischievous tongue.

לֹעֵג לָרָשׁ, חֵרֵף עֹשֵׂהוּ; שָׂמֵחַ לְאֵיד, לֹא יִנָּקֶה
lo'eg larosh cheref osehu; sameach le'eid, lo yinnakeh
Whoso mocketh the poor blasphemeth his Maker; and he that is glad at calamity shall not be unpunished.

עֲטֶרֶת זְקֵנִים, בְּנֵי בָנִים; וְתִפְאֶרֶת בָּנִים אֲבוֹתָם
'ateret zekenim benei vanim; vetif'eret banim avotam
Children's children are the crown of old men; and the glory of children are their fathers.

לֹא-נָאוָה לְנָבָל שְׂפַת-יֶתֶר; אַף, כִּי-לְנָדִיב שְׂפַת-שָׁקֶר
lo-navah lenaval sefat-yeter; af, ki-lenadiv sefat-shaker
Overbearing speech becometh not a churl; much less do lying lips a prince.

אֶבֶן-חֵן הַשֹּׁחַד, בְּעֵינֵי בְעָלָיו; אֶל-כָּל-אֲשֶׁר יִפְנֶה יַשְׂכִּיל
'even-chen hashochad be'einei ve'alav; el-kol-'asher yifneh yaskil
A gift is as a precious stone in the eyes of him that hath it; whithersoever he turneth, he prospereth.

מְכַסֶּה-פֶּשַׁע, מְבַקֵּשׁ אַהֲבָה; וְשֹׁנֶה בְדָבָר, מַפְרִיד אַלּוּף
mechasseh-pesha mevakkesh ahavah; veshoneh vedavar, mafrid alluf
He that covereth a transgression seeketh love; but he that harpeth on a matter estrangeth a familiar friend.

תֵּחַת גְּעָרָה בְמֵבִין--מֵהַכּוֹת כְּסִיל מֵאָה
techat ge'arah vemevin; mehakkot kesil me'ah
A rebuke entereth deeper into a man of understanding than a hundred stripes into a fool.

אַךְ-מְרִי יְבַקֶּשׁ-רָע; וּמַלְאָךְ אַכְזָרִי, יְשֻׁלַּח-בּוֹ
'ach-meri yevakkesh-ra'; umal'ach achzari, yeshullach-bo
A rebellious man seeketh only evil; therefore a cruel messenger shall be sent against him.

פָּגוֹשׁ דֹּב שַׁכּוּל בְּאִישׁ; וְאַל-כְּסִיל, בְּאִוַּלְתּוֹ
pagosh dov shakkul be'ish; ve'al-kesil, be'ivvalto
Let a bear robbed of her whelps meet a man, rather than a fool in his folly.

מֵשִׁיב רָעָה, תַּחַת טוֹבָה--לֹא-תָמוּשׁ רָעָה, מִבֵּיתוֹ
meshiv ra'ah tachat tovah; lo-tamush ra'ah, mibbeito
Whoso rewardeth evil for good, evil shall not depart from his house.

פּוֹטֵר מַיִם, רֵאשִׁית מָדוֹן; וְלִפְנֵי הִתְגַּלַּע, הָרִיב נְטוֹשׁ
poter mayim reshit madon; velifnei hitgalla', hariv netosh
The beginning of strife is as when one letteth out water; therefore leave off contention, before the quarrel break out.

מִשְׁלֵי

נֶפֶשׁ עָמֵל, עָמְלָה לּוֹ: כִּי-אָכַף עָלָיו פִּיהוּ
nefesh amel amelah lo; ki-'achaf alav pihu
The hunger of the labouring man laboureth for him; for his mouth compelleth him.

אִישׁ בְּלִיַּעַל, כֹּרֶה רָעָה; וְעַל-שְׂפָתוֹ, כְּאֵשׁ צָרָבֶת
'ish beliya'al koreh ra'ah; ve'al-sefato, ke'esh tzaravet
An ungodly man diggeth up evil, and in his lips there is as a burning fire.

אִישׁ תַּהְפֻּכוֹת, יְשַׁלַּח מָדוֹן; וְנִרְגָּן, מַפְרִיד אַלּוּף
'ish tahpuchot yeshallach madon; venirgan, mafrid alluf
A froward man soweth strife; and a whisperer separateth familiar friends.

אִישׁ חָמָס, יְפַתֶּה רֵעֵהוּ; וְהוֹלִיכוֹ, בְּדֶרֶךְ לֹא-טוֹב
'ish chamas yefatteh re'ehu; veholicho, bederech lo-tov
A man of violence enticeth his neighbour, and leadeth him into a way that is not good.

עֹצֶה עֵינָיו, לַחְשֹׁב תַּהְפֻּכוֹת; קֹרֵץ שְׂפָתָיו, כִּלָּה רָעָה
'otzeh einav lachshov tahpuchot; koretz sefatav, killah ra'ah
He that shutteth his eyes, it is to devise froward things; he that biteth his lips bringeth evil to pass.

עֲטֶרֶת תִּפְאֶרֶת שֵׂיבָה; בְּדֶרֶךְ צְדָקָה, תִּמָּצֵא
'ateret tif'eret seivah; bederech tzedakah, timmatze
The hoary head is a crown of glory, it is found in the way of righteousness.

טוֹב אֶרֶךְ אַפַּיִם, מִגִּבּוֹר; וּמֹשֵׁל בְּרוּחוֹ, מִלֹּכֵד עִיר
tov erech appayim miggibbor; umoshel berucho, milloched ir
He that is slow to anger is better than the mighty; and he that ruleth his spirit than he that taketh a city.

בַּחֵיק, יוּטַל אֶת-הַגּוֹרָל; וּמֵיְהוָה, כָּל-מִשְׁפָּטוֹ
bacheik yutal et-haggoral; umehashem, kol-mishpato
The lot is cast into the lap; but the whole disposing thereof is of the LORD.

יז

טוֹב פַּת חֲרֵבָה, וְשַׁלְוָה-בָהּ--מִבַּיִת, מָלֵא זִבְחֵי-רִיב
Tov pat charevah veshalvah-vah; mibbayit, malei zivchei-riv
Better is a dry morsel and quietness therewith, than a house full of feasting with strife.

עֶבֶד-מַשְׂכִּיל--יִמְשֹׁל, בְּבֵן מֵבִישׁ
'eved-maskil, yimshol beven mevish
A servant that dealeth wisely shall have rule over a son that dealeth shamefully,

וּבְתוֹךְ אַחִים, יַחֲלֹק נַחֲלָה
uvetoch achim, yachalok nachalah
and shall have part of the inheritance among the brethren.

מִשְׁלֵי

חֲמַת-מֶלֶךְ מַלְאֲכֵי-מָוֶת; וְאִישׁ חָכָם יְכַפְּרֶנָּה
chamat-melech mal'achei-mavet; ve'ish chacham yechapperennah
The wrath of a king is as messengers of death; but a wise man will pacify it.

בְּאוֹר-פְּנֵי-מֶלֶךְ חַיִּים; וּרְצוֹנוֹ, כְּעָב מַלְקוֹשׁ
be'or-penei-melech chayim; uretzono, ke'av malkosh
In the light of the king's countenance is life; and his favour is as a cloud of the latter rain.

קְנֹה-חָכְמָה--מַה-טּוֹב מֵחָרוּץ; וּקְנוֹת בִּינָה, נִבְחָר מִכָּסֶף
kenoh-chochmah mah-tov mecharutz; ukenot binah, nivchar mikkasef
How much better is it to get wisdom than gold! yea, to get understanding is rather to be chosen than silver.

מְסִלַּת יְשָׁרִים, סוּר מֵרָע; שֹׁמֵר נַפְשׁוֹ, נֹצֵר דַּרְכּוֹ
mesillat yesharim sur mera'; shomer nafsho, notzer darko
The highway of the upright is to depart from evil; he that keepeth his way preserveth his soul.

לִפְנֵי-שֶׁבֶר גָּאוֹן; וְלִפְנֵי כִשָּׁלוֹן, גֹּבַהּ רוּחַ
lifnei-shever ga'on; velifnei chishalon, govah ruach
Pride goeth before destruction, and a haughty spirit before a fall.

טוֹב שְׁפַל-רוּחַ, אֶת-עֲנָוִים; מֵחַלֵּק שָׁלָל, אֶת-גֵּאִים
tov shefal-ruach et-'anavim; mechallek shalal, et-ge'im
Better it is to be of a lowly spirit with the humble, than to divide the spoil with the proud.

מַשְׂכִּיל עַל-דָּבָר, יִמְצָא-טוֹב; וּבוֹטֵחַ בַּיהוָה אַשְׁרָיו
maskil al-davor yimtza-tov; uvoteach bahashem ashrav
He that giveth heed unto the word shall find good; and whoso trusteth in the LORD, happy is he.

לַחֲכַם-לֵב, יִקָּרֵא נָבוֹן; וּמֶתֶק שְׂפָתַיִם, יֹסִיף לֶקַח
lachacham-lev yikkarei navon; umetek sefatayim, yosif lekach
The wise in heart is called a man of discernment; and the sweetness of the lips increaseth learning.

מְקוֹר חַיִּים, שֵׂכֶל בְּעָלָיו; וּמוּסַר אֱוִלִים אִוֶּלֶת
mekor chayim sechel be'alav; umusar evilim ivvelet
Understanding is a fountain of life unto him that hath it; but folly is the chastisement of fools.

לֵב חָכָם, יַשְׂכִּיל פִּיהוּ; וְעַל-שְׂפָתָיו, יֹסִיף לֶקַח
lev chacham yaskil pihu; ve'al-sefatav, yosif lekach
The heart of the wise teacheth his mouth, and addeth learning to his lips.

צוּף-דְּבַשׁ, אִמְרֵי-נֹעַם; מָתוֹק לַנֶּפֶשׁ, וּמַרְפֵּא לָעָצֶם
tzuf-devash imrei-no'am; matok lannefesh umarpei la'atzem
Pleasant words are as a honeycomb, sweet to the soul, and health to the bones.

יֵשׁ דֶּרֶךְ יָשָׁר, לִפְנֵי-אִישׁ; וְאַחֲרִיתָהּ, דַּרְכֵי-מָוֶת
yesh derech yashar lifnei-'ish; ve'acharitah, darchei-mavet
There is a way which seemeth right unto a man, but the end thereof are the ways of death.

מִשְׁלֵי

כָּל־דַּרְכֵי־אִישׁ, זַךְ בְּעֵינָיו; וְתֹכֵן רוּחוֹת יְהוָה
kol-darchei-'ish zach be'einav; vetochen ruchot hashem
All the ways of a man are clean in his own eyes; but the LORD weigheth the spirits.

גֹּל אֶל־יְהוָה מַעֲשֶׂיךָ; וְיִכֹּנוּ, מַחְשְׁבֹתֶיךָ
gol el-hashem ma'aseicha; veyikkonu, machshevoteicha
Commit thy works unto the LORD, and thy thoughts shall be established.

כֹּל פָּעַל יְהוָה, לַמַּעֲנֵהוּ; וְגַם־רָשָׁע, לְיוֹם רָעָה
kol pa'al hashem lamma'anehu; vegam-rasha', leyom ra'ah
The LORD hath made every things for His own purpose, yea, even the wicked for the day of evil.

תּוֹעֲבַת יְהוָה, כָּל־גְּבַהּ־לֵב; יָד לְיָד, לֹא יִנָּקֶה
to'avat hashem kol-gevah-lev; yad leyad, lo yinnakeh
Every one that is proud in heart is an abomination to the LORD; my hand upon it! he shall not be unpunished.

בְּחֶסֶד וֶאֱמֶת, יְכֻפַּר עָוֹן; וּבְיִרְאַת יְהוָה, סוּר מֵרָע
bechesed ve'emet yechuppar avon; uveyir'at hashem sur mera
By mercy and truth iniquity is expiated; and by the fear of the LORD men depart from evil.

בִּרְצוֹת יְהוָה, דַּרְכֵי־אִישׁ; גַּם־אוֹיְבָיו, יַשְׁלִם אִתּוֹ
birtzot hashem darchei-'ish; gam-'oyevav, yashlim itto
When a man's ways please the LORD, He maketh even his enemies to be at peace with him.

טוֹב־מְעַט, בִּצְדָקָה--מֵרֹב תְּבוּאוֹת, בְּלֹא מִשְׁפָּט
tov-me'at bitzdakah; merov tevu'ot, belo mishpat
Better is a little with righteousness than great revenues with injustice.

לֵב אָדָם, יְחַשֵּׁב דַּרְכּוֹ; וַיהוָה, יָכִין צַעֲדוֹ
lev adam yechashev darko; vahashem, yachin tza'ado
A man's heart deviseth his way; but the LORD directeth his steps.

קֶסֶם עַל־שִׂפְתֵי־מֶלֶךְ; בְּמִשְׁפָּט, לֹא יִמְעַל־פִּיו
kesem al-siftei-melech; bemishpat, lo yim'al-piv
A divine sentence is in the lips of the king; his mouth trespasseth not in judgment.

פֶּלֶס, וּמֹאזְנֵי מִשְׁפָּט--לַיהוָה; מַעֲשֵׂהוּ, כָּל־אַבְנֵי־כִיס
peles umozenei mishpat lahashem ma'asehu, kol-'avnei-chis
A just balance and scales are the LORD'S; all the weights of the bag are His work.

תּוֹעֲבַת מְלָכִים, עֲשׂוֹת רֶשַׁע: כִּי בִצְדָקָה, יִכּוֹן כִּסֵּא
to'avat melachim asot resha'; ki vitzdakah, yikkon kisse
It is an abomination to kings to commit wickedness; for the throne is established by righteousness.

רְצוֹן מְלָכִים, שִׂפְתֵי־צֶדֶק; וְדֹבֵר יְשָׁרִים יֶאֱהָב
retzon melachim siftei-tzedek; vedover yesharim ye'ehav
Righteous lips are the delight of kings; and they love him that speaketh right.

מִשְׁלֵי

אֹרַח חַיִּים, לְמַעְלָה לְמַשְׂכִּיל--לְמַעַן סוּר, מִשְּׁאוֹל מָטָּה
'orach chayim lema'lah lemaskil; lema'an sur, mishe'ol mattah
The path of life goeth upward for the wise, that he may depart from the nether-world beneath.

בֵּית גֵּאִים, יִסַּח יְהוָה; וְיַצֵּב, גְּבוּל אַלְמָנָה
beit ge'im yissach hashem veyatzev, gevul almanah
The LORD will pluck up the house of the proud; but He will establish the border of the widow.

תּוֹעֲבַת יְהוָה, מַחְשְׁבוֹת רָע; וּטְהֹרִים, אִמְרֵי-נֹעַם
to'avat hashem machshevot ra'; utehorim, imrei-no'am
The thoughts of wickedness are an abomination to the LORD; but words of pleasantness are pure.

עֹכֵר בֵּיתוֹ, בּוֹצֵעַ בָּצַע; וְשׂוֹנֵא מַתָּנֹת יִחְיֶה
'ocher beito botzea batza'; vesonei mattanot yichyeh
He that is greedy of gain troubleth his own house; but he that hateth gifts shall live.

לֵב צַדִּיק, יֶהְגֶּה לַעֲנוֹת; וּפִי רְשָׁעִים, יַבִּיעַ רָעוֹת
lev tzaddik yehgeh la'anot; ufi resha'im, yabbia ra'ot
The heart of the righteous studieth to answer; but the mouth of the wicked poureth out evil things.

רָחוֹק יְהוָה, מֵרְשָׁעִים; וּתְפִלַּת צַדִּיקִים יִשְׁמָע
rachok hashem meresha'im; utefillat tzaddikim yishma
The LORD is far from the wicked; but He heareth the prayer of the righteous.

מְאוֹר-עֵינַיִם, יְשַׂמַּח-לֵב; שְׁמוּעָה טוֹבָה, תְּדַשֶּׁן-עָצֶם
me'or-'einayim yesammach-lev; shemu'ah tovah, tedashen-'atzem
The light of the eyes rejoiceth the heart; and a good report maketh the bones fat.

אֹזֶן--שֹׁמַעַת, תּוֹכַחַת חַיִּים: בְּקֶרֶב חֲכָמִים תָּלִין
'ozen, shoma'at tochachat chayim; bekerev chachamim talin
The ear that hearkeneth to the reproof of life abideth among the wise.

פּוֹרֵעַ מוּסָר, מֹאֵס נַפְשׁוֹ; וְשׁוֹמֵעַ תּוֹכַחַת, קוֹנֶה לֵּב
porea musar mo'es nafsho; veshomea tochachat, koneh lev
He that refuseth correction despiseth his own soul; but he that hearkeneth to reproof getteth understanding.

יִרְאַת יְהוָה, מוּסַר חָכְמָה; וְלִפְנֵי כָבוֹד עֲנָוָה
yir'at hashem musar chochmah velifnei chavod anavah
The fear of the LORD is the instruction of wisdom; and before honour goeth humility.

טז

לְאָדָם מַעַרְכֵי-לֵב; וּמֵיְהוָה, מַעֲנֵה לָשׁוֹן
Le'adam ma'archei-lev; umehashem, ma'aneh lashon
The preparations of the heart are man's, but the answer of the tongue is from the LORD.

מִשְׁלֵי

לֹא יֶאֱהַב־לֵץ, הוֹכֵחַ לוֹ; אֶל־חֲכָמִים, לֹא יֵלֵךְ
lo ye'ehav-letz hocheach lo; el-chachamim, lo yelech
A scorner loveth not to be reproved; he will not go unto the wise.

לֵב שָׂמֵחַ, יֵיטִב פָּנִים; וּבְעַצְּבַת־לֵב, רוּחַ נְכֵאָה
lev sameach yeitiv panim; uve'atzevat-lev ruach neche'ah
A merry heart maketh a cheerful countenance; but by sorrow of heart the spirit is broken.

לֵב נָבוֹן, יְבַקֶּשׁ־דָּעַת; וּפִי כְסִילִים, יִרְעֶה אִוֶּלֶת
lev navon yevakkesh-da'at; ufi chesilim, yir'eh ivvelet
The heart of him that hath discernment seeketh knowledge; but the mouth of fools feedeth on folly.

כָּל־יְמֵי עָנִי רָעִים; וְטוֹב־לֵב, מִשְׁתֶּה תָמִיד
kol-yemei ani ra'im; vetov-lev, mishteh tamid
All the days of the poor are evil; but he that is of a merry heart hath a continual feast.

טוֹב־מְעַט, בְּיִרְאַת יְהוָה--מֵאוֹצָר רָב, וּמְהוּמָה בוֹ
tov-me'at beyir'at hashem me'otzar rav, umehumah vo
Better is little with the fear of the LORD, than great treasure and turmoil therewith.

טוֹב אֲרֻחַת יָרָק, וְאַהֲבָה־שָׁם--מִשּׁוֹר אָבוּס, וְשִׂנְאָה־בוֹ
tov aruchat yarak ve'ahavah-sham; mishor avus, vesin'ah-vo
Better is a dinner of herbs where love is, than a stalled ox and hatred therewith.

אִישׁ חֵמָה, יְגָרֶה מָדוֹן; וְאֶרֶךְ אַפַּיִם, יַשְׁקִיט רִיב
'ish chemah yegareh madon; ve'erech appayim, yashkit riv
A wrathful man stirreth up discord; but he that is slow to anger appeaseth strife.

דֶּרֶךְ עָצֵל, כִּמְשֻׂכַת חָדֶק; וְאֹרַח יְשָׁרִים סְלֻלָה
derech atzel kimsuchat chadek; ve'orach yesharim selulah
The way of the sluggard is as though hedged by thorns; but the path of the upright is even.

בֵּן חָכָם, יְשַׂמַּח־אָב; וּכְסִיל אָדָם, בּוֹזֶה אִמּוֹ
ben chachom yesammach-'av; uchesil adam, bozeh immo
A wise son maketh a glad father; but a foolish man despiseth his mother.

אִוֶּלֶת, שִׂמְחָה לַחֲסַר־לֵב; וְאִישׁ תְּבוּנָה, יְיַשֶּׁר־לָכֶת
'ivvelet simchah lachasar-lev; ve'ish tevunah, yeyasher-lachet
Folly is joy to him that lacketh understanding; but a man of discernment walketh straightforwards.

הָפֵר מַחֲשָׁבוֹת, בְּאֵין סוֹד; וּבְרֹב יוֹעֲצִים תָּקוּם
hafer machashavot be'ein sod; uverov yo'atzim takum
For want of counsel purposes are frustrated; but in the multitude of counsellors they are established.

שִׂמְחָה לָאִישׁ, בְּמַעֲנֵה־פִיו; וְדָבָר בְּעִתּוֹ מַה־טּוֹב
simchah la'ish bema'aneh-fiv; vedavar be'itto mah-tov
A man hath joy in the answer of his mouth; and a word in due season, how good is it!

מִשְׁלֵי

טו

מַעֲנֶה-רַּךְ, יָשִׁיב חֵמָה; וּדְבַר-עֶצֶב, יַעֲלֶה-אָף
Ma'aneh-rach yashiv chemah; udevar-'etzev, ya'aleh-'af
A soft answer turneth away wrath; but a grievous word stirreth up anger.

לְשׁוֹן חֲכָמִים, תֵּיטִיב דָּעַת; וּפִי כְסִילִים, יַבִּיעַ אִוֶּלֶת
leshon chachamim teitiv da'at; ufi chesilim, yabbia ivvelet
The tongue of the wise useth knowledge aright; but the mouth of fools poureth out foolishness.

בְּכָל-מָקוֹם, עֵינֵי יְהוָה; צֹפוֹת, רָעִים וְטוֹבִים
bechol-makom einei hashem tzofot, ra'im vetovim
The eyes of the LORD are in every place, keeping watch upon the evil and the good.

מַרְפֵּא לָשׁוֹן, עֵץ חַיִּים; וְסֶלֶף בָּהּ, שֶׁבֶר בְּרוּחַ
marpei lashon etz chayim; veselef bah, shever beruach
A soothing tongue is a tree of life; but perverseness therein is a wound to the spirit.

אֱוִיל--יִנְאַץ, מוּסַר אָבִיו; וְשֹׁמֵר תּוֹכַחַת יַעְרִים
'evil, yin'atz musar aviv; veshomer tochachat ya'rim
A fool despiseth his father's correction; but he that regardeth reproof is prudent.

בֵּית צַדִּיק, חֹסֶן רָב; וּבִתְבוּאַת רָשָׁע נֶעְכָּרֶת
beit tzaddik chosen rav; uvitvu'at rasha ne'karet
In the house of the righteous is much treasure; but in the revenues of the wicked is trouble.

שִׂפְתֵי חֲכָמִים, יְזָרוּ דָעַת; וְלֵב כְּסִילִים לֹא-כֵן
siftei chachamim yezaru da'at; velev kesilim lo-chen
The lips of the wise disperse knowledge; but the heart of the foolish is not stedfast.

זֶבַח רְשָׁעִים, תּוֹעֲבַת יְהוָה; וּתְפִלַּת יְשָׁרִים רְצוֹנוֹ
zevach resha'im to'avat hashem utefillat yesharim retzono
The sacrifice of the wicked is an abomination to the LORD; but the prayer of the upright is His delight.

תּוֹעֲבַת יְהוָה, דֶּרֶךְ רָשָׁע; וּמְרַדֵּף צְדָקָה יֶאֱהָב
to'avat hashem derech rasha'; umeraddef tzedakah ye'ehav
The way of the wicked is an abomination to the LORD; but He loveth him that followeth after righteousness.

מוּסָר רָע, לְעֹזֵב אֹרַח; שׂוֹנֵא תוֹכַחַת יָמוּת
musar ra le'ozev orach; sonei tochachat yamut
There is grievous correction for him that forsaketh the way; and he that hateth reproof shall die.

שְׁאוֹל וַאֲבַדּוֹן, נֶגֶד יְהוָה; אַף, כִּי-לִבּוֹת בְּנֵי-אָדָם
she'ol va'avaddon neged hashem af, ki-libbot benei-'adam
The nether-world and Destruction are before the LORD; how much more then the hearts of the children of men!

מִשְׁלֵי

עֲטֶרֶת חֲכָמִים עָשְׁרָם; אִוֶּלֶת כְּסִילִים אִוֶּלֶת
'ateret chachamim osheram; ivvelet kesilim ivvelet
The crown of the wise is their riches; but the folly of fools remaineth folly.

מַצִּיל נְפָשׁוֹת, עֵד אֱמֶת; וְיָפִחַ כְּזָבִים מִרְמָה
matzil nefashot ed emet; veyafiach kezavim mirmah
A true witness delivereth souls; but he that breatheth forth lies is all deceit.

בְּיִרְאַת יְהוָה, מִבְטַח-עֹז; וּלְבָנָיו, יִהְיֶה מַחְסֶה
beyir'at hashem mivtach-'oz; ulevanav, yihyeh machseh
In the fear of the LORD a man hath strong confidence; and his children shall have a place of refuge.

יִרְאַת יְהוָה, מְקוֹר חַיִּים--לָסוּר, מִמֹּקְשֵׁי מָוֶת
yir'at hashem mekor chayim; lasur, mimmokeshei mavet
The fear of the LORD is a fountain of life, to depart from the snares of death.

בְּרָב-עָם הַדְרַת-מֶלֶךְ; וּבְאֶפֶס לְאֹם, מְחִתַּת רָזוֹן
berav-'am hadrat-melech; uve'efes le'om, mechittat razon
In the multitude of people is the king's glory; but in the want of people is the ruin of the prince.

אֶרֶךְ אַפַּיִם, רַב-תְּבוּנָה; וּקְצַר-רוּחַ, מֵרִים אִוֶּלֶת
'erech appayim rav-tevunah; uketzar-ruach, merim ivvelet
He that is slow to anger is of great understanding; but he that is hasty of spirit exalteth folly.

חַיֵּי בְשָׂרִים, לֵב מַרְפֵּא; וּרְקַב עֲצָמוֹת קִנְאָה
chayei vesarim lev marpe; urekav atzamot kin'ah
A tranquil heart is the life of the flesh; but envy is the rottenness of the bones.

עֹשֵׁק דָּל, חֵרֵף עֹשֵׂהוּ; וּמְכַבְּדוֹ, חֹנֵן אֶבְיוֹן
'oshek-dal cheref osehu; umechabbedo, chonen evyon
He that oppresseth the poor blasphemeth his Maker; but he that is gracious unto the needy honoureth Him.

בְּרָעָתוֹ, יִדָּחֶה רָשָׁע; וְחֹסֶה בְמוֹתוֹ צַדִּיק
bera'ato yiddacheh rasha'; vechoseh vemoto tzaddik
The wicked is thrust down in his misfortune; but the righteous, even when he is brought to death, hath hope.

בְּלֵב נָבוֹן, תָּנוּחַ חָכְמָה; וּבְקֶרֶב כְּסִילִים, תִּוָּדֵעַ
belev navon tanuach chochmah uvekerev kesilim, tivvadea
In the heart of him that hath discernment wisdom resteth; but in the inward part of fools it maketh itself known.

צְדָקָה תְרוֹמֵם-גּוֹי; וְחֶסֶד לְאֻמִּים חַטָּאת
tzedakah teromem-goy; vechesed le'ummim chattat
Righteousness exalteth a nation; but sin is a reproach to any people.

רְצוֹן-מֶלֶךְ, לְעֶבֶד מַשְׂכִּיל; וְעֶבְרָתוֹ, תִּהְיֶה מֵבִישׁ
retzon-melech le'eved maskil; ve'evrato, tihyeh mevish
The king's favour is toward a servant that dealeth wisely; but his wrath striketh him that dealeth shamefully.

מִשְׁלֵי

יֵשׁ דֶּרֶךְ יָשָׁר, לִפְנֵי-אִישׁ; וְאַחֲרִיתָהּ, דַּרְכֵי-מָוֶת
yesh derech yashar lifnei-'ish; ve'acharitah, darchei-mavet
There is a way which seemeth right unto a man, but the end thereof are the ways of death.

גַּם-בִּשְׂחֹק יִכְאַב-לֵב; וְאַחֲרִיתָהּ שִׂמְחָה תוּגָה
gam-bischok yich'av-lev; ve'acharitah simchah tugah
Even in laughter the heart acheth; and the end of mirth is heaviness.

מִדְּרָכָיו יִשְׂבַּע, סוּג לֵב; וּמֵעָלָיו, אִישׁ טוֹב
midderachav yisba sug lev; ume'alav, ish tov
The dissembler in heart shall have his fill from his own ways; and a good man shall be satisfied from himself.

פֶּתִי, יַאֲמִין לְכָל-דָּבָר; וְעָרוּם, יָבִין לַאֲשֻׁרוֹ
peti ya'amin lechol-davar; ve'arum, yavin la'ashuro
The thoughtless believeth every word; but the prudent man looketh well to his going.

חָכָם יָרֵא, וְסָר מֵרָע; וּכְסִיל, מִתְעַבֵּר וּבוֹטֵחַ
chacham yarei vesar mera'; uchesil, mit'abber uvoteach
A wise man feareth, and departeth from evil; but the fool behaveth overbearingly, and is confident.

קְצַר-אַפַּיִם, יַעֲשֶׂה אִוֶּלֶת; וְאִישׁ מְזִמּוֹת, יִשָּׂנֵא
ketzar-'appayim ya'aseh ivvelet; ve'ish mezimmot, yissane
He that is soon angry dealeth foolishly; and a man of wicked devices is hated.

נָחֲלוּ פְתָאיִם אִוֶּלֶת; וַעֲרוּמִים, יַכְתִּרוּ דָעַת
nachalu fetayim ivvelet; va'arumim, yachtiru da'at
The thoughtless come into possession of folly; but the prudent are crowned with knowledge.

שַׁחוּ רָעִים, לִפְנֵי טוֹבִים; וּרְשָׁעִים, עַל-שַׁעֲרֵי צַדִּיק
shachu ra'im lifnei tovim; uresha'im, al-sha'arei tzaddik
The evil bow before the good, and the wicked at the gates of the righteous.

גַּם-לְרֵעֵהוּ, יִשָּׂנֵא רָשׁ; וְאֹהֲבֵי עָשִׁיר רַבִּים
gam-lere'ehu yissanei rash; ve'ohavei ashir rabbim
The poor is hated even of his own neighbour; but the rich hath many friends.

בָּז-לְרֵעֵהוּ חוֹטֵא; וּמְחוֹנֵן עֲנָוִים אַשְׁרָיו
baz-lere'ehu chote; umechonen anavim ashrav
He that despiseth his neighbour sinneth; but he that is gracious unto the humble, happy is he.

הֲלוֹא-יִתְעוּ, חֹרְשֵׁי רָע; וְחֶסֶד וֶאֱמֶת, חֹרְשֵׁי טוֹב
halo-yit'u choreshei ra'; vechesed ve'emet, choreshei tov
Shall they not go astray that devise evil? But mercy and truth shall be for them that devise good.

בְּכָל-עֶצֶב, יִהְיֶה מוֹתָר; וּדְבַר-שְׂפָתַיִם, אַךְ-לְמַחְסוֹר
bechol-'etzev yihyeh motar; udevar-sefatayim, ach-lemachsor
In all labour there is profit; but the talk of the lips tendeth only to penury.

מִשְׁלֵי

יד

חַכְמוֹת נָשִׁים, בָּנְתָה בֵיתָהּ; וְאִוֶּלֶת, בְּיָדֶיהָ תֶהֶרְסֶנּוּ
Chachmot nashim banetah veitah; ve'ivvelet, beyadeiha tehersennu
Every wise woman buildeth her house; but the foolish plucketh it down with her hands.

הוֹלֵךְ בְּיָשְׁרוֹ, יְרֵא יְהוָה; וּנְלוֹז דְּרָכָיו בּוֹזֵהוּ
holech beyoshero yerei hashem uneloz derachav bozehu
He that walketh in his uprightness feareth the LORD; but he that is perverse in his ways despiseth Him.

בְּפִי-אֱוִיל, חֹטֶר גַּאֲוָה; וְשִׂפְתֵי חֲכָמִים, תִּשְׁמוּרֵם
befi-'evil choter ga'avah; vesiftei chachamim, tishmurem
In the mouth of the foolish is a rod of pride; but the lips of the wise shall preserve them.

בְּאֵין אֲלָפִים, אֵבוּס בָּר; וְרָב-תְּבוּאוֹת, בְּכֹחַ שׁוֹר
be'ein alafim evus bar; verav-tevu'ot, bechoach shor
Where no oxen are, the crib is clean; but much increase is by the strength of the ox.

עֵד אֱמוּנִים, לֹא יְכַזֵּב; וְיָפִיחַ כְּזָבִים, עֵד שָׁקֶר
'ed emunim lo yechazzev; veyafiach kezavim, ed shaker
A faithful witness will not lie; but a false witness breatheth forth lies.

בִּקֶּשׁ-לֵץ חָכְמָה וָאָיִן; וְדַעַת לְנָבוֹן נָקָל
bikkesh-letz chochmah va'ayin; veda'at lenavon nakal
A scorner seeketh wisdom, and findeth it not; but knowledge is easy unto him that hath discernment.

לֵךְ מִנֶּגֶד, לְאִישׁ כְּסִיל; וּבַל-יָדַעְתָּ, שִׂפְתֵי-דָעַת
lech minneged le'ish kesil; uval-yada'ta, siftei-da'at
Go from the presence of a foolish man, for thou wilt not perceive the lips of knowledge.

חָכְמַת עָרוּם, הָבִין דַּרְכּוֹ; וְאִוֶּלֶת כְּסִילִים מִרְמָה
chochemat arum havin darko; ve'ivvelet kesilim mirmah
The wisdom of the prudent is to look well to his way; but the folly of fools is deceit.

אֱוִלִים, יָלִיץ אָשָׁם; וּבֵין יְשָׁרִים רָצוֹן
'evilim yalitz asham; uvein yesharim ratzon
Amends pleadeth for fools; but among the upright there is good will.

לֵב--יוֹדֵעַ, מָרַּת נַפְשׁוֹ; וּבְשִׂמְחָתוֹ, לֹא-יִתְעָרַב זָר
lev, yodea marrat nafsho; uvesimchato, lo-yit'arav zar
The heart knoweth its own bitterness; and with its joy no stranger can intermeddle.

בֵּית רְשָׁעִים, יִשָּׁמֵד; וְאֹהֶל יְשָׁרִים יַפְרִיחַ
beit resha'im yishamed; ve'ohel yesharim yafriach
The house of the wicked shall be overthrown; but the tent of the upright shall flourish.

מִשְׁלֵי

תּוֹרַת חָכָם, מְקוֹר חַיִּים--לָסוּר, מִמֹּקְשֵׁי מָוֶת

torat chacham mekor chayim; lasur, mimmokeshei mavet
The teaching of the wise is a fountain of life, to depart from the snares of death.

שֵׂכֶל-טוֹב, יִתֶּן-חֵן; וְדֶרֶךְ בֹּגְדִים אֵיתָן

sechel-tov yitten-chen; vederech bogedim eitan
Good understanding giveth grace; but the way of the faithless is harsh.

כָּל-עָרוּם, יַעֲשֶׂה בְדָעַת; וּכְסִיל, יִפְרֹשׂ אִוֶּלֶת

kol-'arum ya'aseh veda'at; uchesil, yifros ivvelet
Every prudent man dealeth with forethought; but a fool unfoldeth folly.

מַלְאָךְ רָשָׁע, יִפֹּל בְּרָע; וְצִיר אֱמוּנִים מַרְפֵּא

mal'ach rasho yippol bera'; vetzir emunim marpe
A wicked messenger falleth into evil; but a faithful ambassador is health.

רֵישׁ וְקָלוֹן, פּוֹרֵעַ מוּסָר; וְשֹׁמֵר תּוֹכַחַת יְכֻבָּד

reish vekalon porea musar; veshomer tochachat yechubbad
Poverty and shame shall be to him that refuseth instruction; but he that regardeth reproof shall be honoured.

תַּאֲוָה נִהְיָה, תֶּעֱרַב לְנָפֶשׁ; וְתוֹעֲבַת כְּסִילִים, סוּר מֵרָע

ta'avah nihyah te'erav lenafesh; veto'avat kesilim, sur mera
The desire accomplished is sweet to the soul; and it is an abomination to fools to depart from evil.

הוֹלֵךְ אֶת-חֲכָמִים יֶחְכָּם; וְרֹעֶה כְסִילִים יֵרוֹעַ

holech et-chachamim yechkam; vero'eh chesilim yeroa
He that walketh with wise men shall be wise; but the companion of fools shall smart for it.

חַטָּאִים, תְּרַדֵּף רָעָה; וְאֶת-צַדִּיקִים, יְשַׁלֶּם-טוֹב

chatta'im teraddef ra'ah; ve'et-tzaddikim, yeshallem-tov
Evil pursueth sinners; but to the righteous good shall be repaid.

טוֹב--יַנְחִיל בְּנֵי-בָנִים; וְצָפוּן לַצַּדִּיק, חֵיל חוֹטֵא

tov, yanchil benei-vanim; vetzafun latzaddik, cheil chote
A good man leaveth an inheritance to his children's children; and the wealth of the sinner is laid up for the righteous.

רָב-אֹכֶל, נִיר רָאשִׁים; וְיֵשׁ נִסְפֶּה, בְּלֹא מִשְׁפָּט

rav-'ochel nir rashim; veyesh nispeh, belo mishpat
Much food is in the tillage of the poor; but there is that is swept away by want of righteousness.

חוֹשֵׂךְ שִׁבְטוֹ, שׂוֹנֵא בְנוֹ; וְאֹהֲבוֹ, שִׁחֲרוֹ מוּסָר

chosech shivto sonei veno; ve'ohavo, shicharo musar
He that spareth his rod hateth his son; but he that loveth him chasteneth him betimes.

צַדִּיק--אֹכֵל, לְשֹׂבַע נַפְשׁוֹ; וּבֶטֶן רְשָׁעִים תֶּחְסָר

tzaddik, ochel lesova nafsho; uveten resha'im techsar
The righteous eateth to the satisfying of his desire; but the belly of the wicked shall want.

מִשְׁלֵי

מִפְּרִי פִי־אִישׁ, יֹאכַל טוֹב; וְנֶפֶשׁ בֹּגְדִים חָמָס
mipperi fi-'ish yochal tov; venefesh bogedim chamas
A man shall eat good from the fruit of his mouth; but the desire of the faithless is violence.

נֹצֵר פִּיו, שֹׁמֵר נַפְשׁוֹ; פֹּשֵׂק שְׂפָתָיו, מְחִתָּה־לוֹ
notzer piv shomer nafsho; posek sefatav, mechittah-lo
He that guardeth his mouth keepeth his life; but for him that openeth wide his lips there shall be ruin.

מִתְאַוָּה וָאַיִן, נַפְשׁוֹ עָצֵל; וְנֶפֶשׁ חָרֻצִים תְּדֻשָּׁן
mit'avvah va'ayin nafsho atzel; venefesh charutzim tedushan
The soul of the sluggard desireth, and hath nothing; but the soul of the diligent shall be abundantly gratified.

דְּבַר־שֶׁקֶר, יִשְׂנָא צַדִּיק; וְרָשָׁע, יַבְאִישׁ וְיַחְפִּיר
devar-sheker yisna tzaddik; verasha', yav'ish veyachpir
A righteous man hateth lying; but a wicked man behaveth vilely and shamefully.

צְדָקָה, תִּצֹּר תָּם־דָּרֶךְ; וְרִשְׁעָה, תְּסַלֵּף חַטָּאת
tzedakah titzor tam-darech; verish'ah, tesallef chattat
Righteousness guardeth him that is upright in the way; but wickedness overthroweth the sinner.

יֵשׁ מִתְעַשֵּׁר, וְאֵין כֹּל; מִתְרוֹשֵׁשׁ, וְהוֹן רָב
yesh mit'asher ve'ein kol mitroshesh, vehon rav
There is that pretendeth himself rich, yet hath nothing; there is that pretendeth himself poor, yet hath great wealth.

כֹּפֶר נֶפֶשׁ־אִישׁ עָשְׁרוֹ; וְרָשׁ, לֹא־שָׁמַע גְּעָרָה
kofer nefesh-'ish oshero; verash, lo-shama ge'arah
The ransom of a man's life are his riches; but the poor heareth no threatening.

אוֹר־צַדִּיקִים יִשְׂמָח; וְנֵר רְשָׁעִים יִדְעָךְ
'or-tzaddikim yismach; vener resha'im yid'ach
The light of the righteous rejoiceth; but the lamp of the wicked shall be put out.

רַק־בְּזָדוֹן, יִתֵּן מַצָּה; וְאֶת־נוֹעָצִים חָכְמָה
rak-bezadon yitten matzah; ve'et-no'atzim chochmah
By pride cometh only contention; but with the well-advised is wisdom.

הוֹן, מֵהֶבֶל יִמְעָט; וְקֹבֵץ עַל־יָד יַרְבֶּה
hon mehevel yim'at; vekovetz al-yad yarbeh
Wealth gotten by vanity shall be diminished; but he that gathereth little by little shall increase.

תּוֹחֶלֶת מְמֻשָּׁכָה, מַחֲלָה־לֵב; וְעֵץ חַיִּים, תַּאֲוָה בָאָה
tochelet memushachah machalah-lev; ve'etz chayim, ta'avah va'ah
Hope deferred maketh the heart sick; but desire fulfilled is a tree of life.

בָּז לְדָבָר, יֵחָבֶל לוֹ; וִירֵא מִצְוָה, הוּא יְשֻׁלָּם
baz ledavar yechavel lo; viyrei mitzvah, hu yeshullam
Whoso despiseth the word shall suffer thereby; but he that feareth the commandment shall be rewarded.

מִשְׁלֵי

שְׂפַת-אֱמֶת, תִּכּוֹן לָעַד; וְעַד-אַרְגִּיעָה, לְשׁוֹן שָׁקֶר
sefat-'emet tikkon la'ad; ve'ad-'argi'ah, leshon shaker
The lip of truth shall be established for ever; but a lying tongue is but for a moment.

מִרְמָה, בְּלֶב-חֹרְשֵׁי רָע; וּלְיֹעֲצֵי שָׁלוֹם שִׂמְחָה
mirmah belev-choreshei ra'; uleyo'atzei shalom simchah
Deceit is in the heart of them that devise evil; but to the counsellors of peace is joy.

לֹא-יְאֻנֶּה לַצַּדִּיק כָּל-אָוֶן; וּרְשָׁעִים, מָלְאוּ רָע
lo-ye'unneh latzaddik kol-'aven; uresha'im, male'u ra
There shall no mischief befall the righteous; but the wicked are filled with evil.

תּוֹעֲבַת יְהוָה, שִׂפְתֵי-שָׁקֶר; וְעֹשֵׂי אֱמוּנָה רְצוֹנוֹ
to'avat hashem siftei-shaker; ve'osei emunah retzono
Lying lips are an abomination to the LORD; but they that deal truly are His delight.

אָדָם עָרוּם, כֹּסֶה דָּעַת; וְלֵב כְּסִילִים, יִקְרָא אִוֶּלֶת
'adam arum koseh da'at; velev kesilim, yikra ivvelet
A prudent man concealeth knowledge; but the heart of fools proclaimeth foolishness.

יַד-חָרוּצִים תִּמְשׁוֹל; וּרְמִיָּה, תִּהְיֶה לָמַס
yad-charutzim timshol; uremiyah, tihyeh lamas
The hand of the diligent shall bear rule; but the slothful shall be under tribute.

דְּאָגָה בְלֶב-אִישׁ יַשְׁחֶנָּה; וְדָבָר טוֹב יְשַׂמְּחֶנָּה
de'agah velev-'ish yashchennah; vedavar tov yesammechennah
Care in the heart of a man boweth it down; but a good word maketh it glad.

יָתֵר מֵרֵעֵהוּ צַדִּיק; וְדֶרֶךְ רְשָׁעִים תַּתְעֵם
yater mere'ehu tzaddik; vederech resha'im tat'em
The righteous is guided by his friend; but the way of the wicked leadeth them astray.

לֹא-יַחֲרֹךְ רְמִיָּה צֵידוֹ; וְהוֹן-אָדָם יָקָר חָרוּץ
lo-yacharoch remiyah tzeido; vehon-'adam yakar charutz
The slothful man shall not hunt his prey; but the precious substance of men is to be diligent.

בְּאֹרַח-צְדָקָה חַיִּים; וְדֶרֶךְ נְתִיבָה אַל-מָוֶת
be'orach-tzedakah chayim; vederech netivah al-mavet
In the way of righteousness is life, and in the pathway thereof there is no death.

יג

בֵּן חָכָם, מוּסַר אָב; וְלֵץ, לֹא-שָׁמַע גְּעָרָה
Ben chacham musar av; veletz, lo-shama ge'arah
A wise son is instructed of his father; but a scorner heareth not rebuke.

מִשְׁלֵי

לְפִי-שִׂכְלוֹ, יְהֻלַּל-אִישׁ; וְנַעֲוֵה-לֵב, יִהְיֶה לָבוּז
lefi-sichlo yehullal-'ish; vena'aveh-lev, yihyeh lavuz
A man shall be commended according to his intelligence; but he that is of a distorted understanding shall be despised.

טוֹב נִקְלֶה, וְעֶבֶד לוֹ--מִמִּתְכַּבֵּד, וַחֲסַר-לָחֶם
tov nikleh ve'eved lo; mimmetakkabbed, vachasar-lachem
Better is he that is lightly esteemed, and hath a servant, than he that playeth the man of rank, and lacketh bread.

יוֹדֵעַ צַדִּיק, נֶפֶשׁ בְּהֶמְתּוֹ; וְרַחֲמֵי רְשָׁעִים, אַכְזָרִי
yodea tzaddik nefesh behemto; verachamei resha'im, achzari
A righteous man regardeth the life of his beast; but the tender mercies of the wicked are cruel.

עֹבֵד אַדְמָתוֹ, יִשְׂבַּע-לָחֶם; וּמְרַדֵּף רֵיקִים חֲסַר-לֵב
'oved admato yisba'-lachem; umeraddef reikim chasar-lev
He that tilleth his ground shall have plenty of bread; but he that followeth after vain things is void of understanding.

חָמַד רָשָׁע, מְצוֹד רָעִים; וְשֹׁרֶשׁ צַדִּיקִים יִתֵּן
chamad rasha metzod ra'im; veshoresh tzaddikim yitten
The wicked desireth the prey of evil men; but the root of the righteous yieldeth fruit.

בְּפֶשַׁע שְׂפָתַיִם, מוֹקֵשׁ רָע; וַיֵּצֵא מִצָּרָה צַדִּיק
befesha sefatayim mokesh ra'; vayetzei mitzarah tzaddik
In the transgression of the lips is a snare to the evil man; but the righteous cometh out of trouble.

מִפְּרִי פִי-אִישׁ, יִשְׂבַּע-טוֹב
mipperi fi-'ish yisba'-tov
A man shall be satisfied with good by the fruit of his mouth,

וּגְמוּל יְדֵי-אָדָם, יָשִׁיב לוֹ
ugemul yedei-'adam, yashiv lo
and the doings of a man's hands shall be rendered unto him.

דֶּרֶךְ אֱוִיל, יָשָׁר בְּעֵינָיו; וְשֹׁמֵעַ לְעֵצָה חָכָם
derech evil yashar be'einav; veshomea le'etzah chacham
The way of a fool is straight in his own eyes; but he that is wise hearkeneth unto counsel.

אֱוִיל--בַּיּוֹם, יִוָּדַע כַּעְסוֹ; וְכֹסֶה קָלוֹן עָרוּם
'evil, bayom yivvada ka'so; vechoseh kalon arum
A fool's vexation is presently known; but a prudent man concealeth shame.

יָפִיחַ אֱמוּנָה, יַגִּיד צֶדֶק; וְעֵד שְׁקָרִים מִרְמָה
yafiach emunah yaggid tzedek; ve'ed shekarim mirmah
He that breatheth forth truth uttereth righteousness; but a false witness deceit.

יֵשׁ בּוֹטֶה, כְּמַדְקְרוֹת חָרֶב; וּלְשׁוֹן חֲכָמִים מַרְפֵּא
yesh boteh kemadkerot charev; uleshon chachamim marpe
There is that speaketh like the piercings of a sword; but the tongue of the wise is health.

מִשְׁלֵי

בּוֹטֵחַ בְּעָשְׁרוֹ, הוּא יִפּוֹל; וְכֶעָלֶה, צַדִּיקִים יִפְרָחוּ
boteach be'oshero hu yippol; veche'aleh, tzaddikim yifrachu
He that trusteth in his riches shall fall; but the righteous shall flourish as foliage.

עֹכֵר בֵּיתוֹ, יִנְחַל-רוּחַ; וְעֶבֶד אֱוִיל, לַחֲכַם-לֵב
'ocher beito yinchal-ruach; ve'eved evil, lachacham-lev
He that troubleth his own house shall inherit the wind; and the foolish shall be servant to the wise of heart.

פְּרִי-צַדִּיק, עֵץ חַיִּים; וְלֹקֵחַ נְפָשׂוֹת חָכָם
peri-tzaddik etz chayim; velokeach nefasot chacham
The fruit of the righteous is a tree of life; and he that is wise winneth souls.

הֵן צַדִּיק, בָּאָרֶץ יְשֻׁלָּם; אַף, כִּי-רָשָׁע וְחוֹטֵא
hen tzaddik ba'aretz yeshullam; af, ki-rasha vechotei
Behold, the righteous shall be requited in the earth; how much more the wicked and the sinner!

יב

אֹהֵב מוּסָר, אֹהֵב דָּעַת; וְשׂוֹנֵא תוֹכַחַת בָּעַר
Ohev musar ohev da'at; vesonei tochachat ba'ar
Whoso loveth knowledge loveth correction; but he that is brutish hateth reproof.

טוֹב--יָפִיק רָצוֹן, מֵיְהוָה; וְאִישׁ מְזִמּוֹת יַרְשִׁיעַ
tov, yafik ratzon mehashem; ve'ish mezimmot yarshia
A good man shall obtain favour of the LORD; but a man of wicked devices will He condemn.

לֹא-יִכּוֹן אָדָם בְּרֶשַׁע; וְשֹׁרֶשׁ צַדִּיקִים, בַּל-יִמּוֹט
lo-yikkon adam beresha'; veshoresh tzaddikim, bal-yimmot
A man shall not be established by wickedness; but the root of the righteous shall never be moved.

אֵשֶׁת-חַיִל, עֲטֶרֶת בַּעְלָהּ; וּכְרָקָב בְּעַצְמוֹתָיו מְבִישָׁה
'eshet-chayil ateret ba'lah; ucherakav be'atzmotav mevishah
A virtuous woman is a crown to her husband; but she that doeth shamefully is as rottenness in his bones.

מַחְשְׁבוֹת צַדִּיקִים מִשְׁפָּט; תַּחְבֻּלוֹת רְשָׁעִים מִרְמָה
machshevot tzaddikim mishpat; tachbulot resha'im mirmah
The thoughts of the righteous are right; but the counsels of the wicked are deceit.

דִּבְרֵי רְשָׁעִים אֱרָב-דָּם; וּפִי יְשָׁרִים, יַצִּילֵם
divrei resha'im erov-dam; ufi yesharim, yatzilem
The words of the wicked are to lie in wait for blood; but the mouth of the upright shall deliver them.

הָפוֹךְ רְשָׁעִים וְאֵינָם; וּבֵית צַדִּיקִים יַעֲמֹד
hafoch resha'im ve'einam; uveit tzaddikim ya'amod
The wicked are overthrown, and are not; but the house of the righteous shall stand.

מִשְׁלֵי

גֹּמֵל נַפְשׁוֹ, אִישׁ חָסֶד; וְעֹכֵר שְׁאֵרוֹ, אַכְזָרִי
gomel nafsho ish chased; ve'ocher she'ero, achzari
The merciful man doeth good to his own soul; but he that is cruel troubleth his own flesh.

רָשָׁע--עֹשֶׂה פְעֻלַּת-שָׁקֶר; וְזֹרֵעַ צְדָקָה, שֶׂכֶר אֱמֶת
rasha', oseh fe'ullat-shaker; vezorea tzedakah, secher emet
The wicked earneth deceitful wages; but he that soweth righteousness hath a sure reward.

כֵּן-צְדָקָה לְחַיִּים; וּמְרַדֵּף רָעָה לְמוֹתוֹ
ken-tzedakah lechayim; umeraddef ra'ah lemoto
Stedfast righteousness tendeth to life; but he that pursueth evil pursueth it to his own death.

תּוֹעֲבַת יְהוָה, עִקְּשֵׁי-לֵב; וּרְצוֹנוֹ, תְּמִימֵי דָרֶךְ
to'avat hashem ikkeshei-lev; uretzono, temimei darech
They that are perverse in heart are an abomination to the LORD; but such as are upright in their way are His delight.

יָד לְיָד, לֹא-יִנָּקֶה רָּע; וְזֶרַע צַדִּיקִים נִמְלָט
yad leyad lo-yinnakeh ra'; vezera tzaddikim nimlat
My hand upon it! the evil man shall not be unpunished; but the seed of the righteous shall escape.

נֶזֶם זָהָב, בְּאַף חֲזִיר--אִשָּׁה יָפָה, וְסָרַת טָעַם
nezem zahov be'af chazir; ishah yafah, vesarat ta'am
As a ring of gold in a swine's snout, so is a fair woman that turneth aside from discretion.

תַּאֲוַת צַדִּיקִים אַךְ-טוֹב; תִּקְוַת רְשָׁעִים עֶבְרָה
ta'avat tzaddikim ach-tov; tikvat resha'im evrah
The desire of the righteous is only good; but the expectation of the wicked is wrath.

יֵשׁ מְפַזֵּר, וְנוֹסָף עוֹד
yesh mefazzer venosaf od
There is that scattereth, and yet increaseth;

וְחוֹשֵׂךְ מִיֹּשֶׁר, אַךְ-לְמַחְסוֹר
vechosech miyosher, ach-lemachsor
and there is that withholdeth more than is meet, but it tendeth only to want.

נֶפֶשׁ-בְּרָכָה תְדֻשָּׁן; וּמַרְוֶה, גַּם-הוּא יוֹרֶא
nefesh-berachah tedushan; umarveh, gam-hu yore
The beneficent soul shall be made rich, and he that satisfieth abundantly shall be satisfied also himself.

מֹנֵעַ בָּר, יִקְּבֻהוּ לְאוֹם; וּבְרָכָה, לְרֹאשׁ מַשְׁבִּיר
monea bar yikkevuhu le'om; uverachah, lerosh mashbir
He that withholdeth corn, the people shall curse him; but blessing shall be upon the head of him that selleth it.

שֹׁחֵר טוֹב, יְבַקֵּשׁ רָצוֹן; וְדֹרֵשׁ רָעָה תְבוֹאֶנּוּ
shocher tov yevakkesh ratzon; vedoresh ra'ah tevo'ennu
He that diligently seeketh good seeketh favour; but he that searcheth for evil, it shall come unto him.

מִשְׁלֵי

צִדְקַת יְשָׁרִים, תַּצִּילֵם; וּבְהַוַּת, בֹּגְדִים יִלָּכֵדוּ
tzidkat yesharim tatzilem; uvehavvat, bogedim yillachedu
The righteousness of the upright shall deliver them; but the faithless shall be trapped in their own crafty device.

בְּמוֹת אָדָם רָשָׁע, תֹּאבַד תִּקְוָה; וְתוֹחֶלֶת אוֹנִים אָבָדָה
bemot adam rasha tovad tikvah; vetochelet onim avadah
When a wicked man dieth, his expectation shall perish, and the hope of strength perisheth.

צַדִּיק, מִצָּרָה נֶחֱלָץ; וַיָּבֹא רָשָׁע תַּחְתָּיו
tzaddik mitzarah nechelatz; vayavo rasha tachtav
The righteous is delivered out of trouble, and the wicked cometh in his stead.

בְּפֶה--חָנֵף, יַשְׁחִת רֵעֵהוּ
befeh, chanef yashchit re'ehu
With his mouth the impious man destroyeth his neighbour;

וּבְדַעַת, צַדִּיקִים יֵחָלֵצוּ
uveda'at, tzaddikim yechaletzu
but through knowledge shall the righteous be delivered.

בְּטוּב צַדִּיקִים, תַּעֲלֹץ קִרְיָה; וּבַאֲבֹד רְשָׁעִים רִנָּה
betuv tzaddikim ta'alotz kiryah; uva'avod resha'im rinnah
When it goeth well with the righteous, the city rejoiceth; and when the wicked perish, there is joy.

בְּבִרְכַּת יְשָׁרִים, תָּרוּם קָרֶת; וּבְפִי רְשָׁעִים, תֵּהָרֵס
bevirkat yesharim tarum karet; uvefi resha'im, tehares
By the blessing of the upright a city is exalted; but it is overthrown by the mouth of the wicked.

בָּז-לְרֵעֵהוּ חֲסַר-לֵב; וְאִישׁ תְּבוּנוֹת יַחֲרִישׁ
baz-lere'ehu chasar-lev; ve'ish tevunot yacharish
He that despiseth his neighbour lacketh understanding; but a man of discernment holdeth his peace.

הוֹלֵךְ רָכִיל, מְגַלֶּה-סּוֹד; וְנֶאֱמַן-רוּחַ, מְכַסֶּה דָבָר
holech rachil megalleh-sod; vene'eman-ruach, mechasseh davar
He that goeth about as a talebearer revealeth secrets; but he that is of a faithful spirit concealeth a matter.

בְּאֵין תַּחְבֻּלוֹת, יִפָּל-עָם; וּתְשׁוּעָה, בְּרֹב יוֹעֵץ
be'ein tachbulot yippol-'am; utshu'ah, berov yo'etz
Where no wise direction is, a people falleth; but in the multitude of counsellors there is safety.

רַע-יֵרוֹעַ, כִּי-עָרַב זָר; וְשֹׂנֵא תֹקְעִים בּוֹטֵחַ
ra'-yeroa ki-'arav zar; vesonei toke'im boteach
He that is surety for a stranger shall smart for it; but he that hateth them that strike hands is secure.

אֵשֶׁת-חֵן, תִּתְמֹךְ כָּבוֹד; וְעָרִיצִים, יִתְמְכוּ-עֹשֶׁר
'eshet-chen titmoch kavod; ve'aritzim, yitmechu-'osher
A gracious woman obtaineth honour; and strong men obtain riches.

מִשְׁלֵי

יְרְאַת יְהוָה, תּוֹסִיף יָמִים; וּשְׁנוֹת רְשָׁעִים תִּקְצֹרְנָה
yir'at hashem tosif yamim; ushenot resha'im tiktzorenah
The fear of the LORD prolongeth days; but the years of the wicked shall be shortened.

תּוֹחֶלֶת צַדִּיקִים שִׂמְחָה; וְתִקְוַת רְשָׁעִים תֹּאבֵד
tochelet tzaddikim simchah; vetikvat resha'im toved
The hope of the righteous is gladness; but the expectation of the wicked shall perish.

מָעוֹז לַתֹּם, דֶּרֶךְ יְהוָה; וּמְחִתָּה, לְפֹעֲלֵי אָוֶן
ma'oz lattom derech hashem umechittah, lefo'alei aven
The way of the LORD is a stronghold to the upright, but ruin to the workers of iniquity.

צַדִּיק, לְעוֹלָם בַּל-יִמּוֹט; וּרְשָׁעִים, לֹא יִשְׁכְּנוּ-אָרֶץ
tzaddik le'olam bal-yimmot; uresha'im, lo yishkenu-'aretz
The righteous shall never be moved; but the wicked shall not inhabit the land.

פִּי-צַדִּיק, יָנוּב חָכְמָה; וּלְשׁוֹן תַּהְפֻּכוֹת, תִּכָּרֵת
pi-tzaddik yanuv chochmah uleshon tahpuchot, tikkaret
The mouth of the righteous buddeth with wisdom; but the froward tongue shall be cut off.

שִׂפְתֵי צַדִּיק, יֵדְעוּן רָצוֹן; וּפִי רְשָׁעִים, תַּהְפֻּכוֹת
siftei tzaddik yede'un ratzon; ufi resha'im, tahpuchot
The lips of the righteous know what is acceptable; but the mouth of the wicked is all frowardness.

יא

מֹאזְנֵי מִרְמָה, תּוֹעֲבַת יְהוָה; וְאֶבֶן שְׁלֵמָה רְצוֹנוֹ
Mozenei mirmah to'avat hashem ve'even shelemah retzono
A false balance is an abomination to the LORD; but a perfect weight is His delight.

בָּא-זָדוֹן, וַיָּבֹא קָלוֹן; וְאֶת-צְנוּעִים חָכְמָה
ba-zadon vayavo kalon; ve'et-tzenu'im chochmah
When pride cometh, then cometh shame; but with the lowly is wisdom.

תֻּמַּת יְשָׁרִים תַּנְחֵם; וְסֶלֶף בֹּגְדִים יְשָׁדֵּם
tummat yesharim tanchem; veselef bogedim yeshaddem
The integrity of the upright shall guide them; but the perverseness of the faithless shall destroy them.

לֹא-יוֹעִיל הוֹן, בְּיוֹם עֶבְרָה; וּצְדָקָה, תַּצִּיל מִמָּוֶת
lo-yo'il hon beyom evrah; utzedakah, tatzil mimmavet
Riches profit not in the day of wrath; but righteousness delivereth from death.

צִדְקַת תָּמִים, תְּיַשֵּׁר דַּרְכּוֹ; וּבְרִשְׁעָתוֹ, יִפֹּל רָשָׁע
tzidkat tamim teyasher darko; uverish'ato, yippol rasha
The righteousness of the sincere shall make straight his way; but the wicked shall fall by his own wickedness.

מִשְׁלֵי

הוֹן עָשִׁיר, קִרְיַת עֻזּוֹ; מְחִתַּת דַּלִּים רֵישָׁם
hon ashir kiryat uzzo; mechittat dallim reisham
The rich man's wealth is his strong city; the ruin of the poor is their poverty.

פְּעֻלַּת צַדִּיק לְחַיִּים; תְּבוּאַת רָשָׁע לְחַטָּאת
pe'ullat tzaddik lechayim; tevu'at rasha lechattat
The wages of the righteous is life; the increase of the wicked is sin.

אֹרַח לְחַיִּים, שׁוֹמֵר מוּסָר; וְעֹזֵב תּוֹכַחַת מַתְעֶה
'orach lechayim shomer musar; ve'ozev tochachat mat'eh
He is in the way of life that heedeth instruction; but he that forsaketh reproof erreth.

מְכַסֶּה שִׂנְאָה, שִׂפְתֵי-שָׁקֶר; וּמוֹצִא דִבָּה, הוּא כְסִיל
mechasseh sin'ah siftei-shaker; umotzi dibbah, hu chesil
He that hideth hatred is of lying lips; and he that uttereth a slander is a fool.

בְּרֹב דְּבָרִים, לֹא יֶחְדַּל-פָּשַׁע; וְחוֹשֵׂךְ שְׂפָתָיו מַשְׂכִּיל
berov devarim lo yechdal-pasha'; vechosech sefatav maskil
In the multitude of words there wanteth not transgression; but he that refraineth his lips is wise.

כֶּסֶף נִבְחָר, לְשׁוֹן צַדִּיק; לֵב רְשָׁעִים כִּמְעָט
kesef nivchor leshon tzaddik; lev resha'im kim'at
The tongue of the righteous is as choice silver; the heart of the wicked is little worth.

שִׂפְתֵי צַדִּיק, יִרְעוּ רַבִּים; וֶאֱוִילִים, בַּחֲסַר-לֵב יָמוּתוּ
siftei tzaddik yir'u rabbim; ve'evilim, bachasar-lev yamutu
The lips of the righteous feed many; but the foolish die for want of understanding.

בִּרְכַּת יְהוָה, הִיא תַעֲשִׁיר; וְלֹא-יוֹסִף עֶצֶב עִמָּהּ
birkat hashem hi ta'ashir; velo-yosif etzev immah
The blessing of the LORD, it maketh rich, and toil addeth nothing thereto.

כִּשְׂחוֹק לִכְסִיל, עֲשׂוֹת זִמָּה; וְחָכְמָה, לְאִישׁ תְּבוּנָה
kischok lichsil asot zimmah; vechochemah, le'ish tevunah
It is as sport to a fool to do wickedness, and so is wisdom to a man of discernment.

מְגוֹרַת רָשָׁע, הִיא תְבוֹאֶנּוּ; וְתַאֲוַת צַדִּיקִים יִתֵּן
megorat rasho hi tevo'ennu; veta'avat tzaddikim yitten
The fear of the wicked, it shall come upon him; and the desire of the righteous shall be granted.

כַּעֲבוֹר סוּפָה, וְאֵין רָשָׁע; וְצַדִּיק, יְסוֹד עוֹלָם
ka'avor sufah ve'ein rasha'; vetzaddik, yesod olam
When the whirlwind passeth, the wicked is no more; but the righteous is an everlasting foundation.

כַּחֹמֶץ, לַשִּׁנַּיִם--וְכֶעָשָׁן לָעֵינָיִם: כֵּן הֶעָצֵל, לְשֹׁלְחָיו
kachometz lashinnayim, veche'ashan la'einayim; ken he'atzel, lesholechav
As vinegar to the teeth, and as smoke to the eyes, so is the sluggard to them that send him.

מִשְׁלֵי

רָאשׁ--עֹשֶׂה כַף-רְמִיָּה; וְיַד חָרוּצִים תַּעֲשִׁיר
rash, oseh chaf-remiyah; veyad charutzim ta'ashir
He becometh poor that dealeth with a slack hand; but the hand of the diligent maketh rich.

אֹגֵר בַּקַּיִץ, בֵּן מַשְׂכִּיל; נִרְדָּם בַּקָּצִיר, בֵּן מֵבִישׁ
'oger bakkayitz ben maskil; nirdam bakkatzir, ben mevish
A wise son gathereth in summer; but a son that doeth shamefully sleepeth in harvest.

בְּרָכוֹת, לְרֹאשׁ צַדִּיק; וּפִי רְשָׁעִים, יְכַסֶּה חָמָס
berachot lerosh tzaddik; ufi resha'im, yechasseh chamas
Blessings are upon the head of the righteous; but the mouth of the wicked concealeth violence.

זֵכֶר צַדִּיק, לִבְרָכָה; וְשֵׁם רְשָׁעִים יִרְקָב
zecher tzaddik livrachah; veshem resha'im yirkav
The memory of the righteous shall be for a blessing; but the name of the wicked shall rot.

חֲכַם-לֵב, יִקַּח מִצְוֹת; וֶאֱוִיל שְׂפָתַיִם, יִלָּבֵט
chacham-lev yikkach mitzvot; ve'evil sefatayim, yillavet
The wise in heart will receive commandments; but a prating fool shall fall.

הוֹלֵךְ בַּתֹּם, יֵלֶךְ בֶּטַח; וּמְעַקֵּשׁ דְּרָכָיו, יִוָּדֵעַ
holech battom yelech betach; ume'akkesh derachav, yivvadea
He that walketh uprightly walketh securely; but he that perverteth his ways shall be found out.

קֹרֵץ עַיִן, יִתֵּן עַצָּבֶת; וֶאֱוִיל שְׂפָתַיִם, יִלָּבֵט
koretz ayin yitten atzavet; ve'evil sefatayim, yillavet
He that winketh with the eye causeth sorrow; and a prating fool shall fall.

מְקוֹר חַיִּים, פִּי צַדִּיק; וּפִי רְשָׁעִים, יְכַסֶּה חָמָס
mekor chayim pi tzaddik; ufi resha'im, yechasseh chamas
The mouth of the righteous is a fountain of life; but the mouth of the wicked concealeth violence.

שִׂנְאָה, תְּעוֹרֵר מְדָנִים; וְעַל כָּל-פְּשָׁעִים, תְּכַסֶּה אַהֲבָה
sin'ah te'orer medanim; ve'al kol-pesha'im, techasseh ahavah
Hatred stirreth up strifes; but love covereth all transgressions.

בְּשִׂפְתֵי נָבוֹן, תִּמָּצֵא חָכְמָה
besiftei navon timmatzei chochmah
In the lips of him that hath discernment wisdom is found;

וְשֵׁבֶט, לְגֵו חֲסַר-לֵב
veshevet, legev chasar-lev
but a rod is for the back of him that is void of understanding.

חֲכָמִים יִצְפְּנוּ-דָעַת; וּפִי-אֱוִיל, מְחִתָּה קְרֹבָה
chachamim yitzpenu-da'at; ufi-'evil mechittah kerovah
Wise men lay up knowledge; but the mouth of the foolish is an imminent ruin.

מִשְׁלֵי

כִּי-בִי, יִרְבּוּ יָמֶיךָ; וְיוֹסִיפוּ לְךָ, שְׁנוֹת חַיִּים
ki-vi yirbu yameicha; veyosifu lecha, shenot chayim
For by me thy days shall be multiplied, and the years of thy life shall be increased.

אִם-חָכַמְתָּ, חָכַמְתָּ לָּךְ; וְלַצְתָּ, לְבַדְּךָ תִשָּׂא
'im-chachamta chachamta lach; velatzta, levaddecha tissa
If thou art wise, thou art wise for thyself; and if thou scornest, thou alone shalt bear it.'

אֵשֶׁת כְּסִילוּת, הֹמִיָּה; פְּתַיּוּת, וּבַל-יָדְעָה מָּה
'eshet kesilut homiyah; petayut, uval-yade'ah mah
The woman Folly is riotous; she is thoughtless, and knoweth nothing.

וְיָשְׁבָה, לְפֶתַח בֵּיתָהּ--עַל-כִּסֵּא, מְרֹמֵי קָרֶת
veyashevah lefetach beitah; al-kissa, meromei karet
And she sitteth at the door of her house, on a seat in the high places of the city,

לִקְרֹא לְעֹבְרֵי-דָרֶךְ; הַמְיַשְּׁרִים, אֹרְחוֹתָם
likro le'overei-darech; hamyasherim, orechotam
To call to them that pass by, who go right on their ways:

מִי-פֶתִי, יָסֻר הֵנָּה; וַחֲסַר-לֵב, וְאָמְרָה לּוֹ
mi-feti yasur hennah; vachasar-lev, ve'amerah lo
'Whoso is thoughtless, let him turn in hither'; and as for him that lacketh understanding, she saith to him:

מַיִם-גְּנוּבִים יִמְתָּקוּ; וְלֶחֶם סְתָרִים יִנְעָם
mayim-genuvim yimtaku; velechem setarim yin'am
'Stolen waters are sweet, and bread eaten in secret is pleasant.'

וְלֹא-יָדַע, כִּי-רְפָאִים שָׁם; בְּעִמְקֵי שְׁאוֹל קְרֻאֶיהָ
velo-yada ki-refa'im sham; be'imkei she'ol keru'eiha
But he knoweth not that the shades are there; that her guests are in the depths of the nether-world.

|

מִשְׁלֵי, שְׁלֹמֹה: בֵּן חָכָם, יְשַׂמַּח-אָב; וּבֵן כְּסִיל, תּוּגַת אִמּוֹ
Mishlei, shelomoh ben chacham yesammach-'av; uven kesil, tugat immo
The proverbs of Solomon. A wise son maketh a glad father; but a foolish son is the grief of his mother.

לֹא-יוֹעִילוּ, אוֹצְרוֹת רֶשַׁע; וּצְדָקָה, תַּצִּיל מִמָּוֶת
lo-yo'ilu otzerot resha'; utzedakah, tatzil mimmavet
Treasures of wickedness profit nothing; but righteousness delivereth from death.

לֹא-יַרְעִיב יְהוָה, נֶפֶשׁ צַדִּיק; וְהַוַּת רְשָׁעִים יֶהְדֹּף
lo-yar'iv hashem nefesh tzaddik; vehavvat resha'im yehdof
The LORD will not suffer the soul of the righteous to famish; but He thrusteth away the desire of the wicked.

מִשְׁלֵי

ט

חָכְמוֹת, בָּנְתָה בֵיתָהּ; חָצְבָה עַמּוּדֶיהָ שִׁבְעָה
Chachemot banetah veitah; chatzevah ammudeiha shiv'ah
Wisdom hath builded her house, she hath hewn out her seven pillars;

טָבְחָה טִבְחָהּ, מָסְכָה יֵינָהּ; אַף, עָרְכָה שֻׁלְחָנָהּ
tavechah tivchah masechah yeinah; af, arechah shulchanah
She hath prepared her meat, she hath mingled her wine; she hath also furnished her table.

שָׁלְחָה נַעֲרֹתֶיהָ תִקְרָא--עַל-גַּפֵּי, מְרֹמֵי קָרֶת
shalechah na'aroteiha tikra; al-gappei, meromei karet
She hath sent forth her maidens, she calleth, upon the highest places of the city:

מִי-פֶתִי, יָסֻר הֵנָּה; חֲסַר-לֵב, אָמְרָה לּוֹ
mi-feti yasur hennah; chasar-lev, amerah lo
'Whoso is thoughtless, let him turn in hither'; as for him that lacketh understanding, she saith to him:

לְכוּ, לַחֲמוּ בְלַחֲמִי; וּשְׁתוּ, בְּיַיִן מָסָכְתִּי
lechu lachamu velachami; ushetu, beyayin masacheti
'Come, eat of my bread, and drink of the wine which I have mingled.

עִזְבוּ פְתָאיִם וִחְיוּ; וְאִשְׁרוּ, בְּדֶרֶךְ בִּינָה
'izvu fetayim vichyu; ve'ishru, bederech binah
Forsake all thoughtlessness, and live; and walk in the way of understanding.

יֹסֵר, לֵץ--לֹקֵחַ לוֹ קָלוֹן
yoser letz, lokeach lo kalon
He that correcteth a scorner getteth to himself shame,

וּמוֹכִיחַ לְרָשָׁע מוּמוֹ
umochiach lerasha mumo
and he that reproveth a wicked man, it becometh unto him a blot.

אַל-תּוֹכַח לֵץ, פֶּן-יִשְׂנָאֶךָּ; הוֹכַח לְחָכָם, וְיֶאֱהָבֶךָּ
'al-tochach letz pen-yisna'eka; hochach lechacham, veye'ehaveka
Reprove not a scorner, lest he hate thee; reprove a wise man, and he will love thee.

תֵּן לְחָכָם, וְיֶחְכַּם-עוֹד; הוֹדַע לְצַדִּיק, וְיוֹסֶף לֶקַח
ten lechacham veyechkam-'od; hoda letzaddik, veyosef lekach
Give to a wise man, and he will be yet wiser; teach a righteous man, and he will increase in learning.

תְּחִלַּת חָכְמָה, יִרְאַת יְהוָה; וְדַעַת קְדֹשִׁים בִּינָה
techillat chochmah yir'at hashem veda'at kedoshim binah
The fear of the LORD is the beginning of wisdom, and the knowledge of the All-holy is understanding.

מִשְׁלֵי

עַד-לֹא עָשָׂה, אֶרֶץ וְחוּצוֹת; וְרֹאשׁ, עָפְרוֹת תֵּבֵל
'ad-lo asah eretz vechutzot; verosh, aferot tevel
While as yet He had not made the earth, nor the fields, nor the beginning of the dust of the world.

בַּהֲכִינוֹ שָׁמַיִם, שָׁם אָנִי; בְּחוּקוֹ חוּג, עַל-פְּנֵי תְהוֹם
bahachino shamayim sham ani; bechuko chug, al-penei tehom
When He established the heavens, I was there; when He set a circle upon the face of the deep,

בְּאַמְּצוֹ שְׁחָקִים מִמָּעַל; בַּעֲזוֹז, עִינוֹת תְּהוֹם
be'ammetzo shechakim mimma'al; ba'azoz, inot tehom
When He made firm the skies above, when the fountains of the deep showed their might,

בְּשׂוּמוֹ לַיָּם, חֻקּוֹ, וּמַיִם, לֹא יַעַבְרוּ-פִיו
besumo layam chukko, umayim lo ya'avru-fiv
When He gave to the sea His decree, that the waters should not transgress His commandment,

בְּחוּקוֹ, מוֹסְדֵי אָרֶץ
bechuko, mosedei aretz
when He appointed the foundations of the earth;

וָאֶהְיֶה אֶצְלוֹ, אָמוֹן: וָאֶהְיֶה שַׁעֲשׁוּעִים, יוֹם יוֹם; מְשַׂחֶקֶת לְפָנָיו בְּכָל-עֵת
va'ehyeh etzlo, amon va'ehyeh sha'ashu'im yom yom; mesacheket lefanav bechol-'et
Then I was by Him, as a nursling; and I was daily all delight, playing always before Him,

מְשַׂחֶקֶת, בְּתֵבֵל אַרְצוֹ; וְשַׁעֲשֻׁעַי, אֶת-בְּנֵי אָדָם
mesacheket betevel artzo; vesha'ashu'ai, et-benei adam
Playing in His habitable earth, and my delights are with the sons of men.

וְעַתָּה בָנִים, שִׁמְעוּ-לִי; וְאַשְׁרֵי, דְּרָכַי יִשְׁמֹרוּ
ve'attah vanim shim'u-li; ve'ashrei, derachai yishmoru
Now therefore, ye children, hearken unto me; for happy are they that keep my ways.

שִׁמְעוּ מוּסָר וַחֲכָמוּ; וְאַל-תִּפְרָעוּ
shim'u musar vachachamu, ve'al-tifra'u
Hear instruction, and be wise, and refuse it not.

אַשְׁרֵי אָדָם, שֹׁמֵעַ-לִי: לִשְׁקֹד עַל-דַּלְתֹתַי, יוֹם יוֹם--לִשְׁמֹר, מְזוּזֹת פְּתָחָי
'ashrei adam shomea li lishkod al-daltotai yom yom; lishmor, mezuzot petachai
Happy is the man that hearkeneth to me, watching daily at my gates, waiting at the posts of my doors.

כִּי מֹצְאִי, מָצָא חַיִּים; וַיָּפֶק רָצוֹן, מֵיְהוָה
ki motze'i matza chayim; vayafek ratzon, mehashem
For whoso findeth me findeth life, and obtaineth favour of the LORD.

וְחֹטְאִי, חֹמֵס נַפְשׁוֹ; כָּל-מְשַׂנְאַי, אָהֲבוּ מָוֶת
vechot'i chomes nafsho; kol-mesan'ai, ahavu mavet
But he that misseth me wrongeth his own soul; all they that hate me love death.'

מִשְׁלֵי

לִי-עֵצָה, וְתוּשִׁיָּה; אֲנִי בִינָה, לִי גְבוּרָה
li-'etzah vetushiyah; ani vinah, li gevurah
Counsel is mine, and sound wisdom; I am understanding, power is mine.

בִּי, מְלָכִים יִמְלֹכוּ; וְרוֹזְנִים, יְחֹקְקוּ צֶדֶק
bi melachim yimlochu; verozenim, yechokeku tzedek
By me kings reign, and princes decree justice.

בִּי, שָׂרִים יָשֹׂרוּ; וּנְדִיבִים, כָּל-שֹׁפְטֵי צֶדֶק
bi sarim yasoru; unedivim, kol-shofetei tzedek
By me princes rule, and nobles, even all the judges of the earth.

אֲנִי, אֹהֲבַי אֵהָב; וּמְשַׁחֲרַי, יִמְצָאֻנְנִי
'ani ohavai ehav; umeshacharai, yimtza'uneni
I love them that love me, and those that seek me earnestly shall find me.

עֹשֶׁר-וְכָבוֹד אִתִּי; הוֹן עָתֵק, וּצְדָקָה
'osher-vechavod itti; hon atek, utzedakah
Riches and honour are with me; yea, enduring riches and righteousness.

טוֹב פִּרְיִי, מֵחָרוּץ וּמִפָּז; וּתְבוּאָתִי, מִכֶּסֶף נִבְחָר
tov piryi mecharutz umippaz; utevu'ati, mikkesef nivchar
My fruit is better than gold, yea, than fine gold; and my produce than choice silver.

בְּאֹרַח-צְדָקָה אֲהַלֵּךְ; בְּתוֹךְ, נְתִיבוֹת מִשְׁפָּט
be'orach-tzedakah ahallech; betoch, netivot mishpat
I walk in the way of righteousness, in the midst of the paths of justice;

לְהַנְחִיל אֹהֲבַי יֵשׁ; וְאֹצְרֹתֵיהֶם אֲמַלֵּא
lehanchil ohavai yesh; ve'otzeroteihem amalle
That I may cause those that love me to inherit substance, and that I may fill their treasuries.

יְהוָה--קָנָנִי, רֵאשִׁית דַּרְכּוֹ: קֶדֶם מִפְעָלָיו מֵאָז
hashem kanani reshit darko; kedem mif'alav me'az
The LORD made me as the beginning of His way, the first of His works of old.

מֵעוֹלָם, נִסַּכְתִּי מֵרֹאשׁ--מִקַּדְמֵי-אָרֶץ
me'olam nissachti merosh, mikkadmei-'aretz
I was set up from everlasting, from the beginning, or ever the earth was.

בְּאֵין-תְּהֹמוֹת חוֹלָלְתִּי; בְּאֵין מַעְיָנוֹת, נִכְבַּדֵּי-מָיִם
be'ein-tehomot cholaleti; be'ein ma'yanot, nichbaddei-mayim
When there were no depths, I was brought forth; when there were no fountains abounding with water.

בְּטֶרֶם הָרִים הָטְבָּעוּ; לִפְנֵי גְבָעוֹת חוֹלָלְתִּי
beterem harim hoteba'u; lifnei geva'ot cholaleti
Before the mountains were settled, before the hills was I brought forth;

מִשְׁלֵי

בְּרֹאשׁ-מְרֹמִים עֲלֵי-דָרֶךְ; בֵּית נְתִיבוֹת נִצָּבָה
berosh-meromim alei-darech; beit netivot nitzavah
In the top of high places by the way, where the paths meet, she standeth;

לְיַד-שְׁעָרִים לְפִי-קָרֶת; מְבוֹא פְתָחִים תָּרֹנָּה
leyad-she'arim lefi-karet; mevo fetachim taronnah
Beside the gates, at the entry of the city, at the coming in at the doors, she crieth aloud:

אֲלֵיכֶם אִישִׁים אֶקְרָא; וְקוֹלִי, אֶל-בְּנֵי אָדָם
'aleichem ishim ekra; vekoli, el-benei adam
'Unto you, O men, I call, and my voice is to the sons of men.

הָבִינוּ פְתָאיִם עָרְמָה; וּכְסִילִים, הָבִינוּ לֵב
havinu fetayim aremah; uchesilim, havinu lev
O ye thoughtless, understand prudence, and, ye fools, be ye of an understanding heart.

שִׁמְעוּ, כִּי-נְגִידִים אֲדַבֵּר; וּמִפְתַּח שְׂפָתַי, מֵישָׁרִים
shim'u ki-negidim adabber; umiftach sefatai, meisharim
Hear, for I will speak excellent things, and the opening of my lips shall be right things.

כִּי-אֱמֶת, יֶהְגֶּה חִכִּי; וְתוֹעֲבַת שְׂפָתַי רֶשַׁע
ki-'emet yehgeh chikki; veto'avat sefatai resha
For my mouth shall utter truth, and wickedness is an abomination to my lips.

בְּצֶדֶק כָּל-אִמְרֵי-פִי: אֵין בָּהֶם, נִפְתָּל וְעִקֵּשׁ
betzedek kol-'imrei-fi; ein bahem, niftal ve'ikkesh
All the words of my mouth are in righteousness, there is nothing perverse or crooked in them.

כֻּלָּם נְכֹחִים, לַמֵּבִין; וִישָׁרִים, לְמֹצְאֵי דָעַת
kullam nechochim lammevin; viysharim, lemotze'ei da'at
They are all plain to him that understandeth, and right to them that find knowledge.

קְחוּ-מוּסָרִי וְאַל-כָּסֶף; וְדַעַת, מֵחָרוּץ נִבְחָר
kechu-musari ve'al-kasef; veda'at, mecharutz nivchar
Receive my instruction, and not silver, and knowledge rather than choice gold.

כִּי-טוֹבָה חָכְמָה, מִפְּנִינִים; וְכָל-חֲפָצִים, לֹא יִשְׁווּ-בָהּ
ki-tovah chochmah mippeninim; vechol-chafatzim, lo yishvu-vah
For wisdom is better than rubies, and all things desirable are not to be compared unto her.

אֲנִי-חָכְמָה, שָׁכַנְתִּי עָרְמָה; וְדַעַת מְזִמּוֹת אֶמְצָא
'ani-chochmah shachanti oremah; veda'at mezimmot emtza
I wisdom dwell with prudence, and find out knowledge of devices.

יִרְאַת יְהוָה, שְׂנֹאת-רָע: גֵּאָה וְגָאוֹן וְדֶרֶךְ רָע, וּפִי תַהְפֻּכוֹת שָׂנֵאתִי.
yir'at hashem senot ra ge'ah vega'on vederech ra ufi tahpuchot saneti
The fear of the LORD is to hate evil; pride, and arrogancy, and the evil way, and the froward mouth, do I hate.

מִשְׁלֵי

לְכָה נִרְוֶה דֹדִים, עַד-הַבֹּקֶר; נִתְעַלְּסָה, בָּאֳהָבִים
lechah nirveh dodim ad-habboker; nit'allesah, bo'ohavim
Come, let us take our fill of love until the morning; let us solace ourselves with loves.

כִּי אֵין הָאִישׁ בְּבֵיתוֹ; הָלַךְ, בְּדֶרֶךְ מֵרָחוֹק
ki ein ha'ish beveito; halach, bederech merachok
For my husband is not at home, he is gone a long journey;

צְרוֹר-הַכֶּסֶף, לָקַח בְּיָדוֹ; לְיוֹם הַכֵּסֶא, יָבֹא בֵיתוֹ
tzeror-hakkesef lakach beyado; leyom hakkese, yavo veito
He hath taken the bag of money with him; he will come home at the full moon.'

הִטַּתּוּ, בְּרֹב לִקְחָהּ; בְּחֵלֶק שְׂפָתֶיהָ, תַּדִּיחֶנּוּ
hittattu berov likchah; bechelek sefateiha, taddichennu
With her much fair speech she causeth him to yield, with the blandishment of her lips she enticeth him away.

הוֹלֵךְ אַחֲרֶיהָ, פִּתְאֹם: כְּשׁוֹר, אֶל-טֶבַח יָבֹא; וּכְעֶכֶס, אֶל-מוּסַר אֱוִיל
holech achareiha, pit'om keshor el-tavach yavo; uche'eches, el-musar evil
He goeth after her straightway, as an ox that goeth to the slaughter, or as one in fetters to the correction of the fool;

עַד יְפַלַּח חֵץ, כְּבֵדוֹ--כְּמַהֵר צִפּוֹר אֶל-פָּח; וְלֹא-יָדַע, כִּי-בְנַפְשׁוֹ הוּא.
'ad yefallach chetz kevedo, kemaher tzippor el-pach; velo-yada', ki-venafsho hu
Till an arrow strike through his liver; as a bird hasteneth to the snare--and knoweth not that it is at the cost of his life.

וְעַתָּה בָנִים, שִׁמְעוּ-לִי; וְהַקְשִׁיבוּ, לְאִמְרֵי-פִי
ve'attah vanim shim'u-li; vehakshivu, le'imrei-fi
Now therefore, O ye children, hearken unto me, and attend to the words of my mouth.

אַל-יֵשְׂטְ אֶל-דְּרָכֶיהָ לִבֶּךָ; אַל-תֵּתַע, בִּנְתִיבוֹתֶיהָ
'al-yest el-deracheiha libbecha; al-teta bintivoteiha
Let not thy heart decline to her ways, go not astray in her paths.

כִּי-רַבִּים חֲלָלִים הִפִּילָה; וַעֲצֻמִים, כָּל-הֲרֻגֶיהָ
ki-rabbim chalalim hippilah; va'atzumim, kol-harugeiha
For she hath cast down many wounded; yea, a mighty host are all her slain.

דַּרְכֵי שְׁאוֹל בֵּיתָהּ; יֹרְדוֹת, אֶל-חַדְרֵי-מָוֶת
darchei she'ol beitah; yoredot, el-chadrei-mavet
Her house is the way to the nether-world, going down to the chambers of death.

ח

הֲלֹא-חָכְמָה תִקְרָא; וּתְבוּנָה, תִּתֵּן קוֹלָהּ
Halo-chochmah tikra; utevunah, titten kolah
Doth not wisdom call, and understanding put forth her voice?

מִשְׁלֵי

כִּי, בְּחַלּוֹן בֵּיתִי--בְּעַד אֶשְׁנַבִּי נִשְׁקָפְתִּי
ki bechallon beiti; be'ad eshnabbi nishkafeti
For at the window of my house I looked forth through my lattice;

וָאֵרֶא בַפְּתָאיִם, אָבִינָה בַבָּנִים--נַעַר חֲסַר-לֵב
va'erei vappetayim, avinah vabbanim, na'ar chasar-lev
And I beheld among the thoughtless ones, I discerned among the youths, a young man void of understanding,

עֹבֵר בַּשּׁוּק, אֵצֶל פִּנָּהּ; וְדֶרֶךְ בֵּיתָהּ יִצְעָד
'over bashuk etzel pinnah; vederech beitah yitz'ad
Passing through the street near her corner, and he went the way to her house;

בְּנֶשֶׁף-בְּעֶרֶב יוֹם; בְּאִישׁוֹן לַיְלָה, וַאֲפֵלָה
beneshef-be'erev yom; be'ishon laylah, va'afelah
In the twilight, in the evening of the day, in the blackness of night and the darkness.

וְהִנֵּה אִשָּׁה, לִקְרָאתוֹ; שִׁית זוֹנָה, וּנְצֻרַת לֵב
vehinneh ishah likrato; shit zonah, unetzurat lev
And, behold, there met him a woman with the attire of a harlot, and wily of heart.

הֹמִיָּה הִיא וְסֹרָרֶת; בְּבֵיתָהּ, לֹא-יִשְׁכְּנוּ רַגְלֶיהָ
homiyah hi vesoraret; beveitah, lo-yishkenu ragleiha
She is riotous and rebellious, her feet abide not in her house;

פַּעַם, בַּחוּץ--פַּעַם בָּרְחֹבוֹת; וְאֵצֶל כָּל-פִּנָּה תֶאֱרֹב
pa'am bachutz, pa'am barechovot; ve'etzel kol-pinnah te'erov
Now she is in the streets, now in the broad places, and lieth in wait at every corner.

וְהֶחֱזִיקָה בּוֹ, וְנָשְׁקָה לּוֹ; הֵעֵזָה פָנֶיהָ, וַתֹּאמַר לוֹ
vehechezikah bo venashekah-lo; he'ezah faneiha, vattomar lo
So she caught him, and kissed him, and with an impudent face she said unto him:

זִבְחֵי שְׁלָמִים עָלָי; הַיּוֹם, שִׁלַּמְתִּי נְדָרָי
zivchei shelamim alai; hayom, shillamti nedarai
'Sacrifices of peace-offerings were due from me; this day have I paid my vows.

עַל-כֵּן, יָצָאתִי לִקְרָאתֶךָ; לְשַׁחֵר פָּנֶיךָ, וָאֶמְצָאֶךָּ
'al-ken yatzati likratecha; leshacher paneicha, va'emtza'eka
Therefore came I forth to meet thee, to seek thy face, and I have found thee.

מַרְבַדִּים, רָבַדְתִּי עַרְשִׂי; חֲטֻבוֹת, אֵטוּן מִצְרָיִם
marvaddim ravadti arsi; chatuvot, etun mitzrayim
I have decked my couch with coverlets, with striped cloths of the yarn of Egypt.

נַפְתִּי מִשְׁכָּבִי--מֹר אֲהָלִים, וְקִנָּמוֹן
nafti mishkavi; mor ahalim, vekinnamon
I have perfumed my bed with myrrh, aloes, and cinnamon.

מִשְׁלֵי

לֹא-יָבוּזוּ לַגַּנָּב, כִּי יִגְנוֹב--לְמַלֵּא נַפְשׁוֹ, כִּי יִרְעָב
lo-yavuzu laggannov ki yignov; lemallei nafsho, ki yir'av
Men do not despise a thief, if he steal to satisfy his soul when he is hungry;

וְנִמְצָא, יְשַׁלֵּם שִׁבְעָתָיִם: אֶת-כָּל-הוֹן בֵּיתוֹ יִתֵּן
venimtza yeshallem shiv'atayim; et-kol-hon beito yitten
But if he be found, he must restore sevenfold, he must give all the substance of his house.

נֹאֵף אִשָּׁה חֲסַר-לֵב; מַשְׁחִית נַפְשׁוֹ, הוּא יַעֲשֶׂנָּה
no'ef ishah chasar-lev; mashchit nafsho, hu ya'asennah
He that committeth adultery with a woman lacketh understanding; he doeth it that would destroy his own soul.

נֶגַע-וְקָלוֹן יִמְצָא; וְחֶרְפָּתוֹ, לֹא תִמָּחֶה
nega'-vekalon yimtza; vecherpato, lo timmacheh
Wounds and dishonour shall he get, and his reproach shall not be wiped away.

כִּי-קִנְאָה חֲמַת-גָּבֶר; וְלֹא-יַחְמוֹל, בְּיוֹם נָקָם
ki-kin'ah chamat-gaver; velo-yachmol, beyom nakam
For jealousy is the rage of a man, and he will not spare in the day of vengeance.

לֹא-יִשָּׂא, פְּנֵי כָל-כֹּפֶר; וְלֹא-יֹאבֶה, כִּי תַרְבֶּה-שֹׁחַד
lo-yissa penei chol-kofer; velo-yoveh, ki tarbeh-shochad
He will not regard any ransom; neither will he rest content, though thou givest many gifts.

ז

בְּנִי, שְׁמֹר אֲמָרָי; וּמִצְוֹתַי, תִּצְפֹּן אִתָּךְ
Beni shemor amarai; umitzvotai, titzpon ittach
My son, keep my words, and lay up my commandments with thee.

שְׁמֹר מִצְוֹתַי וֶחְיֵה; וְתוֹרָתִי, כְּאִישׁוֹן עֵינֶיךָ
shemor mitzvotai vechyeh; vetorati, ke'ishon eineicha
Keep my commandments and live, and my teaching as the apple of thine eye.

קָשְׁרֵם עַל-אֶצְבְּעֹתֶיךָ; כָּתְבֵם, עַל-לוּחַ לִבֶּךָ
kosherem al-'etzbe'oteicha; kotevem, al-luach libbecha
Bind them upon thy fingers, write them upon the table of thy heart.

אֱמֹר לַחָכְמָה, אֲחֹתִי אָתְּ; וּמֹדָע, לַבִּינָה תִקְרָא
'emor lachochmah achoti at; umoda', labbinah tikra
Say unto wisdom: 'Thou art my sister', and call understanding thy kinswoman;

לִשְׁמָרְךָ, מֵאִשָּׁה זָרָה; מִנָּכְרִיָּה, אֲמָרֶיהָ הֶחֱלִיקָה
lishmarecha me'ishah zarah; minnocheriyah, amareiha hechelikah
That they may keep thee from the strange woman, from the alien woman that maketh smooth her words.

מִשְׁלֵי

יָפִיחַ כְּזָבִים, עֵד שָׁקֶר; וּמְשַׁלֵּחַ מְדָנִים, בֵּין אַחִים
yafiach kezavim ed shaker; umeshalleach medanim, bein achim
A false witness that breatheth out lies, and he that soweth discord among brethren.

נְצֹר בְּנִי, מִצְוַת אָבִיךָ; וְאַל-תִּטֹּשׁ, תּוֹרַת אִמֶּךָ
netzor beni mitzvat avicha; ve'al-tittosh, torat immecha
My son, keep the commandment of thy father, and forsake not the teaching of thy mother;

קָשְׁרֵם עַל-לִבְּךָ תָמִיד; עָנְדֵם, עַל-גַּרְגְּרֹתֶךָ
kosherem al-libbecha tamid; ondem, al-gargerotecha
Bind them continually upon thy heart, tie them about thy neck.

בְּהִתְהַלֶּכְךָ, תַּנְחֶה אֹתָךְ--בְּשָׁכְבְּךָ, תִּשְׁמֹר עָלֶיךָ
behit'hallechcha tancheh otach, beshachebecha tishmor aleicha
When thou walkest, it shall lead thee, when thou liest down, it shall watch over thee;

וַהֲקִיצוֹתָ, הִיא תְשִׂיחֶךָ
vahakitzota, hi tesichecha
and when thou awakest, it shall talk with thee.

כִּי נֵר מִצְוָה, וְתוֹרָה אוֹר; וְדֶרֶךְ חַיִּים, תּוֹכְחוֹת מוּסָר
ki ner mitzvah vetorah or; vederech chayim, tochechot musar
For the commandment is a lamp, and the teaching is light, and reproofs of instruction are the way of life;

לִשְׁמָרְךָ, מֵאֵשֶׁת רָע; מֵחֶלְקַת, לָשׁוֹן נָכְרִיָּה
lishmorecha me'eshet ra'; mechelkat, lashon nocheriyah
To keep thee from the evil woman, from the smoothness of the alien tongue.

אַל-תַּחְמֹד יָפְיָהּ, בִּלְבָבֶךָ; וְאַל-תִּקָּחֲךָ, בְּעַפְעַפֶּיהָ
'al-tachmod yafeyah bilvavecha; ve'al-tikkachacha, be'af'appeiha
Lust not after her beauty in thy heart; neither let her captivate thee with her eyelids.

כִּי בְעַד-אִשָּׁה זוֹנָה, עַד-כִּכַּר-לָחֶם: וְאֵשֶׁת אִישׁ--נֶפֶשׁ יְקָרָה תָצוּד
ki ve'ad-'ishah zonah, ad-kikkar lachem ve'eshet ish; nefesh yekarah tatzud
For on account of a harlot a man is brought to a loaf of bread, but the adulteress hunteth for the precious life.

הֲיַחְתֶּה אִישׁ אֵשׁ בְּחֵיקוֹ; וּבְגָדָיו, לֹא תִשָּׂרַפְנָה
hayachteh ish esh becheiko; uvegadav, lo tissarafnah
Can a man take fire in his bosom, and his clothes not be burned?

אִם-יְהַלֵּךְ אִישׁ, עַל-הַגֶּחָלִים; וְרַגְלָיו, לֹא תִכָּוֶינָה
'im-yehallech ish al-haggechalim; veraglav, lo tikkaveinah
Or can one walk upon hot coals, and his feet not be scorched?

כֵּן--הַבָּא, אֶל-אֵשֶׁת רֵעֵהוּ: לֹא-יִנָּקֶה, כָּל-הַנֹּגֵעַ בָּהּ
ken, habba el-'eshet re'ehu; lo yinnakeh, kol-hannogea bah
So he that goeth in to his neighbour's wife; whosoever toucheth her shall not go unpunished.

מִשְׁלֵי

אֲשֶׁר אֵין-לָהּ קָצִין--שֹׁטֵר וּמֹשֵׁל
'asher ein-lah katzin, shoter umoshel
Which having no chief, overseer, or ruler,

תָּכִין בַּקַּיִץ לַחְמָהּ; אָגְרָה בַקָּצִיר, מַאֲכָלָהּ
tachin bakkayitz lachmah; agerah vakkatzir, ma'achalah
Provideth her bread in the summer, and gatherest her food in the harvest.

עַד-מָתַי עָצֵל תִּשְׁכָּב; מָתַי, תָּקוּם מִשְּׁנָתֶךָ
'ad-matai atzel tishkav; matai, takum mishenatecha
How long wilt thou sleep, O sluggard? When wilt thou arise out of thy sleep?

מְעַט שֵׁנוֹת, מְעַט תְּנוּמוֹת; מְעַט, חִבֻּק יָדַיִם לִשְׁכָּב
me'at shenot me'at tenumot; me'at chibbuk yadayim lishkav
'Yet a little sleep, a little slumber, a little folding of the hands to sleep'--

וּבָא-כִמְהַלֵּךְ רֵאשֶׁךָ; וּמַחְסֹרְךָ, כְּאִישׁ מָגֵן
uva-chimhallech reshecha; umachsorecha, ke'ish magen
So shall thy poverty come as a runner, and thy want as an armed man.

אָדָם בְּלִיַּעַל, אִישׁ אָוֶן; הוֹלֵךְ, עִקְּשׁוּת פֶּה
'adam beliya'al ish aven; holech, ikkeshut peh
A base person, a man of iniquity, is he that walketh with a froward mouth;

קֹרֵץ בְּעֵינָו, מֹלֵל בְּרַגְלָו; מֹרֶה, בְּאֶצְבְּעֹתָיו
koretz be'einav molel beraglav; moreh, be'etzbe'otav
That winketh with his eyes, that scrapeth with his feet, that pointeth with his fingers;

תַּהְפֻּכוֹת, בְּלִבּוֹ--חֹרֵשׁ רָע בְּכָל-עֵת; מִדְיָנִים יְשַׁלֵּחַ
tahpuchot belibbo, choresh ra bechol-'et; midyanim yeshalleach
Frowardness is in his heart, he deviseth evil continually; he soweth discord.

עַל-כֵּן--פִּתְאֹם, יָבוֹא אֵידוֹ; פֶּתַע יִשָּׁבֵר, וְאֵין מַרְפֵּא
'al-ken, pit'om yavo eido; peta yishaver, ve'ein marpe
Therefore shall his calamity come suddenly; on a sudden shall he be broken, and that without remedy

שֶׁשׁ-הֵנָּה, שָׂנֵא יְהוָה; וְשֶׁבַע, תּוֹעֲבַת נַפְשׁוֹ
shesh-hennah sanei hashem vesheva', to'avat nafsho
There are six things which the LORD hateth, yea, seven which are an abomination unto Him:

עֵינַיִם רָמוֹת, לְשׁוֹן שָׁקֶר; וְיָדַיִם, שֹׁפְכוֹת דָּם-נָקִי
'einayim ramot leshon shaker; veyadayim, shofechot dam-naki
Haughty eyes, a lying tongue, and hands that shed innocent blood;

לֵב--חֹרֵשׁ, מַחְשְׁבוֹת אָוֶן; רַגְלַיִם מְמַהֲרוֹת, לָרוּץ לָרָעָה
lev, choresh machshevot aven; raglayim memaharot, larutz lara'ah
A heart that deviseth wicked thoughts, feet that are swift in running to evil;

מִשְׁלֵי

וְלָמָּה תִשְׁגֶּה בְנִי בְזָרָה; וּתְחַבֵּק, חֵק נָכְרִיָּה
velammah tishgeh veni vezarah; utechabbek, chek nacheriyah
Why then wilt thou, my son, be ravished with a strange woman, and embrace the bosom of an alien?

כִּי נֹכַח, עֵינֵי יְהוָה--דַּרְכֵי-אִישׁ; וְכָל-מַעְגְּלֹתָיו מְפַלֵּס
ki nochach einei hashem darchei-'ish; vechol-ma'gelotav mefalles
For the ways of man are before the eyes of the LORD, and He maketh even all his paths.

עֲווֹנוֹתָיו--יִלְכְּדֻנוֹ אֶת-הָרָשָׁע; וּבְחַבְלֵי חַטָּאתוֹ, יִתָּמֵךְ
'avonotav, yilkeduno et-harasha'; uvechavlei chattato, yittamech
His own iniquities shall ensnare the wicked, and he shall be holden with the cords of his sin.

הוּא--יָמוּת, בְּאֵין מוּסָר; וּבְרֹב אִוַּלְתּוֹ יִשְׁגֶּה
hu, yamut be'ein musar; uverov ivvalto yishgeh
He shall die for lack of instruction; and in the greatness of his folly he shall reel.

I

בְּנִי, אִם-עָרַבְתָּ לְרֵעֶךָ; תָּקַעְתָּ לַזָּר כַּפֶּיךָ
Beni im-'aravta lere'echa; taka'ta lazzar kappeicha
My son, if thou art become surety for thy neighbour, if thou hast struck thy hands for a stranger--

נוֹקַשְׁתָּ בְאִמְרֵי-פִיךָ; נִלְכַּדְתָּ, בְּאִמְרֵי-פִיךָ
nokashta ve'imrei-ficha; nilkadta, be'imrei-ficha
Thou art snared by the words of thy mouth, thou art caught by the words of thy mouth--

עֲשֵׂה זֹאת אֵפוֹא בְּנִי, וְהִנָּצֵל--כִּי בָאתָ בְכַף-רֵעֶךָ
'aseh zot efo beni vehinnatzel, ki vata vechaf-re'echa
Do this now, my son, and deliver thyself, seeing thou art come into the hand of thy neighbour;

לֵךְ הִתְרַפֵּס, וּרְהַב רֵעֶיךָ
lech hitrappes, urehav re'eicha
go, humble thyself, and urge thy neighbour.

אַל-תִּתֵּן שֵׁנָה לְעֵינֶיךָ; וּתְנוּמָה, לְעַפְעַפֶּיךָ
'al-titten shenah le'eineicha; utenumah, le'af'appeicha
Give not sleep to thine eyes, nor slumber to thine eyelids.

הִנָּצֵל, כִּצְבִי מִיָּד; וּכְצִפּוֹר, מִיַּד יָקוּשׁ
hinnatzel kitzvi miyad; uchetzippor, miyad yakush
Deliver thyself as a gazelle from the hand [of the hunter], and as a bird from the hand of the fowler.

לֵךְ-אֶל-נְמָלָה עָצֵל; רְאֵה דְרָכֶיהָ וַחֲכָם
lech-'el-nemalah atzel; re'eh deracheiha vachacham
Go to the ant, thou sluggard; consider her ways, and be wise;

מִשְׁלֵי

הַרְחֵק מֵעָלֶיהָ דַרְכֶּךָ; וְאַל-תִּקְרַב, אֶל-פֶּתַח בֵּיתָהּ
harchek me'aleiha darkecha; ve'al-tikrav, el-petach beitah
Remove thy way far from her, and come not nigh the door of her house;

פֶּן-תִּתֵּן לַאֲחֵרִים הוֹדֶךָ; וּשְׁנֹתֶיךָ, לְאַכְזָרִי
pen-titten la'acherim hodecha; ushenoteicha, le'achzari
Lest thou give thy vigour unto others, and thy years unto the cruel;

פֶּן-יִשְׂבְּעוּ זָרִים כֹּחֶךָ; וַעֲצָבֶיךָ, בְּבֵית נָכְרִי
pen-yisbe'u zarim kochecha; va'atzaveicha, beveit nacheri
Lest strangers be filled with thy strength, and thy labours be in the house of an alien;

וְנָהַמְתָּ בְאַחֲרִיתֶךָ; בִּכְלוֹת בְּשָׂרְךָ, וּשְׁאֵרֶךָ
venahamta ve'acharitecha; bichlot besarecha, ushe'erecha
And thou moan, when thine end cometh, when thy flesh and thy body are consumed,

וְאָמַרְתָּ--אֵיךְ, שָׂנֵאתִי מוּסָר; וְתוֹכַחַת, נָאַץ לִבִּי
ve'amarta, eich saneti musar; vetochachat, na'atz libbi
And say: 'How have I hated instruction, and my heart despised reproof;

וְלֹא-שָׁמַעְתִּי, בְּקוֹל מוֹרָי; וְלִמְלַמְּדַי, לֹא-הִטִּיתִי אָזְנִי
velo-shama'ti bekol morai; velimlammedai, lo-hittiti ozeni
Neither have I hearkened to the voice of my teachers, nor inclined mine ear to them that instructed me!

כִּמְעַט, הָיִיתִי בְכָל-רָע--בְּתוֹךְ קָהָל וְעֵדָה
kim'at hayiti vechal-ra'; betoch kahal ve'edah
I was well nigh in all evil in the midst of the congregation and assembly.'

שְׁתֵה-מַיִם מִבּוֹרֶךָ; וְנֹזְלִים, מִתּוֹךְ בְּאֵרֶךָ
sheteh-mayim mibborecha; venozelim, mittoch be'erecha
Drink waters out of thine own cistern, and running waters out of thine own well.

יָפוּצוּ מַעְיְנֹתֶיךָ חוּצָה; בָּרְחֹבוֹת, פַּלְגֵי-מָיִם
yafutzu ma'yenoteicha chutzah; barechovot, palgei-mayim
Let thy springs be dispersed abroad, and courses of water in the streets.

יִהְיוּ-לְךָ לְבַדֶּךָ; וְאֵין לְזָרִים אִתָּךְ
yihyu-lecha levaddecha; ve'ein lezarim ittach
Let them be only thine own, and not strangers' with thee.

יְהִי-מְקוֹרְךָ בָרוּךְ; וּשְׂמַח, מֵאֵשֶׁת נְעוּרֶךָ
yehi-mekorecha varuch; usemach, me'eshet ne'urecha
Let thy fountain be blessed; and have joy of the wife of thy youth.

אַיֶּלֶת אֲהָבִים, וְיַעֲלַת-חֵן: דַּדֶּיהָ, יְרַוֻּךָ בְכָל-עֵת; בְּאַהֲבָתָהּ, תִּשְׁגֶּה תָמִיד
'ayelet ahavim, veya'alat-chen daddeiha yeravvucha vechol-'et; be'ahavatah, tishgeh tamid
A lovely hind and a graceful doe, let her breasts satisfy thee at all times; with her love be thou ravished always.

מִשְׁלֵי

הָסֵר מִמְּךָ, עִקְּשׁוּת פֶּה; וּלְזוּת שְׂפָתַיִם, הַרְחֵק מִמֶּךָּ
haser mimmecha ikkeshut peh; ulezut sefatayim, harchek mimmeka
Put away from thee a froward mouth, and perverse lips put far from thee.

עֵינֶיךָ, לְנֹכַח יַבִּיטוּ; וְעַפְעַפֶּיךָ, יַיְשִׁרוּ נֶגְדֶּךָ
'eineicha lenochach yabbitu; ve'af'appeicha, yayshiru negdecha
Let thine eyes look right on, and let thine eyelids look straight before thee.

פַּלֵּס, מַעְגַּל רַגְלֶךָ; וְכָל-דְּרָכֶיךָ יִכֹּנוּ
palles ma'gal raglecha; vechol-deracheicha yikkonu
Make plain the path of thy feet, and let all thy ways be established.

אַל-תֵּט-יָמִין וּשְׂמֹאול; הָסֵר רַגְלְךָ מֵרָע
'al-tet-yamin usmol; haser raglecha mera
Turn not to the right hand nor to the left; remove thy foot from evil.

ה

בְּנִי, לְחָכְמָתִי הַקְשִׁיבָה; לִתְבוּנָתִי, הַט-אָזְנֶךָ
Beni lechochemati hakshivah; litvunati, hat-'azenecha
My son, attend unto my wisdom; incline thine ear to my understanding;

לִשְׁמֹר מְזִמּוֹת; וְדַעַת, שְׂפָתֶיךָ יִנְצֹרוּ
lishmor mezimmot; veda'at, sefateicha yintzoru
That thou mayest preserve discretion, and that thy lips may keep knowledge.

כִּי נֹפֶת תִּטֹּפְנָה, שִׂפְתֵי זָרָה; וְחָלָק מִשֶּׁמֶן חִכָּהּ
ki nofet tittofenah siftei zarah; vechalak mishemen chikkah
For the lips of a strange woman drop honey, and her mouth is smoother than oil;

וְאַחֲרִיתָהּ, מָרָה כַלַּעֲנָה; חַדָּה, כְּחֶרֶב פִּיּוֹת
ve'acharitah marah challa'anah; chaddah, kecherev piyot
But her end is bitter as wormwood, sharp as a two-edged sword.

רַגְלֶיהָ, יֹרְדוֹת מָוֶת; שְׁאוֹל, צְעָדֶיהָ יִתְמֹכוּ
ragleiha yoredot mavet; she'ol, tze'adeiha yitmochu
Her feet go down to death; her steps take hold on the nether-world;

אֹרַח חַיִּים, פֶּן-תְּפַלֵּס; נָעוּ מַעְגְּלֹתֶיהָ, לֹא תֵדָע
'orach chayim pen-tefalles; na'u ma'geloteiha, lo teda
Lest she should walk the even path of life, her ways wander, but she knoweth it not.

וְעַתָּה בָנִים, שִׁמְעוּ-לִי; וְאַל-תָּסוּרוּ, מֵאִמְרֵי-פִי
ve'attah vanim shim'u-li; ve'al-tasuru, me'imrei-fi
Now therefore, O ye children, hearken unto me, and depart not from the words of my mouth.

מִשְׁלֵי

בְּלֶכְתְּךָ, לֹא-יֵצַר צַעֲדֶךָ; וְאִם-תָּרוּץ, לֹא תִכָּשֵׁל
belechtecha lo-yetzar tza'adecha; ve'im-tarutz, lo tikkashel
When thou goest, thy step shall not be straitened; and if thou runnest, thou shalt not stumble.

הַחֲזֵק בַּמּוּסָר אַל-תֶּרֶף; נִצְּרֶהָ, כִּי-הִיא חַיֶּיךָ
hachazek bammusar al-teref; nitzereha, ki-hi chayeicha
Take fast hold of instruction, let her not go; keep her, for she is thy life.

בְּאֹרַח רְשָׁעִים, אַל-תָּבֹא; וְאַל-תְּאַשֵּׁר, בְּדֶרֶךְ רָעִים
be'orach resha'im al-tavo; ve'al-te'asher, bederech ra'im
Enter not into the path of the wicked, and walk not in the way of evil men.

פְּרָעֵהוּ אַל-תַּעֲבָר-בּוֹ; שְׂטֵה מֵעָלָיו וַעֲבוֹר
pera'ehu al-ta'avar-bo; seteh me'alav va'avor
Avoid it, pass not by it; turn from it, and pass on.

כִּי לֹא יִשְׁנוּ, אִם-לֹא יָרֵעוּ; וְנִגְזְלָה שְׁנָתָם, אִם-לֹא יַכְשִׁילוּ
ki lo yishnu im-lo yare'u; venigzelah shenatam, im-lo yachshilu
For they sleep not, except they have done evil; and their sleep is taken away, unless they cause some to fall.

כִּי לָחֲמוּ, לֶחֶם רֶשַׁע; וְיֵין חֲמָסִים יִשְׁתּוּ
ki lachamu lechem resha'; veyein chamasim yishtu
For they eat the bread of wickedness, and drink the wine of violence.

וְאֹרַח צַדִּיקִים, כְּאוֹר נֹגַהּ: הוֹלֵךְ וָאוֹר, עַד-נְכוֹן הַיּוֹם
ve'orach tzaddikim ke'or nogah; holech va'or, ad-nechon hayom
But the path of the righteous is as the light of dawn, that shineth more and more unto the perfect day.

דֶּרֶךְ רְשָׁעִים, כָּאֲפֵלָה: לֹא יָדְעוּ, בַּמֶּה יִכָּשֵׁלוּ
derech resha'im ka'afelah; lo yade'u, bammeh yikkashelu
The way of the wicked is as darkness; they know not at what they stumble.

בְּנִי, לִדְבָרַי הַקְשִׁיבָה; לַאֲמָרַי, הַט-אָזְנֶךָ
beni lidvarai hakshivah; la'amarai, hat-'ozenecha
My son, attend to my words; incline thine ear unto my sayings.

אַל-יַלִּיזוּ מֵעֵינֶיךָ; שָׁמְרֵם, בְּתוֹךְ לְבָבֶךָ
'al-yallizu me'eineicha; shomerem, betoch levavecha
Let them not depart from thine eyes; keep them in the midst of thy heart.

כִּי-חַיִּים הֵם, לְמֹצְאֵיהֶם; וּלְכָל-בְּשָׂרוֹ מַרְפֵּא
ki-chayim hem lemotze'eihem; ulechol-besaro marpe
For they are life unto those that find them, and health to all their flesh.

מִכָּל-מִשְׁמָר, נְצֹר לִבֶּךָ: כִּי-מִמֶּנּוּ, תּוֹצְאוֹת חַיִּים
mikkol-mishmar netzor libbecha; ki-mimmennu, totze'ot chayim
Above all that thou guardest keep thy heart; for out of it are the issues of life.

מִשְׁלֵי

ד

שִׁמְעוּ בָנִים, מוּסַר אָב; וְהַקְשִׁיבוּ, לָדַעַת בִּינָה
Shim'u vanim musar av; vehakshivu, lada'at binah
Hear, ye children, the instruction of a father, and attend to know understanding.

כִּי לֶקַח טוֹב, נָתַתִּי לָכֶם; תּוֹרָתִי, אַל-תַּעֲזֹבוּ
ki lekach tov natatti lachem; torati, al-ta'azovu
For I give you good doctrine; forsake ye not my teaching.

כִּי-בֵן, הָיִיתִי לְאָבִי; רַךְ וְיָחִיד, לִפְנֵי אִמִּי
ki-ven hayiti le'avi; rach veyachid, lifnei immi
For I was a son unto my father, tender and an only one in the sight of my mother.

וַיֹּרֵנִי--וַיֹּאמֶר לִי, יִתְמָךְ-דְּבָרַי לִבֶּךָ; שְׁמֹר מִצְוֺתַי וֶחְיֵה
vayoreni, vayomer li, yitmoch-devarai libbecha; shemor mitzvotai vechyeh
And he taught me, and said unto me: 'Let thy heart hold fast my words, keep my commandments, and live;

קְנֵה חָכְמָה, קְנֵה בִינָה; אַל-תִּשְׁכַּח וְאַל-תֵּט, מֵאִמְרֵי-פִי
keneh chochmah keneh vinah; al-tishkach ve'al-tet, me'imrei-fi
Get wisdom, get understanding; forget not, neither decline from the words of my mouth;

אַל-תַּעַזְבֶהָ וְתִשְׁמְרֶךָּ; אֱהָבֶהָ וְתִצְּרֶךָּ
'al-ta'azveha vetishmereka; ehaveha vetitzereka
Forsake her not, and she will preserve thee; love her, and she will keep thee.

רֵאשִׁית חָכְמָה, קְנֵה חָכְמָה; וּבְכָל-קִנְיָנְךָ, קְנֵה בִינָה
reshit chochmah keneh chochmah uvechol-kinyanecha, keneh vinah
The beginning of wisdom is: Get wisdom; yea, with all thy getting get understanding.

סַלְסְלֶהָ וּתְרוֹמְמֶךָּ; תְּכַבֵּדְךָ, כִּי תְחַבְּקֶנָּה
salseleha uteromemeka; techabbedecha, ki techabbekennah
Extol her, and she will exalt thee; she will bring thee to honour, when thou dost embrace her.

תִּתֵּן לְרֹאשְׁךָ, לִוְיַת-חֵן; עֲטֶרֶת תִּפְאֶרֶת תְּמַגְּנֶךָּ
titten leroshecha livyat-chen; ateret tif'eret temaggeneka
She will give to thy head a chaplet of grace; a crown of glory will she bestow on thee.'

שְׁמַע בְּנִי, וְקַח אֲמָרָי; וְיִרְבּוּ לְךָ, שְׁנוֹת חַיִּים
shema beni vekach amarai; veyirbu lecha, shenot chayim
Hear, O my son, and receive my sayings; and the years of thy life shall be many.

בְּדֶרֶךְ חָכְמָה, הֹרֵתִיךָ; הִדְרַכְתִּיךָ, בְּמַעְגְּלֵי-יֹשֶׁר
bederech chochmah horeticha; hidrachticha, bema'gelei-yosher
I have taught thee in the way of wisdom; I have led thee in paths of uprightness.

מִשְׁלֵי

אִם-תִּשְׁכַּב לֹא-תִפְחָד; וְשָׁכַבְתָּ, וְעָרְבָה שְׁנָתֶךָ
'im-tishkav lo-tifchad; veshachavta, ve'arevah shenatecha
When thou liest down, thou shalt not be afraid; yea, thou shalt lie down, and thy sleep shall be sweet.

אַל-תִּירָא, מִפַּחַד פִּתְאֹם; וּמִשֹּׁאַת רְשָׁעִים, כִּי תָבֹא
'al-tira mippachad pit'om; umisho'at resha'im, ki tavo
Be not afraid of sudden terror, neither of the destruction of the wicked, when it cometh;

כִּי-יְהוָה, יִהְיֶה בְכִסְלֶךָ; וְשָׁמַר רַגְלְךָ מִלָּכֶד
ki-hashem yihyeh vechislecha; veshamar raglecha millached
For the LORD will be thy confidence, and will keep thy foot from being caught.

אַל-תִּמְנַע-טוֹב מִבְּעָלָיו--בִּהְיוֹת לְאֵל יָדְךָ לַעֲשׂוֹת
'al-timna'-tov mibbe'alav; bihyot le'el yadecha la'asot
Withhold not good from him to whom it is due, when it is in the power of thy hand to do it.

אַל-תֹּאמַר לְרֵעֲךָ, לֵךְ וָשׁוּב--וּמָחָר אֶתֵּן; וְיֵשׁ אִתָּךְ
'al-tomar lere'acha lech vashuv umachar etten, veyesh ittach
Say not unto thy neighbour: 'Go, and come again, and to-morrow I will give'; when thou hast it by thee.

אַל-תַּחֲרֹשׁ עַל-רֵעֲךָ רָעָה; וְהוּא-יוֹשֵׁב לָבֶטַח אִתָּךְ
'al-tacharosh al-re'acha ra'ah; vehu-yoshev lavetach ittach
Devise not evil against thy neighbour, seeing he dwelleth securely by thee.

אַל-תָּרִיב עִם-אָדָם חִנָּם--אִם-לֹא גְמָלְךָ רָעָה
al-tariv im-'adam chinnam; im-lo gemalecha ra'ah
Strive not with a man without cause, if he have done thee no harm.

אַל-תְּקַנֵּא, בְּאִישׁ חָמָס; וְאַל-תִּבְחַר, בְּכָל-דְּרָכָיו
'al-tekannei be'ish chamas; ve'al-tivchar, bechol-derachav
Envy thou not the man of violence, and choose none of his ways.

כִּי תוֹעֲבַת יְהוָה נָלוֹז; וְאֶת-יְשָׁרִים סוֹדוֹ
ki to'avat hashem naloz; ve'et-yesharim sodo
For the perverse is an abomination to the LORD; but His counsel is with the upright.

מְאֵרַת יְהוָה, בְּבֵית רָשָׁע; וּנְוֵה צַדִּיקִים יְבָרֵךְ
me'erat hashem beveit rasha'; uneveh tzaddikim yevarech
The curse of the LORD is in the house of the wicked; but He blesseth the habitation of the righteous.

אִם-לַלֵּצִים הוּא-יָלִיץ; וְלַעֲנָוִים, יִתֶּן-חֵן
'im-lalletzim hu-yalitz; vela'anavim, yitten-chen
If it concerneth the scorners, He scorneth them, but unto the humble He giveth grace.

כָּבוֹד, חֲכָמִים יִנְחָלוּ; וּכְסִילִים, מֵרִים קָלוֹן
kavod chachamim yinchalu; uchesilim, merim kalon
The wise shall inherit honour; but as for the fools, they carry away shame.

מִשְׁלֵי

כִּי אֶת אֲשֶׁר יֶאֱהַב יְהוָה יוֹכִיחַ; וּכְאָב, אֶת-בֵּן יִרְצֶה
ki et asher ye'ehav hashem yochiach; uche'av, et-ben yirtzeh
For whom the LORD loveth He correcteth, even as a father the son in whom he delighteth.

אַשְׁרֵי אָדָם, מָצָא חָכְמָה; וְאָדָם, יָפִיק תְּבוּנָה.
'ashrei adam matza chochmah ve'adam, yafik tevunah
Happy is the man that findeth wisdom, and the man that obtaineth understanding.

כִּי טוֹב סַחְרָהּ, מִסְּחַר-כָּסֶף; וּמֵחָרוּץ, תְּבוּאָתָהּ
ki tov sachrah missechar-kasef; umecharutz, tevu'atah
For the merchandise of it is better than the merchandise of silver, and the gain thereof than fine gold.

יְקָרָה הִיא, מִפְּנִינִים; וְכָל-חֲפָצֶיךָ, לֹא יִשְׁווּ-בָהּ
yekarah hi mippeninim; vechol-chafatzeicha, lo yishvu-vah
She is more precious than rubies; and all the things thou canst desire are not to be compared unto her.

אֹרֶךְ יָמִים, בִּימִינָהּ; בִּשְׂמֹאולָהּ, עֹשֶׁר וְכָבוֹד
'orech yamim biyminah; bismolah, osher vechavod
Length of days is in her right hand; in her left hand are riches and honour.

דְּרָכֶיהָ דַרְכֵי-נֹעַם; וְכָל-נְתִיבוֹתֶיהָ שָׁלוֹם
deracheiha darchei-no'am; vechol-netivoteiha shalom
Her ways are ways of pleasantness, and all her paths are peace.

עֵץ-חַיִּים הִיא, לַמַּחֲזִיקִים בָּהּ; וְתֹמְכֶיהָ מְאֻשָּׁר
'etz-chayim hi lammachazikim bah; vetomcheiha me'ushar
She is a tree of life to them that lay hold upon her, and happy is every one that holdest her fast.

יְהוָה--בְּחָכְמָה יָסַד-אָרֶץ; כּוֹנֵן שָׁמַיִם, בִּתְבוּנָה
hashem bechochmah yasad-'aretz; konen shamayim, bitvunah
The LORD by wisdom founded the earth; by understanding He established the heavens.

בְּדַעְתּוֹ, תְּהוֹמוֹת נִבְקָעוּ; וּשְׁחָקִים, יִרְעֲפוּ-טָל
beda'to tehomot nivka'u; ushechakim, yir'afu-tal
By His knowledge the depths were broken up, and the skies drop down the dew.

בְּנִי, אַל-יָלֻזוּ מֵעֵינֶיךָ; נְצֹר תֻּשִׁיָּה, וּמְזִמָּה
beni al-yaluzu me'eineicha; netzor tushiyah, umezimmah
My son, let not them depart from thine eyes; keep sound wisdom and discretion;

וְיִהְיוּ חַיִּים לְנַפְשֶׁךָ; וְחֵן, לְגַרְגְּרֹתֶיךָ
veyihyu chayim lenafshecha; vechen, legargeroteicha
So shall they be life unto thy soul, and grace to thy neck.

אָז תֵּלֵךְ לָבֶטַח דַּרְכֶּךָ; וְרַגְלְךָ, לֹא תִגּוֹף
'az telech lavetach darkecha; veraglecha, lo tiggof
Then shalt thou walk in thy way securely, and thou shalt not dash thy foot.

מִשְׁלֵי

ג

בְּנִי, תּוֹרָתִי אַל-תִּשְׁכָּח; וּמִצְוֺתַי, יִצֹּר לִבֶּךָ
Beni torati al-tishkach; umitzvotai, yitzor libbecha
My son, forget not my teaching; but let thy heart keep my commandments;

כִּי אֹרֶךְ יָמִים, וּשְׁנוֹת חַיִּים--וְשָׁלוֹם, יוֹסִיפוּ לָךְ
ki orech yamim ushenot chayim; veshalom, yosifu lach
For length of days, and years of life, and peace, will they add to thee.

חֶסֶד וֶאֱמֶת, אַל-יַעַזְבֻךָ: קָשְׁרֵם עַל-גַּרְגְּרוֹתֶיךָ; כָּתְבֵם, עַל-לוּחַ לִבֶּךָ
chesed ve'emet, al-ya'azvucha kosherem al-gargeroteicha; kotevem, al-luach libbecha
Let not kindness and truth forsake thee; bind them about thy neck, write them upon the table of thy heart;

וּמְצָא-חֵן וְשֵׂכֶל-טוֹב--בְּעֵינֵי אֱלֹהִים וְאָדָם
umetza-chen vesechel-tov; be'einei elohim ve'adam
So shalt thou find grace and good favour in the sight of God and man.

בְּטַח אֶל-יְהוָה, בְּכָל-לִבֶּךָ; וְאֶל-בִּינָתְךָ, אַל-תִּשָּׁעֵן
betach el-hashem bechol-libbecha; ve'el-binatcha, al-tisha'en
Trust in the LORD with all thy heart, and lean not upon thine own understanding.

בְּכָל-דְּרָכֶיךָ דָעֵהוּ; וְהוּא, יְיַשֵּׁר אֹרְחֹתֶיךָ
bechol-deracheicha da'ehu; vehu, yeyasher orchoteicha
In all thy ways acknowledge Him, and He will direct thy paths.

אַל-תְּהִי חָכָם בְּעֵינֶיךָ; יְרָא אֶת-יְהוָה, וְסוּר מֵרָע
'al-tehi chacham be'eineicha; yera et-hashem vesur mera
Be not wise in thine own eyes; fear the LORD, and depart from evil;

רִפְאוּת, תְּהִי לְשָׁרֶּךָ; וְשִׁקּוּי, לְעַצְמוֹתֶיךָ
rif'ut tehi lesharrecha; veshikkui, le'atzmoteicha
It shall be health to thy navel, and marrow to thy bones.

כַּבֵּד אֶת-יְהוָה, מֵהוֹנֶךָ; וּמֵרֵאשִׁית, כָּל-תְּבוּאָתֶךָ
kabbed et-hashem mehonecha; umereshit, kol-tevu'atecha
Honour the LORD with thy substance, and with the first-fruits of all thine increase;

וְיִמָּלְאוּ אֲסָמֶיךָ שָׂבָע; וְתִירוֹשׁ, יְקָבֶיךָ יִפְרֹצוּ
veyimmale'u asameicha sava'; vetirosh, yekaveicha yifrotzu
So shall thy barns be filled with plenty, and thy vats shall overflow with new wine.

מוּסַר יְהוָה, בְּנִי אַל-תִּמְאָס; וְאַל-תָּקֹץ, בְּתוֹכַחְתּוֹ
musar hashem beni al-tim'as; ve'al-takotz, betochachto
My son, despise not the chastening of the LORD, neither spurn thou His correction;

מִשְׁלֵי

לְהַצִּילְךָ, מִדֶּרֶךְ רָע; מֵאִישׁ, מְדַבֵּר תַּהְפֻּכוֹת
lehatzilecha midderech ra'; me'ish, medabber tahpuchot
To deliver thee from the way of evil, from the men that speak froward things;

הַעֹזְבִים, אָרְחוֹת יֹשֶׁר--לָלֶכֶת, בְּדַרְכֵי-חֹשֶׁךְ
ha'ozevim orechot yosher; lalechet, bedarchei-choshech
Who leave the paths of uprightness, to walk in the ways of darkness;

הַשְּׂמֵחִים, לַעֲשׂוֹת רָע; יָגִילוּ, בְּתַהְפֻּכוֹת רָע
hassemechim la'asot ra'; yagilu, betahpuchot ra
Who rejoice to do evil, and delight in the frowardness of evil;

אֲשֶׁר אָרְחֹתֵיהֶם עִקְּשִׁים; וּנְלוֹזִים, בְּמַעְגְּלוֹתָם
'asher orechoteihem ikkeshim; unelozim, bema'gelotam
Who are crooked in their ways, and perverse in their paths;

לְהַצִּילְךָ, מֵאִשָּׁה זָרָה; מִנָּכְרִיָּה, אֲמָרֶיהָ הֶחֱלִיקָה
lehatzilecha me'ishah zarah; minnocheriyah, amareiha hechelikah
To deliver thee from the strange woman, even from the alien woman that maketh smooth her words;

הַעֹזֶבֶת, אַלּוּף נְעוּרֶיהָ; וְאֶת-בְּרִית אֱלֹהֶיהָ שָׁכֵחָה
ha'ozevet alluf ne'ureiha; ve'et-berit eloheiha shachechah
That forsaketh the lord of her youth, and forgetteth the covenant of her God.

כִּי שָׁחָה אֶל-מָוֶת בֵּיתָהּ; וְאֶל-רְפָאִים, מַעְגְּלֹתֶיהָ
ki shachah el-mavet beitah; ve'el-refa'im, ma'geloteiha
For her house sinketh down unto death, and her paths unto the shades;

כָּל-בָּאֶיהָ, לֹא יְשׁוּבוּן; וְלֹא-יַשִּׂיגוּ, אָרְחוֹת חַיִּים
kol-ba'eiha lo yeshuvun; velo-yassigu, orechot chayim
None that go unto her return, neither do they attain unto the paths of life;

לְמַעַן--תֵּלֵךְ, בְּדֶרֶךְ טוֹבִים; וְאָרְחוֹת צַדִּיקִים תִּשְׁמֹר
lema'an, telech bederech tovim; ve'orechot tzaddikim tishmor
That thou mayest walk in the way of good men, and keep the paths of the righteous.

כִּי-יְשָׁרִים יִשְׁכְּנוּ-אָרֶץ; וּתְמִימִים, יִוָּתְרוּ בָהּ
ki-yesharim yishkenu-'aretz; utemimim, yivvateru vah
For the upright shall dwell in the land, and the whole-hearted shall remain in it.

וּרְשָׁעִים, מֵאֶרֶץ יִכָּרֵתוּ; וּבוֹגְדִים, יִסְּחוּ מִמֶּנָּה
uresha'im me'eretz yikkaretu; uvogedim, yissechu mimmennah
But the wicked shall be cut off from the land, and the faithless shall be plucked up out of it.

מִשְׁלֵי

ב

בְּנִי, אִם-תִּקַּח אֲמָרָי; וּמִצְוֹתַי, תִּצְפֹּן אִתָּךְ
Beni im-tikkach amarai; umitzvotai, titzpon ittach
My son, if thou wilt receive my words, and lay up my commandments with thee;

לְהַקְשִׁיב לַחָכְמָה אָזְנֶךָ; תַּטֶּה לִבְּךָ, לַתְּבוּנָה
lehakshiv lachachemah ozenecha; tatteh libbecha, lattevunah
So that thou make thine ear attend unto wisdom, and thy heart incline to discernment;

כִּי אִם לַבִּינָה תִקְרָא; לַתְּבוּנָה, תִּתֵּן קוֹלֶךָ
ki im labbinah tikra; lattevunah, titten kolecha
Yea, if thou call for understanding, and lift up thy voice for discernment;

אִם-תְּבַקְשֶׁנָּה כַכָּסֶף; וְכַמַּטְמוֹנִים תַּחְפְּשֶׂנָּה
'im-tevakshennah chakkasef; vechammatmonim tachpesennah
If thou seek her as silver, and search for her as for hid treasures;

אָז--תָּבִין, יִרְאַת יְהוָה; וְדַעַת אֱלֹהִים תִּמְצָא
'az, tavin yir'at hashem veda'at elohim timtza
Then shalt thou understand the fear of the LORD, and find the knowledge of God.

כִּי-יְהוָה, יִתֵּן חָכְמָה; מִפִּיו, דַּעַת וּתְבוּנָה
ki-hashem yitten chochmah mippiv, da'at utevunah
For the LORD giveth wisdom, out of His mouth cometh knowledge and discernment;

יִצְפֹּן לַיְשָׁרִים, תּוּשִׁיָּה; מָגֵן, לְהֹלְכֵי תֹם
yitzpon laysharim tushiyah; magen, leholechei tom
He layeth up sound wisdom for the upright, He is a shield to them that walk in integrity;

לִנְצֹר, אָרְחוֹת מִשְׁפָּט; וְדֶרֶךְ חֲסִידָו יִשְׁמֹר
lintzor arechot mishpat; vederech chasidav yishmor
That He may guard the paths of justice, and preserve the way of His godly ones.

אָז--תָּבִין, צֶדֶק וּמִשְׁפָּט; וּמֵישָׁרִים, כָּל-מַעְגַּל-טוֹב
'az, tavin tzedek umishpat; umeisharim, kol-ma'gal-tov
Then shalt thou understand righteousness and justice, and equity, yea, every good path.

כִּי-תָבוֹא חָכְמָה בְלִבֶּךָ; וְדַעַת, לְנַפְשְׁךָ יִנְעָם
ki-tavo chochmah velibbecha; veda'at, lenafshecha yin'am
For wisdom shall enter into thy heart, and knowledge shall be pleasant unto thy soul;

מְזִמָּה, תִּשְׁמֹר עָלֶיךָ; תְּבוּנָה תִנְצְרֶכָּה
mezimmah tishmor aleicha, tevunah tintzerekkah
Discretion shall watch over thee, discernment shall guard thee;

מִשְׁלֵי

תָּשׁוּבוּ, לְתוֹכַחְתִּי: הִנֵּה אַבִּיעָה לָכֶם רוּחִי; אוֹדִיעָה דְבָרַי אֶתְכֶם
tashuvu, letochachti hinneh abbi'ah lachem ruchi; odi'ah devarai etchem
Turn you at my reproof; behold, I will pour out my spirit unto you, I will make known my words unto you.

יַעַן קָרָאתִי, וַתְּמָאֵנוּ; נָטִיתִי יָדִי, וְאֵין מַקְשִׁיב
ya'an karati vattema'enu; natiti yadi, ve'ein makshiv
Because I have called, and ye refused, I have stretched out my hand, and no man attended,

וַתִּפְרְעוּ כָל-עֲצָתִי; וְתוֹכַחְתִּי, לֹא אֲבִיתֶם
vattifre'u chol-'atzati; vetochachti, lo avitem
But ye have set at nought all my counsel, and would none of my reproof;

גַּם-אֲנִי, בְּאֵידְכֶם אֶשְׂחָק; אֶלְעַג, בְּבֹא פַחְדְּכֶם
gam-'ani be'eidechem eschak; el'ag, bevo fachdechem
I also, in your calamity, will laugh, I will mock when your dread cometh;

בְּבֹא כְשׁוֹאָה, פַּחְדְּכֶם--וְאֵידְכֶם, כְּסוּפָה יֶאֱתֶה
bevo chesho'ah pachdechem, ve'eidechem kesufah ye'eteh
When your dread cometh as a storm, and your calamity cometh on as a whirlwind;

בְּבֹא עֲלֵיכֶם, צָרָה וְצוּקָה
bevo aleichem, tzarah vetzukah
when trouble and distress come upon you.

אָז יִקְרָאֻנְנִי, וְלֹא אֶעֱנֶה; יְשַׁחֲרֻנְנִי, וְלֹא יִמְצָאֻנְנִי
'az yikra'uneni velo e'eneh; yeshacharuneni, velo yimtza'uneni
Then will they call me, but I will not answer, they will seek me earnestly, but they shall not find me.

תַּחַת, כִּי-שָׂנְאוּ דָעַת; וְיִרְאַת יְהוָה, לֹא בָחָרוּ
tachat ki-sane'u da'at; veyir'at hashem lo vacharu
For that they hated knowledge, and did not choose the fear of the LORD;

לֹא-אָבוּ לַעֲצָתִי; נָאֲצוּ, כָּל-תּוֹכַחְתִּי
lo-'avu la'atzati; na'atzu, kol-tochachti
They would none of my counsel, they despised all my reproof.

וְיֹאכְלוּ, מִפְּרִי דַרְכָּם; וּמִמֹּעֲצֹתֵיהֶם יִשְׂבָּעוּ
veyochelu mipperi darkam; umimmo'atzoteihem yisba'u
Therefore shall they eat of the fruit of their own way, and be filled with their own devices.

כִּי מְשׁוּבַת פְּתָיִם תַּהַרְגֵם; וְשַׁלְוַת כְּסִילִים תְּאַבְּדֵם
ki meshuvat petayim tahargem; veshalvat kesilim te'abbedem
For the waywardness of the thoughtless shall slay them, and the confidence of fools shall destroy them.

וְשֹׁמֵעַ לִי, יִשְׁכָּן-בֶּטַח; וְשַׁאֲנַן, מִפַּחַד רָעָה
veshomea li yishkon-betach; vesha'anan, mippachad ra'ah
But whoso hearkeneth unto me shall dwell securely, and shall be quiet without fear of evil.'

מִשְׁלֵי

נִבְלָעֵם, כִּשְׁאוֹל חַיִּים; וּתְמִימִים, כְּיוֹרְדֵי בוֹר
nivla'em kish'ol chayim; utemimim, keyoredei vor
Let us swallow them up alive as the grave, and whole, as those that go down into the pit;

כָּל-הוֹן יָקָר נִמְצָא; נְמַלֵּא בָתֵּינוּ שָׁלָל
kol-hon yakar nimtza; nemallei vatteinu shalal
We shall find all precious substance, we shall fill our houses with spoil;

גּוֹרָלְךָ, תַּפִּיל בְּתוֹכֵנוּ; כִּיס אֶחָד, יִהְיֶה לְכֻלָּנוּ
goralcha tappil betochenu; kis echad, yihyeh lechullanu
Cast in thy lot among us; let us all have one purse'--

בְּנִי--אַל-תֵּלֵךְ בְּדֶרֶךְ אִתָּם; מְנַע רַגְלְךָ, מִנְּתִיבָתָם
beni, al-telech bederech ittam; mena raglecha, minnetivatam
My son, walk not thou in the way with them, restrain thy foot from their path;

כִּי רַגְלֵיהֶם, לָרַע יָרוּצוּ; וִימַהֲרוּ, לִשְׁפָּךְ-דָּם
ki ragleihem lara yarutzu; vimaharu, lishpoch-dam
For their feet run to evil, and they make haste to shed blood.

כִּי-חִנָּם, מְזֹרָה הָרָשֶׁת--בְּעֵינֵי, כָל-בַּעַל כָּנָף
ki-chinnam mezorah harashet; be'einei, chol-ba'al kanaf
For in vain the net is spread in the eyes of any bird;

וְהֵם, לְדָמָם יֶאֱרֹבוּ; יִצְפְּנוּ, לְנַפְשֹׁתָם
vehem ledamam ye'erovu; yitzpenu, lenafshotam
And these lie in wait for their own blood, they lurk for their own lives.

כֵּן--אָרְחוֹת, כָּל-בֹּצֵעַ בָּצַע; אֶת-נֶפֶשׁ בְּעָלָיו יִקָּח
ken, orechot kol-botzea batza'; et-nefesh be'alav yikkach
So are the ways of every one that is greedy of gain; it taketh away the life of the owners thereof.

חָכְמוֹת, בַּחוּץ תָּרֹנָּה; בָּרְחֹבוֹת, תִּתֵּן קוֹלָהּ
chachemot bachutz taronnah; barechovot, titten kolah
Wisdom crieth aloud in the streets, she uttereth her voice in the broad places;

בְּרֹאשׁ הֹמִיּוֹת, תִּקְרָא: בְּפִתְחֵי שְׁעָרִים בָּעִיר--אֲמָרֶיהָ תֹאמֵר
berosh homiyot, tikra befitchei she'arim ba'ir, amareiha tomer
She calleth at the head of the noisy streets, at the entrances of the gates, in the city, she uttereth her words:

עַד-מָתַי, פְּתָיִם--תְּאֵהֲבוּ-פֶתִי
'ad-matai petayim te'ehavu feti
'How long, ye thoughtless, will ye love thoughtlessness?

וְלֵצִים--לָצוֹן, חָמְדוּ לָהֶם; וּכְסִילִים, יִשְׂנְאוּ-דָעַת
veletzim, latzon chamedu lahem; uchesilim, yisne'u-da'at
And how long will scorners delight them in scorning, and fools hate knowledge?

מִשְׁלֵי

מִשְׁלֵי א

מִשְׁלֵי, שְׁלֹמֹה בֶן-דָּוִד--מֶלֶךְ, יִשְׂרָאֵל
Mishlei shelomoh ven-david; melech, yisra'el
The proverbs of Solomon the son of David, king of Israel;

לָדַעַת חָכְמָה וּמוּסָר; לְהָבִין, אִמְרֵי בִינָה
lada'at chochmah umusar; lehavin, imrei vinah
To know wisdom and instruction; to comprehend the words of understanding;

לָקַחַת, מוּסַר הַשְׂכֵּל; צֶדֶק וּמִשְׁפָּט, וּמֵישָׁרִים
lakachat musar haskel; tzedek umishpat, umeisharim
To receive the discipline of wisdom, justice, and right, and equity;

לָתֵת לִפְתָאיִם עָרְמָה; לְנַעַר, דַּעַת וּמְזִמָּה
latet liftayim oremah; lena'ar, da'at umezimmah
To give prudence to the simple, to the young man knowledge and discretion;

יִשְׁמַע חָכָם, וְיוֹסֶף לֶקַח; וְנָבוֹן, תַּחְבֻּלוֹת יִקְנֶה
yishma chachom veyosef lekach; venavon, tachbulot yikneh
That the wise man may hear, and increase in learning, and the man of understanding may attain unto wise counsels;

לְהָבִין מָשָׁל, וּמְלִיצָה; דִּבְרֵי חֲכָמִים, וְחִידֹתָם
lehavin mashol umelitzah; divrei chachamim, vechidotam
To understand a proverb, and a figure; the words of the wise, and their dark sayings.

יִרְאַת יְהוָה, רֵאשִׁית דָּעַת; חָכְמָה וּמוּסָר, אֱוִילִים בָּזוּ
yir'at hashem reshit da'at; chochmah umusar, evilim bazu
The fear of the LORD is the beginning of knowledge; but the foolish despise wisdom and discipline.

שְׁמַע בְּנִי, מוּסַר אָבִיךָ; וְאַל-תִּטֹּשׁ, תּוֹרַת אִמֶּךָ
shema beni musar avicha; ve'al-tittosh, torat immecha
Hear, my son, the instruction of thy father, and forsake not the teaching of thy mother;

כִּי, לִוְיַת חֵן הֵם לְרֹאשֶׁךָ; וַעֲנָקִים, לְגַרְגְּרֹתֶיךָ
ki livyat chen hem leroshecha; va'anakim, legargeroteicha
For they shall be a chaplet of grace unto thy head, and chains about thy neck.

בְּנִי-- אִם-יְפַתּוּךָ חַטָּאִים, אַל-תֹּבֵא
beni im-yefattucha chatta'im, al-tove
My son, if sinners entice thee, consent thou not.

אִם-יֹאמְרוּ, לְכָה אִתָּנוּ: נֶאֶרְבָה לְדָם; נִצְפְּנָה לְנָקִי חִנָּם
'im-yomeru lechah ittanu ne'ervah ledam; nitzpenah lenaki chinnam
If they say: 'Come with us, let us lie in wait for blood, let us lurk for the innocent without cause;

תְּהִלִּים

כֹּל הַנְּשָׁמָה, תְּהַלֵּל יָהּ: הַלְלוּ-יָהּ
kol hanneshamah tehallel yah, halelu-yah
Let every thing that hath breath praise the LORD. Hallelujah.

תְּהִלִּים

כִּי-רוֹצֶה יְהוָה בְּעַמּוֹ; יְפָאֵר עֲנָוִים, בִּישׁוּעָה
ki-rotzeh hashem be'ammo; yefa'er anavim, biyshu'ah
For the LORD taketh pleasure in His people; He adorneth the humble with salvation.

יַעְלְזוּ חֲסִידִים בְּכָבוֹד; יְרַנְּנוּ, עַל-מִשְׁכְּבוֹתָם
ya'lezu chasidim bechavod; yerannenu, al-mishkevotam
Let the saints exult in glory; let them sing for joy upon their beds.

רוֹמְמוֹת אֵל, בִּגְרוֹנָם; וְחֶרֶב פִּיפִיּוֹת בְּיָדָם
romemot el bigronam; vecherev pifiyot beyadam
Let the high praises of God be in their mouth, and a two-edged sword in their hand;

לַעֲשׂוֹת נְקָמָה, בַּגּוֹיִם; תּוֹכֵחֹת, בַּלְאֻמִּים
la'asot nekamah baggoyim; tochechot, bal-'ummim
To execute vengeance upon the nations, and chastisements upon the peoples;

לֶאְסֹר מַלְכֵיהֶם בְּזִקִּים; וְנִכְבְּדֵיהֶם, בְּכַבְלֵי בַרְזֶל
le'esor malcheihem bezikkim; venichbedeihem, bechavlei varzel
To bind their kings with chains, and their nobles with fetters of iron;

לַעֲשׂוֹת בָּהֶם, מִשְׁפָּט כָּתוּב--הָדָר הוּא, לְכָל-חֲסִידָיו: הַלְלוּ-יָהּ
la'asot bahem mishpat katuv, hadar hu lechol-chasidav, halelu-yah
To execute upon them the judgment written; He is the glory of all His saints. Hallelujah.

קנ

הַלְלוּ-יָהּ: הַלְלוּ-אֵל בְּקָדְשׁוֹ; הַלְלוּהוּ, בִּרְקִיעַ עֻזּוֹ
Halelu yah. Halelu-'el bekodesho; haleluhu, birkia uzzo
Hallelujah. Praise God in His sanctuary; praise Him in the firmament of His power.

הַלְלוּהוּ בִגְבוּרֹתָיו; הַלְלוּהוּ, כְּרֹב גֻּדְלוֹ
haleluhu vigvurotav; haleluhu, kerov gudlo
Praise Him for His mighty acts; praise Him according to His abundant greatness.

הַלְלוּהוּ, בְּתֵקַע שׁוֹפָר; הַלְלוּהוּ, בְּנֵבֶל וְכִנּוֹר
haleluhu beteka shofar; haleluhu, benevel vechinnor
Praise Him with the blast of the horn; praise Him with the psaltery and harp.

הַלְלוּהוּ, בְתֹף וּמָחוֹל; הַלְלוּהוּ, בְּמִנִּים וְעֻגָב
haleluhu vetof umachol; haleluhu, beminnim ve'ugav
Praise Him with the timbrel and dance; praise Him with stringed instruments and the pipe.

הַלְלוּהוּ בְצִלְצְלֵי-שָׁמַע; הַלְלוּהוּ, בְּצִלְצְלֵי תְרוּעָה
haleluhu vetziltzelei-shama'; haleluhu, betziltzelei teru'ah
Praise Him with the loud-sounding cymbals; praise Him with the clanging cymbals.

תְּהִלִים

אֵשׁ וּבָרָד, שֶׁלֶג וְקִיטוֹר; רוּחַ סְעָרָה, עֹשָׂה דְבָרוֹ
'esh uvarod sheleg vekitor; ruach se'arah, osah devaro
Fire and hail, snow and vapour, stormy wind, fulfilling His word;

הֶהָרִים וְכָל-גְּבָעוֹת; עֵץ פְּרִי, וְכָל-אֲרָזִים
heharim vechol-geva'ot; etz peri, vechol-'arazim
Mountains and all hills, fruitful trees and all cedars;

הַחַיָּה וְכָל-בְּהֵמָה; רֶמֶשׂ, וְצִפּוֹר כָּנָף
hachayah vechol-behemah; remes, vetzippor kanaf
Beasts and all cattle, creeping things and winged fowl;

מַלְכֵי-אֶרֶץ, וְכָל-לְאֻמִּים; שָׂרִים, וְכָל-שֹׁפְטֵי אָרֶץ
malchei-'eretz vechol-le'ummim; sarim, vechol-shofetei aretz
Kings of the earth and all peoples, princes and all judges of the earth;

בַּחוּרִים וְגַם-בְּתוּלוֹת; זְקֵנִים, עִם-נְעָרִים
bachurim vegam-betulot; zekenim, im-ne'arim
Both young men and maidens, old men and children;

יְהַלְלוּ, אֶת-שֵׁם יְהוָה--כִּי-נִשְׂגָּב שְׁמוֹ לְבַדּוֹ: הוֹדוֹ, עַל-אֶרֶץ וְשָׁמָיִם
yehalelu et-shem hashem ki-nisgav shemo levaddo; hodo, al-'eretz veshamayim
Let them praise the name of the LORD, for His name alone is exalted; His glory is above the earth and heaven.

וַיָּרֶם קֶרֶן לְעַמּוֹ, תְּהִלָּה לְכָל-חֲסִידָיו
vayarem keren le'ammo tehillah lechol-chasidav
And He hath lifted up a horn for His people, a praise for all His saints,

לִבְנֵי יִשְׂרָאֵל, עַם קְרֹבוֹ: הַלְלוּ-יָהּ
livnei yisra'el am-kerovo, halelu-yah
even for the children of Israel, a people near unto Him. Hallelujah.

קמט

הַלְלוּ-יָהּ: שִׁירוּ לַיהוָה, שִׁיר חָדָשׁ; תְּהִלָּתוֹ, בִּקְהַל חֲסִידִים
Halelu yah. Shiru lahashem shir chadash; tehillato, bik'hal chasidim
Hallelujah. Sing unto the LORD a new song, and His praise in the assembly of the saints.

יִשְׂמַח יִשְׂרָאֵל בְּעֹשָׂיו; בְּנֵי-צִיּוֹן, יָגִילוּ בְמַלְכָּם
yismach yisra'el be'osav; benei-tziyon, yagilu vemalkam
Let Israel rejoice in his Maker; let the children of Zion be joyful in their King.

יְהַלְלוּ שְׁמוֹ בְמָחוֹל; בְּתֹף וְכִנּוֹר, יְזַמְּרוּ-לוֹ
yehalelu shemo vemachol; betof vechinnor, yezammeru-lo
Let them praise His name in the dance; let them sing praises unto Him with the timbrel and harp.

תְּהִלִים

מַשְׁלִיךְ קַרְחוֹ כְפִתִּים; לִפְנֵי קָרָתוֹ, מִי יַעֲמֹד
mashlich karcho chefittim; lifnei karato, mi ya'amod
He casteth forth His ice like crumbs; who can stand before His cold?

יִשְׁלַח דְּבָרוֹ וְיַמְסֵם; יַשֵּׁב רוּחוֹ, יִזְּלוּ-מָיִם
yishlach devaro veyamsem; yashev rucho, yizzelu-mayim
He sendeth forth His word, and melteth them; He causeth His wind to blow, and the waters flow.

מַגִּיד דְּבָרָו לְיַעֲקֹב; חֻקָּיו וּמִשְׁפָּטָיו, לְיִשְׂרָאֵל
maggid devarav leya'akov; chukkav umishpatav, leyisra'el
He declareth His word unto Jacob, His statutes and His ordinances unto Israel.

לֹא עָשָׂה כֵן, לְכָל-גּוֹי--וּמִשְׁפָּטִים בַּל-יְדָעוּם: הַלְלוּ-יָהּ
lo asah chen lechol-goy, umishpatim bal-yeda'um, halelu-yah
He hath not dealt so with any nation; and as for His ordinances, they have not known them. Hallelujah.

קמח

הַלְלוּ-יָהּ: הַלְלוּ אֶת-יְהוָה, מִן-הַשָּׁמַיִם; הַלְלוּהוּ, בַּמְּרוֹמִים
Halelu yah. Halelu et-hashem min-hashamayim; haleluhu, bammeromim
Hallelujah. Praise ye the LORD from the heavens; praise Him in the heights.

הַלְלוּהוּ כָל-מַלְאָכָיו; הַלְלוּהוּ, כָּל-צְבָאָו
haleluhu chol-mal'achav; haleluhu, kol-tzeva'av
Praise ye Him, all His angels; praise ye Him, all His hosts.

הַלְלוּהוּ, שֶׁמֶשׁ וְיָרֵחַ; הַלְלוּהוּ, כָּל-כּוֹכְבֵי אוֹר
haleluhu shemesh veyareach; haleluhu, kol-kochevei or
Praise ye Him, sun and moon; praise Him, all ye stars of light.

הַלְלוּהוּ, שְׁמֵי הַשָּׁמָיִם; וְהַמַּיִם, אֲשֶׁר מֵעַל הַשָּׁמָיִם
haleluhu shemei hashamayim; vehammayim, asher me'al hashamayim
Praise Him, ye heavens of heavens, and ye waters that are above the heavens.

יְהַלְלוּ, אֶת-שֵׁם יְהוָה: כִּי הוּא צִוָּה וְנִבְרָאוּ
yehalelu et-shem hashem ki hu tzivvah venivra'u
Let them praise the name of the LORD; for He commanded, and they were created.

וַיַּעֲמִידֵם לָעַד לְעוֹלָם; חָק-נָתַן, וְלֹא יַעֲבוֹר
vaya'amidem la'ad le'olam; chak-natan, velo ya'avor
He hath also established them for ever and ever; He hath made a decree which shall not be transgressed.

הַלְלוּ אֶת-יְהוָה, מִן-הָאָרֶץ-- תַּנִּינִים, וְכָל-תְּהֹמוֹת
halelu et-hashem min-ha'aretz; tanninim, vechol-tehomot
Praise the LORD from the earth, ye sea-monsters, and all deeps;

תְּהִלִּים

גָּדוֹל אֲדוֹנֵינוּ וְרַב-כֹּחַ; לִתְבוּנָתוֹ, אֵין מִסְפָּר
gadol adoneinu verav-koach; litvunato, ein mispar
Great is our Lord, and mighty in power; His understanding is infinite.

מְעוֹדֵד עֲנָוִים יְהוָה; מַשְׁפִּיל רְשָׁעִים עֲדֵי-אָרֶץ
me'oded anavim hashem mashpil resha'im adei-'aretz
The LORD upholdeth the humble; He bringeth the wicked down to the ground.

עֱנוּ לַיהוָה בְּתוֹדָה; זַמְּרוּ לֵאלֹהֵינוּ בְכִנּוֹר
'enu lahashem betodah; zammeru le'eloheinu vechinnor
Sing unto the LORD with thanksgiving, sing praises upon the harp unto our God;

הַמְכַסֶּה שָׁמַיִם, בְּעָבִים--הַמֵּכִין לָאָרֶץ מָטָר; הַמַּצְמִיחַ הָרִים חָצִיר
hamchasseh shamayim be'avim, hammechin la'aretz matar; hammatzmiach harim chatzir
Who covereth the heaven with clouds, who prepareth rain for the earth, who maketh the mountains to spring with grass.

נוֹתֵן לִבְהֵמָה לַחְמָהּ; לִבְנֵי עֹרֵב, אֲשֶׁר יִקְרָאוּ
noten livhemah lachmah; livnei orev, asher yikra'u
He giveth to the beast his food, and to the young ravens which cry.

לֹא בִגְבוּרַת הַסּוּס יֶחְפָּץ; לֹא-בְשׁוֹקֵי הָאִישׁ יִרְצֶה
lo vigvurat hassus yechpatz; lo-veshokei ha'ish yirtzeh
He delighteth not in the strength of the horse; He taketh no pleasure in the legs of a man.

רוֹצֶה יְהוָה, אֶת-יְרֵאָיו--אֶת-הַמְיַחֲלִים לְחַסְדּוֹ
rotzeh hashem et-yere'av; et-hamyachalim lechasdo
The LORD taketh pleasure in them that fear Him, in those that wait for His mercy.

שַׁבְּחִי יְרוּשָׁלִַם, אֶת-יְהוָה; הַלְלִי אֱלֹהַיִךְ צִיּוֹן
shabbechi yerushalayim et-hashem haleli elohayich tziyon
Glorify the LORD, O Jerusalem; praise thy God, O Zion.

כִּי-חִזַּק, בְּרִיחֵי שְׁעָרָיִךְ; בֵּרַךְ בָּנַיִךְ בְּקִרְבֵּךְ
ki-chizzak berichei she'arayich; berach banayich bekirbech
For He hath made strong the bars of thy gates; He hath blessed thy children within thee.

הַשָּׂם-גְּבוּלֵךְ שָׁלוֹם; חֵלֶב חִטִּים, יַשְׂבִּיעֵךְ
hassam-gevulech shalom; chelev chittim, yasbi'ech
He maketh thy borders peace; He giveth thee in plenty the fat of wheat.

הַשֹּׁלֵחַ אִמְרָתוֹ אָרֶץ; עַד-מְהֵרָה, יָרוּץ דְּבָרוֹ
hasholeach imrato aretz; ad-meherah, yarutz devaro
He sendeth out His commandment upon earth; His word runneth very swiftly.

הַנֹּתֵן שֶׁלֶג כַּצָּמֶר; כְּפוֹר, כָּאֵפֶר יְפַזֵּר
hannoten sheleg katzamer; kefor, ka'efer yefazzer
He giveth snow like wool; He scattereth the hoar-frost like ashes.

תְּהִלִּים

עֹשֶׂה, שָׁמַיִם וָאָרֶץ--אֶת-הַיָּם וְאֶת-כָּל-אֲשֶׁר-בָּם; הַשֹּׁמֵר אֱמֶת לְעוֹלָם
'oseh shamayim va'aretz, et-hayam ve'et-kol-'asher-bam; hashomer emet le'olam
Who made heaven and earth, the sea, and all that in them is; who keepeth truth for ever;

עֹשֶׂה מִשְׁפָּט, לָעֲשׁוּקִים--נֹתֵן לֶחֶם, לָרְעֵבִים; יְהוָה, מַתִּיר אֲסוּרִים
'oseh mishpat la'ashukim, noten lechem lare'evim; hashem mattir asurim
Who executeth justice for the oppressed; who giveth bread to the hungry. The LORD looseth the prisoners;

יְהוָה, פֹּקֵחַ עִוְרִים--יְהוָה, זֹקֵף כְּפוּפִים; יְהוָה, אֹהֵב צַדִּיקִים
hashem pokeach ivrim, hashem zokef kefufim; hashem ohev tzaddikim
The LORD openeth the eyes of the blind; the LORD raiseth up them that are bowed down; the LORD loveth the righteous;

יְהוָה, שֹׁמֵר אֶת-גֵּרִים--יָתוֹם וְאַלְמָנָה יְעוֹדֵד
hashem shomer et-gerim, yatom ve'almanah ye'oded
The LORD preserveth the strangers; He upholdeth the fatherless and the widow;

וְדֶרֶךְ רְשָׁעִים יְעַוֵּת
vederech resha'im ye'avvet
but the way of the wicked He maketh crooked.

יִמְלֹךְ יְהוָה, לְעוֹלָם--אֱלֹהַיִךְ צִיּוֹן, לְדֹר וָדֹר
yimloch hashem le'olam, elohayich tziyon ledor vador
The LORD will reign for ever, thy God, O Zion, unto all generations.

הַלְלוּ-יָהּ
halelu-yah
Hallelujah.

קמז

הַלְלוּ-יָהּ: כִּי-טוֹב, זַמְּרָה אֱלֹהֵינוּ--כִּי-נָעִים, נָאוָה תְהִלָּה
Halelu yah ki-tov zammerah eloheinu; ki-na'im navah tehillah
Hallelujah; for it is good to sing praises unto our God; for it is pleasant, and praise is comely.

בּוֹנֵה יְרוּשָׁלִַם יְהוָה; נִדְחֵי יִשְׂרָאֵל יְכַנֵּס
boneh yerushalayim hashem nidchei yisra'el yechannes
The LORD doth build up Jerusalem, He gathereth together the dispersed of Israel;

הָרֹפֵא, לִשְׁבוּרֵי לֵב; וּמְחַבֵּשׁ, לְעַצְּבוֹתָם
harofei lishvurei lev; umechabbesh, le'atzevotam
Who healeth the broken in heart, and bindeth up their wounds.

מוֹנֶה מִסְפָּר, לַכּוֹכָבִים; לְכֻלָּם, שֵׁמוֹת יִקְרָא
moneh mispar lakkochavim; lechullam, shemot yikra
He counteth the number of the stars; He giveth them all their names.

תְּהִלִּים

פּוֹתֵחַ אֶת-יָדֶךָ; וּמַשְׂבִּיעַ לְכָל-חַי רָצוֹן
poteach et-yadecha; umasbia lechol-chai ratzon
Thou openest Thy hand, and satisfiest every living thing with favour.

צַדִּיק יְהוָה, בְּכָל-דְּרָכָיו; וְחָסִיד, בְּכָל-מַעֲשָׂיו
tzaddik hashem bechol-derachav; vechasid, bechol-ma'asav
The LORD is righteous in all His ways, and gracious in all His works.

קָרוֹב יְהוָה, לְכָל-קֹרְאָיו--לְכֹל אֲשֶׁר יִקְרָאֻהוּ בֶאֱמֶת
karov hashem lechol-kore'av; lechol asher yikra'uhu ve'emet
The LORD is nigh unto all them that call upon Him, to all that call upon Him in truth.

רְצוֹן-יְרֵאָיו יַעֲשֶׂה; וְאֶת-שַׁוְעָתָם יִשְׁמַע, וְיוֹשִׁיעֵם
retzon-yere'av ya'aseh; ve'et-shav'atam yishma', veyoshi'em
He will fulfil the desire of them that fear Him; He also will hear their cry, and will save them.

שׁוֹמֵר יְהוָה, אֶת-כָּל-אֹהֲבָיו; וְאֵת כָּל-הָרְשָׁעִים יַשְׁמִיד
shomer hashem et-kol-'ohavav; ve'et kol-haresha'im yashmid
The LORD preserveth all them that love Him; but all the wicked will He destroy.

תְּהִלַּת יְהוָה, יְדַבֶּר-פִּי: וִיבָרֵךְ כָּל-בָּשָׂר, שֵׁם קָדְשׁוֹ--לְעוֹלָם וָעֶד
tehillat hashem yedabber-pi viyvarech kol-basar shem kodsho le'olam va'ed
My mouth shall speak the praise of the LORD; and let all flesh bless His holy name for ever and ever.

קמו

הַלְלוּ-יָהּ: הַלְלִי נַפְשִׁי, אֶת-יְהוָה
Halelu-yah haleli nafshi, et-hashem
Hallelujah. Praise the LORD, O my soul.

אֲהַלְלָה יְהוָה בְּחַיָּי; אֲזַמְּרָה לֵאלֹהַי בְּעוֹדִי
'ahalelah hashem bechayai; azammerah lelohai be'odi
I will praise the LORD while I live; I will sing praises unto my God while I have my being.

אַל-תִּבְטְחוּ בִנְדִיבִים-- בְּבֶן-אָדָם, שֶׁאֵין לוֹ תְשׁוּעָה
'al-tivtechu vindivim; beven-'adam she'ein lo teshu'ah
Put not your trust in princes, nor in the son of man, in whom there is no help.

תֵּצֵא רוּחוֹ, יָשֻׁב לְאַדְמָתוֹ; בַּיּוֹם הַהוּא, אָבְדוּ עֶשְׁתֹּנֹתָיו
tetzei rucho yashuv le'admato; bayom hahu, avedu eshtonotav
His breath goeth forth, he returneth to his dust; in that very day his thoughts perish.

אַשְׁרֵי--שֶׁאֵל יַעֲקֹב בְּעֶזְרוֹ: שִׂבְרוֹ, עַל-יְהוָה אֱלֹהָיו
'ashrei, she'el ya'akov be'ezro; sivro, al-hashem elohav
Happy is he whose help is the God of Jacob, whose hope is in the LORD his God,

תְּהִלִים

דּוֹר לְדוֹר, יְשַׁבַּח מַעֲשֶׂיךָ; וּגְבוּרֹתֶיךָ יַגִּידוּ
dor ledor yeshabbach ma'aseicha; ugevuroteicha yaggidu
One generation shall laud Thy works to another, and shall declare Thy mighty acts.

הֲדַר, כְּבוֹד הוֹדֶךָ--וְדִבְרֵי נִפְלְאֹתֶיךָ אָשִׂיחָה
hadar kevod hodecha; vedivrei nifle'oteicha asichah
The glorious splendour of Thy majesty, and Thy wondrous works, will I rehearse.

וֶעֱזוּז נוֹרְאֹתֶיךָ יֹאמֵרוּ; וּגְדֻלָּתְךָ אֲסַפְּרֶנָּה
ve'ezuz nore'oteicha yomeru; ugedullatecha asapperennah
And men shall speak of the might of Thy tremendous acts; and I will tell of Thy greatness.

זֵכֶר רַב-טוּבְךָ יַבִּיעוּ; וְצִדְקָתְךָ יְרַנֵּנוּ
zecher rav-tuvecha yabbi'u; vetzidkatecha yerannenu
They shall utter the fame of Thy great goodness, and shall sing of Thy righteousness.

חַנּוּן וְרַחוּם יְהוָה; אֶרֶךְ אַפַּיִם, וּגְדָל-חָסֶד
channun verachum hashem erech appayim, ugedol-chased
The LORD is gracious, and full of compassion; slow to anger, and of great mercy.

טוֹב-יְהוָה לַכֹּל; וְרַחֲמָיו, עַל-כָּל-מַעֲשָׂיו
tov-hashem lakkol; verachamav, al-kol-ma'asav
The LORD is good to all; and His tender mercies are over all His works.

יוֹדוּךָ יְהוָה, כָּל-מַעֲשֶׂיךָ; וַחֲסִידֶיךָ, יְבָרְכוּכָה
yoducha hashem kol-ma'aseicha; vachasideicha, yevarachuchah
All Thy works shall praise Thee, O LORD; and Thy saints shall bless Thee.

כְּבוֹד מַלְכוּתְךָ יֹאמֵרוּ; וּגְבוּרָתְךָ יְדַבֵּרוּ
kevod malchutecha yomeru; ugevuratecha yedabberu
They shall speak of the glory of Thy kingdom, and talk of Thy might;

לְהוֹדִיעַ, לִבְנֵי הָאָדָם--גְּבוּרֹתָיו; וּכְבוֹד, הֲדַר מַלְכוּתוֹ
lehodia livnei ha'adam gevurotav; uchevod, hadar malchuto
To make known to the sons of men His mighty acts, and the glory of the majesty of His kingdom.

מַלְכוּתְךָ, מַלְכוּת כָּל-עֹלָמִים; וּמֶמְשַׁלְתְּךָ, בְּכָל-דּוֹר וָדֹר
malchutcha, malchut kol-'olamim; umemsheltecha, bechol-dor vador
Thy kingdom is a kingdom for all ages, and Thy dominion endureth throughout all generations.

סוֹמֵךְ יְהוָה, לְכָל-הַנֹּפְלִים; וְזוֹקֵף, לְכָל-הַכְּפוּפִים
somech hashem lechol-hannofelim; vezokef, lechol-hakkefufim
The LORD upholdeth all that fall, and raiseth up all those that are bowed down.

עֵינֵי-כֹל, אֵלֶיךָ יְשַׂבֵּרוּ; וְאַתָּה נוֹתֵן-לָהֶם אֶת-אָכְלָם בְּעִתּוֹ
'einei-chol eleicha yesabberu; ve'attah noten-lahem et-'achelam be'itto
The eyes of all wait for Thee, and Thou givest them their food in due season.

תְּהִלִּים

פְּצֵנִי וְהַצִּילֵנִי, מִיַּד בְּנֵי-נֵכָר
petzeni vehatzileni miyad benei-nechar
Rescue me, and deliver me out of the hand of strangers,

אֲשֶׁר פִּיהֶם, דִּבֶּר-שָׁוְא; וִימִינָם, יְמִין שָׁקֶר
asher pihem dibber-shav; viyminam, yemin shaker
whose mouth speaketh falsehood, and their right hand is a right hand of lying.

אֲשֶׁר בָּנֵינוּ, כִּנְטִעִים--מְגֻדָּלִים בִּנְעוּרֵיהֶם
'asher baneinu kinti'im meguddalim bin'ureihem
We whose sons are as plants grown up in their youth;

בְּנוֹתֵינוּ כְזָוִיֹּת--מְחֻטָּבוֹת, תַּבְנִית הֵיכָל
benoteinu chezaviyot; mechuttavot, tavnit heichal
whose daughters are as corner-pillars carved after the fashion of a palace;

מְזָוֵינוּ מְלֵאִים--מְפִיקִים מִזַּן, אֶל-זַן
mezaveinu mele'im mefikim mizzan, el-zan
Whose garners are full, affording all manner of store;

צֹאונֵנוּ מַאֲלִיפוֹת, מְרֻבָּבוֹת--בְּחוּצוֹתֵינוּ
tzonenu ma'alifot merubbavot, bechutzoteinu
whose sheep increase by thousands and ten thousands in our fields;

אַלּוּפֵינוּ, מְסֻבָּלִים: אֵין-פֶּרֶץ, וְאֵין יוֹצֵאת; וְאֵין צְוָחָה, בִּרְחֹבֹתֵינוּ
'allufeinu, mesubbalim ein-peretz ve'ein yotzet; ve'ein tzevachah, birchovoteinu
Whose oxen are well laden; with no breach, and no going forth, and no outcry in our broad places;

אַשְׁרֵי הָעָם, שֶׁכָּכָה לּוֹ: אַשְׁרֵי הָעָם, שֶׁיְהוָה אֱלֹהָיו
'ashrei ha'am shekkachah lo; ashrei ha'am, shehashem elohav
Happy is the people that is in such a case. Yea, happy is the people whose God is the LORD.

קמה

תְּהִלָּה, לְדָוִד: אֲרוֹמִמְךָ אֱלוֹהַי הַמֶּלֶךְ; וַאֲבָרְכָה שִׁמְךָ, לְעוֹלָם וָעֶד
Tehillah, ledavid aromimcha elohai hammelech; va'avarachah shimcha, le'olam va'ed
[A Psalm of] praise; of David. I will extol Thee, my God, O King; and I will bless Thy name for ever and ever.

בְּכָל-יוֹם אֲבָרְכֶךָּ; וַאֲהַלְלָה שִׁמְךָ, לְעוֹלָם וָעֶד
bechol-yom avaracheka; va'ahalelah shimcha, le'olam va'ed
Every day will I bless Thee; and I will praise Thy name for ever and ever.

גָּדוֹל יְהוָה וּמְהֻלָּל מְאֹד; וְלִגְדֻלָּתוֹ, אֵין חֵקֶר
gadol hashem umehullal me'od; veligdullato, ein cheker
Great is the LORD, and highly to be praised; and His greatness is unsearchable.

תְּהִלִים

קמד

לְדָוִד: בָּרוּךְ יְהוָה, צוּרִי--הַמְלַמֵּד יָדַי לַקְרָב; אֶצְבְּעוֹתַי, לַמִּלְחָמָה
Ledavid. baruch hashem tzuri, hamlammed yadai lakrav; etzbe'otai, lammilchamah
[A Psalm] of David. Blessed be the LORD my Rock, who traineth my hands for war, and my fingers for battle;

חַסְדִּי וּמְצוּדָתִי, מִשְׂגַּבִּי וּמְפַלְטִי-לִי
chasdi umetzudati misgabbi umefalti li
My lovingkindness, and my fortress, my high tower, and my deliverer;

מָגִנִּי, וּבוֹ חָסִיתִי; הָרוֹדֵד עַמִּי תַחְתָּי
maginni uvo chasiti; haroded ammi tachtai
my shield, and He in whom I take refuge; who subdueth my people under me.

יְהוָה--מָה-אָדָם, וַתֵּדָעֵהוּ: בֶּן-אֱנוֹשׁ, וַתְּחַשְּׁבֵהוּ
hashem mah-'adom vatteda'ehu; ben-'enosh, vattechashevehu
LORD, what is man, that Thou takest knowledge of him? or the son of man, that Thou makest account of him?

אָדָם, לַהֶבֶל דָּמָה; יָמָיו, כְּצֵל עוֹבֵר
'adom lahevel damah; yamav, ketzel over
Man is like unto a breath; his days are as a shadow that passeth away.

יְהוָה, הַט-שָׁמֶיךָ וְתֵרֵד; גַּע בֶּהָרִים וְיֶעֱשָׁנוּ
hashem hat-shameicha vetered; ga beharim veye'eshanu
O LORD, bow Thy heavens, and come down; touch the mountains, that they may smoke.

בְּרוֹק בָּרָק, וּתְפִיצֵם; שְׁלַח חִצֶּיךָ, וּתְהֻמֵּם
berok barak utefitzem; shelach chitzeicha, utehummem
Cast forth lightning, and scatter them; send out Thine arrows, and discomfit them.

שְׁלַח יָדֶיךָ, מִמָּרוֹם: פְּצֵנִי וְהַצִּילֵנִי, מִמַּיִם רַבִּים; מִיַּד, בְּנֵי נֵכָר
shelach yadeicha, mimmarom petzeni vehatzileni mimmayim rabbim; miyad, benei nechar
Stretch forth Thy hands from on high; rescue me, and deliver me out of many waters, out of the hand of strangers;

אֲשֶׁר פִּיהֶם, דִּבֶּר-שָׁוְא; וִימִינָם, יְמִין שָׁקֶר
'asher pihem dibber-shav; viminam, yemin shaker
Whose mouth speaketh falsehood, and their right hand is a right hand of lying.

אֱלֹהִים--שִׁיר חָדָשׁ, אָשִׁירָה לָּךְ; בְּנֵבֶל עָשׂוֹר, אֲזַמְּרָה-לָּךְ
'elohim, shir chadosh ashirah lach; benevel asor, azammerah-lach
O God, I will sing a new song unto Thee, upon a psaltery of ten strings will I sing praises unto Thee;

הַנּוֹתֵן תְּשׁוּעָה, לַמְּלָכִים: הַפּוֹצֶה, אֶת-דָּוִד עַבְדּוֹ--מֵחֶרֶב רָעָה
hannoten teshu'ah, lammelachim happotzeh et-david avdo, mecherev ra'ah
Who givest salvation unto kings, who rescuest David Thy servant from the hurtful sword.

תְּהִלִּים

זָכַרְתִּי יָמִים, מִקֶּדֶם-- הָגִיתִי בְכָל-פָּעֳלֶךָ
zacharti yamim mikkedem, hagiti vechal-po'olecha
I remember the days of old; I meditate on all Thy doing;

בְּמַעֲשֵׂה יָדֶיךָ אֲשׂוֹחֵחַ
bema'aseh yadeicha asocheach
I muse on the work of Thy hands.

פֵּרַשְׂתִּי יָדַי אֵלֶיךָ; נַפְשִׁי, כְּאֶרֶץ-עֲיֵפָה לְךָ סֶלָה
perasti yadai eleicha; nafshi ke'eretz-'ayefah lecha selah
I spread forth my hands unto Thee; my soul [thirsteth] after Thee, as a weary land. Selah

מַהֵר עֲנֵנִי, יְהוָה-- כָּלְתָה רוּחִי: אַל-תַּסְתֵּר פָּנֶיךָ מִמֶּנִּי
maher aneni hashem kaletah ruchi al-taster paneicha mimmenni
Answer me speedily, O LORD, my spirit faileth; hide not Thy face from me;

וְנִמְשַׁלְתִּי, עִם-יֹרְדֵי בוֹר
venimshalti, im-yoredei vor
lest I become like them that go down into the pit.

הַשְׁמִיעֵנִי בַבֹּקֶר, חַסְדֶּךָ-- כִּי-בְךָ בָטָחְתִּי
hashmi'eni vabboker chasdecha ki-vecha vatacheti
Cause me to hear Thy lovingkindness in the morning, for in Thee do I trust;

הוֹדִיעֵנִי, דֶּרֶךְ-זוּ אֵלֵךְ-- כִּי-אֵלֶיךָ, נָשָׂאתִי נַפְשִׁי
hodi'eni, derech-zu elech; ki-'eleicha nasati nafshi
cause me to know the way wherein I should walk, for unto Thee have I lifted up my soul.

הַצִּילֵנִי מֵאֹיְבַי יְהוָה-- אֵלֶיךָ כִסִּתִי
hatzileni me'oyevai hashem eleicha chissiti
Deliver me from mine enemies, O LORD; with Thee have I hidden myself.

לַמְּדֵנִי, לַעֲשׂוֹת רְצוֹנֶךָ-- כִּי-אַתָּה אֱלוֹהָי: רוּחֲךָ טוֹבָה; תַּנְחֵנִי, בְּאֶרֶץ מִישׁוֹר.
lammedeni la'asot retzonecha ki-'attah elohai ruchacha tovah; tancheni, be'eretz mishor
Teach me to do Thy will, for Thou art my God; let Thy good spirit lead me in an even land.

לְמַעַן-שִׁמְךָ יְהוָה תְּחַיֵּנִי; בְּצִדְקָתְךָ, תּוֹצִיא מִצָּרָה נַפְשִׁי
lema'an-shimcha hashem techayeni; betzidkatecha totzi mitzarah nafshi
For Thy name's sake, O LORD, quicken me; in Thy righteousness bring my soul out of trouble.

וּבְחַסְדְּךָ, תַּצְמִית אֹיְבָי: וְהַאֲבַדְתָּ, כָּל-צֹרְרֵי נַפְשִׁי-- כִּי, אֲנִי עַבְדֶּךָ
uvechasdecha tatzmit oyevai veha'avadta kol-tzorarei nafshi; ki, ani avdecha
And in Thy mercy cut off mine enemies, and destroy all them that harass my soul; for I am Thy servant.

תְּהִלִּים

הַבֵּיט יָמִין, וּרְאֵה--וְאֵין-לִי מַכִּיר: אָבַד מָנוֹס מִמֶּנִּי; אֵין דּוֹרֵשׁ לְנַפְשִׁי
habbeit yamin ure'eh ve'ein-li makkir avad manos mimmenni; ein doresh lenafshi
Look on my right hand, and see, for there is no man that knoweth me; I have no way to flee; no man careth for my soul.

זָעַקְתִּי אֵלֶיךָ, יְהוָה: אָמַרְתִּי, אַתָּה מַחְסִי; חֶלְקִי, בְּאֶרֶץ הַחַיִּים
za'akti eleicha, hashem amarti attah machsi; chelki, be'eretz hachayim
I have cried unto Thee, O LORD; I have said: 'Thou art my refuge, my portion in the land of the living.'

הַקְשִׁיבָה, אֶל-רִנָּתִי--כִּי-דַלּוֹתִי-מְאֹד: הַצִּילֵנִי מֵרֹדְפַי--כִּי אָמְצוּ מִמֶּנִּי
hakshivah el-rinnati ki-dalloti me'od hatzileni merodefai; ki ametzu mimmenni
Attend unto my cry; for I am brought very low; deliver me from my persecutors; for they are too strong for me.

הוֹצִיאָה מִמַּסְגֵּר, נַפְשִׁי--לְהוֹדוֹת אֶת-שְׁמֶךָ
hotzi'ah mimmasger nafshi lehodot et-shemecha
Bring my soul out of prison, that I may give thanks unto Thy name;

בִּי, יַכְתִּרוּ צַדִּיקִים--כִּי תִגְמֹל עָלָי
bi yachtiru tzaddikim; ki tigmol alai
the righteous shall crown themselves because of me; for Thou wilt deal bountifully with me.

קמג

מִזְמוֹר, לְדָוִד: יְהוָה, שְׁמַע תְּפִלָּתִי--הַאֲזִינָה אֶל-תַּחֲנוּנַי
Mizmor, ledavid hashem shema tefillati, ha'azinah el-tachanunai
A Psalm of David. O LORD, hear my prayer, give ear to my supplications;

בֶּאֱמֻנָתְךָ עֲנֵנִי, בְּצִדְקָתֶךָ
be'emunatecha aneni, betzidkatecha
in Thy faithfulness answer me, and in Thy righteousness.

וְאַל-תָּבוֹא בְמִשְׁפָּט, אֶת-עַבְדֶּךָ: כִּי לֹא-יִצְדַּק לְפָנֶיךָ כָל-חָי
ve'al-tavo vemishpot et-'avdecha; ki lo-yitzdak lefaneicha chol-chai
And enter not into judgment with Thy servant; for in Thy sight shall no man living be justified.

כִּי רָדַף אוֹיֵב, נַפְשִׁי--דִּכָּא לָאָרֶץ, חַיָּתִי
ki radaf oyev nafshi, dikka la'aretz chayati
For the enemy hath persecuted my soul; he hath crushed my life down to the ground;

הוֹשִׁיבַנִי בְמַחֲשַׁכִּים, כְּמֵתֵי עוֹלָם
hoshivani vemachashakkim, kemetei olam
he hath made me to dwell in darkness, as those that have been long dead.

וַתִּתְעַטֵּף עָלַי רוּחִי; בְּתוֹכִי, יִשְׁתּוֹמֵם לִבִּי
vattit'attef alai ruchi; betochi, yishtomem libbi
And my spirit fainteth within me; my heart within me is appalled.

תְּהִלִּים

יֶהֶלְמֵנִי צַדִּיק חֶסֶד, וְיוֹכִיחֵנִי--שֶׁמֶן רֹאשׁ, אַל-יָנִי רֹאשִׁי
yehelmeni-tzaddik chesed veyochicheni, shemen rosh al-yani roshi
Let the righteous smite me in kindness, and correct me; oil so choice let not my head refuse;

כִּי-עוֹד וּתְפִלָּתִי, בְּרָעוֹתֵיהֶם
ki-'od utefillati, bera'oteihem
for still is my prayer because of their wickedness.

נִשְׁמְטוּ בִידֵי-סֶלַע, שֹׁפְטֵיהֶם; וְשָׁמְעוּ אֲמָרַי, כִּי נָעֵמוּ
nishmetu videi-sela shofeteihem; veshame'u amarai, ki na'emu
Their judges are thrown down by the sides of the rock; and they shall hear my words, that they are sweet.

כְּמוֹ פֹלֵחַ וּבֹקֵעַ בָּאָרֶץ--נִפְזְרוּ עֲצָמֵינוּ, לְפִי שְׁאוֹל
kemo foleach uvokea ba'aretz; nifzeru atzameinu, lefi she'ol
As when one cleaveth and breaketh up the earth, our bones are scattered at the grave's mouth.

כִּי אֵלֶיךָ, יְהוִה אֲדֹנָי עֵינָי; בְּכָה חָסִיתִי, אַל-תְּעַר נַפְשִׁי
ki eleicha hashem adonai einai; bechah chasiti, al-te'ar nafshi
For mine eyes are unto Thee, O GOD the Lord; in Thee have I taken refuge, O pour not out my soul.

שָׁמְרֵנִי--מִידֵי פַח, יָקְשׁוּ לִי; וּמֹקְשׁוֹת, פֹּעֲלֵי אָוֶן
shomereni, midei fach yakeshu li; umokeshot, po'alei aven
Keep me from the snare which they have laid for me, and from the gins of the workers of iniquity.

יִפְּלוּ בְמַכְמֹרָיו רְשָׁעִים; יַחַד אָנֹכִי, עַד-אֶעֱבוֹר
yippelu vemachmorav resha'im; yachad anochi, ad-'e'evor
Let the wicked fall into their own nets, whilst I withal escape.

קמב

מַשְׂכִּיל לְדָוִד; בִּהְיוֹתוֹ בַמְּעָרָה תְפִלָּה
Maskil ledavid; bihyoto vamme'arah tefillah
Maschil of David, when he was in the cave; a Prayer.

קוֹלִי, אֶל-יְהוָה אֶזְעָק; קוֹלִי, אֶל-יְהוָה אֶתְחַנָּן
koli el-hashem ez'ak; koli, el-hashem etchannan
With my voice I cry unto the LORD; with my voice I make supplication unto the LORD.

אֶשְׁפֹּךְ לְפָנָיו שִׂיחִי; צָרָתִי, לְפָנָיו אַגִּיד
'eshpoch lefanav sichi; tzarati, lefanav aggid
I pour out my complaint before Him, I declare before Him my trouble;

בְּהִתְעַטֵּף עָלַי, רוּחִי--וְאַתָּה, יָדַעְתָּ נְתִיבָתִי: בְּאֹרַח-זוּ אֲהַלֵּךְ--טָמְנוּ פַח לִי
behit'attef alai ruchi, ve'attah yada'ta netivati be'orach-zu ahallech; tamenu fach li
When my spirit fainteth within me--Thou knowest my path--in the way wherein I walk have they hidden a snare for me.

תְּהִלִּים

אַל-תִּתֵּן יְהוָה, מַאֲוַיֵּי רָשָׁע; זְמָמוֹ אַל-תָּפֵק, יָרוּמוּ סֶלָה
'al-titten hashem ma'avayei rasha'; zemamo al-tafek, yarumu selah
Grant not, O LORD, the desires of the wicked; further not his evil device, so that they exalt themselves. Selah

רֹאשׁ מְסִבָּי--עֲמַל שְׂפָתֵימוֹ יְכַסֵּימוֹ
rosh mesibbai; amal sefateimo yechassemo
As for the head of those that compass me about, let the mischief of their own lips cover them.

יִמּוֹטוּ עֲלֵיהֶם, גֶּחָלִים: בָּאֵשׁ יַפִּלֵם; בְּמַהֲמֹרוֹת, בַּל-יָקוּמוּ
yimmotu aleihem, gechalim ba'esh yappilem; bemahamorot, bal-yakumu
Let burning coals fall upon them; let them be cast into the fire, into deep pits, that they rise not up again.

אִישׁ לָשׁוֹן, בַּל-יִכּוֹן בָּאָרֶץ: אִישׁ-חָמָס רָע--יְצוּדֶנּוּ, לְמַדְחֵפֹת
'ish lashon bal-yikkon ba'aretz ish-chamas ra'; yetzudennu, lemadchefot
A slanderer shall not be established in the earth; the violent and evil man shall be hunted with thrust upon thrust.

יָדַעְתִּי--כִּי-יַעֲשֶׂה יְהוָה, דִּין עָנִי: מִשְׁפַּט, אֶבְיֹנִים
yada'ti, ki-ya'aseh hashem din ani; mishpat, evyonim
I know that the LORD will maintain the cause of the poor, and the right of the needy.

אַךְ צַדִּיקִים, יוֹדוּ לִשְׁמֶךָ; יֵשְׁבוּ יְשָׁרִים, אֶת-פָּנֶיךָ
'ach tzaddikim yodu lishmecha; yeshevu yesharim, et-paneicha
Surely the righteous shall give thanks unto Thy name; the upright shall dwell in Thy presence.

קמא

מִזְמוֹר, לְדָוִד: יְהוָה קְרָאתִיךָ, חוּשָׁה לִּי; הַאֲזִינָה קוֹלִי, בְּקָרְאִי-לָךְ
Mizmor, ledavid hashem keraticha chushah li; ha'azinah koli, bekare'i-lach
A Psalm of David. LORD, I have called Thee; make haste unto me; give ear unto my voice, when I call unto Thee.

תִּכּוֹן תְּפִלָּתִי קְטֹרֶת לְפָנֶיךָ; מַשְׂאַת כַּפַּי, מִנְחַת-עָרֶב
tikkon tefillati ketoret lefaneicha; mas'at kappai, minchat-'arev
Let my prayer be set forth as incense before Thee, the lifting up of my hands as the evening sacrifice.

שִׁיתָה יְהוָה, שָׁמְרָה לְפִי; נִצְּרָה, עַל-דַּל שְׂפָתָי
shitah hashem shamerah lefi; nitzerah, al-dal sefatai
Set a guard, O LORD, to my mouth; keep watch at the door of my lips.

אַל-תַּט-לִבִּי לְדָבָר רָע
'al-tat-libbi ledavar ra
Incline not my heart to any evil thing,

לְהִתְעוֹלֵל עֲלִלוֹת בְּרֶשַׁע--אֶת-אִישִׁים פֹּעֲלֵי-אָוֶן; וּבַל-אֶלְחַם, בְּמַנְעַמֵּיהֶם
lehit'olel alilot beresha', et-'ishim po'alei-'aven; uval-'elcham, beman'ammeihem
to be occupied in deeds of wickedness with men that work iniquity; and let me not eat of their dainties.

תְּהִלִּים

חָקְרֵנִי אֵל, וְדַע לְבָבִי; בְּחָנֵנִי, וְדַע שַׂרְעַפָּי
chakereni el veda levavi; bechaneni, veda sar'appai
Search me, O God, and know my heart, try me, and know my thoughts;

וּרְאֵה, אִם-דֶּרֶךְ-עֹצֶב בִּי; וּנְחֵנִי, בְּדֶרֶךְ עוֹלָם
ure'eh, im-derech-'otzev bi; unecheni, bederech olam
And see if there be any way in me that is grievous, and lead me in the way everlasting.

קמ

לַמְנַצֵּחַ, מִזְמוֹר לְדָוִד
Lamnatzeach, mizmor ledavid
For the Leader. A Psalm of David.

חַלְּצֵנִי יְהוָה, מֵאָדָם רָע; מֵאִישׁ חֲמָסִים תִּנְצְרֵנִי
challetzeni hashem me'adam ra'; me'ish chamasim tintzereni
Deliver me, O LORD, from the evil man; preserve me from the violent man;

אֲשֶׁר חָשְׁבוּ רָעוֹת בְּלֵב; כָּל-יוֹם, יָגוּרוּ מִלְחָמוֹת
'asher chashevu ra'ot belev; kol-yom, yaguru milchamot
Who devise evil things in their heart; every day do they stir up wars.

שָׁנְנוּ לְשׁוֹנָם, כְּמוֹ-נָחָשׁ: חֲמַת עַכְשׁוּב--תַּחַת שְׂפָתֵימוֹ סֶלָה
shananu leshonam kemo-nachash chamat achshuv; tachat sefateimo selah
They have sharpened their tongue like a serpent; vipers' venom is under their lips. Selah

שָׁמְרֵנִי יְהוָה, מִידֵי רָשָׁע--מֵאִישׁ חֲמָסִים תִּנְצְרֵנִי
shmereni hashem miydei rasha', me'ish chamasim tintzereni
Keep me, O LORD, from the hands of the wicked; preserve me from the violent man;

אֲשֶׁר חָשְׁבוּ, לִדְחוֹת פְּעָמָי
asher chashevu, lidchot pe'amai
who have purposed to make my steps slip.

טָמְנוּ גֵאִים, פַּח לִי--וַחֲבָלִים, פָּרְשׂוּ רֶשֶׁת לְיַד-מַעְגָּל; מֹקְשִׁים שָׁתוּ-לִי סֶלָה
tamenu-ge'im pach li, vachavalim, paresu reshet leyad-ma'gal; mokeshim shatu-li selah
The proud have hid a snare for me, and cords; they have spread a net by the wayside; they have set gins for me. Selah

אָמַרְתִּי לַיהוָה, אֵלִי אָתָּה; הַאֲזִינָה יְהוָה, קוֹל תַּחֲנוּנָי
'amarti lahashem eli attah; ha'azinah hashem kol tachanunai
I have said unto the LORD: 'Thou art my God'; give ear, O LORD, unto the voice of my supplications.

יְהוִה אֲדֹנָי, עֹז יְשׁוּעָתִי; סַכֹּתָה לְרֹאשִׁי, בְּיוֹם נָשֶׁק
hashem adonai oz yeshu'ati; sakkotah leroshi, beyom nashek
O GOD the Lord, the strength of my salvation, who hast screened my head in the day of battle,

תְּהִלִים

אוֹדְךָ--עַל כִּי נוֹרָאוֹת, נִפְלֵיתִי
'odecha, al ki nora'ot, nifleiti
I will give thanks unto Thee, for I am fearfully and wonderfully made;

נִפְלָאִים מַעֲשֶׂיךָ; וְנַפְשִׁי, יֹדַעַת מְאֹד
nifla'im ma'aseicha; venafshi, yoda'at me'od
wonderful are Thy works; and that my soul knoweth right well.

לֹא-נִכְחַד עָצְמִי, מִמֶּךָּ: אֲשֶׁר-עֻשֵּׂיתִי בַסֵּתֶר; רֻקַּמְתִּי, בְּתַחְתִּיּוֹת אָרֶץ
lo-nichchad otzemi, mimmeka asher-'usseiti vasseter; rukkamti, betachtiyot aretz
My frame was not hidden from Thee, when I was made in secret, and curiously wrought in the lowest parts of the earth.

גָּלְמִי, רָאוּ עֵינֶיךָ, וְעַל-סִפְרְךָ, כֻּלָּם יִכָּתֵבוּ
golemi ra'u eineicha, ve'al-sifrecha kullam yikkatevu
Thine eyes did see mine unformed substance, and in Thy book they were all written--

יָמִים יֻצָּרוּ; וְלוֹ אֶחָד בָּהֶם
yamim yutzaru; velo echad bahem
even the days that were fashioned, when as yet there was none of them.

וְלִי--מַה-יָּקְרוּ רֵעֶיךָ אֵל; מֶה עָצְמוּ, רָאשֵׁיהֶם
veli, mah-yakeru re'eicha el; meh atzemu rasheihem
How weighty also are Thy thoughts unto me, O God! How great is the sum of them!

אֶסְפְּרֵם, מֵחוֹל יִרְבּוּן
'esperem mechol yirbun
If I would count them, they are more in number than the sand;

הֱקִיצֹתִי, וְעוֹדִי עִמָּךְ
hekitzoti, ve'odi immach
were I to come to the end of them, I would still be with Thee.

אִם-תִּקְטֹל אֱלוֹהַּ רָשָׁע; וְאַנְשֵׁי דָמִים, סוּרוּ מֶנִּי
'im-tiktol eloah rasha'; ve'anshei damim, suru menni
If Thou but wouldest slay the wicked, O God--depart from me therefore, ye men of blood;

אֲשֶׁר יֹמְרוּךָ, לִמְזִמָּה; נָשֻׂא לַשָּׁוְא עָרֶיךָ
'asher yomerucha limzimmah; nasu lashav areicha
Who utter Thy name with wicked thought, they take it for falsehood, even Thine enemies--

הֲלוֹא-מְשַׂנְאֶיךָ יְהוָה אֶשְׂנָא; וּבִתְקוֹמְמֶיךָ, אֶתְקוֹטָט
halo-mesan'eicha hashem esna; uvitkomemeicha, etkotat
Do not I hate them, O LORD, that hate Thee? And do not I strive with those that rise up against Thee?

תַּכְלִית שִׂנְאָה שְׂנֵאתִים; לְאוֹיְבִים, הָיוּ לִי
tachlit sin'ah senetim; le'oyevim, hayu li
I hate them with utmost hatred; I count them mine enemies.

תְּהִלִּים

אַתָּה יָדַעְתָּ, שִׁבְתִּי וְקוּמִי; בַּנְתָּה לְרֵעִי, מֵרָחוֹק
'attah yada'ta shivti vekumi; bantah lere'i, merachok
Thou knowest my downsitting and mine uprising, Thou understandest my thought afar off.

אָרְחִי וְרִבְעִי זֵרִיתָ; וְכָל-דְּרָכַי הִסְכַּנְתָּה
'orechi veriv'i zerita; vechol-derachai hiskantah
Thou measurest my going about and my lying down, and art acquainted with all my ways.

כִּי אֵין מִלָּה, בִּלְשׁוֹנִי; הֵן יְהוָה, יָדַעְתָּ כֻלָּהּ
ki ein millah bilshoni; hen hashem yada'ta chullah
For there is not a word in my tongue, but, lo, O LORD, Thou knowest it altogether.

אָחוֹר וָקֶדֶם צַרְתָּנִי; וַתָּשֶׁת עָלַי כַּפֶּכָה
'achor vakedem tzartani; vattashet alai kappechah
Thou hast hemmed me in behind and before, and laid Thy hand upon me.

פְּלִיאָה דַעַת מִמֶּנִּי; נִשְׂגְּבָה, לֹא-אוּכַל לָהּ
peli'ah da'at mimmenni; nisgevah, lo-'uchal lah
Such knowledge is too wonderful for me; too high, I cannot attain unto it.

אָנָה, אֵלֵךְ מֵרוּחֶךָ; וְאָנָה, מִפָּנֶיךָ אֶבְרָח
'anah elech meruchecha; ve'anah, mippaneicha evrach
Whither shall I go from Thy spirit? or whither shall I flee from Thy presence?

אִם אֶסַּק שָׁמַיִם, שָׁם אָתָּה; וְאַצִּיעָה שְּׁאוֹל הִנֶּךָּ
'im-'essak shamayim sham attah; ve'atzi'ah she'ol hinneka
If I ascend up into heaven, Thou art there; if I make my bed in the nether-world, behold, Thou art there.

אֶשָּׂא כַנְפֵי-שָׁחַר; אֶשְׁכְּנָה, בְּאַחֲרִית יָם
'essa chanfei-shachar; eshkenah, be'acharit yam
If I take the wings of the morning, and dwell in the uttermost parts of the sea;

גַּם-שָׁם, יָדְךָ תַנְחֵנִי; וְתֹאחֲזֵנִי יְמִינֶךָ
gam-sham yadecha tancheni; vetochazeni yeminecha
Even there would Thy hand lead me, and Thy right hand would hold me.

וָאֹמַר, אַךְ-חֹשֶׁךְ יְשׁוּפֵנִי; וְלַיְלָה, אוֹר בַּעֲדֵנִי
va'omar ach-choshech yeshufeni; velaylah, or ba'adeni
And if I say: 'Surely the darkness shall envelop me, and the light about me shall be night';

גַּם-חֹשֶׁךְ, לֹא-יַחְשִׁיךְ מִמֶּךָ וְלַיְלָה, כַּיּוֹם יָאִיר--כַּחֲשֵׁיכָה, כָּאוֹרָה
gam-choshech lo-yachshich mimmecha velaylah kayom ya'ir; kachasheichah, ka'orah
Even the darkness is not too dark for Thee, but the night shineth as the day; the darkness is even as the light.

כִּי-אַתָּה, קָנִיתָ כִלְיֹתָי; תְּסֻכֵּנִי, בְּבֶטֶן אִמִּי
ki-'attah kanita chilyotai; tesukkeni, beveten immi
For Thou hast made my reins; Thou hast knit me together in my mother's womb.

תְּהִלִּים

אֶשְׁתַּחֲוֶה אֶל-הֵיכַל קָדְשְׁךָ, וְאוֹדֶה אֶת-שְׁמֶךָ--עַל-חַסְדְּךָ וְעַל-אֲמִתֶּךָ
'eshtachaveh el-heichal kodshecha ve'odeh et-shemecha, al-chasdecha ve'al-'amittecha
I will bow down toward Thy holy temple, and give thanks unto Thy name for Thy mercy and for Thy truth;

כִּי-הִגְדַּלְתָּ עַל-כָּל-שִׁמְךָ, אִמְרָתֶךָ
ki-higdalta al-kol-shimcha, imratecha
for Thou hast magnified Thy word above all Thy name.

בְּיוֹם קָרָאתִי, וַתַּעֲנֵנִי; תַּרְהִבֵנִי בְנַפְשִׁי עֹז
beyom karati vatta'aneni; tarhiveni venafshi oz
In the day that I called, Thou didst answer me; Thou didst encourage me in my soul with strength.

יוֹדוּךָ יְהוָה, כָּל-מַלְכֵי-אָרֶץ: כִּי שָׁמְעוּ, אִמְרֵי-פִיךָ
yoducha hashem kol-malchei-'aretz; ki shame'u, imrei-ficha
All the kings of the earth shall give Thee thanks, O LORD, for they have heard the words of Thy mouth.

וְיָשִׁירוּ, בְּדַרְכֵי יְהוָה: כִּי-גָדוֹל, כְּבוֹד יְהוָה
veyashiru bedarchei hashem ki gadol, kevod hashem
Yea, they shall sing of the ways of the LORD; for great is the glory of the LORD.

כִּי-רָם יְהוָה, וְשָׁפָל יִרְאֶה; וְגָבֹהַּ, מִמֶּרְחָק יְיֵדָע
ki-ram hashem veshafal yir'eh; vegavoha, mimmerchak yeyeda
For though the LORD be high, yet regardeth He the lowly, and the haughty He knoweth from afar.

אִם-אֵלֵךְ, בְּקֶרֶב צָרָה--תְּחַיֵּנִי
'im-'elech bekerev tzarah, techayeni
Though I walk in the midst of trouble, Thou quickenest me;

עַל אַף אֹיְבַי, תִּשְׁלַח יָדֶךָ; וְתוֹשִׁיעֵנִי יְמִינֶךָ
al af oyevai tishlach yadecha; vetoshi'eni yeminecha
Thou stretchest forth Thy hand against the wrath of mine enemies, and Thy right hand doth save me.

יְהוָה, יִגְמֹר בַּעֲדִי
hashem yigmor ba'adi
The LORD will accomplish that which concerneth me;

יְהוָה, חַסְדְּךָ לְעוֹלָם; מַעֲשֵׂי יָדֶיךָ אַל-תֶּרֶף
hashem chasdecha le'olam; ma'asei yadeicha al-teref
Thy mercy, O LORD, endureth for ever; forsake not the work of Thine own hands.

קלט

לַמְנַצֵּחַ, לְדָוִד מִזְמוֹר: יְהוָה חֲקַרְתַּנִי, וַתֵּדָע
Lamnatzeach ledavid mizmor; hashem chakartani, vatteda
For the Leader. A Psalm of David. O LORD, Thou hast searched me, and known me.

תְּהִלִים

עַל-עֲרָבִים בְּתוֹכָהּ--תָּלִינוּ, כִּנֹּרוֹתֵינוּ
'al-'aravim betochah; talinu, kinnoroteinu
Upon the willows in the midst thereof we hanged up our harps.

כִּי שָׁם שְׁאֵלוּנוּ שׁוֹבֵינוּ, דִּבְרֵי-שִׁיר--וְתוֹלָלֵינוּ שִׂמְחָה
ki sham she'elunu shoveinu divrei-shir vetolaleinu simchah
For there they that led us captive asked of us words of song, and our tormentors asked of us mirth:

שִׁירוּ לָנוּ, מִשִּׁיר צִיּוֹן
shiru lanu, mishir tziyon
'Sing us one of the songs of Zion.'

אֵיךְ--נָשִׁיר אֶת-שִׁיר-יְהוָה: עַל, אַדְמַת נֵכָר
'eich, nashir et-shir-hashem al, admat nechar
How shall we sing the LORD'S song in a foreign land?

אִם-אֶשְׁכָּחֵךְ יְרוּשָׁלִָם-- תִּשְׁכַּח יְמִינִי
'im-'eshkachech yerushalayim, tishkach yemini
If I forget thee, O Jerusalem, let my right hand forget her cunning.

תִּדְבַּק-לְשׁוֹנִי, לְחִכִּי-- אִם-לֹא אֶזְכְּרֵכִי: אִם-לֹא אַעֲלֶה, אֶת-יְרוּשָׁלִַם--עַל, רֹאשׁ שִׂמְחָתִי
tidbak-leshoni lechikki im-lo ezkerechi im-lo a'aleh et-yerushalayim; al, rosh simchati
Let my tongue cleave to the roof of my mouth, if I remember thee not; if I set not Jerusalem above my chiefest joy.

זְכֹר יְהוָה, לִבְנֵי אֱדוֹם-- אֵת, יוֹם יְרוּשָׁלִָם: הָאֹמְרִים
zechor hashem livnei edom, et yom yerushalayim ha'omerim
Remember, O LORD, against the children of Edom the day of Jerusalem; who said:

עָרוּ עָרוּ-- עַד, הַיְסוֹד בָּהּ
aru aru; ad, haysod bah
'Rase it, rase it, even to the foundation thereof.'

בַּת-בָּבֶל, הַשְּׁדוּדָה: אַשְׁרֵי שֶׁיְשַׁלֶּם-לָךְ-- אֶת-גְּמוּלֵךְ, שֶׁגָּמַלְתְּ לָנוּ
bat-bavel, hashedudah ashrei sheyshallem-lach; et-gemulech, sheggamalt lanu
O daughter of Babylon, that art to be destroyed; happy shall he be, that repayeth thee as thou hast served us.

אַשְׁרֵי, שֶׁיֹּאחֵז וְנִפֵּץ אֶת-עֹלָלַיִךְ-- אֶל-הַסָּלַע
'ashrei sheyochez venippetz et-'olalayich, el-hassala
Happy shall he be, that taketh and dasheth thy little ones against the rock.

קלח

לְדָוִד: אוֹדְךָ בְכָל-לִבִּי; נֶגֶד אֱלֹהִים אֲזַמְּרֶךָּ
Ledavid odecha vechol-libbi; neged elohim azammereka
[A Psalm] of David. I will give Thee thanks with my whole heart, in the presence of the mighty will I sing praises unto Thee.

תְּהִלִּים

לְמַכֵּה, מְלָכִים גְּדֹלִים: כִּי לְעוֹלָם חַסְדּוֹ
lemakkeh melachim gedolim; ki le'olam chasdo
To Him that smote great kings; for His mercy endureth for ever;

וַיַּהֲרֹג, מְלָכִים אַדִּירִים: כִּי לְעוֹלָם חַסְדּוֹ
vayaharog melachim addirim; ki le'olam chasdo
And slew mighty kings, for His mercy endureth for ever.

לְסִיחוֹן, מֶלֶךְ הָאֱמֹרִי: כִּי לְעוֹלָם חַסְדּוֹ
lesichon melech ha'emori; ki le'olam chasdo
Sihon king of the Amorites, for His mercy endureth for ever;

וּלְעוֹג, מֶלֶךְ הַבָּשָׁן: כִּי לְעוֹלָם חַסְדּוֹ
ule'og melech habbashan; ki le'olam chasdo
And Og king of Bashan, for His mercy endureth for ever;

וְנָתַן אַרְצָם לְנַחֲלָה: כִּי לְעוֹלָם חַסְדּוֹ
venatan artzam lenachalah; ki le'olam chasdo
And gave their land for a heritage, for His mercy endureth for ever;

נַחֲלָה, לְיִשְׂרָאֵל עַבְדּוֹ: כִּי לְעוֹלָם חַסְדּוֹ
nachalah leyisra'el avdo; ki le'olam chasdo
Even a heritage unto Israel His servant, for His mercy endureth for ever.

שֶׁבְּשִׁפְלֵנוּ, זָכַר לָנוּ: כִּי לְעוֹלָם חַסְדּוֹ
shebbeshiflenu zachar lanu; ki le'olam chasdo
Who remembered us in our low estate, for His mercy endureth for ever;

וַיִּפְרְקֵנוּ מִצָּרֵינוּ: כִּי לְעוֹלָם חַסְדּוֹ
vayifrekenu mitzareinu; ki le'olam chasdo
And hath delivered us from our adversaries, for His mercy endureth for ever.

נֹתֵן לֶחֶם, לְכָל-בָּשָׂר: כִּי לְעוֹלָם חַסְדּוֹ
noten lechem lechol-basar; ki le'olam chasdo
Who giveth food to all flesh, for His mercy endureth for ever.

הוֹדוּ, לְאֵל הַשָּׁמָיִם: כִּי לְעוֹלָם חַסְדּוֹ
hodu le'el hashamayim; ki le'olam chasdo
O give thanks unto the God of heaven, for His mercy endureth for ever.

קלז

עַל נַהֲרוֹת, בָּבֶל--שָׁם יָשַׁבְנוּ, גַּם-בָּכִינוּ: בְּזָכְרֵנוּ, אֶת-צִיּוֹן
Al naharot bavel, sham yashavnu gam-bachinu; bezochrenu, et-tziyon
By the rivers of Babylon, there we sat down, yea, we wept, when we remembered Zion.

תְּהִלִּים

לְעֹשֵׂה הַשָּׁמַיִם, בִּתְבוּנָה: כִּי לְעוֹלָם חַסְדּוֹ
le'oseh hashamayim bitvunah; ki le'olam chasdo
To Him that by understanding made the heavens, for His mercy endureth for ever.

לְרֹקַע הָאָרֶץ, עַל-הַמָּיִם: כִּי לְעוֹלָם חַסְדּוֹ
leroka ha'aretz al-hammayim; ki le'olam chasdo
To Him that spread forth the earth above the waters, for His mercy endureth for ever.

לְעֹשֵׂה, אוֹרִים גְּדֹלִים: כִּי לְעוֹלָם חַסְדּוֹ
le'oseh orim gedolim; ki le'olam chasdo
To Him that made great lights, for His mercy endureth for ever;

אֶת-הַשֶּׁמֶשׁ, לְמֶמְשֶׁלֶת בַּיּוֹם: כִּי לְעוֹלָם חַסְדּוֹ
'et-hashemesh lememshelet bayom; ki le'olam chasdo
The sun to rule by day, for His mercy endureth for ever;

אֶת-הַיָּרֵחַ וְכוֹכָבִים, לְמֶמְשְׁלוֹת בַּלָּיְלָה: כִּי לְעוֹלָם חַסְדּוֹ
'et-hayareach vechochavim lememshelot ballayelah; ki le'olam chasdo
The moon and stars to rule by night, for His mercy endureth for ever.

לְמַכֵּה מִצְרַיִם, בִּבְכוֹרֵיהֶם: כִּי לְעוֹלָם חַסְדּוֹ
lemakkeh mitzrayim bivchoreihem; ki le'olam chasdo
To Him that smote Egypt in their first-born, for His mercy endureth for ever;

וַיּוֹצֵא יִשְׂרָאֵל, מִתּוֹכָם: כִּי לְעוֹלָם חַסְדּוֹ
vayotzei yisra'el mittocham; ki le'olam chasdo
And brought out Israel from among them, for His mercy endureth for ever;

בְּיָד חֲזָקָה, וּבִזְרוֹעַ נְטוּיָה: כִּי לְעוֹלָם חַסְדּוֹ
beyad chazakah uvizroa netuyah; ki le'olam chasdo
With a strong hand, and with an outstretched arm, for His mercy endureth for ever.

לְגֹזֵר יַם-סוּף, לִגְזָרִים: כִּי לְעוֹלָם חַסְדּוֹ
legozer yam-suf ligzarim; ki le'olam chasdo
To Him who divided the Red Sea in sunder, for His mercy endureth for ever;

וְהֶעֱבִיר יִשְׂרָאֵל בְּתוֹכוֹ: כִּי לְעוֹלָם חַסְדּוֹ
vehe'evir yisra'el betocho; ki le'olam chasdo
And made Israel to pass through the midst of it, for His mercy endureth for ever;

וְנִעֵר פַּרְעֹה וְחֵילוֹ בְיַם-סוּף: כִּי לְעוֹלָם חַסְדּוֹ
veni'er par'oh vecheilo veyam-suf; ki le'olam chasdo
But overthrew Pharaoh and his host in the Red Sea, for His mercy endureth for ever.

לְמוֹלִיךְ עַמּוֹ, בַּמִּדְבָּר: כִּי לְעוֹלָם חַסְדּוֹ
lemolich ammo bammidbar; ki le'olam chasdo
To Him that led His people through the wilderness, for His mercy endureth for ever.

תְּהִלִּים

פֶּה-לָהֶם, וְלֹא יְדַבֵּרוּ; עֵינַיִם לָהֶם, וְלֹא יִרְאוּ
peh-lahem velo yedabberu; einayim lahem, velo yir'u
They have mouths, but they speak not; eyes have they, but they see not;

אָזְנַיִם לָהֶם, וְלֹא יַאֲזִינוּ; אַף, אֵין-יֶשׁ-רוּחַ בְּפִיהֶם
'ozenayim lahem velo ya'azinu; af, ein-yesh-ruach befihem
They have ears, but they hear not; neither is there any breath in their mouths.

כְּמוֹהֶם, יִהְיוּ עֹשֵׂיהֶם--כֹּל אֲשֶׁר-בֹּטֵחַ בָּהֶם
kemohem yihyu oseihem; kol asher-boteach bahem
They that make them shall be like unto them; yea, every one that trusteth in them.

בֵּית יִשְׂרָאֵל, בָּרְכוּ אֶת-יְהוָה; בֵּית אַהֲרֹן, בָּרְכוּ אֶת-יְהוָה
beit yisra'el barachu et-hashem beit aharon, barachu et-hashem
O house of Israel, bless ye the LORD; O house of Aaron, bless ye the LORD;

בֵּית הַלֵּוִי, בָּרְכוּ אֶת-יְהוָה; יִרְאֵי יְהוָה, בָּרְכוּ אֶת-יְהוָה
beit hallevi barachu et-hashem yir'ei hashem barachu et-hashem
O house of Levi, bless ye the LORD; ye that fear the LORD, bless ye the LORD.

בָּרוּךְ יְהוָה, מִצִּיּוֹן--שֹׁכֵן יְרוּשָׁלִָם:
baruch hashem mitziyon, shochen yerushalayim
Blessed be the LORD out of Zion, who dwelleth at Jerusalem.

הַלְלוּ-יָהּ
halelu-yah
Hallelujah

קלו

הוֹדוּ לַיהוָה כִּי-טוֹב: כִּי לְעוֹלָם חַסְדּוֹ
Hodu lahashem ki-tov; ki le'olam chasdo
O give thanks unto the LORD, for He is good, for His mercy endureth for ever.

הוֹדוּ, לֵאלֹהֵי הָאֱלֹהִים: כִּי לְעוֹלָם חַסְדּוֹ
hodu lelohei ha'elohim; ki le'olam chasdo
O give thanks unto the God of gods, for His mercy endureth for ever.

הוֹדוּ, לַאֲדֹנֵי הָאֲדֹנִים: כִּי לְעוֹלָם חַסְדּוֹ
hodu la'adonei ha'adonim; ki le'olam chasdo
O give thanks unto the Lord of lords, for His mercy endureth for ever.

לְעֹשֵׂה נִפְלָאוֹת גְּדֹלוֹת לְבַדּוֹ: כִּי לְעוֹלָם חַסְדּוֹ
le'oseh nifla'ot gedolot levaddo; ki le'olam chasdo
To Him who alone doeth great wonders, for His mercy endureth for ever.

תְּהִלִּים

כִּי אֲנִי יָדַעְתִּי, כִּי-גָדוֹל יְהוָה; וַאֲדֹנֵינוּ, מִכָּל-אֱלֹהִים
ki ani yada'ti ki-gadol hashem va'adoneinu, mikkol-'elohim
For I know that the LORD is great, and that our Lord is above all gods.

כֹּל אֲשֶׁר-חָפֵץ יְהוָה, עָשָׂה: בַּשָּׁמַיִם וּבָאָרֶץ--בַּיַּמִּים, וְכָל-תְּהֹמוֹת
kol asher-chafetz hashem asah bashamayim uva'aretz; bayammim, vechol-tehomot
Whatsoever the LORD pleased, that hath He done, in heaven and in earth, in the seas and in all deeps;

מַעֲלֶה נְשִׂאִים, מִקְצֵה הָאָרֶץ: בְּרָקִים לַמָּטָר עָשָׂה
ma'aleh nesi'im miktzeh ha'aretz berakim lammatar asah
Who causeth the vapours to ascend from the ends of the earth; He maketh lightnings for the rain;

מוֹצֵא-רוּחַ, מֵאוֹצְרוֹתָיו
motze-ruach me'otzerotav
He bringeth forth the wind out of His treasuries.

שֶׁהִכָּה, בְּכוֹרֵי מִצְרָיִם--מֵאָדָם, עַד-בְּהֵמָה
shehikkah bechorei mitzrayim; me'adam, ad-behemah
Who smote the first-born of Egypt, both of man and beast.

שָׁלַח, אֹתֹת וּמֹפְתִים--בְּתוֹכֵכִי מִצְרָיִם: בְּפַרְעֹה, וּבְכָל-עֲבָדָיו
shalach otot umofetim betochechi mitzrayim; befar'oh, uvechol-'avadav
He sent signs and wonders into the midst of thee, O Egypt, upon Pharaoh, and upon all his servants.

שֶׁהִכָּה, גּוֹיִם רַבִּים; וְהָרַג, מְלָכִים עֲצוּמִים
shehikkah goyim rabbim; veharag, melachim atzumim
Who smote many nations, and slew mighty kings:

לְסִיחוֹן, מֶלֶךְ הָאֱמֹרִי, וּלְעוֹג, מֶלֶךְ הַבָּשָׁן; וּלְכֹל, מַמְלְכוֹת כְּנָעַן
lesichon melech ha'emori, ule'og melech habbashan; ulechol, mamlechot kena'an
Sihon king of the Amorites, and Og king of Bashan, and all the kingdoms of Canaan;

וְנָתַן אַרְצָם נַחֲלָה--נַחֲלָה, לְיִשְׂרָאֵל עַמּוֹ
venatan artzam nachalah; nachalah, leyisra'el ammo
And gave their land for a heritage, a heritage unto Israel His people.

יְהוָה, שִׁמְךָ לְעוֹלָם; יְהוָה, זִכְרְךָ לְדֹר-וָדֹר
hashem shimcha le'olam; hashem zichrecha ledor-vador
O LORD, Thy name endureth for ever; thy memorial, O LORD, throughout all generations.

כִּי-יָדִין יְהוָה עַמּוֹ; וְעַל-עֲבָדָיו, יִתְנֶחָם
ki-yadin hashem ammo; ve'al-'avadav, yitnecham
For the LORD will judge His people, and repent Himself for His servants.

עֲצַבֵּי הַגּוֹיִם, כֶּסֶף וְזָהָב; מַעֲשֵׂה, יְדֵי אָדָם
'atzabbei haggoyim kesef vezahav; ma'aseh, yedei adam
The idols of the nations are silver and gold, the work of men's hands.

תְּהִלִּים

שֶׁיֹּרֵד, עַל-פִּי מִדּוֹתָיו
sheyored, al-pi middotav
that cometh down upon the collar of his garments;

כְּטַל-חֶרְמוֹן--שֶׁיֹּרֵד, עַל-הַרְרֵי צִיּוֹן
ketal-chermon, sheyored al-harerei tziyon
Like the dew of Hermon, that cometh down upon the mountains of Zion;

כִּי שָׁם צִוָּה יְהוָה, אֶת-הַבְּרָכָה--חַיִּים, עַד-הָעוֹלָם
ki sham tzivvah hashem et-habberachah; chayim, ad-ha'olam
for there the LORD commanded the blessing, even life for ever.

קלד

שִׁיר, הַמַּעֲלוֹת: הִנֵּה בָּרְכוּ אֶת-יְהוָה, כָּל-עַבְדֵי יְהוָה
Shir, hamma'alot hinneh barachu et-hashem kol-'avdei hashem
A Song of Ascents. Behold, bless ye the LORD, all ye servants of the LORD,

הָעֹמְדִים בְּבֵית-יְהוָה, בַּלֵּילוֹת
ha'omedim beveit-hashem balleilot
that stand in the house of the LORD in the night seasons.

שְׂאוּ-יְדֵכֶם קֹדֶשׁ; וּבָרְכוּ, אֶת-יְהוָה
se'u-yedechem kodesh; uvarachu et-hashem
Lift up your hands to the sanctuary, and bless ye the LORD.

יְבָרֶכְךָ יְהוָה, מִצִּיּוֹן: עֹשֵׂה, שָׁמַיִם וָאָרֶץ
Yevarechecha hashem, mitziyon. Oseh, shamayim va'aretz
The LORD bless thee out of Zion; even He that made heaven and earth.

קלה

הַלְלוּ-יָהּ: הַלְלוּ, אֶת-שֵׁם יְהוָה; הַלְלוּ, עַבְדֵי יְהוָה
Halelu yah halelu et-shem hashem halelu avdei hashem
Hallelujah. Praise ye the name of the LORD; give praise, O ye servants of the LORD,

שֶׁעֹמְדִים, בְּבֵית יְהוָה--בְּחַצְרוֹת, בֵּית אֱלֹהֵינוּ
she'omedim beveit hashem bechatzrot, beit eloheinu
Ye that stand in the house of the LORD, in the courts of the house of our God.

הַלְלוּ-יָהּ, כִּי-טוֹב יְהוָה; זַמְּרוּ לִשְׁמוֹ, כִּי נָעִים
halelu-yah ki-tov hashem zammeru lishmo, ki na'im
Praise ye the LORD, for the LORD is good; sing praises unto His name, for it is pleasant.

כִּי-יַעֲקֹב, בָּחַר לוֹ יָהּ; יִשְׂרָאֵל, לִסְגֻלָּתוֹ
ki-ya'akov, bachar lo yah; yisra'el, lisgullato
For the LORD hath chosen Jacob unto Himself, and Israel for His own treasure.

תְּהִלִים

נִשְׁבַּע-יְהוָה, לְדָוִד אֱמֶת--לֹא-יָשׁוּב מִמֶּנָּה: מִפְּרִי בִטְנְךָ--אָשִׁית, לְכִסֵּא-לָךְ
nishba'-hashem ledavid emet lo-yashuv mimmennah mipperi vitnecha; ashit, lechisse-lach
The LORD swore unto David in truth; He will not turn back from it: 'Of the fruit of thy body will I set upon thy throne.

אִם-יִשְׁמְרוּ בָנֶיךָ, בְּרִיתִי--וְעֵדֹתִי זוֹ, אֲלַמְּדֵם
'im-yishmeru vaneicha beriti ve'edoti zo, alammedem
If thy children keep My covenant and My testimony that I shall teach them,

גַּם-בְּנֵיהֶם עֲדֵי-עַד--יֵשְׁבוּ, לְכִסֵּא-לָךְ
gam-beneihem adei-'ad; yeshevu, lechisse-lach
their children also for ever shall sit upon thy throne.'

כִּי-בָחַר יְהוָה בְּצִיּוֹן; אִוָּהּ, לְמוֹשָׁב לוֹ
ki-vachar hashem betziyon; ivvah, lemoshav lo
For the LORD hath chosen Zion; He hath desired it for His habitation:

זֹאת-מְנוּחָתִי עֲדֵי-עַד: פֹּה-אֵשֵׁב, כִּי אִוִּתִיהָ
zot-menuchati adei-'ad; poh-'eshev, ki ivvitiha
'This is My resting-place for ever; here will I dwell; for I have desired it.

צֵידָהּ, בָּרֵךְ אֲבָרֵךְ; אֶבְיוֹנֶיהָ, אַשְׂבִּיעַ לָחֶם
tzeidah barech avarech; evyoneiha, asbia lachem
I will abundantly bless her provision; I will give her needy bread in plenty.

וְכֹהֲנֶיהָ, אַלְבִּישׁ יֶשַׁע; וַחֲסִידֶיהָ, רַנֵּן יְרַנֵּנוּ
vechohaneiha albish yesha'; vachasideiha, rannen yerannenu
Her priests also will I clothe with salvation; and her saints shall shout aloud for joy.

שָׁם אַצְמִיחַ קֶרֶן לְדָוִד; עָרַכְתִּי נֵר, לִמְשִׁיחִי
sham atzmiach keren ledavid; arachti ner, limshichi
There will I make a horn to shoot up unto David, there have I ordered a lamp for Mine anointed.

אוֹיְבָיו, אַלְבִּישׁ בֹּשֶׁת; וְעָלָיו, יָצִיץ נִזְרוֹ
'oyevav albish boshet; ve'alav, yatzitz nizro
His enemies will I clothe with shame; but upon himself shall his crown shine.'

קלג

שִׁיר הַמַּעֲלוֹת, לְדָוִד: הִנֵּה מַה-טּוֹב, וּמַה-נָּעִים-- שֶׁבֶת אַחִים גַּם-יָחַד
Shir hamma'alot, ledavid hinneh mah-tov umah-na'im; shevet achim gam-yachad
A Song of Ascents; of David. Behold, how good and how pleasant it is for brethren to dwell together in unity!

כַּשֶּׁמֶן הַטּוֹב, עַל-הָרֹאשׁ--יֹרֵד, עַל-הַזָּקָן זְקַן-אַהֲרֹן
kashemen hattov al-harosh, yored, al-hazzakan zekan-'aharon
It is like the precious oil upon the head, coming down upon the beard; even Aaron's beard,

תְּהִלִּים

יַחֵל יִשְׂרָאֵל, אֶל-יְהוָה--מֵעַתָּה, וְעַד-עוֹלָם
yachel yisra'el el-hashem me'attah, ve'ad-'olam
O Israel, hope in the LORD from this time forth and for ever.

קלב

שִׁיר, הַמַּעֲלוֹת: זְכוֹר-יְהוָה לְדָוִד-- אֵת, כָּל-עֻנּוֹתוֹ
Shir, hamma'alot zechor-hashem ledavid; et kol-'unnoto
A Song of Ascents. LORD, remember unto David all his affliction;

אֲשֶׁר נִשְׁבַּע, לַיהוָה; נָדַר, לַאֲבִיר יַעֲקֹב
'asher nishba lahashem nadar, la'avir ya'akov
How he swore unto the LORD, and vowed unto the Mighty One of Jacob:

אִם-אָבֹא, בְּאֹהֶל בֵּיתִי; אִם-אֶעֱלֶה, עַל-עֶרֶשׂ יְצוּעָי
'im-'avo be'ohel beiti; im-'e'eleh, al-'eres yetzu'ai
'Surely I will not come into the tent of my house, nor go up into the bed that is spread for me;

אִם אֶתֵּן שְׁנַת לְעֵינָי; לְעַפְעַפַּי תְּנוּמָה
'im-'etten shenat le'einai; le'af'appai tenumah
I will not give sleep to mine eyes, nor slumber to mine eyelids;

עַד-אֶמְצָא מָקוֹם, לַיהוָה; מִשְׁכָּנוֹת, לַאֲבִיר יַעֲקֹב
'ad-'emtza makom lahashem mishkanot, la'avir ya'akov
Until I find out a place for the LORD, a dwelling-place for the Mighty One of Jacob.'

הִנֵּה-שְׁמַעֲנוּהָ בְאֶפְרָתָה; מְצָאנוּהָ, בִּשְׂדֵי-יָעַר
hinneh-shema'anuha ve'efratah; metzanuha, bisdei-ya'ar
Lo, we heard of it as being in Ephrath; we found it in the field of the wood.

נָבוֹאָה לְמִשְׁכְּנוֹתָיו; נִשְׁתַּחֲוֶה, לַהֲדֹם רַגְלָיו
navo'ah lemishkenotav; nishtachaveh, lahadom raglav
Let us go into His dwelling-place; let us worship at His footstool.

קוּמָה יְהוָה, לִמְנוּחָתֶךָ: אַתָּה, וַאֲרוֹן עֻזֶּךָ
kumah hashem limnuchatecha; attah, va'aron uzzecha
Arise, O LORD, unto Thy resting-place; Thou, and the ark of Thy strength.

כֹּהֲנֶיךָ יִלְבְּשׁוּ-צֶדֶק; וַחֲסִידֶיךָ יְרַנֵּנוּ
kohaneicha yilbeshu-tzedek; vachasideicha yerannenu
Let Thy priests be clothed with righteousness; and let Thy saints shout for joy.

בַּעֲבוּר, דָּוִד עַבְדֶּךָ-- אַל-תָּשֵׁב, פְּנֵי מְשִׁיחֶךָ
ba'avur david avdecha; al-tashev, penei meshichecha
For Thy servant David's sake turn not away the face of Thine anointed.

תְּהִלִּים

קל

שִׁיר הַמַּעֲלוֹת: מִמַּעֲמַקִּים קְרָאתִיךָ יְהוָה
Shir hamma'alot; mimma'amakkim keraticha hashem
A Song of Ascents. Out of the depths have I called Thee, O LORD.

אֲדֹנָי, שִׁמְעָה בְקוֹלִי: תִּהְיֶינָה אָזְנֶיךָ, קַשֻּׁבוֹת--לְקוֹל, תַּחֲנוּנָי
'adonai shim'ah vekoli tihyeinah azeneicha kashuvot; lekol, tachanunai
Lord, hearken unto my voice; let Thine ears be attentive to the voice of my supplications.

אִם-עֲוֹנוֹת תִּשְׁמָר-יָהּ--אֲדֹנָי, מִי יַעֲמֹד
'im-'avonot tishmar-yah; adonai, mi ya'amod
If Thou, LORD, shouldest mark iniquities, O Lord, who could stand?

כִּי-עִמְּךָ הַסְּלִיחָה--לְמַעַן, תִּוָּרֵא
ki-'immecha hasselichah; lema'an, tivvare
For with Thee there is forgiveness, that Thou mayest be feared.

קִוִּיתִי יְהוָה, קִוְּתָה נַפְשִׁי; וְלִדְבָרוֹ הוֹחָלְתִּי
kivviti hashem kivvetah nafshi; velidvaro hochaleti
I wait for the LORD, my soul doth wait, and in His word do I hope.

נַפְשִׁי לַאדֹנָי--מִשֹּׁמְרִים לַבֹּקֶר, שֹׁמְרִים לַבֹּקֶר
nafshi la'adonai; mishomerim labboker, shomerim labboker
My soul waiteth for the Lord, more than watchmen for the morning; yea, more than watchmen for the morning.

יַחֵל יִשְׂרָאֵל, אֶל-יְהוָה: כִּי-עִם-יְהוָה הַחֶסֶד; וְהַרְבֵּה עִמּוֹ פְדוּת
yachel yisra'el, el-hashem ki-'im-hashem hachesed; veharbeh immo fedut
O Israel, hope in the LORD; for with the LORD there is mercy, and with Him is plenteous redemption.

וְהוּא, יִפְדֶּה אֶת-יִשְׂרָאֵל--מִכֹּל, עֲוֹנֹתָיו
vehu yifdeh et-yisra'el; mikkol avonotav
And He will redeem Israel from all his iniquities.

קלא

שִׁיר הַמַּעֲלוֹת, לְדָוִד: יְהוָה, לֹא-גָבַהּ לִבִּי--וְלֹא-רָמוּ עֵינַי
Shir hamma'alot, ledavid: hashem lo-gavah libbi velo-ramu einai
A Song of Ascents; of David. LORD, my heart is not haughty, nor mine eyes lofty;

וְלֹא-הִלַּכְתִּי, בִּגְדֹלוֹת וּבְנִפְלָאוֹת מִמֶּנִּי
velo-hillachti bigdolot uvenifla'ot mimmenni
neither do I exercise myself in things too great, or in things too wonderful for me.

אִם-לֹא שִׁוִּיתִי, וְדוֹמַמְתִּי--נַפְשִׁי: כְּגָמֻל, עֲלֵי אִמּוֹ; כַּגָּמֻל עָלַי נַפְשִׁי
'im-lo shivviti vedomamti, nafshi kegamul alei immo; kaggamul alai nafshi
Surely I have stilled and quieted my soul; like a weaned child with his mother; my soul is with me like a weaned child.

תְּהִלִּים

הִנֵּה כִי-כֵן, יְבֹרַךְ גָּבֶר--יְרֵא יְהוָה
hinneh chi-chen yevorach gaver, yerei hashem
Behold, surely thus shall the man be blessed that feareth the LORD.

יְבָרֶכְךָ יְהוָה, מִצִּיּוֹן: וּרְאֵה, בְּטוּב יְרוּשָׁלָיִם--כֹּל, יְמֵי חַיֶּיךָ
yevarechcha hashem mitziyon ure'eh betuv yerushalayim; kol yemei chayeicha
The LORD bless thee out of Zion; and see thou the good of Jerusalem all the days of thy life;

וּרְאֵה-בָנִים לְבָנֶיךָ: שָׁלוֹם, עַל-יִשְׂרָאֵל
ure'eh-vanim levaneicha; shalom, al-yisra'el
And see thy children's children. Peace be upon Israel!

קכט

שִׁיר, הַמַּעֲלוֹת: רַבַּת, צְרָרוּנִי מִנְּעוּרַי--יֹאמַר-נָא, יִשְׂרָאֵל
Shir, hamma'a lot: rabbat tzeraruni minne'urai; yomar-na yisra'el
A Song of Ascents. 'Much have they afflicted me from my youth up', let Israel now say;

רַבַּת, צְרָרוּנִי מִנְּעוּרָי; גַּם, לֹא-יָכְלוּ לִי
rabbat tzeraruni minne'urai; gam lo-yachelu li
'Much have they afflicted me from my youth up; but they have not prevailed against me.

עַל-גַּבִּי, חָרְשׁוּ חֹרְשִׁים; הֶאֱרִיכוּ, לְמַעֲנִיתָם
'al-gabbi chareshu choreshim; he'erichu, lema'anitam
The plowers plowed upon my back; they made long their furrows.

יְהוָה צַדִּיק; קִצֵּץ, עֲבוֹת רְשָׁעִים
hashem tzaddik; kitzetz, avot resha'im
The LORD is righteous; He hath cut asunder the cords of the wicked.'

יֵבֹשׁוּ, וְיִסֹּגוּ אָחוֹר-- כֹּל, שֹׂנְאֵי צִיּוֹן
yevoshu veyissogu achor; kol sone'ei tziyon
Let them be ashamed and turned backward, all they that hate Zion.

יִהְיוּ, כַּחֲצִיר גַּגּוֹת-- שֶׁקַּדְמַת שָׁלַף יָבֵשׁ
yihyu kachatzir gaggot; shekkadmat shalaf yavesh
Let them be as the grass upon the housetops, which withereth afore it springeth up;

שֶׁלֹּא מִלֵּא כַפּוֹ קוֹצֵר; וְחִצְנוֹ מְעַמֵּר
shello millei chappo kotzer, vechitzno me'ammer
Wherewith the reaper filleth not his hand, nor he that bindeth sheaves his bosom.

וְלֹא אָמְרוּ, הָעֹבְרִים-- בִּרְכַּת-יְהוָה אֲלֵיכֶם; בֵּרַכְנוּ אֶתְכֶם, בְּשֵׁם יְהוָה
velo ameru ha'overim, birkat-hashem aleichem; berachnu etchem, beshem hashem
Neither do they that go by say: 'The blessing of the LORD be upon you; we bless you in the name of the LORD.'

תְּהִלִים

הָלוֹךְ יֵלֵךְ, וּבָכֹה--נֹשֵׂא מֶשֶׁךְ-הַזָּרַע: בֹּא-יָבֹא בְרִנָּה--נֹשֵׂא, אֲלֻמֹּתָיו
haloch yelech uvachoh nosei meshech-hazzara bo-yavo verinnah; nose, alummotav
Though he goeth on his way weeping that beareth the measure of seed, he shall come home with joy, bearing his sheaves.

קכז

שִׁיר הַמַּעֲלוֹת, לִשְׁלֹמֹה: אִם-יְהוָה, לֹא-יִבְנֶה בַיִת--שָׁוְא עָמְלוּ בוֹנָיו בּוֹ
Shir hamma'alot, lishlomoh im-hashem lo-yivneh vayit, shav amelu vonav bo
A Song of Ascents; of Solomon. Except the LORD build the house, they labour in vain that build it;

אִם-יְהוָה לֹא-יִשְׁמָר-עִיר, שָׁוְא שָׁקַד שׁוֹמֵר
im-hashem lo-yishmor-'ir, shav shakad shomer
except the LORD keep the city, the watchman waketh but in vain.

שָׁוְא לָכֶם מַשְׁכִּימֵי קוּם, מְאַחֲרֵי-שֶׁבֶת--אֹכְלֵי, לֶחֶם הָעֲצָבִים; כֵּן יִתֵּן לִידִידוֹ שֵׁנָא
shav lachem mashkimei kum me'acharei-shevet, ochelei lechem ha'atzavim; ken yitten lidido shena
It is vain for you that ye rise early, and sit up late, ye that eat the bread of toil; so He giveth unto His beloved in sleep.

הִנֵּה נַחֲלַת יְהוָה בָּנִים: שָׂכָר, פְּרִי הַבָּטֶן
hinneh nachalat hashem banim; sachar, peri habbaten
Lo, children are a heritage of the LORD; the fruit of the womb is a reward.

כְּחִצִּים בְּיַד-גִּבּוֹר--כֵּן, בְּנֵי הַנְּעוּרִים
kechitzim beyad-gibbor; ken, benei hanne'urim
As arrows in the hand of a mighty man, so are the children of one's youth.

אַשְׁרֵי הַגֶּבֶר--אֲשֶׁר מִלֵּא אֶת-אַשְׁפָּתוֹ, מֵהֶם
'ashrei haggever, asher millei et-'ashpato, mehem
Happy is the man that hath his quiver full of them;

לֹא-יֵבֹשׁוּ--כִּי-יְדַבְּרוּ אֶת-אוֹיְבִים בַּשָּׁעַר
lo-yevoshu; ki-yedabberu et-'oyevim basha'ar
they shall not be put to shame, when they speak with their enemies in the gate.

קכח

שִׁיר, הַמַּעֲלוֹת: אַשְׁרֵי, כָּל-יְרֵא יְהוָה--הַהֹלֵךְ, בִּדְרָכָיו
Shir, hamma'alot ashrei kol-yerei hashem haholech, bidrachav
A Song of Ascents. Happy is every one that feareth the LORD, that walketh in His ways.

יְגִיעַ כַּפֶּיךָ, כִּי תֹאכֵל; אַשְׁרֶיךָ, וְטוֹב לָךְ
yegia kappeicha ki tochel; ashreicha, vetov lach
When thou eatest the labour of thy hands, happy shalt thou be, and it shall be well with thee.

אֶשְׁתְּךָ, כְּגֶפֶן פֹּרִיָּה--בְּיַרְכְּתֵי בֵיתֶךָ: בָּנֶיךָ, כִּשְׁתִלֵי זֵיתִים--סָבִיב, לְשֻׁלְחָנֶךָ
'eshtecha kegefen poriyah beyarketei veitecha baneicha kishtilei zeitim; saviv, leshulchanecha
Thy wife shall be as a fruitful vine, in the innermost parts of thy house; thy children like olive plants, round about thy table.

תְּהִלִים

כִּי לֹא יָנוּחַ, שֵׁבֶט הָרֶשַׁע--עַל, גּוֹרַל הַצַּדִּיקִים
ki lo yanuach shevet haresha', al goral hatzaddikim
For the rod of wickedness shall not rest upon the lot of the righteous;

לְמַעַן, לֹא-יִשְׁלְחוּ הַצַּדִּיקִים בְּעַוְלָתָה יְדֵיהֶם
lema'an lo-yishlechu hatzaddikim be'avlatah yedeihem
that the righteous put not forth their hands unto iniquity.

הֵיטִיבָה יְהוָה, לַטּוֹבִים; וְלִישָׁרִים, בְּלִבּוֹתָם
heitivah hashem lattovim; velisharim, belibbotam
Do good, O LORD, unto the good, and to them that are upright in their hearts.

וְהַמַּטִּים עֲקַלְקַלּוֹתָם--יוֹלִיכֵם יְהוָה, אֶת-פֹּעֲלֵי הָאָוֶן
vehammattim akalkallotam, yolichem hashem et-po'alei ha'aven
But as for such as turn aside unto their crooked ways, the LORD will lead them away with the workers of iniquity.

שָׁלוֹם, עַל-יִשְׂרָאֵל
shalom, al-yisra'el
Peace be upon Israel.

קכו

שִׁיר, הַמַּעֲלוֹת: בְּשׁוּב יְהוָה, אֶת-שִׁיבַת צִיּוֹן--הָיִינוּ, כְּחֹלְמִים
Shir, hamma'alot beshuv hashem et-shivat tziyon; hayinu, kecholemim
A Song of Ascents. When the LORD brought back those that returned to Zion, we were like unto them that dream.

אָז יִמָּלֵא שְׂחוֹק, פִּינוּ--וּלְשׁוֹנֵנוּ רִנָּה
'az yimmalei sechok pinu uleshonenu rinnah
Then was our mouth filled with laughter, and our tongue with singing;

אָז, יֹאמְרוּ בַגּוֹיִם--הִגְדִּיל יְהוָה, לַעֲשׂוֹת עִם-אֵלֶּה
az yomeru vaggoyim; higdil hashem la'asot im-'elleh
then said they among the nations: 'The LORD hath done great things with these.'

הִגְדִּיל יְהוָה, לַעֲשׂוֹת עִמָּנוּ--הָיִינוּ שְׂמֵחִים
higdil hashem la'asot immanu, hayinu semechim
The LORD hath done great things with us; we are rejoiced.

שׁוּבָה יְהוָה, אֶת-שְׁבִיתֵנוּ--כַּאֲפִיקִים בַּנֶּגֶב
shuvah hashem et-shevitenu; ka'afikim bannegev
Turn our captivity, O LORD, as the streams in the dry land.

הַזֹּרְעִים בְּדִמְעָה--בְּרִנָּה יִקְצֹרוּ
hazzore'im bedim'ah, berinnah yiktzoru
They that sow in tears shall reap in joy.

תְּהִלִּים

רַבַּת, שָׂבְעָה-לָּהּ נַפְשֵׁנוּ: הַלַּעַג הַשַּׁאֲנַנִּים; הַבּוּז, לִגְאֵי יוֹנִים
rabbat save'ah-lah nafshenu halla'ag hasha'anannim; habbuz, lig'eyonim
Our soul is full sated with the scorning of those that are at ease, and with the contempt of the proud oppressors.

קכד

שִׁיר הַמַּעֲלוֹת, לְדָוִד: לוּלֵי יְהוָה, שֶׁהָיָה לָנוּ--יֹאמַר-נָא, יִשְׂרָאֵל
Shir hamma'alot, ledavid: lulei hashem shehayah lanu; yomar-na yisra'el
A Song of Ascents; of David. 'If it had not been the LORD who was for us', let Israel now say;

לוּלֵי יְהוָה, שֶׁהָיָה לָנוּ--בְּקוּם עָלֵינוּ אָדָם
lulei hashem shehayah lanu; bekum aleinu adam
'If it had not been the LORD who was for us, when men rose up against us,

אֲזַי, חַיִּים בְּלָעוּנוּ--בַּחֲרוֹת אַפָּם בָּנוּ
'azai chayim bela'unu; bacharot appam banu
Then they had swallowed us up alive, when their wrath was kindled against us;

אֲזַי, הַמַּיִם שְׁטָפוּנוּ--נַחְלָה, עָבַר עַל-נַפְשֵׁנוּ
'azai hammayim shetafunu; nachlah, avar al-nafshenu
Then the waters had overwhelmed us, the stream had gone over our soul;

אֲזַי, עָבַר עַל-נַפְשֵׁנוּ--הַמַּיִם, הַזֵּידוֹנִים
'azai avar al-nafshenu; hammayim, hazzeidonim
Then the proud waters had gone over our soul.'

בָּרוּךְ יְהוָה--שֶׁלֹּא נְתָנָנוּ טֶרֶף, לְשִׁנֵּיהֶם
baruch hashem shello netananu teref, leshinneihem
Blessed be the LORD, who hath not given us as a prey to their teeth.

נַפְשֵׁנוּ--כְּצִפּוֹר נִמְלְטָה, מִפַּח יוֹקְשִׁים: הַפַּח נִשְׁבָּר, וַאֲנַחְנוּ נִמְלָטְנוּ
nafshenu, ketzippor nimletah mippach yokeshim happach nishbar, va'anachnu nimlatenu
Our soul is escaped as a bird out of the snare of the fowlers; the snare is broken, and we are escaped.

עֶזְרֵנוּ, בְּשֵׁם יְהוָה--עֹשֵׂה, שָׁמַיִם וָאָרֶץ
'ezrenu beshem hashem oseh, shamayim va'aretz
Our help is in the name of the LORD, who made heaven and earth.

קכה

שִׁיר, הַמַּעֲלוֹת: הַבֹּטְחִים בַּיהוָה--כְּהַר-צִיּוֹן לֹא-יִמּוֹט, לְעוֹלָם יֵשֵׁב
Shir, hamma'a lot: habbotechim bahashem; kehar-tziyon lo-yimmot, le'olam yeshev
A Song of Ascents. They that trust in the LORD are as mount Zion, which cannot be moved, but abideth for ever.

יְרוּשָׁלִַם-- הָרִים, סָבִיב לָהּ: וַיהוָה, סָבִיב לְעַמּוֹ--מֵעַתָּה, וְעַד-עוֹלָם
yerushalayim, harim saviv lah vahashem saviv le'ammo; me'attah, ve'ad-'olam
As the mountains are round about Jerusalem, so the LORD is round about His people, from this time forth and for ever.

תְּהִלִים

שֶׁשָּׁם עָלוּ שְׁבָטִים, שִׁבְטֵי־יָהּ
shesham alu shevatim shivtei-yah
Whither the tribes went up, even the tribes of the LORD,

עֵדוּת לְיִשְׂרָאֵל: לְהֹדוֹת, לְשֵׁם יְהוָה
edut leyisra'el; lehodot, leshem hashem
as a testimony unto Israel, to give thanks unto the name of the LORD.

כִּי שָׁמָּה, יָשְׁבוּ כִסְאוֹת לְמִשְׁפָּט: כִּסְאוֹת, לְבֵית דָּוִד
ki shammah yashevu chis'ot lemishpat; kis'ot, leveit david
For there were set thrones for judgment, the thrones of the house of David.

שַׁאֲלוּ, שְׁלוֹם יְרוּשָׁלִָם; יִשְׁלָיוּ, אֹהֲבָיִךְ
sha'alu shelom yerushalayim; yishlayu, ohavayich
Pray for the peace of Jerusalem; may they prosper that love thee.

יְהִי־שָׁלוֹם בְּחֵילֵךְ; שַׁלְוָה, בְּאַרְמְנוֹתָיִךְ
yehi-shalom becheilech; shalvah, be'armenotayich
Peace be within thy walls, and prosperity within thy palaces.

לְמַעַן, אַחַי וְרֵעָי--אֲדַבְּרָה־נָּא שָׁלוֹם בָּךְ
lema'an achai vere'ai; adabberah-na shalom bach
For my brethren and companions' sakes, I will now say: 'Peace be within thee.'

לְמַעַן, בֵּית־יְהוָה אֱלֹהֵינוּ--אֲבַקְשָׁה טוֹב לָךְ
lema'an beit-hashem eloheinu; avakshah tov lach
For the sake of the house of the LORD our God I will seek thy good.

קכג

שִׁיר, הַמַּעֲלוֹת: אֵלֶיךָ, נָשָׂאתִי אֶת־עֵינַי--הַיֹּשְׁבִי, בַּשָּׁמָיִם
Shir, hamma'alot: eleicha nasati et-'einai; hayoshevi, bashamayim
A Song of Ascents. Unto Thee I lift up mine eyes, O Thou that art enthroned in the heavens.

הִנֵּה כְעֵינֵי עֲבָדִים, אֶל־יַד אֲדוֹנֵיהֶם--כְּעֵינֵי שִׁפְחָה, אֶל־יַד גְּבִרְתָּהּ
hinneh che'einei avadim el-yad adoneihem, ke'einei shifchah el-yad gevirtah
Behold, as the eyes of servants unto the hand of their master, as the eyes of a maiden unto the hand of her mistress;

כֵּן עֵינֵינוּ, אֶל־יְהוָה אֱלֹהֵינוּ--עַד, שֶׁיְּחָנֵּנוּ
ken eineinu el-hashem eloheinu; ad, sheyechannenu
so our eyes look unto the LORD our God, until He be gracious unto us.

חָנֵּנוּ יְהוָה חָנֵּנוּ: כִּי־רַב, שָׂבַעְנוּ בוּז
chonnenu hashem chonnenu ki-rav, sava'nu vuz
Be gracious unto us, O LORD, be gracious unto us; for we are full sated with contempt.

תְּהִלִּים

קכא

שִׁיר, לַמַּעֲלוֹת: אֶשָּׂא עֵינַי, אֶל-הֶהָרִים-- מֵאַיִן, יָבֹא עֶזְרִי
Shir, lamma'alot: essa einai el-heharim; me'ayin, yavo ezri
A Song of Ascents. I will lift up mine eyes unto the mountains: from whence shall my help come?

עֶזְרִי, מֵעִם יְהוָה-- עֹשֵׂה, שָׁמַיִם וָאָרֶץ
'ezri me'im hashem oseh, shamayim va'aretz
My help cometh from the LORD, who made heaven and earth.

אַל-יִתֵּן לַמּוֹט רַגְלֶךָ; אַל-יָנוּם, שֹׁמְרֶךָ
'al-yitten lammot raglecha; al-yanum, shomerecha
He will not suffer thy foot to be moved; He that keepeth thee will not slumber.

הִנֵּה לֹא-יָנוּם, וְלֹא יִישָׁן-- שׁוֹמֵר, יִשְׂרָאֵל
hinneh lo-yanum velo yishan; shomer, yisra'el
Behold, He that keepeth Israel doth neither slumber nor sleep.

יְהוָה שֹׁמְרֶךָ; יְהוָה צִלְּךָ, עַל-יַד יְמִינֶךָ
hashem shomerecha; hashem tzillecha, al-yad yeminecha
The LORD is thy keeper; the LORD is thy shade upon thy right hand.

יוֹמָם, הַשֶּׁמֶשׁ לֹא-יַכֶּכָּה; וְיָרֵחַ בַּלָּיְלָה
yomam, hashemesh lo-yakkekkah, veyareach ballayelah
The sun shall not smite thee by day, nor the moon by night.

יְהוָה, יִשְׁמָרְךָ מִכָּל-רָע: יִשְׁמֹר, אֶת-נַפְשֶׁךָ
hashem yishmorecha mikkol-ra'; yishmor, et-nafshecha
The LORD shall keep thee from all evil; He shall keep thy soul.

יְהוָה, יִשְׁמָר-צֵאתְךָ וּבוֹאֶךָ-- מֵעַתָּה, וְעַד-עוֹלָם
hashem yishmor-tzetecha uvo'echa; me'attah, ve'ad-'olam
The LORD shall guard thy going out and thy coming in, from this time forth and for ever.

קכב

שִׁיר הַמַּעֲלוֹת, לְדָוִד: שָׂמַחְתִּי, בְּאֹמְרִים לִי-- בֵּית יְהוָה נֵלֵךְ
Shir hamma'alot, ledavid samachti be'omerim li; beit hashem nelech
A Song of Ascents; of David. I rejoiced when they said unto me: 'Let us go unto the house of the LORD.'

עֹמְדוֹת, הָיוּ רַגְלֵינוּ-- בִּשְׁעָרַיִךְ, יְרוּשָׁלִָם
'omedot hayu ragleinu; bish'arayich, yerushalayim
Our feet are standing within thy gates, O Jerusalem;

יְרוּשָׁלִַם הַבְּנוּיָה-- כְּעִיר, שֶׁחֻבְּרָה-לָּהּ יַחְדָּו
yerushalayim habbenuyah; ke'ir, shechubberah-lah yachdav
Jerusalem, that art builded as a city that is compact together;

תְּהִלִּים

תָּאַבְתִּי לִישׁוּעָתְךָ יְהוָה; וְתוֹרָתְךָ, שַׁעֲשֻׁעָי
ta'avti lishu'atecha hashem vetoratecha, sha'ashu'ai
I have longed for Thy salvation, O LORD; and Thy law is my delight.

תְּחִי-נַפְשִׁי, וּתְהַלְלֶךָּ; וּמִשְׁפָּטֶךָ יַעְזְרֻנִי
techi-nafshi utehaleleka; umishpatecha ya'azruni
Let my soul live, and it shall praise Thee; and let Thine ordinances help me.

תָּעִיתִי--כְּשֶׂה אֹבֵד, בַּקֵּשׁ עַבְדֶּךָ: כִּי מִצְוֺתֶיךָ, לֹא שָׁכָחְתִּי
ta'iti, keseh oved bakkesh avdecha; ki mitzvoteicha, lo shachacheti
I have gone astray like a lost sheep; seek Thy servant; for I have not forgotten Thy commandments.

קכ

שִׁיר, הַמַּעֲלוֹת: אֶל-יְהוָה, בַּצָּרָתָה לִּי--קָרָאתִי, וַיַּעֲנֵנִי
Shir, hamma'alot el-hashem batzaratah li; karati, vaya'aneni
A Song of Ascents. In my distress I called unto the LORD, and He answered me.

יְהוָה--הַצִּילָה נַפְשִׁי, מִשְּׂפַת-שֶׁקֶר: מִלָּשׁוֹן רְמִיָּה
hashem hatzilah nafshi missefat-sheker; millashon remiyah
O LORD, deliver my soul from lying lips, from a deceitful tongue.

מַה-יִּתֵּן לְךָ, וּמַה-יֹּסִיף לָךְ--לָשׁוֹן רְמִיָּה
mah-yitten lecha umah-yosif lach, lashon remiyah
What shall be given unto thee, and what shall be done more unto thee, thou deceitful tongue?

חִצֵּי גִבּוֹר שְׁנוּנִים; עִם, גַּחֲלֵי רְתָמִים
chitzei gibbor shenunim; im, gachalei retamim
Sharp arrows of the mighty, with coals of broom.

אוֹיָה-לִי, כִּי-גַרְתִּי מֶשֶׁךְ; שָׁכַנְתִּי, עִם-אָהֳלֵי קֵדָר
'oyah-li ki-garti meshech; shachanti, im-'oholei kedar
Woe is me, that I sojourn with Meshech, that I dwell beside the tents of Kedar!

רַבַּת, שָׁכְנָה-לָּהּ נַפְשִׁי--עִם, שׂוֹנֵא שָׁלוֹם
rabbat shachenah-lah nafshi; im, sonei shalom
My soul hath full long had her dwelling with him that hateth peace.

אֲנִי-שָׁלוֹם, וְכִי אֲדַבֵּר; הֵמָּה, לַמִּלְחָמָה
'ani-shalom vechi adabber; hemmah, lammilchamah
I am all peace; but when I speak, they are for war.

תְּהִלִּים

שָׂשׂ אָנֹכִי, עַל-אִמְרָתֶךָ--כְּמוֹצֵא, שָׁלָל רָב
sas anochi al-'imratecha; kemotze, shalal rav
I rejoice at Thy word, as one that findeth great spoil.

שֶׁקֶר שָׂנֵאתִי, וַאֲתַעֵבָה; תּוֹרָתְךָ אָהָבְתִּי
sheker saneti va'ata'evah; toratecha ahaveti
I hate and abhor falsehood; Thy law do I love.

שֶׁבַע בַּיּוֹם, הִלַּלְתִּיךָ--עַל, מִשְׁפְּטֵי צִדְקֶךָ
sheva bayom hillalticha; al, mishpetei tzidkecha
Seven times a day do I praise Thee, because of Thy righteous ordinances.

שָׁלוֹם רָב, לְאֹהֲבֵי תוֹרָתֶךָ; וְאֵין-לָמוֹ מִכְשׁוֹל
shalom rav le'ohavei toratecha; ve'ein-lamo michshol
Great peace have they that love Thy law; and there is no stumbling for them.

שִׂבַּרְתִּי לִישׁוּעָתְךָ יְהוָה; וּמִצְוֹתֶיךָ עָשִׂיתִי
sibbarti lishu'atecha hashem umitzvoteicha asiti
I have hoped for Thy salvation, O LORD, and have done Thy commandments.

שָׁמְרָה נַפְשִׁי, עֵדֹתֶיךָ; וָאֹהֲבֵם מְאֹד
shamerah nafshi edoteicha; va'ohavem me'od
My soul hath observed Thy testimonies; and I love them exceedingly.

שָׁמַרְתִּי פִקּוּדֶיךָ, וְעֵדֹתֶיךָ: כִּי כָל-דְּרָכַי נֶגְדֶּךָ
shamarti fikkudeicha ve'edoteicha; ki chol-derachai negdecha
I have observed Thy precepts and Thy testimonies; for all my ways are before Thee.

תִּקְרַב רִנָּתִי לְפָנֶיךָ יְהוָה; כִּדְבָרְךָ הֲבִינֵנִי
tikrav rinnati lefaneicha hashem kidvarecha havineni
TAV. Let my cry come near before Thee, O LORD; give me understanding according to Thy word.

תָּבוֹא תְחִנָּתִי לְפָנֶיךָ; כְּאִמְרָתְךָ, הַצִּילֵנִי
tavo techinnati lefaneicha; ke'imratecha, hatzileni
Let my supplication come before Thee; deliver me according to Thy word.

תַּבַּעְנָה שְׂפָתַי תְּהִלָּה: כִּי תְלַמְּדֵנִי חֻקֶּיךָ
tabba'nah sefatai tehillah; ki telammedeni chukkeicha
Let my lips utter praise: because Thou teachest me Thy statutes.

תַּעַן לְשׁוֹנִי, אִמְרָתֶךָ: כִּי כָל-מִצְוֹתֶיךָ צֶּדֶק
ta'an leshoni imratecha; ki chol-mitzvoteicha tzedek
Let my tongue sing of Thy word; for all Thy commandments are righteousness.

תְּהִי-יָדְךָ לְעָזְרֵנִי: כִּי פִקּוּדֶיךָ בָחָרְתִּי
tehi-yadecha le'azereni; ki fikkudeicha vachareti
Let Thy hand be ready to help me; for I have chosen Thy precepts.

תְּהִלִים

קָרוֹב אַתָּה יְהוָה; וְכָל-מִצְוֹתֶיךָ אֱמֶת
karov attah hashem vechol-mitzvoteicha emet
Thou art nigh, O LORD; and all Thy commandments are truth.

קֶדֶם יָדַעְתִּי, מֵעֵדֹתֶיךָ: כִּי לְעוֹלָם יְסַדְתָּם
kedem yada'ti me'edoteicha; ki le'olam yesadtam
Of old have I known from Thy testimonies that Thou hast founded them for ever.

רְאֵה-עָנְיִי וְחַלְּצֵנִי: כִּי-תוֹרָתְךָ, לֹא שָׁכָחְתִּי
re'eh-'oneyi vechalletzeni; ki-toratecha, lo shachachti
RESH. O see mine affliction, and rescue me; for I do not forget Thy law.

רִיבָה רִיבִי, וּגְאָלֵנִי; לְאִמְרָתְךָ חַיֵּנִי
rivah rivi uge'aleni; le'imratecha chayeni
Plead Thou my cause, and redeem me; quicken me according to Thy word.

רָחוֹק מֵרְשָׁעִים יְשׁוּעָה: כִּי חֻקֶּיךָ, לֹא דָרָשׁוּ
rachok meresha'im yeshu'ah; ki-chukkeicha lo darashu
Salvation is far from the wicked; for they seek not Thy statutes.

רַחֲמֶיךָ רַבִּים יְהוָה; כְּמִשְׁפָּטֶיךָ חַיֵּנִי
rachameicha rabbim hashem kemishpateicha chayeni
Great are Thy compassions, O LORD; quicken me as Thou art wont.

רַבִּים, רֹדְפַי וְצָרָי; מֵעֵדְוֺתֶיךָ, לֹא נָטִיתִי
rabbim rodefai vetzarai; me'edteicha, lo natiti
Many are my persecutors and mine adversaries; yet have I not turned aside from Thy testimonies.

רָאִיתִי בֹגְדִים, וָאֶתְקוֹטָטָה--אֲשֶׁר אִמְרָתְךָ, לֹא שָׁמָרוּ
ra'iti vogedim va'etkotatah; asher imratecha, lo shamaru
I beheld them that were faithless, and strove with them; because they observed not Thy word.

רְאֵה, כִּי-פִקּוּדֶיךָ אָהָבְתִּי; יְהוָה, כְּחַסְדְּךָ חַיֵּנִי
re'eh ki-fikkudeicha ahaveti; hashem kechasdecha chayeni
O see how I love Thy precepts; quicken me, O LORD, according to Thy lovingkindness.

רֹאשׁ-דְּבָרְךָ אֱמֶת; וּלְעוֹלָם, כָּל-מִשְׁפַּט צִדְקֶךָ
rosh-devarecha emet; ule'olam, kol-mishpat tzidkecha
The beginning of Thy word is truth; and all Thy righteous ordinance endureth for ever.

שָׂרִים, רְדָפוּנִי חִנָּם; וּמִדְּבָרְךָ, פָּחַד לִבִּי
sarim redafuni chinnam; umiddevarecha, pachad libbi
SHIN. Princes have persecuted me without a cause; but my heart standeth in awe of Thy words.

תְּהִלִים

צִמְּתַתְנִי קִנְאָתִי: כִּי-שָׁכְחוּ דְבָרֶיךָ צָרָי
tzimmetatni kin'ati; ki-shachechu devareicha tzarai
My zeal hath undone me, because mine adversaries have forgotten Thy words.

צְרוּפָה אִמְרָתְךָ מְאֹד; וְעַבְדְּךָ אֲהֵבָהּ
tzerufah imratcha me'od, ve'avdecha ahevah
Thy word is tried to the uttermost, and Thy servant loveth it.

צָעִיר אָנֹכִי וְנִבְזֶה; פִּקֻּדֶיךָ, לֹא שָׁכָחְתִּי
tza'ir anochi venivzeh; pikkudeicha, lo shachachti
I am small and despised; yet have I not forgotten Thy precepts.

צִדְקָתְךָ צֶדֶק לְעוֹלָם; וְתוֹרָתְךָ אֱמֶת
tzidkatecha tzedek le'olam; vetoratecha emet
Thy righteousness is an everlasting righteousness, and Thy law is truth.

צַר-וּמָצוֹק מְצָאוּנִי; מִצְוֹתֶיךָ, שַׁעֲשֻׁעָי
tzar-umatzok metza'uni; mitzvoteicha, sha'ashu'ai
Trouble and anguish have overtaken me; yet Thy commandments are my delight.

צֶדֶק עֵדְו‍ֹתֶיךָ לְעוֹלָם; הֲבִינֵנִי וְאֶחְיֶה
tzedek edoteicha le'olam, havineni ve'echyeh
Thy testimonies are righteous for ever; give me understanding, and I shall live.

קָרָאתִי בְכָל-לֵב, עֲנֵנִי יְהוָה; חֻקֶּיךָ אֶצֹּרָה
karati vechal-lev aneni hashem chukkeicha etzorah
KOPH. I have called with my whole heart; answer me, O LORD; I will keep Thy statutes.

קְרָאתִיךָ הוֹשִׁיעֵנִי; וְאֶשְׁמְרָה, עֵדֹתֶיךָ
keraticha hoshi'eni; ve'eshmerah, edoteicha
I have called Thee, save me, and I will observe Thy testimonies.

קִדַּמְתִּי בַנֶּשֶׁף, וָאֲשַׁוֵּעָה; לדבריך (לִדְבָרְךָ) יִחָלְתִּי
kiddamti vanneshef va'ashavve'ah; lidvarecha yichaleti
I rose early at dawn, and cried; I hoped in Thy word.

קִדְּמוּ עֵינַי, אַשְׁמֻרוֹת--לָשִׂיחַ, בְּאִמְרָתֶךָ
kiddemu einai ashmurot; lasiach, be'imratecha
Mine eyes forestalled the night-watches, that I might meditate in Thy word.

קוֹלִי, שִׁמְעָה כְחַסְדֶּךָ; יְהוָה, כְּמִשְׁפָּטֶךָ חַיֵּנִי
koli shim'ah chechasdecha; hashem kemishpatecha chayeni
Hear my voice according unto Thy lovingkindness; quicken me, O LORD, as Thou art wont.

קָרְבוּ, רֹדְפֵי זִמָּה; מִתּוֹרָתְךָ רָחָקוּ
karevu rodefei zimmah; mittoratecha rachaku
They draw nigh that follow after wickedness; they are far from Thy law.

תְּהִלִּים

עַל-כֵּן, אָהַבְתִּי מִצְוֹתֶיךָ--מִזָּהָב וּמִפָּז
'al-ken ahavti mitzvoteicha; mizzahav umippaz
Therefore I love Thy commandments above gold, yea, above fine gold.

עַל-כֵּן, כָּל-פִּקּוּדֵי כֹל יִשָּׁרְתִּי; כָּל-אֹרַח שֶׁקֶר שָׂנֵאתִי
'al-ken kol-pikkudei chol yishareti; kol-'orach sheker saneti
Therefore I esteem all [Thy] precepts concerning all things to be right; every false way I hate.

פְּלָאוֹת עֵדְוֹתֶיךָ; עַל-כֵּן, נְצָרָתַם נַפְשִׁי
pela'ot edoteicha; al-ken, netzaratam nafshi
PE. Thy testimonies are wonderful; therefore doth my soul keep them.

פֵּתַח דְּבָרֶיךָ יָאִיר; מֵבִין פְּתָיִים
petach devareicha ya'ir, mevin petayim
The opening of Thy words giveth light; it giveth understanding unto the simple.

פִּי-פָעַרְתִּי, וָאֶשְׁאָפָה: כִּי לְמִצְוֹתֶיךָ יָאָבְתִּי
pi-fa'arti va'esh'afah; ki lemitzvoteicha ya'aveti
I opened wide my mouth, and panted; for I longed for Thy commandments.

פְּנֵה-אֵלַי וְחָנֵּנִי--כְּמִשְׁפָּט, לְאֹהֲבֵי שְׁמֶךָ
peneh-'elai vechonneni kemishpat, le'ohavei shemecha
Turn Thee towards me, and be gracious unto me, as is Thy wont to do unto those that love Thy name.

פְּעָמַי, הָכֵן בְּאִמְרָתֶךָ; וְאַל-תַּשְׁלֶט-בִּי כָל-אָוֶן
pe'amai hachen be'imratecha; ve'al-tashlet-bi chol-'aven
Order my footsteps by Thy word; and let not any iniquity have dominion over me.

פְּדֵנִי, מֵעֹשֶׁק אָדָם; וְאֶשְׁמְרָה, פִּקּוּדֶיךָ
pedeni me'oshek adam; ve'eshmerah, pikkudeicha
Redeem me from the oppression of man, and I will observe Thy precepts.

פָּנֶיךָ, הָאֵר בְּעַבְדֶּךָ; וְלַמְּדֵנִי, אֶת-חֻקֶּיךָ
paneicha ha'er be'avdecha; velammedeni, et-chukkeicha
Make Thy face to shine upon Thy servant; and teach me Thy statutes.

פַּלְגֵי-מַיִם, יָרְדוּ עֵינָי-- עַל, לֹא-שָׁמְרוּ תוֹרָתֶךָ
palgei-mayim yaredu einai; al, lo-shameru toratecha
Mine eyes run down with rivers of water, because they observe not Thy law.

צַדִּיק אַתָּה יְהוָה; וְיָשָׁר, מִשְׁפָּטֶיךָ
tzaddik attah hashem veyashar, mishpateicha
TZADE. Righteous art Thou, O LORD, and upright are Thy judgments.

צִוִּיתָ, צֶדֶק עֵדֹתֶיךָ; וֶאֱמוּנָה מְאֹד
tzivvita tzedek edoteicha; ve'emunah me'od
Thou hast commanded Thy testimonies in righteousness and exceeding faithfulness.

תְּהִלִּים

סוּרוּ-מִמֶּנִּי מְרֵעִים; וְאֶצְּרָה, מִצְוֹת אֱלֹהָי
suru-mimmenni mere'im; ve'etzerah, mitzvot elohai
Depart from me, ye evildoers; that I may keep the commandments of my God.

סָמְכֵנִי כְאִמְרָתְךָ וְאֶחְיֶה; וְאַל-תְּבִישֵׁנִי, מִשִּׂבְרִי
samecheni che'imratecha ve'echyeh; ve'al-tevisheni, missivri
Uphold me according unto Thy word, that I may live; and put me not to shame in my hope.

סְעָדֵנִי וְאִוָּשֵׁעָה; וְאֶשְׁעָה בְחֻקֶּיךָ תָמִיד
se'adeni ve'ivvashe'ah; ve'esh'ah vechukkeicha tamid
Support Thou me, and I shall be saved; and I will occupy myself with Thy statutes continually.

סָלִיתָ, כָּל-שׁוֹגִים מֵחֻקֶּיךָ: כִּי-שֶׁקֶר, תַּרְמִיתָם
salita kol-shogim mechukkeicha; ki-sheker, tarmitam
Thou hast made light of all them that err from Thy statutes; for their deceit is vain.

סִגִים--הִשְׁבַּתָּ כָל-רִשְׁעֵי-אָרֶץ; לָכֵן, אָהַבְתִּי עֵדֹתֶיךָ
sigim, hishbata chol-rish'ei-'aretz; lachen, ahavti edoteicha
Thou puttest away all the wicked of the earth like dross; therefore I love Thy testimonies.

סָמַר מִפַּחְדְּךָ בְשָׂרִי; וּמִמִּשְׁפָּטֶיךָ יָרֵאתִי
samar mippachdecha vesari; umimmishpateicha yareti
My flesh shuddereth for fear of Thee; and I am afraid of Thy judgments.

עָשִׂיתִי, מִשְׁפָּט וָצֶדֶק; בַּל-תַּנִּיחֵנִי, לְעֹשְׁקָי
'asiti mishpat vatzedek; bal-tannicheni, le'oshekai
AIN. I have done justice and righteousness; leave me not to mine oppressors.

עֲרֹב עַבְדְּךָ לְטוֹב; אַל-יַעַשְׁקֻנִי זֵדִים
'arov avdecha letov; al-ya'ashkuni zedim
Be surety for Thy servant for good; let not the proud oppress me.

עֵינַי, כָּלוּ לִישׁוּעָתֶךָ; וּלְאִמְרַת צִדְקֶךָ
'einai kalu lishu'atecha; ule'imrat tzidkecha
Mine eyes fail for Thy salvation, and for Thy righteous word.

עֲשֵׂה עִם-עַבְדְּךָ כְחַסְדֶּךָ; וְחֻקֶּיךָ לַמְּדֵנִי
'aseh im-'avdecha chechasdecha, vechukkeicha lammedeni
Deal with Thy servant according unto Thy mercy, and teach me Thy statutes.

עַבְדְּךָ-אָנִי הֲבִינֵנִי; וְאֵדְעָה, עֵדֹתֶיךָ
'avdecha-'ani havineni; ve'ede'ah, edoteicha
I am Thy servant, give me understanding, that I may know Thy testimonies.

עֵת, לַעֲשׂוֹת לַיהוָה--הֵפֵרוּ, תּוֹרָתֶךָ
'et la'asot lahashem heferu, toratecha
It is time for the LORD to work; they have made void Thy law.

תְּהִלִּים

מַה-נִּמְלְצוּ לְחִכִּי, אִמְרָתֶךָ--מִדְּבַשׁ לְפִי
mah-nimletzu lechikki imratecha, middevash lefi
How sweet are Thy words unto my palate! yea, sweeter than honey to my mouth!

מִפִּקּוּדֶיךָ אֶתְבּוֹנָן; עַל כֵּן, שָׂנֵאתִי כָּל-אֹרַח שָׁקֶר
mippikkudeicha etbonan; al-ken, saneti kol-'orach shaker
From Thy precepts I get understanding; therefore I hate every false way.

נֵר-לְרַגְלִי דְבָרֶךָ; וְאוֹר, לִנְתִיבָתִי
ner-leragli devarecha; ve'or, lintivati
NUN. Thy word is a lamp unto my feet, and a light unto my path.

נִשְׁבַּעְתִּי וָאֲקַיֵּמָה--לִשְׁמֹר, מִשְׁפְּטֵי צִדְקֶךָ
nishba'ti va'akayemah; lishmor, mishpetei tzidkecha
I have sworn, and have confirmed it, to observe Thy righteous ordinances.

נַעֲנֵיתִי עַד-מְאֹד; יְהוָה, חַיֵּנִי כִדְבָרֶךָ
na'aneiti ad-me'od; hashem chayeni chidvarecha
I am afflicted very much; quicken me, O LORD, according unto Thy word.

נִדְבוֹת פִּי, רְצֵה-נָא יְהוָה; וּמִשְׁפָּטֶיךָ לַמְּדֵנִי
nidvot pi retzeh-na hashem umishpateicha lammedeni
Accept, I beseech Thee, the freewill-offerings of my mouth, O LORD, and teach me Thine ordinances.

נַפְשִׁי בְכַפִּי תָמִיד; וְתוֹרָתְךָ, לֹא שָׁכָחְתִּי
nafshi vechappi tamid; vetoratecha, lo shachacheti
My soul is continually in my hand; yet have I not forgotten Thy law.

נָתְנוּ רְשָׁעִים פַּח לִי; וּמִפִּקּוּדֶיךָ, לֹא תָעִיתִי
natenu resha'im pach li; umippikkudeicha, lo ta'iti
The wicked have laid a snare for me; yet went I not astray from Thy precepts.

נָחַלְתִּי עֵדְוֺתֶיךָ לְעוֹלָם: כִּי-שְׂשׂוֹן לִבִּי הֵמָּה
nachalti edoteicha le'olam; ki-seson libbi hemmah
Thy testimonies have I taken as a heritage for ever; for they are the rejoicing of my heart.

נָטִיתִי לִבִּי, לַעֲשׂוֹת חֻקֶּיךָ--לְעוֹלָם עֵקֶב
natiti libbi la'asot chukkeicha, le'olam ekev
I have inclined my heart to perform Thy statutes, for ever, at every step.

סֵעֲפִים שָׂנֵאתִי; וְתוֹרָתְךָ אָהָבְתִּי
se'afim saneti; vetoratecha ahavti
SAMECH. I hate them that are of a double mind; but Thy law do I love.

סִתְרִי וּמָגִנִּי אָתָּה; לִדְבָרְךָ יִחָלְתִּי
sitri umaginni attah; lidvarecha yichaleti
Thou art my covert and my shield; in Thy word do I hope.

תְּהִלִּים

לְמִשְׁפָּטֶיךָ, עָמְדוּ הַיּוֹם: כִּי הַכֹּל עֲבָדֶיךָ
lemishpateicha amedu hayom; ki hakkol avadeicha
They stand this day according to Thine ordinances; for all things are Thy servants.

לוּלֵי תוֹרָתְךָ, שַׁעֲשֻׁעָי--אָז, אָבַדְתִּי בְעָנְיִי
lulei toratecha sha'ashu'ai; az, avadti ve'oneyi
Unless Thy law had been my delight, I should then have perished in mine affliction.

לְעוֹלָם, לֹא-אֶשְׁכַּח פִּקּוּדֶיךָ: כִּי בָם, חִיִּיתָנִי
le'olam lo-'eshkach pikkudeicha; ki vam, chiyitani
I will never forget Thy precepts; for with them Thou hast quickened me.

לְךָ-אֲנִי, הוֹשִׁיעֵנִי: כִּי פִקּוּדֶיךָ דָרָשְׁתִּי
lecha-'ani hoshi'eni; ki fikkudeicha darasheti
I am Thine, save me; for I have sought Thy precepts.

לִי קִוּוּ רְשָׁעִים לְאַבְּדֵנִי; עֵדֹתֶיךָ, אֶתְבּוֹנָן
li kivvu resha'im le'abbedeni; edoteicha, etbonan
The wicked have waited for me to destroy me; but I will consider Thy testimonies.

לְכָל-תִּכְלָה, רָאִיתִי קֵץ; רְחָבָה מִצְוָתְךָ מְאֹד
lechol tichlah ra'iti ketz; rechavah mitzvatecha me'od
I have seen an end to every purpose; but Thy commandment is exceeding broad.

מָה-אָהַבְתִּי תוֹרָתֶךָ: כָּל-הַיּוֹם, הִיא שִׂיחָתִי
mah-'ahavti toratecha; kol-hayom, hi sichati
MEM. O how love I Thy law! It is my meditation all the day.

מֵאֹיְבַי, תְּחַכְּמֵנִי מִצְוֺתֶךָ: כִּי לְעוֹלָם הִיא-לִי
me'oyevai techakkemeni mitzvotecha; ki le'olam hi-li
Thy commandments make me wiser than mine enemies: for they are ever with me.

מִכָּל-מְלַמְּדַי הִשְׂכַּלְתִּי: כִּי עֵדְוֺתֶיךָ, שִׂיחָה לִי
mikkol-melammedai hiskalti; ki edoteicha, sichah li
I have more understanding than all my teachers; for Thy testimonies are my meditation.

מִזְּקֵנִים אֶתְבּוֹנָן: כִּי פִקּוּדֶיךָ נָצָרְתִּי
mizzekenim etbonan; ki fikkudeicha natzareti
I understand more than mine elders, because I have kept Thy precepts.

מִכָּל-אֹרַח רָע, כָּלִאתִי רַגְלָי--לְמַעַן, אֶשְׁמֹר דְּבָרֶךָ
mikkol-'orach ra kaliti raglai; lema'an, eshmor devarecha
I have refrained my feet from every evil way, in order that I might observe Thy word.

מִמִּשְׁפָּטֶיךָ לֹא-סָרְתִּי: כִּי-אַתָּה, הוֹרֵתָנִי
mimmishpateicha lo-sareti; ki-'attah, horetani
I have not turned aside from Thine ordinances; for Thou hast instructed me.

תְּהִלִים

יָשׁוּבוּ לִי יְרֵאֶיךָ; וְיֹדְעֵי, עֵדֹתֶיךָ
yashuvu li yere'eicha; veyode'ei, edoteicha
Let those that fear Thee return unto me, and they that know Thy testimonies.

יְהִי-לִבִּי תָמִים בְּחֻקֶּיךָ--לְמַעַן, לֹא אֵבוֹשׁ
yehi-libbi tamim bechukkeicha; lema'an, lo evosh
Let my heart be undivided in Thy statutes, in order that I may not be put to shame.

כָּלְתָה לִתְשׁוּעָתְךָ נַפְשִׁי; לִדְבָרְךָ יִחָלְתִּי
kaletah litshu'atecha nafshi; lidvarecha yichaleti
CAPH. My soul pineth for Thy salvation; in Thy word do I hope.

כָּלוּ עֵינַי, לְאִמְרָתֶךָ--לֵאמֹר, מָתַי תְּנַחֲמֵנִי
kalu einai le'imratecha; lemor, matai tenachameni
Mine eyes fail for Thy word, saying: 'When wilt Thou comfort me?'

כִּי-הָיִיתִי, כְּנֹאד בְּקִיטוֹר--חֻקֶּיךָ, לֹא שָׁכָחְתִּי
ki-hayiti kenod bekitor; chukkeicha, lo shachacheti
For I am become like a wine-skin in the smoke; yet do I not forget Thy statutes.

כַּמָּה יְמֵי-עַבְדֶּךָ; מָתַי תַּעֲשֶׂה בְרֹדְפַי מִשְׁפָּט
kammah yemei-'avdecha; matai ta'aseh verodefai mishpat
How many are the days of Thy servant? When wilt Thou execute judgment on them that persecute me?

כָּרוּ-לִי זֵדִים שִׁיחוֹת--אֲשֶׁר, לֹא כְתוֹרָתֶךָ
karu-li zedim shichot; asher, lo chetoratecha
The proud have digged pits for me, which is not according to Thy law.

כָּל-מִצְוֺתֶיךָ אֱמוּנָה; שֶׁקֶר רְדָפוּנִי עָזְרֵנִי
kol-mitzvoteicha emunah; sheker redafuni ozereni
All Thy commandments are faithful; they persecute me for nought; help Thou me.

כִּמְעַט, כִּלּוּנִי בָאָרֶץ; וַאֲנִי, לֹא-עָזַבְתִּי פִקֻּדֶיךָ
kim'at killuni va'aretz; va'ani, lo-'azavti fikkudeicha
They had almost consumed me upon earth; but as for me, I forsook not Thy precepts.

כְּחַסְדְּךָ חַיֵּנִי; וְאֶשְׁמְרָה, עֵדוּת פִּיךָ
kechasdecha chayeni; ve'eshmerah, edut picha
Quicken me after Thy lovingkindness, and I will observe the testimony of Thy mouth.

לְעוֹלָם יְהוָה--דְּבָרְךָ, נִצָּב בַּשָּׁמָיִם
le'olam hashem devarecha, nitzav bashamayim
LAMED. For ever, O LORD, Thy word standeth fast in heaven.

לְדֹר וָדֹר, אֱמוּנָתֶךָ; כּוֹנַנְתָּ אֶרֶץ, וַתַּעֲמֹד
ledor vador emunatecha; konanta eretz, vatta'amod
Thy faithfulness is unto all generations; Thou hast established the earth, and it standeth.

תְּהִלִים

טֶרֶם אֶעֱנֶה, אֲנִי שֹׁגֵג; וְעַתָּה, אִמְרָתְךָ שָׁמָרְתִּי
terem e'eneh ani shogeg; ve'attah, imratecha shamareti
Before I was afflicted, I did err; but now I observe Thy word.

טוֹב-אַתָּה וּמֵטִיב; לַמְּדֵנִי חֻקֶּיךָ
tov-'attah umetiv, lammedeni chukkeicha
Thou art good, and doest good; teach me Thy statutes.

טָפְלוּ עָלַי שֶׁקֶר זֵדִים; אֲנִי, בְּכָל-לֵב אֶצֹּר פִּקּוּדֶיךָ
tafelu alai sheker zedim; ani, bechol-lev etzor pikkudeicha
The proud have forged a lie against me; but I with my whole heart will keep Thy precepts.

טָפַשׁ כַּחֵלֶב לִבָּם; אֲנִי, תּוֹרָתְךָ שִׁעֲשָׁעְתִּי
tafash kachelev libbam; ani, toratecha shi'asha'eti
Their heart is gross like fat; but I delight in Thy law.

טוֹב-לִי כִי-עֻנֵּיתִי--לְמַעַן, אֶלְמַד חֻקֶּיךָ
tov-li chi-'unneiti; lema'an, elmad chukkeicha
It is good for me that I have been afflicted, in order that I might learn Thy statutes.

טוֹב-לִי תוֹרַת-פִּיךָ--מֵאַלְפֵי, זָהָב וָכָסֶף
tov-li torat-picha; me'alfei, zahav vachasef
The law of Thy mouth is better unto me than thousands of gold and silver.

יָדֶיךָ עָשׂוּנִי, וַיְכוֹנְנוּנִי; הֲבִינֵנִי, וְאֶלְמְדָה מִצְוֹתֶיךָ
yadeicha asuni vaychonenuni; havineni, ve'elmedah mitzvoteicha
IOD. Thy hands have made me and fashioned me; give me understanding, that I may learn Thy commandments.

יְרֵאֶיךָ, יִרְאוּנִי וְיִשְׂמָחוּ: כִּי לִדְבָרְךָ יִחָלְתִּי
yere'eicha yir'uni veyismachu; ki lidvarecha yichaleti
They that fear Thee shall see me and be glad, because I have hope in Thy word.

יָדַעְתִּי יְהוָה, כִּי-צֶדֶק מִשְׁפָּטֶיךָ; וֶאֱמוּנָה, עִנִּיתָנִי
yada'ti hashem ki-tzedek mishpateicha; ve'emunah, innitani
I know, O LORD, that Thy judgments are righteous, and that in faithfulness Thou hast afflicted me.

יְהִי-נָא חַסְדְּךָ לְנַחֲמֵנִי--כְּאִמְרָתְךָ לְעַבְדֶּךָ
yehi-na chasdecha lenachameni; ke'imratecha le'avdecha
Let, I pray Thee, Thy lovingkindness be ready to comfort me, according to Thy promise unto Thy servant.

יְבֹאוּנִי רַחֲמֶיךָ וְאֶחְיֶה: כִּי-תוֹרָתְךָ, שַׁעֲשֻׁעָי
yevo'uni rachameicha ve'echyeh; ki-toratecha, sha'ashu'ai
Let Thy tender mercies come unto me, that I may live; for Thy law is my delight.

יֵבֹשׁוּ זֵדִים, כִּי-שֶׁקֶר עִוְּתוּנִי; אֲנִי, אָשִׂיחַ בְּפִקּוּדֶיךָ
yevoshu zedim ki-sheker ivvetuni; ani, asiach befikkudeicha
Let the proud be put to shame, for they have distorted my cause with falsehood; but I will meditate in Thy precepts.

תְּהִלִּים

זָכַרְתִּי בַלַּיְלָה שִׁמְךָ יְהוָה; וָאֶשְׁמְרָה, תּוֹרָתֶךָ
zacharti vallaylah shimcha hashem va'eshmerah, toratecha
I have remembered Thy name, O LORD, in the night, and have observed Thy law.

זֹאת הָיְתָה-לִּי: כִּי פִקֻּדֶיךָ נָצָרְתִּי
zot hayetah-li; ki fikkudeicha natzareti
This I have had, that I have kept Thy precepts.

חֶלְקִי יְהוָה אָמַרְתִּי--לִשְׁמֹר דְּבָרֶיךָ
chelki hashem amarti, lishmor devareicha
HETH. My portion is the LORD, I have said that I would observe Thy words.

חִלִּיתִי פָנֶיךָ בְכָל-לֵב; חָנֵּנִי, כְּאִמְרָתֶךָ
chilliti faneicha vechal-lev; chonneni ke'imratecha
I have entreated Thy favour with my whole heart; be gracious unto me according to Thy word.

חִשַּׁבְתִּי דְרָכָי; וָאָשִׁיבָה רַגְלַי, אֶל-עֵדֹתֶיךָ
chishavti derachai; va'ashivah raglai, el-'edoteicha
I considered my ways, and turned my feet unto Thy testimonies.

חַשְׁתִּי, וְלֹא הִתְמַהְמָהְתִּי--לִשְׁמֹר, מִצְוֹתֶיךָ
chashti velo hitmahmaheti; lishmor, mitzvoteicha
I made haste, and delayed not, to observe Thy commandments.

חֶבְלֵי רְשָׁעִים עִוְּדֻנִי; תּוֹרָתְךָ, לֹא שָׁכָחְתִּי
chevlei resha'im ivveduni; toratcha, lo shachacheti
The bands of the wicked have enclosed me; but I have not forgotten Thy law.

חֲצוֹת-לַיְלָה--אָקוּם, לְהוֹדוֹת לָךְ: עַל, מִשְׁפְּטֵי צִדְקֶךָ
chatzot-laylah, akum lehodot lach; al, mishpetei tzidkecha
At midnight I will rise to give thanks unto Thee because of Thy righteous ordinances.

חָבֵר אָנִי, לְכָל-אֲשֶׁר יְרֵאוּךָ; וּלְשֹׁמְרֵי, פִּקּוּדֶיךָ
chaver ani lechol-'asher yere'ucha; uleshomerei, pikkudeicha
I am a companion of all them that fear Thee, and of them that observe Thy precepts.

חַסְדְּךָ יְהוָה, מָלְאָה הָאָרֶץ; חֻקֶּיךָ לַמְּדֵנִי
chasdecha hashem male'ah ha'aretz, chukkeicha lammedeni
The earth, O LORD, is full of Thy mercy; teach me Thy statutes.

טוֹב, עָשִׂיתָ עִם-עַבְדְּךָ--יְהוָה, כִּדְבָרֶךָ
tov asita im-'avdecha; hashem kidvarecha
TETH. Thou hast dealt well with Thy servant, O LORD, according unto Thy word.

טוּב טַעַם וָדַעַת לַמְּדֵנִי: כִּי בְמִצְוֹתֶיךָ הֶאֱמָנְתִּי
tuv ta'am vada'at lammedeni; ki vemitzvoteicha he'emaneti
Teach me good discernment and knowledge; for I have believed in Thy commandments.

תְּהִלִים

וְאַל-תַּצֵּל מִפִּי דְבַר-אֱמֶת עַד-מְאֹד: כִּי לְמִשְׁפָּטֶךָ, יִחָלְתִּי
ve'al-tatzel mippi devar-'emet ad-me'od; ki lemishpatecha yichalti
And take not the word of truth utterly out of my mouth; for I hope in Thine ordinances;

וְאֶשְׁמְרָה תוֹרָתְךָ תָמִיד--לְעוֹלָם וָעֶד
ve'eshmerah toratecha tamid, le'olam va'ed
So shall I observe Thy law continually for ever and ever;

וְאֶתְהַלְּכָה בָרְחָבָה: כִּי פִקֻּדֶיךָ דָרָשְׁתִּי
ve'et'hallechah varechavah; ki fikkudeicha darasheti
And I will walk at ease, for I have sought Thy precepts;

וַאֲדַבְּרָה בְעֵדֹתֶיךָ, נֶגֶד מְלָכִים; וְלֹא אֵבוֹשׁ
va'adabberah ve'edoteicha neged melachim, velo evosh
I will also speak of Thy testimonies before kings, and will not be ashamed.

וְאֶשְׁתַּעֲשַׁע בְּמִצְוֹתֶיךָ, אֲשֶׁר אָהָבְתִּי
ve'eshta'asha bemitzvoteicha, asher ahaveti
And I will delight myself in Thy commandments, which I have loved.

וְאֶשָּׂא-כַפַּי--אֶל-מִצְוֹתֶיךָ, אֲשֶׁר אָהָבְתִּי; וְאָשִׂיחָה בְחֻקֶּיךָ
ve'essa-chappai, el-mitzvoteicha asher ahaveti, ve'asichah vechukkeicha
I will lift up my hands also unto Thy commandments, which I have loved; and I will meditate in Thy statutes.

זְכֹר-דָּבָר, לְעַבְדֶּךָ-- עַל, אֲשֶׁר יִחַלְתָּנִי
zechor-davar le'ovdecha al, asher yichaltani
ZAIN. Remember the word unto Thy servant, because Thou hast made me to hope.

זֹאת נֶחָמָתִי בְעָנְיִי: כִּי אִמְרָתְךָ חִיָּתְנִי
zot nechamati ve'aneyi; ki imratecha chiyateni
This is my comfort in my affliction, that Thy word hath quickened me.

זֵדִים, הֱלִיצֻנִי עַד-מְאֹד; מִתּוֹרָתְךָ, לֹא נָטִיתִי
zedim helitzuni ad-me'od; mittoratecha, lo natiti
The proud have had me greatly in derision; yet have I not turned aside from Thy law.

זָכַרְתִּי מִשְׁפָּטֶיךָ מֵעוֹלָם יְהוָה; וָאֶתְנֶחָם
zacharti mishpateicha me'olam hashem va'etnecham
I have remembered Thine ordinances which are of old, O LORD, and have comforted myself.

זַלְעָפָה אֲחָזַתְנִי, מֵרְשָׁעִים-- עֹזְבֵי, תּוֹרָתֶךָ
zal'afah achazatni meresha'im; ozevei, toratecha
Burning indignation hath taken hold upon me, because of the wicked that forsake Thy law.

זְמִרוֹת, הָיוּ-לִי חֻקֶּיךָ-- בְּבֵית מְגוּרָי
zemirot hayu-li chukkeicha, beveit megurai
Thy statutes have been my songs in the house of my pilgrimage.

תְּהִלִים

דֶּרֶךְ־מִצְוֹתֶיךָ אָרוּץ: כִּי תַרְחִיב לִבִּי
derech-mitzvoteicha arutz; ki tarchiv libbi
I will run the way of Thy commandments, for Thou dost enlarge my heart.

הוֹרֵנִי יְהוָה, דֶּרֶךְ חֻקֶּיךָ; וְאֶצְּרֶנָּה עֵקֶב
horeni hashem derech chukkeicha, ve'etzerennah ekev
HE. Teach me, O LORD, the way of Thy statutes; and I will keep it at every step.

הֲבִינֵנִי, וְאֶצְּרָה תוֹרָתֶךָ; וְאֶשְׁמְרֶנָּה בְכָל־לֵב
havineni ve'etzerah toratecha, ve'eshmerennah vechol-lev
Give me understanding, that I keep Thy law and observe it with my whole heart.

הַדְרִיכֵנִי, בִּנְתִיב מִצְוֹתֶיךָ: כִּי־בוֹ חָפָצְתִּי
hadricheni bintiv mitzvoteicha; ki-vo chafatzeti
Make me to tread in the path of Thy commandments; for therein do I delight.

הַט־לִבִּי, אֶל־עֵדְוֹתֶיךָ; וְאַל אֶל־בָּצַע
hat-libbi el-'edoteicha, ve'al el-batza
Incline my heart unto Thy testimonies, and not to covetousness.

הַעֲבֵר עֵינַי, מֵרְאוֹת שָׁוְא; בִּדְרָכֶךָ חַיֵּנִי
ha'aver einai mere'ot shav; bidrachecha chayeni
Turn away mine eyes from beholding vanity, and quicken me in Thy ways.

הָקֵם לְעַבְדְּךָ, אִמְרָתֶךָ--אֲשֶׁר, לְיִרְאָתֶךָ
hakem le'avdecha imratecha; asher, leyir'atecha
Confirm Thy word unto Thy servant, which pertaineth unto the fear of Thee.

הַעֲבֵר חֶרְפָּתִי, אֲשֶׁר יָגֹרְתִּי: כִּי מִשְׁפָּטֶיךָ טוֹבִים
ha'aver cherpati asher yagoreti; ki mishpateicha tovim
Turn away my reproach which I dread; for Thine ordinances are good.

הִנֵּה, תָּאַבְתִּי לְפִקֻּדֶיךָ; בְּצִדְקָתְךָ חַיֵּנִי
hinneh ta'avti lefikkudeicha; betzidkatecha chayeni
Behold, I have longed after Thy precepts; quicken me in Thy righteousness.

וִיבֹאֻנִי חֲסָדֶךָ יְהוָה; תְּשׁוּעָתְךָ, כְּאִמְרָתֶךָ
viyvo'uni chasadecha hashem teshu'atecha, ke'imratecha
VAV. Let Thy mercies also come unto me, O LORD, even Thy salvation, according to Thy word;

וְאֶעֱנֶה חֹרְפִי דָבָר: כִּי־בָטַחְתִּי, בִּדְבָרֶךָ
ve'e'eneh chorefi davar; ki-vatachti bidvarecha
That I may have an answer for him that taunteth me; for I trust in Thy word.

תְּהִלִים

גָּרְסָה נַפְשִׁי לְתַאֲבָה--אֶל-מִשְׁפָּטֶיךָ בְכָל-עֵת
garesah nafshi leta'avah; el-mishpateicha vechal-'et
My soul breaketh for the longing that it hath unto Thine ordinances at all times.

גָּעַרְתָּ, זֵדִים אֲרוּרִים--הַשֹּׁגִים, מִמִּצְוֺתֶיךָ
ga'arta zedim arurim; hashogim mimmitzvoteicha
Thou hast rebuked the proud that are cursed, that do err from Thy commandments.

גַּל מֵעָלַי, חֶרְפָּה וָבוּז: כִּי עֵדֹתֶיךָ נָצָרְתִּי
gal me'alai cherpah vavuz; ki edoteicha natzarti
Take away from me reproach and contempt; for I have kept Thy testimonies.

גַּם יָשְׁבוּ שָׂרִים, בִּי נִדְבָּרוּ--עַבְדְּךָ, יָשִׂיחַ בְּחֻקֶּיךָ
gam yashevu sarim bi nidbaru; avdecha, yasiach bechukkeicha
Even though princes sit and talk against me, thy servant doth meditate in Thy statutes.

גַּם-עֵדֹתֶיךָ, שַׁעֲשֻׁעָי--אַנְשֵׁי עֲצָתִי
gam-'edoteicha sha'ashu'ai, anshei atzati
Yea, Thy testimonies are my delight, they are my counsellors.

דָּבְקָה לֶעָפָר נַפְשִׁי; חַיֵּנִי, כִּדְבָרֶךָ
davekah le'afar nafshi; chayeni, kidvarecha
DALETH. My soul cleaveth unto the dust; quicken Thou me according to Thy word.

דְּרָכַי סִפַּרְתִּי, וַתַּעֲנֵנִי; לַמְּדֵנִי חֻקֶּיךָ
derachai sipparti vatta'aneni, lammedeni chukkeicha
I told of my ways, and Thou didst answer me; teach me Thy statutes.

דֶּרֶךְ-פִּקּוּדֶיךָ הֲבִינֵנִי; וְאָשִׂיחָה, בְּנִפְלְאוֹתֶיךָ
derech-pikkudeicha havineni; ve'asichah, benifle'oteicha
Make me to understand the way of Thy precepts, that I may talk of Thy wondrous works.

דָּלְפָה נַפְשִׁי, מִתּוּגָה; קַיְּמֵנִי, כִּדְבָרֶךָ
dalefah nafshi mittugah; kayemeni, kidvarecha
My soul melteth away for heaviness; sustain me according unto Thy word.

דֶּרֶךְ-שֶׁקֶר, הָסֵר מִמֶּנִּי; וְתוֹרָתְךָ חָנֵּנִי
derech-sheker haser mimmenni; vetoratecha chonneni
Remove from me the way of falsehood; and grant me Thy law graciously.

דֶּרֶךְ-אֱמוּנָה בָחָרְתִּי; מִשְׁפָּטֶיךָ שִׁוִּיתִי
derech-'emunah vachareti; mishpateicha shivviti
I have chosen the way of faithfulness; Thine ordinances have I set [before me].

דָּבַקְתִּי בְעֵדְוֺתֶיךָ; יְהוָה, אַל-תְּבִישֵׁנִי
davakti ve'edoteicha; hashem al-tevisheni
I cleave unto Thy testimonies; O LORD, put me not to shame.

תְּהִלִים

אֶת-חֻקֶּיךָ אֶשְׁמֹר; אַל-תַּעַזְבֵנִי עַד-מְאֹד
'et-chukkeicha eshmor; al-ta'azveni ad-me'od
I will observe Thy statutes; O forsake me not utterly.

בַּמֶּה יְזַכֶּה-נַּעַר, אֶת-אָרְחוֹ-- לִשְׁמֹר, כִּדְבָרֶךָ
bammeh yezakkeh-na'ar et-'arecho; lishmor, kidvarecha
BETH. Wherewithal shall a young man keep his way pure? By taking heed thereto according to Thy word.

בְּכָל-לִבִּי דְרַשְׁתִּיךָ; אַל-תַּשְׁגֵּנִי, מִמִּצְוֺתֶיךָ
bechol-libbi derashticha; al-tashgeni, mimmitzvoteicha
With my whole heart have I sought Thee; O let me not err from Thy commandments.

בְּלִבִּי, צָפַנְתִּי אִמְרָתֶךָ-- לְמַעַן, לֹא אֶחֱטָא-לָךְ.
belibbi tzafanti imratecha; lema'an, lo echeta-lach
Thy word have I laid up in my heart, that I might not sin against Thee.

בָּרוּךְ אַתָּה יְהוָה-- לַמְּדֵנִי חֻקֶּיךָ
baruch attah hashem lammedeni chukkeicha
Blessed art Thou, O LORD; teach me Thy statutes.

בִּשְׂפָתַי סִפַּרְתִּי-- כֹּל, מִשְׁפְּטֵי-פִיךָ
bisfatai sipparti; kol mishpetei-ficha
With my lips have I told all the ordinances of Thy mouth.

בְּדֶרֶךְ עֵדְוֺתֶיךָ שַׂשְׂתִּי-- כְּעַל כָּל-הוֹן
bederech edoteicha sasti, ke'al kol-hon
I have rejoiced in the way of Thy testimonies, as much as in all riches.

בְּפִקּוּדֶיךָ אָשִׂיחָה; וְאַבִּיטָה, אֹרְחֹתֶיךָ
befikkudeicha asichah; ve'abbitah, orchoteicha
I will meditate in Thy precepts, and have respect unto Thy ways.

בְּחֻקֹּתֶיךָ אֶשְׁתַּעֲשָׁע; לֹא אֶשְׁכַּח דְּבָרֶךָ
bechukkoteicha eshta'asha'; lo eshkach devarecha
I will delight myself in Thy statutes; I will not forget Thy word.

גְּמֹל עַל-עַבְדְּךָ אֶחְיֶה; וְאֶשְׁמְרָה דְבָרֶךָ
gemol al-'avdecha echyeh, ve'eshmerah devarecha
GIMEL. Deal bountifully with Thy servant that I may live, and I will observe Thy word.

גַּל-עֵינַי וְאַבִּיטָה-- נִפְלָאוֹת, מִתּוֹרָתֶךָ
gal-'einai ve'abbitah; nifla'ot, mittoratecha
Open Thou mine eyes, that I may behold wondrous things out of Thy law.

גֵּר אָנֹכִי בָאָרֶץ; אַל-תַּסְתֵּר מִמֶּנִּי, מִצְוֺתֶיךָ
ger anochi va'aretz; al-taster mimmenni, mitzvoteicha
I am a sojourner in the earth; hide not Thy commandments from me.

תְּהִלִּים

בָּרוּךְ הַבָּא, בְּשֵׁם יְהוָה; בֵּרַכְנוּכֶם, מִבֵּית יְהוָה
baruch habba beshem hashem berachnuchem, mibbeit hashem
Blessed be he that cometh in the name of the LORD; we bless you out of the house of the LORD.

אֵל, יְהוָה--וַיָּאֶר-לָנוּ: אִסְרוּ-חַג בַּעֲבֹתִים--עַד קַרְנוֹת, הַמִּזְבֵּחַ
'el hashem vaya'er lanu isru-chag ba'avotim; ad-karnot, hammizbeach
The LORD is God, and hath given us light; order the festival procession with boughs, even unto the horns of the altar.

אֵלִי אַתָּה וְאוֹדֶךָּ; אֱלֹהַי, אֲרוֹמְמֶךָּ
'eli attah ve'odeka; elohai, aromemeka
Thou art my God, and I will give thanks unto Thee; Thou art my God, I will exalt Thee.

הוֹדוּ לַיהוָה כִּי-טוֹב: כִּי לְעוֹלָם חַסְדּוֹ
hodu lahashem ki-tov; ki le'olam chasdo
O give thanks unto the LORD, for He is good, for His mercy endureth for ever.

קיט

אַשְׁרֵי תְמִימֵי-דָרֶךְ--הַהֹלְכִים, בְּתוֹרַת יְהוָה
Ashrei temimei-darech; haholechim, betorat hashem
ALEPH. Happy are they that are upright in the way, who walk in the law of the LORD.

אַשְׁרֵי, נֹצְרֵי עֵדֹתָיו; בְּכָל-לֵב יִדְרְשׁוּהוּ
'ashrei notzerei edotav, bechol-lev yidreshuhu
Happy are they that keep His testimonies, that seek Him with the whole heart.

אַף, לֹא-פָעֲלוּ עַוְלָה; בִּדְרָכָיו הָלָכוּ
'af lo-fa'alu avlah; bidrachav halachu
Yea, they do no unrighteousness; they walk in His ways.

אַתָּה, צִוִּיתָה פִקֻּדֶיךָ--לִשְׁמֹר מְאֹד
'attah tzivvitah fikkudeicha, lishmor me'od
Thou hast ordained Thy precepts, that we should observe them diligently.

אַחֲלַי, יִכֹּנוּ דְרָכָי--לִשְׁמֹר חֻקֶּיךָ
'achalai yikkonu derachai, lishmor chukkeicha
Oh that my ways were directed to observe Thy statutes!

אָז לֹא-אֵבוֹשׁ--בְּהַבִּיטִי, אֶל-כָּל-מִצְוֹתֶיךָ
'az lo-'evosh; behabbiti, el-kol-mitzvoteicha
Then should I not be ashamed, when I have regard unto all Thy commandments.

אוֹדְךָ, בְּיֹשֶׁר לֵבָב--בְּלָמְדִי, מִשְׁפְּטֵי צִדְקֶךָ
'odecha beyosher levav; belomedi, mishpetei tzidkecha
I will give thanks unto Thee with uprightness of heart, when I learn Thy righteous ordinances.

תְּהִלִּים

עָזִּי וְזִמְרָת יָהּ; וַיְהִי-לִי, לִישׁוּעָה
'ozzi vezimrat yah; vayhi-li, liyshu'ah
The LORD is my strength and song; and He is become my salvation.

קוֹל, רִנָּה וִישׁוּעָה--בְּאָהֳלֵי צַדִּיקִים; יְמִין יְהוָה, עֹשָׂה חָיִל
kol rinnah vishu'ah, be'oholei tzaddikim; yemin hashem osah chayil
The voice of rejoicing and salvation is in the tents of the righteous; the right hand of the LORD doeth valiantly.

יְמִין יְהוָה, רוֹמֵמָה; יְמִין יְהוָה, עֹשָׂה חָיִל
yemin hashem romemah; yemin hashem osah chayil
The right hand of the LORD is exalted; the right hand of the LORD doeth valiantly.

לֹא-אָמוּת כִּי-אֶחְיֶה; וַאֲסַפֵּר, מַעֲשֵׂי יָהּ
lo amut ki-'echyeh; va'asapper, ma'asei yah
I shall not die, but live, and declare the works of the LORD.

יַסֹּר יִסְּרַנִּי יָּהּ; וְלַמָּוֶת, לֹא נְתָנָנִי
yassor yisseranni yah; velammavet, lo netanani
The LORD hath chastened me sore; but He hath not given me over unto death.

פִּתְחוּ-לִי שַׁעֲרֵי-צֶדֶק; אָבֹא-בָם, אוֹדֶה יָהּ
pitchu-li sha'arei-tzedek; avo-vam odeh yah
Open to me the gates of righteousness; I will enter into them, I will give thanks unto the LORD.

זֶה-הַשַּׁעַר לַיהוָה; צַדִּיקִים, יָבֹאוּ בוֹ
zeh-hasha'ar lahashem tzaddikim, yavo'u vo
This is the gate of the LORD; the righteous shall enter into it.

אוֹדְךָ, כִּי עֲנִיתָנִי; וַתְּהִי-לִי, לִישׁוּעָה
'odecha ki anitani; vattehi-li, lishu'ah
I will give thanks unto Thee, for Thou hast answered me, and art become my salvation.

אֶבֶן, מָאֲסוּ הַבּוֹנִים--הָיְתָה, לְרֹאשׁ פִּנָּה
'even ma'asu habbonim; hayetah, lerosh pinnah
The stone which the builders rejected is become the chief corner-stone.

מֵאֵת יְהוָה, הָיְתָה זֹּאת; הִיא נִפְלָאת בְּעֵינֵינוּ
me'et hashem hayetah zot; hi niflat be'eineinu
This is the LORD'S doing; it is marvellous in our eyes.

זֶה-הַיּוֹם, עָשָׂה יְהוָה; נָגִילָה וְנִשְׂמְחָה בוֹ
zeh-hayom asah hashem nagilah venismechah vo
This is the day which the LORD hath made; we will rejoice and be glad in it.

אָנָּא יְהוָה, הוֹשִׁיעָה נָּא; אָנָּא יְהוָה, הַצְלִיחָה נָּא
'anna hashem hoshi'ah na; anna hashem hatzlichah na
We beseech Thee, O LORD, save now! We beseech Thee, O LORD, make us now to prosper!

תְּהִלִּים

יֹאמְרוּ-נָא בֵית-אַהֲרֹן: כִּי לְעוֹלָם חַסְדּוֹ
yomeru-na veit-'aharon; ki le'olam chasdo
So let the house of Aaron now say, for His mercy endureth for ever.

יֹאמְרוּ-נָא יִרְאֵי יְהוָה: כִּי לְעוֹלָם חַסְדּוֹ
yomeru-na yir'ei hashem ki le'olam chasdo
So let them now that fear the LORD say, for His mercy endureth for ever.

מִן-הַמֵּצַר, קָרָאתִי יָּהּ; עָנָנִי בַמֶּרְחָב יָהּ
min-hammetzar karati yah; anani vammerchav yah
Out of my straits I called upon the LORD; He answered me with great enlargement.

יְהוָה לִי, לֹא אִירָא; מַה-יַּעֲשֶׂה לִי אָדָם
hashem li lo ira; mah-ya'aseh li adam
The LORD is for me; I will not fear; what can man do unto me?

יְהוָה לִי, בְּעֹזְרָי; וַאֲנִי, אֶרְאֶה בְשֹׂנְאָי
hashem li be'ozerai; va'ani, er'eh vesone'ai
The LORD is for me as my helper; and I shall gaze upon them that hate me.

טוֹב, לַחֲסוֹת בַּיהוָה--מִבְּטֹחַ, בָּאָדָם
tov, lachasot bahashem; mibbetoach, ba'adam
It is better to take refuge in the LORD than to trust in man.

טוֹב, לַחֲסוֹת בַּיהוָה--מִבְּטֹחַ, בִּנְדִיבִים
tov, lachasot bahashem; mibbetoach, bindivim
It is better to take refuge in the LORD than to trust in princes.

כָּל-גּוֹיִם סְבָבוּנִי; בְּשֵׁם יְהוָה, כִּי אֲמִילַם
kol-goyim sevavuni; beshem hashem ki amilam
All nations compass me about; verily, in the name of the LORD I will cut them off.

סַבּוּנִי גַם-סְבָבוּנִי; בְּשֵׁם יְהוָה, כִּי אֲמִילַם
sabbuni gam-sevavuni; beshem hashem ki amilam
They compass me about, yea, they compass me about; verily, in the name of the LORD I will cut them off.

סַבּוּנִי כִדְבוֹרִים--דֹּעֲכוּ, כְּאֵשׁ קוֹצִים
sabbuni chidvorim, do'achu ke'esh kotzim
They compass me about like bees; they are quenched as the fire of thorns;

בְּשֵׁם יְהוָה, כִּי אֲמִילַם
beshem hashem ki amilam
verily, in the name of the LORD I will cut them off.

דַּחֹה דְחִיתַנִי לִנְפֹּל; וַיהוָה עֲזָרָנִי
dachoh dechitani linpol; vahashem azarani
Thou didst thrust sore at me that I might fall; but the LORD helped me.

תְּהִלִּים

נְדָרַי, לַיהוָה אֲשַׁלֵּם; נֶגְדָה-נָּא, לְכָל-עַמּוֹ
nedarai lahashem ashallem; negdah-na, lechol-'ammo
My vows will I pay unto the LORD, yea, in the presence of all His people.

יָקָר, בְּעֵינֵי יְהוָה--הַמָּוְתָה, לַחֲסִידָיו
yakar be'einei hashem hammavetah, lechasidav
Precious in the sight of the LORD is the death of His saints.

אָנָּה יְהוָה, כִּי-אֲנִי עַבְדֶּךָ: אֲנִי-עַבְדְּךָ, בֶּן-אֲמָתֶךָ; פִּתַּחְתָּ, לְמוֹסֵרָי
'annah hashem ki-'ani avdecha ani-'avdecha ben-'amatecha; pittachta, lemoserai
I beseech Thee, O LORD, for I am Thy servant; I am Thy servant, the son of Thy handmaid; Thou hast loosed my bands.

לְךָ-אֶזְבַּח, זֶבַח תּוֹדָה; וּבְשֵׁם יְהוָה אֶקְרָא
lecha-'ezbach zevach todah; uveshem hashem ekra
I will offer to thee the sacrifice of thanksgiving, and will call upon the name of the LORD.

נְדָרַי, לַיהוָה אֲשַׁלֵּם; נֶגְדָה-נָּא, לְכָל-עַמּוֹ
nedarai lahashem ashallem; negdah-na, lechol-'ammo
I will pay my vows unto the LORD, yea, in the presence of all His people;

בְּחַצְרוֹת, בֵּית יְהוָה-- בְּתוֹכֵכִי יְרוּשָׁלִָם: הַלְלוּ-יָהּ
bechatzrot beit hashem betochechi yerushalayim, halelu-yah
In the courts of the LORD'S house, in the midst of thee, O Jerusalem. Hallelujah.

קיז

הַלְלוּ אֶת-יְהוָה, כָּל-גּוֹיִם; שַׁבְּחוּהוּ, כָּל-הָאֻמִּים
Halelu et-hashem kol-goyim; shabbechuhu, kol-ha'ummim
O praise the LORD, all ye nations; laud Him, all ye peoples.

כִּי גָבַר עָלֵינוּ, חַסְדּוֹ-- וֶאֱמֶת-יְהוָה לְעוֹלָם: הַלְלוּ-יָהּ
ki gavar aleinu chasdo, ve'emet-hashem le'olam, halelu-yah
For His mercy is great toward us; and the truth of the LORD endureth for ever. Hallelujah.

קיח

הוֹדוּ לַיהוָה כִּי-טוֹב: כִּי לְעוֹלָם חַסְדּוֹ
Hodu lahashem ki-tov; ki le'olam chasdo
'O give thanks unto the LORD, for He is good, for His mercy endureth for ever.'

יֹאמַר-נָא יִשְׂרָאֵל: כִּי לְעוֹלָם חַסְדּוֹ
yomar-na yisra'el; ki le'olam chasdo
So let Israel now say, for His mercy endureth for ever,

תְּהִלִּים

כִּי-הִטָּה אָזְנוֹ לִי; וּבְיָמַי אֶקְרָא
ki-hittah ozeno li; uveyamai ekra
Because He hath inclined His ear unto me, therefore will I call upon Him all my days.

אֲפָפוּנִי, חֶבְלֵי-מָוֶת--וּמְצָרֵי שְׁאוֹל מְצָאוּנִי; צָרָה וְיָגוֹן אֶמְצָא
'afafuni chevlei-mavet, umetzarei she'ol metza'uni; tzarah veyagon emtza
The cords of death compassed me, and the straits of the nether-world got hold upon me; I found trouble and sorrow.

וּבְשֵׁם-יְהוָה אֶקְרָא: אָנָּה יְהוָה, מַלְּטָה נַפְשִׁי
uveshem-hashem ekra; annah hashem malletah nafshi
But I called upon the name of the LORD: 'I beseech thee, O LORD, deliver my soul.'

חַנּוּן יְהוָה וְצַדִּיק; וֵאלֹהֵינוּ מְרַחֵם
channun hashem vetzaddik; ve'eloheinu merachem
Gracious is the LORD, and righteous; yea, our God is compassionate.

שֹׁמֵר פְּתָאיִם יְהוָה; דַּלֹּתִי, וְלִי יְהוֹשִׁיעַ
shomer petayim hashem dalloti, veli yehoshia
The LORD preserveth the simple; I was brought low, and He saved me.

שׁוּבִי נַפְשִׁי, לִמְנוּחָיְכִי: כִּי-יְהוָה, גָּמַל עָלָיְכִי
shuvi nafshi limnuchayechi; ki-hashem gamal alayechi
Return, O my soul, unto thy rest; for the LORD hath dealt bountifully with thee.

כִּי חִלַּצְתָּ נַפְשִׁי, מִמָּוֶת: אֶת-עֵינִי מִן-דִּמְעָה; אֶת-רַגְלִי מִדֶּחִי
ki chillatzta nafshi, mimmavet et-'eini min-dim'ah; et-ragli middechi
For Thou hast delivered my soul from death, mine eyes from tears, and my feet from stumbling.

אֶתְהַלֵּךְ, לִפְנֵי יְהוָה--בְּאַרְצוֹת, הַחַיִּים
'et'hallech lifnei hashem be'artzot, hachayim
I shall walk before the LORD in the lands of the living.

הֶאֱמַנְתִּי, כִּי אֲדַבֵּר; אֲנִי, עָנִיתִי מְאֹד
he'emanti ki adabber; ani, aniti me'od
I trusted even when I spoke: 'I am greatly afflicted.'

אֲנִי, אָמַרְתִּי בְחָפְזִי: כָּל-הָאָדָם כֹּזֵב
'ani amarti vechofezi; kol-ha'adam kozev
I said in my haste: 'All men are liars.'

מָה-אָשִׁיב לַיהוָה--כָּל-תַּגְמוּלוֹהִי עָלָי
mah-'ashiv lahashem kol-tagmulohi alai
How can I repay unto the LORD all His bountiful dealings toward me?

כּוֹס-יְשׁוּעוֹת אֶשָּׂא; וּבְשֵׁם יְהוָה אֶקְרָא
kos-yeshu'ot essa; uveshem hashem ekra
I will lift up the cup of salvation, and call upon the name of the LORD.

תְּהִלִּים

יִשְׂרָאֵל, בְּטַח בַּיהוָה; עֶזְרָם וּמָגִנָּם הוּא
yisra'el betach bahashem; ezram umaginnam hu
O Israel, trust thou in the LORD! He is their help and their shield!

בֵּית אַהֲרֹן, בִּטְחוּ בַיהוָה; עֶזְרָם וּמָגִנָּם הוּא
beit aharon bitchu vahashem; ezram umaginnam hu
O house of Aaron, trust ye in the LORD! He is their help and their shield!

יִרְאֵי יְהוָה, בִּטְחוּ בַיהוָה; עֶזְרָם וּמָגִנָּם הוּא
yir'ei hashem bitchu vahashem; ezram umaginnam hu
Ye that fear the LORD, trust in the LORD! He is their help and their shield.

יְהוָה, זְכָרָנוּ יְבָרֵךְ: יְבָרֵךְ, אֶת-בֵּית יִשְׂרָאֵל; יְבָרֵךְ, אֶת-בֵּית אַהֲרֹן
hashem zecharanu yevarech yevarech et-beit yisra'el; yevarech, et-beit aharon
The LORD hath been mindful of us, He will bless--He will bless the house of Israel; He will bless the house of Aaron.

יְבָרֵךְ, יִרְאֵי יְהוָה--הַקְּטַנִּים, עִם-הַגְּדֹלִים
yevarech yir'ei hashem hakketannim, im-haggedolim
He will bless them that fear the LORD, both small and great.

יֹסֵף יְהוָה עֲלֵיכֶם; עֲלֵיכֶם, וְעַל בְּנֵיכֶם
yosef hashem aleichem; aleichem, ve'al-beneichem
The LORD increase you more and more, you and your children.

בְּרוּכִים אַתֶּם, לַיהוָה--עֹשֵׂה, שָׁמַיִם וָאָרֶץ
beruchim attem lahashem oseh, shamayim va'aretz
Blessed be ye of the LORD who made heaven and earth.

הַשָּׁמַיִם שָׁמַיִם, לַיהוָה; וְהָאָרֶץ, נָתַן לִבְנֵי-אָדָם
hashamayim shamayim lahashem veha'aretz, natan livnei-'adam
The heavens are the heavens of the LORD; but the earth hath He given to the children of men.

לֹא הַמֵּתִים, יְהַלְלוּ-יָהּ; וְלֹא, כָּל-יֹרְדֵי דוּמָה
lo hammetim yehalelu-yah; velo, kol-yoredei dumah
The dead praise not the LORD, neither any that go down into silence;

וַאֲנַחְנוּ, נְבָרֵךְ יָהּ--מֵעַתָּה וְעַד-עוֹלָם: הַלְלוּ-יָהּ
va'anachnu nevarech yah, me'attah ve'ad-'olam, halelu-yah
But we will bless the LORD from this time forth and for ever. Hallelujah.

קטז

אָהַבְתִּי, כִּי-יִשְׁמַע יְהוָה--אֶת-קוֹלִי, תַּחֲנוּנָי
Ahavti ki-yishma hashem et-koli, tachanunai
I love that the LORD should hear my voice and my supplications.

תְּהִלִים

הֶהָרִים, תִּרְקְדוּ כְאֵילִים; גְּבָעוֹת, כִּבְנֵי-צֹאן
heharim tirkedu che'eilim; geva'ot, kivnei-tzon
Ye mountains, that ye skip like rams; ye hills, like young sheep?

מִלִּפְנֵי אָדוֹן, חוּלִי אָרֶץ; מִלִּפְנֵי, אֱלוֹהַּ יַעֲקֹב
millifnei adon chuli aretz; millifnei, eloah ya'akov
Tremble, thou earth, at the presence of the Lord, at the presence of the God of Jacob;

הַהֹפְכִי הַצּוּר אֲגַם-מָיִם; חַלָּמִישׁ, לְמַעְיְנוֹ-מָיִם
hahofechi hatzur agam-mayim; challamish, lema'yeno-mayim
Who turned the rock into a pool of water, the flint into a fountain of waters.

קטו

לֹא לָנוּ יְהוָה, לֹא-לָנוּ: כִּי-לְשִׁמְךָ, תֵּן כָּבוֹד--עַל-חַסְדְּךָ, עַל-אֲמִתֶּךָ
Lo lanu hashem lo lanu ki-leshimcha ten kavod; al-chasdecha, al-'amittecha
Not unto us, O LORD, not unto us, but unto Thy name give glory, for Thy mercy, and for Thy truth's sake.

לָמָּה, יֹאמְרוּ הַגּוֹיִם: אַיֵּה-נָא, אֱלֹהֵיהֶם
lammah yomeru haggoyim; ayeh-na, eloheihem
Wherefore should the nations say: 'Where is now their God?'

וֵאלֹהֵינוּ בַשָּׁמָיִם--כֹּל אֲשֶׁר-חָפֵץ עָשָׂה
Ve'eloheinu vashamayim; kol asher-chafetz asah
But our God is in the heavens; whatsoever pleased Him He hath done.

עֲצַבֵּיהֶם, כֶּסֶף וְזָהָב; מַעֲשֵׂה, יְדֵי אָדָם
'atzabbeihem kesef vezahav; ma'aseh, yedei adam
Their idols are silver and gold, the work of men's hands.

פֶּה-לָהֶם, וְלֹא יְדַבֵּרוּ; עֵינַיִם לָהֶם, וְלֹא יִרְאוּ
peh-lahem velo yedabberu; einayim lahem, velo yir'u
They have mouths, but they speak not; eyes have they, but they see not;

אָזְנַיִם לָהֶם, וְלֹא יִשְׁמָעוּ; אַף לָהֶם, וְלֹא יְרִיחוּן
'ozenayim lahem velo yishma'u; af lahem, velo yerichun
They have ears, but they hear not; noses have they, but they smell not;

יְדֵיהֶם, וְלֹא יְמִישׁוּן--רַגְלֵיהֶם, וְלֹא יְהַלֵּכוּ; לֹא-יֶהְגּוּ, בִּגְרוֹנָם
yedeihem velo yemishun, ragleihem velo yehallechu; lo-yehgu, bigronam
They have hands, but they handle not; feet have they, but they walk not; neither speak they with their throat.

כְּמוֹהֶם, יִהְיוּ עֹשֵׂיהֶם--כֹּל אֲשֶׁר-בֹּטֵחַ בָּהֶם
kemohem yihyu oseihem; kol asher-boteach bahem
They that make them shall be like unto them; yea, every one that trusteth in them.

תְּהִלִּים

רָם עַל-כָּל-גּוֹיִם יְהוָה; עַל הַשָּׁמַיִם כְּבוֹדוֹ
ram al-kol-goyim hashem al hashamayim kevodo
The LORD is high above all nations, His glory is above the heavens.

מִי, כַּיהוָה אֱלֹהֵינוּ--הַמַּגְבִּיהִי לָשָׁבֶת
mi kahashem eloheinu; hammagbihi lashavet
Who is like unto the LORD our God, that is enthroned on high,

הַמַּשְׁפִּילִי לִרְאוֹת--בַּשָּׁמַיִם וּבָאָרֶץ
hammashpili lir'ot; bashamayim uva'aretz
That looketh down low upon heaven and upon the earth?

מְקִימִי מֵעָפָר דָּל; מֵאַשְׁפֹּת, יָרִים אֶבְיוֹן
mekimi me'afar dal; me'ashpot, yarim evyon
Who raiseth up the poor out of the dust, and lifteth up the needy out of the dunghill;

לְהוֹשִׁיבִי עִם-נְדִיבִים; עִם, נְדִיבֵי עַמּוֹ
lehoshivi im-nedivim; im, nedivei ammo
That He may set him with princes, even with the princes of His people.

מוֹשִׁיבִי, עֲקֶרֶת הַבַּיִת--אֵם-הַבָּנִים שְׂמֵחָה הַלְלוּ-יָהּ
moshivi akeret habbayit, em-habbanim semechah, halelu-yah
Who maketh the barren woman to dwell in her house as a joyful mother of children. Hallelujah.

קיד

בְּצֵאת יִשְׂרָאֵל, מִמִּצְרָיִם; בֵּית יַעֲקֹב, מֵעַם לֹעֵז
Betzet yisra'el mimmitzrayim; beit ya'akov, me'am lo'ez
When Israel came forth out of Egypt, the house of Jacob from a people of strange language;

הָיְתָה יְהוּדָה לְקָדְשׁוֹ; יִשְׂרָאֵל, מַמְשְׁלוֹתָיו
hayetah yehudah lekodsho yisra'el, mamshelotav
Judah became His sanctuary, Israel His dominion.

הַיָּם רָאָה, וַיָּנֹס; הַיַּרְדֵּן, יִסֹּב לְאָחוֹר
hayam ra'ah vayanos; hayarden, yissov le'achor
The sea saw it, and fled; the Jordan turned backward.

הֶהָרִים, רָקְדוּ כְאֵילִים; גְּבָעוֹת, כִּבְנֵי-צֹאן
heharim rakedu che'eilim; geva'ot, kivnei-tzon
The mountains skipped like rams, the hills like young sheep.

מַה-לְּךָ הַיָּם, כִּי תָנוּס; הַיַּרְדֵּן, תִּסֹּב לְאָחוֹר
mah-lecha hayom ki tanus; hayarden, tissov le'achor
What aileth thee, O thou sea, that thou fleest? thou Jordan, that thou turnest backward?

תְּהִלִים

זָרַח בַּחֹשֶׁךְ אוֹר, לַיְשָׁרִים; חַנּוּן וְרַחוּם וְצַדִּיק
zarach bachoshech or layesharim; channun verachum vetzaddik
Unto the upright He shineth as a light in the darkness, gracious, and full of compassion, and righteous.

טוֹב-אִישׁ, חוֹנֵן וּמַלְוֶה; יְכַלְכֵּל דְּבָרָיו בְּמִשְׁפָּט
tov-'ish chonen umalveh; yechalkel devarav bemishpat
Well is it with the man that dealeth graciously and lendeth, that ordereth his affairs rightfully.

כִּי-לְעוֹלָם לֹא-יִמּוֹט; לְזֵכֶר עוֹלָם, יִהְיֶה צַדִּיק
ki-le'olam lo-yimmot; lezecher olam, yihyeh tzaddik
For he shall never be moved; the righteous shall be had in everlasting remembrance.

מִשְּׁמוּעָה רָעָה, לֹא יִירָא; נָכוֹן לִבּוֹ, בָּטֻחַ בַּיהוָה
mishemu'ah ra'ah lo yira; nachon libbo, batuach bahashem
He shall not be afraid of evil tidings; his heart is stedfast, trusting in the LORD.

סָמוּךְ לִבּוֹ, לֹא יִירָא; עַד אֲשֶׁר-יִרְאֶה בְצָרָיו
samuch libbo lo yira; ad asher-yir'eh vetzarav
His heart is established, he shall not be afraid, until he gaze upon his adversaries.

פִּזַּר, נָתַן לָאֶבְיוֹנִים--צִדְקָתוֹ, עֹמֶדֶת לָעַד
pizzar natan la'evyonim, tzidkato omedet la'ad
He hath scattered abroad, he hath given to the needy; his righteousness endureth for ever;

קַרְנוֹ, תָּרוּם בְּכָבוֹד
karno, tarum bechavod
his horn shall be exalted in honour.

רָשָׁע יִרְאֶה, וְכָעָס--שִׁנָּיו יַחֲרֹק וְנָמָס; תַּאֲוַת רְשָׁעִים תֹּאבֵד
rasha yir'eh vecha'as, shinnav yacharok venamas; ta'avat resha'im toved
The wicked shall see it, and be vexed; he shall gnash with his teeth, and melt away; the desire of the wicked shall perish.

קיג

הַלְלוּ-יָהּ: הַלְלוּ, עַבְדֵי יְהוָה; הַלְלוּ, אֶת-שֵׁם יְהוָה
Halelu yah halelu avdei hashem halelu et-shem hashem
Hallelujah. Praise, O ye servants of the LORD, praise the name of the LORD.

יְהִי שֵׁם יְהוָה מְבֹרָךְ-- מֵעַתָּה, וְעַד-עוֹלָם
yehi shem hashem mevorach; me'attah, ve'ad-'olam
Blessed be the name of the LORD from this time forth and for ever.

מִמִּזְרַח-שֶׁמֶשׁ עַד-מְבוֹאוֹ-- מְהֻלָּל, שֵׁם יְהוָה
mimmizrach-shemesh ad-mevo'o; mehullal, shem hashem
From the rising of the sun unto the going down thereof the LORD'S name is to be praised.

תְּהִלִּים

זֵכֶר עָשָׂה, לְנִפְלְאֹתָיו; חַנּוּן וְרַחוּם יְהוָה
zecher asah lenifle'otav; channun verachum hashem
He hath made a memorial for His wonderful works; the LORD is gracious and full of compassion.

טֶרֶף, נָתַן לִירֵאָיו; יִזְכֹּר לְעוֹלָם בְּרִיתוֹ
teref natan lire'av; yizkor le'olam berito
He hath given food unto them that fear Him; He will ever be mindful of His covenant.

כֹּחַ מַעֲשָׂיו, הִגִּיד לְעַמּוֹ--לָתֵת לָהֶם, נַחֲלַת גּוֹיִם
koach ma'asav higgid le'ammo; latet lahem, nachalat goyim
He hath declared to His people the power of His works, in giving them the heritage of the nations.

מַעֲשֵׂי יָדָיו, אֱמֶת וּמִשְׁפָּט; נֶאֱמָנִים, כָּל-פִּקּוּדָיו
ma'asei yadav emet umishpat; ne'emanim, kol-pikkudav
The works of His hands are truth and justice; all His precepts are sure.

סְמוּכִים לָעַד לְעוֹלָם; עֲשׂוּיִם, בֶּאֱמֶת וְיָשָׁר
semuchim la'ad le'olam; asuyim, be'emet veyashar
They are established for ever and ever, they are done in truth and uprightness.

פְּדוּת, שָׁלַח לְעַמּוֹ--צִוָּה-לְעוֹלָם בְּרִיתוֹ; קָדוֹשׁ וְנוֹרָא שְׁמוֹ
pedut shalach le'ammo, tzivvah-le'olam berito; kadosh venora shemo
He hath sent redemption unto His people; He hath commanded His covenant for ever; Holy and awful is His name.

רֵאשִׁית חָכְמָה, יִרְאַת יְהוָה
reshit chochmah yir'at hashem
The fear of the LORD is the beginning of wisdom;

שֵׂכֶל טוֹב, לְכָל-עֹשֵׂיהֶם; תְּהִלָּתוֹ, עֹמֶדֶת לָעַד
sechel tov lechol-'oseihem; tehillato, omedet la'ad
a good understanding have all they that do thereafter; His praise endureth for ever.

קיב

הַלְלוּ-יָהּ: אַשְׁרֵי-אִישׁ, יָרֵא אֶת-יְהוָה; בְּמִצְוֹתָיו, חָפֵץ מְאֹד
Halelu yah ashrei-'ish yarei et-hashem bemitzvotav, chafetz me'od
Hallelujah. Happy is the man that feareth the LORD, that delighteth greatly in His commandments.

גִּבּוֹר בָּאָרֶץ, יִהְיֶה זַרְעוֹ; דּוֹר יְשָׁרִים יְבֹרָךְ
gibbor ba'aretz yihyeh zar'o; dor yesharim yevorach
His seed shall be mighty upon earth; the generation of the upright shall be blessed.

הוֹן-וָעֹשֶׁר בְּבֵיתוֹ; וְצִדְקָתוֹ, עֹמֶדֶת לָעַד
hon-va'osher beveito; vetzidkato, omedet la'ad
Wealth and riches are in his house; and his merit endureth for ever.

תְּהִלִּים

מַטֵּה-עֻזְּךָ--יִשְׁלַח יְהוָה, מִצִּיּוֹן; רְדֵה, בְּקֶרֶב אֹיְבֶיךָ
matteh-'uzzecha, yishlach hashem mitziyon; redeh, bekerev oyeveicha
The rod of Thy strength the LORD will send out of Zion: 'Rule thou in the midst of thine enemies.'

עַמְּךָ נְדָבֹת, בְּיוֹם חֵילֶךָ
'ammecha nedavot beyom cheilecha
Thy people offer themselves willingly in the day of thy warfare;

בְּהַדְרֵי-קֹדֶשׁ, מֵרֶחֶם מִשְׁחָר; לְךָ, טַל יַלְדֻתֶיךָ
behadrei-kodesh merechem mishchar; lecha, tal yalduteicha
in adornments of holiness, from the womb of the dawn, thine is the dew of thy youth.

נִשְׁבַּע יְהוָה, וְלֹא יִנָּחֵם
nishba hashem velo yinnachem
The LORD hath sworn, and will not repent:

אַתָּה-כֹהֵן לְעוֹלָם עַל-דִּבְרָתִי, מַלְכִּי-צֶדֶק
attah-chohen le'olam; al-divrati, malki-tzedek
'Thou art a priest for ever after the manner of Melchizedek.'

אֲדֹנָי עַל-יְמִינְךָ; מָחַץ בְּיוֹם-אַפּוֹ מְלָכִים
'adonai al-yeminecha; machatz beyom-'appo melachim
The Lord at thy right hand doth crush kings in the day of His wrath.

יָדִין בַּגּוֹיִם, מָלֵא גְוִיּוֹת; מָחַץ רֹאשׁ, עַל-אֶרֶץ רַבָּה
yadin baggoyim malei geviyot; machatz rosh, al-'eretz rabbah
He will judge among the nations; He filleth it with dead bodies, He crusheth the head over a wide land.

מִנַּחַל, בַּדֶּרֶךְ יִשְׁתֶּה; עַל-כֵּן, יָרִים רֹאשׁ
minnachal badderech yishteh; al-ken, yarim rosh
He will drink of the brook in the way; therefore will he lift up the head.

קיא

הַלְלוּ-יָהּ: אוֹדֶה יְהוָה, בְּכָל-לֵבָב; בְּסוֹד יְשָׁרִים וְעֵדָה
Halelu yah: odeh hashem bechol-levav; besod yesharim ve'edah
Hallelujah. I will give thanks unto the LORD with my whole heart, in the council of the upright, and in the congregation.

גְּדֹלִים, מַעֲשֵׂי יְהוָה; דְּרוּשִׁים, לְכָל-חֶפְצֵיהֶם
gedolim ma'asei hashem derushim, lechol-cheftzeihem
The works of the LORD are great, sought out of all them that have delight therein.

הוֹד-וְהָדָר פָּעֳלוֹ; וְצִדְקָתוֹ, עֹמֶדֶת לָעַד
hod-vehadar po'olo; vetzidkato, omedet la'ad
His work is glory and majesty; and His righteousness endureth for ever.

תְּהִלִּים

כִּי-עָנִי וְאֶבְיוֹן אָנֹכִי; וְלִבִּי, חָלַל בְּקִרְבִּי

ki-'ani ve'evyon anochi; velibbi, chalal bekirbi
For I am poor and needy, and my heart is wounded within me.

כְּצֵל-כִּנְטוֹתוֹ נֶהֱלָכְתִּי; נִנְעַרְתִּי, כָּאַרְבֶּה

ketzel-kintoto nehelacheti; nin'arti, ka'arbeh
I am gone like the shadow when it lengtheneth; I am shaken off as the locust.

בִּרְכַּי, כָּשְׁלוּ מִצּוֹם; וּבְשָׂרִי, כָּחַשׁ מִשָּׁמֶן

birkai kashelu mitzom; uvesari, kachash mishamen
My knees totter through fasting; and my flesh is lean, and hath no fatness.

וַאֲנִי, הָיִיתִי חֶרְפָּה לָהֶם; יִרְאוּנִי, יְנִיעוּן רֹאשָׁם

va'ani hayiti cherpah lahem; yir'uni, yeni'un rosham
I am become also a taunt unto them; when they see me, they shake their head.

עָזְרֵנִי, יְהוָה אֱלֹהָי; הוֹשִׁיעֵנִי כְחַסְדֶּךָ

'ozereni hashem elohai; hoshi'eni chechasdecha
Help me, O LORD my God; O save me according to Thy mercy;

וְיֵדְעוּ, כִּי-יָדְךָ זֹּאת; אַתָּה יְהוָה עֲשִׂיתָהּ

veyede'u ki-yadecha zot; attah hashem asitah
That they may know that this is Thy hand; that Thou, LORD, hast done it.

יְקַלְלוּ-הֵמָּה, וְאַתָּה תְבָרֵךְ: קָמוּ, וַיֵּבֹשׁוּ--וְעַבְדְּךָ יִשְׂמָח

yekalelu-hemmah ve'attah tevarech kamu vayevoshu, ve'avdecha yismach
Let them curse, but bless Thou; when they arise, they shall be put to shame, but Thy servant shall rejoice.

יִלְבְּשׁוּ שׂוֹטְנַי כְּלִמָּה; וְיַעֲטוּ כַמְעִיל בָּשְׁתָּם

yilbeshu sotenai kelimmah; veya'atu cham'il bashetam
Mine adversaries shall be clothed with confusion, and shall put on their own shame as a robe.

אוֹדֶה יְהוָה מְאֹד בְּפִי; וּבְתוֹךְ רַבִּים אֲהַלְלֶנּוּ

'odeh hashem me'od befi; uvetoch rabbim ahalelennu
I will give great thanks unto the LORD with my mouth; yea, I will praise Him among the multitude;

כִּי-יַעֲמֹד, לִימִין אֶבְיוֹן--לְהוֹשִׁיעַ, מִשֹּׁפְטֵי נַפְשׁוֹ

ki-ya'amod limin evyon; lehoshia', mishofetei nafsho
Because He standeth at the right hand of the needy, to save him from them that judge his soul.

קי

לְדָוִד, מִזְמוֹר: נְאֻם יְהוָה, לַאדֹנִי, שֵׁב לִימִינִי; עַד-אָשִׁית אֹיְבֶיךָ, הֲדֹם לְרַגְלֶיךָ

Ledavid, mizmor: Ne'um hashem ladoni, shev limini; ad-'ashit oyeveicha, hadom leragleicha
A Psalm of David. The LORD saith unto my lord: 'Sit thou at My right hand, until I make thine enemies thy footstool.'

תְּהִלִּים

יְהִי-אַחֲרִיתוֹ לְהַכְרִית; בְּדוֹר אַחֵר, יִמַּח שְׁמָם
yehi-'acharito lehachrit; bedor acher, yimmach shemam
Let his posterity be cut off; in the generation following let their name be blotted out.

יִזָּכֵר, עֲו‍ֹן אֲבֹתָיו--אֶל-יְהוָה
yizzacher avon avotav el-hashem
Let the iniquity of his fathers be brought to remembrance unto the LORD;

וְחַטַּאת אִמּוֹ, אַל-תִּמָּח
vechattat immo, al-timmach
and let not the sin of his mother be blotted out.

יִהְיוּ נֶגֶד-יְהוָה תָּמִיד; וְיַכְרֵת מֵאֶרֶץ זִכְרָם
yihyu neged-hashem tamid; veyachret me'eretz zichram
Let them be before the LORD continually, that He may cut off the memory of them from the earth.

יַעַן--אֲשֶׁר לֹא זָכַר, עֲשׂוֹת חָסֶד: וַיִּרְדֹּף, אִישׁ-עָנִי וְאֶבְיוֹן
ya'an, asher lo zachar asot chased vayirdof ish-'ani ve'evyon
Because that he remembered not to do kindness, but persecuted the poor and needy man,

וְנִכְאֵה לֵבָב; לְמוֹתֵת
venich'eh levav lemotet
and the broken in heart he was ready to slay.

וַיֶּאֱהַב קְלָלָה, וַתְּבוֹאֵהוּ; וְלֹא-חָפֵץ בִּבְרָכָה, וַתִּרְחַק מִמֶּנּוּ
vaye'ehav kelalah vattevo'ehu; velo-chafetz bivrachah, vattirchak mimmennu
Yea, he loved cursing, and it came unto him; and he delighted not in blessing, and it is far from him.

וַיִּלְבַּשׁ קְלָלָה, כְּמַדּוֹ
vayilbash kelalah, kemaddo
He clothed himself also with cursing as with his raiment,

וַתָּבֹא כַמַּיִם בְּקִרְבּוֹ; וְכַשֶּׁמֶן, בְּעַצְמוֹתָיו.
vattavo chammayim bekirbo; vechashemen, be'atzmotav
and it is come into his inward parts like water, and like oil into his bones.

תְּהִי-לוֹ, כְּבֶגֶד יַעְטֶה; וּלְמֵזַח, תָּמִיד יַחְגְּרֶהָ
tehi-lo keveged ya'teh; ulemezach, tamid yachgereha
Let it be unto him as the garment which he putteth on, and for the girdle wherewith he is girded continually.'

זֹאת פְּעֻלַּת שֹׂטְנַי, מֵאֵת יְהוָה; וְהַדֹּבְרִים רָע, עַל-נַפְשִׁי
zot pe'ullat sotenai me'et hashem vehaddoverim ra', al-nafshi
This would mine adversaries effect from the LORD, and they that speak evil against my soul.

וְאַתָּה, יְהוִה אֲדֹנָי--עֲשֵׂה-אִתִּי, לְמַעַן שְׁמֶךָ; כִּי-טוֹב חַסְדְּךָ, הַצִּילֵנִי
ve'attah hashem adonai, aseh-'itti lema'an shemecha; ki-tov chasdecha, hatzileni
But Thou, O GOD the Lord, deal with me for Thy name's sake; because Thy mercy is good, deliver Thou me.

תְּהִלִים

כִּי פִי רָשָׁע, וּפִי-מִרְמָה--עָלַי פָּתָחוּ
ki fi rasha ufi-mirmah alai patachu
For the mouth of the wicked and the mouth of deceit have they opened against me;

דִּבְּרוּ אִתִּי, לְשׁוֹן שָׁקֶר
dibberu itti, leshon shaker
they have spoken unto me with a lying tongue.

וְדִבְרֵי שִׂנְאָה סְבָבוּנִי; וַיִּלָּחֲמוּנִי חִנָּם
vedivrei sin'ah sevavuni; vayillachamuni chinnam
They compassed me about also with words of hatred, and fought against me without a cause.

תַּחַת-אַהֲבָתִי יִשְׂטְנוּנִי; וַאֲנִי תְפִלָּה
tachat-'ahavati yistenuni, va'ani tefillah
In return for my love they are my adversaries; but I am all prayer.

וַיָּשִׂימוּ עָלַי רָעָה, תַּחַת טוֹבָה; וְשִׂנְאָה, תַּחַת אַהֲבָתִי
vayasimu alai ra'ah tachat tovah; vesin'ah, tachat ahavati
And they have laid upon me evil for good, and hatred for my love:

הַפְקֵד עָלָיו רָשָׁע; וְשָׂטָן, יַעֲמֹד עַל-יְמִינוֹ
hafked alav rasha'; vesatan, ya'amod al-yemino
'Set Thou a wicked man over him; and let an adversary stand at his right hand.

בְּהִשָּׁפְטוֹ, יֵצֵא רָשָׁע; וּתְפִלָּתוֹ, תִּהְיֶה לַחֲטָאָה
behishafeto yetzei rasha'; utefillato, tihyeh lachata'ah
When he is judged, let him go forth condemned; and let his prayer be turned into sin.

יִהְיוּ-יָמָיו מְעַטִּים; פְּקֻדָּתוֹ, יִקַּח אַחֵר
yihyu-yamav me'attim; pekuddato, yikkach acher
Let his days be few; let another take his charge.

יִהְיוּ-בָנָיו יְתוֹמִים; וְאִשְׁתּוֹ, אַלְמָנָה
yihyu-vanav yetomim; ve'ishto almanah
Let his children be fatherless, and his wife a widow.

וְנוֹעַ יָנוּעוּ בָנָיו וְשִׁאֵלוּ; וְדָרְשׁוּ, מֵחָרְבוֹתֵיהֶם
venoa yanu'u vanav veshi'elu; vedareshu, mechorvoteihem
Let his children be vagabonds, and beg; and let them seek their bread out of their desolate places.

יְנַקֵּשׁ נוֹשֶׁה, לְכָל-אֲשֶׁר-לוֹ; וְיָבֹזּוּ זָרִים יְגִיעוֹ
yenakkesh nosheh lechol-'asher-lo; veyavozzu zarim yegi'o
Let the creditor distrain all that he hath; and let strangers make spoil of his labour.

אַל-יְהִי-לוֹ, מֹשֵׁךְ חָסֶד; וְאַל-יְהִי חוֹנֵן, לִיתוֹמָיו
'al-yehi-lo moshech chased; ve'al-yehi chonen, litomav
Let there be none to extend kindness unto him; neither let there be any to be gracious unto his fatherless children.

תְּהִלִים

כִּי-גָדֹל מֵעַל-שָׁמַיִם חַסְדֶּךָ; וְעַד-שְׁחָקִים אֲמִתֶּךָ
ki-gadol me'al-shamayim chasdecha; ve'ad-shechakim amittecha
For Thy mercy is great above the heavens, and Thy truth reacheth unto the skies.

רוּמָה עַל-שָׁמַיִם אֱלֹהִים; וְעַל כָּל-הָאָרֶץ כְּבוֹדֶךָ
rumah al-shamayim elohim; ve'al kol-ha'aretz kevodecha
Be Thou exalted, O God, above the heavens; and Thy glory be above all the earth.

לְמַעַן, יֵחָלְצוּן יְדִידֶיךָ; הוֹשִׁיעָה יְמִינְךָ וַעֲנֵנִי
lema'an yechaletzun yedideicha; hoshi'ah yeminecha va'aneni
That Thy beloved may be delivered, save with Thy right hand, and answer me.

אֱלֹהִים, דִּבֶּר בְּקָדְשׁוֹ--אֶעְלֹזָה: אֲחַלְּקָה שְׁכֶם; וְעֵמֶק סֻכּוֹת אֲמַדֵּד
'elohim dibber bekodesho, e'lozah achallekah shechem; ve'emek sukkot amadded
God spoke in His holiness, that I would exult; that I would divide Shechem, and mete out the valley of Succoth.

לִי גִלְעָד, לִי מְנַשֶּׁה, וְאֶפְרַיִם, מָעוֹז רֹאשִׁי; יְהוּדָה, מְחֹקְקִי
li gil'ad li menasheh, ve'efrayim ma'oz roshi; yehudah, mechokeki
Gilead is mine, Manasseh is mine; Ephraim also is the defence of my head; Judah is my sceptre.

מוֹאָב, סִיר רַחְצִי--עַל-אֱדוֹם, אַשְׁלִיךְ נַעֲלִי; עֲלֵי-פְלֶשֶׁת, אֶתְרוֹעָע
mo'av sir rachtzi, al-'edom ashlich na'ali; alei-feleshet, etro'a
Moab is my washpot; upon Edom do I cast my shoe; over Philistia do I cry aloud.

מִי יֹבִלֵנִי, עִיר מִבְצָר; מִי נָחַנִי עַד-אֱדוֹם
mi yovileni ir mivtzar; mi nachani ad-'edom
Who will bring me into the fortified city? Who will lead me unto Edom?

הֲלֹא-אֱלֹהִים זְנַחְתָּנוּ; וְלֹא-תֵצֵא אֱלֹהִים, בְּצִבְאוֹתֵינוּ
halo-'elohim zenachtanu; velo-tetzei elohim, betziv'oteinu
Hast not Thou cast us off, O God? and Thou goest not forth, O God, with our hosts?

הָבָה-לָּנוּ עֶזְרָת מִצָּר; וְשָׁוְא, תְּשׁוּעַת אָדָם
havah-lanu ezrat mitzar; veshav, teshu'at adam
Give us help against the adversary; for vain is the help of man.

בֵּאלֹהִים נַעֲשֶׂה-חָיִל; וְהוּא, יָבוּס צָרֵינוּ
Be'elohim na'aseh-chayil; vehu, yavus tzareinu
Through God we shall do valiantly; for He it is that will tread down our adversaries.

קט

לַמְנַצֵּחַ, לְדָוִד מִזְמוֹר: אֱלֹהֵי תְהִלָּתִי, אַל-תֶּחֱרַשׁ
Lamnatzeach ledavid mizmor; elohei tehillati, al-techerash
For the Leader. A Psalm of David. O God of my praise, keep not silence;

תְּהִלִּים

וַיּוֹשֶׁב שָׁם רְעֵבִים; וַיְכוֹנְנוּ, עִיר מוֹשָׁב
vayoshev sham re'evim; vaychonenu, ir moshav
And there He maketh the hungry to dwell, and they establish a city of habitation;

וַיִּזְרְעוּ שָׂדוֹת, וַיִּטְּעוּ כְרָמִים; וַיַּעֲשׂוּ, פְּרִי תְבוּאָה
vayizre'u sadot vayitte'u cheramim; vaya'asu, peri tevu'ah
And sow fields, and plant vineyards, which yield fruits of increase.

וַיְבָרְכֵם וַיִּרְבּוּ מְאֹד; וּבְהֶמְתָּם, לֹא יַמְעִיט
vayvarachem vayirbu me'od; uvehemtam, lo yam'it
He blesseth them also, so that they are multiplied greatly, and suffereth not their cattle to decrease.

וַיִּמְעֲטוּ וַיָּשֹׁחוּ--מֵעֹצֶר רָעָה וְיָגוֹן
vayim'atu vayashochu; me'otzer ra'ah veyagon
Again, they are minished and dwindle away through oppression of evil and sorrow.

שֹׁפֵךְ בּוּז, עַל-נְדִיבִים; וַיַּתְעֵם, בְּתֹהוּ לֹא-דָרֶךְ
shofech buz al-nedivim; vayat'em, betohu lo-darech
He poureth contempt upon princes, and causeth them to wander in the waste, where there is no way.

וַיְשַׂגֵּב אֶבְיוֹן מֵעוֹנִי; וַיָּשֶׂם כַּצֹּאן, מִשְׁפָּחוֹת
vaysaggev evyon me'oni; vayasem katzon, mishpachot
Yet setteth He the needy on high from affliction, and maketh his families like a flock.

יִרְאוּ יְשָׁרִים וְיִשְׂמָחוּ; וְכָל-עַוְלָה, קָפְצָה פִּיהָ
yir'u yesharim veyismachu; vechol-'avlah, kafetzah piha
The upright see it, and are glad; and all iniquity stoppeth her mouth.

מִי-חָכָם וְיִשְׁמָר-אֵלֶּה; וְיִתְבּוֹנְנוּ, חַסְדֵי יְהוָה
mi-chacham veyishmor-'elleh; veyitbonenu, chasdei hashem
Whoso is wise, let him observe these things, and let them consider the mercies of the LORD.

קח

שִׁיר מִזְמוֹר לְדָוִד. נָכוֹן לִבִּי אֱלֹהִים; אָשִׁירָה וַאֲזַמְּרָה, אַף-כְּבוֹדִי
Shir mizmor ledavid. Nachon libbi elohim; ashirah va'azammerah, af-kevodi
A Song, a Psalm of David. My heart is steadfast, O God; I will sing, yea, I will sing praises, even with my glory.

עוּרָה, הַנֵּבֶל וְכִנּוֹר; אָעִירָה שָּׁחַר
'urah hannevel vechinnor, a'irah shachar
Awake, psaltery and harp; I will awake the dawn.

אוֹדְךָ בָעַמִּים יְהוָה; וַאֲזַמֶּרְךָ, בַּלְאֻמִּים
'odecha va'ammim hashem va'azammercha, bal-'ummim
I will give thanks unto Thee, O LORD, among the peoples; and I will sing praises unto Thee among the nations.

תְּהִלִים

הֵמָּה רָאוּ, מַעֲשֵׂי יְהוָה; וְנִפְלְאוֹתָיו, בִּמְצוּלָה
hemmah ra'u ma'asei hashem venifle'otav, bimtzulah
These saw the works of the LORD, and His wonders in the deep;

וַיֹּאמֶר--וַיַּעֲמֵד, רוּחַ סְעָרָה; וַתְּרוֹמֵם גַּלָּיו
vayomer, vaya'amed ruach se'arah; vatteromem gallav
For He commanded, and raised the stormy wind, which lifted up the waves thereof;

יַעֲלוּ שָׁמַיִם, יֵרְדוּ תְהוֹמוֹת; נַפְשָׁם, בְּרָעָה תִתְמוֹגָג
ya'alu shamayim yeredu tehomot; nafsham, bera'ah titmogag
They mounted up to the heaven, they went down to the deeps; their soul melted away because of trouble;

יָחוֹגּוּ וְיָנוּעוּ, כַּשִּׁכּוֹר; וְכָל-חָכְמָתָם, תִּתְבַּלָּע
yachoggu veyanu'u kashikkor; vechol-chachematam, titballa
They reeled to and fro, and staggered like a drunken man, and all their wisdom was swallowed up--

וַיִּצְעֲקוּ אֶל-יְהוָה, בַּצַּר לָהֶם; וּמִמְּצוּקֹתֵיהֶם, יוֹצִיאֵם
vayitz'aku el-hashem batzar lahem; umimmetzukoteihem, yotzi'em
They cried unto the LORD in their trouble, and He brought them out of their distresses.

יָקֵם סְעָרָה, לִדְמָמָה; וַיֶּחֱשׁוּ, גַּלֵּיהֶם
yakem se'arah lidmamah; vayecheshu, galleihem
He made the storm a calm, so that the waves thereof were still.

וַיִּשְׂמְחוּ כִי-יִשְׁתֹּקוּ; וַיַּנְחֵם, אֶל-מְחוֹז חֶפְצָם
vayismechu chi-yishtoku; vayanchem, el-mechoz cheftzam
Then were they glad because they were quiet, and He led them unto their desired haven.

יוֹדוּ לַיהוָה חַסְדּוֹ; וְנִפְלְאוֹתָיו, לִבְנֵי אָדָם
yodu lahashem chasdo; venifle'otav, livnei adam
Let them give thanks unto the LORD for His mercy, and for His wonderful works to the children of men!

וִירוֹמְמוּהוּ, בִּקְהַל-עָם; וּבְמוֹשַׁב זְקֵנִים יְהַלְלוּהוּ
viromemuhu bik'hal-'am; uvemoshav zekenim yehaleluhu
Let them exalt Him also in the assembly of the people, and praise Him in the seat of the elders.

יָשֵׂם נְהָרוֹת לְמִדְבָּר; וּמֹצָאֵי מַיִם, לְצִמָּאוֹן
yasem neharot lemidbar; umotza'ei mayim, letzimma'on
He turneth rivers into a wilderness, and watersprings into a thirsty ground;

אֶרֶץ פְּרִי, לִמְלֵחָה; מֵרָעַת, יוֹשְׁבֵי בָהּ
'eretz peri limlechah; mera'at, yoshevei vah
A fruitful land into a salt waste, for the wickedness of them that dwell therein.

יָשֵׂם מִדְבָּר לַאֲגַם-מַיִם; וְאֶרֶץ צִיָּה, לְמֹצָאֵי מָיִם
yasem midbar la'agam-mayim; ve'eretz tziyah, lemotza'ei mayim
He turneth a wilderness into a pool of water, and a dry land into watersprings.

תְּהִלִּים

וַיַּכְנַע בֶּעָמָל לִבָּם; כָּשְׁלוּ, וְאֵין עֹזֵר
vayachna be'amal libbam; kashelu, ve'ein ozer
Therefore He humbled their heart with travail, they stumbled, and there was none to help--

וַיִּזְעֲקוּ אֶל-יְהוָה, בַּצַּר לָהֶם; מִמְּצֻקוֹתֵיהֶם, יוֹשִׁיעֵם
vayiz'aku el-hashem batzar lahem; mimmetzukoteihem, yoshi'em
They cried unto the LORD in their trouble, and He saved them out of their distresses.

יוֹצִיאֵם, מֵחֹשֶׁךְ וְצַלְמָוֶת; וּמוֹסְרוֹתֵיהֶם יְנַתֵּק
yotzi'em mechoshech vetzalmavet; umoseroteihem yenattek
He brought them out of darkness and the shadow of death, and broke their bands in sunder.

יוֹדוּ לַיהוָה חַסְדּוֹ; וְנִפְלְאוֹתָיו, לִבְנֵי אָדָם
yodu lahashem chasdo; venifle'otav, livnei adam
Let them give thanks unto the LORD for His mercy, and for His wonderful works to the children of men!

כִּי-שִׁבַּר, דַּלְתוֹת נְחֹשֶׁת; וּבְרִיחֵי בַרְזֶל גִּדֵּעַ
ki-shibbar daltot nechoshet; uverichei varzel giddea
For He hath broken the gates of brass, and cut the bars of iron in sunder.

אֱוִלִים, מִדֶּרֶךְ פִּשְׁעָם; וּמֵעֲוֹנֹתֵיהֶם, יִתְעַנּוּ
'evilim midderech pish'am; ume'avonoteihem, yit'annu
Crazed because of the way of their transgression, and afflicted because of their iniquities--

כָּל-אֹכֶל, תְּתַעֵב נַפְשָׁם; וַיַּגִּיעוּ, עַד-שַׁעֲרֵי מָוֶת
kol-'ochel teta'ev nafsham; vayaggi'u, ad-sha'arei mavet
Their soul abhorred all manner of food, and they drew near unto the gates of death--

וַיִּזְעֲקוּ אֶל-יְהוָה, בַּצַּר לָהֶם; מִמְּצֻקוֹתֵיהֶם יוֹשִׁיעֵם
vayiz'aku el-hashem batzar lahem; mimmetzukoteihem, yoshi'em
They cried unto the LORD in their trouble, and He saved them out of their distresses;

יִשְׁלַח דְּבָרוֹ, וְיִרְפָּאֵם; וִימַלֵּט, מִשְּׁחִיתוֹתָם
yishlach devaro veyirpa'em; viymallet, mishechitotam
He sent His word, and healed them, and delivered them from their graves.

יוֹדוּ לַיהוָה חַסְדּוֹ; וְנִפְלְאוֹתָיו, לִבְנֵי אָדָם
yodu lahashem chasdo; venifle'otav, livnei adam
Let them give thanks unto the LORD for His mercy, and for His wonderful works to the children of men!

וְיִזְבְּחוּ, זִבְחֵי תוֹדָה; וִיסַפְּרוּ מַעֲשָׂיו בְּרִנָּה
veyizbechu zivchei todah; visapperu ma'asav berinnah
And let them offer the sacrifices of thanksgiving, and declare His works with singing.

יוֹרְדֵי הַיָּם, בָּאֳנִיּוֹת; עֹשֵׂי מְלָאכָה, בְּמַיִם רַבִּים
yoredei hayam bo'oniyot; osei melachah, bemayim rabbim
They that go down to the sea in ships, that do business in great waters--

תְּהִלִּים

קז

הֹדוּ לַיהוָה כִּי-טוֹב: כִּי לְעוֹלָם חַסְדּוֹ
Hodu lahashem ki-tov; ki le'olam chasdo
'O give thanks unto the LORD, for He is good, for His mercy endureth for ever.'

יֹאמְרוּ, גְּאוּלֵי יְהוָה--אֲשֶׁר גְּאָלָם, מִיַּד-צָר
yomeru ge'ulei hashem asher ge'alam, miyad-tzar
So let the redeemed of the LORD say, whom He hath redeemed from the hand of the adversary;

וּמֵאֲרָצוֹת, קִבְּצָם: מִמִּזְרָח וּמִמַּעֲרָב; מִצָּפוֹן וּמִיָּם
ume'aratzot, kibbetzam mimmizrach umimma'arav; mitzafon umiyam
And gathered them out of the lands, from the east and from the west, from the north and from the sea.

תָּעוּ בַמִּדְבָּר, בִּישִׁימוֹן דָּרֶךְ; עִיר מוֹשָׁב, לֹא מָצָאוּ
ta'u vammidbar biyshimon darech; ir moshav, lo matza'u
They wandered in the wilderness in a desert way; they found no city of habitation.

רְעֵבִים גַּם-צְמֵאִים--נַפְשָׁם, בָּהֶם תִּתְעַטָּף
re'evim gam-tzeme'im; nafsham, bahem tit'attaf
Hungry and thirsty, their soul fainted in them.

וַיִּצְעֲקוּ אֶל-יְהוָה, בַּצַּר לָהֶם; מִמְּצוּקוֹתֵיהֶם, יַצִּילֵם
vayitz'aku el-hashem batzar lahem; mimmetzukoteihem, yatzilem
Then they cried unto the LORD in their trouble, and He delivered them out of their distresses.

וַיַּדְרִיכֵם, בְּדֶרֶךְ יְשָׁרָה--לָלֶכֶת, אֶל-עִיר מוֹשָׁב
vayadrichem bederech yesharah; lalechet, el-'ir moshav
And He led them by a straight way, that they might go to a city of habitation.

יוֹדוּ לַיהוָה חַסְדּוֹ; וְנִפְלְאוֹתָיו, לִבְנֵי אָדָם
yodu lahashem chasdo; venifle'otav, livnei adam
Let them give thanks unto the LORD for His mercy, and for His wonderful works to the children of men!

כִּי-הִשְׂבִּיעַ, נֶפֶשׁ שֹׁקֵקָה; וְנֶפֶשׁ רְעֵבָה, מִלֵּא-טוֹב
ki-hisbia nefesh shokekah; venefesh re'evah mille-tov
For He hath satisfied the longing soul, and the hungry soul He hath filled with good.

יֹשְׁבֵי, חֹשֶׁךְ וְצַלְמָוֶת; אֲסִירֵי עֳנִי וּבַרְזֶל
yoshevei choshech vetzalmavet; asirei oni uvarzel
Such as sat in darkness and in the shadow of death, being bound in affliction and iron--

כִּי-הִמְרוּ אִמְרֵי-אֵל; וַעֲצַת עֶלְיוֹן נָאָצוּ
ki-himru imrei-'el; va'atzat elyon na'atzu
Because they rebelled against the words of God, and contemned the counsel of the Most High.

תְּהִלִים

וַיִּטְמְאוּ בְמַעֲשֵׂיהֶם; וַיִּזְנוּ, בְּמַעַלְלֵיהֶם
vayitme'u vema'aseihem; vayiznu, bema'aleleihem
Thus were they defiled with their works, and went astray in their doings.

וַיִּחַר-אַף יְהוָה בְּעַמּוֹ; וַיְתָעֵב, אֶת-נַחֲלָתוֹ
vayichar-'af hashem be'ammo; vayta'ev, et-nachalato
Therefore was the wrath of the LORD kindled against His people, and He abhorred His inheritance.

וַיִּתְּנֵם בְּיַד-גּוֹיִם; וַיִּמְשְׁלוּ בָהֶם, שֹׂנְאֵיהֶם
vayittenem beyad-goyim; vayimshelu vahem, sone'eihem
And He gave them into the hand of the nations; and they that hated them ruled over them.

וַיִּלְחָצוּם אוֹיְבֵיהֶם; וַיִּכָּנְעוּ, תַּחַת יָדָם.
vayilchatzum oyeveihem; vayikkane'u, tachat yadam
Their enemies also oppressed them, and they were subdued under their hand.

פְּעָמִים רַבּוֹת, יַצִּילֵם: וְהֵמָּה, יַמְרוּ בַעֲצָתָם; וַיָּמֹכּוּ, בַּעֲוֹנָם
pe'amim rabbot, yatzilem vehemmah yamru va'atzatam; vayamokku, ba'avonam
Many times did He deliver them; but they were rebellious in their counsel, and sank low through their iniquity.

וַיַּרְא, בַּצַּר לָהֶם-- בְּשָׁמְעוֹ, אֶת-רִנָּתָם
vayar batzar lahem; beshame'o, et-rinnatam
Nevertheless He looked upon their distress, when He heard their cry;

וַיִּזְכֹּר לָהֶם בְּרִיתוֹ; וַיִּנָּחֵם, כְּרֹב חֲסָדָו
vayizkor lahem berito; vayinnachem, kerov chasadav
And He remembered for them His covenant, and repented according to the multitude of His mercies.

וַיִּתֵּן אוֹתָם לְרַחֲמִים-- לִפְנֵי, כָּל-שׁוֹבֵיהֶם
vayitten otam lerachamim; lifnei kol-shoveihem
He made them also to be pitied of all those that carried them captive.

הוֹשִׁיעֵנוּ, יְהוָה אֱלֹהֵינוּ, וְקַבְּצֵנוּ, מִן-הַגּוֹיִם
hoshi'enu hashem eloheinu, vekabbetzenu min-haggoyim
Save us, O LORD our God, and gather us from among the nations,

לְהֹדוֹת, לְשֵׁם קָדְשֶׁךָ; לְהִשְׁתַּבֵּחַ, בִּתְהִלָּתֶךָ
lehodot leshem kodshecha lehishtabbeach, bit'hillatecha
that we may give thanks unto Thy holy name, that we may triumph in Thy praise.

בָּרוּךְ יְהוָה אֱלֹהֵי יִשְׂרָאֵל, מִן-הָעוֹלָם וְעַד הָעוֹלָם
baruch-hashem elohei yisra'el min-ha'olam ve'ad ha'olam
Blessed be the LORD, the God of Israel, from everlasting even to everlasting,

וְאָמַר כָּל-הָעָם אָמֵן: הַלְלוּ-יָהּ
ve'amar kol-ha'am amen, halelu-yah
and let all the people say: 'Amen.' Hallelujah.

תְּהִלִּים

וַיִּצָּמְדוּ, לְבַעַל פְּעוֹר; וַיֹּאכְלוּ, זִבְחֵי מֵתִים
vayitzamedu leva'al pe'or; vayochelu, zivchei metim
They joined themselves also unto Baal of Peor, and ate the sacrifices of the dead.

וַיַּכְעִיסוּ, בְּמַעַלְלֵיהֶם; וַתִּפְרָץ-בָּם, מַגֵּפָה
vayach'isu bema'aleleihem; vattifrotz-bam, maggefah
Thus they provoked Him with their doings, and the plague broke in upon them.

וַיַּעֲמֹד פִּינְחָס, וַיְפַלֵּל; וַתֵּעָצַר, הַמַּגֵּפָה
vaya'amod pinchas vayfallel; vatte'atzar, hammaggefah
Then stood up Phinehas, and wrought judgment, and so the plague was stayed.

וַתֵּחָשֶׁב לוֹ, לִצְדָקָה; לְדֹר וָדֹר, עַד-עוֹלָם
vattechashev lo litzdakah; ledor vador, ad-'olam
And that was counted unto him for righteousness, unto all generations for ever.

וַיַּקְצִיפוּ, עַל-מֵי מְרִיבָה; וַיֵּרַע לְמֹשֶׁה, בַּעֲבוּרָם
vayaktzifu al-mei merivah; vayera lemosheh, ba'avuram
They angered Him also at the waters of Meribah, and it went ill with Moses because of them;

כִּי-הִמְרוּ אֶת-רוּחוֹ; וַיְבַטֵּא, בִּשְׂפָתָיו
ki-himru et-rucho; vayvatte, bisfatav
For they embittered his spirit, and he spoke rashly with his lips.

לֹא-הִשְׁמִידוּ, אֶת-הָעַמִּים-- אֲשֶׁר אָמַר יְהוָה לָהֶם
lo-hishmidu et-ha'ammim; asher amar hashem lahem
They did not destroy the peoples, as the LORD commanded them;

וַיִּתְעָרְבוּ בַגּוֹיִם; וַיִּלְמְדוּ, מַעֲשֵׂיהֶם
vayit'arevu vaggoyim; vayilmedu, ma'aseihem
But mingled themselves with the nations, and learned their works;

וַיַּעַבְדוּ אֶת-עֲצַבֵּיהֶם; וַיִּהְיוּ לָהֶם לְמוֹקֵשׁ
vaya'avdu et-'atzabbeihem; vayihyu lahem lemokesh
And they served their idols, which became a snare unto them;

וַיִּזְבְּחוּ אֶת-בְּנֵיהֶם, וְאֶת-בְּנוֹתֵיהֶם-- לַשֵּׁדִים
vayizbechu et-beneihem ve'et-benoteihem, lashedim
Yea, they sacrificed their sons and their daughters unto demons,

וַיִּשְׁפְּכוּ דָם נָקִי, דַּם-בְּנֵיהֶם וּבְנוֹתֵיהֶם
vayishpechu dam naki dam-beneihem uvenoteihem
And shed innocent blood, even the blood of their sons and of their daughters,

אֲשֶׁר זִבְּחוּ, לַעֲצַבֵּי כְנָעַן; וַתֶּחֱנַף הָאָרֶץ, בַּדָּמִים
asher zibbechu la'atzabbei chena'an; vattechenaf ha'aretz, baddamim
whom they sacrificed unto the idols of Canaan; and the land was polluted with blood.

תְּהִלִּים

תִּפְתַּח-אֶרֶץ, וַתִּבְלַע דָּתָן; וַתְּכַס, עַל-עֲדַת אֲבִירָם
tiftach-'eretz vattivla datan; vattechas, al-'adat aviram
The earth opened and swallowed up Dathan, and covered the company of Abiram.

וַתִּבְעַר-אֵשׁ בַּעֲדָתָם; לֶהָבָה, תְּלַהֵט רְשָׁעִים
vattiv'ar-'esh ba'adatam; lehavah, telahet resha'im
And a fire was kindled in their company; the flame burned up the wicked.

יַעֲשׂוּ-עֵגֶל בְּחֹרֵב; וַיִּשְׁתַּחֲווּ, לְמַסֵּכָה
ya'asu-'egel bechorev; vayishtachavu, lemassechah
They made a calf in Horeb, and worshipped a molten image.

וַיָּמִירוּ אֶת-כְּבוֹדָם; בְּתַבְנִית שׁוֹר, אֹכֵל עֵשֶׂב
vayamiru et-kevodam; betavnit shor, ochel esev
Thus they exchanged their glory for the likeness of an ox that eateth grass.

שָׁכְחוּ, אֵל מוֹשִׁיעָם--עֹשֶׂה גְדֹלוֹת בְּמִצְרָיִם
shachechu el moshi'am; oseh gedolot bemitzrayim
They forgot God their saviour, who had done great things in Egypt;

נִפְלָאוֹת, בְּאֶרֶץ חָם; נוֹרָאוֹת, עַל-יַם-סוּף
nifla'ot be'eretz cham; nora'ot, al-yam-suf
Wondrous works in the land of Ham, terrible things by the Red Sea.

וַיֹּאמֶר, לְהַשְׁמִידָם: לוּלֵי, מֹשֶׁה בְחִירוֹ--עָמַד בַּפֶּרֶץ לְפָנָיו
vayomer, lehashmidam lulei mosheh vechiro, amad bapperetz lefanav
Therefore He said that He would destroy them, had not Moses His chosen stood before Him in the breach,

לְהָשִׁיב חֲמָתוֹ, מֵהַשְׁחִית
lehashiv chamato, mehashchit
to turn back His wrath, lest He should destroy them.

וַיִּמְאֲסוּ, בְּאֶרֶץ חֶמְדָּה; לֹא-הֶאֱמִינוּ, לִדְבָרוֹ
vayim'asu be'eretz chemdah; lo-he'eminu, lidvaro
Moreover, they scorned the desirable land, they believed not His word;

וַיֵּרָגְנוּ בְאָהֳלֵיהֶם; לֹא שָׁמְעוּ, בְּקוֹל יְהוָה
vayeragenu ve'oholeihem; lo shame'u, bekol hashem
And they murmured in their tents, they hearkened not unto the voice of the LORD.

וַיִּשָּׂא יָדוֹ לָהֶם--לְהַפִּיל אוֹתָם, בַּמִּדְבָּר
vayissa yado lahem; lehappil otam, bammidbar
Therefore He swore concerning them, that He would overthrow them in the wilderness;

וּלְהַפִּיל זַרְעָם, בַּגּוֹיִם; וּלְזָרוֹתָם, בָּאֲרָצוֹת
ulehappil zar'am baggoyim; ulezarotam, ba'aratzot
And that He would cast out their seed among the nations, and scatter them in the lands.

תְּהִלִּים

חָטָאנוּ עִם-אֲבוֹתֵינוּ; הֶעֱוִינוּ הִרְשָׁעְנוּ
chatanu im-'avoteinu, he'evinu hirsha'enu
We have sinned with our fathers, we have done iniquitously, we have dealt wickedly.

אֲבוֹתֵינוּ בְמִצְרַיִם, לֹא-הִשְׂכִּילוּ נִפְלְאוֹתֶיךָ--לֹא זָכְרוּ, אֶת-רֹב חֲסָדֶיךָ
'avoteinu vemitzrayim lo-hiskilu nifle'oteicha, lo zacheru et-rov chasadeicha
Our fathers in Egypt gave no heed unto Thy wonders; they remembered not the multitude of Thy mercies;

וַיַּמְרוּ עַל-יָם בְּיַם-סוּף
vayamru al-yam beyam-suf
but were rebellious at the sea, even at the Red Sea.

וַיּוֹשִׁיעֵם, לְמַעַן שְׁמוֹ--לְהוֹדִיעַ, אֶת-גְּבוּרָתוֹ
vayoshi'em lema'an shemo; lehodia', et-gevurato
Nevertheless He saved them for His name's sake, that He might make His mighty power to be known.

וַיִּגְעַר בְּיַם-סוּף, וַיֶּחֱרָב; וַיּוֹלִיכֵם בַּתְּהֹמוֹת, כַּמִּדְבָּר
vayig'ar beyam-suf vayecherav; vayolichem battehomot, kammidbar
And He rebuked the Red Sea, and it was dried up; and He led them through the depths, as through a wilderness.

וַיּוֹשִׁיעֵם, מִיַּד שׂוֹנֵא; וַיִּגְאָלֵם, מִיַּד אוֹיֵב
vayoshi'em miyad sone; vayig'alem, miyad oyev
And He saved them from the hand of him that hated them, and redeemed them from the hand of the enemy.

וַיְכַסּוּ-מַיִם צָרֵיהֶם; אֶחָד מֵהֶם, לֹא נוֹתָר
vaychassu-mayim tzareihem; echad mehem, lo notar
And the waters covered their adversaries; there was not one of them left.

וַיַּאֲמִינוּ בִדְבָרָיו; יָשִׁירוּ, תְּהִלָּתוֹ
vaya'aminu vidvarav; yashiru, tehillato
Then believed they His words; they sang His praise.

מִהֲרוּ, שָׁכְחוּ מַעֲשָׂיו; לֹא-חִכּוּ, לַעֲצָתוֹ
miharu shachechu ma'asav; lo-chikku, la'atzato
They soon forgot His works; they waited not for His counsel;

וַיִּתְאַוּוּ תַאֲוָה, בַּמִּדְבָּר; וַיְנַסּוּ-אֵל, בִּישִׁימוֹן
vayit'avvu ta'avah bammidbar; vaynassu-'el, biyshimon
But lusted exceedingly in the wilderness, and tried God in the desert.

וַיִּתֵּן לָהֶם, שֶׁאֱלָתָם; וַיְשַׁלַּח רָזוֹן בְּנַפְשָׁם
vayitten lahem she'elatam; vayshallach razon benafsham
And He gave them their request; but sent leanness into their soul.

וַיְקַנְאוּ לְמֹשֶׁה, בַּמַּחֲנֶה; לְאַהֲרֹן, קְדוֹשׁ יְהוָה
vaykan'u lemosheh bammachaneh; le'aharon, kedosh hashem
They were jealous also of Moses in the camp, and of Aaron the holy one of the LORD.

תְּהִלִּים

פָּתַח צוּר, וַיָּזוּבוּ מָיִם; הָלְכוּ, בַּצִּיּוֹת נָהָר
patach tzur vayazuvu mayim; halechu, batziyot nahar
He opened the rock, and waters gushed out; they ran, a river in the dry places.

כִּי-זָכַר, אֶת-דְּבַר קָדְשׁוֹ; אֶת-אַבְרָהָם עַבְדּוֹ
ki-zachar et-devar kodsho et-'avraham avdo
For He remembered His holy word unto Abraham His servant;

וַיּוֹצִא עַמּוֹ בְשָׂשׂוֹן; בְּרִנָּה, אֶת-בְּחִירָיו
vayotzi ammo vesason; berinnah, et-bechirav
And He brought forth His people with joy, His chosen ones with singing.

וַיִּתֵּן לָהֶם, אַרְצוֹת גּוֹיִם; וַעֲמַל לְאֻמִּים יִירָשׁוּ
vayitten lahem artzot goyim; va'amal le'ummim yirashu
And He gave them the lands of the nations, and they took the labour of the peoples in possession;

בַּעֲבוּר, יִשְׁמְרוּ חֻקָּיו--וְתוֹרֹתָיו יִנְצֹרוּ; הַלְלוּ-יָהּ
ba'avur yishmeru chukkav vetorotav yintzoru, halelu-yah
That they might keep His statutes, and observe His laws. Hallelujah.

קו

הַלְלוּ-יָהּ: הוֹדוּ לַיהוָה כִּי-טוֹב--כִּי לְעוֹלָם חַסְדּוֹ
Haleluyah: hodu lahashem ki-tov; ki le'olam chasdo
Hallelujah. O give thanks unto the LORD; for He is good; for His mercy endureth for ever.

מִי--יְמַלֵּל, גְּבוּרוֹת יְהוָה; יַשְׁמִיעַ, כָּל-תְּהִלָּתוֹ
mi, yemallel gevurot hashem yashmia', kol-tehillato
Who can express the mighty acts of the LORD, or make all His praise to be heard?

אַשְׁרֵי, שֹׁמְרֵי מִשְׁפָּט; עֹשֵׂה צְדָקָה בְכָל-עֵת
'ashrei shomerei mishpat; oseh tzedakah vechol-'et
Happy are they that keep justice, that do righteousness at all times.

זָכְרֵנִי יְהוָה, בִּרְצוֹן עַמֶּךָ; פָּקְדֵנִי, בִּישׁוּעָתֶךָ
zachereni hashem birtzon ammecha; pokideni, bishu'atecha
Remember me, O LORD, when Thou favourest Thy people; O think of me at Thy salvation;

לִרְאוֹת, בְּטוֹבַת בְּחִירֶיךָ--לִשְׂמֹחַ, בְּשִׂמְחַת גּוֹיֶךָ
lir'ot betovat bechireicha, lismoach besimchat goyecha
That I may behold the prosperity of Thy chosen, that I may rejoice in the gladness of Thy nation,

לְהִתְהַלֵּל, עִם-נַחֲלָתֶךָ
lehit'hallel, im-nachalatecha
that I may glory with Thine inheritance.

תְּהִלִּים

הָפַךְ אֶת-מֵימֵיהֶם לְדָם; וַיָּמֶת, אֶת-דְּגָתָם
hafach et-meimeihem ledam; vayamet, et-degatam
He turned their waters into blood, and slew their fish.

שָׁרַץ אַרְצָם צְפַרְדְּעִים; בְּחַדְרֵי, מַלְכֵיהֶם
sharatz artzam tzefarde'im; bechadrei, malcheihem
Their land swarmed with frogs, in the chambers of their kings.

אָמַר, וַיָּבֹא עָרֹב; כִּנִּים, בְּכָל-גְּבוּלָם
'amar vayavo arov; kinnim, bechol-gevulam
He spoke, and there came swarms of flies, and gnats in all their borders.

נָתַן גִּשְׁמֵיהֶם בָּרָד; אֵשׁ לֶהָבוֹת בְּאַרְצָם
natan gishmeihem barad; esh lehavot be'artzam
He gave them hail for rain, and flaming fire in their land.

וַיַּךְ גַּפְנָם, וּתְאֵנָתָם; וַיְשַׁבֵּר, עֵץ גְּבוּלָם
vayach gafnom ute'enatam; vayshabber, etz gevulam
He smote their vines also and their fig-trees; and broke the trees of their borders.

אָמַר, וַיָּבֹא אַרְבֶּה; וְיֶלֶק, וְאֵין מִסְפָּר
'amar vayavo arbeh; veyelek, ve'ein mispar
He spoke, and the locust came, and the canker-worm without number,

וַיֹּאכַל כָּל-עֵשֶׂב בְּאַרְצָם; וַיֹּאכַל, פְּרִי אַדְמָתָם
vayochal kol-'esev be'artzam; vayochal, peri admatam
And did eat up every herb in their land, and did eat up the fruit of their ground.

וַיַּךְ כָּל-בְּכוֹר בְּאַרְצָם; רֵאשִׁית, לְכָל-אוֹנָם
vayach kol-bechor be'artzam; reshit, lechol-'onam
He smote also all the first-born in their land, the first-fruits of all their strength.

וַיּוֹצִיאֵם, בְּכֶסֶף וְזָהָב; וְאֵין בִּשְׁבָטָיו כּוֹשֵׁל
vayotzi'em bechesef vezahav; ve'ein bishvatav koshel
And He brought them forth with silver and gold; and there was none that stumbled among His tribes.

שָׂמַח מִצְרַיִם בְּצֵאתָם: כִּי-נָפַל פַּחְדָּם עֲלֵיהֶם
samach mitzrayim betzetam; ki-nafal pachdam aleihem
Egypt was glad when they departed; for the fear of them had fallen upon them.

פָּרַשׂ עָנָן לְמָסָךְ; וְאֵשׁ, לְהָאִיר לָיְלָה
paras anan lemasach; ve'esh, leha'ir laylah
He spread a cloud for a screen; and fire to give light in the night.

שָׁאַל, וַיָּבֵא שְׂלָו; וְלֶחֶם שָׁמַיִם, יַשְׂבִּיעֵם
sha'al vayavei selav; velechem shamayim, yasbi'em
They asked, and He brought quails, and gave them in plenty the bread of heaven.

תְּהִלִּים

שָׁלַח לִפְנֵיהֶם אִישׁ; לְעֶבֶד, נִמְכַּר יוֹסֵף
shalach lifneihem ish; le'eved, nimkar yosef
He sent a man before them; Joseph was sold for a servant;

עִנּוּ בַכֶּבֶל רַגְלוֹ; בַּרְזֶל, בָּאָה נַפְשׁוֹ
'innu vakkevel raglo; barzel, ba'ah nafsho
His feet they hurt with fetters, his person was laid in iron;

עַד-עֵת בֹּא-דְבָרוֹ--אִמְרַת יְהוָה צְרָפָתְהוּ
'ad-'et bo-devaro; imrat hashem tzerafatehu
Until the time that his word came to pass, the word of the LORD tested him.

שָׁלַח מֶלֶךְ, וַיַּתִּירֵהוּ; מֹשֵׁל עַמִּים, וַיְפַתְּחֵהוּ
shalach melech vayattirehu; moshel ammim, vayfattechehu
The king sent and loosed him; even the ruler of the peoples, and set him free.

שָׂמוֹ אָדוֹן לְבֵיתוֹ; וּמֹשֵׁל, בְּכָל-קִנְיָנוֹ
samo adon leveito; umoshel, bechol-kinyano
He made him lord of his house, and ruler of all his possessions;

לֶאְסֹר שָׂרָיו בְּנַפְשׁוֹ; וּזְקֵנָיו יְחַכֵּם
le'sor sarav benafsho; uzekenav yechakkem
To bind his princes at his pleasure, and teach his elders wisdom.

וַיָּבֹא יִשְׂרָאֵל מִצְרָיִם; וְיַעֲקֹב, גָּר בְּאֶרֶץ-חָם
vayavo yisra'el mitzrayim; veya'akov, gar be'eretz-cham
Israel also came into Egypt; and Jacob sojourned in the land of Ham.

וַיֶּפֶר אֶת-עַמּוֹ מְאֹד; וַיַּעֲצִמֵהוּ, מִצָּרָיו
vayefer et-'ammo me'od; vaya'atzimehu mitzarav
And He increased His people greatly, and made them too mighty for their adversaries.

הָפַךְ לִבָּם, לִשְׂנֹא עַמּוֹ; לְהִתְנַכֵּל, בַּעֲבָדָיו
hafach libbam lisno ammo; lehitnakkel, ba'avadav
He turned their heart to hate His people, to deal craftily with His servants.

שָׁלַח, מֹשֶׁה עַבְדּוֹ; אַהֲרֹן, אֲשֶׁר בָּחַר-בּוֹ
shalach mosheh avdo; aharon, asher bachar-bo
He sent Moses His servant, and Aaron whom He had chosen.

שָׂמוּ-בָם, דִּבְרֵי אֹתוֹתָיו; וּמֹפְתִים, בְּאֶרֶץ חָם
samu-vam divrei ototav; umofetim, be'eretz cham
They wrought among them His manifold signs, and wonders in the land of Ham.

שָׁלַח חֹשֶׁךְ, וַיַּחְשִׁךְ; וְלֹא-מָרוּ, אֶת-דְּבָרוֹ
shalach choshech vayachshich; velo-maru, et-devaro
He sent darkness, and it was dark; and they rebelled not against His word.

תְּהִלִים

זִכְרוּ--נִפְלְאוֹתָיו אֲשֶׁר-עָשָׂה; מֹפְתָיו, וּמִשְׁפְּטֵי-פִיו
zichru, nifle'otav asher-'asah; mofetav, umishpetei-fiv
Remember His marvellous works that He hath done, His wonders, and the judgments of His mouth;

זֶרַע, אַבְרָהָם עַבְדּוֹ: בְּנֵי יַעֲקֹב בְּחִירָיו
zera avraham avdo; benei ya'akov bechirav
O ye seed of Abraham His servant, ye children of Jacob, His chosen ones.

הוּא, יְהוָה אֱלֹהֵינוּ; בְּכָל-הָאָרֶץ, מִשְׁפָּטָיו
hu hashem eloheinu; bechol-ha'aretz, mishpatav
He is the LORD our God; His judgments are in all the earth.

זָכַר לְעוֹלָם בְּרִיתוֹ; דָּבָר צִוָּה, לְאֶלֶף דּוֹר
zachar le'olam berito; davar tzivvah, le'elef dor
He hath remembered His covenant for ever, the word which He commanded to a thousand generations;

אֲשֶׁר כָּרַת, אֶת-אַבְרָהָם; וּשְׁבוּעָתוֹ לְיִשְׂחָק
'asher karat et-'avraham; ushevu'ato leyischak
[The covenant] which He made with Abraham, and His oath unto Isaac;

וַיַּעֲמִידֶהָ לְיַעֲקֹב לְחֹק; לְיִשְׂרָאֵל, בְּרִית עוֹלָם
vaya'amideha leya'akov lechok; leyisra'el, berit olam
And He established it unto Jacob for a statute, to Israel for an everlasting covenant;

לֵאמֹר--לְךָ, אֶתֵּן אֶת-אֶרֶץ-כְּנָעַן: חֶבֶל, נַחֲלַתְכֶם
lemor, lecha, etten et-'eretz-kena'an; chevel, nachalatchem
Saying: 'Unto thee will I give the land of Canaan, the lot of your inheritance.'

בִּהְיוֹתָם, מְתֵי מִסְפָּר; כִּמְעַט, וְגָרִים בָּהּ
bihyotom metei mispar; kim'at, vegarim bah
When they were but a few men in number. Yea, very few, and sojourners in it,

וַיִּתְהַלְּכוּ, מִגּוֹי אֶל-גּוֹי; מִמַּמְלָכָה, אֶל-עַם אַחֵר
vayit'hallechu miggoy el-goy; mimmamlachah, el-'am acher
And when they went about from nation to nation, from one kingdom to another people,

לֹא-הִנִּיחַ אָדָם לְעָשְׁקָם; וַיּוֹכַח עֲלֵיהֶם מְלָכִים
lo-hinniach adam le'ashekam; vayochach aleihem melachim
He suffered no man to do them wrong, yea, for their sake He reproved kings:

אַל-תִּגְּעוּ בִמְשִׁיחָי; וְלִנְבִיאַי, אַל-תָּרֵעוּ
'al-tigge'u vimshichai; velinvi'ai al-tare'u
'Touch not Mine anointed ones, and do My prophets no harm.'

וַיִּקְרָא רָעָב, עַל-הָאָרֶץ; כָּל-מַטֵּה-לֶחֶם שָׁבָר
vayikra ra'ov al-ha'aretz; kol-matteh-lechem shavar
And He called a famine upon the land; He broke the whole staff of bread.

תְּהִלִּים

תַּסְתִּיר פָּנֶיךָ, יִבָּהֵלוּן: תֹּסֵף רוּחָם, יִגְוָעוּן; וְאֶל-עֲפָרָם יְשׁוּבוּן
tastir paneicha yibbahelun tosef rucham yigva'un; ve'el-'afaram yeshuvun
Thou hidest Thy face, they vanish; Thou withdrawest their breath, they perish, and return to their dust.

תְּשַׁלַּח רוּחֲךָ, יִבָּרֵאוּן; וּתְחַדֵּשׁ, פְּנֵי אֲדָמָה
teshallach ruchacha yibbare'un; utechaddesh, penei adamah
Thou sendest forth Thy spirit, they are created; and Thou renewest the face of the earth.

יְהִי כְבוֹד יְהוָה לְעוֹלָם; יִשְׂמַח יְהוָה בְּמַעֲשָׂיו
yehi chevod hashem le'olam; yismach hashem bema'asav
May the glory of the LORD endure for ever; let the LORD rejoice in His works!

הַמַּבִּיט לָאָרֶץ, וַתִּרְעָד; יִגַּע בֶּהָרִים וְיֶעֱשָׁנוּ
hammabbit la'aretz vattir'ad; yigga beharim veye'eshanu
Who looketh on the earth, and it trembleth; He toucheth the mountains, and they smoke.

אָשִׁירָה לַיהוָה בְּחַיָּי; אֲזַמְּרָה לֵאלֹהַי בְּעוֹדִי
'ashirah lahashem bechayai; azammerah le'elohai be'odi
I will sing unto the LORD as long as I live; I will sing praise to my God while I have any being.

יֶעֱרַב עָלָיו שִׂיחִי; אָנֹכִי, אֶשְׂמַח בַּיהוָה
ye'erav alav sichi; anochi, esmach bahashem
Let my musing be sweet unto Him; as for me, I will rejoice in the LORD.

יִתַּמּוּ חַטָּאִים מִן-הָאָרֶץ, וּרְשָׁעִים עוֹד אֵינָם--בָּרְכִי נַפְשִׁי, אֶת-יְהוָה; הַלְלוּ-יָהּ
yittammu chatta'im min-ha'aretz uresha'im od einam, barechi nafshi et-hashem halelu-yah
Let sinners cease out of the earth, and let the wicked be no more. Bless the LORD, O my soul. Hallelujah.

קה

הוֹדוּ לַיהוָה, קִרְאוּ בִשְׁמוֹ; הוֹדִיעוּ בָעַמִּים, עֲלִילוֹתָיו
Hodu lahashem kir'u bishmo; hodi'u va'ammim, alilotav
O give thanks unto the LORD, call upon His name; make known His doings among the peoples.

שִׁירוּ-לוֹ, זַמְּרוּ-לוֹ; שִׂיחוּ, בְּכָל-נִפְלְאוֹתָיו
shiru-lo zammeru-lo; sichu, bechol-nifle'otav
Sing unto Him, sing praises unto Him; speak ye of all His marvellous works.

הִתְהַלְלוּ, בְּשֵׁם קָדְשׁוֹ; יִשְׂמַח, לֵב מְבַקְשֵׁי יְהוָה
hit'halelu beshem kodsho yismach, lev mevakshei hashem
Glory ye in His holy name; let the heart of them rejoice that seek the LORD.

דִּרְשׁוּ יְהוָה וְעֻזּוֹ; בַּקְּשׁוּ פָנָיו תָּמִיד
dirshu hashem ve'uzzo; bakkeshu fanav tamid
Seek ye the LORD and His strength; seek His face continually.

תְּהִלִּים

הָרִים הַגְּבֹהִים, לַיְּעֵלִים; סְלָעִים, מַחְסֶה לַשְׁפַנִּים

harim haggevohim laye'elim; sela'im, machseh lashfannim
The high mountains are for the wild goats; the rocks are a refuge for the conies.

עָשָׂה יָרֵחַ, לְמוֹעֲדִים; שֶׁמֶשׁ, יָדַע מְבוֹאוֹ

'asah yareach lemo'adim; shemesh, yada mevo'o
Who appointedst the moon for seasons; the sun knoweth his going down.

תָּשֶׁת-חֹשֶׁךְ, וִיהִי לָיְלָה--בּוֹ-תִרְמֹשׂ, כָּל-חַיְתוֹ-יָעַר

tashet-choshech vihi layelah; bo-tirmos, kol-chayto-ya'ar
Thou makest darkness, and it is night, wherein all the beasts of the forest do creep forth.

הַכְּפִירִים, שֹׁאֲגִים לַטָּרֶף; וּלְבַקֵּשׁ מֵאֵל אָכְלָם

hakkefirim sho'agim lattaref; ulevakkesh me'el ochelam
The young lions roar after their prey, and seek their food from God.

תִּזְרַח הַשֶּׁמֶשׁ, יֵאָסֵפוּן; וְאֶל-מְעוֹנֹתָם, יִרְבָּצוּן

tizrach hashemesh ye'asefun; ve'el-me'onotam, yirbatzun
The sun ariseth, they slink away, and couch in their dens.

יֵצֵא אָדָם לְפָעֳלוֹ; וְלַעֲבֹדָתוֹ עֲדֵי-עָרֶב

yetzei adam lefo'olo; vela'avodato adei-'arev
Man goeth forth unto his work and to his labour until the evening.

מָה-רַבּוּ מַעֲשֶׂיךָ, יְהוָה--כֻּלָּם, בְּחָכְמָה עָשִׂיתָ; מָלְאָה הָאָרֶץ, קִנְיָנֶךָ

mah-rabbu ma'aseicha hashem kullom bechochmah asita; male'ah ha'aretz, kinyanecha
How manifold are Thy works, O LORD! In wisdom hast Thou made them all; the earth is full of Thy creatures.

זֶה, הַיָּם גָּדוֹל--וּרְחַב יָדָיִם: שָׁם-רֶמֶשׂ, וְאֵין מִסְפָּר; חַיּוֹת קְטַנּוֹת, עִם-גְּדֹלוֹת

zeh hayam gadol urechav yadayim sham-remes ve'ein mispar; chayot ketannot, im-gedolot
Yonder sea, great and wide, therein are creeping things innumerable, living creatures, both small and great.

שָׁם, אֳנִיּוֹת יְהַלֵּכוּן; לִוְיָתָן, זֶה-יָצַרְתָּ לְשַׂחֶק-בּוֹ

sham oniyot yehallechun; livyatan, zeh-yatzarta lesachek-bo
There go the ships; there is leviathan, whom Thou hast formed to sport therein.

כֻּלָּם, אֵלֶיךָ יְשַׂבֵּרוּן--לָתֵת אָכְלָם בְּעִתּוֹ

kullom eleicha yesabberun; latet ochelam be'itto
All of them wait for Thee, that Thou mayest give them their food in due season.

תִּתֵּן לָהֶם, יִלְקֹטוּן; תִּפְתַּח יָדְךָ, יִשְׂבְּעוּן טוֹב

titten lahem yilkotun; tiftach yadecha, yisbe'un tov
Thou givest it unto them, they gather it; Thou openest Thy hand, they are satisfied with good.

תְּהִלִים

תְּהוֹם, כַּלְּבוּשׁ כִּסִּיתוֹ; עַל-הָרִים, יַעַמְדוּ מָיִם
tehom kallevush kissito; al-harim, ya'amdu-mayim
Thou didst cover it with the deep as with a vesture; the waters stood above the mountains.

מִן-גַּעֲרָתְךָ יְנוּסוּן; מִן-קוֹל רַעַמְךָ, יֵחָפֵזוּן
min-ga'aratecha yenusun; min-kol ra'amcha, yechafezun
At Thy rebuke they fled, at the voice of Thy thunder they hasted away--

יַעֲלוּ הָרִים, יֵרְדוּ בְקָעוֹת-- אֶל-מְקוֹם, זֶה יָסַדְתָּ לָהֶם
ya'alu harim yeredu veka'ot; el-mekom, zeh yasadta lahem
The mountains rose, the valleys sank down--unto the place which Thou hadst founded for them;

גְּבוּל-שַׂמְתָּ, בַּל-יַעֲבֹרוּן; בַּל-יְשֻׁבוּן, לְכַסּוֹת הָאָרֶץ
gevul-samta bal-ya'avorun; bal-yeshuvun, lechassot ha'aretz
Thou didst set a bound which they should not pass over, that they might not return to cover the earth.

הַמְשַׁלֵּחַ מַעְיָנִים, בַּנְּחָלִים; בֵּין הָרִים, יְהַלֵּכוּן
hamshalleach ma'yanim bannechalim; bein harim, yehallechun
Who sendest forth springs into the valleys; they run between the mountains;

יַשְׁקוּ, כָּל-חַיְתוֹ שָׂדָי; יִשְׁבְּרוּ פְרָאִים צְמָאָם
yashku kol-chayto sadai; yishberu fera'im tzema'am
They give drink to every beast of the field, the wild asses quench their thirst.

עֲלֵיהֶם, עוֹף-הַשָּׁמַיִם יִשְׁכּוֹן; מִבֵּין עֳפָאיִם, יִתְּנוּ-קוֹל
'aleihem of-hashamayim yishkon; mibbein ofayim, yittenu-kol
Beside them dwell the fowl of the heaven, from among the branches they sing.

מַשְׁקֶה הָרִים, מֵעֲלִיּוֹתָיו; מִפְּרִי מַעֲשֶׂיךָ, תִּשְׂבַּע הָאָרֶץ
mashkeh harim me'aliyotav; mipperi ma'aseicha, tisba ha'aretz
Who waterest the mountains from Thine upper chambers; the earth is full of the fruit of Thy works.

מַצְמִיחַ חָצִיר, לַבְּהֵמָה, וְעֵשֶׂב, לַעֲבֹדַת הָאָדָם; לְהוֹצִיא לֶחֶם, מִן-הָאָרֶץ
matzmiach chatzir labbehemah, ve'esev la'avodat ha'adam; lehotzi lechem, min-ha'aretz
Who causeth the grass to spring up for the cattle, and herb for the service of man; to bring forth bread out of the earth,

וְיַיִן, יְשַׂמַּח לְבַב-אֱנוֹשׁ-- לְהַצְהִיל פָּנִים מִשָּׁמֶן; וְלֶחֶם, לְבַב-אֱנוֹשׁ יִסְעָד
veyayin yesammach levav-'enosh, lehatzhil panim mishamen; velechem, levav-'enosh yis'ad
And wine that maketh glad the heart of man, making the face brighter than oil, and bread that stayeth man's heart.

יִשְׂבְּעוּ, עֲצֵי יְהוָה-- אַרְזֵי לְבָנוֹן, אֲשֶׁר נָטָע
yisbe'u atzei hashem arzei levanon, asher nata
The trees of the LORD have their fill, the cedars of Lebanon, which He hath planted;

אֲשֶׁר-שָׁם, צִפֳּרִים יְקַנֵּנוּ; חֲסִידָה, בְּרוֹשִׁים בֵּיתָהּ
'asher-sham tzipporim yekannenu; chasidah, beroshim beitah
Wherein the birds make their nests; as for the stork, the fir-trees are her house.

תְּהִלִּים

לְשֹׁמְרֵי בְרִיתוֹ; וּלְזֹכְרֵי פִקֻּדָיו, לַעֲשׂוֹתָם
leshomerei verito; ulezocherei fikkudav, la'asotam
To such as keep His covenant, and to those that remember His precepts to do them.

יְהוָה--בַּשָּׁמַיִם, הֵכִין כִּסְאוֹ; וּמַלְכוּתוֹ, בַּכֹּל מָשָׁלָה
hashem bashamayim hechin kis'o; umalchuto, bakkol mashalah
The LORD hath established His throne in the heavens; and His kingdom ruleth over all.

בָּרְכוּ יְהוָה, מַלְאָכָיו: גִּבֹּרֵי כֹחַ, עֹשֵׂי דְבָרוֹ; לִשְׁמֹעַ, בְּקוֹל דְּבָרוֹ
barachu hashem mal'achav gibborei choach osei devaro; lishmoa', bekol devaro
Bless the LORD, ye angels of His, ye mighty in strength, that fulfil His word, hearkening unto the voice of His word.

בָּרְכוּ יְהוָה, כָּל-צְבָאָיו--מְשָׁרְתָיו, עֹשֵׂי רְצוֹנוֹ
barachu hashem kol-tzeva'av; mesharetav, osei retzono
Bless the LORD, all ye His hosts; ye ministers of His, that do His pleasure.

בָּרְכוּ יְהוָה, כָּל-מַעֲשָׂיו--בְּכָל-מְקֹמוֹת מֶמְשַׁלְתּוֹ; בָּרְכִי נַפְשִׁי, אֶת-יְהוָה
barachu hashem kol-ma'asav, bechol-mekomot memshalto; barachi nafshi, et-hashem
Bless the LORD, all ye His works, in all places of His dominion; bless the LORD, O my soul.

קד

בָּרְכִי נַפְשִׁי, אֶת-יְהוָה: יְהוָה אֱלֹהַי, גָּדַלְתָּ מְּאֹד; הוֹד וְהָדָר לָבָשְׁתָּ
Barachi nafshi, et-hashem hashem elohai gadalta me'od; hod vehadar lavashta
Bless the LORD, O my soul. O LORD my God, Thou art very great; Thou art clothed with glory and majesty.

עֹטֶה-אוֹר, כַּשַּׂלְמָה; נוֹטֶה שָׁמַיִם, כַּיְרִיעָה
'oteh-'or kassalmah; noteh shamayim, kayri'ah
Who coverest Thyself with light as with a garment, who stretchest out the heavens like a curtain;

הַמְקָרֶה בַמַּיִם, עֲלִיּוֹתָיו
hamkareh vammayim, aliyotav
Who layest the beams of Thine upper chambers in the waters,

הַשָּׂם-עָבִים רְכוּבוֹ; הַמְהַלֵּךְ, עַל-כַּנְפֵי-רוּחַ
hassam-'avim rechuvo; hamehallech, al-kanfei-ruach
who makest the clouds Thy chariot, who walkest upon the wings of the wind;

עֹשֶׂה מַלְאָכָיו רוּחוֹת; מְשָׁרְתָיו, אֵשׁ לֹהֵט
'oseh mal'achav ruchot; mesharetav, esh lohet
Who makest winds Thy messengers, the flaming fire Thy ministers.

יָסַד-אֶרֶץ, עַל-מְכוֹנֶיהָ; בַּל-תִּמּוֹט, עוֹלָם וָעֶד
yasad-'eretz al-mechoneiha; bal-timmot, olam va'ed
Who didst establish the earth upon its foundations, that it should not be moved for ever and ever;

תְּהִלִּים

יוֹדִיעַ דְּרָכָיו לְמֹשֶׁה; לִבְנֵי יִשְׂרָאֵל, עֲלִילוֹתָיו
yodia derachav lemosheh; livnei yisra'el, alilotav
He made known His ways unto Moses, His doings unto the children of Israel.

רַחוּם וְחַנּוּן יְהוָה; אֶרֶךְ אַפַּיִם וְרַב-חָסֶד
rachum vechannun hashem erech appayim verav-chased
The LORD is full of compassion and gracious, slow to anger, and plenteous in mercy.

לֹא-לָנֶצַח יָרִיב; וְלֹא לְעוֹלָם יִטּוֹר
lo-lanetzach yariv; velo le'olam yittor
He will not always contend; neither will He keep His anger for ever.

לֹא כַחֲטָאֵינוּ, עָשָׂה לָנוּ; וְלֹא כַעֲוֺנֹתֵינוּ, גָּמַל עָלֵינוּ
lo chachata'einu asah lanu; velo cha'avonoteinu, gamal aleinu
He hath not dealt with us after our sins, nor requited us according to our iniquities.

כִּי כִגְבֹהַּ שָׁמַיִם, עַל-הָאָרֶץ-- גָּבַר חַסְדּוֹ, עַל-יְרֵאָיו
ki chigvoah shamayim al-ha'aretz; gavar chasdo, al-yere'av
For as the heaven is high above the earth, so great is His mercy toward them that fear Him.

כִּרְחֹק מִזְרָח, מִמַּעֲרָב-- הִרְחִיק מִמֶּנּוּ, אֶת-פְּשָׁעֵינוּ
kirchok mizrach mimma'arav; hirchik mimmennu, et-pesha'einu
As far as the east is from the west, so far hath He removed our transgressions from us.

כְּרַחֵם אָב, עַל-בָּנִים-- רִחַם יְהוָה, עַל-יְרֵאָיו
kerachem av al-banim; richam hashem al-yere'av
Like as a father hath compassion upon his children, so hath the LORD compassion upon them that fear Him.

כִּי-הוּא, יָדַע יִצְרֵנוּ; זָכוּר, כִּי-עָפָר אֲנָחְנוּ
ki-hu yada yitzrenu; zachur, ki-'afar anachenu
For He knoweth our frame; He remembereth that we are dust.

אֱנוֹשׁ, כֶּחָצִיר יָמָיו; כְּצִיץ הַשָּׂדֶה, כֵּן יָצִיץ
'enosh kechatzir yamav; ketzitz hassadeh, ken yatzitz
As for man, his days are as grass; as a flower of the field, so he flourisheth.

כִּי רוּחַ עָבְרָה-בּוֹ וְאֵינֶנּוּ; וְלֹא-יַכִּירֶנּוּ עוֹד מְקוֹמוֹ
ki ruach averah-bo ve'einennu; velo-yakkirennu od mekomo
For the wind passeth over it, and it is gone; and the place thereof knoweth it no more.

וְחֶסֶד יְהוָה, מֵעוֹלָם וְעַד-עוֹלָם--עַל-יְרֵאָיו
vechesed hashem me'olam ve'ad-'olam al-yere'av
But the mercy of the LORD is from everlasting to everlasting upon them that fear Him,

וְצִדְקָתוֹ, לִבְנֵי בָנִים
vetzidkato, livnei vanim
and His righteousness unto children's children;

תְּהִלִים

לְפָנִים, הָאָרֶץ יָסַדְתָּ; וּמַעֲשֵׂה יָדֶיךָ שָׁמָיִם
lefanim ha'aretz yasadta; uma'aseh yadeicha shamayim
Of old Thou didst lay the foundation of the earth; and the heavens are the work of Thy hands.

הֵמָּה, יֹאבֵדוּ--וְאַתָּה תַעֲמֹד: וְכֻלָּם, כַּבֶּגֶד יִבְלוּ
hemmah yovedu ve'attah ta'amod vechullom kabbeged yivlu
They shall perish, but Thou shalt endure; yea, all of them shall wax old like a garment;

כַּלְּבוּשׁ תַּחֲלִיפֵם וְיַחֲלֹפוּ
kallevush tachalifem veyachalofu
as a vesture shalt Thou change them, and they shall pass away;

וְאַתָּה-הוּא; וּשְׁנוֹתֶיךָ, לֹא יִתָּמּוּ
ve'attah-hu; ushnoteicha, lo yittammu
But Thou art the selfsame, and Thy years shall have no end.

בְּנֵי-עֲבָדֶיךָ יִשְׁכּוֹנוּ; וְזַרְעָם, לְפָנֶיךָ יִכּוֹן
benei-'avadeicha yishkonu; vezar'am, lefaneicha yikkon
The children of Thy servants shall dwell securely, and their seed shall be established before Thee.'

קג

לְדָוִד: בָּרְכִי נַפְשִׁי, אֶת-יְהוָה; וְכָל-קְרָבַי, אֶת-שֵׁם קָדְשׁוֹ
Ledavid: barechi nafshi et-hashem vechol-keravai, et-shem kodsho
[A Psalm] of David. Bless the LORD, O my soul; and all that is within me, bless His holy name.

בָּרְכִי נַפְשִׁי, אֶת-יְהוָה; וְאַל-תִּשְׁכְּחִי, כָּל-גְּמוּלָיו
barechi nafshi et-hashem ve'al-tishkechi, kol-gemulav
Bless the LORD, O my soul, and forget not all His benefits;

הַסֹּלֵחַ לְכָל-עֲוֺנֵכִי; הָרֹפֵא, לְכָל-תַּחֲלוּאָיְכִי
hassoleach lechol-'avonechi; harofe, lechol-tachalu'ayechi
Who forgiveth all thine iniquity; who healeth all thy diseases;

הַגּוֹאֵל מִשַּׁחַת חַיָּיְכִי; הַמְעַטְּרֵכִי, חֶסֶד וְרַחֲמִים
haggo'el mishachat chayayechi; ham'atterechi, chesed verachamim
Who redeemeth thy life from the pit; who encompasseth thee with lovingkindness and tender mercies;

הַמַּשְׂבִּיעַ בַּטּוֹב עֶדְיֵךְ; תִּתְחַדֵּשׁ כַּנֶּשֶׁר נְעוּרָיְכִי
hammasbiya battov edyech; titchaddesh kannesher ne'uraychi
Who satisfieth thine old age with good things; so that thy youth is renewed like the eagle.

עֹשֵׂה צְדָקוֹת יְהוָה; וּמִשְׁפָּטִים, לְכָל-עֲשׁוּקִים
'oseh tzedakot hashem umishpatim, lechol-'ashukim
The LORD executeth righteousness, and acts of justice for all that are oppressed.

תְּהִלִים

אַתָּה תָקוּם, תְּרַחֵם צִיּוֹן: כִּי-עֵת לְחֶנְנָהּ, כִּי-בָא מוֹעֵד
'attah takum terachem tziyon; ki-'et lechenenah, ki-va mo'ed
Thou wilt arise, and have compassion upon Zion; for it is time to be gracious unto her, for the appointed time is come.

כִּי-רָצוּ עֲבָדֶיךָ, אֶת-אֲבָנֶיהָ; וְאֶת-עֲפָרָהּ, יְחֹנֵנוּ
ki-ratzu avadeicha et-'avaneiha; ve'et-'afarah yechonenu
For Thy servants take pleasure in her stones, and love her dust.

וְיִירְאוּ גוֹיִם, אֶת-שֵׁם יְהוָה; וְכָל-מַלְכֵי הָאָרֶץ, אֶת-כְּבוֹדֶךָ
veyire'u goyim et-shem hashem vechol-malchei ha'aretz, et-kevodecha
So the nations will fear the name of the LORD, and all the kings of the earth Thy glory;

כִּי-בָנָה יְהוָה צִיּוֹן-- נִרְאָה, בִּכְבוֹדוֹ
ki-vanah hashem tziyon; nir'ah, bichvodo
When the LORD hath built up Zion, when He hath appeared in His glory;

פָּנָה, אֶל-תְּפִלַּת הָעַרְעָר; וְלֹא-בָזָה, אֶת-תְּפִלָּתָם
panah el-tefillat ha'ar'ar; velo-vazah, et-tefillatam
When He hath regarded the prayer of the destitute, and hath not despised their prayer.

תִּכָּתֶב זֹאת, לְדוֹר אַחֲרוֹן; וְעַם נִבְרָא, יְהַלֶּל-יָהּ
tikkatev zot ledor acharon; ve'am nivra, yehallel-yah
This shall be written for the generation to come; and a people which shall be created shall praise the LORD.

כִּי-הִשְׁקִיף, מִמְּרוֹם קָדְשׁוֹ; יְהוָה, מִשָּׁמַיִם אֶל-אֶרֶץ הִבִּיט
ki-hishkif mimmerom kodsho hashem mishamayim el-'eretz hibbit
For He hath looked down from the height of His sanctuary; from heaven did the LORD behold the earth;

לִשְׁמֹעַ, אֶנְקַת אָסִיר; לְפַתֵּחַ, בְּנֵי תְמוּתָה
lishmoa enkat asir; lefatteach, benei temutah
To hear the groaning of the prisoner; to loose those that are appointed to death;

לְסַפֵּר בְּצִיּוֹן, שֵׁם יְהוָה; וּתְהִלָּתוֹ, בִּירוּשָׁלִָם
lesapper betziyon shem hashem utehillato, biyerushalayim
That men may tell of the name of the LORD in Zion, and His praise in Jerusalem;

בְּהִקָּבֵץ עַמִּים יַחְדָּו; וּמַמְלָכוֹת, לַעֲבֹד אֶת-יְהוָה
behikkavetz ammim yachdav; umamlachot, la'avod et-hashem
When the peoples are gathered together, and the kingdoms, to serve the LORD.

עִנָּה בַדֶּרֶךְ כֹּחִי; קִצַּר יָמָי
'innah vadderech kochi, kitzar yamai
He weakened my strength in the way; He shortened my days.

אֹמַר--אֵלִי, אַל תַּעֲלֵנִי בַּחֲצִי יָמָי: בְּדוֹר דּוֹרִים שְׁנוֹתֶיךָ
'omar, eli, al-ta'aleni bachatzi yamai; bedor dorim shenoteicha
I say: 'O my God, take me not away in the midst of my days, Thou whose years endure throughout all generations.

תְּהִלִּים

אַל-תַּסְתֵּר פָּנֶיךָ, מִמֶּנִּי--בְּיוֹם צַר-לִי
'al-taster paneicha mimmenni beyom tzar li
Hide not Thy face from me in the day of my distress;

הַטֵּה-אֵלַי אָזְנֶךָ; בְּיוֹם אֶקְרָא, מַהֵר עֲנֵנִי
hatteh-'elai oznecha; beyom ekra, maher aneni
incline Thine ear unto me; in the day when I call answer me speedily.

כִּי-כָלוּ בְעָשָׁן יָמָי; וְעַצְמוֹתַי, כְּמוֹ-קֵד נִחָרוּ
ki-chalu ve'ashan yamai; ve'atzmotai, kemo-ked nicharu
For my days are consumed like smoke, and my bones are burned as a hearth.

הוּכָּה-כָעֵשֶׂב וַיִּבַשׁ לִבִּי: כִּי-שָׁכַחְתִּי, מֵאֲכֹל לַחְמִי
hukah-cha'esev vayivash libbi; ki-shachachti, me'achol lachmi
My heart is smitten like grass, and withered; for I forget to eat my bread.

מִקּוֹל אַנְחָתִי--דָּבְקָה עַצְמִי, לִבְשָׂרִי
mikkol anchati; davekah atzmi, livsari
By reason of the voice of my sighing my bones cleave to my flesh.

דָּמִיתִי, לִקְאַת מִדְבָּר; הָיִיתִי, כְּכוֹס חֳרָבוֹת
damiti lik'at midbar; hayiti, kechos choravot
I am like a pelican of the wilderness; I am become as an owl of the waste places.

שָׁקַדְתִּי וָאֶהְיֶה--כְּצִפּוֹר, בּוֹדֵד עַל-גָּג
shakadti va'ehyeh; ketzippor, boded al-gag
I watch, and am become like a sparrow that is alone upon the housetop.

כָּל-הַיּוֹם, חֵרְפוּנִי אוֹיְבָי; מְהוֹלָלַי, בִּי נִשְׁבָּעוּ
kol-hayom cherefuni oyevai; meholalai, bi nishba'u
Mine enemies taunt me all the day; they that are mad against me do curse by me.

כִּי-אֵפֶר, כַּלֶּחֶם אָכָלְתִּי; וְשִׁקֻּוַי, בִּבְכִי מָסָכְתִּי
ki-'efer kallechem achaleti; veshikkuvai, bivchi masacheti
For I have eaten ashes like bread, and mingled my drink with weeping,

מִפְּנֵי-זַעַמְךָ וְקִצְפֶּךָ--כִּי נְשָׂאתַנִי, וַתַּשְׁלִיכֵנִי
mippenei-za'amcha vekitzpecha; ki nesatani, vattashlicheni
Because of Thine indignation and Thy wrath; for Thou hast taken me up, and cast me away.

יָמַי, כְּצֵל נָטוּי; וַאֲנִי, כָּעֵשֶׂב אִיבָשׁ
yamai ketzel natui; va'ani, ka'esev ivash
My days are like a lengthening shadow; and I am withered like grass.

וְאַתָּה יְהוָה, לְעוֹלָם תֵּשֵׁב; וְזִכְרְךָ, לְדֹר וָדֹר
ve'attah hashem le'olam teshev; vezichrecha, ledor vador
But Thou, O LORD, sittest enthroned for ever; and Thy name is unto all generations.

תְּהִלִים

לֹא-אָשִׁית, לְנֶגֶד עֵינַי--דְּבַר-בְּלִיָּעַל: עֲשֹׂה-סֵטִים שָׂנֵאתִי; לֹא יִדְבַּק בִּי
lo-'ashit leneged einai, devar-beliya'al asoh-setim saneti; lo yidbak bi
I will set no base thing before mine eyes; I hate the doing of things crooked; it shall not cleave unto me.

לֵבָב עִקֵּשׁ, יָסוּר מִמֶּנִּי; רָע, לֹא אֵדָע
levav ikkesh yasur mimmenni; ra', lo eda
A perverse heart shall depart from me; I will know no evil thing.

מְלָשְׁנִי בַסֵּתֶר, רֵעֵהוּ--אוֹתוֹ אַצְמִית
melasheni vasseter re'ehu oto atzmit
Whoso slandereth his neighbour in secret, him will I destroy;

גְּבַהּ-עֵינַיִם, וּרְחַב לֵבָב--אֹתוֹ, לֹא אוּכָל
gevah-'einayim urechav levav; oto, lo uchal
whoso is haughty of eye and proud of heart, him will I not suffer.

עֵינַי, בְּנֶאֶמְנֵי-אֶרֶץ--לָשֶׁבֶת עִמָּדִי
'einai bene'emnei-'eretz lashevet immadi
Mine eyes are upon the faithful of the land, that they may dwell with me;

הֹלֵךְ, בְּדֶרֶךְ תָּמִים--הוּא, יְשָׁרְתֵנִי
holech bederech tamim; hu, yeshareteni
he that walketh in a way of integrity, he shall minister unto me.

לֹא-יֵשֵׁב, בְּקֶרֶב בֵּיתִי--עֹשֵׂה רְמִיָּה
lo-yeshev bekerev beiti oseh remiyah
He that worketh deceit shall not dwell within my house;

דֹּבֵר שְׁקָרִים--לֹא-יִכּוֹן, לְנֶגֶד עֵינָי
dover shekarim; lo-yikkon, leneged einai
he that speaketh falsehood shall not be established before mine eyes.

לַבְּקָרִים, אַצְמִית כָּל-רִשְׁעֵי-אָרֶץ; לְהַכְרִית מֵעִיר-יְהוָה, כָּל-פֹּעֲלֵי אָוֶן
labbekarim, atzmit kol-rish'ei-'aretz; lehachrit me'ir-hashem kol-po'alei aven
Morning by morning will I destroy all the wicked of the land; to cut off all the workers of iniquity from the city of the LORD.

קב

תְּפִלָּה, לְעָנִי כִי-יַעֲטֹף--וְלִפְנֵי יְהוָה, יִשְׁפֹּךְ שִׂיחוֹ
Tefillah le'ani chi-ya'atof; velifnei hashem yishpoch sicho
A Prayer of the afflicted, when he fainteth, and poureth out his complaint before the LORD.

יְהוָה, שִׁמְעָה תְפִלָּתִי; וְשַׁוְעָתִי, אֵלֶיךָ תָבוֹא
hashem shim'ah tefillati; veshav'ati, eleicha tavo
O LORD, hear my prayer, and let my cry come unto Thee.

תְּהִלִּים

וְנֹקֵם, עַל-עֲלִילוֹתָם
venokem, al-'alilotam
though Thou tookest vengeance of their misdeeds.

רוֹמְמוּ, יְהוָה אֱלֹהֵינוּ, וְהִשְׁתַּחֲווּ, לְהַר קָדְשׁוֹ: כִּי-קָדוֹשׁ, יְהוָה אֱלֹהֵינוּ
romemu hashem eloheinu, vehishtachavu lehar kodsho ki-kadosh, hashem eloheinu
Exalt ye the LORD our God, and worship at His holy hill; for the LORD our God is holy.

ק

מִזְמוֹר לְתוֹדָה: הָרִיעוּ לַיהוָה, כָּל-הָאָרֶץ
Mizmor letodah; hari'u lahashem kol-ha'aretz
A Psalm of thanksgiving. Shout unto the LORD, all the earth.

עִבְדוּ אֶת-יְהוָה בְּשִׂמְחָה; בֹּאוּ לְפָנָיו, בִּרְנָנָה
'ivdu et-hashem besimchah; bo'u lefanav, birnanah
Serve the LORD with gladness; come before His presence with singing.

דְּעוּ--כִּי יְהוָה, הוּא אֱלֹהִים: הוּא-עָשָׂנוּ
de'u, ki-hashem hu elohim hu-'asanu
Know ye that the LORD He is God; it is He that hath made us,

וְלוֹ אֲנַחְנוּ--עַמּוֹ, וְצֹאן מַרְעִיתוֹ
velo anachnu; ammo, vetzon mar'ito
and we are His, His people, and the flock of His pasture.

בֹּאוּ שְׁעָרָיו, בְּתוֹדָה--חֲצֵרֹתָיו בִּתְהִלָּה; הוֹדוּ-לוֹ, בָּרְכוּ שְׁמוֹ
bo'u she'arav betodah, chatzerotav bit'hillah; hodu-lo, barachu shemo
Enter into His gates with thanksgiving, and into His courts with praise; give thanks unto Him, and bless His name.

כִּי-טוֹב יְהוָה, לְעוֹלָם חַסְדּוֹ; וְעַד-דֹּר וָדֹר, אֱמוּנָתוֹ
ki-tov hashem le'olam chasdo; ve'ad-dor vador, emunato
For the LORD is good; His mercy endureth for ever; and His faithfulness unto all generations.

קא

לְדָוִד, מִזְמוֹר: חֶסֶד-וּמִשְׁפָּט אָשִׁירָה; לְךָ יְהוָה אֲזַמֵּרָה
Ledavid, mizmor: chesed-umishpat ashirah; lecha hashem azammerah
A Psalm of David. I will sing of mercy and justice; unto Thee, O LORD, will I sing praises.

אַשְׂכִּילָה, בְּדֶרֶךְ תָּמִים--מָתַי, תָּבוֹא אֵלָי
'askilah bederech tamim, matai tavo elai
I will give heed unto the way of integrity; oh when wilt Thou come unto me?

אֶתְהַלֵּךְ בְּתָם-לְבָבִי, בְּקֶרֶב בֵּיתִי
et'hallech betom-levavi, bekerev beiti
I will walk within my house in the integrity of my heart.

תְּהִלִּים

יִשְׁפֹּט-תֵּבֵל בְּצֶדֶק; וְעַמִּים, בְּמֵישָׁרִים
yishpot-tevel betzedek; ve'ammim, bemeisharim
He will judge the world with righteousness, and the peoples with equity.

צט

יְהוָה מָלָךְ, יִרְגְּזוּ עַמִּים; יֹשֵׁב כְּרוּבִים, תָּנוּט הָאָרֶץ
Hashem maloch yirgezu ammim; yoshev keruvim, tanut ha'aretz
The LORD reigneth; let the peoples tremble; He is enthroned upon the cherubim; let the earth quake.

יְהוָה, בְּצִיּוֹן גָּדוֹל; וְרָם הוּא, עַל-כָּל-הָעַמִּים
hashem betziyon gadol; veram hu, al-kol-ha'ammim
The LORD is great in Zion; and He is high above all the peoples.

יוֹדוּ שִׁמְךָ, גָּדוֹל וְנוֹרָא; קָדוֹשׁ הוּא
yodu shimcha gadol venora, kadosh hu
Let them praise Thy name as great and awful; Holy is He.

וְעֹז מֶלֶךְ, מִשְׁפָּט אָהֵב: אַתָּה, כּוֹנַנְתָּ מֵישָׁרִים
ve'oz melech mishpat ahev attah konanta meisharim
The strength also of the king who loveth justice--Thou hast established equity,

מִשְׁפָּט וּצְדָקָה, בְּיַעֲקֹב אַתָּה עָשִׂיתָ
mishpat utzedakah, beya'akov attah asita
Thou hast executed justice and righteousness in Jacob.

רוֹמְמוּ, יְהוָה אֱלֹהֵינוּ, וְהִשְׁתַּחֲווּ, לַהֲדֹם רַגְלָיו: קָדוֹשׁ הוּא
romemu hashem eloheinu, vehishtachavu lahadom raglav, kadosh hu
Exalt ye the LORD our God, and prostrate yourselves at His footstool; Holy is He.

מֹשֶׁה וְאַהֲרֹן, בְּכֹהֲנָיו, וּשְׁמוּאֵל, בְּקֹרְאֵי שְׁמוֹ
mosheh ve'aharon bechohanav, ushemu'el bekore'ei shemo
Moses and Aaron among His priests, and Samuel among them that call upon His name,

קֹרִאים אֶל-יְהוָה, וְהוּא יַעֲנֵם
korim el-hashem vehu ya'anem
did call upon the LORD, and He answered them.

בְּעַמּוּד עָנָן, יְדַבֵּר אֲלֵיהֶם; שָׁמְרוּ עֵדֹתָיו, וְחֹק נָתַן-לָמוֹ
be'ammud anan yedabber aleihem; shameru edotav, vechok natan-lamo
He spoke unto them in the pillar of cloud; they kept His testimonies, and the statute that He gave them.

יְהוָה אֱלֹהֵינוּ, אַתָּה עֲנִיתָם: אֵל נֹשֵׂא, הָיִיתָ לָהֶם
hashem eloheinu attah anitam el nosei hayita lahem
O LORD our God, Thou didst answer them; a forgiving God wast Thou unto them,

תְּהִלִּים

צח

מִזְמוֹר, שִׁירוּ לַיהוָה שִׁיר חָדָשׁ--כִּי-נִפְלָאוֹת עָשָׂה
Mizmor shiru lahashem shir chadash ki-nifla'ot asah
A Psalm. O sing unto the LORD a new song; for He hath done marvellous things;

הוֹשִׁיעָה-לּוֹ יְמִינוֹ, וּזְרוֹעַ קָדְשׁוֹ
hoshi'ah-lo yemino, uzroa kodsho
His right hand, and His holy arm, hath wrought salvation for Him.

הוֹדִיעַ יְהוָה, יְשׁוּעָתוֹ; לְעֵינֵי הַגּוֹיִם, גִּלָּה צִדְקָתוֹ
hodia hashem yeshu'ato; le'einei haggoyim, gillah tzidkato
The LORD hath made known His salvation; His righteousness hath He revealed in the sight of the nations.

זָכַר חַסְדּוֹ, וֶאֱמוּנָתוֹ--לְבֵית יִשְׂרָאֵל
zachar chasdo ve'emunato leveit yisra'el
He hath remembered His mercy and His faithfulness toward the house of Israel;

רָאוּ כָל-אַפְסֵי-אָרֶץ--אֵת, יְשׁוּעַת אֱלֹהֵינוּ
ra'u chol-'afsei-'aretz; et, yeshu'at eloheinu
all the ends of the earth have seen the salvation of our God.

הָרִיעוּ לַיהוָה, כָּל-הָאָרֶץ; פִּצְחוּ וְרַנְּנוּ וְזַמֵּרוּ
hari'u lahashem kol-ha'aretz; pitzchu verannenu vezammeru
Shout unto the LORD, all the earth; break forth and sing for joy, yea, sing praises.

זַמְּרוּ לַיהוָה בְּכִנּוֹר; בְּכִנּוֹר, וְקוֹל זִמְרָה
zammeru lahashem bechinnor; bechinnor, vekol zimrah
Sing praises unto the LORD with the harp; with the harp and the voice of melody.

בַּחֲצֹצְרוֹת, וְקוֹל שׁוֹפָר--הָרִיעוּ, לִפְנֵי הַמֶּלֶךְ יְהוָה
bachatzotzerot vekol shofar; hari'u, lifnei hammelech hashem
With trumpets and sound of the horn shout ye before the King, the LORD.

יִרְעַם הַיָּם, וּמְלֹאוֹ; תֵּבֵל, וְיֹשְׁבֵי בָהּ
yir'am hayam umelo'o; tevel, veyoshevei vah
Let the sea roar, and the fulness thereof; the world, and they that dwell therein;

נְהָרוֹת יִמְחֲאוּ-כָף; יַחַד, הָרִים יְרַנֵּנוּ
neharot yimcha'u-chaf; yachad, harim yerannenu
Let the floods clap their hands; let the mountains sing for joy together;

לִפְנֵי יְהוָה--כִּי בָא, לִשְׁפֹּט הָאָרֶץ
lifnei-hashem ki va lishpot ha'aretz
Before the LORD, for He is come to judge the earth;

תְּהִלִּים

עָנָן וַעֲרָפֶל סְבִיבָיו; צֶדֶק וּמִשְׁפָּט, מְכוֹן כִּסְאוֹ
'anan va'arafel sevivav; tzedek umishpat, mechon kis'o
Clouds and darkness are round about Him; righteousness and justice are the foundation of His throne.

אֵשׁ, לְפָנָיו תֵּלֵךְ; וּתְלַהֵט סָבִיב צָרָיו
'esh lefanav telech; utelahet saviv tzarav
A fire goeth before Him, and burneth up His adversaries round about.

הֵאִירוּ בְרָקָיו תֵּבֵל; רָאֲתָה וַתָּחֵל הָאָרֶץ
he'iru verakav tevel; ra'atah vattachel ha'aretz
His lightnings lighted up the world; the earth saw, and trembled.

הָרִים--כַּדּוֹנַג, נָמַסּוּ מִלִּפְנֵי יְהוָה: מִלִּפְנֵי, אֲדוֹן כָּל-הָאָרֶץ
harim, kaddonag, namassu millifnei hashem millifnei, adon kol-ha'aretz
The mountains melted like wax at the presence of the LORD, at the presence of the Lord of the whole earth.

הִגִּידוּ הַשָּׁמַיִם צִדְקוֹ; וְרָאוּ כָל-הָעַמִּים כְּבוֹדוֹ
higgidu hashamayim tzidko; vera'u chol-ha'ammim kevodo
The heavens declared His righteousness, and all the peoples saw His glory.

יֵבֹשׁוּ, כָּל-עֹבְדֵי פֶסֶל--הַמִּתְהַלְלִים בָּאֱלִילִים
yevoshu kol-'ovedei fesel, hammit'halelim ba'elilim
Ashamed be all they that serve graven images, that boast themselves of things of nought;

הִשְׁתַּחֲווּ-לוֹ, כָּל-אֱלֹהִים
hishtachavu-lo kol-'elohim
bow down to Him, all ye gods.

שָׁמְעָה וַתִּשְׂמַח, צִיּוֹן, וַתָּגֵלְנָה, בְּנוֹת יְהוּדָה--לְמַעַן מִשְׁפָּטֶיךָ יְהוָה
shame'ah vattismach tziyon, vattagelnah benot yehudah; lema'an mishpateicha hashem
Zion heard and was glad, and the daughters of Judah rejoiced; because of Thy judgments, O LORD.

כִּי-אַתָּה יְהוָה, עֶלְיוֹן עַל-כָּל-הָאָרֶץ; מְאֹד נַעֲלֵיתָ, עַל-כָּל-אֱלֹהִים
ki-'attah hashem elyon al-kol-ha'aretz; me'od na'aleita, al-kol-'elohim
For Thou, LORD, art most high above all the earth; Thou art exalted far above all gods.

אֹהֲבֵי יְהוָה, שִׂנְאוּ-רָע: שֹׁמֵר, נַפְשׁוֹת חֲסִידָיו; מִיַּד רְשָׁעִים, יַצִּילֵם
'ohavei hashem sin'u ra shomer nafshot chasidav; miyad resha'im, yatzilem
O ye that love the LORD, hate evil; He preserveth the souls of His saints; He delivered them out of the hand of the wicked.

אוֹר, זָרֻעַ לַצַּדִּיק; וּלְיִשְׁרֵי-לֵב שִׂמְחָה
'or zarua latzaddik; uleyishrei-lev simchah
Light is sown for the righteous, and gladness for the upright in heart.

שִׂמְחוּ צַדִּיקִים, בַּיהוָה; וְהוֹדוּ, לְזֵכֶר קָדְשׁוֹ
simchu tzaddikim bahashem; vehodu, lezecher kodsho
Be glad in the LORD, ye righteous; and give thanks to His holy name.

תְּהִלִּים

הוֹד-וְהָדָר לְפָנָיו; עֹז וְתִפְאֶרֶת, בְּמִקְדָּשׁוֹ
hod-vehadar lefanav; oz vetif'eret, bemikdasho
Honour and majesty are before Him; strength and beauty are in His sanctuary.

הָבוּ לַיהוָה, מִשְׁפְּחוֹת עַמִּים; הָבוּ לַיהוָה, כָּבוֹד וָעֹז
havu lashem mishpechot ammim; havu lashem kavod va'oz
Ascribe unto the LORD, ye kindreds of the peoples, ascribe unto the LORD glory and strength.

הָבוּ לַיהוָה, כְּבוֹד שְׁמוֹ; שְׂאוּ-מִנְחָה, וּבֹאוּ לְחַצְרוֹתָיו
havu lashem kevod shemo; se'u-minchah, uvo'u lechatzrotav
Ascribe unto the LORD the glory due unto His name; bring an offering, and come into His courts.

הִשְׁתַּחֲווּ לַיהוָה, בְּהַדְרַת-קֹדֶשׁ; חִילוּ מִפָּנָיו, כָּל-הָאָרֶץ
hishtachavu lashem behadrat-kodesh; chilu mippanav, kol-ha'aretz
O worship the LORD in the beauty of holiness; tremble before Him, all the earth.

אִמְרוּ בַגּוֹיִם, יְהוָה מָלָךְ--אַף-תִּכּוֹן תֵּבֵל, בַּל-תִּמּוֹט
'imru vaggoyim hashem malach, af-tikkon tevel bal-timmot
Say among the nations: 'The LORD reigneth.' The world also is established that it cannot be moved;

יָדִין עַמִּים, בְּמֵישָׁרִים
yadin ammim, bemeisharim
He will judge the peoples with equity.

יִשְׂמְחוּ הַשָּׁמַיִם, וְתָגֵל הָאָרֶץ; יִרְעַם הַיָּם, וּמְלֹאוֹ
yismechu hashamayim vetagel ha'aretz; yir'am hayam, umelo'o
Let the heavens be glad, and let the earth rejoice; let the sea roar, and the fulness thereof;

יַעֲלֹז שָׂדַי, וְכָל-אֲשֶׁר-בּוֹ; אָז יְרַנְּנוּ, כָּל-עֲצֵי-יָעַר
ya'aloz sadai vechol-'asher-bo; az yerannenu, kol-'atzei-ya'ar
Let the field exult; and all that is therein; then shall all the trees of the wood sing for joy;

לִפְנֵי יְהוָה, כִּי בָא--כִּי בָא, לִשְׁפֹּט הָאָרֶץ
lifnei hashem ki va, ki va lishpot ha'aretz
Before the LORD, for He is come; for He is come to judge the earth;

יִשְׁפֹּט-תֵּבֵל בְּצֶדֶק; וְעַמִּים, בֶּאֱמוּנָתוֹ
yishpot-tevel betzedek; ve'ammim, be'emunato
He will judge the world with righteousness, and the peoples in His faithfulness.

צז

יְהוָה מָלָךְ, תָּגֵל הָאָרֶץ; יִשְׂמְחוּ, אִיִּים רַבִּים
Hashem malach tagel ha'aretz; yismechu, iyim rabbim
The LORD reigneth; let the earth rejoice; let the multitude of isles be glad.

תְּהִלִּים

הַיּוֹם, אִם-בְּקֹלוֹ תִשְׁמָעוּ
hayom, im-bekolo tishma'u
To-day, if ye would but hearken to His voice!

אַל-תַּקְשׁוּ לְבַבְכֶם, כִּמְרִיבָה; כְּיוֹם מַסָּה, בַּמִּדְבָּר
'al-takshu levavchem kimrivah; keyom massah, bammidbar
'Harden not your heart, as at Meribah, as in the day of Massah in the wilderness;

אֲשֶׁר נִסּוּנִי, אֲבוֹתֵיכֶם: בְּחָנוּנִי, גַּם-רָאוּ פָעֳלִי
'asher nissuni avoteichem; bechanuni, gam-ra'u fo'oli
When your fathers tried Me, proved Me, even though they saw My work.

אַרְבָּעִים שָׁנָה, אָקוּט בְּדוֹר--וָאֹמַר
'arba'im shanah akut bedor, va'omar
For forty years was I wearied with that generation, and said:

עַם תֹּעֵי לֵבָב הֵם; וְהֵם, לֹא-יָדְעוּ דְרָכָי
am to'ei levav hem; vehem, lo-yade'u derachai
It is a people that do err in their heart, and they have not known My ways;

אֲשֶׁר-נִשְׁבַּעְתִּי בְאַפִּי; אִם-יְבֹאוּן, אֶל-מְנוּחָתִי
'asher-nishba'ti ve'appi; im-yevo'un, el-menuchati
Wherefore I swore in My wrath, that they should not enter into My rest.'

צו

שִׁירוּ לַיהוָה, שִׁיר חָדָשׁ; שִׁירוּ לַיהוָה, כָּל-הָאָרֶץ
Shiru lahashem shir chadash; shiru lahashem kol-ha'aretz
O sing unto the LORD a new song; sing unto the LORD, all the earth.

שִׁירוּ לַיהוָה, בָּרְכוּ שְׁמוֹ; בַּשְּׂרוּ מִיּוֹם-לְיוֹם, יְשׁוּעָתוֹ
shiru lahashem barachu shemo; basseru miyom-leyom, yeshu'ato
Sing unto the LORD, bless His name; proclaim His salvation from day to day.

סַפְּרוּ בַגּוֹיִם כְּבוֹדוֹ; בְּכָל-הָעַמִּים, נִפְלְאוֹתָיו
sapperu vaggoyim kevodo; bechol-ha'ammim, nifle'otav
Declare His glory among the nations, His marvellous works among all the peoples.

כִּי גָדוֹל יְהוָה וּמְהֻלָּל מְאֹד; נוֹרָא הוּא, עַל-כָּל-אֱלֹהִים
ki gadol hashem umehullal me'od; nora hu, al-kol-'elohim
For great is the LORD, and highly to be praised; He is to be feared above all gods.

כִּי, כָּל-אֱלֹהֵי הָעַמִּים אֱלִילִים; וַיהוָה, שָׁמַיִם עָשָׂה
ki kol-'elohei ha'ammim elilim; vahashem, shamayim asah
For all the gods of the peoples are things of nought; but the LORD made the heavens.

תְּהִלִים

יָגוֹדּוּ, עַל-נֶפֶשׁ צַדִּיק; וְדָם נָקִי יַרְשִׁיעוּ
yagoddu al-nefesh tzaddik; vedam naki yarshi'u
They gather themselves together against the soul of the righteous, and condemn innocent blood.

וַיְהִי יְהוָה לִי לְמִשְׂגָּב; וֵאלֹהַי, לְצוּר מַחְסִי
vayhi hashem li lemisgav; velohai, letzur machsi
But the LORD hath been my high tower, and my God the rock of my refuge.

וַיָּשֶׁב עֲלֵיהֶם, אֶת אוֹנָם--וּבְרָעָתָם יַצְמִיתֵם
vayashev aleihem et-'onam, uvera'atam yatzmitem
And He hath brought upon them their own iniquity, and will cut them off in their own evil;

יַצְמִיתֵם, יְהוָה אֱלֹהֵינוּ
yatzmitem, hashem eloheinu
the LORD our God will cut them off.

צה

לְכוּ, נְרַנְּנָה לַיהוָה; נָרִיעָה, לְצוּר יִשְׁעֵנוּ
Lechu nerannenah lahashem nari'ah, letzur yish'enu
O come, let us sing unto the LORD; let us shout for joy to the Rock of our salvation.

נְקַדְּמָה פָנָיו בְּתוֹדָה; בִּזְמִרוֹת, נָרִיעַ לוֹ
nekaddemah fanav betodah; bizmirot, naria lo
Let us come before His presence with thanksgiving, let us shout for joy unto Him with psalms.

כִּי אֵל גָּדוֹל יְהוָה; וּמֶלֶךְ גָּדוֹל, עַל-כָּל-אֱלֹהִים
ki el gadol hashem umelech gadol, al-kol-'elohim
For the LORD is a great God, and a great King above all gods;

אֲשֶׁר בְּיָדוֹ, מֶחְקְרֵי-אָרֶץ; וְתוֹעֲפֹת הָרִים לוֹ
'asher beyado mechkerei-'aretz; veto'afot harim lo
In whose hand are the depths of the earth; the heights of the mountains are His also.

אֲשֶׁר-לוֹ הַיָּם, וְהוּא עָשָׂהוּ; וְיַבֶּשֶׁת, יָדָיו יָצָרוּ
'asher-lo hayom vehu asahu; veyabbeshet, yadav yatzaru
The sea is His, and He made it; and His hands formed the dry land.

בֹּאוּ, נִשְׁתַּחֲוֶה וְנִכְרָעָה; נִבְרְכָה, לִפְנֵי-יְהוָה עֹשֵׂנוּ
bo'u nishtachaveh venichra'ah; nivrechah, lifnei-hashem osenu
O come, let us bow down and bend the knee; let us kneel before the LORD our Maker;

כִּי הוּא אֱלֹהֵינוּ--וַאֲנַחְנוּ עַם מַרְעִיתוֹ, וְצֹאן יָדוֹ
ki hu eloheinu, va'anachnu am mar'ito vetzon yado
For He is our God, and we are the people of His pasture, and the flock of His hand.

תְּהִלִּים

הֲנֹטַע אֹזֶן, הֲלֹא יִשְׁמָע; אִם-יֹצֵר עַיִן, הֲלֹא יַבִּיט
hanota ozen halo yishma'; im-yotzer ayin, halo yabbit
He that planted the ear, shall He not hear? He that formed the eye, shall He not see?

הֲיֹסֵר גּוֹיִם, הֲלֹא יוֹכִיחַ: הַמְלַמֵּד אָדָם דָּעַת
hayoser goyim halo yochiach; hamlammed adam da'at
He that instructeth nations, shall not He correct? even He that teacheth man knowledge?

יְהוָה--יֹדֵעַ, מַחְשְׁבוֹת אָדָם: כִּי-הֵמָּה הָבֶל
hashem yodea machshevot adam; ki-hemmah havel
The LORD knoweth the thoughts of man, that they are vanity.

אַשְׁרֵי, הַגֶּבֶר אֲשֶׁר-תְּיַסְּרֶנּוּ יָּהּ; וּמִתּוֹרָתְךָ תְלַמְּדֶנּוּ
'ashrei haggever asher-teyasserennu yah; umittoratecha telammedennu
Happy is the man whom Thou instructest, O LORD, and teachest out of Thy law;

לְהַשְׁקִיט לוֹ, מִימֵי רָע--עַד יִכָּרֶה לָרָשָׁע שָׁחַת
lehashkit lo mimei ra'; ad yikkareh larasha shachat
That Thou mayest give him rest from the days of evil, until the pit be digged for the wicked.

כִּי, לֹא-יִטֹּשׁ יְהוָה עַמּוֹ; וְנַחֲלָתוֹ, לֹא יַעֲזֹב
ki lo-yittosh hashem ammo; venachalato, lo ya'azov
For the LORD will not cast off His people, neither will He forsake His inheritance.

כִּי-עַד-צֶדֶק, יָשׁוּב מִשְׁפָּט; וְאַחֲרָיו, כָּל-יִשְׁרֵי-לֵב
ki-'ad-tzedek yashuv mishpat; ve'acharav, kol-yishrei-lev
For right shall return unto justice, and all the upright in heart shall follow it.

מִי-יָקוּם לִי, עִם-מְרֵעִים; מִי-יִתְיַצֵּב לִי, עִם-פֹּעֲלֵי אָוֶן
mi-yakum li im-mere'im; mi-yityatzev li im-po'alei aven
Who will rise up for me against the evil-doers? Who will stand up for me against the workers of iniquity?

לוּלֵי יְהוָה, עֶזְרָתָה לִּי-- כִּמְעַט, שָׁכְנָה דוּמָה נַפְשִׁי
lulei hashem ezratah li; kim'at shachenah dumah nafshi
Unless the LORD had been my help, my soul had soon dwelt in silence.

אִם-אָמַרְתִּי, מָטָה רַגְלִי; חַסְדְּךָ יְהוָה, יִסְעָדֵנִי
'im-'amarti matah ragli; chasdecha hashem yis'adeni
If I say: 'My foot slippeth', Thy mercy, O LORD, holdeth me up.

בְּרֹב שַׂרְעַפַּי בְּקִרְבִּי-- תַּנְחוּמֶיךָ, יְשַׁעַשְׁעוּ נַפְשִׁי.
berov sar'appai bekirbi; tanchumeicha, yesha'ash'u nafshi
When my cares are many within me, Thy comforts delight my soul.

הַיְחָבְרְךָ, כִּסֵּא הַוּוֹת; יֹצֵר עָמָל עֲלֵי-חֹק
haychaverecha kissei havvot; yotzer amal alei-chok
Shall the seat of wickedness have fellowship with Thee, which frameth mischief by statute?

תְּהִלִים

נָשְׂאוּ נְהָרוֹת, יְהוָה--נָשְׂאוּ נְהָרוֹת קוֹלָם; יִשְׂאוּ נְהָרוֹת דָּכְיָם
nase'u neharot hashem nase'u neharot kolam; yis'u neharot docheyam
The floods have lifted up, O LORD, the floods have lifted up their voice; the floods lift up their roaring.

מִקֹּלוֹת, מַיִם רַבִּים--אַדִּירִים מִשְׁבְּרֵי-יָם; אַדִּיר בַּמָּרוֹם יְהוָה
mikkolot mayim rabbim, addirim mishberei-yam; addir bammarom hashem
Above the voices of many waters, the mighty breakers of the sea, the LORD on high is mighty.

עֵדֹתֶיךָ, נֶאֶמְנוּ מְאֹד--לְבֵיתְךָ נַאֲוָה-קֹדֶשׁ: יְהוָה, לְאֹרֶךְ יָמִים
'edoteicha ne'emnu me'od, leveitecha na'avah-kodesh; hashem le'orech yamim
Thy testimonies are very sure, holiness becometh Thy house, O LORD, for evermore.

צד

אֵל-נְקָמוֹת יְהוָה; אֵל נְקָמוֹת הוֹפִיעַ
El-nekamot hashem el nekamot hofiya
O LORD, Thou God to whom vengeance belongeth, Thou God to whom vengeance belongeth, shine forth.

הִנָּשֵׂא, שֹׁפֵט הָאָרֶץ; הָשֵׁב גְּמוּל, עַל-גֵּאִים
hinnasei shofet ha'aretz; hashev gemul, al-ge'im
Lift up Thyself, Thou Judge of the earth; render to the proud their recompense.

עַד-מָתַי רְשָׁעִים יְהוָה: עַד-מָתַי, רְשָׁעִים יַעֲלֹזוּ
'ad-matai resha'im hashem ad-matai, resha'im ya'alozu
LORD, how long shall the wicked, how long shall the wicked exult?

יַבִּיעוּ יְדַבְּרוּ עָתָק; יִתְאַמְּרוּ, כָּל-פֹּעֲלֵי אָוֶן
yabbi'u yedabberu atak; yit'ammeru, kol-po'alei aven
They gush out, they speak arrogancy; all the workers of iniquity bear themselves loftily.

עַמְּךָ יְהוָה יְדַכְּאוּ; וְנַחֲלָתְךָ יְעַנּוּ
'ammecha hashem yedakke'u; venachalatecha ye'annu
They crush Thy people, O LORD, and afflict Thy heritage.

אַלְמָנָה וְגֵר יַהֲרֹגוּ; וִיתוֹמִים יְרַצֵּחוּ
'almanah veger yaharogu; vitomim yeratzechu
They slay the widow and the stranger, and murder the fatherless.

וַיֹּאמְרוּ, לֹא יִרְאֶה-יָּהּ; וְלֹא-יָבִין, אֱלֹהֵי יַעֲקֹב
vayomeru lo yir'eh-yah; velo-yavin, elohei ya'akov
And they say: 'The LORD will not see, neither will the God of Jacob give heed.'

בִּינוּ, בֹּעֲרִים בָּעָם; וּכְסִילִים, מָתַי תַּשְׂכִּילוּ
binu bo'arim ba'am; uchesilim, matai taskilu
Consider, ye brutish among the people; and ye fools, when will ye understand?

תְּהִלִּים

כִּי הִנֵּה אֹיְבֶיךָ, יְהוָה--כִּי-הִנֵּה אֹיְבֶיךָ יֹאבֵדוּ: יִתְפָּרְדוּ, כָּל-פֹּעֲלֵי אָוֶן.
ki hinneh oyeveicha hashem ki-hinneh oyeveicha yovedu; yitparedu, kol-po'alei aven
For, lo, Thine enemies, O LORD, for, lo, Thine enemies shall perish: all the workers of iniquity shall be scattered.

וַתָּרֶם כִּרְאֵים קַרְנִי; בַּלֹּתִי, בְּשֶׁמֶן רַעֲנָן
vattarem kir'eim karni; balloti, beshemen ra'anan
But my horn hast Thou exalted like the horn of the wild-ox; I am anointed with rich oil.

וַתַּבֵּט עֵינִי, בְּשׁוּרָי
vattabbet eini, beshurai
Mine eye also hath gazed on them that lie in wait for me,

בַּקָּמִים עָלַי מְרֵעִים--תִּשְׁמַעְנָה אָזְנָי
bakkamim alai mere'im, tishma'nah azenai
mine ears have heard my desire of the evil-doers that rise up against me.

צַדִּיק, כַּתָּמָר יִפְרָח; כְּאֶרֶז בַּלְּבָנוֹן יִשְׂגֶּה
tzaddik kattamar yifrach; ke'erez ballevanon yisgeh
The righteous shall flourish like the palm-tree; he shall grow like a cedar in Lebanon.

שְׁתוּלִים, בְּבֵית יְהוָה; בְּחַצְרוֹת אֱלֹהֵינוּ יַפְרִיחוּ
shetulim beveit hashem bechatzrot eloheinu yafrichu
Planted in the house of the LORD, they shall flourish in the courts of our God.

עוֹד, יְנוּבוּן בְּשֵׂיבָה; דְּשֵׁנִים וְרַעֲנַנִּים יִהְיוּ
'od yenuvun beseivah; deshenim vera'anannim yihyu
They shall still bring forth fruit in old age; they shall be full of sap and richness;

לְהַגִּיד, כִּי-יָשָׁר יְהוָה; צוּרִי, וְלֹא-עַוְלָתָה בּוֹ
lehaggid ki-yashar hashem tzuri, velo-'avlatah bo
To declare that the LORD is upright, my Rock, in whom there is no unrighteousness.

צג

יְהוָה מָלָךְ, גֵּאוּת לָבֵשׁ: לָבֵשׁ יְהוָה, עֹז הִתְאַזָּר
Hashem malach ge'ut lavesh lavesh hashem oz hit'azzar
The LORD reigneth; He is clothed in majesty; the LORD is clothed, He hath girded Himself with strength;

אַף-תִּכּוֹן תֵּבֵל, בַּל-תִּמּוֹט
af-tikkon tevel, bal-timmot
yea, the world is established, that it cannot be moved.

נָכוֹן כִּסְאֲךָ מֵאָז; מֵעוֹלָם אָתָּה
nachon kis'acha me'az; me'olam attah
Thy throne is established of old; Thou art from everlasting.

תְּהִלִּים

אֹרֶךְ יָמִים, אַשְׂבִּיעֵהוּ; וְאַרְאֵהוּ, בִּישׁוּעָתִי
'orech yamim asbi'ehu; ve'ar'ehu, bishu'ati
With long life will I satisfy him, and make him to behold My salvation.'

צב

מִזְמוֹר שִׁיר, לְיוֹם הַשַּׁבָּת
Mizmor shir, leyom hashabbat
A Psalm, a Song. For the sabbath day.

טוֹב, לְהֹדוֹת לַיהוָה; וּלְזַמֵּר לְשִׁמְךָ עֶלְיוֹן
tov, lehodot lahashem ulezammer leshimcha elyon
It is a good thing to give thanks unto the LORD, and to sing praises unto Thy name, O Most High;

לְהַגִּיד בַּבֹּקֶר חַסְדֶּךָ; וֶאֱמוּנָתְךָ, בַּלֵּילוֹת
lehaggid babboker chasdecha; ve'emunatecha, balleilot
To declare Thy lovingkindness in the morning, and Thy faithfulness in the night seasons,

עֲלֵי-עָשׂוֹר, וַעֲלֵי-נָבֶל; עֲלֵי הִגָּיוֹן בְּכִנּוֹר
'alei-'asor va'alei-navel; alei higgayon bechinnor
With an instrument of ten strings, and with the psaltery; with a solemn sound upon the harp.

כִּי שִׂמַּחְתַּנִי יְהוָה בְּפָעֳלֶךָ; בְּמַעֲשֵׂי יָדֶיךָ אֲרַנֵּן
ki simmachtani hashem befo'olecha; bema'asei yadeicha arannen
For Thou, LORD, hast made me glad through Thy work; I will exult in the works of Thy hands.

מַה-גָּדְלוּ מַעֲשֶׂיךָ יְהוָה; מְאֹד, עָמְקוּ מַחְשְׁבֹתֶיךָ
mah-gadelu ma'aseicha hashem me'od, ameku machshevoteicha
How great are Thy works, O LORD! Thy thoughts are very deep.

אִישׁ-בַּעַר, לֹא יֵדָע; וּכְסִיל, לֹא-יָבִין אֶת-זֹאת
'ish-ba'ar lo yeda'; uchesil, lo-yavin et-zot
A brutish man knoweth not, neither doth a fool understand this.

בִּפְרֹחַ רְשָׁעִים, כְּמוֹ עֵשֶׂב, וַיָּצִיצוּ, כָּל-פֹּעֲלֵי אָוֶן
bifroach resha'im kemo esev, vayatzitzu kol-po'alei aven
When the wicked spring up as the grass, and when all the workers of iniquity do flourish;

לְהִשָּׁמְדָם עֲדֵי-עַד
lehishamedam adei-'ad
it is that they may be destroyed for ever.

וְאַתָּה מָרוֹם--לְעֹלָם יְהוָה
ve'attah marom, le'olam hashem
But Thou, O LORD, art on high for evermore.

תְּהִלִּים

לֹא-תִירָא, מִפַּחַד לָיְלָה; מֵחֵץ, יָעוּף יוֹמָם
lo-tira mippachad layelah; mechetz, ya'uf yomam
Thou shalt not be afraid of the terror by night, nor of the arrow that flieth by day;

מִדֶּבֶר, בָּאֹפֶל יַהֲלֹךְ; מִקֶּטֶב, יָשׁוּד צָהֳרָיִם
middever ba'ofel yahaloch; mikketev, yashud tzohorayim
Of the pestilence that walketh in darkness, nor of the destruction that wasteth at noonday.

יִפֹּל מִצִּדְּךָ, אֶלֶף--וּרְבָבָה מִימִינֶךָ: אֵלֶיךָ, לֹא יִגָּשׁ
yippol mitziddecha elef, urevavah miminecha; eleicha, lo yiggash
A thousand may fall at thy side, and ten thousand at thy right hand; it shall not come nigh thee.

רַק, בְּעֵינֶיךָ תַבִּיט; וְשִׁלֻּמַת רְשָׁעִים תִּרְאֶה
rak be'eineicha tabbit; veshillumat resha'im tir'eh
Only with thine eyes shalt thou behold, and see the recompense of the wicked.

כִּי-אַתָּה יְהוָה מַחְסִי; עֶלְיוֹן, שַׂמְתָּ מְעוֹנֶךָ
ki-'attah hashem machsi; elyon, samta me'onecha
For thou hast made the LORD who is my refuge, even the Most High, thy habitation.

לֹא-תְאֻנֶּה אֵלֶיךָ רָעָה; וְנֶגַע, לֹא-יִקְרַב בְּאָהֳלֶךָ
lo-te'unneh eleicha ra'ah; venega', lo-yikrav be'oholecha
There shall no evil befall thee, neither shall any plague come nigh thy tent.

כִּי מַלְאָכָיו, יְצַוֶּה-לָּךְ; לִשְׁמָרְךָ, בְּכָל-דְּרָכֶיךָ
ki mal'achav yetzavveh-lach; lishmorcha, bechol-deracheicha
For He will give His angels charge over thee, to keep thee in all thy ways.

עַל-כַּפַּיִם יִשָּׂאוּנְךָ: פֶּן-תִּגֹּף בָּאֶבֶן רַגְלֶךָ
'al-kappayim yissa'unecha; pen-tiggof ba'even raglecha
They shall bear thee upon their hands, lest thou dash thy foot against a stone.

עַל-שַׁחַל וָפֶתֶן, תִּדְרֹךְ; תִּרְמֹס כְּפִיר וְתַנִּין
'al-shachal vafeten tidroch; tirmos kefir vetannin
Thou shalt tread upon the lion and asp; the young lion and the serpent shalt thou trample under feet.

כִּי בִי חָשַׁק, וַאֲפַלְּטֵהוּ
ki vi chashak va'afalletehu
'Because he hath set his love upon Me, therefore will I deliver him;

אֲשַׂגְּבֵהוּ, כִּי-יָדַע שְׁמִי
asaggevehu, ki-yada shemi
I will set him on high, because he hath known My name.

יִקְרָאֵנִי, וְאֶעֱנֵהוּ--עִמּוֹ-אָנֹכִי בְצָרָה; אֲחַלְּצֵהוּ, וַאֲכַבְּדֵהוּ
yikra'eni ve'e'enehu, immo-'anochi vetzarah; achalletzehu, va'achabbedehu
He shall call upon Me, and I will answer him; I will be with him in trouble; I will rescue him, and bring him to honour.

תְּהִלִּים

לִמְנוֹת יָמֵינוּ, כֵּן הוֹדַע; וְנָבִא, לְבַב חָכְמָה
limnot yameinu ken hoda'; venavi, levav chochmah
So teach us to number our days, that we may get us a heart of wisdom.

שׁוּבָה יְהוָה, עַד-מָתָי; וְהִנָּחֵם, עַל-עֲבָדֶיךָ
shuvah hashem ad-matai; vehinnachem, al-'avadeicha
Return, O LORD; how long? And let it repent Thee concerning Thy servants.

שַׂבְּעֵנוּ בַבֹּקֶר חַסְדֶּךָ; וּנְרַנְּנָה וְנִשְׂמְחָה, בְּכָל-יָמֵינוּ
sabbe'enu vabboker chasdecha; unerannenah venismechah, bechol-yameinu
O satisfy us in the morning with Thy mercy; that we may rejoice and be glad all our days.

שַׂמְּחֵנוּ, כִּימוֹת עִנִּיתָנוּ: שְׁנוֹת, רָאִינוּ רָעָה
sammechenu kimot innitanu; shenot, ra'inu ra'ah
Make us glad according to the days wherein Thou hast afflicted us, according to the years wherein we have seen evil.

יֵרָאֶה אֶל-עֲבָדֶיךָ פָעֳלֶךָ; וַהֲדָרְךָ, עַל-בְּנֵיהֶם
yera'eh el-'avadeicha fa'olecha; vahadarecha, al-beneihem
Let Thy work appear unto Thy servants, and Thy glory upon their children.

וִיהִי, נֹעַם אֲדֹנָי אֱלֹהֵינוּ--עָלֵינוּ
vihi no'am adonai eloheinu, aleinu
And let the graciousness of the Lord our God be upon us;

וּמַעֲשֵׂה יָדֵינוּ, כּוֹנְנָה עָלֵינוּ; וּמַעֲשֵׂה יָדֵינוּ, כּוֹנְנֵהוּ
uma'aseh yadeinu konenah aleinu; uma'aseh yadeinu, konenehu
establish Thou also upon us the work of our hands; yea, the work of our hands establish Thou it.

צא

יֹשֵׁב, בְּסֵתֶר עֶלְיוֹן; בְּצֵל שַׁדַּי, יִתְלוֹנָן
Yoshev beseter elyon; betzel shaddai, yitlonan
O thou that dwellest in the covert of the Most High, and abidest in the shadow of the Almighty;

אֹמַר--לַיהוָה, מַחְסִי וּמְצוּדָתִי; אֱלֹהַי, אֶבְטַח-בּוֹ
'omar, lahashem machsi umetzudati; elohai, evtach-bo
I will say of the LORD, who is my refuge and my fortress, my God, in whom I trust,

כִּי הוּא יַצִּילְךָ, מִפַּח יָקוּשׁ; מִדֶּבֶר הַוּוֹת
ki hu yatzilecha mippach yakush, middever havvot
That He will deliver thee from the snare of the fowler, and from the noisome pestilence.

בְּאֶבְרָתוֹ, יָסֶךְ לָךְ--וְתַחַת-כְּנָפָיו תֶּחְסֶה; צִנָּה וְסֹחֵרָה אֲמִתּוֹ
be'evrato yasech lach vetachat-kenafav techseh; tzinnah vesocherah amitto
He will cover thee with His pinions, and under His wings shalt thou take refuge; His truth is a shield and a buckler.

תְּהִלִּים

בְּטֶרֶם, הָרִים יֻלָּדוּ--וַתְּחוֹלֵל אֶרֶץ וְתֵבֵל
beterem harim yulladu, vattecholel eretz vetevel
Before the mountains were brought forth, or ever Thou hadst formed the earth and the world,

וּמֵעוֹלָם עַד-עוֹלָם, אַתָּה אֵל
ume'olam ad-'olam, attah el
even from everlasting to everlasting, Thou art God.

תָּשֵׁב אֱנוֹשׁ, עַד-דַּכָּא; וַתֹּאמֶר, שׁוּבוּ בְנֵי-אָדָם
tashev enosh ad-dakka; vattomer, shuvu venei-'adam
Thou turnest man to contrition; and sayest: 'Return, ye children of men.'

כִּי אֶלֶף שָׁנִים, בְּעֵינֶיךָ--כְּיוֹם אֶתְמוֹל, כִּי יַעֲבֹר; וְאַשְׁמוּרָה בַלָּיְלָה.
ki elef shanim be'eineicha, keyom etmol ki ya'avor; ve'ashmurah vallayelah
For a thousand years in Thy sight are but as yesterday when it is past, and as a watch in the night.

זְרַמְתָּם, שֵׁנָה יִהְיוּ; בַּבֹּקֶר, כֶּחָצִיר יַחֲלֹף
zeramtom shenah yihyu; babboker, kechatzir yachalof
Thou carriest them away as with a flood; they are as a sleep; in the morning they are like grass which groweth up.

בַּבֹּקֶר, יָצִיץ וְחָלָף; לָעֶרֶב, יְמוֹלֵל וְיָבֵשׁ
babboker yatzitz vechalaf; la'erev, yemolel veyavesh
In the morning it flourisheth, and groweth up; in the evening it is cut down, and withereth.

כִּי-כָלִינוּ בְאַפֶּךָ; וּבַחֲמָתְךָ נִבְהָלְנוּ.
ki-chalinu ve'appecha; uvachamatecha nivhalenu
For we are consumed in Thine anger, and by Thy wrath are we hurried away.

שַׁתָּ עֲוֺנֹתֵינוּ לְנֶגְדֶּךָ; עֲלֻמֵנוּ, לִמְאוֹר פָּנֶיךָ
shattah avonoteinu lenegdecha; alumenu, lim'or paneicha
Thou hast set our iniquities before Thee, our secret sins in the light of Thy countenance.

כִּי כָל-יָמֵינוּ, פָּנוּ בְעֶבְרָתֶךָ; כִּלִּינוּ שָׁנֵינוּ כְמוֹ-הֶגֶה
ki chol-yameinu panu ve'evratecha; killinu shaneinu chemo-hegeh
For all our days are passed away in Thy wrath; we bring our years to an end as a tale that is told.

יְמֵי-שְׁנוֹתֵינוּ בָהֶם שִׁבְעִים שָׁנָה, וְאִם בִּגְבוּרֹת שְׁמוֹנִים שָׁנָה
yemei-shenoteinu vahem shiv'im shanah ve'im bigvurot shemonim shanah
The days of our years are threescore years and ten, or even by reason of strength fourscore years;

וְרָהְבָּם, עָמָל וָאָוֶן: כִּי-גָז חִישׁ, וַנָּעֻפָה
verohebam amal va'aven; ki-gaz chish, vanna'ufah
yet is their pride but travail and vanity; for it is speedily gone, and we fly away.

מִי-יוֹדֵעַ, עֹז אַפֶּךָ; וּכְיִרְאָתְךָ, עֶבְרָתֶךָ
mi-yodea oz appecha; ucheyir'atecha, evratecha
Who knoweth the power of Thine anger, and Thy wrath according to the fear that is due unto Thee?

תְּהִלִּים

אַף-תָּשִׁיב, צוּר חַרְבּוֹ; וְלֹא הֲקֵימֹתוֹ, בַּמִּלְחָמָה
'af-tashiv tzur charbo; velo hakeimoto, bammilchamah
Yea, Thou turnest back the edge of his sword, and hast not made him to stand in the battle.

הִשְׁבַּתָּ מִטְּהָרוֹ; וְכִסְאוֹ, לָאָרֶץ מִגַּרְתָּה
hishbata mittoharo; vechis'o, la'aretz miggartah
Thou hast made his brightness to cease, and cast his throne down to the ground.

הִקְצַרְתָּ, יְמֵי עֲלוּמָיו; הֶעֱטִיתָ עָלָיו בּוּשָׁה סֶלָה
hiktzarta yemei alumav; he'etita alav bushah selah
The days of his youth hast Thou shortened; Thou hast covered him with shame. Selah

עַד-מָה יְהוָה, תִּסָּתֵר לָנֶצַח; תִּבְעַר כְּמוֹ-אֵשׁ חֲמָתֶךָ
'ad-mah hashem tissater lanetzach; tiv'ar kemo-'esh chamatecha
How long, O LORD, wilt Thou hide Thyself for ever? How long shall Thy wrath burn like fire?

זְכָר-אֲנִי מֶה-חָלֶד; עַל-מַה-שָּׁוְא, בָּרָאתָ כָל-בְּנֵי-אָדָם
zechor-'ani meh-chaled; al-mah-shav, barata chol-benei-'adam
O remember how short my time is; for what vanity hast Thou created all the children of men!

מִי גֶבֶר יִחְיֶה, וְלֹא יִרְאֶה-מָּוֶת; יְמַלֵּט נַפְשׁוֹ מִיַּד-שְׁאוֹל סֶלָה
mi gever yichyeh velo yir'eh-mavet; yemallet nafsho miyad-she'ol selah
What man is he that liveth and shall not see death, that shall deliver his soul from the power of the grave? Selah

אַיֵּה, חֲסָדֶיךָ הָרִאשֹׁנִים אֲדֹנָי: נִשְׁבַּעְתָּ לְדָוִד, בֶּאֱמוּנָתֶךָ
'ayeh chasadeicha harishonim adonai; nishba'ta ledavid, be'emunatecha
Where are Thy former mercies, O Lord, which Thou didst swear unto David in Thy faithfulness?

זְכֹר אֲדֹנָי, חֶרְפַּת עֲבָדֶיךָ; שְׂאֵתִי בְחֵיקִי, כָּל-רַבִּים עַמִּים
zechor adonai cherpat avadeicha; se'eti vecheiki, kol-rabbim ammim
Remember, Lord, the taunt of Thy servants; how I do bear in my bosom [the taunt of] so many peoples;

אֲשֶׁר חֵרְפוּ אוֹיְבֶיךָ יְהוָה: אֲשֶׁר חֵרְפוּ, עִקְּבוֹת מְשִׁיחֶךָ
'asher cherefu oyeveicha hashem asher cherefu, ikkevot meshichecha
Wherewith Thine enemies have taunted, O LORD, wherewith they have taunted the footsteps of Thine anointed.

בָּרוּךְ יְהוָה לְעוֹלָם: אָמֵן וְאָמֵן
baruch hashem le'olam, amen ve'amen
Blessed be the LORD for evermore. Amen, and Amen.

צ

תְּפִלָּה, לְמֹשֶׁה אִישׁ-הָאֱלֹהִים: אֲדֹנָי--מָעוֹן אַתָּה, הָיִיתָ לָּנוּ; בְּדֹר וָדֹר
Tefillah lemosheh ish-ha'elohim adonai, ma'on attah hayita lanu, bedor vador
A Prayer of Moses the man of God. Lord, Thou hast been our dwelling-place in all generations.

תְּהִלִּים

אִם-חֻקֹּתַי יְחַלֵּלוּ; וּמִצְוֹתַי, לֹא יִשְׁמֹרוּ
'im-chukkotai yechallelu; umitzvotai, lo yishmoru
If they profane My statutes, and keep not My commandments;

וּפָקַדְתִּי בְשֵׁבֶט פִּשְׁעָם; וּבִנְגָעִים עֲוֹנָם
ufakadti veshevet pish'am; uvinga'im avonam
Then will I visit their transgression with the rod, and their iniquity with strokes.

וְחַסְדִּי, לֹא-אָפִיר מֵעִמּוֹ; וְלֹא-אֲשַׁקֵּר, בֶּאֱמוּנָתִי
vechasdi lo-'afir me'immo; velo-'ashakker, be'emunati
But My mercy will I not break off from him, nor will I be false to My faithfulness.

לֹא-אֲחַלֵּל בְּרִיתִי; וּמוֹצָא שְׂפָתַי, לֹא אֲשַׁנֶּה
lo-'achallel beriti; umotza sefatai, lo ashanneh
My covenant will I not profane, nor alter that which is gone out of My lips.

אַחַת, נִשְׁבַּעְתִּי בְקָדְשִׁי: אִם-לְדָוִד אֲכַזֵּב
'achat nishba'ti vekodeshi; im-ledavid achazzev
Once have I sworn by My holiness: Surely I will not be false unto David;

זַרְעוֹ, לְעוֹלָם יִהְיֶה; וְכִסְאוֹ כַשֶּׁמֶשׁ נֶגְדִּי
zar'o le'olam yihyeh; vechis'o chashemesh negdi
His seed shall endure for ever, and his throne as the sun before Me.

כְּיָרֵחַ, יִכּוֹן עוֹלָם; וְעֵד בַּשַּׁחַק, נֶאֱמָן סֶלָה
keyareach yikkon olam; ve'ed bashachak, ne'eman selah
It shall be established for ever as the moon; and be stedfast as the witness in sky.' Selah

וְאַתָּה זָנַחְתָּ, וַתִּמְאָס; הִתְעַבַּרְתָּ, עִם-מְשִׁיחֶךָ
ve'attah zanachta vattim'as; hit'abbarta, im-meshichecha
But Thou hast cast off and rejected, Thou hast been wroth with Thine anointed.

נֵאַרְתָּה, בְּרִית עַבְדֶּךָ; חִלַּלְתָּ לָאָרֶץ נִזְרוֹ
ne'artah berit avdecha; chillalta la'aretz nizro
Thou hast abhorred the covenant of Thy servant; Thou hast profaned his crown even to the ground.

פָּרַצְתָּ כָל-גְּדֵרֹתָיו; שַׂמְתָּ מִבְצָרָיו מְחִתָּה
paratzta chol-gederotav; samta mivtzarav mechittah
Thou hast broken down all his fences; Thou hast brought his strongholds to ruin.

שַׁסֻּהוּ, כָּל-עֹבְרֵי דָרֶךְ; הָיָה חֶרְפָּה, לִשְׁכֵנָיו
shassuhu kol-'overei darech; hayah cherpah, lishchenav
All that pass by the way spoil him; he is become a taunt to his neighbours.

הֲרִימוֹתָ, יְמִין צָרָיו; הִשְׂמַחְתָּ, כָּל-אוֹיְבָיו
harimota yemin tzarav; hismachta, kol-'oyevav
Thou hast exalted the right hand of his adversaries; Thou hast made all his enemies to rejoice.

תְּהִלִּים

שִׁוִּיתִי עֵזֶר עַל-גִּבּוֹר; הֲרִימוֹתִי בָחוּר מֵעָם
shivviti ezer al-gibbor; harimoti vachur me'am
'I have laid help upon one that is mighty; I have exalted one chosen out of the people.

מָצָאתִי, דָּוִד עַבְדִּי; בְּשֶׁמֶן קָדְשִׁי מְשַׁחְתִּיו
matzati david avdi; beshemen kodshi meshachtiv
I have found David My servant; with My holy oil have I anointed him;

אֲשֶׁר יָדִי, תִּכּוֹן עִמּוֹ; אַף-זְרוֹעִי תְאַמְּצֶנּוּ
'asher yadi tikkon immo; af-zero'i te'ammetzennu
With whom My hand shall be established; Mine arm also shall strengthen him.

לֹא-יַשִּׁיא אוֹיֵב בּוֹ; וּבֶן-עַוְלָה, לֹא יְעַנֶּנּוּ
lo-yashi oyev bo; uven-'avlah, lo ye'annennu
The enemy shall not exact from him; nor the son of wickedness afflict him.

וְכַתּוֹתִי מִפָּנָיו צָרָיו; וּמְשַׂנְאָיו אֶגּוֹף
vechattoti mippanav tzarav; umesan'av eggof
And I will beat to pieces his adversaries before him, and smite them that hate him.

וֶאֱמוּנָתִי וְחַסְדִּי עִמּוֹ; וּבִשְׁמִי, תָּרוּם קַרְנוֹ
ve'emunati vechasdi immo; uvishmi, tarum karno
But My faithfulness and My mercy shall be with him; and through My name shall his horn be exalted.

וְשַׂמְתִּי בַיָּם יָדוֹ; וּבַנְּהָרוֹת יְמִינוֹ
vesamti vayam yado; uvanneharot yemino
I will set his hand also on the sea, and his right hand on the rivers.

הוּא יִקְרָאֵנִי, אָבִי אָתָּה; אֵלִי, וְצוּר יְשׁוּעָתִי
hu yikra'eni avi attah; eli, vetzur yeshu'ati
He shall call unto Me: Thou art my Father, my God, and the rock of my salvation.

אַף-אָנִי, בְּכוֹר אֶתְּנֵהוּ; עֶלְיוֹן, לְמַלְכֵי-אָרֶץ
'af-'ani bechor ettenehu; elyon, lemalchei-'aretz
I also will appoint him first-born, the highest of the kings of the earth.

לְעוֹלָם, אֶשְׁמָר-לוֹ חַסְדִּי; וּבְרִיתִי, נֶאֱמֶנֶת לוֹ
le'olam, 'eshmor-lo chasdi; uveriti, ne'emenet lo
For ever will I keep for him My mercy, and My covenant shall stand fast with him.

וְשַׂמְתִּי לָעַד זַרְעוֹ; וְכִסְאוֹ, כִּימֵי שָׁמָיִם
vesamti la'ad zar'o; vechis'o, kimei shamayim
His seed also will I make to endure for ever, and his throne as the days of heaven.

אִם-יַעַזְבוּ בָנָיו, תּוֹרָתִי; וּבְמִשְׁפָּטַי, לֹא יֵלֵכוּן
'im-ya'azvu vanav torati; uvemishpatai, lo yelechun
If his children forsake My law, and walk not in Mine ordinances;

תְּהִלִּים

יְהוָה, אֱלֹהֵי צְבָאוֹת--מִי-כָמוֹךָ חֲסִין יָהּ; וֶאֱמוּנָתְךָ, סְבִיבוֹתֶיךָ
hashem elohei tzeva'ot, mi-chamocha chasin yah; ve'emunatecha, sevivoteicha
O LORD God of hosts, who is a mighty one, like unto Thee, O LORD? And Thy faithfulness is round about Thee.

אַתָּה מוֹשֵׁל, בְּגֵאוּת הַיָּם; בְּשׂוֹא גַלָּיו, אַתָּה תְשַׁבְּחֵם
'attah moshel bege'ut hayam; beso gallav, attah teshabbechem
Thou rulest the proud swelling of the sea; when the waves thereof arise, Thou stillest them.

אַתָּה דִכִּאתָ כֶחָלָל רָהַב; בִּזְרוֹעַ עֻזְּךָ, פִּזַּרְתָּ אוֹיְבֶיךָ
'attah dikkita chechalal rahav; bizroa uzzecha, pizzarta oyeveicha
Thou didst crush Rahab, as one that is slain; Thou didst scatter Thine enemies with the arm of Thy strength.

לְךָ שָׁמַיִם, אַף-לְךָ אָרֶץ; תֵּבֵל וּמְלֹאָהּ, אַתָּה יְסַדְתָּם
lecha shamayim af-lecha aretz; tevel umelo'ah, attah yesadtam
Thine are the heavens, Thine also the earth; the world and the fulness thereof, Thou hast founded them.

צָפוֹן וְיָמִין, אַתָּה בְרָאתָם; תָּבוֹר וְחֶרְמוֹן, בְּשִׁמְךָ יְרַנֵּנוּ
tzafon veyamin attah veratam; tavor vechermon, beshimcha yerannenu
The north and the south, Thou hast created them; Tabor and Hermon rejoice in Thy name.

לְךָ זְרוֹעַ, עִם-גְּבוּרָה; תָּעֹז יָדְךָ, תָּרוּם יְמִינֶךָ
lecha zeroa im-gevurah; ta'oz yadecha, tarum yeminecha
Thine is an arm with might; strong is Thy hand, and exalted is Thy right hand.

צֶדֶק וּמִשְׁפָּט, מְכוֹן כִּסְאֶךָ; חֶסֶד וֶאֱמֶת, יְקַדְּמוּ פָנֶיךָ
tzedek umishpot mechon kis'echa; chesed ve'emet, yekaddemu faneicha
Righteousness and justice are the foundation of Thy throne; mercy and truth go before Thee.

אַשְׁרֵי הָעָם, יוֹדְעֵי תְרוּעָה; יְהוָה, בְּאוֹר-פָּנֶיךָ יְהַלֵּכוּן
'ashrei ha'om yode'ei teru'ah; hashem be'or-paneicha yehallechun
Happy is the people that know the joyful shout; they walk, O LORD, in the light of Thy countenance.

בְּשִׁמְךָ, יְגִילוּן כָּל-הַיּוֹם; וּבְצִדְקָתְךָ יָרוּמוּ
beshimcha yegilun kol-hayom; uvetzidkatecha yarumu
In Thy name do they rejoice all the day; and through Thy righteousness are they exalted.

כִּי-תִפְאֶרֶת עֻזָּמוֹ אָתָּה; וּבִרְצוֹנְךָ, תָּרוּם קַרְנֵנוּ
ki-tif'eret uzzamo attah; uvirtzonecha, tarum karnenu
For Thou art the glory of their strength; and in Thy favour our horn is exalted.

כִּי לַיהוָה, מָגִנֵּנוּ; וְלִקְדוֹשׁ יִשְׂרָאֵל מַלְכֵּנוּ
ki lahashem maginnenu; velikdosh yisra'el malkenu
For of the LORD is our shield; and the Holy One of Israel is our king.

אָז דִּבַּרְתָּ בְחָזוֹן, לַחֲסִידֶיךָ--וַתֹּאמֶר
'az dibbarta-vechazon lachasideicha, vattomer
Then Thou spokest in vision to Thy godly ones, and saidst:

תְּהִלִים

סַבּוּנִי כַמַּיִם, כָּל-הַיּוֹם; הִקִּיפוּ עָלַי יָחַד
sabbuni chammayim kol-hayom; hikkifu alai yachad
They came round about me like water all the day; they compassed me about together.

הִרְחַקְתָּ מִמֶּנִּי, אֹהֵב וָרֵעַ; מְיֻדָּעַי מַחְשָׁךְ
hirchakta mimmenni ohev varea'; meyudda'ai machshach
Friend and companion hast Thou put far from me, and mine acquaintance into darkness.

פט

מַשְׂכִּיל, לְאֵיתָן הָאֶזְרָחִי
Maskil, le'eitan ha'ezrachi
Maschil of Ethan the Ezrahite.

חַסְדֵי יְהוָה, עוֹלָם אָשִׁירָה; לְדֹר וָדֹר, אוֹדִיעַ אֱמוּנָתְךָ בְּפִי
chasdei hashem olam ashirah; ledor vador odia emunatecha befi
I will sing of the mercies of the LORD for ever; to all generations will I make known Thy faithfulness with my mouth.

כִּי-אָמַרְתִּי--עוֹלָם, חֶסֶד יִבָּנֶה; שָׁמַיִם, תָּכִן אֱמוּנָתְךָ בָהֶם
ki-'amarti, olam chesed yibbaneh; shamayim tachin emunatecha vahem
For I have said: 'For ever is mercy built; in the very heavens Thou dost establish Thy faithfulness.

כָּרַתִּי בְרִית, לִבְחִירִי; נִשְׁבַּעְתִּי, לְדָוִד עַבְדִּי
karatti verit livchiri; nishba'ti, ledavid avdi
I have made a covenant with My chosen, I have sworn unto David My servant:

עַד-עוֹלָם, אָכִין זַרְעֶךָ; וּבָנִיתִי לְדֹר-וָדוֹר כִּסְאֲךָ סֶלָה
'ad-'olam achin zar'echa; uvaniti ledor-vador kis'acha selah
For ever will I establish thy seed, and build up thy throne to all generations.' Selah

וְיוֹדוּ שָׁמַיִם פִּלְאֲךָ יְהוָה; אַף-אֱמוּנָתְךָ, בִּקְהַל קְדֹשִׁים
veyodu shamayim pil'acha hashem af-'emunatecha, bik'hal kedoshim
So shall the heavens praise Thy wonders, O LORD, Thy faithfulness also in the assembly of the holy ones.

כִּי מִי בַשַּׁחַק, יַעֲרֹךְ לַיהוָה
ki mi vashachak ya'aroch lahashem
For who in the skies can be compared unto the LORD,

יִדְמֶה לַיהוָה, בִּבְנֵי אֵלִים
yidmeh lahashem bivnei elim
who among the sons of might can be likened unto the LORD,

אֵל נַעֲרָץ, בְּסוֹד-קְדֹשִׁים רַבָּה; וְנוֹרָא, עַל-כָּל-סְבִיבָיו
'el na'aratz besod-kedoshim rabbah; venora, al-kol-sevivav
A God dreaded in the great council of the holy ones, and feared of all them that are about Him?

תְּהִלִּים

עָלַי, סָמְכָה חֲמָתֶךָ; וְכָל־מִשְׁבָּרֶיךָ, עִנִּיתָ סֶּלָה
'alai samechah chamatecha; vechol-mishbareicha, innita selah
Thy wrath lieth hard upon me, and all Thy waves Thou pressest down. Selah

הִרְחַקְתָּ מְיֻדָּעַי, מִמֶּנִּי: שַׁתַּנִי תוֹעֵבוֹת לָמוֹ
hirchakta meyudda'ai, mimmenni shattani to'evot lamo
Thou hast put mine acquaintance far from me; Thou hast made me an abomination unto them;

כָּלֻא, וְלֹא אֵצֵא
kalu, velo etze
I am shut up, and I cannot come forth.

עֵינִי דָאֲבָה, מִנִּי־עֹנִי
'eini da'avah, minni oni
Mine eye languisheth by reason of affliction;

קְרָאתִיךָ יְהוָה בְּכָל־יוֹם; שִׁטַּחְתִּי אֵלֶיךָ כַפָּי
keraticha hashem bechol-yom; shittachti eleicha chappai
I have called upon Thee, O LORD, every day, I have spread forth my hands unto Thee.

הֲלַמֵּתִים תַּעֲשֶׂה־פֶּלֶא: אִם־רְפָאִים, יָקוּמוּ יוֹדוּךָ סֶּלָה
halammetim ta'aseh-pele; im-refa'im, yakumu yoducha selah
Wilt Thou work wonders for the dead? Or shall the shades arise and give Thee thanks? Selah

הַיְסֻפַּר בַּקֶּבֶר חַסְדֶּךָ; אֱמוּנָתְךָ, בָּאֲבַדּוֹן
haysuppar bakkever chasdecha; emunatecha, ba'avaddon
Shall Thy mercy be declared in the grave? or Thy faithfulness in destruction?

הֲיִוָּדַע בַּחֹשֶׁךְ פִּלְאֶךָ; וְצִדְקָתְךָ, בְּאֶרֶץ נְשִׁיָּה
hayivvada bachoshech pil'echa; vetzidkatecha, be'eretz neshiyah
Shall Thy wonders be known in the dark? and Thy righteousness in the land of forgetfulness?

וַאֲנִי, אֵלֶיךָ יְהוָה שִׁוַּעְתִּי; וּבַבֹּקֶר, תְּפִלָּתִי תְקַדְּמֶךָּ
va'ani eleicha hashem shivva'ti; uvabboker, tefillati tekaddemeka
But as for me, unto Thee, O LORD, do I cry, and in the morning doth my prayer come to meet Thee.

לָמָה יְהוָה, תִּזְנַח נַפְשִׁי; תַּסְתִּיר פָּנֶיךָ מִמֶּנִּי
lamah hashem tiznach nafshi; tastir paneicha mimmenni
LORD, why castest Thou off my soul? Why hidest Thou Thy face from me?

עָנִי אֲנִי וְגֹוֵעַ מִנֹּעַר; נָשָׂאתִי אֵמֶיךָ אָפוּנָה
'ani ani vegoa minno'ar; nasati emeicha afunah
I am afflicted and at the point of death from my youth up; I have borne Thy terrors, I am distracted.

עָלַי, עָבְרוּ חֲרוֹנֶיךָ; בִּעוּתֶיךָ, צִמְּתוּתֻנִי
'alai averu charoneicha; bi'uteicha, tzimmetutuni
Thy fierce wrath is gone over me; Thy terrors have cut me off.

תְּהִלִּים

יְהוָה--יִסְפֹּר, בִּכְתוֹב עַמִּים: זֶה יֻלַּד-שָׁם סֶלָה
hashem yispor bichtov ammim; zeh yullad-sham selah
The LORD shall count in the register of the peoples: 'This one was born there.' Selah

וְשָׁרִים כְּחֹלְלִים--כָּל-מַעְיָנַי בָּךְ
vesharim kecholelim; kol-ma'yanai bach
And whether they sing or dance, all my thoughts are in thee.

פח

שִׁיר מִזְמוֹר, לִבְנֵי-קֹרַח: לַמְנַצֵּחַ
Shir mizmor, livnei korach lamnatzeach
A Song, a Psalm of the sons of Korah; for the Leader;

עַל-מָחֲלַת לְעַנּוֹת; מַשְׂכִּיל, לְהֵימָן הָאֶזְרָחִי
al-machalat le'annot; maskil, leheiman ha'ezrachi
upon Mahalath Leannoth. Maschil of Heman the Ezrahite.

יְהוָה, אֱלֹהֵי יְשׁוּעָתִי--יוֹם-צָעַקְתִּי בַלַּיְלָה נֶגְדֶּךָ
hashem elohei yeshu'ati; yom-tza'akti vallaylah negdecha
O LORD, God of my salvation, what time I cry in the night before Thee,

תָּבוֹא לְפָנֶיךָ, תְּפִלָּתִי; הַטֵּה-אָזְנְךָ, לְרִנָּתִי.
tavo lefaneicha tefillati; hatteh-'ozenecha, lerinnati
Let my prayer come before Thee, incline Thine ear unto my cry.

כִּי-שָׂבְעָה בְרָעוֹת נַפְשִׁי; וְחַיַּי, לִשְׁאוֹל הִגִּיעוּ
ki-save'ah vera'ot nafshi; vechayai, lish'ol higgi'u
For my soul is sated with troubles, and my life draweth nigh unto the grave.

נֶחְשַׁבְתִּי, עִם-יוֹרְדֵי בוֹר; הָיִיתִי, כְּגֶבֶר אֵין-אֱיָל
nechshavti im-yoredei vor; hayiti, kegever ein-'eyal
I am counted with them that go down into the pit; I am become as a man that hath no help;

בַּמֵּתִים, חָפְשִׁי: כְּמוֹ חֲלָלִים, שֹׁכְבֵי קֶבֶר
bammetim, chafeshi kemo chalalim shochevei kever
Set apart among the dead, like the slain that lie in the grave,

אֲשֶׁר לֹא זְכַרְתָּם עוֹד; וְהֵמָּה, מִיָּדְךָ נִגְזָרוּ
asher lo zechartam od; vehemmah, miyadecha nigzaru
whom Thou rememberest no more; and they are cut off from Thy hand.

שַׁתַּנִי, בְּבוֹר תַּחְתִּיּוֹת; בְּמַחֲשַׁכִּים, בִּמְצֹלוֹת
shattani bevor tachtiyot; bemachashakkim, bimtzolot
Thou hast laid me in the nethermost pit, in dark places, in the deeps.

תְּהִלִּים

וַעֲדַת עָרִיצִים, בִּקְשׁוּ נַפְשִׁי; וְלֹא שָׂמוּךָ לְנֶגְדָּם
va'adat aritzim bikshu nafshi; velo samucha lenegdam
and the company of violent men have sought after my soul, and have not set Thee before them.

וְאַתָּה אֲדֹנָי, אֵל-רַחוּם וְחַנּוּן; אֶרֶךְ אַפַּיִם, וְרַב-חֶסֶד וֶאֱמֶת
ve'attah adonai el-rachum vechannun; erech appayim, verav-chesed ve'emet
But Thou, O Lord, art a God full of compassion and gracious, slow to anger, and plenteous in mercy and truth.

פְּנֵה אֵלַי, וְחָנֵּנִי: תְּנָה-עֻזְּךָ לְעַבְדֶּךָ; וְהוֹשִׁיעָה, לְבֶן-אֲמָתֶךָ
peneh elai, vechonneni tenah-'uzzecha le'ovdecha vehoshi'ah, leven-'amatecha
O turn unto me, and be gracious unto me; give Thy strength unto Thy servant, and save the son of Thy handmaid.

עֲשֵׂה-עִמִּי אוֹת, לְטוֹבָה: וְיִרְאוּ שֹׂנְאַי וְיֵבֹשׁוּ
'aseh-'immi ot, letovah veyir'u sone'ai veyevoshu
Work in my behalf a sign for good; that they that hate me may see it, and be put to shame,

כִּי-אַתָּה יְהוָה, עֲזַרְתַּנִי וְנִחַמְתָּנִי
ki-'attah hashem azartani venichamtani
because Thou, LORD, hast helped me, and comforted me.

פז

לִבְנֵי-קֹרַח, מִזְמוֹר שִׁיר: יְסוּדָתוֹ, בְּהַרְרֵי-קֹדֶשׁ
Livnei-korach mizmor shir; yesudato, beharerei-kodesh
A Psalm of the sons of Korah; a Song. His foundation is in the holy mountains.

אֹהֵב יְהוָה, שַׁעֲרֵי צִיּוֹן--מִכֹּל, מִשְׁכְּנוֹת יַעֲקֹב
'ohev hashem sha'arei tziyon; mikkol mishkenot ya'akov
The LORD loveth the gates of Zion more than all the dwellings of Jacob.

נִכְבָּדוֹת, מְדֻבָּר בָּךְ-- עִיר הָאֱלֹהִים סֶלָה
nichbadot medubbar bach; ir ha'elohim selah
Glorious things are spoken of thee, O city of God. Selah

אַזְכִּיר, רַהַב וּבָבֶל--לְיֹדְעָי
'azkir rahav uvavel, leyode'ai
'I will make mention of Rahab and Babylon as among them that know Me;

הִנֵּה פְלֶשֶׁת וְצֹר עִם-כּוּשׁ; זֶה, יֻלַּד-שָׁם
hinneh feleshet vetzor im-kush; zeh, yullad-sham
behold Philistia, and Tyre, with Ethiopia; this one was born there.'

וּלְצִיּוֹן, יֵאָמַר--אִישׁ וְאִישׁ, יֻלַּד-בָּהּ; וְהוּא יְכוֹנְנֶהָ עֶלְיוֹן
ulatziyon ye'amar, ish ve'ish yullad-bah; vehu yechoneneha elyon
But of Zion it shall be said: 'This man and that was born in her; and the Most High Himself doth establish her.'

תְּהִלִּים

שַׂמֵּחַ, נֶפֶשׁ עַבְדֶּךָ: כִּי אֵלֶיךָ אֲדֹנָי, נַפְשִׁי אֶשָּׂא
sammeach nefesh avdecha; ki eleicha adonai, nafshi essa
Rejoice the soul of Thy servant; for unto Thee, O Lord, do I lift up my soul.

כִּי-אַתָּה אֲדֹנָי, טוֹב וְסַלָּח; וְרַב-חֶסֶד, לְכָל-קֹרְאֶיךָ
ki-'attah adonai tov vesallach; verav-chesed, lechol-kore'eicha
For Thou, Lord, art good, and ready to pardon, and plenteous in mercy unto all them that call upon Thee.

הַאֲזִינָה יְהוָה, תְּפִלָּתִי; וְהַקְשִׁיבָה, בְּקוֹל תַּחֲנוּנוֹתָי
ha'azinah hashem tefillati; vehakshivah, bekol tachanunotai
Give ear, O LORD, unto my prayer; and attend unto the voice of my supplications.

בְּיוֹם צָרָתִי, אֶקְרָאֶךָּ: כִּי תַעֲנֵנִי
beyom tzarati ekra'eka, ki ta'aneni
In the day of my trouble I call upon Thee; for Thou wilt answer me.

אֵין-כָּמוֹךָ בָאֱלֹהִים אֲדֹנָי; וְאֵין כְּמַעֲשֶׂיךָ
'ein-kamocha va'elohim adonai, ve'ein kema'aseicha
There is none like unto Thee among the gods, O Lord, and there are no works like Thine.

כָּל-גּוֹיִם, אֲשֶׁר עָשִׂיתָ--יָבוֹאוּ וְיִשְׁתַּחֲווּ לְפָנֶיךָ אֲדֹנָי
kol-goyim asher asita, yavo'u veyishtachavu lefaneicha adonai
All nations whom Thou hast made shall come and prostrate themselves before Thee, O Lord;

וִיכַבְּדוּ לִשְׁמֶךָ
vichabbedu lishmecha
and they shall glorify Thy name.

כִּי-גָדוֹל אַתָּה, וְעֹשֵׂה נִפְלָאוֹת; אַתָּה אֱלֹהִים לְבַדֶּךָ
ki-gadol attah ve'oseh nifla'ot; attah elohim levaddecha
For Thou art great, and doest wondrous things; Thou art God alone.

הוֹרֵנִי יְהוָה, דַּרְכֶּךָ--אֲהַלֵּךְ בַּאֲמִתֶּךָ; יַחֵד לְבָבִי, לְיִרְאָה שְׁמֶךָ
horeni hashem darkecha, ahallech ba'amittecha; yached levavi, leyir'ah shemecha
Teach me, O LORD, Thy way, that I may walk in Thy truth; make one my heart to fear Thy name.

אוֹדְךָ, אֲדֹנָי אֱלֹהַי--בְּכָל-לְבָבִי; וַאֲכַבְּדָה שִׁמְךָ לְעוֹלָם
'odecha adonai elohai bechol-levavi; va'achabbedah shimcha le'olam
I will thank Thee, O Lord my God, with my whole heart; and I will glorify Thy name for evermore.

כִּי-חַסְדְּךָ, גָּדוֹל עָלָי; וְהִצַּלְתָּ נַפְשִׁי, מִשְּׁאוֹל תַּחְתִּיָּה
ki-chasdecha gadol alai; vehitzalta nafshi, mishe'ol tachtiyah
For great is Thy mercy toward me; and Thou hast delivered my soul from the lowest nether-world.

אֱלֹהִים, זֵדִים קָמוּ-עָלַי
'elohim zedim kamu-'alai
O God, the proud are risen up against me,

תְּהִלִּים

הַרְאֵנוּ יְהוָה חַסְדֶּךָ; וְיֶשְׁעֲךָ, תִּתֶּן-לָנוּ
har'enu hashem chasdecha; veyesh'acha, titten-lanu
Show us Thy mercy, O LORD, and grant us Thy salvation.

אֶשְׁמְעָה--מַה-יְדַבֵּר, הָאֵל יְהוָה: כִּי, יְדַבֵּר שָׁלוֹם--אֶל-עַמּוֹ וְאֶל-חֲסִידָיו
'eshme'ah, mah-yedabber ha'el hashem ki yedabber shalom, el-'ammo ve'el-chasidav
I will hear what God the LORD will speak; for He will speak peace unto His people, and to His saints;

וְאַל-יָשׁוּבוּ לְכִסְלָה
ve'al-yashuvu lechislah
but let them not turn back to folly.

אַךְ קָרוֹב לִירֵאָיו יִשְׁעוֹ; לִשְׁכֹּן כָּבוֹד בְּאַרְצֵנוּ
'ach karov lire'av yish'o; lishkon kavod be'artzenu
Surely His salvation is nigh them that fear Him; that glory may dwell in our land.

חֶסֶד-וֶאֱמֶת נִפְגָּשׁוּ; צֶדֶק וְשָׁלוֹם נָשָׁקוּ
chesed-ve'emet nifgashu; tzedek veshalom nashaku
Mercy and truth are met together; righteousness and peace have kissed each other.

אֱמֶת, מֵאֶרֶץ תִּצְמָח; וְצֶדֶק, מִשָּׁמַיִם נִשְׁקָף
'emet me'eretz titzmach; vetzedek, mishamayim nishkaf
Truth springeth out of the earth; and righteousness hath looked down from heaven.

גַּם-יְהוָה, יִתֵּן הַטּוֹב; וְאַרְצֵנוּ, תִּתֵּן יְבוּלָהּ
gam-hashem yitten hattov; ve'artzenu, titten yevulah
Yea, the LORD will give that which is good; and our land shall yield her produce.

צֶדֶק, לְפָנָיו יְהַלֵּךְ; וְיָשֵׂם לְדֶרֶךְ פְּעָמָיו
tzedek lefanav yehallech; veyasem lederech pe'amav
Righteousness shall go before Him, and shall make His footsteps a way.

פו

תְּפִלָּה, לְדָוִד: הַטֵּה-יְהוָה אָזְנְךָ עֲנֵנִי--כִּי-עָנִי וְאֶבְיוֹן אָנִי
Tefillah, ledavid: hatteh-hashem azenecha aneni; ki-'ani ve'evyon ani
A Prayer of David. Incline Thine ear, O LORD, and answer me; for I am poor and needy.

שָׁמְרָה נַפְשִׁי, כִּי-חָסִיד אָנִי: הוֹשַׁע עַבְדְּךָ, אַתָּה אֱלֹהַי--הַבּוֹטֵחַ אֵלֶיךָ
shamerah nafshi ki-chasid ani hosha avdecha attah elohai; habboteach eleicha
Keep my soul, for I am godly; O Thou my God, save Thy servant that trusteth in Thee.

חָנֵּנִי אֲדֹנָי: כִּי אֵלֶיךָ אֶקְרָא, כָּל-הַיּוֹם
chonneni adonai; ki eleicha ekra, kol-hayom
Be gracious unto me, O Lord; for unto Thee do I cry all the day.

תְּהִלִּים

כִּי שֶׁמֶשׁ, וּמָגֵן--יְהוָה אֱלֹהִים
ki shemesh umagen hashem elohim
For the LORD God is a sun and a shield

חֵן וְכָבוֹד, יִתֵּן יְהוָה
chen vechavod yitten hashem
the LORD giveth grace and glory;

לֹא יִמְנַע-טוֹב, לַהֹלְכִים בְּתָמִים
lo yimna'-tov, laholechim betamim
no good thing will He withhold from them that walk uprightly.

יְהוָה צְבָאוֹת--אַשְׁרֵי אָדָם, בֹּטֵחַ בָּךְ
hashem tzeva'ot; ashrei adam, boteach bach
O LORD of hosts, happy is the man that trusteth in Thee.

פה

לַמְנַצֵּחַ לִבְנֵי-קֹרַח מִזְמוֹר
Lamnatzeach livnei-korach mizmor
For the Leader. A Psalm of the sons of Korah.

רָצִיתָ יְהוָה אַרְצֶךָ; שַׁבְתָּ, שְׁבִית יַעֲקֹב
ratzita hashem artzecha; shavta, shevit ya'akov
LORD, Thou hast been favourable unto Thy land, Thou hast turned the captivity of Jacob.

נָשָׂאתָ, עֲוֺן עַמֶּךָ; כִּסִּיתָ כָל-חַטָּאתָם סֶלָה
nasata avon ammecha; kissita chol-chattatam selah
Thou hast forgiven the iniquity of Thy people, Thou hast pardoned all their sin. Selah

אָסַפְתָּ כָל-עֶבְרָתֶךָ; הֱשִׁיבוֹתָ, מֵחֲרוֹן אַפֶּךָ
'asafta chol-'evratecha; heshivota, mecharon appecha
Thou hast withdrawn all Thy wrath; Thou hast turned from the fierceness of Thine anger.

שׁוּבֵנוּ, אֱלֹהֵי יִשְׁעֵנוּ; וְהָפֵר כַּעַסְךָ עִמָּנוּ
shuvenu elohei yish'enu; vehafer ka'ascha immanu
Restore us, O God of our salvation, and cause Thine indignation toward us to cease.

הַלְעוֹלָם תֶּאֱנַף-בָּנוּ; תִּמְשֹׁךְ אַפְּךָ, לְדֹר וָדֹר
hale'olam te'enaf-banu; timshoch appecha, ledor vador
Wilt Thou be angry with us for ever? Wilt Thou draw out Thine anger to all generations?

הֲלֹא-אַתָּה, תָּשׁוּב תְּחַיֵּנוּ; וְעַמְּךָ, יִשְׂמְחוּ-בָךְ
halo-'attah tashuv techayenu; ve'ammecha, yismechu-vach
Wilt Thou not quicken us again, that Thy people may rejoice in Thee?

תְּהִלִּים

מַה-יְּדִידוֹת מִשְׁכְּנוֹתֶיךָ--יְהוָה צְבָאוֹת
mah-yedidot mishkenoteicha, hashem tzeva'ot
How lovely are Thy tabernacles, O LORD of hosts!

נִכְסְפָה וְגַם-כָּלְתָה, נַפְשִׁי-- לְחַצְרוֹת יְהוָה: לִבִּי וּבְשָׂרִי-- יְרַנְּנוּ, אֶל אֵל-חָי
nichsefah vegam-kaletah nafshi lechatzrot hashem libbi uvesari; yerannenu, el el-chai
My soul yearneth, yea, even pineth for the courts of the LORD; my heart and my flesh sing for joy unto the living God.

גַּם-צִפּוֹר מָצְאָה בַיִת, וּדְרוֹר קֵן לָהּ--אֲשֶׁר-שָׁתָה אֶפְרֹחֶיהָ
gam-tzippor matze'ah vayit uderor ken lah asher-shatah efrocheiha
Yea, the sparrow hath found a house, and the swallow a nest for herself, where she may lay her young;

אֶת-מִזְבְּחוֹתֶיךָ, יְהוָה צְבָאוֹת-- מַלְכִּי, וֵאלֹהָי
et-mizbechoteicha hashem tzeva'ot; malki, velohai
Thine altars, O LORD of hosts, my King, and my God--.

אַשְׁרֵי, יוֹשְׁבֵי בֵיתֶךָ--עוֹד, יְהַלְלוּךָ סֶּלָה
'ashrei yoshevei veitecha; od, yehalelucha selah
Happy are they that dwell in Thy house, they are ever praising Thee. Selah

אַשְׁרֵי אָדָם, עוֹז-לוֹ בָךְ; מְסִלּוֹת, בִּלְבָבָם
'ashrei adam oz-lo vach; mesillot, bilvavam
Happy is the man whose strength is in Thee; in whose heart are the highways.

עֹבְרֵי, בְּעֵמֶק הַבָּכָא-- מַעְיָן יְשִׁיתוּהוּ; גַּם-בְּרָכוֹת, יַעְטֶה מוֹרֶה
'overei be'emek habbacha ma'yan yeshituhu; gam-berachot, ya'teh moreh
Passing through the valley of Baca they make it a place of springs; yea, the early rain clotheth it with blessings.

יֵלְכוּ, מֵחַיִל אֶל-חָיִל; יֵרָאֶה אֶל-אֱלֹהִים בְּצִיּוֹן
yelechu mechayil el-chayil; yera'eh el-'elohim betziyon
They go from strength to strength, every one of them appeareth before God in Zion.

יְהוָה אֱלֹהִים צְבָאוֹת, שִׁמְעָה תְפִלָּתִי; הַאֲזִינָה אֱלֹהֵי יַעֲקֹב סֶלָה
hashem elohim tzeva'ot shim'ah tefillati; ha'azinah elohei ya'akov selah
O LORD God of hosts, hear my prayer; give ear, O God of Jacob. Selah

מָגִנֵּנוּ, רְאֵה אֱלֹהִים; וְהַבֵּט, פְּנֵי מְשִׁיחֶךָ
maginnenu re'eh elohim; vehabbet, penei meshichecha
Behold, O God our shield, and look upon the face of Thine anointed.

כִּי טוֹב-יוֹם בַּחֲצֵרֶיךָ, מֵאָלֶף
ki tov-yom bachatzereicha, me'alef
For a day in Thy courts is better than a thousand;

בָּחַרְתִּי--הִסְתּוֹפֵף, בְּבֵית אֱלֹהַי; מִדּוּר, בְּאָהֳלֵי-רֶשַׁע
bacharti, histofef beveit elohai; middur, be'oholei-resha
I had rather stand at the threshold of the house of my God, than to dwell in the tents of wickedness.

תְּהִלִּים

עֲשֵׂה-לָהֶם כְּמִדְיָן; כְּסִיסְרָא כְיָבִין, בְּנַחַל קִישׁוֹן
'aseh-lahem kemidyan; kesisera cheyavin, benachal kishon
Do Thou unto them as unto Midian; as to Sisera, as to Jabin, at the brook Kishon;

נִשְׁמְדוּ בְעֵין-דֹּאר; הָיוּ דֹּמֶן, לָאֲדָמָה
nishmedu ve'ein-dor; hayu domen, la'adamah
Who were destroyed at En-dor; they became as dung for the earth.

שִׁיתֵמוֹ נְדִיבֵימוֹ, כְּעֹרֵב וְכִזְאֵב; וּכְזֶבַח וּכְצַלְמֻנָּע, כָּל-נְסִיכֵימוֹ
shitemo nedivemo ke'orev vechiz'ev; uchezevach uchetzalmunna', kol-nesichemo
Make their nobles like Oreb and Zeeb, and like Zebah and Zalmunna all their princes;

אֲשֶׁר אָמְרוּ, נִירְשָׁה לָּנוּ--אֵת, נְאוֹת אֱלֹהִים
'asher ameru nirashah lanu; et, ne'ot elohim
Who said: 'Let us take to ourselves in possession the habitations of God.'

אֱלֹהַי, שִׁיתֵמוֹ כַגַּלְגַּל; כְּקַשׁ, לִפְנֵי-רוּחַ
'elohai, shitemo chaggalgal; kekash, lifnei-ruach
O my God, make them like the whirling dust; as stubble before the wind.

כְּאֵשׁ תִּבְעַר-יָעַר; וּכְלֶהָבָה, תְּלַהֵט הָרִים
ke'esh tiv'ar-ya'ar; uchelehavah, telahet harim
As the fire that burneth the forest, and as the flame that setteth the mountains ablaze;

כֵּן, תִּרְדְּפֵם בְּסַעֲרֶךָ; וּבְסוּפָתְךָ תְבַהֲלֵם
ken tirdefem besa'arecha; uvesufatecha tevahalem
So pursue them with Thy tempest, and affright them with Thy storm.

מַלֵּא פְנֵיהֶם קָלוֹן; וִיבַקְשׁוּ שִׁמְךָ יְהוָה
mallei feneihem kalon; viyvakshu shimcha hashem
Fill their faces with shame; that they may seek Thy name, O LORD.

יֵבֹשׁוּ וְיִבָּהֲלוּ עֲדֵי-עַד; וְיַחְפְּרוּ וְיֹאבֵדוּ
yevoshu veyibbahalu adei-'ad, veyachperu veyovedu
Let them be ashamed and affrighted for ever; yea, let them be abashed and perish;

וְיֵדְעוּ--כִּי-אַתָּה שִׁמְךָ יְהוָה לְבַדֶּךָ: עֶלְיוֹן, עַל-כָּל-הָאָרֶץ
veyede'u, ki-'attah shimcha hashem levaddecha; elyon, al-kol-ha'aretz
That they may know that it is Thou alone whose name is the LORD, the Most High over all the earth.

פד

לַמְנַצֵּחַ עַל-הַגִּתִּית; לִבְנֵי-קֹרַח מִזְמוֹר
Lamnatzeach al-haggittit; livnei-korach mizmor
For the Leader; upon the Gittith. A Psalm of the sons of Korah.

תְּהִלִּים

קוּמָה אֱלֹהִים, שָׁפְטָה הָאָרֶץ: כִּי-אַתָּה תִנְחַל, בְּכָל-הַגּוֹיִם
kumah elohim shafetah ha'aretz; ki-'attah tinchal, bechol-haggoyim
Arise, O God, judge the earth; for Thou shalt possess all the nations.

פג

שִׁיר מִזְמוֹר לְאָסָף
Shir mizmor le'asaf
A Song, a Psalm of Asaph.

אֱלֹהִים אַל-דֳּמִי-לָךְ; אַל-תֶּחֱרַשׁ וְאַל-תִּשְׁקֹט אֵל
'elohim al-domi-lach; al-techerash ve'al-tishkot el
O God, keep not Thou silence; hold not Thy peace, and be not still, O God.

כִּי-הִנֵּה אוֹיְבֶיךָ, יֶהֱמָיוּן; וּמְשַׂנְאֶיךָ, נָשְׂאוּ רֹאשׁ
ki-hinneh oyeveicha yehemayun; umesan'eicha, nase'u rosh
For, lo, Thine enemies are in an uproar; and they that hate Thee have lifted up the head.

עַל-עַמְּךָ, יַעֲרִימוּ סוֹד; וְיִתְיָעֲצוּ, עַל-צְפוּנֶיךָ
'al-'ammecha ya'arimu sod; veyitya'atzu, al-tzefuneicha
They hold crafty converse against Thy people, and take counsel against Thy treasured ones.

אָמְרוּ--לְכוּ, וְנַכְחִידֵם מִגּוֹי
'ameru, lechu venachchidem miggoy
They have said: 'Come, and let us cut them off from being a nation;

וְלֹא-יִזָּכֵר שֵׁם-יִשְׂרָאֵל עוֹד
velo-yizzacher shem-yisra'el od
that the name of Israel may be no more in remembrance.'

כִּי נוֹעֲצוּ לֵב יַחְדָּו; עָלֶיךָ, בְּרִית יִכְרֹתוּ
ki no'atzu lev yachdav; aleicha, berit yichrotu
For they have consulted together with one consent; against Thee do they make a covenant;

אָהֳלֵי אֱדוֹם, וְיִשְׁמְעֵאלִים; מוֹאָב וְהַגְרִים
'aholei edom veyishme'elim, mo'av vehagrim
The tents of Edom and the Ishmaelites; Moab, and the Hagrites;

גְּבָל וְעַמּוֹן, וַעֲמָלֵק; פְּלֶשֶׁת, עִם-יֹשְׁבֵי צוֹר
geval ve'ammon va'amalek; peleshet, im-yoshevei tzor
Gebal, and Ammon, and Amalek; Philistia with the inhabitants of Tyre;

גַּם-אַשּׁוּר, נִלְוָה עִמָּם; הָיוּ זְרוֹעַ לִבְנֵי-לוֹט סֶלָה
gam-'ashur nilvah immam; hayu zeroa livnei-lot selah
Assyria also is joined with them; they have been an arm to the children of Lot. Selah

תְּהִלִּים

לוּ--עַמִּי, שֹׁמֵעַ לִי; יִשְׂרָאֵל, בִּדְרָכַי יְהַלֵּכוּ
lu, ammi shomea li; yisra'el, bidrachai yehallechu
Oh that My people would hearken unto Me, that Israel would walk in My ways!

כִּמְעַט, אוֹיְבֵיהֶם אַכְנִיעַ; וְעַל צָרֵיהֶם, אָשִׁיב יָדִי
kim'at oyeveihem achnia'; ve'al tzareihem, ashiv yadi
I would soon subdue their enemies, and turn My hand against their adversaries.

מְשַׂנְאֵי יְהוָה, יְכַחֲשׁוּ-לוֹ; וִיהִי עִתָּם לְעוֹלָם
mesan'ei hashem yechachashu-lo; vihi ittam le'olam
The haters of the LORD should dwindle away before Him; and their punishment should endure for ever.

וַיַּאֲכִילֵהוּ, מֵחֵלֶב חִטָּה; וּמִצּוּר, דְּבַשׁ אַשְׂבִּיעֶךָ
vaya'achilehu mechelev chittah; umitzur, devash asbi'echa
They should also be fed with the fat of wheat; and with honey out of the rock would I satisfy thee.'

פב

מִזְמוֹר, לְאָסָף: אֱלֹהִים, נִצָּב בַּעֲדַת-אֵל; בְּקֶרֶב אֱלֹהִים יִשְׁפֹּט
Mizmor, le'asaf: elohim, nitzav ba'adat-'el; bekerev elohim yishpot
A Psalm of Asaph. God standeth in the congregation of God; in the midst of the judges He judgeth:

עַד-מָתַי תִּשְׁפְּטוּ-עָוֶל; וּפְנֵי רְשָׁעִים, תִּשְׂאוּ-סֶלָה
'ad-matai tishpetu-'avel; ufenei resha'im, tis'u-selah
'How long will ye judge unjustly, and respect the persons of the wicked? Selah

שִׁפְטוּ-דַל וְיָתוֹם; עָנִי וָרָשׁ הַצְדִּיקוּ
shiftu-dal veyatom; ani varash hatzdiku
Judge the poor and fatherless; do justice to the afflicted and destitute.

פַּלְּטוּ-דַל וְאֶבְיוֹן; מִיַּד רְשָׁעִים הַצִּילוּ
palletu-dal ve'evyon; miyad resha'im hatzilu
Rescue the poor and needy; deliver them out of the hand of the wicked.

לֹא יָדְעוּ, וְלֹא יָבִינוּ--בַּחֲשֵׁכָה יִתְהַלָּכוּ; יִמּוֹטוּ, כָּל-מוֹסְדֵי אָרֶץ
lo yade'u velo yavinu, bachashechah yit'hallachu; yimmotu, kol-mosedei aretz
They know not, neither do they understand; they go about in darkness; all the foundations of the earth are moved.

אֲנִי-אָמַרְתִּי, אֱלֹהִים אַתֶּם; וּבְנֵי עֶלְיוֹן כֻּלְּכֶם
'ani-'amarti elohim attem; uvenei elyon kullechem
I said: Ye are godlike beings, and all of you sons of the Most High.

אָכֵן, כְּאָדָם תְּמוּתוּן; וּכְאַחַד הַשָּׂרִים תִּפֹּלוּ
'achen ke'adam temutun; uche'achad hassarim tippolu
Nevertheless ye shall die like men, and fall like one of the princes.'

תְּהִלִּים

תִּקְעוּ בַחֹדֶשׁ שׁוֹפָר; בַּכֵּסֶה, לְיוֹם חַגֵּנוּ
tik'u vachodesh shofar; bakkeseh, leyom chaggenu
Blow the horn at the new moon, at the full moon for our feast-day.

כִּי חֹק לְיִשְׂרָאֵל הוּא; מִשְׁפָּט, לֵאלֹהֵי יַעֲקֹב
ki chok leyisra'el hu; mishpat, lelohei ya'akov
For it is a statute for Israel, an ordinance of the God of Jacob.

עֵדוּת, בִּיהוֹסֵף שָׂמוֹ--בְּצֵאתוֹ, עַל-אֶרֶץ מִצְרָיִם
'edut bihosef samo, betzeto al-'eretz mitzrayim
He appointed it in Joseph for a testimony, when He went forth against the land of Egypt.

שְׂפַת לֹא-יָדַעְתִּי אֶשְׁמָע
sefat lo-yada'ti eshma
The speech of one that I knew not did I hear:

הֲסִירוֹתִי מִסֵּבֶל שִׁכְמוֹ; כַּפָּיו, מִדּוּד תַּעֲבֹרְנָה
hasiroti missevel shichmo; kappav, middud ta'avorenah
'I removed his shoulder from the burden; his hands were freed from the basket.

בַּצָּרָה קָרָאתָ, וָאֲחַלְּצֶךָּ: אֶעֶנְךָ, בְּסֵתֶר רַעַם
batzarah karata, va'achalletzeka e'encha beseter ra'am
Thou didst call in trouble, and I rescued thee; I answered thee in the secret place of thunder;

אֶבְחָנְךָ עַל-מֵי מְרִיבָה סֶלָה
evchonecha al-mei merivah selah
I proved thee at the waters of Meribah. Selah

שְׁמַע עַמִּי, וְאָעִידָה בָּךְ; יִשְׂרָאֵל, אִם-תִּשְׁמַע-לִי
shema ammi ve'a'idah bach; yisra'el, im-tishma'-li
Hear, O My people, and I will admonish thee: O Israel, if thou wouldest hearken unto Me!

לֹא-יִהְיֶה בְךָ, אֵל זָר; וְלֹא תִשְׁתַּחֲוֶה, לְאֵל נֵכָר
lo-yihyeh vecha el zar; velo tishtachaveh, le'el nechar
There shall no strange god be in thee; neither shalt thou worship any foreign god.

אָנֹכִי, יְהוָה אֱלֹהֶיךָ--הַמַּעַלְךָ, מֵאֶרֶץ מִצְרָיִם; הַרְחֶב-פִּיךָ, וַאֲמַלְאֵהוּ
'anochi hashem eloheicha, hamma'alcha me'eretz mitzrayim; harchev-picha, va'amal'ehu
I am the LORD thy God, who brought thee up out of the land of Egypt; open thy mouth wide, and I will fill it.

וְלֹא-שָׁמַע עַמִּי לְקוֹלִי; וְיִשְׂרָאֵל, לֹא-אָבָה לִי
velo-shama ammi lekoli; veyisra'el, lo-'avah li
But My people hearkened not to My voice; and Israel would none of Me.

וָאֲשַׁלְּחֵהוּ, בִּשְׁרִירוּת לִבָּם; יֵלְכוּ, בְּמוֹעֲצוֹתֵיהֶם
va'ashallechehu bishrirut libbam; yelechu, bemo'atzoteihem
So I let them go after the stubbornness of their heart, that they might walk in their own counsels.

תְּהִלִּים

לָמָּה, פָּרַצְתָּ גְדֵרֶיהָ; וְאָרוּהָ, כָּל-עֹבְרֵי דָרֶךְ.
lammah paratzta gedereiha; ve'aruha, kol-'overei darech
Why hast Thou broken down her fences, so that all they that pass by the way do pluck her?

יְכַרְסְמֶנָּה חֲזִיר מִיָּעַר; וְזִיז שָׂדַי יִרְעֶנָּה
yecharsemennah chazir miya'ar; veziz sadai yir'ennah
The boar out of the wood doth ravage it, that which moveth in the field feedeth on it.

אֱלֹהִים צְבָאוֹת, שׁוּב-נָא: הַבֵּט מִשָּׁמַיִם וּרְאֵה; וּפְקֹד, גֶּפֶן זֹאת
'elohim tzeva'ot shuv-na habbet mishamayim ure'eh; ufekod, gefen zot
O God of hosts, return, we beseech Thee; look from heaven, and behold, and be mindful of this vine,

וְכַנָּה, אֲשֶׁר-נָטְעָה יְמִינֶךָ; וְעַל-בֵּן, אִמַּצְתָּה לָּךְ
vechannah asher-nate'ah yeminecha; ve'al-ben, immatztah lach
And of the stock which Thy right hand hath planted, and the branch that Thou madest strong for Thyself.

שְׂרֻפָה בָאֵשׁ כְּסוּחָה; מִגַּעֲרַת פָּנֶיךָ יֹאבֵדוּ
serufah va'esh kesuchah; migga'arat paneicha yovedu
It is burned with fire, it is cut down; they perish at the rebuke of Thy countenance.

תְּהִי-יָדְךָ, עַל-אִישׁ יְמִינֶךָ; עַל-בֶּן-אָדָם, אִמַּצְתָּ לָּךְ
tehi-yadecha al-'ish yeminecha; al-ben-'adam, immatzta lach
Let Thy hand be upon the man of Thy right hand, upon the son of man whom Thou madest strong for Thyself.

וְלֹא-נָסוֹג מִמֶּךָּ; תְּחַיֵּנוּ, וּבְשִׁמְךָ נִקְרָא
velo-nasog mimmeka; techayenu, uveshimcha nikra
So shall we not turn back from Thee; quicken Thou us, and we will call upon Thy name.

יְהוָה אֱלֹהִים צְבָאוֹת הֲשִׁיבֵנוּ; הָאֵר פָּנֶיךָ, וְנִוָּשֵׁעָה
hashem elohim tzeva'ot hashivenu; ha'er paneicha, venivvashe'ah
O LORD God of hosts, restore us; cause Thy face to shine, and we shall be saved.

פא

לַמְנַצֵּחַ עַל-הַגִּתִּית לְאָסָף
Lamnatzeach al-haggittit le'asaf
For the Leader; upon the Gittith. [A Psalm] of Asaph.

הַרְנִינוּ, לֵאלֹהִים עוּזֵּנוּ; הָרִיעוּ, לֵאלֹהֵי יַעֲקֹב
harninu le'elohim uzzenu; hari'u, le'elohei ya'akov
Sing aloud unto God our strength; shout unto the God of Jacob.

שְׂאוּ-זִמְרָה, וּתְנוּ-תֹף; כִּנּוֹר נָעִים עִם-נָבֶל
se'u-zimrah utenu-tof; kinnor na'im im-navel
Take up the melody, and sound the timbrel, the sweet harp with the psaltery.

תְּהִלִּים

רֹעֵה יִשְׂרָאֵל, הַאֲזִינָה--נֹהֵג כַּצֹּאן יוֹסֵף
ro'eh yisra'el ha'azinah, noheg katzon yosef
Give ear, O Shepherd of Israel, Thou that leadest Joseph like a flock;

יֹשֵׁב הַכְּרוּבִים הוֹפִיעָה
yoshev hakkeruvim hofi'ah
Thou that art enthroned upon the cherubim, shine forth.

לִפְנֵי אֶפְרַיִם, וּבִנְיָמִן וּמְנַשֶּׁה--עוֹרְרָה אֶת-גְּבוּרָתֶךָ; וּלְכָה לִישֻׁעָתָה לָּנוּ
lifnei efrayim uvinyamin umenasheh, orerah et-gevuratecha; ulechah lishu'atah lanu
Before Ephraim and Benjamin and Manasseh, stir up Thy might, and come to save us.

אֱלֹהִים הֲשִׁיבֵנוּ; וְהָאֵר פָּנֶיךָ, וְנִוָּשֵׁעָה
'elohim hashivenu; veha'er paneicha, venivvashe'ah
O God, restore us; and cause Thy face to shine, and we shall be saved.

יְהוָה אֱלֹהִים צְבָאוֹת--עַד-מָתַי עָשַׁנְתָּ, בִּתְפִלַּת עַמֶּךָ
hashem elohim tzeva'ot; ad-matai ashanta, bitfillat ammecha
O LORD God of hosts, how long wilt Thou be angry against the prayer of Thy people?

הֶאֱכַלְתָּם, לֶחֶם דִּמְעָה; וַתַּשְׁקֵמוֹ, בִּדְמָעוֹת שָׁלִישׁ
he'echaltam lechem dim'ah; vattashkemo, bidma'ot shalish
Thou hast fed them with the bread of tears, and given them tears to drink in large measure.

תְּשִׂימֵנוּ מָדוֹן, לִשְׁכֵנֵינוּ; וְאֹיְבֵינוּ, יִלְעֲגוּ-לָמוֹ
tesimenu madon lishcheneinu; ve'oyeveinu, yil'agu-lamo
Thou makest us a strife unto our neighbours; and our enemies mock as they please.

אֱלֹהִים צְבָאוֹת הֲשִׁיבֵנוּ; וְהָאֵר פָּנֶיךָ, וְנִוָּשֵׁעָה
'elohim tzeva'ot hashivenu; veha'er paneicha, venivvashe'ah
O God of hosts, restore us; and cause Thy face to shine, and we shall be saved.

גֶּפֶן, מִמִּצְרַיִם תַּסִּיעַ; תְּגָרֵשׁ גּוֹיִם, וַתִּטָּעֶהָ
gefen mimmitzrayim tassia'; tegaresh goyim, vattitta'eha
Thou didst pluck up a vine out of Egypt; Thou didst drive out the nations, and didst plant it.

פִּנִּיתָ לְפָנֶיהָ; וַתַּשְׁרֵשׁ שָׁרָשֶׁיהָ, וַתְּמַלֵּא-אָרֶץ
pinnita lefaneiha; vattashresh sharasheiha, vattemalle-'aretz
Thou didst clear a place before it, and it took deep root, and filled the land.

כָּסּוּ הָרִים צִלָּהּ; וַעֲנָפֶיהָ, אַרְזֵי-אֵל
kassu harim tzillah; va'anafeiha, arzei-'el
The mountains were covered with the shadow of it, and the mighty cedars with the boughs thereof.

תְּשַׁלַּח קְצִירֶהָ עַד-יָם; וְאֶל-נָהָר, יוֹנְקוֹתֶיהָ
teshallach ketzireha ad-yam; ve'el-nahar, yonekoteiha
She sent out her branches unto the sea, and her shoots unto the River.

תְּהִלִּים

עָזְרֵנוּ, אֱלֹהֵי יִשְׁעֵנוּ--עַל-דְּבַר כְּבוֹד-שְׁמֶךָ
'ozerenu elohei yish'enu, al-devar kevod-shemecha
Help us, O God of our salvation, for the sake of the glory of Thy name;

וְהַצִּילֵנוּ וְכַפֵּר עַל-חַטֹּאתֵינוּ, לְמַעַן שְׁמֶךָ
vehatzilenu vechapper al-chattoteinu, lema'an shemecha
and deliver us, and forgive our sins, for Thy name's sake.

לָמָּה, יֹאמְרוּ הַגּוֹיִם--אַיֵּה אֱלֹהֵיהֶם
lammah yomeru haggoyim ayeh eloheihem
Wherefore should the nations say: 'Where is their God?'

יִוָּדַע בַּגֹּיִים לְעֵינֵינוּ; נִקְמַת, דַּם-עֲבָדֶיךָ הַשָּׁפוּךְ
yivvada baggoyim baggoyim le'eineinu; nikmat, dam-'avadeicha hashafuch
Let the avenging of Thy servants' blood that is shed be made known among the nations in our sight.

תָּבוֹא לְפָנֶיךָ, אֶנְקַת אָסִיר
tavo lefaneicha enkat asir
Let the groaning of the prisoner come before Thee;

כְּגֹדֶל זְרוֹעֲךָ--הוֹתֵר, בְּנֵי תְמוּתָה
kegodel zero'acha; hoter, benei temutah
according to the greatness of Thy power set free those that are appointed to death;

וְהָשֵׁב לִשְׁכֵנֵינוּ שִׁבְעָתַיִם, אֶל-חֵיקָם; חֶרְפָּתָם
vehashev lishcheneinu shiv'atayim el-cheikam; cherpatam
And render unto our neighbours sevenfold into their bosom their reproach,

אֲשֶׁר חֵרְפוּךָ אֲדֹנָי
asher cherefucha adonai
wherewith they have reproached Thee, O Lord.

וַאֲנַחְנוּ עַמְּךָ, וְצֹאן מַרְעִיתֶךָ--נוֹדֶה לְּךָ, לְעוֹלָם
va'anachnu ammecha vetzon mar'itecha nodeh lecha, le'olam
So we that are Thy people and the flock of Thy pasture will give Thee thanks for ever;

לְדוֹר וָדֹר--נְסַפֵּר, תְּהִלָּתֶךָ
ledor vador nesapper, tehillatecha
we will tell of Thy praise to all generations.

פ

לַמְנַצֵּחַ אֶל-שֹׁשַׁנִּים; עֵדוּת לְאָסָף מִזְמוֹר
Lamnatzeach el-shoshannim; edut le'asaf mizmor
For the Leader; upon Shoshannim. A testimony. A Psalm of Asaph.

תְּהִלִּים

עט

מִזְמוֹר, לְאָסָף: אֱלֹהִים, בָּאוּ גוֹיִם בְּנַחֲלָתֶךָ
Mizmor, le'asaf: elohim ba'u goyim benachalatecha
A Psalm of Asaph. O God, the heathen are come into Thine inheritance;

טִמְּאוּ, אֶת הֵיכַל קָדְשֶׁךָ; שָׂמוּ אֶת-יְרוּשָׁלִַם לְעִיִּים
timme'u et-heichal kodshecha samu et-yerushalayim le'iyim
they have defiled Thy holy temple; they have made Jerusalem into heaps.

נָתְנוּ, אֶת-נִבְלַת עֲבָדֶיךָ--מַאֲכָל, לְעוֹף הַשָּׁמָיִם
natenu et-nivlat avadeicha, ma'achol le'of hashamayim
They have given the dead bodies of Thy servants to be food unto the fowls of the heaven,

בְּשַׂר חֲסִידֶיךָ, לְחַיְתוֹ-אָרֶץ
besar chasideicha, lechayto-'aretz
the flesh of Thy saints unto the beasts of the earth.

שָׁפְכוּ דָמָם, כַּמַּיִם--סְבִיבוֹת יְרוּשָׁלִָם; וְאֵין קוֹבֵר
shafechu damam kammayim, sevivot yerushalayim, ve'ein kover
They have shed their blood like water round about Jerusalem, with none to bury them.

הָיִינוּ חֶרְפָּה, לִשְׁכֵנֵינוּ; לַעַג וָקֶלֶס, לִסְבִיבוֹתֵינוּ
hayinu cherpah lishcheneinu; la'ag vakeles, lisvivoteinu
We are become a taunt to our neighbours, a scorn and derision to them that are round about us.

עַד-מָה יְהוָה, תֶּאֱנַף לָנֶצַח; תִּבְעַר כְּמוֹ-אֵשׁ, קִנְאָתֶךָ
'ad-mah hashem te'enaf lanetzach; tiv'ar kemo-'esh, kin'atecha
How long, O LORD, wilt Thou be angry for ever? How long will Thy jealousy burn like fire?

שְׁפֹךְ חֲמָתְךָ--אֶל הַגּוֹיִם, אֲשֶׁר לֹא-יְדָעוּךָ: וְעַל מַמְלָכוֹת--אֲשֶׁר בְּשִׁמְךָ, לֹא קָרָאוּ.
shefoch chamatecha el-haggoyim asher lo-yeda'ucha ve'al mamlachot; asher beshimcha, lo kara'u
Pour out Thy wrath upon the nations that know Thee not, and upon the kingdoms that call not upon Thy name.

כִּי, אָכַל אֶת-יַעֲקֹב; וְאֶת-נָוֵהוּ הֵשַׁמּוּ
ki achal et-ya'akov; ve'et-navehu heshammu
For they have devoured Jacob, and laid waste his habitation.

אַל-תִּזְכָּר-לָנוּ, עֲוֺנֹת רִאשֹׁנִים
'al-tizkor-lanu avonot rishonim
Remember not against us the iniquities of our forefathers;

מַהֵר, יְקַדְּמוּנוּ רַחֲמֶיךָ--כִּי דַלּוֹנוּ מְאֹד
maher yekaddemunu rachameicha; ki dallonu me'od
let Thy compassions speedily come to meet us; for we are brought very low.

תְּהִלִּים

וַיִּתֵּן לַשְּׁבִי עֻזּוֹ; וְתִפְאַרְתּוֹ בְיַד-צָר
vayitten lashevi uzzo; vetif'arto veyad-tzar
And delivered His strength into captivity, and His glory into the adversary's hand.

וַיַּסְגֵּר לַחֶרֶב עַמּוֹ; וּבְנַחֲלָתוֹ, הִתְעַבָּר
vayasger lacherev ammo; uvenachalato, hit'abbar
He gave His people over also unto the sword; and was wroth with His inheritance.

בַּחוּרָיו אָכְלָה-אֵשׁ; וּבְתוּלֹתָיו, לֹא הוּלָּלוּ
bachurav achelah-'esh; uvetulotav, lo hullalu
Fire devoured their young men; and their virgins had no marriage-song.

כֹּהֲנָיו, בַּחֶרֶב נָפָלוּ; וְאַלְמְנֹתָיו, לֹא תִבְכֶּינָה
kohanav bacherev nafalu; ve'almenotav, lo tivkeinah
Their priests fell by the sword; and their widows made no lamentation.

וַיִּקַץ כְּיָשֵׁן אֲדֹנָי; כְּגִבּוֹר, מִתְרוֹנֵן מִיָּיִן
vayikatz keyashen adonai; kegibbor, mitronen miyayin
Then the Lord awaked as one asleep, like a mighty man recovering from wine.

וַיַּךְ-צָרָיו אָחוֹר; חֶרְפַּת עוֹלָם, נָתַן לָמוֹ
vayach-tzarav achor; cherpat olam, natan lamo
And He smote His adversaries backward; He put upon them a perpetual reproach.

וַיִּמְאַס, בְּאֹהֶל יוֹסֵף; וּבְשֵׁבֶט אֶפְרַיִם, לֹא בָחָר
vayim'as be'ohel yosef; uveshevet efrayim, lo vachar
Moreover He abhorred the tent of Joseph, and chose not the tribe of Ephraim;

וַיִּבְחַר, אֶת-שֵׁבֶט יְהוּדָה; אֶת-הַר צִיּוֹן, אֲשֶׁר אָהֵב
vayivchar et-shevet yehudah; et-har tziyon, asher ahev
But chose the tribe of Judah, the mount Zion which He loved.

וַיִּבֶן כְּמוֹ-רָמִים, מִקְדָּשׁוֹ; כְּאֶרֶץ, יְסָדָהּ לְעוֹלָם
vayiven kemo-ramim mikdasho; ke'eretz, yesadah le'olam
And He built His sanctuary like the heights, like the earth which He hath founded for ever.

וַיִּבְחַר, בְּדָוִד עַבְדּוֹ; וַיִּקָּחֵהוּ, מִמִּכְלְאֹת צֹאן
vayivchar bedavid avdo; vayikkachehu, mimmichle'ot tzon
He chose David also His servant, and took him from the sheepfolds;

מֵאַחַר עָלוֹת, הֱבִיאוֹ: לִרְעוֹת, בְּיַעֲקֹב עַמּוֹ; וּבְיִשְׂרָאֵל, נַחֲלָתוֹ
me'achar alot, hevi'o lir'ot beya'akov ammo; uveyisra'el, nachalato
From following the ewes that give suck He brought him, to be shepherd over Jacob His people, and Israel His inheritance.

וַיִּרְעֵם, כְּתֹם לְבָבוֹ; וּבִתְבוּנוֹת כַּפָּיו יַנְחֵם
vayir'em ketom levavo; uvitvunot kappav yanchem
So he shepherded them according to the integrity of his heart; and lead them by the skilfulness of his hands.

תְּהִלִים

יְפַלֵּס נָתִיב, לְאַפּוֹ: לֹא-חָשַׂךְ מִמָּוֶת נַפְשָׁם; וְחַיָּתָם, לַדֶּבֶר הִסְגִּיר
yefalles nativ, le'appo lo-chasach mimmavet nafsham; vechayatam, laddever hisgir
He levelled a path for His anger; He spared not their soul from death, but gave their life over to the pestilence;

וַיַּךְ כָּל-בְּכוֹר בְּמִצְרָיִם; רֵאשִׁית אוֹנִים, בְּאָהֳלֵי-חָם
vayach kol-bechor bemitzrayim; reshit onim, be'aholei-cham
And smote all the first-born in Egypt, the first-fruits of their strength in the tents of Ham;

וַיַּסַּע כַּצֹּאן עַמּוֹ; וַיְנַהֲגֵם כַּעֵדֶר, בַּמִּדְבָּר
vayassa katzon ammo; vaynahagem ka'eder, bammidbar
But He made His own people to go forth like sheep, and guided them in the wilderness like a flock.

וַיַּנְחֵם לָבֶטַח, וְלֹא פָחָדוּ; וְאֶת-אוֹיְבֵיהֶם, כִּסָּה הַיָּם
vayanchem lavetach velo fachadu; ve'et-'oyeveihem, kissah hayam
And He led them safely, and they feared not; but the sea overwhelmed their enemies.

וַיְבִיאֵם, אֶל-גְּבוּל קָדְשׁוֹ; הַר-זֶה, קָנְתָה יְמִינוֹ
vayvi'em el-gevul kodsho har-zeh, kanetah yemino
And He brought them to His holy border, to the mountain, which His right hand had gotten.

וַיְגָרֶשׁ מִפְּנֵיהֶם, גּוֹיִם--וַיַּפִּילֵם, בְּחֶבֶל נַחֲלָה
vaygaresh mippeneihem goyim, vayappilem bechevel nachalah
He drove out the nations also before them, and allotted them for an inheritance by line,

וַיַּשְׁכֵּן בְּאָהֳלֵיהֶם, שִׁבְטֵי יִשְׂרָאֵל
vayashken be'oholeihem, shivtei yisra'el
and made the tribes of Israel to dwell in their tents.

וַיְנַסּוּ וַיַּמְרוּ, אֶת-אֱלֹהִים עֶלְיוֹן; וְעֵדוֹתָיו, לֹא שָׁמָרוּ
vaynassu vayamru et-'elohim elyon; ve'edotav, lo shamaru
Yet they tried and provoked God, the Most High, and kept not His testimonies;

וַיִּסֹּגוּ וַיִּבְגְּדוּ, כַּאֲבוֹתָם; נֶהְפְּכוּ, כְּקֶשֶׁת רְמִיָּה
vayissogu vayivgedu ka'avotam; nehpechu, kekeshet remiyah
But turned back, and dealt treacherously like their fathers; they were turned aside like a deceitful bow.

וַיַּכְעִיסוּהוּ בְּבָמוֹתָם; וּבִפְסִילֵיהֶם, יַקְנִיאוּהוּ
vayach'isuhu bevamotam; uvifsileihem, yakni'uhu
For they provoked Him with their high places, and moved Him to jealousy with their graven images.

שָׁמַע אֱלֹהִים, וַיִּתְעַבָּר; וַיִּמְאַס מְאֹד, בְּיִשְׂרָאֵל
shama elohim vayit'abbar; vayim'as me'od, beyisra'el
God heard, and was wroth, and He greatly abhorred Israel;

וַיִּטֹּשׁ, מִשְׁכַּן שִׁלוֹ; אֹהֶל, שִׁכֵּן בָּאָדָם
vayittosh mishkan shilo; ohel, shikken ba'adam
And He forsook the tabernacle of Shiloh, the tent which He had made to dwell among men;

תְּהִלִים

וְהִרְבָּה, לְהָשִׁיב אַפּוֹ; וְלֹא-יָעִיר, כָּל-חֲמָתוֹ
vehirbah lehashiv appo; velo-ya'ir kol-chamato
yea, many a time doth He turn His anger away, and doth not stir up all His wrath.

וַיִּזְכֹּר, כִּי-בָשָׂר הֵמָּה; רוּחַ הוֹלֵךְ, וְלֹא יָשׁוּב
vayizkor ki-vasar hemmah; ruach holech, velo yashuv
So He remembered that they were but flesh, a wind that passeth away, and cometh not again.

כַּמָּה, יַמְרוּהוּ בַמִּדְבָּר; יַעֲצִיבוּהוּ, בִּישִׁימוֹן
kammah yamruhu vammidbar; ya'atzivuhu, biyshimon
How oft did they rebel against Him in the wilderness, and grieve Him in the desert!

וַיָּשׁוּבוּ וַיְנַסּוּ אֵל; וּקְדוֹשׁ יִשְׂרָאֵל הִתְווּ
vayashuvu vaynassu el; ukedosh yisra'el hitvu
And still again they tried God, and set bounds to the Holy One of Israel.

לֹא-זָכְרוּ אֶת-יָדוֹ; יוֹם, אֲשֶׁר-פָּדָם מִנִּי-צָר
lo-zacheru et-yado; yom, asher-padam minni-tzar
They remembered not His hand, nor the day when He redeemed them from the adversary.

אֲשֶׁר-שָׂם בְּמִצְרַיִם, אֹתוֹתָיו; וּמוֹפְתָיו, בִּשְׂדֵה-צֹעַן
'asher-sam bemitzrayim ototav; umofetav, bisdeh-tzo'an
How He set His signs in Egypt, and His wonders in the field of Zoan;

וַיַּהֲפֹךְ לְדָם, יְאֹרֵיהֶם; וְנֹזְלֵיהֶם, בַּל-יִשְׁתָּיוּן
vayahafoch ledam ye'oreihem; venozeleihem, bal-yishtayun
And turned their rivers into blood, so that they could not drink their streams.

יְשַׁלַּח בָּהֶם עָרֹב, וַיֹּאכְלֵם; וּצְפַרְדֵּעַ, וַתַּשְׁחִיתֵם
yeshallach bahem arov vayochelem; utzefardea', vattashchitem
He sent among them swarms of flies, which devoured them; and frogs, which destroyed them.

וַיִּתֵּן לֶחָסִיל יְבוּלָם; וִיגִיעָם, לָאַרְבֶּה
vayitten lechasil yevulam; vigi'am, la'arbeh
He gave also their increase unto the caterpillar, and their labour unto the locust.

יַהֲרֹג בַּבָּרָד גַּפְנָם; וְשִׁקְמוֹתָם, בַּחֲנָמַל
yaharog babbarad gafnam; veshikmotam, bachanamal
He destroyed their vines with hail, and their sycamore-trees with frost.

וַיַּסְגֵּר לַבָּרָד בְּעִירָם; וּמִקְנֵיהֶם, לָרְשָׁפִים
vayasger labbarad be'iram; umikneihem, lareshafim
He gave over their cattle also to the hail, and their flocks to fiery bolts.

יְשַׁלַּח-בָּם, חֲרוֹן אַפּוֹ--עֶבְרָה וָזַעַם וְצָרָה; מִשְׁלַחַת, מַלְאֲכֵי רָעִים
yeshallach-bam charon appo, evrah vaza'am vetzarah; mishlachat, mal'achei ra'im
He sent forth upon them the fierceness of His anger, wrath, and indignation, and trouble, a sending of messengers of evil.

תְּהִלִים

וַיַּפֵּל, בְּקֶרֶב מַחֲנֵהוּ; סָבִיב, לְמִשְׁכְּנֹתָיו
vayappel bekerev machanehu; saviv, lemishkenotav
And He let it fall in the midst of their camp, round about their dwellings.

וַיֹּאכְלוּ וַיִּשְׂבְּעוּ מְאֹד; וְתַאֲוָתָם, יָבִא לָהֶם
vayochelu vayisbe'u me'od; veta'avatam, yavi lahem
So they did eat, and were well filled; and He gave them that which they craved.

לֹא-זָרוּ מִתַּאֲוָתָם; עוֹד, אָכְלָם בְּפִיהֶם
lo-zaru mitta'avatam; od, ochelam befihem
They were not estranged from their craving, their food was yet in their mouths,

וְאַף אֱלֹהִים, עָלָה בָהֶם
ve'af elohim alah vahem
When the anger of God went up against them,

וַיַּהֲרֹג, בְּמִשְׁמַנֵּיהֶם; וּבַחוּרֵי יִשְׂרָאֵל הִכְרִיעַ
vayaharog bemishmanneihem; uvachurei yisra'el hichria
and slew of the lustieth among them, and smote down the young men of Israel.

בְּכָל-זֹאת חָטְאוּ-עוֹד; וְלֹא-הֶאֱמִינוּ, בְּנִפְלְאוֹתָיו
bechol-zot chate'u-'od; velo-he'eminu, benifle'otav
For all this they sinned still, and believed not in His wondrous works.

וַיְכַל-בַּהֶבֶל יְמֵיהֶם; וּשְׁנוֹתָם, בַּבֶּהָלָה
vaychal-bahevel yemeihem; ushenotam, babbehalah
Therefore He ended their days as a breath, and their years in terror.

אִם-הֲרָגָם וּדְרָשׁוּהוּ; וְשָׁבוּ, וְשִׁחֲרוּ-אֵל
'im-haragam uderashuhu; veshavu, veshicharu-'el
When He slew them, then they would inquire after Him, and turn back and seek God earnestly.

וַיִּזְכְּרוּ, כִּי-אֱלֹהִים צוּרָם; וְאֵל עֶלְיוֹן, גֹּאֲלָם
vayizkeru ki-'elohim tzuram; ve'el elyon go'alam
And they remembered that God was their Rock, and the Most High God their redeemer.

וַיְפַתּוּהוּ בְּפִיהֶם; וּבִלְשׁוֹנָם, יְכַזְּבוּ-לוֹ
vayifattuhu befihem; uvilshonam, yechazzevu-lo
But they beguiled Him with their mouth, and lied unto Him with their tongue.

וְלִבָּם, לֹא-נָכוֹן עִמּוֹ; וְלֹא נֶאֶמְנוּ, בִּבְרִיתוֹ
velibbom lo-nachon immo; velo ne'emnu, bivrito
For their heart was not stedfast with Him, neither were they faithful in His covenant.

וְהוּא רַחוּם, יְכַפֵּר עָו‍ֹן–וְלֹא-יַשְׁחִית
vehu rachum yechapper avon velo-yashchit
But He, being full of compassion, forgiveth iniquity, and destroyeth not;

תְּהִלִים

וַיּוֹסִיפוּ עוֹד, לַחֲטֹא-לוֹ--לַמְרוֹת עֶלְיוֹן, בַּצִּיָּה
vayosifu od lachato-lo; lamrot elyon, batziyah
Yet went they on still to sin against Him, to rebel against the Most High in the desert.

וַיְנַסּוּ-אֵל בִּלְבָבָם--לִשְׁאָל-אֹכֶל לְנַפְשָׁם
vaynassu-'el bilvavam; lish'ol-'ochel lenafsham
And they tried God in their heart by asking food for their craving.

וַיְדַבְּרוּ, בֵּאלֹהִים: אָמְרוּ, הֲיוּכַל אֵל--לַעֲרֹךְ שֻׁלְחָן, בַּמִּדְבָּר
vaydabberu, be'elohim ameru hayuchal el; la'aroch shulchan, bammidbar
Yea, they spoke against God; they said: 'Can God prepare a table in the wilderness?

הֵן הִכָּה-צוּר, וַיָּזוּבוּ מַיִם--וּנְחָלִים יִשְׁטֹפוּ
hen hikkah-tzur vayazuvu mayim unechalim yishtofu
Behold, He smote the rock, that waters gushed out, and streams overflowed;

הֲגַם-לֶחֶם, יוּכַל תֵּת; אִם-יָכִין שְׁאֵר לְעַמּוֹ
hagam-lechem yuchal tet; im-yachin she'er le'ammo
can He give bread also? or will He provide flesh for His people?'

לָכֵן, שָׁמַע יְהוָה--וַיִּתְעַבָּר: וְאֵשׁ, נִשְּׂקָה בְיַעֲקֹב; וְגַם-אַף, עָלָה בְיִשְׂרָאֵל
lachen shama hashem vayit'abbar ve'esh nissekah veya'akov; vegam-'af, alah veyisra'el
Therefore the LORD heard, and was wroth; and a fire was kindled against Jacob, and anger also went up against Israel;

כִּי לֹא הֶאֱמִינוּ, בֵּאלֹהִים; וְלֹא בָטְחוּ, בִּישׁוּעָתוֹ
ki lo he'eminu be'elohim; velo vatechu, bishu'ato
Because they believed not in God, and trusted not in His salvation.

וַיְצַו שְׁחָקִים מִמָּעַל; וְדַלְתֵי שָׁמַיִם פָּתָח
vaytzav shechakim mimma'al; vedaltei shamayim patach
And He commanded the skies above, and opened the doors of heaven;

וַיַּמְטֵר עֲלֵיהֶם מָן לֶאֱכֹל; וּדְגַן-שָׁמַיִם, נָתַן לָמוֹ
vayamter aleihem man le'echol; udegan-shamayim, natan lamo
And He caused manna to rain upon them for food, and gave them of the corn of heaven.

לֶחֶם אַבִּירִים, אָכַל אִישׁ; צֵידָה שָׁלַח לָהֶם לָשֹׂבַע
lechem abbirim achal ish; tzeidah shalach lahem lasova
Man did eat the bread of the mighty; He sent them provisions to the full.

יַסַּע קָדִים, בַּשָּׁמָיִם; וַיְנַהֵג בְּעֻזּוֹ תֵימָן
yassa kadim bashamayim; vaynaheg be'uzzo teiman
He caused the east wind to set forth in heaven; and by His power He brought on the south wind.

וַיַּמְטֵר עֲלֵיהֶם כֶּעָפָר שְׁאֵר; וּכְחוֹל יַמִּים, עוֹף כָּנָף
vayamter aleihem ke'afar she'er; uchechol yammim, of kanaf
He caused flesh also to rain upon them as the dust, and winged fowl as the sand of the seas;

תְּהִלִים

בָּנִים יִוָּלֵדוּ; יָקֻמוּ, וִיסַפְּרוּ לִבְנֵיהֶם
banim yivvaledu; yakumu, vyisapperu livneihem
even the children that should be born; who should arise and tell them to their children,

וְיָשִׂימוּ בֵאלֹהִים, כִּסְלָם: וְלֹא יִשְׁכְּחוּ, מַעַלְלֵי-אֵל; וּמִצְוֺתָיו יִנְצֹרוּ
veyasimu velohim, kislam velo yishkechu ma'alelei-'el; umitzvotav yintzoru
That they might put their confidence in God, and not forget the works of God, but keep His commandments;

וְלֹא יִהְיוּ, כַּאֲבוֹתָם--דּוֹר, סוֹרֵר וּמֹרֶה
velo yihyu ka'avotam, dor sorer umoreh
And might not be as their fathers, a stubborn and rebellious generation;

דּוֹר, לֹא-הֵכִין לִבּוֹ; וְלֹא-נֶאֶמְנָה אֶת-אֵל רוּחוֹ
dor lo-hechin libbo; velo-ne'emnah et-'el rucho
a generation that set not their heart aright, and whose spirit was not stedfast with God.

בְּנֵי-אֶפְרַיִם, נוֹשְׁקֵי רוֹמֵי-קָשֶׁת; הָפְכוּ, בְּיוֹם קְרָב
benei-'efrayim, noshekei romei-kashet; hafechu, beyom kerav
The children of Ephraim were as archers handling the bow, that turned back in the day of battle.

לֹא שָׁמְרוּ, בְּרִית אֱלֹהִים; וּבְתוֹרָתוֹ, מֵאֲנוּ לָלֶכֶת
lo shameru berit elohim; uvtorato, me'anu lalechet
They kept not the covenant of God, and refused to walk in His law;

וַיִּשְׁכְּחוּ עֲלִילוֹתָיו; וְנִפְלְאוֹתָיו, אֲשֶׁר הֶרְאָם
vayishkechu alilotav; venifle'otav, asher her'am
And they forgot His doings, and His wondrous works that He had shown them.

נֶגֶד אֲבוֹתָם, עָשָׂה פֶלֶא; בְּאֶרֶץ מִצְרַיִם שְׂדֵה-צֹעַן
neged avotom asah fele; be'eretz mitzrayim sedeh-tzo'an
Marvellous things did He in the sight of their fathers, in the land of Egypt, in the field of Zoan.

בָּקַע יָם, וַיַּעֲבִירֵם; וַיַּצֶּב-מַיִם כְּמוֹ-נֵד
baka yam vaya'avirem; vayatzev-mayim kemo-ned
He cleaved the sea, and caused them to pass through; and He made the waters to stand as a heap.

וַיַּנְחֵם בֶּעָנָן יוֹמָם; וְכָל-הַלַּיְלָה, בְּאוֹר אֵשׁ
vayanchem be'anan yomam; vechol-hallaylah, be'or esh
By day also He led them with a cloud, and all the night with a light of fire.

יְבַקַּע צֻרִים, בַּמִּדְבָּר; וַיַּשְׁקְ, כִּתְהֹמוֹת רַבָּה
yevakka tzurim bammidbar; vayashk, kit'homot rabbah
He cleaved rocks in the wilderness, and gave them drink abundantly as out of the great deep.

וַיּוֹצִא נוֹזְלִים מִסָּלַע; וַיּוֹרֶד כַּנְּהָרוֹת מָיִם
vayotzi nozelim missala'; vayored kanneharot mayim
He brought streams also out of the rock, and caused waters to run down like rivers.

תְּהִלִים

קוֹל רַעַמְךָ, בַּגַּלְגַּל--הֵאִירוּ בְרָקִים תֵּבֵל; רָגְזָה וַתִּרְעַשׁ הָאָרֶץ
kol ra'amcha baggalgal, he'iru verakim tevel; ragezah vattir'ash ha'aretz
The voice of Thy thunder was in the whirlwind; the lightnings lighted up the world; the earth trembled and shook.

בַּיָּם דַּרְכֶּךָ--וּשְׁבִילְךָ, בְּמַיִם רַבִּים; וְעִקְּבוֹתֶיךָ, לֹא נֹדָעוּ
bayam darkecha, ushevilecha bemayim rabbim; ve'ikkevoteicha, lo noda'u
Thy way was in the sea, and Thy path in the great waters, and Thy footsteps were not known.

נָחִיתָ כַצֹּאן עַמֶּךָ--בְּיַד-מֹשֶׁה וְאַהֲרֹן
nachita chatzon ammecha; beyad-mosheh ve'aharon
Thou didst lead Thy people like a flock, by the hand of Moses and Aaron.

עח

מַשְׂכִּיל, לְאָסָף: הַאֲזִינָה עַמִּי, תּוֹרָתִי; הַטּוּ אָזְנְכֶם, לְאִמְרֵי-פִי
Maskil, le'asaf: ha'azinah ammi torati; hattu azenechem, le'imrei-fi
Maschil of Asaph. Give ear, O my people, to my teaching; incline your ears to the words of my mouth.

אֶפְתְּחָה בְמָשָׁל פִּי; אַבִּיעָה חִידוֹת, מִנִּי-קֶדֶם
'eftechah vemashal pi; abbi'ah chidot, minni-kedem
I will open my mouth with a parable; I will utter dark sayings concerning days of old;

אֲשֶׁר שָׁמַעְנוּ, וַנֵּדָעֵם; וַאֲבוֹתֵינוּ, סִפְּרוּ-לָנוּ
'asher shama'nu vanneda'em; va'avoteinu, sipperu-lanu
That which we have heard and known, and our fathers have told us,

לֹא נְכַחֵד, מִבְּנֵיהֶם--לְדוֹר אַחֲרוֹן, מְסַפְּרִים תְּהִלּוֹת יְהוָה
lo nechached mibbeneihem, ledor acharon, mesapperim tehillot hashem
We will not hide from their children, telling to the generation to come the praises of the LORD,

וֶעֱזוּזוֹ וְנִפְלְאֹתָיו, אֲשֶׁר עָשָׂה
ve'ezuzo venifle'otav, asher asah
and His strength, and His wondrous works that He hath done.

וַיָּקֶם עֵדוּת, בְּיַעֲקֹב, וְתוֹרָה, שָׂם בְּיִשְׂרָאֵל
vayakem edut beya'akov, vetorah sam beyisra'el
For He established a testimony in Jacob, and appointed a law in Israel,

אֲשֶׁר צִוָּה, אֶת-אֲבוֹתֵינוּ--לְהוֹדִיעָם, לִבְנֵיהֶם
asher tzivvah et-'avoteinu; lehodi'am, livneihem
which He commanded our fathers, that they should make them known to their children;

לְמַעַן יֵדְעוּ, דּוֹר אַחֲרוֹן
lema'an yede'u dor acharon
That the generation to come might know them,

תְּהִלִים

וַיְחַפֵּשׂ רוּחִי
vaychappes ruchi
and my spirit maketh diligent search:

הַלְעוֹלָמִים, יִזְנַח אֲדֹנָי; וְלֹא־יֹסִיף לִרְצוֹת עוֹד
hal'olamim yiznach adonai; velo-yosif lirtzot od
'Will the Lord cast off for ever? And will He be favourable no more?

הֶאָפֵס לָנֶצַח חַסְדּוֹ; גָּמַר אֹמֶר, לְדֹר וָדֹר
he'afes lanetzach chasdo; gamar omer, ledor vador
Is His mercy clean gone for ever? Is His promise come to an end for evermore?

הֲשָׁכַח חַנּוֹת אֵל; אִם־קָפַץ בְּאַף, רַחֲמָיו סֶלָה
hashachach channot el; im-kafatz be'af, rachamav selah
Hath God forgotten to be gracious? Hath He in anger shut up his compassions?' Selah

וָאֹמַר, חַלּוֹתִי הִיא--שְׁנוֹת, יְמִין עֶלְיוֹן
va'omar challoti hi; shenot, yemin elyon
And I say: 'This is my weakness, that the right hand of the Most High could change.

אֶזְכּוֹר מַעַלְלֵי־יָהּ: כִּי־אֶזְכְּרָה מִקֶּדֶם פִּלְאֶךָ
ezkor ma'alelei-yah; ki-'ezkerah mikkedem pil'echa
I will make mention of the deeds of the LORD; yea, I will remember Thy wonders of old.

וְהָגִיתִי בְכָל־פָּעֳלֶךָ; וּבַעֲלִילוֹתֶיךָ אָשִׂיחָה
vehagiti vechol-pa'olecha; uva'aliloteicha asichah
I will meditate also upon all Thy work, and muse on Thy doings.'

אֱלֹהִים, בַּקֹּדֶשׁ דַּרְכֶּךָ; מִי־אֵל גָּדוֹל, כֵּאלֹהִים
'elohim bakkodesh darkecha; mi-'el gadol, ke'elohim
O God, Thy way is in holiness; who is a great god like unto God?

אַתָּה הָאֵל, עֹשֵׂה פֶלֶא; הוֹדַעְתָּ בָעַמִּים עֻזֶּךָ
'attah ha'el oseh fele; hoda'ta va'ammim uzzecha
Thou art the God that doest wonders; Thou hast made known Thy strength among the peoples.

גָּאַלְתָּ בִּזְרוֹעַ עַמֶּךָ; בְּנֵי־יַעֲקֹב וְיוֹסֵף סֶלָה
ga'alta bizroa ammecha; benei-ya'akov veyosef selah
Thou hast with Thine arm redeemed Thy people, the sons of Jacob and Joseph. Selah

רָאוּךָ מַּיִם, אֱלֹהִים--רָאוּךָ מַּיִם יָחִילוּ; אַף, יִרְגְּזוּ תְהֹמוֹת
ra'ucha mayim elohim, ra'ucha mayim yachilu; af, yirgezu tehomot
The waters saw Thee, O God; the waters saw Thee, they were in pain; the depths also trembled.

זֹרְמוּ מַיִם, עָבוֹת--קוֹל, נָתְנוּ שְׁחָקִים; אַף־חֲצָצֶיךָ, יִתְהַלָּכוּ
zoremu mayim avot, kol natenu shechakim; af-chatzatzeicha, yit'hallachu
The clouds flooded forth waters; the skies sent out a sound; Thine arrows also went abroad.

תְּהִלִּים

כִּי-חֲמַת אָדָם תּוֹדֶךָּ; שְׁאֵרִית חֵמֹת תַּחְגֹּר
ki-chamat adam todeka; she'erit chemot tachgor
Surely the wrath of man shall praise Thee; the residue of wrath shalt Thou gird upon Thee.

נִדְרוּ וְשַׁלְּמוּ, לַיהוָה אֱלֹהֵיכֶם: כָּל-סְבִיבָיו--יֹבִילוּ שַׁי, לַמּוֹרָא
nidaru veshallemu lahashem eloheichem kol-sevivav; yovilu shai, lammora
Vow, and pay unto the LORD your God; let all that are round about Him bring presents unto Him that is to be feared;

יִבְצֹר, רוּחַ נְגִידִים; נוֹרָא, לְמַלְכֵי-אָרֶץ
yivtzor ruach negidim; nora, lemalchei-'aretz
He minisheth the spirit of princes; He is terrible to the kings of the earth.

עז

לַמְנַצֵּחַ עַל-יְדִיתוּן; לְאָסָף מִזְמוֹר
Lamnatzeach al-yeditun al-yedutun, le'asaf mizmor
For the Leader; for Jeduthun. A Psalm of Asaph.

קוֹלִי אֶל-אֱלֹהִים וְאֶצְעָקָה; קוֹלִי אֶל-אֱלֹהִים, וְהַאֲזִין אֵלָי
koli el-'elohim ve'etz'akah; koli el-'elohim, veha'azin elai
I will lift up my voice unto God, and cry; I will lift up my voice unto God, that He may give ear unto me.

בְּיוֹם צָרָתִי, אֲדֹנָי דָּרָשְׁתִּי
beyom tzarati adonai darasheti
In the day of my trouble I seek the Lord;

יָדִי, לַיְלָה נִגְּרָה--וְלֹא תָפוּג; מֵאֲנָה הִנָּחֵם נַפְשִׁי
yadi laylah niggerah velo tafug; me'anah hinnachem nafshi
with my hand uplifted, [mine eye] streameth in the night without ceasing; my soul refuseth to be comforted.

אֶזְכְּרָה אֱלֹהִים וְאֶהֱמָיָה; אָשִׂיחָה, וְתִתְעַטֵּף רוּחִי סֶלָה
'ezkerah elohim ve'ehemayah; asichah vetit'attef ruchi selah
When I think thereon, O God, I must moan; when I muse thereon, my spirit fainteth. Selah

אָחַזְתָּ, שְׁמֻרוֹת עֵינָי; נִפְעַמְתִּי, וְלֹא אֲדַבֵּר
'achazta shemurot einai; nif'amti, velo adabber
Thou holdest fast the lids of mine eyes; I am troubled, and cannot speak.

חִשַּׁבְתִּי יָמִים מִקֶּדֶם--שְׁנוֹת, עוֹלָמִים
chishavti yamim mikkedem; shenot, olamim
I have pondered the days of old, the years of ancient times.

אֶזְכְּרָה נְגִינָתִי, בַּלָּיְלָה: עִם-לְבָבִי אָשִׂיחָה
'ezkerah neginati, ballayelah im-levavi asichah
In the night I will call to remembrance my song; I will commune with mine own heart;

תְּהִלִּים

וְכָל-קַרְנֵי רְשָׁעִים אֲגַדֵּעַ; תְּרוֹמַמְנָה, קַרְנוֹת צַדִּיק
vechol-karnei resha'im agaddea'; teromamnah, karnot tzaddik
All the horns of the wicked also will I cut off; but the horns of the righteous shall be lifted up.

עו

לַמְנַצֵּחַ בִּנְגִינֹת; מִזְמוֹר לְאָסָף שִׁיר
Lamnatzeach binginot; mizmor le'asaf shir
For the Leader; with string-music. A Psalm of Asaph, a Song.

נוֹדָע בִּיהוּדָה אֱלֹהִים; בְּיִשְׂרָאֵל, גָּדוֹל שְׁמוֹ.
noda biyehudah elohim; beyisra'el, gadol shemo
In Judah is God known; His name is great in Israel.

וַיְהִי בְשָׁלֵם סֻכּוֹ; וּמְעוֹנָתוֹ בְצִיּוֹן
vayhi veshalem sukko; ume'onato vetziyon
In Salem also is set His tabernacle, and His dwelling-place in Zion.

שָׁמָּה, שִׁבַּר רִשְׁפֵי-קָשֶׁת; מָגֵן וְחֶרֶב וּמִלְחָמָה סֶלָה
shammah shibbar rishfei-kashet; magen vecherev umilchamah selah
There He broke the fiery shafts of the bow; the shield, and the sword, and the battle. Selah

נָאוֹר, אַתָּה אַדִּיר--מֵהַרְרֵי-טָרֶף
na'or attah addir, meharerei-taref
Glorious art Thou and excellent, coming down from the mountains of prey.

אֶשְׁתּוֹלְלוּ, אַבִּירֵי לֵב--נָמוּ שְׁנָתָם; וְלֹא-מָצְאוּ כָל-אַנְשֵׁי-חַיִל יְדֵיהֶם
'eshtolelu abbirei lev namu shenatam; velo-matze'u chol-'anshei-chayil yedeihem
The stout-hearted are bereft of sense, they sleep their sleep; and none of the men of might have found their hands.

מִגַּעֲרָתְךָ, אֱלֹהֵי יַעֲקֹב; נִרְדָּם, וְרֶכֶב וָסוּס
migga'aratecha elohei ya'akov; nirdam, verechev vasus
At Thy rebuke, O God of Jacob, they are cast into a dead sleep, the riders also and the horses.

אַתָּה, נוֹרָא אַתָּה--וּמִי-יַעֲמֹד לְפָנֶיךָ; מֵאָז אַפֶּךָ
'attah nora attah, umi-ya'amod lefaneicha, me'az appecha
Thou, even Thou, art terrible; and who may stand in Thy sight when once Thou art angry?

מִשָּׁמַיִם, הִשְׁמַעְתָּ דִּין; אֶרֶץ יָרְאָה וְשָׁקָטָה
mishamayim hishma'ta din; eretz yare'ah veshakatah
Thou didst cause sentence to be heard from heaven; the earth feared, and was still,

בְּקוּם-לַמִּשְׁפָּט אֱלֹהִים--לְהוֹשִׁיעַ כָּל-עַנְוֵי-אֶרֶץ סֶלָה
bekum-lammishpat elohim; lehoshia kol-'anvei-'eretz selah
When God arose to judgment, to save all the humble of the earth. Selah

תְּהִלִים

עה

לַמְנַצֵּחַ אַל-תַּשְׁחֵת; מִזְמוֹר לְאָסָף שִׁיר
Lamnatzeach al-tashchet; mizmor le'asaf shir
For the Leader; Al-tashheth. A Psalm of Asaph, a Song.

הוֹדִינוּ לְךָ, אֱלֹהִים--הוֹדִינוּ, וְקָרוֹב שְׁמֶךָ; סִפְּרוּ, נִפְלְאוֹתֶיךָ
hodinu lecha elohim, hodinu vekarov shemecha; sipperu, nifle'oteicha
We give thanks unto Thee, O God, we give thanks, and Thy name is near; men tell of Thy wondrous works.

כִּי, אֶקַּח מוֹעֵד; אֲנִי, מֵישָׁרִים אֶשְׁפֹּט
ki ekkach mo'ed; ani, meisharim eshpot
'When I take the appointed time, I Myself will judge with equity.

נְמֹגִים, אֶרֶץ וְכָל-יֹשְׁבֶיהָ; אָנֹכִי תִכַּנְתִּי עַמּוּדֶיהָ פֶּלָה
nemogim, eretz vechol-yosheveiha; anochi tikkanti ammudeiha selah
When the earth and all the inhabitants thereof are dissolved, I Myself establish the pillars of it.' Selah

אָמַרְתִּי לַהוֹלְלִים, אַל-תָּהֹלּוּ; וְלָרְשָׁעִים, אַל-תָּרִימוּ קָרֶן
'amarti laholelim al-tahollu; velaresha'im, al-tarimu karen
I say unto the arrogant: 'Deal not arrogantly'; and to the wicked: 'Lift not up the horn.'

אַל-תָּרִימוּ לַמָּרוֹם קַרְנְכֶם; תְּדַבְּרוּ בְצַוָּאר עָתָק
'al-tarimu lammarom karnechem; tedabberu vetzavvar atak
Lift not up your horn on high; speak not insolence with a haughty neck.

כִּי לֹא מִמּוֹצָא, וּמִמַּעֲרָב; וְלֹא, מִמִּדְבַּר הָרִים
ki lo mimmotza umimma'arav; velo, mimmidbar harim
For neither from the east, nor from the west, nor yet from the wilderness, cometh lifting up.

כִּי-אֱלֹהִים שֹׁפֵט; זֶה יַשְׁפִּיל, וְזֶה יָרִים
ki-'elohim shofet; zeh yashpil, vezeh yarim
For God is judge; He putteth down one, and lifteth up another.

כִּי כוֹס בְּיַד-יְהוָה, וְיַיִן חָמַר מָלֵא מֶסֶךְ--וַיַּגֵּר מִזֶּה
ki chos beyad-hashem veyayin chamar malei mesech vayagger mizzeh
For in the hand of the LORD there is a cup, with foaming wine, full of mixture, and He poureth out of the same;

אַךְ-שְׁמָרֶיהָ, יִמְצוּ יִשְׁתּוּ; כֹּל, רִשְׁעֵי-אָרֶץ
ach-shemareiha yimtzu yishtu; kol rish'ei-'aretz
surely the dregs thereof, all the wicked of the earth shall drain them, and drink them.

וַאֲנִי, אַגִּיד לְעֹלָם; אֲזַמְּרָה, לֵאלֹהֵי יַעֲקֹב
va'ani aggid le'olam; azammerah, lelohei ya'akov
But as for me, I will declare for ever, I will sing praises to the God of Jacob.

תְּהִלִּים

וֵאלֹהִים, מַלְכִּי מִקֶּדֶם; פֹּעֵל יְשׁוּעוֹת, בְּקֶרֶב הָאָרֶץ

Ve'elohim malki mikkedem; po'el yeshu'ot, bekerev ha'aretz
Yet God is my King of old, working salvation in the midst of the earth.

אַתָּה פוֹרַרְתָּ בְעָזְּךָ יָם; שִׁבַּרְתָּ רָאשֵׁי תַנִּינִים, עַל-הַמָּיִם

'attah forarta ve'ozzecha yam; shibbarta rashei tanninim, al-hammayim
Thou didst break the sea in pieces by Thy strength; Thou didst shatter the heads of the sea-monsters in the waters.

אַתָּה רִצַּצְתָּ, רָאשֵׁי לִוְיָתָן; תִּתְּנֶנּוּ מַאֲכָל, לְעָם לְצִיִּים

'attah ritzatzta rashei livyatan; tittenennu ma'achal, le'am letziyim
Thou didst crush the heads of leviathan, Thou gavest him to be food to the folk inhabiting the wilderness.

אַתָּה בָקַעְתָּ, מַעְיָן וָנָחַל; אַתָּה הוֹבַשְׁתָּ, נַהֲרוֹת אֵיתָן

'attah vaka'ta ma'yan vanachal; attah hovashta, naharot eitan
Thou didst cleave fountain and brook; Thou driedst up ever-flowing rivers.

לְךָ יוֹם, אַף-לְךָ לָיְלָה; אַתָּה הֲכִינוֹתָ, מָאוֹר וָשָׁמֶשׁ

lecha yom af-lecha layelah; attah hachinota, ma'or vashamesh
Thine is the day, Thine also the night; Thou hast established luminary and sun.

אַתָּה הִצַּבְתָּ, כָּל-גְּבוּלוֹת אָרֶץ; קַיִץ וָחֹרֶף, אַתָּה יְצַרְתָּם

'attah hitzavta kol-gevulot aretz; kayitz vachoref, attah yetzartam
Thou hast set all the borders of the earth; Thou hast made summer and winter.

זְכָר-זֹאת--אוֹיֵב, חֵרֵף יְהוָה; וְעַם נָבָל, נִאֲצוּ שְׁמֶךָ

zechor-zot, oyev cheref hashem ve'am naval, ni'atzu shemecha
Remember this, how the enemy hath reproached the LORD, and how a base people have blasphemed Thy name.

אַל-תִּתֵּן לְחַיַּת, נֶפֶשׁ תּוֹרֶךָ; חַיַּת עֲנִיֶּיךָ, אַל-תִּשְׁכַּח לָנֶצַח

'al-titten lechayat nefesh torecha; chayat aniyeicha, al-tishkach lanetzach
O deliver not the soul of Thy turtle-dove unto the wild beast; forget not the life of Thy poor for ever.

הַבֵּט לַבְּרִית: כִּי מָלְאוּ מַחֲשַׁכֵּי-אֶרֶץ, נְאוֹת חָמָס

habbet labberit; ki male'u machashakkei-'eretz, ne'ot chamas
Look upon the covenant; for the dark places of the land are full of the habitations of violence.

אַל-יָשֹׁב דַּךְ נִכְלָם; עָנִי וְאֶבְיוֹן, יְהַלְלוּ שְׁמֶךָ

'al-yashov dach nichlam; ani ve'evyon, yehalelu shemecha
O let not the oppressed turn back in confusion; let the poor and needy praise Thy name.

קוּמָה אֱלֹהִים, רִיבָה רִיבֶךָ; זְכֹר חֶרְפָּתְךָ מִנִּי-נָבָל, כָּל-הַיּוֹם

kumah elohim rivah rivecha; zechor cherpatecha minni-naval, kol-hayom
Arise, O God, plead Thine own cause; remember Thy reproach all the day at the hand of the base man.

אַל-תִּשְׁכַּח, קוֹל צֹרְרֶיךָ; שְׁאוֹן קָמֶיךָ, עֹלֶה תָמִיד

'al-tishkach kol tzorereicha; she'on kameicha, oleh tamid
Forget not the voice of Thine adversaries, the tumult of those that rise up against Thee which ascendeth continually.

תְּהִלִּים

זְכֹר עֲדָתְךָ, קָנִיתָ קֶּדֶם
zechor adatcha kanita kedem
Remember Thy congregation, which Thou hast gotten of old,

גָּאַלְתָּ, שֵׁבֶט נַחֲלָתֶךָ; הַר-צִיּוֹן, זֶה שָׁכַנְתָּ בּוֹ
ga'alta shevet nachalatecha; har-tziyon, zeh shachanta bo
which Thou hast redeemed to be the tribe of Thine inheritance; and mount Zion, wherein Thou hast dwelt.

הָרִימָה פְעָמֶיךָ, לְמַשֻּׁאוֹת נֶצַח; כָּל-הֵרַע אוֹיֵב בַּקֹּדֶשׁ
harimah fe'ameicha lemashu'ot netzach; kol-hera oyev bakkodesh
Lift up Thy steps because of the perpetual ruins, even all the evil that the enemy hath done in the sanctuary.

שָׁאֲגוּ צֹרְרֶיךָ, בְּקֶרֶב מוֹעֲדֶךָ; שָׂמוּ אוֹתֹתָם אֹתוֹת
sha'agu tzorereicha bekerev mo'adecha; samu ototam otot
Thine adversaries have roared in the midst of Thy meeting-place; they have set up their own signs for signs.

יִוָּדַע, כְּמֵבִיא לְמָעְלָה; בִּסְבָךְ-עֵץ, קַרְדֻּמּוֹת
yivvada kemevi lema'elah; bisavoch-'etz, kardummot
It seemed as when men wield upwards axes in a thicket of trees.

וְעַתָּה, פִּתּוּחֶיהָ יָּחַד--בְּכַשִּׁיל וְכֵילַפּוֹת, יַהֲלֹמוּן
ve'attah pittucheiha yachad; bechashil vecheilappot, yahalomun
And now all the carved work thereof together they strike down with hatchet and hammers.

שִׁלְחוּ בָאֵשׁ, מִקְדָּשֶׁךָ; לָאָרֶץ, חִלְּלוּ מִשְׁכַּן-שְׁמֶךָ
shilchu va'esh mikdashecha; la'aretz, chillelu mishkan-shemecha
They have set Thy sanctuary on fire; they have profaned the dwelling-place of Thy name even to the ground.

אָמְרוּ בְלִבָּם, נִינָם יָחַד
'ameru velibbom ninam yachad
They said in their heart: 'Let us make havoc of them altogether';

שָׂרְפוּ כָל-מוֹעֲדֵי-אֵל בָּאָרֶץ
sarefu chol-mo'adei-'el ba'aretz
they have burned up all the meeting-places of God in the land.

אוֹתֹתֵינוּ, לֹא רָאִינוּ: אֵין-עוֹד נָבִיא; וְלֹא-אִתָּנוּ, יֹדֵעַ עַד-מָה
'ototeinu, lo ra'inu ein-'od navi; velo-'ittanu, yodea ad-mah
We see not our signs; there is no more any prophet; neither is there among us any that knoweth how long.

עַד-מָתַי אֱלֹהִים, יְחָרֶף צָר; יְנָאֵץ אוֹיֵב שִׁמְךָ לָנֶצַח
'ad-matai elohim yecharef tzar; yena'etz oyev shimcha lanetzach
How long, O God, shall the adversary reproach? Shall the enemy blaspheme Thy name for ever?

לָמָּה תָשִׁיב יָדְךָ, וִימִינֶךָ; מִקֶּרֶב חֵיקְךָ כַלֵּה
lammah tashiv yadecha viminecha; mikkerev heikecha challeh
Why withdrawest Thou Thy hand, even Thy right hand? Draw it out of Thy bosom and consume them.

תְּהִלִּים

כַּחֲלוֹם מֵהָקִיץ--אֲדֹנָי, בָּעִיר צַלְמָם תִּבְזֶה
kachalom mehakitz; adonai ba'ir tzalmam tivzeh
As a dream when one awaketh, so, O Lord, when Thou arousest Thyself, Thou wilt despise their semblance.

כִּי, יִתְחַמֵּץ לְבָבִי; וְכִלְיוֹתַי, אֶשְׁתּוֹנָן
ki yitchammetz levavi; vechilyotai, eshtonan
For my heart was in a ferment, and I was pricked in my reins.

וַאֲנִי-בַעַר, וְלֹא אֵדָע; בְּהֵמוֹת, הָיִיתִי עִמָּךְ
va'ani-va'ar velo eda'; behemot, hayiti immach
But I was brutish, and ignorant; I was as a beast before Thee.

וַאֲנִי תָמִיד עִמָּךְ; אָחַזְתָּ, בְּיַד-יְמִינִי
va'ani tamid immach; achazta, beyad-yemini
Nevertheless I am continually with Thee; Thou holdest my right hand.

בַּעֲצָתְךָ תַנְחֵנִי; וְאַחַר, כָּבוֹד תִּקָּחֵנִי
ba'atzatecha tancheni; ve'achar, kavod tikkacheni
Thou wilt guide me with Thy counsel, and afterward receive me with glory.

מִי-לִי בַשָּׁמָיִם; וְעִמְּךָ, לֹא-חָפַצְתִּי בָאָרֶץ
mi-li vashamayim; ve'immecha, lo-chafatzti va'aretz
Whom have I in heaven but Thee? And beside Thee I desire none upon earth.

כָּלָה שְׁאֵרִי, וּלְבָבִי: צוּר-לְבָבִי וְחֶלְקִי--אֱלֹהִים לְעוֹלָם
kalah she'eri, ulevavi tzur-levavi vechelki, elohim le'olam
My flesh and my heart faileth; but God is the rock of my heart and my portion for ever.

כִּי-הִנֵּה רְחֵקֶיךָ יֹאבֵדוּ; הִצְמַתָּה, כָּל-זוֹנֶה מִמֶּךָּ
ki-hinneh rechekeicha yovedu; hitzmattah, kol-zoneh mimmeka
For, lo, they that go far from Thee shall perish; Thou dost destroy all them that go astray from Thee.

וַאֲנִי, קִרְבַת אֱלֹהִים--לִי-טוֹב: שַׁתִּי, בַּאדֹנָי יְהוִה מַחְסִי; לְסַפֵּר, כָּל-מַלְאֲכוֹתֶיךָ
va'ani kiravat elohim, li-tov shatti ba'adonai hashem machsi; lesapper, kol-mal'achoteicha
But as for me, the nearness of God is my good; I have made the Lord GOD my refuge, that I may tell of all Thy works.

עד

מַשְׂכִּיל, לְאָסָף: לָמָה אֱלֹהִים, זָנַחְתָּ לָנֶצַח
Maskil, le'asaf lamah elohim zanachta lanetzach
Maschil of Asaph. Why, O God, hast Thou cast us off for ever?

יֶעְשַׁן אַפְּךָ, בְּצֹאן מַרְעִיתֶךָ
ye'shan appecha, betzon mar'itecha
Why doth Thine anger smoke against the flock of Thy pasture?

תְּהִלִּים

יָמִיקוּ, וִידַבְּרוּ בְרָע עֹשֶׁק; מִמָּרוֹם יְדַבֵּרוּ
yamiku viydabberu vera oshek; mimmarom yedabberu
They scoff, and in wickedness utter oppression; they speak as if there were none on high.

שַׁתּוּ בַשָּׁמַיִם פִּיהֶם; וּלְשׁוֹנָם, תִּהֲלַךְ בָּאָרֶץ
shattu vashamayim pihem; uleshonam, tihalach ba'aretz
They have set their mouth against the heavens, and their tongue walketh through the earth.

לָכֵן, יָשׁוּב עַמּוֹ הֲלֹם; וּמֵי מָלֵא, יִמָּצוּ לָמוֹ
lachen yashuv ammo halom; umei male, yimmatzu lamo
Therefore His people return hither; and waters of fullness are drained out by them.

וְאָמְרוּ, אֵיכָה יָדַע-אֵל; וְיֵשׁ דֵּעָה בְעֶלְיוֹן
ve'ameru, eichah yada'-'el; veyesh de'ah ve'elyon
And they say: 'How doth God know? And is there knowledge in the Most High?'

הִנֵּה-אֵלֶּה רְשָׁעִים; וְשַׁלְוֵי עוֹלָם, הִשְׂגּוּ-חָיִל
hinneh-'elleh resha'im; veshalvei olam, hisgu-chayil
Behold, such are the wicked; and they that are always at ease increase riches.

אַךְ-רִיק, זִכִּיתִי לְבָבִי; וָאֶרְחַץ בְּנִקָּיוֹן כַּפָּי
'ach-rik zikkiti levavi; va'erchatz benikkayon kappai
Surely in vain have I cleansed my heart, and washed my hands in innocency;

וָאֱהִי נָגוּעַ, כָּל-הַיּוֹם; וְתוֹכַחְתִּי, לַבְּקָרִים
va'ehi nagua kol-hayom; vetochachti, labbekarim
For all the day have I been plagued, and my chastisement came every morning.

אִם-אָמַרְתִּי, אֲסַפְּרָה כְמוֹ; הִנֵּה דוֹר בָּנֶיךָ בָגָדְתִּי
'im-'amarti asapperah chemo; hinneh dor baneicha vagadeti
If I had said: 'I will speak thus', behold, I had been faithless to the generation of Thy children.

וָאֲחַשְּׁבָה, לָדַעַת זֹאת; עָמָל הוּא בְעֵינָי
va'achashevah lada'at zot; amal hu ve'einai
And when I pondered how I might know this, it was wearisome in mine eyes;

עַד-אָבוֹא, אֶל-מִקְדְּשֵׁי-אֵל; אָבִינָה, לְאַחֲרִיתָם
'ad-'avo el-mikdeshei-'el; avinah, le'acharitam
Until I entered into the sanctuary of God, and considered their end.

אַךְ בַּחֲלָקוֹת, תָּשִׁית לָמוֹ; הִפַּלְתָּם, לְמַשּׁוּאוֹת
'ach bachalakot tashit lamo; hippaltam, lemashu'ot
Surely Thou settest them in slippery places; Thou hurlest them down to utter ruin.

אֵיךְ הָיוּ לְשַׁמָּה כְרָגַע; סָפוּ תַמּוּ, מִן-בַּלָּהוֹת
'eich hayu leshammah cheraga'; safu tammu, min-ballahot
How are they become a desolation in a moment! They are wholly consumed by terrors.

תְּהִלִּים

וְיִתְבָּרְכוּ בוֹ; כָּל-גּוֹיִם יְאַשְּׁרוּהוּ
veyitbarechu vo; kol-goyim ye'asheruhu
may men also bless themselves by him; may all nations call him happy.

בָּרוּךְ, יְהוָה אֱלֹהִים--אֱלֹהֵי יִשְׂרָאֵל: עֹשֵׂה נִפְלָאוֹת לְבַדּוֹ
baruch hashem elohim elohei yisra'el; oseh nifla'ot levaddo
Blessed be the LORD God, the God of Israel, who only doeth wondrous things;

וּבָרוּךְ, שֵׁם כְּבוֹדוֹ--לְעוֹלָם: וְיִמָּלֵא כְבוֹדוֹ, אֶת-כֹּל הָאָרֶץ--אָמֵן וְאָמֵן
uvaruch shem kevodo, le'olam veyimmalei chevodo et-kol ha'aretz, amen ve'amen
And blessed be His glorious name for ever; and let the whole earth be filled with His glory. Amen, and Amen.

כָּלּוּ תְפִלּוֹת--דָּוִד, בֶּן-יִשָׁי
kallu tefillot; david, ben-yishai
The prayers of David the son of Jesse are ended.

עג

מִזְמוֹר, לְאָסָף: אַךְ טוֹב לְיִשְׂרָאֵל אֱלֹהִים, לְבָרֵי לֵבָב
Mizmor, le'asaf: ach tov leyisra'el elohim, levarei levav
A Psalm of Asaph. Surely God is good to Israel, even to such as are pure in heart.

וַאֲנִי--כִּמְעַט, נָטָיוּ רַגְלָי; כְּאַיִן, שֻׁפְּכוּ אֲשֻׁרָי
va'ani, kim'at natayu raglai; ke'ayin, shuppechu ashurai
But as for me, my feet were almost gone; my steps had well nigh slipped.

כִּי-קִנֵּאתִי, בַּהוֹלְלִים; שְׁלוֹם רְשָׁעִים אֶרְאֶה
ki-kinneti baholelim; shelom resha'im er'eh
For I was envious at the arrogant, when I saw the prosperity of the wicked.

כִּי אֵין חַרְצֻבּוֹת לְמוֹתָם; וּבָרִיא אוּלָם
ki ein chartzubbot lemotam, uvari ulam
For there are no pangs at their death, and their body is sound.

בַּעֲמַל אֱנוֹשׁ אֵינֵמוֹ; וְעִם-אָדָם, לֹא יְנֻגָּעוּ
ba'amal enosh einemo; ve'im-'adam, lo yenugga'u
In the trouble of man they are not; neither are they plagued like men.

לָכֵן, עֲנָקַתְמוֹ גַאֲוָה; יַעֲטָף-שִׁית, חָמָס לָמוֹ
lachen anakatmo ga'avah; ya'ataf-shit, chamas lamo
Therefore pride is as a chain about their neck; violence covereth them as a garment.

יָצָא, מֵחֵלֶב עֵינֵמוֹ; עָבְרוּ, מַשְׂכִּיּוֹת לֵבָב
yatza mechelev einemo; averu, maskiyot levav
Their eyes stand forth from fatness; they are gone beyond the imaginations of their heart.

תְּהִלִּים

וְיֵרְדְּ, מִיָּם עַד-יָם; וּמִנָּהָר, עַד-אַפְסֵי-אָרֶץ
veyerd miyam ad-yam; uminnahar, ad-'afsei-'aretz
May he have dominion also from sea to sea, and from the River unto the ends of the earth.

לְפָנָיו, יִכְרְעוּ צִיִּים; וְאֹיְבָיו, עָפָר יְלַחֵכוּ
lefanav yichre'u tziyim; ve'oyevav, afar yelachechu
Let them that dwell in the wilderness bow before him; and his enemies lick the dust.

מַלְכֵי תַרְשִׁישׁ וְאִיִּים, מִנְחָה יָשִׁיבוּ; מַלְכֵי שְׁבָא וּסְבָא, אֶשְׁכָּר יַקְרִיבוּ
malchei tarshish ve'iyim minchah yashivu; malchei sheva useva, eshkar yakrivu
The kings of Tarshish and of the isles shall render tribute; the kings of Sheba and Seba shall offer gifts.

וְיִשְׁתַּחֲווּ-לוֹ כָל-מְלָכִים; כָּל-גּוֹיִם יַעַבְדוּהוּ
veyishtachavu-lo chol-melachim; kol-goyim ya'avduhu
Yea, all kings shall prostrate themselves before him; all nations shall serve him.

כִּי-יַצִּיל, אֶבְיוֹן מְשַׁוֵּעַ; וְעָנִי, וְאֵין-עֹזֵר לוֹ
ki-yatzil evyon meshavvea'; ve'ani, ve'ein-'ozer lo
For he will deliver the needy when he crieth; the poor also, and him that hath no helper.

יָחֹס, עַל-דַּל וְאֶבְיוֹן; וְנַפְשׁוֹת אֶבְיוֹנִים יוֹשִׁיעַ
yachos al-dal ve'evyon; venafshot evyonim yoshia
He will have pity on the poor and needy, and the souls of the needy he will save.

מִתּוֹךְ וּמֵחָמָס, יִגְאַל נַפְשָׁם; וְיֵיקַר דָּמָם בְּעֵינָיו
mittoch umechamos yig'al nafsham; veyeikar damam be'einav
He will redeem their soul from oppression and violence, and precious will their blood be in his sight;

וִיחִי--וְיִתֶּן-לוֹ, מִזְּהַב שְׁבָא
vichi, veyitten-lo mizzehav sheva
That they may live, and that he may give them of the gold of Sheba,

וְיִתְפַּלֵּל בַּעֲדוֹ תָמִיד; כָּל-הַיּוֹם, יְבָרְכֶנְהוּ
veyitpallel ba'ado tamid; kol-hayom, yevarachenhu
that they may pray for him continually, yea, bless him all the day.

יְהִי פִסַּת-בַּר, בָּאָרֶץ--בְּרֹאשׁ הָרִים
yehi fissat-bar ba'aretz berosh harim
May he be as a rich cornfield in the land upon the top of the mountains;

יִרְעַשׁ כַּלְּבָנוֹן פִּרְיוֹ; וְיָצִיצוּ מֵעִיר, כְּעֵשֶׂב הָאָרֶץ
yir'ash kallevanon piryo; veyatzitzu me'ir, ke'esev ha'aretz
may his fruit rustle like Lebanon; and may they blossom out of the city like grass of the earth.

יְהִי שְׁמוֹ, לְעוֹלָם--לִפְנֵי-שֶׁמֶשׁ יִנּוֹן שְׁמוֹ
yehi shemo le'olam, lifnei-shemesh yinnon shemo
May his name endure for ever; may his name be continued as long as the sun;

תְּהִלִּים

גַּם-אֲנִי, אוֹדְךָ בִכְלִי-נֶבֶל--אֲמִתְּךָ
gam-'ani odecha vichli-nevel amittecha
I also will give thanks unto Thee with the psaltery, even unto Thy truth,

אֱלֹהַי: אֲזַמְּרָה לְךָ בְכִנּוֹר--קְדוֹשׁ, יִשְׂרָאֵל
elohai azammerah lecha vechinnor; kedosh, yisra'el
O my God; I will sing praises unto Thee with the harp, O Thou Holy One of Israel.

תְּרַנֵּנָּה שְׂפָתַי, כִּי אֲזַמְּרָה-לָּךְ; וְנַפְשִׁי, אֲשֶׁר פָּדִיתָ
terannennah sefatai ki azammerah-lach; venafshi, asher padita
My lips shall greatly rejoice when I sing praises unto Thee; and my soul, which Thou hast redeemed.

גַּם-לְשׁוֹנִי--כָּל-הַיּוֹם, תֶּהְגֶּה צִדְקָתֶךָ: כִּי-בֹשׁוּ כִי-חָפְרוּ, מְבַקְשֵׁי רָעָתִי
gam-leshoni, kol-hayom tehgeh tzidkatecha; ki-voshu chi-chaferu, mevakshei ra'ati
My tongue also shall tell of Thy righteousness all the day; for they are ashamed, for they are abashed, that seek my hurt.

עב

לִשְׁלֹמֹה: אֱלֹהִים--מִשְׁפָּטֶיךָ, לְמֶלֶךְ תֵּן; וְצִדְקָתְךָ לְבֶן-מֶלֶךְ
Lishlomoh: elohim, mishpateicha lemelech ten; vetzidkatecha leven-melech
[A Psalm] of Solomon. Give the king Thy judgments, O God, and Thy righteousness unto the king's son;

יָדִין עַמְּךָ בְצֶדֶק; וַעֲנִיֶּיךָ בְמִשְׁפָּט
yadin ammecha vetzedek; va'aniyeicha vemishpat
That he may judge Thy people with righteousness, and Thy poor with justice.

יִשְׂאוּ הָרִים שָׁלוֹם לָעָם; וּגְבָעוֹת, בִּצְדָקָה
yis'u harim shalom la'am; ugeva'ot, bitzdakah
Let the mountains bear peace to the people, and the hills, through righteousness.

יִשְׁפֹּט, עֲנִיֵּי-עָם--יוֹשִׁיעַ, לִבְנֵי אֶבְיוֹן; וִידַכֵּא עוֹשֵׁק
yishpot aniyei-'am, yoshia livnei evyon; viydakkei oshek
May he judge the poor of the people, and save the children of the needy, and crush the oppressor.

יִירָאוּךָ עִם-שָׁמֶשׁ; וְלִפְנֵי יָרֵחַ, דּוֹר דּוֹרִים
yira'ucha im-shamesh; velifnei yareach, dor dorim
They shall fear Thee while the sun endureth, and so long as the moon, throughout all generations.

יֵרֵד, כְּמָטָר עַל-גֵּז; כִּרְבִיבִים, זַרְזִיף אָרֶץ
yered kematar al-gez; kirvivim, zarzif aretz
May he come down like rain upon the mown grass, as showers that water the earth.

יִפְרַח-בְּיָמָיו צַדִּיק; וְרֹב שָׁלוֹם, עַד-בְּלִי יָרֵחַ
yifrach-beyamav tzaddik; verov shalom, ad-beli yareach
In his days let the righteous flourish, and abundance of peace, till the moon be no more.

תְּהִלִּים

יֵעָטוּ חֶרְפָּה, וּכְלִמָּה--מְבַקְשֵׁי, רָעָתִי
ya'atu cherpah uchelimmah; mevakshei, ra'ati
let them be covered with reproach and confusion that seek my hurt.

וַאֲנִי, תָּמִיד אֲיַחֵל; וְהוֹסַפְתִּי, עַל-כָּל-תְּהִלָּתֶךָ
va'ani tamid ayachel; vehosafti, al-kol-tehillatecha
But as for me, I will hope continually, and will praise Thee yet more and more.

פִּי, יְסַפֵּר צִדְקָתֶךָ--כָּל-הַיּוֹם תְּשׁוּעָתֶךָ: כִּי לֹא יָדַעְתִּי סְפֹרוֹת
pi yesapper tzidkatecha, kol-hayom teshu'atecha; ki lo yada'ti seforot
My mouth shall tell of Thy righteousness, and of Thy salvation all the day; for I know not the numbers thereof.

אָבוֹא--בִּגְבֻרוֹת, אֲדֹנָי יְהוִה; אַזְכִּיר צִדְקָתְךָ לְבַדֶּךָ
'avo, bigvurot adonai hashem azkir tzidkatecha levaddecha
I will come with Thy mighty acts, O Lord GOD; I will make mention of Thy righteousness, even of Thine only.

אֱלֹהִים, לִמַּדְתַּנִי מִנְּעוּרָי; וְעַד-הֵנָּה, אַגִּיד נִפְלְאוֹתֶיךָ
'elohim, limmadtani minne'urai; ve'ad-hennah, aggid nifle'oteicha
O God, Thou hast taught me from my youth; and until now do I declare Thy wondrous works.

וְגַם עַד-זִקְנָה, וְשֵׂיבָה--אֱלֹהִים אַל-תַּעַזְבֵנִי
vegam ad-ziknah veseivah elohim al-ta'azveni
And even unto old age and hoary hairs, O God, forsake me not;

עַד-אַגִּיד זְרוֹעֲךָ לְדוֹר; לְכָל-יָבוֹא, גְּבוּרָתֶךָ
ad-'aggid zero'acha ledor; lechol-yavo, gevuratecha
until I have declared Thy strength unto the next generation, Thy might to every one that is to come.

וְצִדְקָתְךָ אֱלֹהִים, עַד-מָרוֹם
vetzidkatecha elohim, ad-marom
Thy righteousness also, O God, which reacheth unto high heaven;

אֲשֶׁר-עָשִׂיתָ גְדֹלוֹת; אֱלֹהִים, מִי כָמוֹךָ
asher-'asita gedolot; elohim, mi chamocha
Thou who hast done great things, O God, who is like unto Thee?

אֲשֶׁר הִרְאִיתַנִי, צָרוֹת רַבּוֹת--וְרָעוֹת:
'asher hir'itani tzarot rabbot, vera'ot
Thou, who hast made me to see many and sore troubles,

תָּשׁוּב תְּחַיֵּינִי; וּמִתְּהֹמוֹת הָאָרֶץ, תָּשׁוּב תַּעֲלֵנִי
tashuv techayeini; umittehomot ha'aretz, tashuv ta'aleni
wilt quicken me again, and bring me up again from the depths of the earth.

תֶּרֶב גְּדֻלָּתִי; וְתִסֹּב תְּנַחֲמֵנִי
terev gedullati, vetissov tenachameni
Thou wilt increase my greatness, and turn and comfort me.

תְּהִלִּים

צִוִּיתָ לְהוֹשִׁיעֵנִי: כִּי-סַלְעִי וּמְצוּדָתִי אַתָּה
tzivvita lehoshi'eni; ki-sal'i umetzudati attah
which Thou hast appointed to save me; for Thou art my rock and my fortress.

אֱלֹהַי--פַּלְּטֵנִי, מִיַּד רָשָׁע; מִכַּף מְעַוֵּל וְחוֹמֵץ
'elohai, palleteni miyad rasha'; mikkaf me'avvel vechometz
O my God, rescue me out of the hand of the wicked, out of the grasp of the unrighteous and ruthless man.

כִּי-אַתָּה תִקְוָתִי; אֲדֹנָי יְהוִה, מִבְטַחִי מִנְּעוּרָי
ki-'attah tikvati; adonai hashem mivtachi minne'urai
For Thou art my hope; O Lord GOD, my trust from my youth.

עָלֶיךָ, נִסְמַכְתִּי מִבֶּטֶן
'aleicha nismachti mibbeten
Upon Thee have I stayed myself from birth;

מִמְּעֵי אִמִּי, אַתָּה גוֹזִי; בְּךָ תְהִלָּתִי תָמִיד
mimme'ei immi attah gozi; becha tehillati tamid
Thou art He that took me out of my mother's womb; my praise is continually of Thee.

כְּמוֹפֵת, הָיִיתִי לְרַבִּים; וְאַתָּה, מַחֲסִי-עֹז
kemofet hayiti lerabbim; ve'attah, machasi-'oz
I am as a wonder unto many; but Thou art my strong refuge.

יִמָּלֵא פִי, תְּהִלָּתֶךָ; כָּל-הַיּוֹם, תִּפְאַרְתֶּךָ
yimmalei fi tehillatecha; kol-hayom, tif'artecha
My mouth shall be filled with Thy praise, and with Thy glory all the day.

אַל-תַּשְׁלִיכֵנִי, לְעֵת זִקְנָה; כִּכְלוֹת כֹּחִי, אַל-תַּעַזְבֵנִי
'al-tashlicheni le'et ziknah; kichlot kochi, al-ta'azveni
Cast me not off in the time of old age; when my strength faileth, forsake me not.

כִּי-אָמְרוּ אוֹיְבַי לִי; וְשֹׁמְרֵי נַפְשִׁי, נוֹעֲצוּ יַחְדָּו
ki-'ameru oyevai li; veshomerei nafshi, no'atzu yachdav
For mine enemies speak concerning me, and they that watch for my soul take counsel together,

לֵאמֹר, אֱלֹהִים עֲזָבוֹ; רִדְפוּ וְתִפְשׂוּהוּ, כִּי-אֵין מַצִּיל
lemor elohim azavo; ridfu vetifsuhu, ki-'ein matzil
Saying: 'God hath forsaken him; pursue and take him; for there is none to deliver.'

אֱלֹהִים, אַל-תִּרְחַק מִמֶּנִּי; אֱלֹהַי, לְעֶזְרָתִי חוּשָׁה
'elohim al-tirchak mimmenni; elohai, le'ezrati chushah
O God, be not far from me; O my God, make haste to help me.

יֵבֹשׁוּ יִכְלוּ, שֹׂטְנֵי נַפְשִׁי
yevoshu yichlu sotenei nafshi
Let them be ashamed and consumed that are adversaries to my soul;

תְּהִלִים

ע

לַמְנַצֵּחַ, לְדָוִד לְהַזְכִּיר
Lamnatzeach, ledavid lehazkir
For the Leader. [A Psalm] of David; to make memorial.

אֱלֹהִים לְהַצִּילֵנִי; יְהוָה, לְעֶזְרָתִי חוּשָׁה
'elohim lehatzileni; hashem le'ezrati chushah
O God, to deliver me, O LORD, to help me, make haste.

יֵבֹשׁוּ וְיַחְפְּרוּ, מְבַקְשֵׁי נַפְשִׁי
yevoshu veyachperu mevakshei nafshi
Let them be ashamed and abashed that seek after my soul;

יִסֹּגוּ אָחוֹר, וְיִכָּלְמוּ; חֲפֵצֵי, רָעָתִי
yissogu achor veyikkalemu; chafetzei, ra'ati
let them be turned backward and brought to confusion that delight in my hurt.

יָשׁוּבוּ, עַל-עֵקֶב בָּשְׁתָּם--הָאֹמְרִים, הֶאָח הֶאָח
yashuvu al-'ekev boshetam; ha'omerim, he'ach he'ach
Let them be turned back by reason of their shame that say: 'Aha, aha.'

יָשִׂישׂוּ וְיִשְׂמְחוּ, בְּךָ--כָּל-מְבַקְשֶׁיךָ
yasisu veyismechu becha, kol-mevaksheicha
Let all those that seek Thee rejoice and be glad in Thee;

וְיֹאמְרוּ תָמִיד, יִגְדַּל אֱלֹהִים--אֹהֲבֵי, יְשׁוּעָתֶךָ
veyomeru tamid yigdal elohim; ohavei, yeshu'atecha
and let such as love Thy salvation say continually: 'Let God be magnified.'

וַאֲנִי, עָנִי וְאֶבְיוֹן--אֱלֹהִים חוּשָׁה-לִּי: עֶזְרִי וּמְפַלְטִי אַתָּה; יְהוָה, אַל-תְּאַחַר
va'ani ani ve'evyon elohim chushah-li ezri umefalti attah; hashem al-te'achar
But I am poor and needy; O God, make haste unto me; Thou art my help and my deliverer; O LORD, tarry not.

עא

בְּךָ-יְהוָה חָסִיתִי; אַל-אֵבוֹשָׁה לְעוֹלָם
Becha-hashem chasiti; al-'evoshah le'olam
In Thee, O LORD, have I taken refuge; let me never be ashamed.

בְּצִדְקָתְךָ, תַּצִּילֵנִי וּתְפַלְּטֵנִי; הַטֵּה-אֵלַי אָזְנְךָ, וְהוֹשִׁיעֵנִי
betzidkatecha, tatzileni utefalleteni; hatteh-'elai ozenecha, vehoshi'eni
Deliver me in Thy righteousness, and rescue me; incline Thine ear unto me, and save me.

הֱיֵה לִי, לְצוּר מָעוֹן לָבוֹא--תָּמִיד
heyeh li letzur ma'on lavo, tamid
Be Thou to me a sheltering rock, whereunto I may continually resort,

תְּהִלִים

תְּהִי-טִירָתָם נְשַׁמָּה; בְּאָהֳלֵיהֶם, אַל-יְהִי יֹשֵׁב
tehi-tiratam neshammah; be'aholeihem, al-yehi yoshev
Let their encampment be desolate; let none dwell in their tents.

כִּי-אַתָּה אֲשֶׁר-הִכִּיתָ רָדָפוּ; וְאֶל-מַכְאוֹב חֲלָלֶיךָ יְסַפֵּרוּ
ki-'attah asher-hikkita radafu; ve'el-mach'ov chalaleicha yesapperu
For they persecute him whom Thou hast smitten; and they tell of the pain of those whom Thou hast wounded.

תְּנָה-עָוֺן, עַל-עֲוֺנָם; וְאַל-יָבֹאוּ, בְּצִדְקָתֶךָ
tenah-'avon al-'avonam; ve'al-yavo'u, betzidkatecha
Add iniquity unto their iniquity; and let them not come into Thy righteousness.

יִמָּחוּ, מִסֵּפֶר חַיִּים; וְעִם צַדִּיקִים, אַל-יִכָּתֵבוּ
yimmachu missefer chayim; ve'im tzaddikim, al-yikkatevu
Let them be blotted out of the book of the living, and not be written with the righteous.

וַאֲנִי, עָנִי וְכוֹאֵב; יְשׁוּעָתְךָ אֱלֹהִים תְּשַׂגְּבֵנִי
va'ani ani vecho'ev; yeshu'atecha elohim tesaggeveni
But I am afflicted and in pain; let Thy salvation, O God, set me up on high.

אֲהַלְלָה שֵׁם-אֱלֹהִים בְּשִׁיר; וַאֲגַדְּלֶנּוּ בְתוֹדָה
'ahalelah shem-'elohim beshir; va'agaddelennu vetodah
I will praise the name of God with a song, and will magnify Him with thanksgiving.

וְתִיטַב לַיהוָה, מִשּׁוֹר פָּר; מַקְרִן מַפְרִיס
vetitav lahashem mishor par, makrin mafris
And it shall please the LORD better than a bullock that hath horns and hoofs.

רָאוּ עֲנָוִים יִשְׂמָחוּ; דֹּרְשֵׁי אֱלֹהִים, וִיחִי לְבַבְכֶם
ra'u anavim yismachu; doreshei elohim, vichi levavchem
The humble shall see it, and be glad; ye that seek after God, let your heart revive.

כִּי-שֹׁמֵעַ אֶל-אֶבְיוֹנִים יְהוָה; וְאֶת-אֲסִירָיו, לֹא בָזָה
ki-shomea el-'evyonim hashem ve'et-'asirav, lo vazah
For the LORD hearkeneth unto the needy, and despiseth not His prisoners.

יְהַלְלוּהוּ, שָׁמַיִם וָאָרֶץ; יַמִּים, וְכָל-רֹמֵשׂ בָּם
yehaleluhu shamayim va'aretz; yammim, vechol-romes bam
Let heaven and earth praise Him, the seas, and every thing that moveth therein.

כִּי אֱלֹהִים, יוֹשִׁיעַ צִיּוֹן, וְיִבְנֶה, עָרֵי יְהוּדָה; וְיָשְׁבוּ שָׁם, וִירֵשׁוּהָ
ki elohim yoshia tziyon, veyivneh arei yehudah; veyashevu sham, viyereshuha
For God will save Zion, and build the cities of Judah; and they shall abide there, and have it in possession.

וְזֶרַע עֲבָדָיו, יִנְחָלוּהָ; וְאֹהֲבֵי שְׁמוֹ, יִשְׁכְּנוּ-בָהּ
vezera avadav yinchaluha; ve'ohavei shemo, yishkenu-vah
The seed also of His servants shall inherit it; and they that love His name shall dwell therein.

תְּהִלִּים

הַצִּילֵנִי מִטִּיט, וְאַל-אֶטְבָּעָה; אִנָּצְלָה מִשֹּׂנְאַי, וּמִמַּעֲמַקֵּי מָיִם
hatzileni mittit ve'al-'etba'ah; innatzelah missone'ai, umimma'amakkei-mayim
Deliver me out of the mire, and let me not sink; let me be delivered from them that hate me, and out of the deep waters.

אַל-תִּשְׁטְפֵנִי, שִׁבֹּלֶת מַיִם--וְאַל-תִּבְלָעֵנִי מְצוּלָה; וְאַל-תֶּאְטַר-עָלַי בְּאֵר פִּיהָ.
'al-tishtefeni shibbolet mayim ve'al-tivla'eni metzulah; ve'al-te'tar-'alai be'er piha
Let not the waterflood overwhelm me, neither let the deep swallow me up; and let not the pit shut her mouth upon me.

עֲנֵנִי יְהוָה, כִּי-טוֹב חַסְדֶּךָ; כְּרֹב רַחֲמֶיךָ, פְּנֵה אֵלָי
'aneni hashem ki-tov chasdecha; kerov rachameicha, peneh elai
Answer me, O LORD, for Thy mercy is good; according to the multitude of Thy compassions turn Thou unto me.

וְאַל-תַּסְתֵּר פָּנֶיךָ, מֵעַבְדֶּךָ: כִּי-צַר-לִי, מַהֵר עֲנֵנִי
ve'al-taster paneicha me'avdecha; ki-tzar-li, maher aneni
And hide not Thy face from Thy servant; for I am in distress; answer me speedily.

קָרְבָה אֶל-נַפְשִׁי גְאָלָהּ; לְמַעַן אֹיְבַי פְּדֵנִי
karevah el-nafshi ge'alah; lema'an oyevai pedeni
Draw nigh unto my soul, and redeem it; ransom me because of mine enemies.

אַתָּה יָדַעְתָּ--חֶרְפָּתִי וּבָשְׁתִּי, וּכְלִמָּתִי; נֶגְדְּךָ, כָּל-צוֹרְרָי
'attah yada'ta, cherpati uvasheti uchelimmati; negdecha, kol-tzorerai
Thou knowest my reproach, and my shame, and my confusion; mine adversaries are all before Thee.

חֶרְפָּה, שָׁבְרָה לִבִּי--וָאָנוּשָׁה: וָאֲקַוֶּה לָנוּד
cherpah shaverah libbi, va'anushah va'akavveh lanud
Reproach hath broken my heart; and I am sore sick; and I looked for some to show compassion,

וָאַיִן; וְלַמְנַחֲמִים, וְלֹא מָצָאתִי
va'ayin; velamnachamim, velo matzati
but there was none; and for comforters, but I found none.

וַיִּתְּנוּ בְּבָרוּתִי רֹאשׁ; וְלִצְמָאִי, יַשְׁקוּנִי חֹמֶץ
vayittenu bevaruti rosh; velitzma'i, yashkuni chometz
Yea, they put poison into my food; and in my thirst they gave me vinegar to drink.

יְהִי-שֻׁלְחָנָם לִפְנֵיהֶם לְפָח; וְלִשְׁלוֹמִים לְמוֹקֵשׁ
yehi-shulchanam lifneihem lefach; velishlomim lemokesh
Let their table before them become a snare; and when they are in peace, let it become a trap.

תֶּחְשַׁכְנָה עֵינֵיהֶם, מֵרְאוֹת; וּמָתְנֵיהֶם, תָּמִיד הַמְעַד
techshachnah eineihem mere'ot; umateneihem, tamid ham'ad
Let their eyes be darkened, that they see not; and make their loins continually to totter.

שְׁפָךְ-עֲלֵיהֶם זַעְמֶךָ; וַחֲרוֹן אַפְּךָ, יַשִּׂיגֵם
shefoch-'aleihem za'mecha; vacharon appecha, yassigem
Pour out Thine indignation upon them, and let the fierceness of Thine anger overtake them.

תְּהִלִּים

אֹיְבַי שֶׁקֶר--אֲשֶׁר לֹא-גָזַלְתִּי, אָז אָשִׁיב
oyevai sheker; asher lo-gazalti, az ashiv
being mine enemies wrongfully, are many; should I restore that which I took not away?

אֱלֹהִים--אַתָּה יָדַעְתָּ, לְאִוַּלְתִּי; וְאַשְׁמוֹתַי, מִמְּךָ לֹא-נִכְחָדוּ
'elohim, attah yada'ta le'ivvalti; ve'ashmotai, mimmecha lo-nichchadu
O God, Thou knowest my folly; and my trespasses are not hid from Thee.

אַל-יֵבֹשׁוּ בִי, קֹוֶיךָ--אֲדֹנָי יְהוִה, צְבָאוֹת
'al-yevoshu vi koycha adonai hashem tzeva'ot
Let not them that wait for Thee be ashamed through me, O Lord GOD of hosts;

אַל-יִכָּלְמוּ בִי מְבַקְשֶׁיךָ--אֱלֹהֵי, יִשְׂרָאֵל
al-yikkalemu vi mevaksheicha; elohei, yisra'el
let not those that seek Thee be brought to confusion through me, O God of Israel.

כִּי-עָלֶיךָ, נָשָׂאתִי חֶרְפָּה; כִּסְּתָה כְלִמָּה פָנָי
ki-'aleicha nasati cherpah; kissetah chelimmah fanai
Because for Thy sake I have borne reproach; confusion hath covered my face.

מוּזָר, הָיִיתִי לְאֶחָי; וְנָכְרִי, לִבְנֵי אִמִּי
muzar hayiti le'echai; venacheri, livnei immi
I am become a stranger unto my brethren, and an alien unto my mother's children.

כִּי-קִנְאַת בֵּיתְךָ אֲכָלָתְנִי; וְחֶרְפּוֹת חוֹרְפֶיךָ, נָפְלוּ עָלָי
ki-kin'at beitecha achalateni; vecherpot chorefeicha, nafelu alai
Because zeal for Thy house hath eaten me up, and the reproaches of them that reproach Thee are fallen upon me.

וָאֶבְכֶּה בַצּוֹם נַפְשִׁי; וַתְּהִי לַחֲרָפוֹת לִי
va'evkeh vatzom nafshi; vattehi lacharafot li
And I wept with my soul fasting, and that became unto me a reproach.

וָאֶתְּנָה לְבוּשִׁי שָׂק; וָאֱהִי לָהֶם לְמָשָׁל
va'ettenah levushi sak; va'ehi lahem lemashal
I made sackcloth also my garment, and I became a byword unto them.

יָשִׂיחוּ בִי, יֹשְׁבֵי שָׁעַר; וּנְגִינוֹת, שׁוֹתֵי שֵׁכָר
yasichu vi yoshevei sha'ar; uneginot, shotei shechar
They that sit in the gate talk of me; and I am the song of the drunkards.

וַאֲנִי תְפִלָּתִי-לְךָ יְהוָה, עֵת רָצוֹן--אֱלֹהִים
va'ani tefillati-lecha hashem et ratzon, elohim
But as for me, let my prayer be unto Thee, O LORD, in an acceptable time; O God,

בְּרָב-חַסְדֶּךָ; עֲנֵנִי, בֶּאֱמֶת יִשְׁעֶךָ
berav-chasdecha; aneni, be'emet yish'echa
in the abundance of Thy mercy, answer me with the truth of Thy salvation.

תְּהִלִים

מִתְרַפֵּס בְּרַצֵּי-כָסֶף; בִּזַּר עַמִּים, קְרָבוֹת יֶחְפָּצוּ
mitrappes beratzei-chasef; bizzar ammim, keravot yechpatzu
every one submitting himself with pieces of silver; He hath scattered the peoples that delight in war!

יֶאֱתָיוּ חַשְׁמַנִּים, מִנִּי מִצְרָיִם; כּוּשׁ תָּרִיץ יָדָיו, לֵאלֹהִים
ye'etayu chashmannim minni mitzrayim; kush taritz yadav, le'elohim
Nobles shall come out of Egypt; Ethiopia shall hasten to stretch out her hands unto God.

מַמְלְכוֹת הָאָרֶץ, שִׁירוּ לֵאלֹהִים; זַמְּרוּ אֲדֹנָי סֶלָה
mamlechot ha'aretz shiru le'elohim; zammeru adonai selah
Sing unto God, ye kingdoms of the earth; O sing praises unto the Lord; Selah

לָרֹכֵב, בִּשְׁמֵי שְׁמֵי-קֶדֶם--הֵן יִתֵּן בְּקוֹלוֹ, קוֹל עֹז
larochev bishmei shemei-kedem; hen yitten bekolo kol oz
To Him that rideth upon the heavens of heavens, which are of old; lo, He uttereth His voice, a mighty voice.

תְּנוּ עֹז, לֵאלֹהִים: עַל-יִשְׂרָאֵל גַּאֲוָתוֹ; וְעֻזּוֹ, בַּשְּׁחָקִים
tenu oz, le'elohim al-yisra'el ga'avato; ve'uzzo, bashechakim
Ascribe ye strength unto God; His majesty is over Israel, and His strength is in the skies.

נוֹרָא אֱלֹהִים, מִמִּקְדָּשֶׁיךָ: אֵל יִשְׂרָאֵל--הוּא נֹתֵן עֹז וְתַעֲצֻמוֹת לָעָם; בָּרוּךְ אֱלֹהִים
nora elohim, mimmikdasheicha el yisra'el, hu noten oz veta'atzumot la'am, baruch elohim
Awful is God out of thy holy places; the God of Israel, He giveth strength and power unto the people; blessed be God.

סט

לַמְנַצֵּחַ עַל-שׁוֹשַׁנִּים לְדָוִד
Lamnatzeach al-shoshannim ledavid
For the Leader; upon Shoshannim. [A Psalm] of David.

הוֹשִׁיעֵנִי אֱלֹהִים-- כִּי בָאוּ מַיִם עַד-נָפֶשׁ
hoshi'eni elohim; ki va'u mayim ad-nafesh
Save me, O God; for the waters are come in even unto the soul.

טָבַעְתִּי, בִּיוֵן מְצוּלָה-- וְאֵין מָעֳמָד; בָּאתִי בְמַעֲמַקֵּי-מַיִם, וְשִׁבֹּלֶת שְׁטָפָתְנִי
tava'ti biven metzulah ve'ein mo'omad; bati vema'amakkei-mayim, veshibbolet shetafatni
I am sunk in deep mire, where there is no standing; I am come into deep waters, and the flood overwhelmeth me.

יָגַעְתִּי בְקָרְאִי, נִחַר גְּרוֹנִי: כָּלוּ עֵינַי--מְיַחֵל, לֵאלֹהָי
yaga'ti vekare'i nichar geroni kalu einai; meyachel, le'elohai
I am weary of my crying; my throat is dried; mine eyes fail while I wait for my God.

רַבּוּ, מִשַּׂעֲרוֹת רֹאשִׁי-- שֹׂנְאַי חִנָּם: עָצְמוּ מַצְמִיתַי
rabbu missa'arot roshi sone'ai chinnam atzemu matzmitai
They that hate me without a cause are more than the hairs of my head; they that would cut me off,

תְּהִלִּים

הָאֵל לָנוּ, אֵל לְמוֹשָׁעוֹת: וְלֵיהוָה אֲדֹנָי--לַמָּוֶת, תֹּצָאוֹת
ha'el lanu el lemosha'ot vele'elohim adonai; lammavet, totza'ot
God is unto us a God of deliverances; and unto GOD the Lord belong the issues of death.

אַךְ-אֱלֹהִים--יִמְחַץ, רֹאשׁ אֹיְבָיו: קָדְקֹד שֵׂעָר--מִתְהַלֵּךְ, בַּאֲשָׁמָיו
'ach-'elohim, yimchatz rosh oyevav kodekod se'ar; mit'hallech, ba'ashamav
Surely God will smite through the head of His enemies, the hairy scalp of him that goeth about in his guiltiness.

אָמַר אֲדֹנָי, מִבָּשָׁן אָשִׁיב; אָשִׁיב, מִמְּצֻלוֹת יָם
'amar adonai mibbashan ashiv; ashiv, mimmetzulot yam
The Lord said: 'I will bring back from Bashan, I will bring them back from the depths of the sea;

לְמַעַן, תִּמְחַץ רַגְלְךָ--בְּדָם: לְשׁוֹן כְּלָבֶיךָ--מֵאֹיְבִים מִנֵּהוּ
lema'an timchatz raglecha, bedam leshon kelaveicha; me'oyevim minnehu
That thy foot may wade through blood, that the tongue of thy dogs may have its portion from thine enemies.'

רָאוּ הֲלִיכוֹתֶיךָ אֱלֹהִים; הֲלִיכוֹת אֵלִי מַלְכִּי בַקֹּדֶשׁ
ra'u halichoteicha elohim; halichot eli malki vakkodesh
They see Thy goings, O God, even the goings of my God, my King, in holiness.

קִדְּמוּ שָׁרִים, אַחַר נֹגְנִים; בְּתוֹךְ עֲלָמוֹת, תּוֹפֵפוֹת
kiddemu sharim achar nogenim; betoch alamot, tofefot
The singers go before, the minstrels follow after, in the midst of damsels playing upon timbrels.

בְּמַקְהֵלוֹת, בָּרְכוּ אֱלֹהִים; אֲדֹנָי, מִמְּקוֹר יִשְׂרָאֵל
bemak'helot barechu elohim; hashem mimmekor yisra'el
'Bless ye God in full assemblies, even the Lord, ye that are from the fountain of Israel.'

שָׁם בִּנְיָמִן, צָעִיר רֹדֵם
sham binyamin tza'ir rodem
There is Benjamin, the youngest, ruling them,

שָׂרֵי יְהוּדָה, רִגְמָתָם; שָׂרֵי זְבֻלוּן, שָׂרֵי נַפְתָּלִי
sarei yehudah rigmatam; sarei zevulun, sarei naftali
the princes of Judah their council, the princes of Zebulun, the princes of Naphtali.

צִוָּה אֱלֹהֶיךָ, עֻזֶּךָ: עוּזָּה אֱלֹהִים--זוּ, פָּעַלְתָּ לָּנוּ
tzivvah eloheicha, uzzecha uzzah elohim; zu, pa'alta lanu
Thy God hath commanded thy strength; be strong, O God, Thou that hast wrought for us

מֵהֵיכָלֶךָ, עַל-יְרוּשָׁלִָם--לְךָ יוֹבִילוּ מְלָכִים שָׁי
meheichalecha al-yerushalayim; lecha yovilu melachim shai
Out of Thy temple at Jerusalem, whither kings shall bring presents unto Thee.

-גְּעַר חַיַּת קָנֶה, עֲדַת אַבִּירִים בְּעֶגְלֵי עַמִּים
ge'ar chayat kaneh adat abbirim be'eglei ammim
Rebuke the wild beast of the reeds, the multitude of the bulls, with the calves of the peoples,

תְּהִלִּים

אֲדֹנָי יִתֶּן-אֹמֶר; הַמְבַשְּׂרוֹת, צָבָא רָב
'adonai yitten-'omer; hamevasserot, tzava rav
The Lord giveth the word; the women that proclaim the tidings are a great host.

מַלְכֵי צְבָאוֹת, יִדֹּדוּן יִדֹּדוּן; וּנְוַת-בַּיִת, תְּחַלֵּק שָׁלָל
malchei tzeva'ot yiddodun yiddodun; unevat bayit, techallek shalal
Kings of armies flee, they flee; and she that tarrieth at home divideth the spoil.

אִם-תִּשְׁכְּבוּן, בֵּין שְׁפַתָּיִם: כַּנְפֵי יוֹנָה, נֶחְפָּה בַכֶּסֶף
'im-tishkevun bein shefattayim kanfei yonah nechpah vakkesef
When ye lie among the sheepfolds, the wings of the dove are covered with silver,

וְאֶבְרוֹתֶיהָ, בִּירַקְרַק חָרוּץ
ve'evroteiha, birakrak charutz
and her pinions with the shimmer of gold.

בְּפָרֵשׂ שַׁדַּי מְלָכִים בָּהּ--תַּשְׁלֵג בְּצַלְמוֹן
befares shaddai melachim bah, tashleg betzalmon
When the Almighty scattereth kings therein, it snoweth in Zalmon.

הַר-אֱלֹהִים הַר-בָּשָׁן: הַר גַּבְנֻנִּים, הַר-בָּשָׁן
har-'elohim har-bashan; har gavnunnim, har-bashan
A mountain of God is the mountain of Bashan; a mountain of peaks is the mountain of Bashan.

לָמָּה, תְּרַצְּדוּן--הָרִים גַּבְנֻנִּים: הָהָר--חָמַד אֱלֹהִים לְשִׁבְתּוֹ
lammah teratzedun harim gavnunnim hahar, chamad elohim leshIvto
Why look ye askance, ye mountains of peaks, at the mountain which God hath desired for His abode?

אַף-יְהוָה, יִשְׁכֹּן לָנֶצַח
af-hashem yishkon lanetzach
Yea, the LORD will dwell therein for ever.

רֶכֶב אֱלֹהִים, רִבֹּתַיִם אַלְפֵי שִׁנְאָן; אֲדֹנָי בָם, סִינַי בַּקֹּדֶשׁ
rechev elohim, ribbotayim alfei shin'an; adonai vam, sinai bakkodesh
The chariots of God are myriads, even thousands upon thousands; the Lord is among them, as in Sinai, in holiness.

עָלִיתָ לַמָּרוֹם, שָׁבִיתָ שֶּׁבִי--לָקַחְתָּ מַתָּנוֹת, בָּאָדָם
'alita lammarom shavita shevi, lakachta mattanot ba'adam;
Thou hast ascended on high, Thou hast led captivity captive; Thou hast received gifts among men,

וְאַף סוֹרְרִים, לִשְׁכֹּן יָהּ אֱלֹהִים
ve'af sorerim, lishkon yah elohim
yea, among the rebellious also, that the LORD God might dwell there.

בָּרוּךְ אֲדֹנָי, יוֹם יוֹם: יַעֲמָס-לָנוּ--הָאֵל יְשׁוּעָתֵנוּ סֶלָה
baruch adonai yom yom ya'amos-lanu, ha'el yeshu'atenu selah
Blessed be the Lord, day by day He beareth our burden, even the God who is our salvation. Selah

תְּהִלִּים

כְּהִמֵּס דּוֹנַג, מִפְּנֵי-אֵשׁ--יֹאבְדוּ רְשָׁעִים, מִפְּנֵי אֱלֹהִים
kehimmes donag mippenei-'esh; yovedu resha'im, mippenei elohim
as wax melteth before the fire, so let the wicked perish at the presence of God.

וְצַדִּיקִים--יִשְׂמְחוּ יַעַלְצוּ, לִפְנֵי אֱלֹהִים; וְיָשִׂישׂוּ בְשִׂמְחָה
vetzaddikim, yismechu ya'altzu lifnei elohim, veyasisu vesimchah
But let the righteous be glad, let them exult before God; yea, let them rejoice with gladness.

שִׁירוּ, לֵאלֹהִים--זַמְּרוּ שְׁמוֹ: סֹלּוּ, לָרֹכֵב בָּעֲרָבוֹת
shiru le'elohim zammeru shemo sollu larochev ba'aravot
Sing unto God, sing praises to His name; extol Him that rideth upon the skies,

בְּיָהּ שְׁמוֹ; וְעִלְזוּ לְפָנָיו
beyah shemo, ve'ilzu lefanav
whose name is the LORD; and exult ye before Him.

אֲבִי יְתוֹמִים, וְדַיַּן אַלְמָנוֹת--אֱלֹהִים, בִּמְעוֹן קָדְשׁוֹ
'avi yetomim vedayan almanot; elohim, bim'on kodsho
A father of the fatherless, and a judge of the widows, is God in His holy habitation.

אֱלֹהִים, מוֹשִׁיב יְחִידִים בַּיְתָה--מוֹצִיא אֲסִירִים, בַּכּוֹשָׁרוֹת
'elohim moshiv yechidim baytah, motzi asirim bakkosharot
God maketh the solitary to dwell in a house; He bringeth out the prisoners into prosperity;

אַךְ סוֹרְרִים, שָׁכְנוּ צְחִיחָה
ach sorarim, shachenu tzechichah
the rebellious dwell but in a parched land.

אֱלֹהִים--בְּצֵאתְךָ, לִפְנֵי עַמֶּךָ; בְּצַעְדְּךָ בִישִׁימוֹן סֶלָה
'elohim, betzetecha lifnei ammecha; betza'decha vishimon selah
O God, when Thou wentest forth before Thy people, when Thou didst march through the wilderness; Selah

אֶרֶץ רָעָשָׁה, אַף-שָׁמַיִם נָטְפוּ--מִפְּנֵי אֱלֹהִים
'eretz ra'ashah af-shamayim natefu mippenei elohim
The earth trembled, the heavens also dropped at the presence of God;

זֶה סִינַי--מִפְּנֵי אֱלֹהִים, אֱלֹהֵי יִשְׂרָאֵל
zeh sinai; mippenei elohim, elohei yisra'el
even yon Sinai trembled at the presence of God, the God of Israel.

גֶּשֶׁם נְדָבוֹת, תָּנִיף אֱלֹהִים; נַחֲלָתְךָ וְנִלְאָה, אַתָּה כוֹנַנְתָּהּ
geshem nedavot tanif elohim; nachalatecha venil'ah, attah chonantah
A bounteous rain didst Thou pour down, O God; when Thine inheritance was weary, Thou didst confirm it.

חַיָּתְךָ יָשְׁבוּ-בָהּ; תָּכִין בְּטוֹבָתְךָ לֶעָנִי אֱלֹהִים
chayatecha yashevu-vah; tachin betovatecha le'ani elohim
Thy flock settled therein; Thou didst prepare in Thy goodness for the poor, O God.

תְּהִלִּים

אֱלֹהִים, יְחָנֵּנוּ וִיבָרְכֵנוּ; יָאֵר פָּנָיו אִתָּנוּ סֶלָה
'elohim, yechannenu vivarechenu; ya'er panav ittanu selah
God be gracious unto us, and bless us; may He cause His face to shine toward us; Selah

לָדַעַת בָּאָרֶץ דַּרְכֶּךָ; בְּכָל-גּוֹיִם, יְשׁוּעָתֶךָ
lada'at ba'aretz darkecha; bechol-goyim, yeshu'atecha
That Thy way may be known upon earth, Thy salvation among all nations.

יוֹדוּךָ עַמִּים אֱלֹהִים: יוֹדוּךָ, עַמִּים כֻּלָּם
yoducha ammim elohim; yoducha, ammim kullam
Let the peoples give thanks unto Thee, O God; let the peoples give thanks unto Thee, all of them.

יִשְׂמְחוּ וִירַנְּנוּ, לְאֻמִּים: כִּי-תִשְׁפֹּט עַמִּים מִישֹׁר
yismechu virannenu, le'ummim ki-tishpot ammim mishor
O let the nations be glad and sing for joy; for Thou wilt judge the peoples with equity,

וּלְאֻמִּים, בָּאָרֶץ תַּנְחֵם סֶלָה
ule'ummim ba'aretz tanchem selah
and lead the nations upon earth. Selah

יוֹדוּךָ עַמִּים אֱלֹהִים: יוֹדוּךָ, עַמִּים כֻּלָּם
yoducha ammim elohim; yoducha, ammim kullam
Let the peoples give thanks unto Thee, O God; let the peoples give thanks unto Thee, all of them.

אֶרֶץ, נָתְנָה יְבוּלָהּ; יְבָרְכֵנוּ, אֱלֹהִים אֱלֹהֵינוּ
'eretz natenah yevulah; yevarechenu, elohim eloheinu
The earth hath yielded her increase; may God, our own God, bless us.

יְבָרְכֵנוּ אֱלֹהִים; וְיִירְאוּ אוֹתוֹ, כָּל-אַפְסֵי-אָרֶץ
yevarechenu elohim; veyire'u oto, kol-'afsei-'aretz
May God bless us; and let all the ends of the earth fear Him.

סח

לַמְנַצֵּחַ לְדָוִד, מִזְמוֹר שִׁיר
Lamnatzeach ledavid, mizmor shir
For the Leader. A Psalm of David, a Song.

יָקוּם אֱלֹהִים, יָפוּצוּ אוֹיְבָיו; וְיָנוּסוּ מְשַׂנְאָיו, מִפָּנָיו
yakum elohim yafutzu oyevav; veyanusu mesan'av, mippanav
Let God arise, let His enemies be scattered; and let them that hate Him flee before Him.

כְּהִנְדֹּף עָשָׁן, תִּנְדֹּף
kehindof ashan, tindof
As smoke is driven away, so drive them away;

תְּהִלִּים

בָּאנוּ-בָאֵשׁ וּבַמַּיִם; וַתּוֹצִיאֵנוּ, לָרְוָיָה
banu-va'esh uvammayim; vattotzi'enu, larevayah
we went through fire and through water; but Thou didst bring us out unto abundance.

אָבוֹא בֵיתְךָ בְעוֹלוֹת; אֲשַׁלֵּם לְךָ נְדָרָי
'avo veitecha ve'olot; ashallem lecha nedarai
I will come into Thy house with burnt-offerings, I will perform unto Thee my vows,

אֲשֶׁר-פָּצוּ שְׂפָתָי; וְדִבֶּר-פִּי, בַּצַּר-לִי
'asher-patzu sefatai; vedibber-pi, batzar-li
Which my lips have uttered, and my mouth hath spoken, when I was in distress.

עֹלוֹת מֵיחִים אַעֲלֶה-לָּךְ, עִם-קְטֹרֶת אֵילִים
'olot mechim a'aleh-lach im-ketoret eilim
I will offer unto Thee burnt-offerings of fatlings, with the sweet smoke of rams;

אֶעֱשֶׂה בָקָר עִם-עַתּוּדִים סֶלָה
e'eseh vakar im-'attudim selah
I will offer bullocks with goats. Selah

לְכוּ-שִׁמְעוּ וַאֲסַפְּרָה, כָּל-יִרְאֵי אֱלֹהִים: אֲשֶׁר עָשָׂה לְנַפְשִׁי
lechu-shim'u va'asapperah kol-yir'ei elohim; asher asah lenafshi
Come, and hearken, all ye that fear God, and I will declare what He hath done for my soul.

אֵלָיו פִּי-קָרָאתִי; וְרוֹמַם, תַּחַת לְשׁוֹנִי
'elav pi-karati; veromam, tachat leshoni
I cried unto Him with my mouth, and He was extolled with my tongue.

אָוֶן, אִם-רָאִיתִי בְלִבִּי-- לֹא יִשְׁמַע אֲדֹנָי
'aven im-ra'iti velibbi; lo yishma adonai
If I had regarded iniquity in my heart, the Lord would not hear;

אָכֵן, שָׁמַע אֱלֹהִים; הִקְשִׁיב, בְּקוֹל תְּפִלָּתִי
'achen shama elohim; hikshiv, bekol tefillati
But verily God hath heard; He hath attended to the voice of my prayer.

בָּרוּךְ אֱלֹהִים-- אֲשֶׁר לֹא-הֵסִיר תְּפִלָּתִי וְחַסְדּוֹ, מֵאִתִּי
baruch elohim; asher lo-hesir tefillati vechasdo, me'itti
Blessed be God, who hath not turned away my prayer, nor His mercy from me.

67

לַמְנַצֵּחַ בִּנְגִינֹת, מִזְמוֹר שִׁיר
Lamnatzech binginot, mizmor shir
For the Leader; with string-music. A Psalm, a Song.

תְּהִלִים

אִמְרוּ לֵאלֹהִים, מַה-נּוֹרָא מַעֲשֶׂיךָ
'imru le'elohim mah-nora ma'aseicha
Say unto God: 'How tremendous is Thy work!

בְּרֹב עֻזְּךָ, יְכַחֲשׁוּ לְךָ אֹיְבֶיךָ
berov uzzecha, yechachashu lecha oyeveicha
Through the greatness of Thy power shall Thine enemies dwindle away before Thee.

כָּל-הָאָרֶץ, יִשְׁתַּחֲווּ לְךָ--וִיזַמְּרוּ-לָךְ; יְזַמְּרוּ שִׁמְךָ סֶלָה
kol-ha'aretz yishtachavu lecha vizammeru-lach; yezammeru shimcha selah
All the earth shall worship Thee, and shall sing praises unto Thee; they shall sing praises to Thy name.' Selah

לְכוּ וּרְאוּ, מִפְעֲלוֹת אֱלֹהִים; נוֹרָא עֲלִילָה, עַל-בְּנֵי אָדָם
lechu ure'u mif'alot elohim; nora alilah, al-benei adam
Come, and see the works of God; He is terrible in His doing toward the children of men.

הָפַךְ יָם, לְיַבָּשָׁה--בַּנָּהָר, יַעַבְרוּ בְרָגֶל; שָׁם, נִשְׂמְחָה-בּוֹ
hafach yam leyabbashah, bannahar ya'avru veragel; sham, nismechah-bo
He turned the sea into dry land; they went through the river on foot; there let us rejoice in Him!

מֹשֵׁל בִּגְבוּרָתוֹ, עוֹלָם--עֵינָיו, בַּגּוֹיִם תִּצְפֶּינָה
moshel bigvurato olam, einav baggoyim titzpeinah
Who ruleth by His might for ever; His eyes keep watch upon the nations

הַסּוֹרְרִים, אַל-יָרוּמוּ לָמוֹ סֶלָה
hassorerim al-yarumu lamo selah
let not the rebellious exalt themselves. Selah

בָּרְכוּ עַמִּים אֱלֹהֵינוּ; וְהַשְׁמִיעוּ, קוֹל תְּהִלָּתוֹ
barechu ammim eloheinu; vehashmi'u, kol tehillato
Bless our God, ye peoples, and make the voice of His praise to be heard;

הַשָּׂם נַפְשֵׁנוּ, בַּחַיִּים; וְלֹא-נָתַן לַמּוֹט רַגְלֵנוּ
hassam nafshenu bachayim; velo-natan lammot raglenu
Who hath set our soul in life, and suffered not our foot to be moved,

כִּי-בְחַנְתָּנוּ אֱלֹהִים; צְרַפְתָּנוּ, כִּצְרָף-כָּסֶף
ki-vechantanu elohim; tzeraftanu, kitzraf-kasef
For Thou, O God, hast tried us; Thou hast refined us, as silver is refined.

הֲבֵאתָנוּ בַמְּצוּדָה; שַׂמְתָּ מוּעָקָה בְמָתְנֵינוּ
havetanu vammetzudah; samta mu'akah vemateneinu
Thou didst bring us into the hold; Thou didst lay constraint upon our loins.

הִרְכַּבְתָּ אֱנוֹשׁ, לְרֹאשֵׁנוּ
hirkavta enosh, leroshenu
Thou hast caused men to ride over our heads;

תְּהִלִּים

וַיִּירְאוּ, יֹשְׁבֵי קְצָוֺת-מֵאוֹתֹתֶיךָ
vayire'u yoshevei ketzavot me'ototeicha
So that they that dwell in the uttermost parts stand in awe of Thy signs;

מוֹצָאֵי בֹקֶר וָעֶרֶב תַּרְנִין
motza'ei-voker va'erev tarnin
Thou makest the outgoings of the morning and evening to rejoice.

פָּקַדְתָּ הָאָרֶץ וַתְּשֹׁקְקֶהָ, רַבַּת תַּעְשְׁרֶנָּה
pakadta ha'aretz vatteshokekeha rabbat ta'sherennah
Thou hast remembered the earth, and watered her, greatly enriching her,

פֶּלֶג אֱלֹהִים, מָלֵא מָיִם; תָּכִין דְּגָנָם, כִּי-כֵן תְּכִינֶהָ
peleg elohim malei mayim; tachin deganam, ki-chen techineha
with the river of God that is full of water; Thou preparest them corn, for so preparest Thou her.

תְּלָמֶיהָ רַוֵּה, נַחֵת גְּדוּדֶהָ
telameiha ravveh nachet gedudeiha
Watering her ridges abundantly, settling down the furrows thereof,

בִּרְבִיבִים תְּמֹגְגֶנָּה, צִמְחָהּ תְּבָרֵךְ
birvivim temogegennah, tzimchah tevarech
Thou makest her soft with showers; Thou blessest the growth thereof.

עִטַּרְתָּ, שְׁנַת טוֹבָתֶךָ; וּמַעְגָּלֶיךָ, יִרְעֲפוּן דָּשֶׁן
'ittarta shenat tovatecha; uma'galeicha, yir'afun dashen
Thou crownest the year with Thy goodness; and Thy paths drop fatness.

יִרְעֲפוּ, נְאוֹת מִדְבָּר; וְגִיל, גְּבָעוֹת תַּחְגֹּרְנָה
yir'afu ne'ot midbar; vegil, geva'ot tachgorenah
The pastures of the wilderness do drop; and the hills are girded with joy.

לָבְשׁוּ כָרִים, הַצֹּאן--וַעֲמָקִים יַעַטְפוּ-בָר; יִתְרוֹעֲעוּ, אַף-יָשִׁירוּ
laveshu charim hatzon, va'amakim ya'atfu-var; yitro'a'u, af-yashiru
The meadows are clothed with flocks; the valleys also are covered over with corn; they shout for joy, yea, they sing.

10

לַמְנַצֵּחַ, שִׁיר מִזְמוֹר: הָרִיעוּ לֵאלֹהִים, כָּל-הָאָרֶץ
Lamnatzeach shir mizmor; hari'u le'elohim kol-ha'aretz
For the Leader. A Song, a Psalm. Shout unto God, all the earth;

זַמְּרוּ כְבוֹד-שְׁמוֹ; שִׂימוּ כָבוֹד, תְּהִלָּתוֹ
zammeru chevod-shemo; simu chavod, tehillato
Sing praises unto the glory of His name; make His praise glorious.

תְּהִלִּים

יִשְׂמַח צַדִּיק בַּיהוָה, וְחָסָה בוֹ; וְיִתְהַלְלוּ, כָּל-יִשְׁרֵי-לֵב
yismach tzaddik bahashem vechasah vo; veyit'halelu, kol-yishrei-lev
The righteous shall be glad in the LORD, and shall take refuge in Him; and all the upright in heart shall glory.

סה

לַמְנַצֵּחַ מִזְמוֹר, לְדָוִד שִׁיר
Lamnatzeach mizmor, ledavid shir
For the Leader. A Psalm. A Song of David.

לְךָ דֻמִיָּה תְהִלָּה אֱלֹהִים בְּצִיּוֹן; וּלְךָ, יְשֻׁלַּם-נֶדֶר
lecha dumiyah tehillah elohim betziyon; ulecha, yeshullam-neder
Praise waiteth for Thee, O God, in Zion; and unto Thee the vow is performed.

שֹׁמֵעַ תְּפִלָּה--עָדֶיךָ, כָּל-בָּשָׂר יָבֹאוּ
shomea tefillah; adeicha, kol-basar yavo'u
O Thou that hearest prayer, unto Thee doth all flesh come.

דִּבְרֵי עֲוֹנֹת, גָּבְרוּ מֶנִּי; פְּשָׁעֵינוּ, אַתָּה תְכַפְּרֵם
divrei avonot gaveru menni; pesha'einu, attah techapperem
The tale of iniquities is too heavy for me; as for our transgressions, Thou wilt pardon them.

אַשְׁרֵי, תִּבְחַר וּתְקָרֵב--יִשְׁכֹּן חֲצֵרֶיךָ
'ashrei tivchar utekarev yishkon chatzereicha
Happy is the man whom Thou choosest, and bringest near, that he may dwell in Thy courts;

נִשְׂבְּעָה, בְּטוּב בֵּיתֶךָ; קְדֹשׁ, הֵיכָלֶךָ
nisbe'ah betuv beitecha; kedosh, heichalecha
may we be satisfied with the goodness of Thy house, the holy place of Thy temple!

נוֹרָאוֹת, בְּצֶדֶק תַּעֲנֵנוּ--אֱלֹהֵי יִשְׁעֵנוּ
nora'ot betzedek ta'anenu elohei yish'enu
With wondrous works dost Thou answer us in righteousness, O God of our salvation;

מִבְטָח כָּל-קַצְוֵי-אֶרֶץ, וְיָם רְחֹקִים
mivtach kol-katzvei-'eretz, veyam rechokim
Thou the confidence of all the ends of the earth, and of the far distant seas;

מֵכִין הָרִים בְּכֹחוֹ; נֶאְזָר, בִּגְבוּרָה
mechin harim bechocho; ne'ezar, bigvurah
Who by Thy strength settest fast the mountains, who art girded about with might;

מַשְׁבִּיחַ, שְׁאוֹן יַמִּים--שְׁאוֹן גַּלֵּיהֶם; וַהֲמוֹן לְאֻמִּים
mashbiach she'on yammim she'on galleihem, vahamon le'ummim
Who stillest the roaring of the seas, the roaring of their waves, and the tumult of the peoples;

תְּהִלִּים

סד

לַמְנַצֵּחַ, מִזְמוֹר לְדָוִד
Lamnatzeach, mizmor ledavid
For the Leader. A Psalm of David.

שְׁמַע-אֱלֹהִים קוֹלִי בְשִׂיחִי; מִפַּחַד אוֹיֵב, תִּצֹּר חַיָּי
shema'-'elohim koli vesichi; mippachad oyev, titzor chayai
Hear my voice, O God, in my complaint; preserve my life from the terror of the enemy.

תַּסְתִּירֵנִי, מִסּוֹד מְרֵעִים; מֵרִגְשַׁת, פֹּעֲלֵי אָוֶן
tastireni missod mere'im; merigshat, po'alei aven
Hide me from the council of evil-doers; from the tumult of the workers of iniquity;

אֲשֶׁר שָׁנְנוּ כַחֶרֶב לְשׁוֹנָם; דָּרְכוּ חִצָּם, דָּבָר מָר
'asher shanenu chacherev leshonam; darechu chitzam, davar mar
Who have whet their tongue like a sword, and have aimed their arrow, a poisoned word;

לִירוֹת בַּמִּסְתָּרִים תָּם; פִּתְאֹם יֹרֻהוּ, וְלֹא יִירָאוּ
lirot bammistarim tam; pit'om yoruhu, velo yira'u
That they may shoot in secret places at the blameless; suddenly do they shoot at him, and fear not.

יְחַזְּקוּ-לָמוֹ, דָּבָר רָע--יְסַפְּרוּ, לִטְמוֹן מוֹקְשִׁים; אָמְרוּ, מִי יִרְאֶה-לָּמוֹ
yechazzeku-lamo davar ra', yesapperu litmon mokeshim; ameru, mi yir'eh-lamo
They encourage one another in an evil matter; they converse of laying snares secretly; they ask, who would see them.

יַחְפְּשׂוּ-עוֹלֹת--תַּמְנוּ, חֵפֶשׂ מְחֻפָּשׂ
yachpesu-'olot, tamnu chefes mechuppas
They search out iniquities, they have accomplished a diligent search;

וְקֶרֶב אִישׁ, וְלֵב עָמֹק
vekerev ish, velev amok
even in the inward thought of every one, and the deep heart.

וַיֹּרֵם, אֱלֹהִים: חֵץ פִּתְאוֹם--הָיוּ, מַכּוֹתָם
vayorem, elohim chetz pit'om; hayu, makkotam
But God doth shoot at them with an arrow suddenly; thence are their wounds.

וַיַּכְשִׁילוּהוּ עָלֵימוֹ לְשׁוֹנָם; יִתְנֹדְדוּ, כָּל-רֹאֵה בָם
vayachshiluhu aleimo leshonam; yitnodedu, kol-ro'eh vam
So they make their own tongue a stumbling unto themselves; all that see them shake the head.

וַיִּירְאוּ, כָּל-אָדָם: וַיַּגִּידוּ, פֹּעַל אֱלֹהִים; וּמַעֲשֵׂהוּ הִשְׂכִּילוּ
vayire'u, kol-'adam vayaggidu po'al elohim, uma'asehu hiskilu
And all men fear; and they declare the work of God, and understand His doing.

תְּהִלִים

כַּמַהּ לְךָ בְשָׂרִי; בְּאֶרֶץ־צִיָּה וְעָיֵף בְּלִי־מָיִם
kamah lecha vesari; be'eretz-tziyah ve'ayef beli-mayim
my flesh longeth for Thee, in a dry and weary land, where no water is.

כֵּן, בַּקֹּדֶשׁ חֲזִיתִךָ--לִרְאוֹת עֻזְּךָ, וּכְבוֹדֶךָ
ken bakkodesh chaziticha; lir'ot uzzecha, uchevodecha
So have I looked for Thee in the sanctuary, to see Thy power and Thy glory.

כִּי־טוֹב חַסְדְּךָ, מֵחַיִּים; שְׂפָתַי יְשַׁבְּחוּנְךָ
ki-tov chasdecha mechayim, sefatai yeshabbechuncha
For Thy lovingkindness is better than life; my lips shall praise Thee.

כֵּן אֲבָרֶכְךָ בְחַיָּי; בְּשִׁמְךָ, אֶשָּׂא כַפָּי
ken avarechcha vechayai; beshimcha essa chappai
So will I bless Thee as long as I live; in Thy name will I lift up my hands.

כְּמוֹ חֵלֶב וָדֶשֶׁן, תִּשְׂבַּע נַפְשִׁי; וְשִׂפְתֵי רְנָנוֹת, יְהַלֶּל־פִּי
kemo chelev vadeshen tisba nafshi; vesiftei renanot, yehallel-pi
My soul is satisfied as with marrow and fatness; and my mouth doth praise Thee with joyful lips;

אִם־זְכַרְתִּיךָ עַל־יְצוּעָי--בְּאַשְׁמֻרוֹת, אֶהְגֶּה־בָּךְ
'im-zecharticha al-yetzu'ai; be'ashmurot, ehgeh-bach
When I remember Thee upon my couch, and meditate on Thee in the night-watches.

כִּי־הָיִיתָ עֶזְרָתָה לִּי; וּבְצֵל כְּנָפֶיךָ אֲרַנֵּן
ki-hayita ezratah li; uvetzel kenafeicha arannen
For Thou hast been my help, and in the shadow of Thy wings do I rejoice.

דָּבְקָה נַפְשִׁי אַחֲרֶיךָ; בִּי, תָּמְכָה יְמִינֶךָ
davekah nafshi achareicha; bi, tamchah yeminecha
My soul cleaveth unto Thee; Thy right hand holdeth me fast.

וְהֵמָּה--לְשׁוֹאָה, יְבַקְשׁוּ נַפְשִׁי; יָבֹאוּ, בְּתַחְתִּיּוֹת הָאָרֶץ
vehemmah, lesho'ah yevakeshu nafshi; yavo'u, betachtiyot ha'aretz
But those that seek my soul, to destroy it, shall go into the nethermost parts of the earth.

יַגִּירֻהוּ, עַל־יְדֵי־חָרֶב; מְנָת שֻׁעָלִים יִהְיוּ
yaggiruhu al-yedei-charev; menat shu'alim yihyu
They shall be hurled to the power of the sword; they shall be a portion for foxes.

וְהַמֶּלֶךְ, יִשְׂמַח בֵּאלֹהִים: יִתְהַלֵּל, כָּל־הַנִּשְׁבָּע בּוֹ
vehammelech yismach be'elohim yit'hallel kol-hannishba bo
But the king shall rejoice in God; every one that sweareth by Him shall glory;

כִּי יִסָּכֵר, פִּי דוֹבְרֵי־שָׁקֶר
ki yissacher, pi doverei-shaker
for the mouth of them that speak lies shall be stopped.

תְּהִלִים

אַךְ לֵאלֹהִים, דּוֹמִי נַפְשִׁי: כִּי-מִמֶּנּוּ, תִּקְוָתִי
'ach le'elohim dommi nafshi; ki-mimmennu, tikvati
Only for God wait thou in stillness, my soul; for from Him cometh my hope.

אַךְ-הוּא צוּרִי, וִישׁוּעָתִי; מִשְׂגַּבִּי, לֹא אֶמּוֹט
'ach-hu tzuri vishu'ati; misgabbi, lo emmot
He only is my rock and my salvation, my high tower, I shall not be moved.

עַל-אֱלֹהִים, יִשְׁעִי וּכְבוֹדִי; צוּר-עֻזִּי מַחְסִי, בֵּאלֹהִים
'al-'elohim yish'i uchevodi; tzur-'uzzi machsi, belohim
Upon God resteth my salvation and my glory; the rock of my strength, and my refuge, is in God.

בִּטְחוּ בוֹ בְכָל-עֵת, עָם--שִׁפְכוּ-לְפָנָיו לְבַבְכֶם; אֱלֹהִים מַחֲסֶה-לָּנוּ סֶלָה
bitchu vo vechal-'et am, shifchu-lefanav levavchem; elohim machaseh-lanu selah
Trust in Him at all times, ye people; pour out your heart before Him; God is a refuge for us. Selah

אַךְ, הֶבֶל בְּנֵי-אָדָם--כָּזָב בְּנֵי-אִישׁ
'ach hevel benei-'adam kazav benei ish
Men of low degree are vanity, and men of high degree are a lie;

בְּמֹאזְנַיִם לַעֲלוֹת; הֵמָּה, מֵהֶבֶל יָחַד
bemozenayim la'alot; hemmah, mehevel yachad
if they be laid in the balances, they are together lighter than vanity.

אַל-תִּבְטְחוּ בְעֹשֶׁק, וּבְגָזֵל אַל-תֶּהְבָּלוּ: חַיִל כִּי-יָנוּב--אַל-תָּשִׁיתוּ לֵב
'al-tivtechu ve'oshek uvegazel al-tehbalu chayil ki-yanuv; al-tashitu lev
Trust not in oppression, and put not vain hope in robbery; if riches increase, set not your heart thereon.

אַחַת, דִּבֶּר אֱלֹהִים--שְׁתַּיִם-זוּ שָׁמָעְתִּי: כִּי עֹז, לֵאלֹהִים
'achat dibber elohim, shetayim-zu shama'eti; ki oz, le'elohim
God hath spoken once, twice have I heard this: that strength belongeth unto God;

וּלְךָ-אֲדֹנָי חָסֶד: כִּי-אַתָּה תְשַׁלֵּם לְאִישׁ כְּמַעֲשֵׂהוּ
ulecha-'adonai chased; ki-'attah teshallem le'ish kema'asehu
Also unto Thee, O Lord, belongeth mercy; for Thou renderest to every man according to his work.

סג

מִזְמוֹר לְדָוִד; בִּהְיוֹתוֹ, בְּמִדְבַּר יְהוּדָה
Mizmor ledavid; bihyoto, bemidbar yehudah
A Psalm of David, when he was in the wilderness of Judah.

אֱלֹהִים, אֵלִי אַתָּה--אֲשַׁחֲרֶךָּ: צָמְאָה לְךָ, נַפְשִׁי
'elohim eli attah, ashachareka tzame'ah lecha nafshi
O God, Thou art my God, earnestly will I seek Thee; my soul thirsteth for Thee,

תְּהִלִּים

אֲגוּרָה בְאָהָלְךָ, עוֹלָמִים; אֶחֱסֶה בְסֵתֶר כְּנָפֶיךָ סֶּלָה
'agurah ve'aholecha olamim; echeseh veseter kenafeicha selah
I will dwell in Thy Tent for ever; I will take refuge in the covert of Thy wings. Selah

כִּי-אַתָּה אֱלֹהִים, שָׁמַעְתָּ לִנְדָרָי; נָתַתָּ יְרֻשַּׁת, יִרְאֵי שְׁמֶךָ
ki-'attah elohim shama'ta lindarai; natata yerushat, yir'ei shemecha
For Thou, O God, hast heard my vows; Thou hast granted the heritage of those that fear Thy name.

יָמִים עַל-יְמֵי-מֶלֶךְ תּוֹסִיף; שְׁנוֹתָיו, כְּמוֹ-דֹר וָדֹר
yamim al-yemei-melech tosif; shenotav, kemo-dor vador
Mayest Thou add days unto the king's days! May his years be as many generations!

יֵשֵׁב עוֹלָם, לִפְנֵי אֱלֹהִים; חֶסֶד וֶאֱמֶת, מַן יִנְצְרֻהוּ
yeshev olom lifnei elohim; chesed ve'emet, man yintzeruhu
May he be enthroned before God for ever! Appoint mercy and truth, that they may preserve him.

כֵּן אֲזַמְּרָה שִׁמְךָ לָעַד--לְשַׁלְּמִי נְדָרַי, יוֹם יוֹם
ken azammerah shimcha la'ad; leshallemi nedarai, yom yom
So will I sing praise unto Thy name for ever, that I may daily perform my vows.

סב

לַמְנַצֵּחַ עַל-יְדוּתוּן--מִזְמוֹר לְדָוִד
Lamnatzeach al-yedutun, mizmor ledavid
For the Leader; for Jeduthun. A Psalm of David.

אַךְ אֶל-אֱלֹהִים, דּוּמִיָּה נַפְשִׁי; מִמֶּנּוּ, יְשׁוּעָתִי
'ach el-'elohim dumiyah nafshi; mimmennu, yeshu'ati
Only for God doth my soul wait in stillness; from Him cometh my salvation.

אַךְ-הוּא צוּרִי, וִישׁוּעָתִי; מִשְׂגַּבִּי, לֹא-אֶמּוֹט רַבָּה
'ach-hu tzuri vishu'ati; misgabbi, lo-'emmot rabbah
He only is my rock and my salvation, my high tower, I shall not be greatly moved.

עַד-אָנָה, תְּהוֹתְתוּ עַל-אִישׁ--תְּרָצְּחוּ כֻלְּכֶם: כְּקִיר נָטוּי; גָּדֵר, הַדְּחוּיָה
'ad-'anah tehotetu al ish teratzechu chullechem kekir natui; gader, haddechuyah
How long will ye set upon a man, that ye may slay him, all of you, as a leaning wall, a tottering fence?

אַךְ מִשְּׂאֵתוֹ, יָעֲצוּ לְהַדִּיחַ--יִרְצוּ כָזָב
'ach misse'eto ya'atzu lehaddiach yirtzu chazav
They only devise to thrust him down from his height, delighting in lies;

בְּפִיו יְבָרֵכוּ; וּבְקִרְבָּם, יְקַלְלוּ-סֶלָה
befiv yevarechu; uvekirbam, yekalelu-selah
they bless with their mouth, but they curse inwardly. Selah

תְּהִלִים

אֱלֹהִים, דִּבֶּר בְּקָדְשׁוֹ--אֶעְלֹזָה: אֲחַלְּקָה שְׁכֶם; וְעֵמֶק סֻכּוֹת אֲמַדֵּד
'elohim dibber bekodesho, e'lozah achallekah shechem; ve'emek sukkot amadded
God spoke in His holiness, that I would exult; that I would divide Shechem, and mete out the valley of Succoth.

לִי גִלְעָד, וְלִי מְנַשֶּׁה, וְאֶפְרַיִם, מָעוֹז רֹאשִׁי; יְהוּדָה, מְחֹקְקִי
li gil'ad veli menasheh, ve'efrayim ma'oz roshi; yehudah, mechokeki
Gilead is mine, and Manasseh is mine; Ephraim also is the defence of my head; Judah is my sceptre.

מוֹאָב, סִיר רַחְצִי--עַל-אֱדוֹם, אַשְׁלִיךְ נַעֲלִי; עָלַי, פְּלֶשֶׁת הִתְרוֹעָעִי
mo'av sir rachtzi, al-'edom ashlich na'ali; alai, peleshet hitro'a'i
Moab is my washpot; upon Edom do I cast my shoe; Philistia, cry aloud because of me!

מִי יֹבִלֵנִי, עִיר מָצוֹר; מִי נָחַנִי עַד-אֱדוֹם
mi yovileni ir matzor; mi nachani ad-'edom
Who will bring me into the fortified city? Who will lead me unto Edom?

הֲלֹא-אַתָּה אֱלֹהִים זְנַחְתָּנוּ; וְלֹא-תֵצֵא אֱלֹהִים, בְּצִבְאוֹתֵינוּ
halo-'attah elohim zenachtanu; velo-tetzei elohim, betziv'oteinu
Hast not Thou, O God, cast us off? And Thou goest not forth, O God, with our hosts.

הָבָה-לָּנוּ עֶזְרָת מִצָּר; וְשָׁוְא, תְּשׁוּעַת אָדָם
havah-lanu ezrat mitzar; veshav, teshu'at adam
Give us help against the adversary; for vain is the help of man.

בֵּאלֹהִים נַעֲשֶׂה-חָיִל; וְהוּא, יָבוּס צָרֵינוּ
Be'elohim na'aseh-chayil; vehu, yavus tzareinu
Through God we shall do valiantly; for He it is that will tread down our adversaries.

סא

לַמְנַצֵּחַ עַל-נְגִינַת לְדָוִד
Lamnatzeach al-neginat ledavid
For the Leader; with string-music. [A Psalm] of David.

שִׁמְעָה אֱלֹהִים, רִנָּתִי; הַקְשִׁיבָה, תְּפִלָּתִי
shim'ah elohim rinnati; hakshivah, tefillati
Hear my cry, O God; attend unto my prayer.

מִקְצֵה הָאָרֶץ, אֵלֶיךָ אֶקְרָא--בַּעֲטֹף לִבִּי; בְּצוּר-יָרוּם מִמֶּנִּי תַנְחֵנִי
miktzeh ha'aretz eleicha ekra ba'atof libbi; betzur-yarum mimmenni tancheni
From the end of the earth will I call unto Thee, when my heart fainteth; lead me to a rock that is too high for me.

כִּי-הָיִיתָ מַחְסֶה לִי; מִגְדַּל-עֹז, מִפְּנֵי אוֹיֵב
ki-hayita machseh li; migdal-'oz, mippenei oyev
For Thou hast been a refuge for me, a tower of strength in the face of the enemy.

תְּהִלִּים

וַאֲנִי, אָשִׁיר עֻזֶּךָ--וַאֲרַנֵּן לַבֹּקֶר, חַסְדֶּךָ
va'ani ashir uzzecha va'arannen labboker, chasdecha
But as for me, I will sing of Thy strength; yea, I will sing aloud of Thy mercy in the morning;

כִּי-הָיִיתָ מִשְׂגָּב לִי; וּמָנוֹס, בְּיוֹם צַר-לִי
ki-hayita misgav li; umanos, beyom tzar-li
for Thou hast been my high tower, and a refuge in the day of my distress.

עֻזִּי, אֵלֶיךָ אֲזַמֵּרָה: כִּי-אֱלֹהִים מִשְׂגַּבִּי, אֱלֹהֵי חַסְדִּי
'uzzi eleicha azammerah; ki-'elohim misgabbi, elohei chasdi
O my strength, unto Thee will I sing praises; for God is my high tower, the God of my mercy.

O

לַמְנַצֵּחַ, עַל-שׁוּשַׁן עֵדוּת; מִכְתָּם לְדָוִד לְלַמֵּד
Lamnatzeach al-shushan edut; michtam ledavid lelammed
For the Leader; upon Shushan Eduth; Michtam of David, to teach;

בְּהַצּוֹתוֹ, אֶת אֲרַם נַהֲרַיִם--וְאֶת-אֲרַם צוֹבָה: וַיָּשָׁב יוֹאָב
behatzoto et aram naharayim ve'et-'aram tzovah vayashov yo'av
when he strove with Aram-naharaim and with Aram-zobah, and Joab returned,

וַיַּךְ אֶת-אֱדוֹם בְּגֵיא-מֶלַח--שְׁנֵים עָשָׂר אָלֶף
vayach et-'edom begei-melach; sheneim asar alef
and smote of Edom in the Valley of Salt twelve thousand.

אֱלֹהִים, זְנַחְתָּנוּ פְרַצְתָּנוּ; אָנַפְתָּ, תְּשׁוֹבֵב לָנוּ
'elohim zenachtanu feratztanu; anafta, teshovev lanu
O God, Thou hast cast us off, Thou hast broken us down; Thou hast been angry; O restore us.

הִרְעַשְׁתָּה אֶרֶץ פְּצַמְתָּהּ; רְפָה שְׁבָרֶיהָ כִי-מָטָה
hir'ashtah eretz petzamtah; refah shevareiha chi-matah
Thou hast made the land to shake, Thou hast cleft it; heal the breaches thereof; for it tottereth.

הִרְאִיתָ עַמְּךָ קָשָׁה; הִשְׁקִיתָנוּ, יַיִן תַּרְעֵלָה
hir'itah ammecha kashah; hishkitanu, yayin tar'elah
Thou hast made Thy people to see hard things; Thou hast made us to drink the wine of staggering.

נָתַתָּה לִּירֵאֶיךָ נֵּס, לְהִתְנוֹסֵס--מִפְּנֵי, קֹשֶׁט סֶלָה
natattah lire'eicha nes lehitnoses; mippenei, koshet selah
Thou hast given a banner to them that fear Thee, that it may be displayed because of the truth. Selah

לְמַעַן, יֵחָלְצוּן יְדִידֶיךָ; הוֹשִׁיעָה יְמִינְךָ וַעֲנֵנִי
lema'an yechaletzun yedideicha; hoshi'ah yeminecha va'aneni
That Thy beloved may be delivered, save with Thy right hand, and answer me.

תְּהִלִּים

הִנֵּה, יַבִּיעוּן בְּפִיהֶם--חֲרָבוֹת, בְּשִׂפְתוֹתֵיהֶם: כִּי-מִי שֹׁמֵעַ
hinneh yabbi'un befihem, charavot besiftoteihem; ki-mi shomea
Behold, they belch out with their mouth; swords are in their lips: 'For who doth hear?'

וְאַתָּה יְהוָה, תִּשְׂחַק-לָמוֹ; תִּלְעַג, לְכָל-גּוֹיִם
ve'attah hashem tischak-lamo; til'ag, lechol-goyim
But Thou, O LORD, shalt laugh at them; Thou shalt have all the nations in derision.

עֻזּוֹ, אֵלֶיךָ אֶשְׁמֹרָה: כִּי-אֱלֹהִים, מִשְׂגַּבִּי
'uzzo eleicha eshmorah; ki-'elohim, misgabbi
Because of his strength, I will wait for Thee; for God is my high tower.

אֱלֹהֵי חַסְדִּי יְקַדְּמֵנִי; אֱלֹהִים, יַרְאֵנִי בְשֹׁרְרָי
'elohei chasdi yekaddemeni; elohim, yar'eni veshorerai
The God of my mercy will come to meet me; God will let me gaze upon mine adversaries.

אַל-תַּהַרְגֵם, פֶּן-יִשְׁכְּחוּ עַמִּי--הֲנִיעֵמוֹ בְחֵילְךָ
'al-tahargem pen-yishkechu ammi, hani'emo vecheilecha
Slay them not, lest my people forget, make them wander to and fro by Thy power,

וְהוֹרִידֵמוֹ: מָגִנֵּנוּ אֲדֹנָי
vehoridemo; maginnenu adonai
and bring them down, O Lord our shield.

חַטַּאת-פִּימוֹ, דְּבַר-שְׂפָתֵימוֹ
chattat-pimo, devar-sefateimo
For the sin of their mouth, and the words of their lips,

וְיִלָּכְדוּ בִגְאוֹנָם; וּמֵאָלָה וּמִכַּחַשׁ יְסַפֵּרוּ
veyillachedu vig'onam; ume'alah umikkachash yesapperu
let them even be taken in their pride, and for cursing and lying which they speak.

כַּלֵּה בְחֵמָה, כַּלֵּה וְאֵינֵמוֹ
kalleh vechemah kalleh ve'einemo
Consume them in wrath, consume them, that they be no more;

וְיֵדְעוּ--כִּי-אֱלֹהִים, מֹשֵׁל בְּיַעֲקֹב; לְאַפְסֵי הָאָרֶץ סֶלָה
veyede'u, ki-'elohim moshel beya'akov; le'afsei ha'aretz selah
and let them know that God ruleth in Jacob, unto the ends of the earth. Selah

וְיָשֻׁבוּ לָעֶרֶב, יֶהֱמוּ כַכָּלֶב; וִיסוֹבְבוּ עִיר
veyashuvu la'erev yehemu chakkalev, viysovevu ir
And they return at evening, they howl like a dog, and go round about the city;

הֵמָּה, יְנִיעוּן לֶאֱכֹל--אִם-לֹא יִשְׂבְּעוּ, וַיָּלִינוּ
hemmah yeni'un le'echol; im-lo yisbe'u, vayalinu
They wander up and down to devour, and tarry all night if they have not their fill.

תְּהִלִּים

יִשְׂמַח צַדִּיק, כִּי-חָזָה נָקָם; פְּעָמָיו יִרְחַץ, בְּדַם הָרָשָׁע
yismach tzaddik ki-chazah nakam; pe'amav yirchatz, bedam harasha
The righteous shall rejoice when he seeth the vengeance; he shall wash his feet in the blood of the wicked.

וְיֹאמַר אָדָם, אַךְ-פְּרִי לַצַּדִּיק; אַךְ יֵשׁ-אֱלֹהִים, שֹׁפְטִים בָּאָרֶץ
veyomar adom ach-peri latzaddik; ach yesh-'elohim, shofetim ba'aretz
And men shall say: 'Verily there is a reward for the righteous; verily there is a God that judgeth in the earth.'

נט

לַמְנַצֵּחַ אַל-תַּשְׁחֵת, לְדָוִד מִכְתָּם: בִּשְׁלֹחַ שָׁאוּל; וַיִּשְׁמְרוּ אֶת-הַבַּיִת, לַהֲמִיתוֹ
Lamnatzeach al-tashchet ledavid michtam bishloach sha'ul; vayishmeru et-habbayit, lahamito
For the Leader; Al-tashheth. [A Psalm] of David; Michtam; when Saul sent, and they watched the house to kill him.

הַצִּילֵנִי מֵאֹיְבַי אֱלֹהָי; מִמִּתְקוֹמְמַי תְּשַׂגְּבֵנִי
hatzileni me'oyevai elohai; mimitkomemai tesaggeveni
Deliver me from mine enemies, O my God; set me on high from them that rise up against me.

הַצִּילֵנִי, מִפֹּעֲלֵי אָוֶן; וּמֵאַנְשֵׁי דָמִים, הוֹשִׁיעֵנִי
hatzileni mippo'alei aven; ume'anshei damim, hoshi'eni
Deliver me from the workers of iniquity, and save me from the men of blood.

כִּי הִנֵּה אָרְבוּ, לְנַפְשִׁי--יָגוּרוּ עָלַי עַזִים
ki hinneh arevu lenafshi, yaguru alai azim
For, lo, they lie in wait for my soul; the impudent gather themselves together against me;

לֹא-פִשְׁעִי וְלֹא-חַטָּאתִי יְהוָה
lo-fish'i velo-chattati hashem
not for my transgression, nor for my sin, O LORD.

בְּלִי-עָו‍ֹן, יְרֻצוּן וְיִכּוֹנָנוּ; עוּרָה לִקְרָאתִי וּרְאֵה
beli-'avon yerutzun veyikkonanu; urah likrati ure'eh
Without my fault, they run and prepare themselves; awake Thou to help me, and behold.

וְאַתָּה יְהוָה-אֱלֹהִים צְבָאוֹת, אֱלֹהֵי יִשְׂרָאֵל-הָקִיצָה-לִפְקֹד כָּל-הַגּוֹיִם
ve'attah hashem-'elohim tzeva'ot elohei yisra'el, hakitzah, lifkod kol-haggoyim
Thou therefore, O LORD God of hosts, the God of Israel, arouse Thyself to punish all the nations;

אַל-תָּחֹן כָּל-בֹּגְדֵי אָוֶן סֶלָה
al-tachon kol-bogedei aven selah
show no mercy to any iniquitous traitors. Selah

יָשׁוּבוּ לָעֶרֶב, יֶהֱמוּ כַכָּלֶב; וִיסוֹבְבוּ עִיר
yashuvu la'erev yehemu chakkalev, visovevu ir
They return at evening, they howl like a dog, and go round about the city.

תְּהִלִים

רוּמָה עַל-שָׁמַיִם אֱלֹהִים; עַל כָּל-הָאָרֶץ כְּבוֹדֶךָ
rumah al-shamayim elohim; al kol-ha'aretz kevodecha
Be Thou exalted, O God, above the heavens; Thy glory be above all the earth.

נח

לַמְנַצֵּחַ אַל-תַּשְׁחֵת, לְדָוִד מִכְתָּם
Lamnatzeach al-tashchet, ledavid michtam
For the Leader; Al-tashheth. [A Psalm] of David; Michtam.

הַאֻמְנָם--אֵלֶם צֶדֶק, תְּדַבֵּרוּן; מֵישָׁרִים תִּשְׁפְּטוּ, בְּנֵי אָדָם
ha'umnam, elem tzedek tedabberun; meisharim tishpetu, benei adam
Do ye indeed speak as a righteous company? Do ye judge with equity the sons of men?

אַף-בְּלֵב, עוֹלֹת תִּפְעָלוּן: בָּאָרֶץ--חֲמַס יְדֵיכֶם, תְּפַלֵּסוּן
'af-belev olot tif'alun ba'aretz chamas yedeichem, tefallesun
Yea, in heart ye work wickedness; ye weigh out in the earth the violence of your hands.

זֹרוּ רְשָׁעִים מֵרָחֶם; תָּעוּ מִבֶּטֶן, דֹּבְרֵי כָזָב
zoru resha'im merachem; ta'u mibbeten, doverei chazav
The wicked are estranged from the womb; the speakers of lies go astray as soon as they are born.

חֲמַת-לָמוֹ, כִּדְמוּת חֲמַת-נָחָשׁ; כְּמוֹ-פֶתֶן חֵרֵשׁ, יַאְטֵם אָזְנוֹ
chamat-lamo, kidmut chamat-nachash; kemo-feten cheresh, ya'tem ozeno
Their venom is like the venom of a serpent; they are like the deaf asp that stoppeth her ear;

אֲשֶׁר לֹא-יִשְׁמַע, לְקוֹל מְלַחֲשִׁים; חוֹבֵר חֲבָרִים מְחֻכָּם
'asher lo-yishma lekol melachashim; chover chavarim mechukkam
Which hearkeneth not to the voice of charmers, or of the most cunning binder of spells.

אֱלֹהִים--הֲרָס שִׁנֵּימוֹ בְּפִימוֹ; מַלְתְּעוֹת כְּפִירִים, נְתֹץ יְהוָה
'elohim, haras-shinneimo befimo; malte'ot kefirim, netotz hashem
Break their teeth, O God, in their mouth; break out the cheek-teeth of the young lions, O LORD.

יִמָּאֲסוּ כְמוֹ-מַיִם, יִתְהַלְּכוּ-לָמוֹ; יִדְרֹךְ חִצָּו, כְּמוֹ יִתְמֹלָלוּ
yimma'asu chemo-mayim yit'hallechu-lamo; yidroch chitzav, kemo yitmolalu
Let them melt away as water that runneth apace; when he aimeth his arrows, let them be as though they were cut off.

כְּמוֹ שַׁבְּלוּל, תֶּמֶס יַהֲלֹךְ; נֵפֶל אֵשֶׁת, בַּל-חָזוּ שָׁמֶשׁ
kemo shabbelul temes yahaloch; nefel eshet, bal-chazu shamesh
Let them be as a snail which melteth and passeth away; like the untimely births of a woman, that have not seen the sun.

בְּטֶרֶם, יָבִינוּ סִּירֹתֵכֶם אָטָד; כְּמוֹ-חַי כְּמוֹ-חָרוֹן, יִשְׂעָרֶנּוּ
beterem yavinu siroteichem atad; kemo-chai kemo-charon, yis'arennu
Before your pots can feel the thorns, He will sweep it away with a whirlwind, the raw and the burning alike.

תְּהִלִּים

אֶקְרָא, לֵאלֹהִים עֶלְיוֹן; לָאֵל, גֹּמֵר עָלָי
'ekra le'elohim elyon; la'el, gomer alai
I will cry unto God Most high; unto God that accomplisheth it for me.

יִשְׁלַח מִשָּׁמַיִם, וְיוֹשִׁיעֵנִי--חֵרֵף שֹׁאֲפִי סֶלָה
yishlach mishamayim veyoshi'eni, cheref sho'afi selah
He will send from heaven, and save me, when he that would swallow me up taunteth; Selah

יִשְׁלַח אֱלֹהִים, חַסְדּוֹ וַאֲמִתּוֹ
yishlach elohim, chasdo va'amitto
God shall send forth His mercy and His truth.

נַפְשִׁי, בְּתוֹךְ לְבָאִם--אֶשְׁכְּבָה לֹהֲטִים
nafshi betoch leva'im eshkevah lohatim
My soul is among lions, I do lie down among them that are aflame;

בְּנֵי-אָדָם--שִׁנֵּיהֶם, חֲנִית וְחִצִּים; וּלְשׁוֹנָם, חֶרֶב חַדָּה
benei-'adam, shinneihem chanit vechitzim; uleshonam, cherev chaddah
even the sons of men, whose teeth are spears and arrows, and their tongue a sharp sword.

רוּמָה עַל-הַשָּׁמַיִם אֱלֹהִים; עַל כָּל-הָאָרֶץ כְּבוֹדֶךָ
rumah al-hashamayim elohim; al kol-ha'aretz kevodecha
Be Thou exalted, O God, above the heavens; Thy glory be above all the earth.

רֶשֶׁת, הֵכִינוּ לִפְעָמַי--כָּפַף נַפְשִׁי
reshet hechinu lif'amai kafaf nafshi
They have prepared a net for my steps, my soul is bowed down;

כָּרוּ לְפָנַי שִׁיחָה; נָפְלוּ בְתוֹכָהּ סֶלָה
karu lefanai shichah; nafelu vetochah selah
they have digged a pit before me, they are fallen into the midst thereof themselves. Selah

נָכוֹן לִבִּי אֱלֹהִים, נָכוֹן לִבִּי; אָשִׁירָה, וַאֲזַמֵּרָה
nachon libbi elohim nachon libbi; ashirah, va'azammerah
My heart is stedfast, O God, my heart is stedfast; I will sing, yea, I will sing praises.

עוּרָה כְבוֹדִי--עוּרָה, הַנֵּבֶל וְכִנּוֹר; אָעִירָה שָּׁחַר
'urah chevodi, urah hannevel vechinnor, a'irah shachar
Awake, my glory; awake, psaltery and harp; I will awake the dawn.

אוֹדְךָ בָעַמִּים אֲדֹנָי; אֲזַמֶּרְךָ, בַּלְאֻמִּים
'odecha va'ammim adonai; azammercha, bal-'ummim
I will give thanks unto Thee, O Lord, among the peoples; I will sing praises unto Thee among the nations.

כִּי-גָדֹל עַד-שָׁמַיִם חַסְדֶּךָ; וְעַד-שְׁחָקִים אֲמִתֶּךָ
ki-gadol ad-shamayim chasdecha; ve'ad-shechakim amittecha
For Thy mercy is great unto the heavens, and Thy truth unto the skies.

תְּהִלִּים

עַל-אָוֶן פַּלֶּט-לָמוֹ; בְּאַף, עַמִּים הוֹרֵד אֱלֹהִים
'al-'aven pallet-lamo; be'af, ammim hored elohim
Because of iniquity cast them out; in anger bring down the peoples, O God.

נֹדִי, סָפַרְתָּה-אָתָּה: שִׂימָה דִמְעָתִי בְנֹאדֶךָ; הֲלֹא, בְּסִפְרָתֶךָ
nodi safartah attah simah dim'ati venodecha; halo, besifratecha
Thou has counted my wanderings; put Thou my tears into Thy bottle; are they not in Thy book?

אָז יָשׁוּבוּ אוֹיְבַי אָחוֹר, בְּיוֹם אֶקְרָא; זֶה-יָדַעְתִּי, כִּי-אֱלֹהִים לִי
'az yashuvu oyevai achor beyom ekra; zeh-yada'ti, ki-'elohim li
Then shall mine enemies turn back in the day that I call; this I know, that God is for me.

בֵּאלֹהִים, אֲהַלֵּל דָּבָר; בַּיהוָה, אֲהַלֵּל דָּבָר
Be'elohim ahallel davar; bahashem, ahallel davar
In God--I will praise His word--in the LORD--I will praise His word--

בֵּאלֹהִים בָּטַחְתִּי, לֹא אִירָא; מַה-יַּעֲשֶׂה אָדָם לִי
Be'elohim batachti lo ira; mah-ya'aseh adam li
In God do I trust, I will not be afraid; what can man do unto me?

עָלַי אֱלֹהִים נְדָרֶיךָ; אֲשַׁלֵּם תּוֹדֹת לָךְ
'alai elohim nedareicha; ashallem todot lach
Thy vows are upon me, O God; I will render thank-offerings unto Thee.

כִּי הִצַּלְתָּ נַפְשִׁי, מִמָּוֶת--הֲלֹא רַגְלַי, מִדֶּחִי
ki hitzalta nafshi mimmavet halo raglai, middechi
For Thou hast delivered my soul from death; hast Thou not delivered my feet from stumbling?

לְהִתְהַלֵּךְ, לִפְנֵי אֱלֹהִים--בְּאוֹר, הַחַיִּים
lehit'hallech lifnei elohim; be'or, hachayim
that I may walk before God in the light of the living.

נז

לַמְנַצֵּחַ אַל-תַּשְׁחֵת, לְדָוִד מִכְתָּם--בְּבָרְחוֹ מִפְּנֵי-שָׁאוּל, בַּמְּעָרָה
Lamnatzeach al-tashchet ledavid michtam; bevarecho mippenei-sha'ul, bamme'arah
For the Leader; Al-tashheth. [A Psalm] of David; Michtam; when he fled from Saul, in the cave.

חָנֵּנִי אֱלֹהִים, חָנֵּנִי--כִּי בְךָ, חָסָיָה נַפְשִׁי
chonneni elohim chonneni ki vecha chasayah nafshi
Be gracious unto me, O God, be gracious unto me, for in Thee hath my soul taken refuge;

וּבְצֵל-כְּנָפֶיךָ אֶחְסֶה--עַד, יַעֲבֹר הַוּוֹת
uvetzel-kenafeicha echseh; ad, ya'avor havvot
yea, in the shadow of Thy wings will I take refuge, until calamities be overpast.

תְּהִלִּים

רַכּוּ דְבָרָיו מִשֶּׁמֶן; וְהֵמָּה פְתִחוֹת
rakku devarav mishemen, vehemmah fetichot
his words were softer than oil, yet were they keen-edged swords.

הַשְׁלֵךְ עַל-יְהוָה, יְהָבְךָ—וְהוּא יְכַלְכְּלֶךָ: לֹא-יִתֵּן לְעוֹלָם מוֹט—לַצַּדִּיק
hashlech al-hashem yehavecha vehu yechalkelecha lo-yitten le'olam mot, latzaddik
Cast thy burden upon the LORD, and He will sustain thee; He will never suffer the righteous to be moved.

וְאַתָּה אֱלֹהִים, תּוֹרִדֵם לִבְאֵר שַׁחַת
ve'attah elohim toridem liv'er shachat
But Thou, O God, wilt bring them down into the nethermost pit;

אַנְשֵׁי דָמִים וּמִרְמָה, לֹא-יֶחֱצוּ יְמֵיהֶם; וַאֲנִי, אֶבְטַח-בָּךְ
anshei damim umirmah lo-yechetzu yemeihem; va'ani, evtach-bach
men of blood and deceit shall not live out half their days; but as for me, I will trust in Thee.

כו

לַמְנַצֵּחַ, עַל-יוֹנַת אֵלֶם רְחֹקִים—לְדָוִד מִכְתָּם: בֶּאֱחֹז אוֹתוֹ פְלִשְׁתִּים בְּגַת
Lamnatzeach al-yonat elem rechokim ledavid michtam; be'echoz oto felishtim begat
For the Leader; upon Jonath-elem-rehokim. [A Psalm] of David; Michtam; when the Philistines took him in Gath.

חָנֵּנִי אֱלֹהִים, כִּי-שְׁאָפַנִי אֱנוֹשׁ; כָּל-הַיּוֹם, לֹחֵם יִלְחָצֵנִי
chonneni elohim ki-she'afani enosh; kol-hayom, lochem yilchatzeni
Be gracious unto me, O God, for man would swallow me up; all the day he fighting oppresseth me.

שָׁאֲפוּ שׁוֹרְרַי, כָּל-הַיּוֹם: כִּי-רַבִּים לֹחֲמִים לִי מָרוֹם
sha'afu shorerai kol-hayom; ki-rabbim lochamim li marom
They that lie in wait for me would swallow me up all the day; for they are many that fight against me, O Most High,

יוֹם אִירָא-אֲנִי, אֵלֶיךָ אֶבְטָח
yom ira; ani, eleicha evtach
In the day that I am afraid, I will put my trust in Thee.

בֵּאלֹהִים, אֲהַלֵּל דְּבָרוֹ: בֵּאלֹהִים בָּטַחְתִּי, לֹא אִירָא; מַה-יַּעֲשֶׂה בָשָׂר לִי
Be'elohim ahallel devaro be'elohim batachti lo ira; mah-ya'aseh vasar li
In God—I will praise His word—in God do I trust, I will not be afraid; what can flesh do unto me?

כָּל-הַיּוֹם, דְּבָרַי יְעַצֵּבוּ; עָלַי כָּל-מַחְשְׁבֹתָם לָרָע
kol-hayom devarai ye'atzevu; alai kol-machshevotam lara
All the day they trouble mine affairs; all their thoughts are against me for evil.

יָגוּרוּ, יִצְפּוֹנוּ—הֵמָּה, עֲקֵבַי יִשְׁמֹרוּ: כַּאֲשֶׁר, קִוּוּ נַפְשִׁי
yaguru yitzponu, hemmah akevai yishmoru; ka'asher, kivvu nafshi
They gather themselves together, they hide themselves, they mark my steps; according as they have waited for my soul.

תְּהִלִים

כִּי לֹא-אוֹיֵב יְחָרְפֵנִי, וְאֶשָּׂא
ki lo-'oyev yecharefeni, ve'essa
For it was not an enemy that taunted me, then I could have borne it;

לֹא-מְשַׂנְאִי, עָלַי הִגְדִּיל; וְאֶסָּתֵר מִמֶּנּוּ
lo-mesan'i alai higdil; ve'essater mimmennu
neither was it mine adversary that did magnify himself against me, then I would have hid myself from him.

וְאַתָּה אֱנוֹשׁ כְּעֶרְכִּי; אַלּוּפִי, וּמְיֻדָּעִי
ve'attah enosh ke'erki; allufi, umeyudda'i
But it was thou, a man mine equal, my companion, and my familiar friend;

אֲשֶׁר יַחְדָּו, נַמְתִּיק סוֹד; בְּבֵית אֱלֹהִים, נְהַלֵּךְ בְּרָגֶשׁ
'asher yachdov namtik sod; beveit elohim, nehallech beragesh
We took sweet counsel together, in the house of God we walked with the throng.

יַשִּׁי מָוֶת, עָלֵימוֹ--יֵרְדוּ שְׁאוֹל חַיִּים
yashi mavet aleimo, yeredu she'ol chayim
May He incite death against them, let them go down alive into the nether-world;

כִּי-רָעוֹת בִּמְגוּרָם בְּקִרְבָּם
ki-ra'ot bimguram bekirbam
for evil is in their dwelling, and within them.

אֲנִי, אֶל-אֱלֹהִים אֶקְרָא; וַיהוָה, יוֹשִׁיעֵנִי
'ani el-'elohim ekra; vahashem, yoshi'eni
As for me, I will call upon God; and the LORD shall save me.

עֶרֶב וָבֹקֶר וְצָהֳרַיִם, אָשִׂיחָה וְאֶהֱמֶה; וַיִּשְׁמַע קוֹלִי
'erev vavoker vetzohorayim asichah ve'ehemeh; vayishma koli
Evening, and morning, and at noon, will I complain, and moan; and He hath heard my voice.

פָּדָה בְשָׁלוֹם נַפְשִׁי, מִקְּרָב-לִי: כִּי-בְרַבִּים, הָיוּ עִמָּדִי
padah veshalom nafshi mikkarav-li; ki-verabbim, hayu immadi
He hath redeemed my soul in peace so that none came nigh me; for they were many that strove with me.

יִשְׁמַע אֵל, וְיַעֲנֵם--וְיֹשֵׁב קֶדֶם, סֶלָה: אֲשֶׁר אֵין חֲלִיפוֹת לָמוֹ; וְלֹא יָרְאוּ אֱלֹהִים
yishma el veya'anem veyoshev kedem, selah asher ein chalifot lamo; velo yare'u elohim
God shall hear, and humble them, even He that is enthroned of old, Selah such as have no changes, and fear not God.

שָׁלַח יָדָיו, בִּשְׁלֹמָיו; חִלֵּל בְּרִיתוֹ
shalach yadav bishlomav, chillel berito
He hath put forth his hands against them that were at peace with him; he hath profaned his covenant.

חָלְקוּ, מַחְמָאֹת פִּיו--וּקְרָב-לִבּוֹ
chaleku machma'ot piv ukrav-libbo
Smoother than cream were the speeches of his mouth, but his heart was war;

תְּהִלִים

הַאֲזִינָה אֱלֹהִים, תְּפִלָּתִי; וְאַל-תִּתְעַלַּם, מִתְּחִנָּתִי
ha'azinah elohim tefillati; ve'al-tit'allam, mittechinnati
Give ear, O God, to my prayer; and hide not Thyself from my supplication.

הַקְשִׁיבָה לִּי וַעֲנֵנִי; אָרִיד בְּשִׂיחִי וְאָהִימָה
hakshivah li va'aneni; arid besichi ve'ahimah
Attend unto me, and hear me; I am distraught in my complaint, and will moan;

מִקּוֹל אוֹיֵב--מִפְּנֵי, עָקַת רָשָׁע
mikkol oyev, mippenei akat rasha'
Because of the voice of the enemy, because of the oppression of the wicked;

כִּי-יָמִיטוּ עָלַי אָוֶן, וּבְאַף יִשְׂטְמוּנִי
ki-yamitu alai aven, uve'af yistemuni
for they cast mischief upon me, and in anger they persecute me.

לִבִּי, יָחִיל בְּקִרְבִּי; וְאֵימוֹת מָוֶת, נָפְלוּ עָלָי
libbi yachil bekirbi; ve'eimot mavet, nafelu alai
My heart doth writhe within me; and the terrors of death are fallen upon me.

יִרְאָה וָרַעַד, יָבֹא בִי; וַתְּכַסֵּנִי, פַּלָּצוּת
yir'ah vara'ad yavo vi; vattechasseni, pallatzut
Fear and trembling come upon me, and horror hath overwhelmed me.

וָאֹמַר--מִי-יִתֶּן-לִי אֵבֶר, כַּיּוֹנָה: אָעוּפָה וְאֶשְׁכֹּנָה
va'omar, mi-yitten-li ever kayonah, a'ufah ve'eshkonah
And I said: 'Oh that I had wings like a dove! then would I fly away, and be at rest.

הִנֵּה, אַרְחִיק נְדֹד; אָלִין בַּמִּדְבָּר סֶלָה
hinneh archik nedod; alin bammidbar selah
Lo, then would I wander far off, I would lodge in the wilderness. Selah

אָחִישָׁה מִפְלָט לִי-- מֵרוּחַ סֹעָה מִסָּעַר
'achishah miflat li; meruach so'ah missa'ar
I would haste me to a shelter from the stormy wind and tempest.'

בַּלַּע אֲדֹנָי, פַּלַּג לְשׁוֹנָם: כִּי-רָאִיתִי חָמָס וְרִיב בָּעִיר
balla adonai pallag leshonam; ki-ra'iti chamas veriv ba'ir
Destroy, O Lord, and divide their tongue; for I have seen violence and strife in the city.

יוֹמָם וָלַיְלָה--יְסוֹבְבֻהָ עַל-חוֹמֹתֶיהָ; וְאָוֶן וְעָמָל בְּקִרְבָּהּ
yomam valaylah, yesovevuha al-chomoteiha; ve'aven ve'amal bekirbah
Day and night they go about it upon the walls thereof; iniquity also and mischief are in the midst of it.

הַוּוֹת בְּקִרְבָּהּ; וְלֹא-יָמִישׁ מֵרְחֹבָהּ, תֹּךְ וּמִרְמָה
havvot bekirbah; velo-yamish merechovah, toch umirmah
Wickedness is in the midst thereof; oppression and guile depart not from her broad place.

תְּהִלִּים

נד

לַמְנַצֵּחַ בִּנְגִינֹת, מַשְׂכִּיל לְדָוִד
Lamnatzeach binginot, maskil ledavid
For the Leader; with string-music. Maschil of David:

בְּבֹא הַזִּיפִים, וַיֹּאמְרוּ לְשָׁאוּל: הֲלֹא דָוִד, מִסְתַּתֵּר עִמָּנוּ
bevo hazzifim vayomeru lesha'ul; halo david, mistatter immanu
when the Ziphites came and said to Saul: 'Doth not David hide himself with us?'

אֱלֹהִים, בְּשִׁמְךָ הוֹשִׁיעֵנִי; וּבִגְבוּרָתְךָ תְדִינֵנִי
'elohim beshimcha hoshi'eni; uvigvuratecha tedineni
O God, save me by Thy name, and right me by Thy might.

אֱלֹהִים, שְׁמַע תְּפִלָּתִי; הַאֲזִינָה, לְאִמְרֵי-פִי
'elohim shema tefillati; ha'azinah, le'imrei-fi
O God, hear my prayer; give ear to the words of my mouth.

כִּי זָרִים, קָמוּ עָלַי--וְעָרִיצִים, בִּקְשׁוּ נַפְשִׁי
ki zarim kamu alai, ve'aritzim bikshu nafshi
For strangers are risen up against me, and violent men have sought after my soul;

לֹא שָׂמוּ אֱלֹהִים לְנֶגְדָּם סֶלָה
lo samu elohim lenegdam selah
they have not set God before them. Selah

הִנֵּה אֱלֹהִים, עֹזֵר לִי; אֲדֹנָי, בְּסֹמְכֵי נַפְשִׁי
hinneh elohim ozer li; adonai, besomechei nafshi
Behold, God is my helper; the Lord is for me as the upholder of my soul.

יָשִׁיב הָרַע, לְשֹׁרְרָי; בַּאֲמִתְּךָ, הַצְמִיתֵם
yashiv hara leshorerai; ba'amittecha, hatzmitem
He will requite the evil unto them that lie in wait for me; destroy Thou them in Thy truth.

בִּנְדָבָה אֶזְבְּחָה-לָּךְ; אוֹדֶה שִּׁמְךָ יְהוָה כִּי-טוֹב
bindavah ezbechah-lach; odeh shimcha hashem ki-tov
With a freewill-offering will I sacrifice unto Thee; I will give thanks unto Thy name, O LORD, for it is good.

כִּי מִכָּל-צָרָה, הִצִּילָנִי; וּבְאֹיְבַי, רָאֲתָה עֵינִי.
ki mikkol-tzarah hitzilani; uve'oyevai, ra'atah eini
For He hath delivered me out of all trouble; and mine eye hath gazed upon mine enemies.

נה

לַמְנַצֵּחַ בִּנְגִינֹת, מַשְׂכִּיל לְדָוִד
Lamnatzeach binginot, maskil ledavid
For the Leader; with string-music. Maschil of David.

תְּהִלִּים

נג

לַמְנַצֵּחַ עַל-מָחֲלַת, מַשְׂכִּיל לְדָוִד
Lamnatzeach al-machalat, maskil ledavid
For the Leader; upon Mahalath. Maschil of David.

אָמַר נָבָל בְּלִבּוֹ, אֵין אֱלֹהִים
'amar naval belibbo ein elohim
The fool hath said in his heart: 'There is no God';

הִשְׁחִיתוּ, וְהִתְעִיבוּ עָוֶל--אֵין עֹשֵׂה-טוֹב
hishchitu, vehit'ivu avel, ein oseh-tov
they have dealt corruptly, and have done abominable iniquity; there is none that doeth good.

אֱלֹהִים--מִשָּׁמַיִם, הִשְׁקִיף עַל-בְּנֵי-אָדָם
'elohim, mishamayim hishkif al-benei adam
God looked forth from heaven upon the children of men,

לִרְאוֹת, הֲיֵשׁ מַשְׂכִּיל--דֹּרֵשׁ, אֶת-אֱלֹהִים
lir'ot hayesh maskil; doresh, et-'elohim
to see if there were any man of understanding, that did seek after God.

כֻּלּוֹ סָג, יַחְדָּו נֶאֱלָחוּ: אֵין עֹשֵׂה-טוֹב; אֵין, גַּם-אֶחָד
kullo sag yachdav ne'elachu ein oseh-tov; ein, gam-'echad
Every one of them is unclean, they are together become impure; there is none that doeth good, no, not one.

הֲלֹא יָדְעוּ, פֹּעֲלֵי-אָוֶן: אֹכְלֵי עַמִּי, אָכְלוּ לֶחֶם; אֱלֹהִים, לֹא קָרָאוּ
halo yade'u po'alei aven ochelei ammi achelu lechem; elohim, lo kara'u
'Shall not the workers of iniquity know it, who eat up My people as they eat bread, and call not upon God?'

שָׁם, פָּחֲדוּ פַחַד--לֹא-הָיָה-פָחַד: כִּי-אֱלֹהִים--פִּזַּר, עַצְמוֹת חֹנָךְ
sham pachadu-fachad lo-hayah fachad ki-'elohim, pizzar atzmot chonach
There are they in great fear, where no fear was; for God hath scattered the bones of him that encampeth against thee;

הֱבִשֹׁתָה, כִּי-אֱלֹהִים מְאָסָם
hevishotah, ki-'elohim me'asam
Thou hast put them to shame, because God hath rejected them.

מִי יִתֵּן מִצִּיּוֹן, יְשֻׁעוֹת יִשְׂרָאֵל
mi yitten mitziyon yeshu'ot yisra'el
Oh that the salvation of Israel were come out of Zion!

בְּשׁוּב אֱלֹהִים, שְׁבוּת עַמּוֹ; יָגֵל יַעֲקֹב, יִשְׂמַח יִשְׂרָאֵל
beshuv elohim shevut ammo; yagel ya'akov, yismach yisra'el
When God turneth the captivity of His people, let Jacob rejoice, let Israel be glad.

תְּהִלִים

מַה-תִּתְהַלֵּל בְּרָעָה, הַגִּבּוֹר; חֶסֶד אֵל, כָּל-הַיּוֹם
mah-tit'hallel bera'ah haggibbor; chesed el, kol-hayom
Why boastest thou thyself of evil, O mighty man? The mercy of God endureth continually.

הַוּוֹת, תַּחְשֹׁב לְשׁוֹנֶךָ; כְּתַעַר מְלֻטָּשׁ, עֹשֵׂה רְמִיָּה
havvot tachshov leshonecha; keta'ar meluttash, oseh remiyah
Thy tongue deviseth destruction; like a sharp razor, working deceitfully.

אָהַבְתָּ רָּע מִטּוֹב; שֶׁקֶר, מִדַּבֵּר צֶדֶק סֶלָה
'ahavta ra mittov; sheker middabber tzedek selah
Thou lovest evil more than good; falsehood rather than speaking righteousness. Selah

אָהַבְתָּ כָל-דִּבְרֵי-בָלַע; לְשׁוֹן מִרְמָה
'ahavta chol-divrei-vala', leshon mirmah
Thou lovest all devouring words, the deceitful tongue.

גַּם-אֵל, יִתָּצְךָ לָנֶצַח: יַחְתְּךָ
gam-'el yittatzecha lanetzach yachtecha
God will likewise break thee for ever, He will take thee up,

וְיִסָּחֲךָ מֵאֹהֶל; וְשֵׁרֶשְׁךָ מֵאֶרֶץ חַיִּים סֶלָה
veyissachacha me'ohel; vesheshcha me'eretz chayim selah
and pluck thee out of thy tent, and root thee out of the land of the living. Selah

וְיִרְאוּ צַדִּיקִים וְיִירָאוּ; וְעָלָיו יִשְׂחָקוּ
veyir'u tzaddikim veyira'u, ve'alav yischaku
The righteous also shall see, and fear, and shall laugh at him:

הִנֵּה הַגֶּבֶר--לֹא יָשִׂים אֱלֹהִים, מָעוּזּוֹ
hinneh haggever, lo yasim elohim, ma'uzzo
'Lo, this is the man that made not God his stronghold;

וַיִּבְטַח, בְּרֹב עָשְׁרוֹ; יָעֹז, בְּהַוָּתוֹ
vayivtach berov ashero; ya'oz, behavvato
but trusted in the abundance of his riches, and strengthened himself in his wickedness.'

וַאֲנִי, כְּזַיִת רַעֲנָן--בְּבֵית אֱלֹהִים; בָּטַחְתִּי בְחֶסֶד-אֱלֹהִים, עוֹלָם וָעֶד
va'ani kezayit ra'anan beveit elohim; batachti vechesed-'elohim, olam va'ed
But as for me, I am like a leafy olive-tree in the house of God; I trust in the mercy of God for ever and ever.

אוֹדְךָ לְעוֹלָם, כִּי עָשִׂיתָ
'odecha le'olam ki asita
I will give Thee thanks for ever, because Thou hast done it;

וַאֲקַוֶּה שִׁמְךָ כִי-טוֹב, נֶגֶד חֲסִידֶיךָ
va'akavveh shimcha chi-tov, neged chasideicha
and I will wait for Thy name, for it is good, in the presence of Thy saints.

תְּהִלִּים

אֲלַמְּדָה פֹשְׁעִים דְּרָכֶיךָ; וְחַטָּאִים, אֵלֶיךָ יָשׁוּבוּ

'alammedah foshe'im deracheicha; vechatta'im, eleicha yashuvu
Then will I teach transgressors Thy ways; and sinners shall return unto Thee.

הַצִּילֵנִי מִדָּמִים, אֱלֹהִים--אֱלֹהֵי תְּשׁוּעָתִי

hatzileni middamim elohim, elohei teshu'ati
Deliver me from bloodguiltiness, O God, Thou God of my salvation;

תְּרַנֵּן לְשׁוֹנִי, צִדְקָתֶךָ

terannen leshoni, tzidkatecha
so shall my tongue sing aloud of Thy righteousness.

אֲדֹנָי, שְׂפָתַי תִּפְתָּח; וּפִי, יַגִּיד תְּהִלָּתֶךָ

'adonai sefatai tiftach; ufi, yaggid tehillatecha
O Lord, open Thou my lips; and my mouth shall declare Thy praise.

כִּי, לֹא-תַחְפֹּץ זֶבַח וְאֶתֵּנָה; עוֹלָה, לֹא תִרְצֶה

ki lo-tachpotz zevach ve'ettenah; olah, lo tirtzeh
For Thou delightest not in sacrifice, else would I give it; Thou hast no pleasure in burnt-offering.

זִבְחֵי אֱלֹהִים, רוּחַ נִשְׁבָּרָה: לֵב-נִשְׁבָּר וְנִדְכֶּה-- אֱלֹהִים, לֹא תִבְזֶה

zivchei elohim ruach nishbarah lev-nishbar venidkeh; elohim, lo tivzeh
The sacrifices of God are a broken spirit; a broken and a contrite heart, O God, Thou wilt not despise.

הֵיטִיבָה בִרְצוֹנְךָ, אֶת-צִיּוֹן; תִּבְנֶה, חוֹמוֹת יְרוּשָׁלִָם

heitivah virtzonecha et-tziyon; tivneh, chomot yerushalayim
Do good in Thy favour unto Zion; build Thou the walls of Jerusalem.

אָז תַּחְפֹּץ זִבְחֵי-צֶדֶק, עוֹלָה וְכָלִיל

'az tachpotz zivchei-tzedek olah vechalil
Then wilt Thou delight in the sacrifices of righteousness, in burnt-offering and whole offering;

אָז יַעֲלוּ עַל-מִזְבַּחֲךָ פָרִים

az ya'alu al-mizbachacha farim
then will they offer bullocks upon Thine altar.

נב

לַמְנַצֵּחַ, מַשְׂכִּיל לְדָוִד

Lamnatzeach, maskil ledavid
For the Leader. Maschil of David;

בְּבוֹא, דּוֹאֵג הָאֲדֹמִי-- וַיַּגֵּד לְשָׁאוּל: וַיֹּאמֶר לוֹ-- בָּא דָוִד, אֶל-בֵּית אֲחִימֶלֶךְ.

bevo do'eg ha'adomi vayagged lesha'ul vayomer lo; ba david, el-beit achimelech
when Doeg the Edomite came and told Saul, and said unto him: 'David is come to the house of Ahimelech.'

תְּהִלִים

הֶרֶב, כַּבְּסֵנִי מֵעֲוֹנִי; וּמֵחַטָּאתִי טַהֲרֵנִי
herev kabbeseni me'avoni; umechattati tahareni
Wash me thoroughly from mine iniquity, and cleanse me from my sin.

כִּי-פְשָׁעַי, אֲנִי אֵדָע; וְחַטָּאתִי נֶגְדִּי תָמִיד
ki-fesha'ai ani eda'; vechattati negdi tamid
For I know my transgressions; and my sin is ever before me.

לְךָ לְבַדְּךָ, חָטָאתִי, וְהָרַע בְּעֵינֶיךָ, עָשִׂיתִי
lecha levaddecha chatati vehara be'eineicha, asiti
Against Thee, Thee only, have I sinned, and done that which is evil in Thy sight;

לְמַעַן, תִּצְדַּק בְּדָבְרֶךָ--תִּזְכֶּה בְשָׁפְטֶךָ
lema'an titzdak bedoverecha, tizkeh veshofetecha
that Thou mayest be justified when Thou speakest, and be in the right when Thou judgest.

הֵן-בְּעָווֹן חוֹלָלְתִּי; וּבְחֵטְא, יֶחֱמַתְנִי אִמִּי
hen-be'avon cholaleti; uvechet, yechematni immi
Behold, I was brought forth in iniquity, and in sin did my mother conceive me.

הֵן-אֱמֶת, חָפַצְתָּ בַטֻּחוֹת; וּבְסָתֻם, חָכְמָה תוֹדִיעֵנִי
hen-'emet chafatzta vattuchot; uvesatum, chochmah todi'eni
Behold, Thou desirest truth in the inward parts; make me, therefore, to know wisdom in mine inmost heart.

תְּחַטְּאֵנִי בְאֵזוֹב וְאֶטְהָר; תְּכַבְּסֵנִי, וּמִשֶּׁלֶג אַלְבִּין
techatte'eni ve'ezov ve'et'har; techabbeseni, umisheleg albin
Purge me with hyssop, and I shall be clean; wash me, and I shall be whiter than snow.

תַּשְׁמִיעֵנִי, שָׂשׂוֹן וְשִׂמְחָה; תָּגֵלְנָה, עֲצָמוֹת דִּכִּיתָ
tashmi'eni sason vesimchah; tagelenah, atzamot dikkita
Make me to hear joy and gladness; that the bones which Thou hast crushed may rejoice.

הַסְתֵּר פָּנֶיךָ, מֵחֲטָאָי; וְכָל-עֲוֹנֹתַי מְחֵה
haster paneicha mechata'ai; vechol-'avonotai mecheh
Hide Thy face from my sins, and blot out all mine iniquities.

לֵב טָהוֹר, בְּרָא-לִי אֱלֹהִים; וְרוּחַ נָכוֹן, חַדֵּשׁ בְּקִרְבִּי
lev tahor bera-li elohim; veruach nachon, chaddesh bekirbi
Create me a clean heart, O God; and renew a stedfast spirit within me.

אַל-תַּשְׁלִיכֵנִי מִלְּפָנֶיךָ; וְרוּחַ קָדְשְׁךָ, אַל-תִּקַּח מִמֶּנִּי
'al-tashlicheni millefaneicha; veruach kodshecha al-tikkach mimmenni
Cast me not away from Thy presence; and take not Thy holy spirit from me.

הָשִׁיבָה לִּי, שְׂשׂוֹן יִשְׁעֶךָ; וְרוּחַ נְדִיבָה תִסְמְכֵנִי
hashivah li seson yish'echa; veruach nedivah tismecheni
Restore unto me the joy of Thy salvation; and let a willing spirit uphold me.

תְּהִלִים

תֵּשֵׁב, בְּאָחִיךָ תְדַבֵּר; בְּבֶן-אִמְּךָ, תִּתֶּן-דֹּפִי
teshev be'achicha tedabber; beven-'immecha, titten-dofi
Thou sittest and speakest against thy brother; thou slanderest thine own mother's son.

אֵלֶּה עָשִׂיתָ, וְהֶחֱרַשְׁתִּי
'elleh asita vehecherashti
These things hast thou done, and should I have kept silence?

דִּמִּיתָ, הֱיוֹת-אֶהְיֶה כָמוֹךָ
dimmita, heyot-'ehyeh chamocha
Thou hadst thought that I was altogether such a one as thyself;

אוֹכִיחֲךָ וְאֶעֶרְכָה לְעֵינֶיךָ
ochichacha ve'e'erchah le'eineicha
but I will reprove thee, and set the cause before thine eyes.

בִּינוּ-נָא זֹאת, שֹׁכְחֵי אֱלוֹהַּ: פֶּן-אֶטְרֹף, וְאֵין מַצִּיל
binu-na zot shochechei eloah; pen-'etrof, ve'ein matzil
Now consider this, ye that forget God, lest I tear in pieces, and there be none to deliver.

זֹבֵחַ תּוֹדָה, יְכַבְּדָנְנִי
zoveach todah, yechabbedaneni
Whoso offereth the sacrifice of thanksgiving honoureth Me;

וְשָׂם דֶּרֶךְ--אַרְאֶנּוּ, בְּיֵשַׁע אֱלֹהִים
vesam derech; ar'ennu, beyesha elohim
and to him that ordereth his way aright will I show the salvation of God.'

נא

לַמְנַצֵּחַ, מִזְמוֹר לְדָוִד
Lamnatzeach, mizmor ledavid
For the Leader. A Psalm of David;

בְּבוֹא-אֵלָיו, נָתָן הַנָּבִיא--כַּאֲשֶׁר-בָּא, אֶל-בַּת-שָׁבַע
bevo-'elav natan hannavi; ka'asher-ba, el-bat-shava
When Nathan the prophet came unto him, after he had gone in to Bath-sheba.

חָנֵּנִי אֱלֹהִים כְּחַסְדֶּךָ
chonneni elohim kechasdecha
Be gracious unto me, O God, according to Thy mercy;

כְּרֹב רַחֲמֶיךָ, מְחֵה פְשָׁעָי
kerov rachameicha, mecheh fesha'ai
according to the multitude of Thy compassions blot out my transgressions.

תְּהִלִּים

לֹא-אֶקַּח מִבֵּיתְךָ פָר; מִמִּכְלְאֹתֶיךָ, עַתּוּדִים
lo-'ekkach mibbeitecha far; mimmichle'oteicha, attudim
I will take no bullock out of thy house, nor he-goats out of thy folds.

כִּי-לִי כָל-חַיְתוֹ-יָעַר; בְּהֵמוֹת, בְּהַרְרֵי-אָלֶף
ki-li chol-chayto-ya'ar; behemot, beharerei-'alef
For every beast of the forest is Mine, and the cattle upon a thousand hills.

יָדַעְתִּי, כָּל-עוֹף הָרִים; וְזִיז שָׂדַי, עִמָּדִי
yada'ti kol-'of harim; veziz sadai, immadi
I know all the fowls of the mountains; and the wild beasts of the field are Mine.

אִם-אֶרְעַב, לֹא-אֹמַר לָךְ: כִּי-לִי תֵבֵל, וּמְלֹאָהּ
'im-'er'av lo-'omar lach; ki-li tevel, umelo'ah
If I were hungry, I would not tell thee; for the world is Mine, and the fulness thereof.

הַאוֹכַל, בְּשַׂר אַבִּירִים; וְדַם עַתּוּדִים אֶשְׁתֶּה
ha'ochal besar abbirim; vedam attudim eshteh
Do I eat the flesh of bulls, or drink the blood of goats?

זְבַח לֵאלֹהִים תּוֹדָה; וְשַׁלֵּם לְעֶלְיוֹן נְדָרֶיךָ
zvach le'elohim todah; veshallem le'elyon nedareicha
Offer unto God the sacrifice of thanksgiving; and pay thy vows unto the Most High;

וּקְרָאֵנִי, בְּיוֹם צָרָה; אֲחַלֶּצְךָ, וּתְכַבְּדֵנִי
ukera'eni beyom tzarah; achalletzcha, utechabbedeni
And call upon Me in the day of trouble; I will deliver thee, and thou shalt honour Me.'

וְלָרָשָׁע, אָמַר אֱלֹהִים
velarasha amar elohim
But unto the wicked God saith:

מַה-לְּךָ, לְסַפֵּר חֻקָּי; וַתִּשָּׂא בְרִיתִי עֲלֵי-פִיךָ
mah-lecha lesapper chukkai; vattissa veriti alei-ficha
'What hast thou to do to declare My statutes, and that thou hast taken My covenant in thy mouth?

וְאַתָּה, שָׂנֵאתָ מוּסָר; וַתַּשְׁלֵךְ דְּבָרַי אַחֲרֶיךָ
ve'attah saneta musar; vattashlech devarai achareicha
Seeing thou hatest instruction, and castest My words behind thee.

אִם-רָאִיתָ גַנָּב, וַתִּרֶץ עִמּוֹ; וְעִם מְנָאֲפִים חֶלְקֶךָ
'im-ra'ita gannav vattiretz immo; ve'im mena'afim chelkecha
When thou sawest a thief, thou hadst company with him, and with adulterers was thy portion.

פִּיךָ, שָׁלַחְתָּ בְרָעָה; וּלְשׁוֹנְךָ, תַּצְמִיד מִרְמָה
picha shalachta vera'ah; uleshonecha, tatzmid mirmah
Thou hast let loose thy mouth for evil, and thy tongue frameth deceit.

תְּהִלִּים

תָּבוֹא, עַד-דּוֹר אֲבוֹתָיו; עַד-נֵצַח, לֹא יִרְאוּ-אוֹר
tavo ad-dor avotav; ad-netzach, lo yir'u-'or
It shall go to the generation of his fathers; they shall never see the light.

אָדָם בִּיקָר, וְלֹא יָבִין; נִמְשַׁל כַּבְּהֵמוֹת נִדְמוּ
'adam bikar velo yavin; nimshal kabbehemot nidmu
Man that is in honour understandeth not; he is like the beasts that perish.

נ

מִזְמוֹר, לְאָסָף: אֵל, אֱלֹהִים יְהוָה--דִּבֶּר
Mizmor, le'asaf el elohim hashem dibber
A Psalm of Asaph. God, God, the LORD, hath spoken,

וַיִּקְרָא-אָרֶץ; מִמִּזְרַח-שֶׁמֶשׁ, עַד-מְבֹאוֹ
vayikra-'aretz; mimmizrach-shemesh, ad-mevo'o
and called the earth from the rising of the sun unto the going down thereof.

מִצִּיּוֹן מִכְלַל-יֹפִי--אֱלֹהִים הוֹפִיעַ
mitziyon michlal-yofi, elohim hofia
Out of Zion, the perfection of beauty, God hath shined forth.

יָבֹא אֱלֹהֵינוּ, וְאַל-יֶחֱרַשׁ: אֵשׁ-לְפָנָיו תֹּאכֵל; וּסְבִיבָיו, נִשְׂעֲרָה מְאֹד
yavo eloheinu, ve'al-yecherash esh-lefanav tochel; usevivav, nis'arah me'od
Our God cometh, and doth not keep silence; a fire devoureth before Him, and round about Him it stormeth mightily.

יִקְרָא אֶל-הַשָּׁמַיִם מֵעָל; וְאֶל-הָאָרֶץ, לָדִין עַמּוֹ
yikra el-hashamayim me'al; ve'el-ha'aretz, ladin ammo
He calleth to the heavens above, and to the earth, that He may judge His people:

אִסְפוּ-לִי חֲסִידָי--כֹּרְתֵי בְרִיתִי עֲלֵי-זָבַח
'isfu-li chasidai; koretei veriti alei-zavach
'Gather My saints together unto Me; those that have made a covenant with Me by sacrifice.'

וַיַּגִּידוּ שָׁמַיִם צִדְקוֹ: כִּי-אֱלֹהִים, שֹׁפֵט הוּא סֶלָה
vayaggidu shamayim tzidko; ki-'elohim shofet hu selah
And the heavens declare His righteousness; for God, He is judge. Selah

שִׁמְעָה עַמִּי, וַאֲדַבֵּרָה--יִשְׂרָאֵל, וְאָעִידָה בָּךְ: אֱלֹהִים אֱלֹהֶיךָ אָנֹכִי
shim'ah ammi va'adabberah, yisra'el ve'a'idah bach; elohim eloheicha anochi
'Hear, O My people, and I will speak; O Israel, and I will testify against thee: God, thy God, am I.

לֹא עַל-זְבָחֶיךָ, אוֹכִיחֶךָ; וְעוֹלֹתֶיךָ לְנֶגְדִּי תָמִיד
lo al-zevacheicha ochichecha; ve'oloteicha lenegdi tamid
I will not reprove thee for thy sacrifices; and thy burnt-offerings are continually before Me.

תְּהִלִים

כִּי יִרְאֶה, חֲכָמִים יָמוּתוּ--יַחַד כְּסִיל וָבַעַר יֹאבֵדוּ; וְעָזְבוּ לַאֲחֵרִים חֵילָם
ki yir'eh chachamim yamutu, yachad kesil vava'ar yovedu; ve'azevu la'acherim cheilam
For he seeth that wise men die, the fool and the brutish together perish, and leave their wealth to others.

קִרְבָּם בָּתֵּימוֹ, לְעוֹלָם--מִשְׁכְּנֹתָם, לְדֹר וָדֹר
kirbam batteimo le'olam, mishkenotom ledor vador
Their inward thought is, that their houses shall continue for ever, and their dwelling-places to all generations;

קָרְאוּ בִשְׁמוֹתָם, עֲלֵי אֲדָמוֹת
kare'u vishmotam, alei adamot
they call their lands after their own names.

וְאָדָם בִּיקָר, בַּל-יָלִין; נִמְשַׁל כַּבְּהֵמוֹת נִדְמוּ
ve'adam bikor bal-yalin; nimshal kabbehemot nidmu
But man abideth not in honour; he is like the beasts that perish.

זֶה דַרְכָּם, כֵּסֶל לָמוֹ; וְאַחֲרֵיהֶם, בְּפִיהֶם יִרְצוּ סֶלָה
zeh darkom kesel lamo; ve'achareihem befihem yirtzu selah
This is the way of them that are foolish, and of those who after them approve their sayings. Selah

כַּצֹּאן, לִשְׁאוֹל שַׁתּוּ--מָוֶת יִרְעֵם
katzon lish'ol shattu mavet yir'em
Like sheep they are appointed for the nether-world; death shall be their shepherd;

וַיִּרְדּוּ בָם יְשָׁרִים, לַבֹּקֶר
vayirdu vam yesharim labboker
and the upright shall have dominion over them in the morning;

וְצוּרָם, לְבַלּוֹת שְׁאוֹל; מִזְּבֻל לוֹ
vetzurom levallot she'ol, mizzevul lo
and their form shall be for the nether-world to wear away, that there be no habitation for it.

אַךְ-אֱלֹהִים--יִפְדֶּה נַפְשִׁי, מִיַּד-שְׁאוֹל: כִּי יִקָּחֵנִי סֶלָה
'ach-'elohim, yifdeh nafshi miyad-she'ol; ki yikkacheni selah
But God will redeem my soul from the power of the nether-world; for He shall receive me. Selah

אַל-תִּירָא, כִּי-יַעֲשִׁר אִישׁ: כִּי-יִרְבֶּה, כְּבוֹד בֵּיתוֹ
'al-tira ki-ya'ashir ish; ki-yirbeh kevod beito
Be not thou afraid when one waxeth rich, when the wealth of his house is increased;

כִּי לֹא בְמוֹתוֹ, יִקַּח הַכֹּל; לֹא-יֵרֵד אַחֲרָיו כְּבוֹדוֹ
ki lo vemoto yikkach hakkol; lo-yered acharav kevodo
For when he dieth he shall carry nothing away; his wealth shall not descend after him.

כִּי-נַפְשׁוֹ, בְּחַיָּיו יְבָרֵךְ; וְיוֹדֻךָ, כִּי-תֵיטִיב לָךְ
ki-nafsho bechayav yevarech; veyoducha, ki-teitiv lach
Though while he lived he blessed his soul: 'Men will praise thee, when thou shalt do well to thyself';

תְּהִלִּים

כִּי זֶה, אֱלֹהִים אֱלֹהֵינוּ--עוֹלָם וָעֶד; הוּא יְנַהֲגֵנוּ עַל-מוּת
ki zeh elohim eloheinu olam va'ed; hu yenahagenu al-mut
For such is God, our God, for ever and ever; He will guide us eternally.

מט

לַמְנַצֵּחַ לִבְנֵי-קֹרַח מִזְמוֹר
Lamnatzeach livnei-korach mizmor
For the Leader; a Psalm of the sons of Korah.

שִׁמְעוּ-זֹאת, כָּל-הָעַמִּים; הַאֲזִינוּ, כָּל-יֹשְׁבֵי חָלֶד
shim'u-zot kol-ha'ammim; ha'azinu, kol-yoshevei chaled
Hear this, all ye peoples; give ear, all ye inhabitants of the world,

גַּם-בְּנֵי אָדָם, גַּם-בְּנֵי-אִישׁ--יַחַד, עָשִׁיר וְאֶבְיוֹן
gam-benei adom gam-benei-'ish; yachad, ashir ve'evyon
Both low and high, rich and poor together.

פִּי, יְדַבֵּר חָכְמוֹת; וְהָגוּת לִבִּי תְבוּנוֹת
pi yedabber chochemot; vehagut libbi tevunot
My mouth shall speak wisdom, and the meditation of my heart shall be understanding.

אַטֶּה לְמָשָׁל אָזְנִי; אֶפְתַּח בְּכִנּוֹר, חִידָתִי
'atteh lemashal azeni; eftach bechinnor, chidati
I will incline mine ear to a parable; I will open my dark saying upon the harp.

לָמָּה אִירָא, בִּימֵי רָע--עֲוֺן עֲקֵבַי יְסוּבֵּנִי
lammah ira bimei ra'; avon akevai yesubeni
Wherefore should I fear in the days of evil, when the iniquity of my supplanters compasseth me about,

הַבֹּטְחִים עַל-חֵילָם; וּבְרֹב עָשְׁרָם יִתְהַלָּלוּ
habbotechim al-cheilam; uverov osheram, yit'hallalu
Of them that trust in their wealth, and boast themselves in the multitude of their riches?

אָח--לֹא פָדֹה יִפְדֶּה אִישׁ; לֹא-יִתֵּן לֵאלֹהִים כָּפְרוֹ
'ach, lo-fadoh yifdeh ish; lo-yitten le'elohim kofero
No man can by any means redeem his brother, nor give to God a ransom for him--

וְיֵקַר, פִּדְיוֹן נַפְשָׁם; וְחָדַל לְעוֹלָם
veyekar pidyon nafsham, vechadal le'olam
For too costly is the redemption of their soul, and must be let alone for ever--

וִיחִי-עוֹד לָנֶצַח; לֹא יִרְאֶה הַשָּׁחַת
vichi-'od lanetzach; lo yir'eh hashachat
That he should still live always, that he should not see the pit.

תְּהִלִּים

אֱלֹהִים בְּאַרְמְנוֹתֶיהָ, נוֹדַע לְמִשְׂגָּב
'elohim be'armenoteiha, noda lemisgav
God in her palaces hath made Himself known for a stronghold.

כִּי-הִנֵּה הַמְּלָכִים, נוֹעֲדוּ; עָבְרוּ יַחְדָּו
ki-hinneh hammelachim no'adu; averu yachdav
For, lo, the kings assembled themselves, they came onward together.

הֵמָּה רָאוּ, כֵּן תָּמָהוּ; נִבְהֲלוּ נֶחְפָּזוּ
hemmah ra'u ken tamahu; nivhalu nechpazu
They saw, straightway they were amazed; they were affrighted, they hasted away.

רְעָדָה, אֲחָזָתַם שָׁם; חִיל, כַּיּוֹלֵדָה
re'adah achazatam sham; chil, kayoledah
Trembling took hold of them there, pangs, as of a woman in travail.

בְּרוּחַ קָדִים--תְּשַׁבֵּר, אֳנִיּוֹת תַּרְשִׁישׁ
beruach kadim; teshabber, oniyot tarshish
With the east wind Thou breakest the ships of Tarshish.

כַּאֲשֶׁר שָׁמַעְנוּ, כֵּן רָאִינוּ--בְּעִיר-יְהוָה צְבָאוֹת, בְּעִיר אֱלֹהֵינוּ
ka'asher shama'nu ken ra'inu, be'ir-hashem tzeva'ot be'ir eloheinu
As we have heard, so have we seen in the city of the LORD of hosts, in the city of our God

אֱלֹהִים יְכוֹנְנֶהָ עַד-עוֹלָם סֶלָה
elohim yechoneneha ad-'olam selah
God establish it for ever. Selah

דִּמִּינוּ אֱלֹהִים חַסְדֶּךָ--בְּקֶרֶב, הֵיכָלֶךָ
dimminu elohim chasdecha; bekerev, heichalecha
We have thought on Thy lovingkindness, O God, in the midst of Thy temple.

כְּשִׁמְךָ אֱלֹהִים--כֵּן תְּהִלָּתְךָ, עַל-קַצְוֵי-אֶרֶץ; צֶדֶק, מָלְאָה יְמִינֶךָ.
keshimcha elohim, ken tehillatecha al-katzvei-'eretz; tzedek, male'ah yeminecha
As is Thy name, O God, so is Thy praise unto the ends of the earth; Thy right hand is full of righteousness.

יִשְׂמַח, הַר צִיּוֹן--תָּגֵלְנָה, בְּנוֹת יְהוּדָה: לְמַעַן, מִשְׁפָּטֶיךָ
yismach har-tziyon, tagelenah benot yehudah; lema'an, mishpateicha
Let mount Zion be glad, let the daughters of Judah rejoice, because of Thy judgments.

סֹבּוּ צִיּוֹן, וְהַקִּיפוּהָ; סִפְרוּ, מִגְדָּלֶיהָ
sobbu tziyon vehakkifuha; sifru, migdaleiha
Walk about Zion, and go round about her; count the towers thereof.

שִׁיתוּ לִבְּכֶם, לְחֵילָה--פַּסְּגוּ אַרְמְנוֹתֶיהָ: לְמַעַן תְּסַפְּרוּ, לְדוֹר אַחֲרוֹן
shitu libbechem lecheilah, passegu armenoteiha; lema'an tesapperu, ledor acharon
Mark ye well her ramparts, traverse her palaces; that ye may tell it to the generation following.

תְּהִלִּים

יִבְחַר-לָנוּ אֶת-נַחֲלָתֵנוּ; אֶת גְּאוֹן יַעֲקֹב אֲשֶׁר-אָהֵב סֶלָה
yivchar-lanu et-nachalatenu; et ge'on ya'akov asher-'ahev selah
He chooseth our inheritance for us, the pride of Jacob whom He loveth. Selah

עָלָה אֱלֹהִים, בִּתְרוּעָה; יְהוָה, בְּקוֹל שׁוֹפָר
'alah elohim bitru'ah; hashem bekol shofar
God is gone up amidst shouting, the LORD amidst the sound of the horn.

זַמְּרוּ אֱלֹהִים זַמֵּרוּ; זַמְּרוּ לְמַלְכֵּנוּ זַמֵּרוּ
zammeru elohim zammeru; zammeru lemalkenu zammeru
Sing praises to God, sing praises; sing praises unto our King, sing praises.

כִּי מֶלֶךְ כָּל-הָאָרֶץ אֱלֹהִים--זַמְּרוּ מַשְׂכִּיל
ki melech kol-ha'aretz elohim, zammeru maskil
For God is the King of all the earth; sing ye praises in a skilful song.

מָלַךְ אֱלֹהִים, עַל-גּוֹיִם; אֱלֹהִים, יָשַׁב עַל-כִּסֵּא קָדְשׁוֹ
malach elohim al-goyim; elohim, yashav al-kissei kodsho
God reigneth over the nations; God sitteth upon His holy throne.

נְדִיבֵי עַמִּים, נֶאֱסָפוּ--עַם, אֱלֹהֵי אַבְרָהָם
nedivei ammim ne'esafu, am elohei avraham
The princes of the peoples are gathered together, the people of the God of Abraham;

כִּי לֵאלֹהִים, מָגִנֵּי-אֶרֶץ--מְאֹד נַעֲלָה
ki le'elohim maginnei-'eretz, me'od na'alah
for unto God belong the shields of the earth; He is greatly exalted.

מח

שִׁיר מִזְמוֹר, לִבְנֵי-קֹרַח
Shir mizmor livnei-korach
A Song; a Psalm of the sons of Korah.

גָּדוֹל יְהוָה וּמְהֻלָּל מְאֹד--בְּעִיר אֱלֹהֵינוּ, הַר-קָדְשׁוֹ
gadol hashem umehullal me'od; be'ir eloheinu, har-kodsho
Great is the LORD, and highly to be praised, in the city of our God, His holy mountain,

יְפֵה נוֹף, מְשׂוֹשׂ כָּל-הָאָרֶץ
yefeh nof mesos kol-ha'aretz
Fair in situation, the joy of the whole earth;

הַר-צִיּוֹן, יַרְכְּתֵי צָפוֹן; קִרְיַת, מֶלֶךְ רָב
har-tziyon yarketei tzafon; kiryat, melech rav
even mount Zion, the uttermost parts of the north, the city of the great King.

תְּהִלִּים

הָמוּ גוֹיִם, מָטוּ מַמְלָכוֹת; נָתַן בְּקוֹלוֹ, תָּמוּג אָרֶץ
hamu goyim matu mamlachot; natan bekolo, tamug aretz
Nations were in tumult, kingdoms were moved; He uttered His voice, the earth melted.

יְהוָה צְבָאוֹת עִמָּנוּ; מִשְׂגָּב-לָנוּ אֱלֹהֵי יַעֲקֹב סֶלָה
hashem tzeva'ot immanu; misgav-lanu elohei ya'akov selah
The LORD of hosts is with us; the God of Jacob is our high tower. Selah

לְכוּ-חֲזוּ, מִפְעֲלוֹת יְהוָה--אֲשֶׁר-שָׂם שַׁמּוֹת בָּאָרֶץ
lechu-chazu mif'alot hashem asher-sam shammot ba'aretz
Come, behold the works of the LORD, who hath made desolations in the earth.

מַשְׁבִּית מִלְחָמוֹת, עַד-קְצֵה הָאָרֶץ
mashbit milchamot ad-ketzeh ha'aretz
He maketh wars to cease unto the end of the earth;

קֶשֶׁת יְשַׁבֵּר, וְקִצֵּץ חֲנִית; עֲגָלוֹת, יִשְׂרֹף בָּאֵשׁ
keshet yeshabber vekitzetz chanit; agalot, yisrof ba'esh
He breaketh the bow, and cutteth the spear in sunder; He burneth the chariots in the fire.

הַרְפּוּ וּדְעוּ, כִּי-אָנֹכִי אֱלֹהִים; אָרוּם בַּגּוֹיִם, אָרוּם בָּאָרֶץ
harpu ude'u ki-'anochi elohim; arum baggoyim, arum ba'aretz
'Let be, and know that I am God; I will be exalted among the nations, I will be exalted in the earth.'

יְהוָה צְבָאוֹת עִמָּנוּ; מִשְׂגָּב-לָנוּ אֱלֹהֵי יַעֲקֹב סֶלָה
hashem tzeva'ot immanu; misgav-lanu elohei ya'akov selah
The LORD of hosts is with us; the God of Jacob is our high tower. Selah

מז

לַמְנַצֵּחַ לִבְנֵי-קֹרַח מִזְמוֹר
Lamnatzeach livnei-korach mizmor
For the Leader; a Psalm for the sons of Korah.

כָּל-הָעַמִּים, תִּקְעוּ-כָף; הָרִיעוּ לֵאלֹהִים, בְּקוֹל רִנָּה
kol-ha'ammim tik'u-chaf; hari'u le'elohim, bekol rinnah
O clap your hands, all ye peoples; shout unto God with the voice of triumph.

כִּי-יְהוָה עֶלְיוֹן נוֹרָא; מֶלֶךְ גָּדוֹל, עַל-כָּל-הָאָרֶץ
ki-hashem elyon nora; melech gadol al-kol-ha'aretz
For the LORD is most high, awful; a great King over all the earth.

יַדְבֵּר עַמִּים תַּחְתֵּינוּ; וּלְאֻמִּים, תַּחַת רַגְלֵינוּ
yadber ammim tachteinu; ule'ummim, tachat ragleinu
He subdueth peoples under us, and nations under our feet.

תְּהִלִּים

כָּל-כְּבוּדָּה בַת-מֶלֶךְ פְּנִימָה; מִמִּשְׁבְּצוֹת זָהָב לְבוּשָׁהּ
kol-kevudah vat-melech penimah; mimmishbetzot zahav levushah
All glorious is the king's daughter within the palace; her raiment is of chequer work inwrought with gold.

לִרְקָמוֹת, תּוּבַל לַמֶּלֶךְ: בְּתוּלוֹת אַחֲרֶיהָ, רֵעוֹתֶיהָ--מוּבָאוֹת לָךְ
lirkamot tuval lammelech betulot achareiha re'oteiha; muva'ot lach
She shall be led unto the king on richly woven stuff; the virgins her companions in her train being brought unto thee.

תּוּבַלְנָה, בִּשְׂמָחֹת וָגִיל; תְּבֹאֶינָה, בְּהֵיכַל מֶלֶךְ
tuvalnah bismachot vagil; tevo'einah, beheichal melech
They shall be led with gladness and rejoicing; they shall enter into the king's palace.

תַּחַת אֲבֹתֶיךָ, יִהְיוּ בָנֶיךָ; תְּשִׁיתֵמוֹ לְשָׂרִים, בְּכָל-הָאָרֶץ
tachat avoteicha yihyu vaneicha; teshitemo lesarim, bechol-ha'aretz
Instead of thy fathers shall be thy sons, whom thou shalt make princes in all the land.

אַזְכִּירָה שִׁמְךָ, בְּכָל-דֹּר וָדֹר; עַל-כֵּן עַמִּים יְהוֹדוּךָ, לְעֹלָם וָעֶד
'azkirah shimcha bechol-dor vador; al-ken ammim yehoducha, le'olam va'ed
I will make thy name to be remembered in all generations; therefore shall the peoples praise thee for ever and ever.

מו

לַמְנַצֵּחַ לִבְנֵי-קֹרַח--עַל-עֲלָמוֹת שִׁיר
Lamnatzeach livnei-korach; al-'alamot shir
For the Leader; [a Psalm] of the sons of Korah; upon Alamoth. A Song.

אֱלֹהִים לָנוּ, מַחֲסֶה וָעֹז; עֶזְרָה בְצָרוֹת, נִמְצָא מְאֹד
'elohim lanu machaseh va'oz; ezrah vetzarot, nimtza me'od
God is our refuge and strength, a very present help in trouble.

עַל-כֵּן לֹא-נִירָא, בְּהָמִיר אָרֶץ; וּבְמוֹט הָרִים, בְּלֵב יַמִּים
'al-ken lo-nira behamir aretz; uvemot harim, belev yammim
Therefore will we not fear, though the earth do change, and though the mountains be moved into the heart of the seas;

יֶהֱמוּ יֶחְמְרוּ מֵימָיו; יִרְעֲשׁוּ הָרִים בְּגַאֲוָתוֹ סֶלָה
yehemu yechmeru meimav; yir'ashu-harim bega'avato selah
Though the waters thereof roar and foam, though the mountains shake at the swelling thereof. Selah

נָהָר--פְּלָגָיו, יְשַׂמְּחוּ עִיר-אֱלֹהִים; קְדֹשׁ, מִשְׁכְּנֵי עֶלְיוֹן
nahar, pelagav, yesammechu ir-'elohim; kedosh, mishkenei elyon
There is a river, the streams whereof make glad the city of God, the holiest dwelling-place of the Most High.

אֱלֹהִים בְּקִרְבָּהּ, בַּל-תִּמּוֹט; יַעְזְרֶהָ אֱלֹהִים, לִפְנוֹת בֹּקֶר
'elohim bekirbah bal-timmot; ya'zereha elohim, lifnot boker
God is in the midst of her, she shall not be moved; God shall help her, at the approach of morning.

תְּהִלִים

חֲגוֹר-חַרְבְּךָ עַל-יָרֵךְ גִּבּוֹר--הוֹדְךָ, וַהֲדָרֶךָ
chagor-charbecha al-yarech gibbor; hodecha, vahadarecha
Gird thy sword upon thy thigh, O mighty one, thy glory and thy majesty.

וַהֲדָרְךָ, צְלַח רְכַב--עַל-דְּבַר-אֱמֶת, וְעַנְוָה-צֶדֶק
vahadarecha tzelach rechav, al-devar-'emet ve'anvah-tzedek
And in thy majesty prosper, ride on, in behalf of truth and meekness and righteousness;

וְתוֹרְךָ נוֹרָאוֹת יְמִינֶךָ
vetorecha nora'ot yeminecha
and let thy right hand teach thee tremendous things.

חִצֶּיךָ, שְׁנוּנִים: עַמִּים, תַּחְתֶּיךָ יִפְּלוּ; בְּלֵב, אוֹיְבֵי הַמֶּלֶךְ
chitzeicha, shenunim ammim tachteicha yippelu; belev, oyevei hammelech
Thine arrows are sharp--the peoples fall under thee--[they sink] into the heart of the king's enemies.

כִּסְאֲךָ אֱלֹהִים, עוֹלָם וָעֶד; שֵׁבֶט מִישֹׁר, שֵׁבֶט מַלְכוּתֶךָ
kis'acha elohim olam va'ed; shevet mishor, shevet malchutecha
Thy throne given of God is for ever and ever; a sceptre of equity is the sceptre of thy kingdom.

אָהַבְתָּ צֶּדֶק, וַתִּשְׂנָא-רֶשַׁע
'ahavta tzedek vattisna resha
Thou hast loved righteousness, and hated wickedness;

עַל-כֵּן מְשָׁחֲךָ אֱלֹהִים אֱלֹהֶיךָ, שֶׁמֶן שָׂשׂוֹן--מֵחֲבֵרֶךָ
al-ken meshachacha elohim eloheicha shemen sason, mechavereicha
therefore God, thy God, hath anointed thee with the oil of gladness above thy fellows.

מֹר-וַאֲהָלוֹת קְצִיעוֹת, כָּל-בִּגְדֹתֶיךָ; מִן-הֵיכְלֵי שֵׁן, מִנִּי שִׂמְּחוּךָ
mor-va'ahalot ketzi'ot kol-bigdoteicha; min-heichelei shen, minni simmechucha
Myrrh, and aloes, and cassia are all thy garments; out of ivory palaces stringed instruments have made thee glad.

בְּנוֹת מְלָכִים, בְּיִקְּרוֹתֶיךָ; נִצְּבָה שֵׁגַל לִימִינְךָ, בְּכֶתֶם אוֹפִיר
benot melachim beyikkeroteicha; nitzevah shegal liminecha, bechetem ofir
Kings' daughters are among thy favourites; at thy right hand doth stand the queen in gold of Ophir.

שִׁמְעִי-בַת וּרְאִי, וְהַטִּי אָזְנֵךְ; וְשִׁכְחִי עַמֵּךְ, וּבֵית אָבִיךְ
shim'i-vat ure'i vehatti ozenech; veshichchi ammech, uveit avich
'Hearken, O daughter, and consider, and incline thine ear; forget also thine own people, and thy father's house;

וְיִתְאָו הַמֶּלֶךְ יָפְיֵךְ: כִּי-הוּא אֲדֹנַיִךְ, וְהִשְׁתַּחֲוִי-לוֹ
veyit'av hammelech yofeyech; ki-hu adonayich, vehishtachavi-lo
So shall the king desire thy beauty; for he is thy lord; and do homage unto him.

וּבַת-צֹר: בְּמִנְחָה, פָּנַיִךְ יְחַלּוּ--עֲשִׁירֵי עָם
uvat-tzor beminchah panayich yechallu, ashirei am
And, O daughter of Tyre, the richest of the people shall entreat thy favour with a gift.'

תְּהִלִים

הֲלֹא אֱלֹהִים, יַחֲקָר-זֹאת: כִּי-הוּא יֹדֵעַ, תַּעֲלֻמוֹת לֵב
halo elohim yachakor-zot; ki-hu yodea', ta'alumot lev
Would not God search this out? For He knoweth the secrets of the heart.

כִּי-עָלֶיךָ, הֹרַגְנוּ כָל-הַיּוֹם; נֶחְשַׁבְנוּ, כְּצֹאן טִבְחָה
ki-'aleicha horagnu chol-hayom; nechshavnu, ketzon tivchah
Nay, but for Thy sake are we killed all the day; we are accounted as sheep for the slaughter.

עוּרָה, לָמָּה תִישַׁן אֲדֹנָי; הָקִיצָה, אַל-תִּזְנַח לָנֶצַח
'urah lammah tishan adonai; hakitzah, al-tiznach lanetzach
Awake, why sleepest Thou, O Lord? Arouse Thyself, cast not off for ever.

לָמָּה-פָנֶיךָ תַסְתִּיר; תִּשְׁכַּח עָנְיֵנוּ וְלַחֲצֵנוּ
lammah-faneicha tastir; tishkach aneyenu velachatzenu
Wherefore hidest Thou Thy face, and forgettest our affliction and our oppression?

כִּי שָׁחָה לֶעָפָר נַפְשֵׁנוּ; דָּבְקָה לָאָרֶץ בִּטְנֵנוּ
ki shachah le'afar nafshenu; davekah la'aretz bitnenu
For our soul is bowed down to the dust; our belly cleaveth unto the earth.

קוּמָה, עֶזְרָתָה לָּנוּ; וּפְדֵנוּ, לְמַעַן חַסְדֶּךָ
kumah ezratah lanu; ufedenu, lema'an chasdecha
Arise for our help, and redeem us for Thy mercy's sake.

מה

לַמְנַצֵּחַ עַל-שֹׁשַׁנִּים, לִבְנֵי-קֹרַח; מַשְׂכִּיל, שִׁיר יְדִידֹת
Lamnatzeach al-shoshannim livnei-korach; maskil, shir yedidot
For the Leader; upon Shoshannim; [a Psalm] of the sons of Korah. Maschil. A Song of loves.

רָחַשׁ לִבִּי, דָּבָר טוֹב
rachash libbi davar tov
My heart overfloweth with a goodly matter;

אֹמֵר אָנִי, מַעֲשַׂי לְמֶלֶךְ; לְשׁוֹנִי, עֵט סוֹפֵר מָהִיר
omer ani ma'asai lemelech; leshoni, et sofer mahir
I say: 'My work is concerning a king'; my tongue is the pen of a ready writer.

יָפְיָפִיתָ, מִבְּנֵי אָדָם--הוּצַק חֵן, בְּשִׂפְתוֹתֶיךָ
yafeyafita mibbenei adam, hutzak chen besefetoteicha
Thou art fairer than the children of men; grace is poured upon thy lips;

עַל-כֵּן בֵּרַכְךָ אֱלֹהִים לְעוֹלָם
al-ken berachecha elohim le'olam
therefore God hath blessed thee for ever.

תְּהִלִּים

אַף-זָנַחְתָּ, וַתַּכְלִימֵנוּ; וְלֹא-תֵצֵא, בְּצִבְאוֹתֵינוּ
'af-zanachta vattachlimenu; velo-tetze, betziv'oteinu
Yet Thou hast cast off, and brought us to confusion; and goest not forth with our hosts.

תְּשִׁיבֵנוּ אָחוֹר, מִנִּי-צָר; וּמְשַׂנְאֵינוּ, שָׁסוּ לָמוֹ
teshivenu achor minni-tzar; umesan'einu, shasu lamo
Thou makest us to turn back from the adversary; and they that hate us spoil at their will.

תִּתְּנֵנוּ, כְּצֹאן מַאֲכָל; וּבַגּוֹיִם, זֵרִיתָנוּ
tittenenu ketzon ma'achal; uvaggoyim, zeritanu
Thou hast given us like sheep to be eaten; and hast scattered us among the nations.

תִּמְכֹּר-עַמְּךָ בְלֹא-הוֹן; וְלֹא-רִבִּיתָ, בִּמְחִירֵיהֶם
timkor-'ammecha velo-hon; velo-ribbita, bimchireihem
Thou sellest Thy people for small gain, and hast not set their prices high.

תְּשִׂימֵנוּ חֶרְפָּה, לִשְׁכֵנֵינוּ; לַעַג וָקֶלֶס, לִסְבִיבוֹתֵינוּ
tesimenu cherpah lishcheneinu; la'ag vakeles, lisvivoteinu
Thou makest us a taunt to our neighbours, a scorn and a derision to them that are round about us.

תְּשִׂימֵנוּ מָשָׁל, בַּגּוֹיִם; מְנוֹד-רֹאשׁ, בַּלְאֻמִּים
tesimenu mashal baggoyim; menod-rosh, bal-'ummim
Thou makest us a byword among the nations, a shaking of the head among the peoples.

כָּל-הַיּוֹם, כְּלִמָּתִי נֶגְדִּי; וּבֹשֶׁת פָּנַי כִּסָּתְנִי
kol-hayom kelimmati negdi; uvoshet panai kissateni
All the day is my confusion before me, and the shame of my face hath covered me,

מִקּוֹל, מְחָרֵף וּמְגַדֵּף; מִפְּנֵי אוֹיֵב, וּמִתְנַקֵּם
mikkol mecharef umegaddef; mippenei oyev, umitnakkem
For the voice of him that taunteth and blasphemeth; by reason of the enemy and the revengeful.

כָּל-זֹאת בָּאַתְנוּ, וְלֹא שְׁכַחֲנוּךָ; וְלֹא-שִׁקַּרְנוּ, בִּבְרִיתֶךָ
kol-zot ba'atnu velo shechachanucha; velo-shikkarnu, bivritecha
All this is come upon us; yet have we not forgotten Thee, neither have we been false to Thy covenant.

לֹא-נָסוֹג אָחוֹר לִבֵּנוּ; וַתֵּט אֲשֻׁרֵינוּ, מִנִּי אָרְחֶךָ
lo-nasog achor libbenu; vattet ashureinu, minni orechecha
Our heart is not turned back, neither have our steps declined from Thy path;

כִּי דִכִּיתָנוּ, בִּמְקוֹם תַּנִּים; וַתְּכַס עָלֵינוּ בְצַלְמָוֶת
ki dikkitanu bimkom tannim; vattechas aleinu vetzalmavet
Though Thou hast crushed us into a place of jackals, and covered us with the shadow of death.

אִם-שָׁכַחְנוּ, שֵׁם אֱלֹהֵינוּ; וַנִּפְרֹשׂ כַּפֵּינוּ, לְאֵל זָר
'im-shachachnu shem eloheinu; vannifros kappeinu, le'el zar
If we had forgotten the name of our God, or spread forth our hands to a strange god;

תְּהִלִּים

מד

לַמְנַצֵּחַ לִבְנֵי-קֹרַח מַשְׂכִּיל
Lamnatzeach livnei-korach maskil
For the Leader; [a Psalm] of the sons of Korah. Maschil.

אֱלֹהִים, בְּאָזְנֵינוּ שָׁמַעְנוּ--אֲבוֹתֵינוּ סִפְּרוּ-לָנוּ: פֹּעַל פָּעַלְתָּ בִימֵיהֶם, בִּימֵי קֶדֶם
'elohim be'azeneinu shama'nu, avoteinu sipperu-lanu; po'al pa'alta viymeihem, biymei kedem
O God, we have heard with our ears, our fathers have told us; a work Thou didst in their days, in the days of old.

אַתָּה, יָדְךָ גּוֹיִם הוֹרַשְׁתָּ--וַתִּטָּעֵם
'attah yadecha goyim horashta vattitta'em
Thou with Thy hand didst drive out the nations, and didst plant them in;

תָּרַע לְאֻמִּים, וַתְּשַׁלְּחֵם
tara le'ummim, vatteshallechem
Thou didst break the peoples, and didst spread them abroad.

כִּי לֹא בְחַרְבָּם, יָרְשׁוּ אָרֶץ, וּזְרוֹעָם, לֹא-הוֹשִׁיעָה-לָּמוֹ
ki lo vecharbam yareshu aretz, uzero'am lo-hoshi'ah lamo
For not by their own sword did they get the land in possession, neither did their own arm save them;

כִּי-יְמִינְךָ וּזְרוֹעֲךָ, וְאוֹר פָּנֶיךָ--כִּי רְצִיתָם
ki-yeminecha uzero'acha ve'or paneicha, ki retzitam
but Thy right hand, and Thine arm, and the light of Thy countenance, because Thou wast favourable unto them.

אַתָּה-הוּא מַלְכִּי אֱלֹהִים; צַוֵּה, יְשׁוּעוֹת יַעֲקֹב
'attah-hu malki elohim; tzavveh, yeshu'ot ya'akov
Thou art my King, O God; command the salvation of Jacob.

בְּךָ, צָרֵינוּ נְנַגֵּחַ; בְּשִׁמְךָ, נָבוּס קָמֵינוּ
becha tzareinu nenaggeach; beshimcha, navus kameinu
Through Thee do we push down our adversaries; through Thy name do we tread them under that rise up against us.

כִּי לֹא בְקַשְׁתִּי אֶבְטָח; וְחַרְבִּי, לֹא תוֹשִׁיעֵנִי
ki lo vekashti evtach; vecharbi, lo toshi'eni
For I trust not in my bow, neither can my sword save me.

כִּי הוֹשַׁעְתָּנוּ, מִצָּרֵינוּ; וּמְשַׂנְאֵינוּ הֱבִישׁוֹתָ
ki hosha'tanu mitzareinu; umesan'einu hevishota
But Thou hast saved us from our adversaries, and hast put them to shame that hate us.

בֵּאלֹהִים, הִלַּלְנוּ כָל-הַיּוֹם; וְשִׁמְךָ, לְעוֹלָם נוֹדֶה סֶלָה
Be'elohim hillalnu chol-hayom; veshimcha le'olam nodeh selah
In God have we gloried all the day, and we will give thanks unto Thy name for ever. Selah

תְּהִלִּים

הוֹחִילִי לֵאלֹהִים, כִּי-עוֹד אוֹדֶנּוּ-- יְשׁוּעֹת פָּנַי, וֵאלֹהָי
hochili le'elohim ki-'od odennu; yeshu'ot panai, ve'elohai
Hope thou in God; for I shall yet praise Him, the salvation of my countenance, and my God.

מג

שָׁפְטֵנִי אֱלֹהִים, וְרִיבָה רִיבִי--מִגּוֹי לֹא-חָסִיד
Shofeteni elohim verivah rivi, miggoy lo-chasid
Be Thou my judge, O God, and plead my cause against an ungodly nation;

מֵאִישׁ מִרְמָה וְעַוְלָה תְפַלְּטֵנִי
me'ish-mirmah ve'avlah tefalleteni
O deliver me from the deceitful and unjust man.

כִּי-אַתָּה, אֱלֹהֵי מָעוּזִּי-- לָמָה זְנַחְתָּנִי
ki-'attah elohei ma'uzzi lamah zenachtani
For Thou art the God of my strength; why hast Thou cast me off?

לָמָּה-קֹדֵר אֶתְהַלֵּךְ, בְּלַחַץ אוֹיֵב
lammah-koder et'hallech, belachatz oyev
Why go I mourning under the oppression of the enemy?

שְׁלַח-אוֹרְךָ וַאֲמִתְּךָ, הֵמָּה יַנְחוּנִי
shelach-'orecha va'amittecha hemmah yanchuni
O send out Thy light and Thy truth; let them lead me;

יְבִיאוּנִי אֶל-הַר-קָדְשְׁךָ, וְאֶל-מִשְׁכְּנוֹתֶיךָ
yevi'uni el-har-kodshecha ve'el-mishkenoteicha
let them bring me unto Thy holy mountain, and to Thy dwelling-places.

וְאָבוֹאָה, אֶל-מִזְבַּח אֱלֹהִים--אֶל-אֵל, שִׂמְחַת גִּילִי: וְאוֹדְךָ בְכִנּוֹר-- אֱלֹהִים אֱלֹהָי
ve'avo'ah el-mizbach elohim, el-'el simchat gili ve'odecha vechinnor, elohim elohai
Then will I go unto the altar of God, unto God, my exceeding joy; and praise Thee upon the harp, O God, my God.

מַה-תִּשְׁתּוֹחֲחִי, נַפְשִׁי-- וּמַה-תֶּהֱמִי עָלָי
mah-tishtochachi nafshi umah-tehemi alai
Why art thou cast down, O my soul? and why moanest thou within me?

הוֹחִילִי לֵאלֹהִים, כִּי-עוֹד אוֹדֶנּוּ-- יְשׁוּעֹת פָּנַי, וֵאלֹהָי
hochili le'elohim ki-'od odennu; yeshu'ot panai, ve'elohai
Hope thou in God; for I shall yet praise Him, the salvation of my countenance, and my God.

תְּהִלִּים

כִּי אֶעֱבֹר בַּסָּךְ, אֶדַּדֵּם עַד־בֵּית אֱלֹהִים
ki e'evor bassach eddaddem, ad-beit elohim
how I passed on with the throng, and led them to the house of God,

בְּקוֹל־רִנָּה וְתוֹדָה; הָמוֹן חוֹגֵג
bekol-rinnah vetodah, hamon chogeg
with the voice of joy and praise, a multitude keeping holyday.

מַה־תִּשְׁתּוֹחֲחִי, נַפְשִׁי־־וַתֶּהֱמִי עָלָי: הוֹחִלִי לֵאלֹהִים
mah-tishtochachi nafshi vattehemi alai hochili le'elohim
Why art thou cast down, O my soul? and why moanest thou within me? Hope thou in God;

כִּי־עוֹד אוֹדֶנּוּ־־יְשׁוּעוֹת פָּנָיו
ki-'od odennu, yeshu'ot panav
for I shall yet praise Him for the salvation of His countenance.

אֱלֹהַי־־עָלַי, נַפְשִׁי תִשְׁתּוֹחָח
'elohai, alai nafshi tishtochach
O my God, my soul is cast down within me;

עַל־כֵּן־־אֶזְכָּרְךָ, מֵאֶרֶץ יַרְדֵּן; וְחֶרְמוֹנִים, מֵהַר מִצְעָר
al-ken, ezkorcha me'eretz yarden; vechermonim, mehar mitz'ar
therefore do I remember Thee from the land of Jordan, and the Hermons, from the hill Mizar.

תְּהוֹם־אֶל־תְּהוֹם קוֹרֵא, לְקוֹל צִנּוֹרֶיךָ; כָּל־מִשְׁבָּרֶיךָ וְגַלֶּיךָ, עָלַי עָבָרוּ
tehom-'el-tehom korei lekol tzinnoreicha; kol-mishbareicha vegalleicha, alai avaru
Deep calleth unto deep at the voice of Thy cataracts; all Thy waves and Thy billows are gone over me.

יוֹמָם, יְצַוֶּה יְהוָה חַסְדּוֹ
yomam yetzavveh hashem chasdo
By day the LORD will command His lovingkindness,

וּבַלַּיְלָה, שִׁירֹה עִמִּי־־תְּפִלָּה, לְאֵל חַיָּי
uvallaylah shiroh shiro immi; tefillah, le'el chayai
and in the night His song shall be with me, even a prayer unto the God of my life.

אוֹמְרָה, לְאֵל סַלְעִי־־לָמָה שְׁכַחְתָּנִי: לָמָּה־קֹדֵר אֵלֵךְ־־בְּלַחַץ אוֹיֵב
'omerah le'el sal'i lamah shechachtani lammah-koder elech, belachatz oyev
I will say unto God my Rock: 'Why hast Thou forgotten me? Why go I mourning under the oppression of the enemy?'

בְּרֶצַח, בְּעַצְמוֹתַי־־חֵרְפוּנִי צוֹרְרָי; בְּאָמְרָם אֵלַי כָּל־הַיּוֹם, אַיֵּה אֱלֹהֶיךָ
beretzach be'atzmotai, cherefuni tzorerai; be'ameram elai kol-hayom, ayeh eloheicha
As with a crushing in my bones, mine adversaries taunt me; while they say unto me all the day: 'Where is thy God?'

מַה־תִּשְׁתּוֹחֲחִי, נַפְשִׁי־־וּמַה־תֶּהֱמִי עָלָי
mah-tishtochachi nafshi umah-tehemi alai
Why art thou cast down, O my soul? and why moanest thou within me?

תְּהִלִּים

דְּבַר-בְּלִיַּעַל, יָצוּק בּוֹ; וַאֲשֶׁר שָׁכַב, לֹא-יוֹסִיף לָקוּם
devar-beliya'al yatzuk bo; va'asher shachav, lo-yosif lakum
'An evil thing cleaveth fast unto him; and now that he lieth, he shall rise up no more.'

גַּם-אִישׁ שְׁלוֹמִי, אֲשֶׁר-בָּטַחְתִּי בוֹ--אוֹכֵל לַחְמִי; הִגְדִּיל עָלַי עָקֵב
gam-'ish shelomi asher-batachti vo ochel lachmi; higdil alai akev
Yea, mine own familiar friend, in whom I trusted, who did eat of my bread, hath lifted up his heel against me.

וְאַתָּה יְהוָה, חָנֵּנִי וַהֲקִימֵנִי; וַאֲשַׁלְּמָה לָהֶם
ve'attah hashem chonneni vahakimeni; va'ashallemah lahem
But Thou, O LORD, be gracious unto me, and raise me up, that I may requite them.

בְּזֹאת יָדַעְתִּי, כִּי-חָפַצְתָּ בִּי: כִּי לֹא-יָרִיעַ אֹיְבִי עָלָי
bezot yada'ti ki-chafatzta bi; ki lo-yaria oyevi alai
By this I know that Thou delightest in me, that mine enemy doth not triumph over me.

וַאֲנִי--בְּתֻמִּי, תָּמַכְתָּ בִּי; וַתַּצִּיבֵנִי לְפָנֶיךָ לְעוֹלָם
va'ani, betummi tamachta bi; vattatziveni lefaneicha le'olam
And as for me, Thou upholdest me because of mine integrity, and settest me before Thy face for ever.

בָּרוּךְ יְהוָה, אֱלֹהֵי יִשְׂרָאֵל--מֵהָעוֹלָם, וְעַד הָעוֹלָם: אָמֵן וְאָמֵן
baruch hashem elohei yisra'el, meha'olam ve'ad ha'olam, amen ve'amen
Blessed be the LORD, the God of Israel, from everlasting and to everlasting. Amen, and Amen.

מב

לַמְנַצֵּחַ, מַשְׂכִּיל לִבְנֵי-קֹרַח
Lamnatzeach, maskil livnei-korach
For the Leader; Maschil of the sons of Korah.

כְּאַיָּל, תַּעֲרֹג עַל-אֲפִיקֵי-מָיִם--כֵּן נַפְשִׁי תַעֲרֹג אֵלֶיךָ אֱלֹהִים
ke'ayal, ta'arog al-'afikei-mayim; ken nafshi ta'arog eleicha elohim
As the hart panteth after the water brooks, so panteth my soul after Thee, O God.

צָמְאָה נַפְשִׁי, לֵאלֹהִים--לְאֵל חָי: מָתַי אָבוֹא; וְאֵרָאֶה, פְּנֵי אֱלֹהִים
tzame'ah nafshi le'elohim le'el chai matai avo; ve'era'eh, penei elohim
My soul thirsteth for God, for the living God: 'When shall I come and appear before God?'

הָיְתָה-לִּי דִמְעָתִי לֶחֶם, יוֹמָם וָלָיְלָה; בֶּאֱמֹר אֵלַי כָּל-הַיּוֹם, אַיֵּה אֱלֹהֶיךָ
hayetah-li dim'ati lechem yomam valayelah; be'emor elai kol-hayom, ayeh eloheicha
My tears have been my food day and night, while they say unto me all the day: 'Where is thy God?'

אֵלֶּה אֶזְכְּרָה, וְאֶשְׁפְּכָה עָלַי נַפְשִׁי
'elleh ezkerah ve'eshpechah alai nafshi
These things I remember, and pour out my soul within me,

עֶזְרָתִי וּמְפַלְטִי אַתָּה; אֱלֹהַי, אַל-תְּאַחַר
ezrati umefalti attah; elohai, al-te'achar
Thou art my help and my deliverer; O my God, tarry not.

מא

לַמְנַצֵּחַ, מִזְמוֹר לְדָוִד
Lamnatzeach, mizmor ledavid
For the Leader. A Psalm of David.

אַשְׁרֵי, מַשְׂכִּיל אֶל-דָּל; בְּיוֹם רָעָה, יְמַלְּטֵהוּ יְהוָה
'ashrei maskil el-dal; beyom ra'ah, yemalletehu hashem
Happy is he that considereth the poor; the LORD will deliver him in the day of evil.

יְהוָה, יִשְׁמְרֵהוּ וִיחַיֵּהוּ--וְאֻשַּׁר בָּאָרֶץ
hashem yishmerehu vichayehu ve'ushar ba'aretz
The LORD preserve him, and keep him alive, let him be called happy in the land;

וְאַל-תִּתְּנֵהוּ, בְּנֶפֶשׁ אֹיְבָיו
ve'al-tittenehu, benefesh oyevav
and deliver not Thou him unto the greed of his enemies.

יְהוָה--יִסְעָדֶנּוּ, עַל-עֶרֶשׂ דְּוָי; כָּל-מִשְׁכָּבוֹ, הָפַכְתָּ בְחָלְיוֹ
hashem yis'adennu al-'eres devai; kol-mishkavo, hafachta vecholiyo
The LORD support him upon the bed of illness; mayest Thou turn all his lying down in his sickness.

אֲנִי-אָמַרְתִּי, יְהוָה חָנֵּנִי; רְפָאָה נַפְשִׁי, כִּי-חָטָאתִי לָךְ
'ani-'amarti hashem chonneni refa'ah nafshi, ki-chatati lach
As for me, I said: 'O LORD, be gracious unto me; heal my soul; for I have sinned against Thee.'

אוֹיְבַי--יֹאמְרוּ רַע לִי; מָתַי יָמוּת, וְאָבַד שְׁמוֹ
'oyevai, yomeru ra li; matai yamut, ve'avad shemo
Mine enemies speak evil of me: 'When shall he die, and his name perish?'

וְאִם-בָּא לִרְאוֹת, שָׁוְא יְדַבֵּר
ve'im-ba lir'ot shav yedabber
And if one come to see me, he speaketh falsehood;

לִבּוֹ, יִקְבָּץ-אָוֶן לוֹ; יֵצֵא לַחוּץ יְדַבֵּר
libbo yikbatz-'aven lo; yetzei lachutz yedabber
his heart gathereth iniquity to itself; when he goeth abroad, he speaketh of it.

יַחַד--עָלַי יִתְלַחֲשׁוּ, כָּל-שֹׂנְאָי; עָלַי--יַחְשְׁבוּ רָעָה לִי
yachad, alai yitlachashu kol-sone'ai; alai yachshevu ra'ah li
All that hate me whisper together against me, against me do they devise my hurt:

תְּהִלִּים

צִדְקָתְךָ לֹא-כִסִּיתִי, בְּתוֹךְ לִבִּי--אֱמוּנָתְךָ וּתְשׁוּעָתְךָ אָמָרְתִּי
tzidkatecha lo-chissiti betoch libbi, emunatecha uteshu'atecha amareti
I have not hid Thy righteousness within my heart; I have declared Thy faithfulness and Thy salvation;

לֹא-כִחַדְתִּי חַסְדְּךָ וַאֲמִתְּךָ, לְקָהָל רָב
lo-chichadti chasdecha va'amittecha, lekahal rav
I have not concealed Thy mercy and Thy truth from the great congregation.

אַתָּה יְהוָה--לֹא-תִכְלָא רַחֲמֶיךָ מִמֶּנִּי; חַסְדְּךָ וַאֲמִתְּךָ, תָּמִיד יִצְּרוּנִי
'attah hashem lo-tichla rachameicha mimmenni; chasdecha va'amittecha, tamid yitzeruni
Thou, O LORD, wilt not withhold Thy compassions from me; let Thy mercy and Thy truth continually preserve me.

כִּי אָפְפוּ-עָלַי רָעוֹת, עַד-אֵין מִסְפָּר--הִשִּׂיגוּנִי עֲוֺנֹתַי, וְלֹא-יָכֹלְתִּי לִרְאוֹת
ki afefu-'alai ra'ot ad-'ein mispar, hissiguni avonotai velo-yacholeti lir'ot
For innumerable evils have compassed me about, mine iniquities have overtaken me, so that I am not able to look up;

עָצְמוּ מִשַּׂעֲרוֹת רֹאשִׁי, וְלִבִּי עֲזָבָנִי
atzemu missa'arot roshi, velibbi azavani
they are more than the hairs of my head, and my heart hath failed me.

רְצֵה יְהוָה, לְהַצִּילֵנִי; יְהוָה, לְעֶזְרָתִי חוּשָׁה
retzeh hashem lehatzileni; hashem le'ezrati chushah
Be pleased, O LORD, to deliver me; O LORD, make haste to help me.

יֵבֹשׁוּ וְיַחְפְּרוּ, יַחַד--מְבַקְשֵׁי נַפְשִׁי, לִסְפּוֹתָהּ
yevoshu veyachperu yachad mevakshei nafshi, lispotah
Let them be ashamed and abashed together that seek after my soul to sweep it away;

יִסֹּגוּ אָחוֹר, וְיִכָּלְמוּ--חֲפֵצֵי, רָעָתִי
yissogu achor veyikkalemu; chafetzei, ra'ati
let them be turned backward and brought to confusion that delight in my hurt.

יָשֹׁמּוּ, עַל-עֵקֶב בָּשְׁתָּם--הָאֹמְרִים לִי, הֶאָח הֶאָח
yashommu al-'ekev boshetam; ha'omerim li, he'ach he'ach
Let them be appalled by reason of their shame that say unto me: 'Aha, aha.'

יָשִׂישׂוּ וְיִשְׂמְחוּ, בְּךָ--כָּל-מְבַקְשֶׁיךָ
yasisu veyismechu becha, kol-mevaksheicha
Let all those that seek Thee rejoice and be glad in Thee;

יֹאמְרוּ תָמִיד, יִגְדַּל יְהוָה--אֹהֲבֵי, תְּשׁוּעָתֶךָ
yomeru tamid yigdal hashem ohavei, teshu'atecha
let such as love Thy salvation say continually: 'The LORD be magnified.'

וַאֲנִי, עָנִי וְאֶבְיוֹן--אֲדֹנָי יַחֲשָׁב-לִי
va'ani ani ve'evyon adonai yachashov li
But, as for me, that am poor and needy, the Lord will account it unto me;

תְּהִלִּים

וַיָּקֶם עַל-סֶלַע רַגְלַי; כּוֹנֵן אֲשֻׁרָי
vayakom al-sela raglai, konen ashurai
and He set my feet upon a rock, He established my goings.

וַיִּתֵּן בְּפִי, שִׁיר חָדָשׁ--תְּהִלָּה לֵאלֹהֵינוּ
vayitten befi shir chadash tehillah le'eloheinu
And He hath put a new song in my mouth, even praise unto our God;

יִרְאוּ רַבִּים וְיִירָאוּ; וְיִבְטְחוּ, בַּיהוָה
yir'u rabbim veyira'u; veyivtechu, bahashem
many shall see, and fear, and shall trust in the LORD.

אַשְׁרֵי הַגֶּבֶר--אֲשֶׁר-שָׂם יְהוָה, מִבְטַחוֹ
'ashrei haggever, asher-sam hashem mivtacho
Happy is the man that hath made the LORD his trust,

וְלֹא-פָנָה אֶל-רְהָבִים, וְשָׂטֵי כָזָב
velo-fanah el-rehavim, vesatei chazav
and hath not turned unto the arrogant, nor unto such as fall away treacherously.

רַבּוֹת עָשִׂיתָ, אַתָּה יְהוָה אֱלֹהַי--נִפְלְאֹתֶיךָ וּמַחְשְׁבֹתֶיךָ, אֵלֵינוּ
rabbot asita attah hashem elohai nifle'oteicha umachshevoteicha, eleinu
Many things hast Thou done, O LORD my God, even Thy wonderful works, and Thy thoughts toward us;

אֵין, עֲרֹךְ אֵלֶיךָ--אַגִּידָה וַאֲדַבֵּרָה; עָצְמוּ, מִסַּפֵּר
ein aroch eleicha, aggidah va'adabberah; atzemu, missapper
there is none to be compared unto Thee! If I would declare and speak of them, they are more than can be told.

זֶבַח וּמִנְחָה, לֹא-חָפַצְתָּ--אָזְנַיִם, כָּרִיתָ לִּי
zevach uminchah lo-chafatzta, azenayim karita li
Sacrifice and meal-offering Thou hast no delight in; mine ears hast Thou opened;

עוֹלָה וַחֲטָאָה, לֹא שָׁאָלְתָּ
olah vachata'ah, lo sha'alta
burnt-offering and sin-offering hast Thou not required.

אָז אָמַרְתִּי, הִנֵּה-בָאתִי: בִּמְגִלַּת-סֵפֶר, כָּתוּב עָלָי
'az amarti hinneh-vati; bimgillat-sefer, katuv alai
Then said I: 'Lo, I am come with the roll of a book which is prescribed for me;

לַעֲשׂוֹת-רְצוֹנְךָ אֱלֹהַי חָפָצְתִּי; וְתוֹרָתְךָ, בְּתוֹךְ מֵעָי
la'asot-retzonecha elohai chafatzeti; vetoratecha, betoch me'ai
I delight to do Thy will, O my God; yea, Thy law is in my inmost parts.'

בִּשַּׂרְתִּי צֶדֶק, בְּקָהָל רָב--הִנֵּה שְׂפָתַי, לֹא אֶכְלָא: יְהוָה, אַתָּה יָדָעְתָּ
bissarti tzedek bekahal rav, hinneh sefatai lo echla; hashem attah yada'eta
I have preached righteousness in the great congregation, lo, I did not refrain my lips; O LORD, Thou knowest.

תְּהִלִּים

מִכָּל-פְּשָׁעַי הַצִּילֵנִי; חֶרְפַּת נָבָל, אַל-תְּשִׂימֵנִי
mikkol-pesha'ai hatzileni; cherpat naval, al-tesimeni
Deliver me from all my transgressions; make me not the reproach of the base.

נֶאֱלַמְתִּי, לֹא אֶפְתַּח-פִּי: כִּי אַתָּה עָשִׂיתָ
ne'elamti lo eftach-pi; ki attah asita
I am dumb, I open not my mouth; because Thou hast done it.

הָסֵר מֵעָלַי נִגְעֶךָ; מִתִּגְרַת יָדְךָ, אֲנִי כָלִיתִי
haser me'alai nig'echa; mittigrat yadecha, ani chaliti
Remove Thy stroke from off me; I am consumed by the blow of Thy hand.

בְּתוֹכָחוֹת עַל-עָוֺן, יִסַּרְתָּ אִישׁ
betochachot al-'avon yissarta ish
With rebukes dost Thou chasten man for iniquity,

וַתֶּמֶס כָּעָשׁ חֲמוּדוֹ; אַךְ הֶבֶל כָּל-אָדָם סֶלָה
vattemes ka'ash chamudo; ach hevel kol-'adam selah
and like a moth Thou makest his beauty to consume away; surely every man is vanity. Selah

שִׁמְעָה תְפִלָּתִי יְהוָה, וְשַׁוְעָתִי הַאֲזִינָה--אֶל-דִּמְעָתִי, אַל-תֶּחֱרַשׁ
shim'ah-tefillati hashem veshav'ati ha'azinah el-dim'ati, al-techerash
Hear my prayer, O LORD, and give ear unto my cry; keep not silence at my tears;

כִּי גֵר אָנֹכִי עִמָּךְ; תּוֹשָׁב, כְּכָל-אֲבוֹתָי
ki ger anochi immach; toshav, kechol-'avotai
for I am a stranger with Thee, a sojourner, as all my fathers were.

הָשַׁע מִמֶּנִּי וְאַבְלִיגָה--בְּטֶרֶם אֵלֵךְ וְאֵינֶנִּי.
hasha mimmenni ve'avligah; beterem elech ve'einenni
Look away from me, that I may take comfort, before I go hence, and be no more.'

מ

לַמְנַצֵּחַ, לְדָוִד מִזְמוֹר
Lamnatzeach, ledavid mizmor
For the Leader. A Psalm of David.

קַוֺּה קִוִּיתִי יְהוָה; וַיֵּט אֵלַי, וַיִּשְׁמַע שַׁוְעָתִי
kavoh kivviti hashem vayet elai, vayishma shav'ati
I waited patiently for the LORD; and He inclined unto me, and heard my cry.

וַיַּעֲלֵנִי, מִבּוֹר שָׁאוֹן--מִטִּיט הַיָּוֵן
vaya'aleni mibbor sha'on mittit hayaven
He brought me up also out of the tumultuous pit, out of the miry clay;

תְּהִלִּים

לט

לַמְנַצֵּחַ לידיתון, מִזְמוֹר לְדָוִד
Lamnatzeach lidutun, mizmor ledavid
For the Leader, for Jeduthun. A Psalm of David.

אָמַרְתִּי--אֶשְׁמְרָה דְרָכַי, מֵחֲטוֹא בִלְשׁוֹנִי
'amarti, eshmerah derachai mechato vilshoni
I said: 'I will take heed to my ways, that I sin not with my tongue;

אֶשְׁמְרָה לְפִי מַחְסוֹם--בְּעֹד רָשָׁע לְנֶגְדִּי
eshmerah lefi machsom; be'od rasha lenegdi
I will keep a curb upon my mouth, while the wicked is before me.'

נֶאֱלַמְתִּי דוּמִיָּה, הֶחֱשֵׁיתִי מִטּוֹב; וּכְאֵבִי נֶעְכָּר
ne'elamti dumiyah hechesheiti mittov; uche'evi ne'kar
I was dumb with silence; I held my peace, had no comfort; and my pain was held in check.

חַם-לִבִּי, בְּקִרְבִּי--בַּהֲגִיגִי תִבְעַר-אֵשׁ; דִּבַּרְתִּי, בִּלְשׁוֹנִי
cham-libbi bekirbi, bahagigi tiv'ar-'esh; dibbarti, bilshoni
My heart waxed hot within me; while I was musing, the fire kindled; then spoke I with my tongue:

הוֹדִיעֵנִי יְהוָה, קִצִּי--וּמִדַּת יָמַי מַה-הִיא; אֵדְעָה, מֶה-חָדֵל אָנִי
hodi'eni hashem kitzi, umiddat yamai mah-hi; ede'ah, meh-chadel ani
'LORD, make me to know mine end, and the measure of my days, what it is; let me know how short-lived I am.

הִנֵּה טְפָחוֹת, נָתַתָּה יָמַי--וְחֶלְדִּי כְאַיִן נֶגְדֶּךָ
hinneh tefachot natattah yamai, vecheldi che'ayin negdecha
Behold, Thou hast made my days as hand-breadths; and mine age is as nothing before Thee;

אַךְ כָּל-הֶבֶל כָּל-אָדָם, נִצָּב סֶלָה
ach kol-hevel kol-'adam, nitzav selah
surely every man at his best estate is altogether vanity. Selah

אַךְ-בְּצֶלֶם, יִתְהַלֶּךְ-אִישׁ--אַךְ-הֶבֶל יֶהֱמָיוּן
'ach-betzelem yit'hallech-'ish, ach-hevel yehemayun
Surely man walketh as a mere semblance; surely for vanity they are in turmoil;

יִצְבֹּר, וְלֹא-יֵדַע מִי-אֹסְפָם
yitzbor, velo-yeda mi-'osefam
he heapeth up riches, and knoweth not who shall gather them.

וְעַתָּה מַה-קִּוִּיתִי אֲדֹנָי--תּוֹחַלְתִּי, לְךָ הִיא
ve'attah mah-kivviti adonai; tochalti, lecha hi
And now, Lord, what wait I for? My hope, it is in Thee.

תְּהִלִּים

וְדֹרְשֵׁי רָעָתִי, דִּבְּרוּ הַוּוֹת; וּמִרְמוֹת, כָּל-הַיּוֹם יֶהְגּוּ
vedoreshei ra'ati dibberu havvot; umirmot, kol-hayom yehgu
and they that seek my hurt speak crafty devices, and utter deceits all the day.

וַאֲנִי כְחֵרֵשׁ, לֹא אֶשְׁמָע; וּכְאִלֵּם, לֹא יִפְתַּח-פִּיו
va'ani checheresh lo eshma'; uche'illem, lo yiftach-piv
But I am as a deaf man, I hear not; and I am as a dumb man that openeth not his mouth.

וָאֱהִי--כְּאִישׁ, אֲשֶׁר לֹא-שֹׁמֵעַ; וְאֵין בְּפִיו, תּוֹכָחוֹת
va'ehi, ke'ish asher lo-shomea'; ve'ein befiv, tochachot
Yea, I am become as a man that heareth not, and in whose mouth are no arguments.

כִּי-לְךָ יְהוָה הוֹחָלְתִּי; אַתָּה תַעֲנֶה, אֲדֹנָי אֱלֹהָי
ki-lecha hashem hochaleti; attah ta'aneh, adonai elohai
For in Thee, O LORD, do I hope; Thou wilt answer, O Lord my God.

כִּי-אָמַרְתִּי, פֶּן-יִשְׂמְחוּ-לִי; בְּמוֹט רַגְלִי, עָלַי הִגְדִּילוּ
ki-'amarti pen-yismechu-li; bemot ragli, alai higdilu
For I said: 'Lest they rejoice over me; when my foot slippeth, they magnify themselves against me.'

כִּי-אֲנִי, לְצֶלַע נָכוֹן; וּמַכְאוֹבִי נֶגְדִּי תָמִיד
ki-'ani letzela nachon; umach'ovi negdi tamid
For I am ready to halt, and my pain is continually before me.

כִּי-עֲוֹנִי אַגִּיד; אֶדְאַג, מֵחַטָּאתִי
ki-'avoni aggid; ed'ag, mechattati
For I do declare mine iniquity; I am full of care because of my sin.

וְאֹיְבַי, חַיִּים עָצֵמוּ; וְרַבּוּ שֹׂנְאַי שָׁקֶר
ve'oyevai chayim atzemu; verabbu sone'ai shaker
But mine enemies are strong in health; and they that hate me wrongfully are multiplied.

וּמְשַׁלְּמֵי רָעָה, תַּחַת טוֹבָה--יִשְׂטְנוּנִי, תַּחַת רָדְפִי-טוֹב
umeshallemei ra'ah tachat tovah; yistenuni, tachat radefi-tov
They also that repay evil for good are adversaries unto me, because I follow the thing that is good.

אַל-תַּעַזְבֵנִי יְהוָה: אֱלֹהַי, אַל-תִּרְחַק מִמֶּנִּי
'al-ta'azveni hashem elohai, al-tirchak mimmenni
Forsake me not, O LORD; O my God, be not far from me.

חוּשָׁה לְעֶזְרָתִי: אֲדֹנָי, תְּשׁוּעָתִי
chushah le'ezrati; adonai, teshu'ati
Make haste to help me, O Lord, my salvation.

תְּהִלִּים

כִּי־חִצֶּיךָ, נִחֲתוּ בִי; וַתִּנְחַת עָלַי יָדֶךָ
ki-chitzeicha nichatu vi; vattinchat alai yadecha
For Thine arrows are gone deep into me, and Thy hand is come down upon me.

אֵין־מְתֹם בִּבְשָׂרִי, מִפְּנֵי זַעְמֶךָ
'ein-metom bivsari mippenei za'mecha
There is no soundness in my flesh because of Thine indignation;

אֵין־שָׁלוֹם בַּעֲצָמַי, מִפְּנֵי חַטָּאתִי
ein-shalom ba'atzamai, mippenei chattati
neither is there any health in my bones because of my sin.

כִּי עֲוֹנֹתַי, עָבְרוּ רֹאשִׁי; כְּמַשָּׂא כָבֵד, יִכְבְּדוּ מִמֶּנִּי
ki avonotai averu roshi; kemassa chaved, yichbedu mimmenni
For mine iniquities are gone over my head; as a heavy burden they are too heavy for me.

הִבְאִישׁוּ נָמַקּוּ, חַבּוּרֹתָי: מִפְּנֵי, אִוַּלְתִּי
hiv'ishu namakku chabburotai; mippenei, ivvalti
My wounds are noisome, they fester, because of my foolishness.

נַעֲוֵיתִי שַׁחֹתִי עַד־מְאֹד; כָּל־הַיּוֹם, קֹדֵר הִלָּכְתִּי
na'aveiti shachoti ad-me'od; kol-hayom, koder hillacheti
I am bent and bowed down greatly; I go mourning all the day.

כִּי־כְסָלַי, מָלְאוּ נִקְלֶה; וְאֵין מְתֹם, בִּבְשָׂרִי
ki-chesalai male'u nikleh; ve'ein metom, bivsari
For my loins are filled with burning; and there is no soundness in my flesh.

נְפוּגוֹתִי וְנִדְכֵּיתִי עַד־מְאֹד; שָׁאַגְתִּי, מִנַּהֲמַת לִבִּי
nefugoti venidkeiti ad-me'od; sha'agti, minnahamat libbi
I am benumbed and sore crushed; I groan by reason of the moaning of my heart.

אֲדֹנָי, נֶגְדְּךָ כָל־תַּאֲוָתִי; וְאַנְחָתִי, מִמְּךָ לֹא־נִסְתָּרָה
'adonai negdecha chol-ta'avati; ve'anchati, mimmecha lo-nistarah
Lord, all my desire is before Thee; and my sighing is not hid from Thee.

לִבִּי סְחַרְחַר, עֲזָבַנִי כֹחִי; וְאוֹר־עֵינַי גַּם־הֵם, אֵין אִתִּי
libbi secharchar azavani chochi; ve'or-'einai gam-hem, ein itti
My heart fluttereth, my strength faileth me; as for the light of mine eyes, it also is gone from me.

אֹהֲבַי, וְרֵעַי--מִנֶּגֶד נִגְעִי יַעֲמֹדוּ; וּקְרוֹבַי, מֵרָחֹק עָמָדוּ
'ohavai vere'ai, minneged nig'i ya'amodu; ukerovai, merachok amadu
My friends and my companions stand aloof from my plague; and my kinsmen stand afar off.

וַיְנַקְשׁוּ, מְבַקְשֵׁי נַפְשִׁי
vaynakshu mevakshei nafshi
They also that seek after my life lay snares for me;

תְּהִלִּים

קַוֵּה אֶל-יְהוָה, וּשְׁמֹר דַּרְכּוֹ, וִירוֹמִמְךָ, לָרֶשֶׁת אָרֶץ
kavveh el-hashem ushemor darko, viromimcha lareshet aretz
Wait for the LORD, and keep His way, and He will exalt thee to inherit the land;

בְּהִכָּרֵת רְשָׁעִים תִּרְאֶה
behikkaret resha'im tir'eh
when the wicked are cut off, thou shalt see it.

רָאִיתִי, רָשָׁע עָרִיץ; וּמִתְעָרֶה, כְּאֶזְרָח רַעֲנָן
ra'iti rasha aritz; umit'areh, ke'ezrach ra'anan
I have seen the wicked in great power, and spreading himself like a leafy tree in its native soil.

וַיַּעֲבֹר, וְהִנֵּה אֵינֶנּוּ; וָאֲבַקְשֵׁהוּ, וְלֹא נִמְצָא
vaya'avor vehinneh einennu; va'avakshehu, velo nimtza
But one passed by, and, lo, he was not; yea, I sought him, but he could not be found.

שְׁמָר-תָּם, וּרְאֵה יָשָׁר: כִּי-אַחֲרִית לְאִישׁ שָׁלוֹם
shemor-tam ure'eh yashar; ki-'acharit le'ish shalom
Mark the man of integrity, and behold the upright; for there is a future for the man of peace.

וּפֹשְׁעִים, נִשְׁמְדוּ יַחְדָּו; אַחֲרִית רְשָׁעִים נִכְרָתָה
ufoshe'im nishmedu yachdav; acharit resha'im nichratah
But transgressors shall be destroyed together; the future of the wicked shall be cut off.

וּתְשׁוּעַת צַדִּיקִים, מֵיְהוָה; מָעוּזָּם, בְּעֵת צָרָה
uteshu'at tzaddikim mehashem; ma'uzzam, be'et tzarah
But the salvation of the righteous is of the LORD; He is their stronghold in the time of trouble.

וַיַּעְזְרֵם יְהוָה, וַיְפַלְּטֵם: יְפַלְּטֵם מֵרְשָׁעִים
vaya'zerem hashem vayefalletem yefalletem meresha'im
And the LORD helpeth them, and delivereth them; He delivereth them from the wicked,

וְיוֹשִׁיעֵם--כִּי-חָסוּ בוֹ
veyoshi'em; ki-chasu vo
and saveth them, because they have taken refuge in Him.

לח

מִזְמוֹר לְדָוִד לְהַזְכִּיר
Mizmor ledavid lehazkir
A Psalm of David, to make memorial.

יְהוָה--אַל-בְּקֶצְפְּךָ תוֹכִיחֵנִי; וּבַחֲמָתְךָ תְיַסְּרֵנִי
hashem al-beketzpecha tochicheni; uvachamatecha teyassereni
O LORD, rebuke me not in Thine anger; neither chasten me in Thy wrath.

תְּהִלִּים

מֵיְהוָה, מִצְעֲדֵי-גֶבֶר כּוֹנָנוּ; וְדַרְכּוֹ יֶחְפָּץ
mehashem mitz'adei-gever konanu, vedarko yechpatz
It is of the LORD that a man's goings are established; and He delighted in his way.

כִּי-יִפֹּל לֹא-יוּטָל: כִּי-יְהוָה, סוֹמֵךְ יָדוֹ
ki-yippol lo-yutal; ki-hashem somech yado
Though he fall, he shall not be utterly cast down; for the LORD upholdeth his hand.

נַעַר, הָיִיתִי--גַּם-זָקַנְתִּי: וְלֹא-רָאִיתִי, צַדִּיק נֶעֱזָב; וְזַרְעוֹ, מְבַקֶּשׁ-לָחֶם
na'ar hayiti, gam-zakanti velo-ra'iti tzaddik ne'ezav; vezar'o, mevakkesh-lachem
I have been young, and now am old; yet have I not seen the righteous forsaken, nor his seed begging bread.

כָּל-הַיּוֹם, חוֹנֵן וּמַלְוֶה; וְזַרְעוֹ, לִבְרָכָה
kol-hayom chonen umalveh; vezar'o, livrachah
All the day long he dealeth graciously, and lendeth; and his seed is blessed.

סוּר מֵרָע, וַעֲשֵׂה-טוֹב; וּשְׁכֹן לְעוֹלָם
sur mero va'aseh-tov, ushechon le'olam
Depart from evil, and do good; and dwell for evermore.

כִּי יְהוָה, אֹהֵב מִשְׁפָּט, וְלֹא-יַעֲזֹב אֶת-חֲסִידָיו
ki hashem ohev mishpat, velo-ya'azov et-chasidav
For the LORD loveth justice, and forsaketh not His saints;

לְעוֹלָם נִשְׁמָרוּ; וְזֶרַע רְשָׁעִים נִכְרָת
le'olam nishmaru; vezera resha'im nichrat
they are preserved for ever; but the seed of the wicked shall be cut off.

צַדִּיקִים יִירְשׁוּ-אָרֶץ; וְיִשְׁכְּנוּ לָעַד עָלֶיהָ
tzaddikim yireshu-'aretz; veyishkenu la'ad aleiha
The righteous shall inherit the land, and dwell therein for ever.

פִּי-צַדִּיק, יֶהְגֶּה חָכְמָה; וּלְשׁוֹנוֹ, תְּדַבֵּר מִשְׁפָּט
pi-tzaddik yehgeh chochmah uleshono, tedabber mishpat
The mouth of the righteous uttereth wisdom, and his tongue speaketh justice.

תּוֹרַת אֱלֹהָיו בְּלִבּוֹ; לֹא תִמְעַד אֲשֻׁרָיו
torat elohav belibbo; lo tim'ad ashurav
The law of his God is in his heart; none of his steps slide.

צוֹפֶה רָשָׁע, לַצַּדִּיק; וּמְבַקֵּשׁ, לַהֲמִיתוֹ
tzofeh rasha latzaddik; umevakkesh, lahamito
The wicked watcheth the righteous, and seeketh to slay him.

יְהוָה, לֹא-יַעַזְבֶנּוּ בְיָדוֹ; וְלֹא יַרְשִׁיעֶנּוּ, בְּהִשָּׁפְטוֹ
hashem lo-ya'azvennu veyado; velo yarshi'ennu, behishafto
The LORD will not leave him in his hand, nor suffer him to be condemned when he is judged.

תְּהִלִים

אֲדֹנָי יִשְׂחַק-לוֹ: כִּי-רָאָה, כִּי-יָבֹא יוֹמוֹ
'adonai yischak-lo; ki-ra'ah, ki-yavo yomo
The Lord doth laugh at him; for He seeth that his day is coming.

חֶרֶב, פָּתְחוּ רְשָׁעִים--וְדָרְכוּ קַשְׁתָּם
cherev patechu resha'im vedarechu kashtam
The wicked have drawn out the sword, and have bent their bow;

לְהַפִּיל, עָנִי וְאֶבְיוֹן; לִטְבוֹחַ, יִשְׁרֵי-דָרֶךְ
lehappil ani ve'evyon; litvoach, yishrei-darech
to cast down the poor and needy, to slay such as are upright in the way;

חַרְבָּם, תָּבוֹא בְלִבָּם; וְקַשְּׁתוֹתָם, תִּשָּׁבַרְנָה
charbom tavo velibbam; vekashetotam, tishavarnah
Their sword shall enter into their own heart, and their bows shall be broken.

טוֹב-מְעַט, לַצַּדִּיק--מֵהֲמוֹן, רְשָׁעִים רַבִּים
tov-me'at latzaddik; mehamon, resha'im rabbim
Better is a little that the righteous hath than the abundance of many wicked.

כִּי זְרוֹעוֹת רְשָׁעִים, תִּשָּׁבַרְנָה; וְסוֹמֵךְ צַדִּיקִים יְהוָה
ki zero'ot resha'im tishavarnah; vesomech tzaddikim hashem
For the arms of the wicked shall be broken; but the LORD upholdeth the righteous.

יוֹדֵעַ יְהוָה, יְמֵי תְמִימִם; וְנַחֲלָתָם, לְעוֹלָם תִּהְיֶה
yodea hashem yemei temimim; venachalatam, le'olam tihyeh
The LORD knoweth the days of them that are wholehearted; and their inheritance shall be for ever.

לֹא-יֵבֹשׁוּ, בְּעֵת רָעָה; וּבִימֵי רְעָבוֹן יִשְׂבָּעוּ
lo-yevoshu be'et ra'ah; uvimei re'avon yisba'u
They shall not be ashamed in the time of evil; and in the days of famine they shall be satisfied.

כִּי רְשָׁעִים, יֹאבֵדוּ, וְאֹיְבֵי יְהוָה, כִּיקַר כָּרִים
ki resha'im yovedu, ve'oyevei hashem kikar karim
For the wicked shall perish, and the enemies of the LORD shall be as the fat of lambs--

כָּלוּ בֶעָשָׁן כָּלוּ
kalu ve'ashan kalu
they shall pass away in smoke, they shall pass away.

לֹוֶה רָשָׁע, וְלֹא יְשַׁלֵּם; וְצַדִּיק, חוֹנֵן וְנוֹתֵן
loh rasho velo yeshallem; vetzaddik, chonen venoten
The wicked borroweth, and payeth not; but the righteous dealeth graciously, and giveth.

כִּי מְבֹרָכָיו, יִירְשׁוּ אָרֶץ; וּמְקֻלָּלָיו, יִכָּרֵתוּ
ki mevorachav yireshu aretz; umekullalav, yikkaretu
For such as are blessed of Him shall inherit the land; and they that are cursed of Him shall be cut off.

תְּהִלִּים

כִּי כֶחָצִיר, מְהֵרָה יִמָּלוּ; וּכְיֶרֶק דֶּשֶׁא, יִבּוֹלוּן
ki chechatzir meherah yimmalu; ucheyerek deshe, yibbolun
For they shall soon wither like the grass, and fade as the green herb.

בְּטַח בַּיהוָה, וַעֲשֵׂה-טוֹב; שְׁכָן-אֶרֶץ, וּרְעֵה אֱמוּנָה
betach bahashem va'aseh-tov; shechan-'eretz, ure'eh emunah
Trust in the LORD, and do good; dwell in the land, and cherish faithfulness.

וְהִתְעַנַּג עַל-יְהוָה; וְיִתֶּן-לְךָ, מִשְׁאֲלֹת לִבֶּךָ
vehit'annag al-hashem veyitten-lecha, mish'alot libbecha
So shalt thou delight thyself in the LORD; and He shall give thee the petitions of thy heart.

גּוֹל עַל-יְהוָה דַּרְכֶּךָ; וּבְטַח עָלָיו, וְהוּא יַעֲשֶׂה
gol al-hashem darkecha; uvetach alav, vehu ya'aseh
Commit thy way unto the LORD; trust also in Him, and He will bring it to pass.

וְהוֹצִיא כָאוֹר צִדְקֶךָ; וּמִשְׁפָּטֶךָ, כַּצָּהֳרָיִם
vehotzi cha'or tzidkecha; umishpatecha, katzohorayim
And He will make thy righteousness to go forth as the light, and thy right as the noonday.

דּוֹם, לַיהוָה--וְהִתְחוֹלֵל-לוֹ
dom lahashem vehitcholel lo
Resign thyself unto the LORD, and wait patiently for Him;

אַל-תִּתְחַר, בְּמַצְלִיחַ דַּרְכּוֹ; בְּאִישׁ, עֹשֶׂה מְזִמּוֹת
al-titchar bematzliach darko; be'ish, oseh mezimmot
fret not thyself because of him who prospereth in his way, because of the man who bringeth wicked devices to pass.

הֶרֶף מֵאַף, וַעֲזֹב חֵמָה; אַל-תִּתְחַר, אַךְ-לְהָרֵעַ
heref me'af va'azov chemah; al-titchar, ach-leharea
Cease from anger, and forsake wrath; fret not thyself, it tendeth only to evil-doing.

כִּי-מְרֵעִים, יִכָּרֵתוּן; וְקֹוֵי יְהוָה, הֵמָּה יִירְשׁוּ-אָרֶץ
ki-mere'im yikkaretun; vekovei hashem hemmah yireshu-'aretz
For evil-doers shall be cut off; but those that wait for the LORD, they shall inherit the land.

וְעוֹד מְעַט, וְאֵין רָשָׁע; וְהִתְבּוֹנַנְתָּ עַל-מְקוֹמוֹ וְאֵינֶנּוּ
ve'od me'at ve'ein rasha'; vehitbonanta al-mekomo ve'einennu
And yet a little while, and the wicked is no more; yea, thou shalt look well at his place, and he is not.

וַעֲנָוִים יִירְשׁוּ-אָרֶץ; וְהִתְעַנְּגוּ, עַל-רֹב שָׁלוֹם
va'anavim yireshu-'aretz; vehit'annegu, al-rov shalom
But the humble shall inherit the land, and delight themselves in the abundance of peace.

זֹמֵם רָשָׁע, לַצַּדִּיק; וְחֹרֵק עָלָיו שִׁנָּיו
zomem rasha latzaddik; vechorek alav shinnav
The wicked plotteth against the righteous, and gnasheth at him with his teeth.

תְּהִלִּים

אָוֶן, יַחְשֹׁב--עַל-מִשְׁכָּבוֹ: יִתְיַצֵּב, עַל-דֶּרֶךְ לֹא-טוֹב; רָע, לֹא יִמְאָס
'aven yachshov, al-mishkavo yityatzev al-derech lo-tov; ra', lo yim'as
He deviseth iniquity upon his bed; he setteth himself in a way that is not good; he abhorreth not evil.

יְהוָה, בְּהַשָּׁמַיִם חַסְדֶּךָ; אֱמוּנָתְךָ, עַד-שְׁחָקִים
hashem behashamayim chasdecha; emunatecha, ad-shechakim
Thy lovingkindness, O LORD, is in the heavens; Thy faithfulness reacheth unto the skies.

צִדְקָתְךָ, כְּהַרְרֵי-אֵל
tzidkatecha kehararei-'el
Thy righteousness is like the mighty mountains;

מִשְׁפָּטֶיךָ, תְּהוֹם רַבָּה; אָדָם וּבְהֵמָה תוֹשִׁיעַ יְהוָה
mishpatecha tehom rabbah; adam-uvehemah toshia hashem
Thy judgments are like the great deep; man and beast Thou preservest, O LORD.

מַה-יָּקָר חַסְדְּךָ, אֱלֹהִים: וּבְנֵי אָדָם--בְּצֵל כְּנָפֶיךָ, יֶחֱסָיוּן
mah-yakar chasdecha, elohim uvenei adam; betzel kenafeicha, yechesayun
How precious is Thy lovingkindness, O God! and the children of men take refuge in the shadow of Thy wings.

יִרְוְיֻן, מִדֶּשֶׁן בֵּיתֶךָ; וְנַחַל עֲדָנֶיךָ תַשְׁקֵם
yirveyun middeshen beitecha; venachal adaneicha tashkem
They are abundantly satisfied with the fatness of Thy house; and Thou makest them drink of the river of Thy pleasures.

כִּי-עִמְּךָ, מְקוֹר חַיִּים; בְּאוֹרְךָ, נִרְאֶה-אוֹר
ki-'immecha mekor chayim; be'orecha, nir'eh-'or
For with Thee is the fountain of life; in Thy light do we see light.

מְשֹׁךְ חַסְדְּךָ, לְיֹדְעֶיךָ; וְצִדְקָתְךָ, לְיִשְׁרֵי-לֵב
meshoch chasdecha leyode'eicha; vetzidkatecha, leyishrei-lev
O continue Thy lovingkindness unto them that know Thee; and Thy righteousness to the upright in heart.

אַל-תְּבוֹאֵנִי, רֶגֶל גַּאֲוָה; וְיַד-רְשָׁעִים, אַל-תְּנִדֵנִי
'al-tevo'eni regel ga'avah; veyad-resha'im, al-tenideni
Let not the foot of pride overtake me, and let not the hand of the wicked drive me away.

שָׁם נָפְלוּ, פֹּעֲלֵי אָוֶן; דֹּחוּ, וְלֹא-יָכְלוּ קוּם
sham nafelu po'alei aven; dochu, velo-yachelu kum
There are the workers of iniquity fallen; they are thrust down, and are not able to rise.

לז

לְדָוִד: אַל-תִּתְחַר בַּמְּרֵעִים; אַל-תְּקַנֵּא, בְּעֹשֵׂי עַוְלָה
Ledavid al-titchar bammere'im; al-tekanne, be'osei avlah
[A Psalm] of David. Fret not thyself because of evil-doers, neither be thou envious against them that work unrighteousness.

תְּהִלִּים

שָׁפְטֵנִי כְצִדְקְךָ, יְהוָה אֱלֹהָי; וְאַל-יִשְׂמְחוּ-לִי
shafeteni chetzidkecha hashem elohai, ve'al-yismechu-li
Judge me, O LORD my God, according to Thy righteousness; and let them not rejoice over me.

אַל-יֹאמְרוּ בְלִבָּם, הֶאָח נַפְשֵׁנוּ; אַל-יֹאמְרוּ, בִּלַּעֲנוּהוּ
'al-yomeru velibbom he'ach nafshenu; al-yomeru, billa'anuhu
Let them not say in their heart: 'Aha, we have our desire'; let them not say: 'We have swallowed him up.'

יֵבֹשׁוּ וְיַחְפְּרוּ, יַחְדָּו--שְׂמֵחֵי רָעָתִי
yevoshu veyachperu yachdav semechei ra'ati
Let them be ashamed and abashed together that rejoice at my hurt;

יִלְבְּשׁוּ-בֹשֶׁת וּכְלִמָּה--הַמַּגְדִּילִים עָלָי
yilbeshu-voshet uchelimmah; hammagdilim alai
let them be clothed with shame and confusion that magnify themselves against me.

יָרֹנּוּ וְיִשְׂמְחוּ, חֲפֵצֵי צִדְקִי
yaronnu veyismechu chafetzei tzidki
Let them shout for joy, and be glad, that delight in my righteousness;

וְיֹאמְרוּ תָמִיד, יִגְדַּל יְהוָה; הֶחָפֵץ, שְׁלוֹם עַבְדּוֹ
veyomeru tamid yigdal hashem hechafetz, shelom avdo
yea, let them say continually: 'Magnified be the LORD, who delighteth in the peace of His servant.'

וּלְשׁוֹנִי, תֶּהְגֶּה צִדְקֶךָ; כָּל-הַיּוֹם, תְּהִלָּתֶךָ
uleshoni tehgeh tzidkecha; kol-hayom tehillatecha
And my tongue shall speak of Thy righteousness, and of Thy praise all the day.

לו

לַמְנַצֵּחַ לְעֶבֶד-יְהוָה לְדָוִד
Lamnatzeach le'eved-hashem ledavid
For the Leader. [A Psalm] of David the servant of the LORD.

נְאֻם-פֶּשַׁע לָרָשָׁע, בְּקֶרֶב לִבִּי; אֵין-פַּחַד אֱלֹהִים, לְנֶגֶד עֵינָיו
ne'um-pesha larasha bekerev libbi; ein-pachad elohim, leneged einav
Transgression speaketh to the wicked, methinks--there is no fear of God before his eyes.

כִּי-הֶחֱלִיק אֵלָיו בְּעֵינָיו; לִמְצֹא עֲוֹנוֹ לִשְׂנֹא
ki-hechelik elav be'einav; limtzo avono lisno
For it flattereth him in his eyes, until his iniquity be found, and he be hated.

דִּבְרֵי-פִיו, אָוֶן וּמִרְמָה; חָדַל לְהַשְׂכִּיל לְהֵיטִיב
divrei-fiv aven umirmah; chadal lehaskil leheitiv
The words of his mouth are iniquity and deceit; he hath left off to be wise, to do good.

תְּהִלִּים

כַּאֲבֶל-אֵם, קֹדֵר שַׁחוֹתִי
ka'avel-'em, koder shachoti
I bowed down mournful, as one that mourneth for his mother.

וּבְצַלְעִי, שָׂמְחוּ וְנֶאֱסָפוּ
uvetzal'i samechu vene'esafu
But when I halt they rejoice, and gather themselves together;

נֶאֶסְפוּ עָלַי נֵכִים, וְלֹא יָדַעְתִּי; קָרְעוּ וְלֹא-דָמּוּ
ne'esfu alai nechim velo yada'ti; kare'u velo-dammu
the abjects gather themselves together against me, and those whom I know not; they tear me, and cease not;

בְּחַנְפֵי, לַעֲגֵי מָעוֹג--חָרֹק עָלַי שִׁנֵּימוֹ
bechanfei la'agei ma'og; charok alai shinneimo
With the profanest mockeries of backbiting they gnash at me with their teeth.

אֲדֹנָי, כַּמָּה תִּרְאֶה: הָשִׁיבָה נַפְשִׁי, מִשֹּׁאֵיהֶם; מִכְּפִירִים, יְחִידָתִי
'adonai kammah tir'eh hashivah nafshi misho'eihem; mikkefirim, yechidati
Lord, how long wilt Thou look on? Rescue my soul from their destructions, mine only one from the lions.

אוֹדְךָ, בְּקָהָל רָב; בְּעַם עָצוּם אֲהַלְלֶךָּ
'odecha bekahal rav; be'am atzum ahaleleka
I will give Thee thanks in the great congregation; I will praise Thee among a numerous people.

אַל-יִשְׂמְחוּ-לִי אֹיְבַי שֶׁקֶר
'al-yismechu-li oyevai sheker
Let not them that are wrongfully mine enemies rejoice over me;

שֹׂנְאַי חִנָּם, יִקְרְצוּ-עָיִן
sone'ai chinnam, yikretzu-'ayin
neither let them wink with the eye that hate me without a cause.

כִּי לֹא שָׁלוֹם, יְדַבֵּרוּ: וְעַל רִגְעֵי-אֶרֶץ--דִּבְרֵי מִרְמוֹת, יַחֲשֹׁבוּן
ki lo shalom, yedabberu ve'al rig'ei-'eretz; divrei mirmot yachashovun
For they speak not peace; but they devise deceitful matters against them that are quiet in the land.

וַיַּרְחִיבוּ עָלַי, פִּיהֶם: אָמְרוּ, הֶאָח הֶאָח; רָאֲתָה עֵינֵנוּ
vayarchivu alai, pihem ameru he'ach he'ach; ra'atah eineinu
Yea, they open their mouth wide against me; they say: 'Aha, aha, our eye hath seen it.'

רָאִיתָה יְהוָה, אַל-תֶּחֱרַשׁ; אֲדֹנָי, אַל-תִּרְחַק מִמֶּנִּי
ra'itah hashem al-techerash; adonai, al-tirchak mimmenni
Thou hast seen, O LORD; keep not silence; O Lord, be not far from me.

הָעִירָה וְהָקִיצָה, לְמִשְׁפָּטִי; אֱלֹהַי וַאדֹנָי לְרִיבִי
ha'irah vehakitzah lemishpati; elohai vadonai lerivi
Rouse Thee, and awake to my judgment, even unto my cause, my God and my Lord.

תְּהִלִּים

יְהִי-דַרְכָּם, חֹשֶׁךְ וַחֲלַקְלַקֹּת; וּמַלְאַךְ יְהוָה, רֹדְפָם
yehi-darkam, choshech vachalaklakkot; umal'ach hashem rodefam
Let their way be dark and slippery, the angel of the LORD pursuing them.

כִּי-חִנָּם טָמְנוּ-לִי, שַׁחַת רִשְׁתָּם; חִנָּם, חָפְרוּ לְנַפְשִׁי
ki-chinnam tamenu-li shachat rishtam; chinnam, chaferu lenafshi
For without cause have they hid for me the pit, even their net, without cause have they digged for my soul.

תְּבוֹאֵהוּ שׁוֹאָה, לֹא-יֵדָע: וְרִשְׁתּוֹ אֲשֶׁר-טָמַן תִּלְכְּדוֹ
tevo'ehu sho'ah lo-yeda verishto asher-taman tilkedo
Let destruction come upon him unawares; and let his net that he hath hid catch himself;

בְּשׁוֹאָה, יִפָּל-בָּהּ
besho'ah, yippal-bah
with destruction let him fall therein.

וְנַפְשִׁי, תָּגִיל בַּיהוָה; תָּשִׂישׂ, בִּישׁוּעָתוֹ
venafshi tagil bahashem; tasis bishu'ato
And my soul shall be joyful in the LORD; it shall rejoice in His salvation.

כָּל עַצְמוֹתַי, תֹּאמַרְנָה--יְהוָה, מִי כָמוֹךָ
kol atzmotai tomarnah hashem mi chamocha
All my bones shall say: 'LORD, who is like unto Thee,

מַצִּיל עָנִי, מֵחָזָק מִמֶּנּוּ; וְעָנִי וְאֶבְיוֹן, מִגֹּזְלוֹ
matzil ani mechazak mimmennu; ve'ani ve'evyon, miggozelo
who deliverest the poor from him that is too strong for him, yea, the poor and the needy from him that spoileth him?'

יְקוּמוּן, עֵדֵי חָמָס: אֲשֶׁר לֹא-יָדַעְתִּי, יִשְׁאָלוּנִי
yekumun edei chamas; asher lo-yada'ti, yish'aluni
Unrighteous witnesses rise up; they ask me of things that I know not.

יְשַׁלְּמוּנִי רָעָה, תַּחַת טוֹבָה: שְׁכוֹל לְנַפְשִׁי
yeshallemuni ra'ah tachat tovah, shechol lenafshi
They repay me evil for good; bereavement is come to my soul.

וַאֲנִי, בַּחֲלוֹתָם לְבוּשִׁי שָׂק
va'ani bachalotam levushi sak
But as for me, when they were sick, my clothing was sackcloth,

עִנֵּיתִי בַצּוֹם נַפְשִׁי; וּתְפִלָּתִי, עַל-חֵיקִי תָשׁוּב
inneiti vatzom nafshi; utefillati, al-cheiki tashuv
I afflicted my soul with fasting; and my prayer, may it return into mine own bosom.

כְּרֵעַ-כְּאָח לִי, הִתְהַלָּכְתִּי
kerea'-ke'ach li hit'hallacheti
I went about as though it had been my friend or my brother;

תְּהִלִּים

קָר֣וֹב יְ֭הוָה לְנִשְׁבְּרֵי־לֵ֑ב; וְֽאֶת־דַּכְּאֵי־ר֥וּחַ יוֹשִֽׁיעַ
karov hashem lenishberei-lev; ve'et-dakke'ei-ruach yoshia
The LORD is nigh unto them that are of a broken heart, and saveth such as are of a contrite spirit.

רַ֭בּוֹת רָע֣וֹת צַדִּ֑יק; וּ֝מִכֻּלָּ֗ם יַצִּילֶ֥נּוּ יְהוָֽה
rabbot ra'ot tzaddik; umikkullam, yatzilennu hashem
Many are the ills of the righteous, but the LORD delivereth him out of them all.

שֹׁמֵ֥ר כָּל־עַצְמוֹתָ֑יו; אַחַ֥ת מֵ֝הֵ֗נָּה לֹ֣א נִשְׁבָּֽרָה
shomer kol-'atzmotav; achat mehennah, lo nishbarah
He keepeth all his bones; not one of them is broken.

תְּמוֹתֵ֣ת רָשָׁ֣ע רָעָ֑ה; וְשֹׂנְאֵ֖י צַדִּ֣יק יֶאְשָֽׁמוּ
temotet rasha ra'ah; vesone'ei tzaddik ye'eshamu
Evil shall kill the wicked; and they that hate the righteous shall be held guilty.

פֹּדֶ֣ה יְ֭הוָה נֶ֣פֶשׁ עֲבָדָ֑יו; וְלֹ֥א יֶ֝אְשְׁמ֗וּ כָּֽל־הַחֹסִ֥ים בּֽוֹ
podeh hashem nefesh avadav; velo ye'shemu, kol-hachosim bo
The LORD redeemeth the soul of His servants; and none of them that take refuge in Him shall be desolate.

לה

לְדָוִ֨ד ׀ רִיבָ֣ה יְ֭הוָה אֶת־יְרִיבַ֑י; לְ֝חַ֗ם אֶת־לֹֽחֲמָֽי
Ledavid rivah hashem et-yerivai; lecham, et-lochamai
A Psalm of David. Strive, O LORD, with them that strive with me; fight against them that fight against me.

הַחֲזֵ֣ק מָגֵ֣ן וְצִנָּ֑ה; וְ֝ק֗וּמָה בְּעֶזְרָתִֽי
hachazek magen vetzinnah; vekumah, be'ezrati
Take hold of shield and buckler, and rise up to my help.

וְהָ֘רֵ֤ק חֲנִ֣ית וּ֭סְגֹר לִקְרַ֣את רֹדְפָ֑י; אֱמֹ֥ר לְ֝נַפְשִׁ֗י יְֽשֻׁעָתֵ֥ךְ אָֽנִי
veharek chanit usegor likrat rodefai; emor lenafshi, yeshu'atech ani
Draw out also the spear, and the battle-axe, against them that pursue me; say unto my soul: 'I am thy salvation.'

יֵבֹ֣שׁוּ וְיִכָּלְמוּ֮ מְבַקְשֵׁ֪י נַ֫פְשִׁ֥י
yevoshu veyikkalemu mevakshei nafshi
Let them be ashamed and brought to confusion that seek after my soul;

יִסֹּ֣גוּ אָח֣וֹר וְיַחְפְּר֑וּ חֹ֝שְׁבֵ֗י רָעָתִֽי
yissogu achor veyachperu; choshevei, ra'ati
let them be turned back and be abashed that devise my hurt.

יִֽהְי֗וּ כְּמֹ֥ץ לִפְנֵי־ר֑וּחַ; וּמַלְאַ֖ךְ יְהוָ֣ה דּוֹחֶֽה
yihyu, kemotz lifnei-ruach; umal'ach hashem docheh
Let them be as chaff before the wind, the angel of the LORD thrusting them.

תְּהִלִּים

זֶה עָנִי קָרָא, וַיהוָה שָׁמֵעַ; וּמִכָּל־צָרוֹתָיו, הוֹשִׁיעוֹ
zeh ani kara vahashem shamea'; umikkal-tzarotav, hoshi'o
This poor man cried, and the LORD heard, and saved him out of all his troubles.

חֹנֶה מַלְאַךְ־יְהוָה סָבִיב לִירֵאָיו; וַיְחַלְּצֵם
choneh mal'ach-hashem saviv lire'av, vaychalletzem
The angel of the LORD encampeth round about them that fear Him, and delivereth them.

טַעֲמוּ וּרְאוּ, כִּי־טוֹב יְהוָה; אַשְׁרֵי הַגֶּבֶר, יֶחֱסֶה־בּוֹ
ta'amu ure'u ki-tov hashem ashrei haggever, yecheseh-bo
O consider and see that the LORD is good; happy is the man that taketh refuge in Him.

יְראוּ אֶת־יְהוָה קְדֹשָׁיו: כִּי־אֵין מַחְסוֹר, לִירֵאָיו
yer'u et-hashem kedoshav; ki-'ein machsor, lire'av
O fear the LORD, ye His holy ones; for there is no want to them that fear Him.

כְּפִירִים, רָשׁוּ וְרָעֵבוּ; וְדֹרְשֵׁי יְהוָה, לֹא־יַחְסְרוּ כָל־טוֹב
kefirim rashu vera'evu; vedoreshei hashem lo-yachseru chol-tov
The young lions do lack, and suffer hunger; but they that seek the LORD want not any good thing.

לְכוּ־בָנִים, שִׁמְעוּ־לִי; יִרְאַת יְהוָה, אֲלַמֶּדְכֶם
lechu-vanim shim'u-li; yir'at hashem alammedchem
Come, ye children, hearken unto me; I will teach you the fear of the LORD.

מִי־הָאִישׁ, הֶחָפֵץ חַיִּים; אֹהֵב יָמִים, לִרְאוֹת טוֹב
mi-ha'ish hechafetz chayim; ohev yamim, lir'ot tov
Who is the man that desireth life, and loveth days, that he may see good therein?

נְצֹר לְשׁוֹנְךָ מֵרָע; וּשְׂפָתֶיךָ, מִדַּבֵּר מִרְמָה
netzor leshonecha mera'; usefateicha, middabber mirmah
Keep thy tongue from evil, and thy lips from speaking guile.

סוּר מֵרָע, וַעֲשֵׂה־טוֹב; בַּקֵּשׁ שָׁלוֹם וְרָדְפֵהוּ
sur mera va'aseh-tov; bakkesh shalom verodefehu
Depart from evil, and do good; seek peace, and pursue it.

עֵינֵי יְהוָה, אֶל־צַדִּיקִים; וְאָזְנָיו, אֶל־שַׁוְעָתָם
'einei hashem el-tzaddikim; ve'azenav, el-shav'atam
The eyes of the LORD are toward the righteous, and His ears are open unto their cry.

פְּנֵי יְהוָה, בְּעֹשֵׂי רָע; לְהַכְרִית מֵאֶרֶץ זִכְרָם
penei hashem be'osei ra'; lehachrit me'eretz zichram
The face of the LORD is against them that do evil, to cut off the remembrance of them from the earth.

צָעֲקוּ, וַיהוָה שָׁמֵעַ; וּמִכָּל־צָרוֹתָם, הִצִּילָם
tza'aku vahashem shamea'; umikkol-tzarotam, hitzilam
They cried, and the LORD heard, and delivered them out of all their troubles.

תְּהִלִּים

הִנֵּה עֵין יְהוָה, אֶל-יְרֵאָיו; לַמְיַחֲלִים לְחַסְדּוֹ
hinneh ein hashem el-yere'av; lamyachalim lechasdo
Behold, the eye of the LORD is toward them that fear Him, toward them that wait for His mercy;

לְהַצִּיל מִמָּוֶת נַפְשָׁם; וּלְחַיּוֹתָם, בָּרָעָב
lehatzil mimmavet nafsham; ulechayotam, bara'av
To deliver their soul from death, and to keep them alive in famine.

נַפְשֵׁנוּ, חִכְּתָה לַיהוָה; עֶזְרֵנוּ וּמָגִנֵּנוּ הוּא
nafshenu chikketah lahashem ezrenu umaginnenu hu
Our soul hath waited for the LORD; He is our help and our shield.

כִּי-בוֹ, יִשְׂמַח לִבֵּנוּ: כִּי בְשֵׁם קָדְשׁוֹ בָטָחְנוּ
ki-vo yismach libbenu; ki veshem kodsho vatachenu
For in Him doth our heart rejoice, because we have trusted in His holy name.

יְהִי-חַסְדְּךָ יְהוָה עָלֵינוּ: כַּאֲשֶׁר, יִחַלְנוּ לָךְ
yehi-chasdecha hashem aleinu; ka'asher, yichalnu lach
Let Thy mercy, O LORD, be upon us, according as we have waited for Thee.

לד

לְדָוִד--בְּשַׁנּוֹתוֹ אֶת-טַעְמוֹ, לִפְנֵי אֲבִימֶלֶךְ; וַיְגָרְשֵׁהוּ, וַיֵּלַךְ
Ledavid, beshannoto et-ta'mo lifnei avimelech; vaygarashehu, vayelach
[A Psalm] of David; when he changed his demeanour before Abimelech, who drove him away, and he departed.

אֲבָרְכָה אֶת-יְהוָה בְּכָל-עֵת; תָּמִיד, תְּהִלָּתוֹ בְּפִי
'avarachah et-hashem bechol-'et; tamid, tehillato befi
I will bless the LORD at all times; His praise shall continually be in my mouth.

בַּיהוָה, תִּתְהַלֵּל נַפְשִׁי; יִשְׁמְעוּ עֲנָוִים וְיִשְׂמָחוּ
bahashem tit'hallel nafshi; yishme'u anavim veyismachu
My soul shall glory in the LORD; the humble shall hear thereof, and be glad.

גַּדְּלוּ לַיהוָה אִתִּי; וּנְרוֹמְמָה שְׁמוֹ יַחְדָּו
gaddelu lahashem itti; uneromemah shemo yachdav
O magnify the LORD with me, and let us exalt His name together.

דָּרַשְׁתִּי אֶת-יְהוָה וְעָנָנִי; וּמִכָּל-מְגוּרוֹתַי הִצִּילָנִי
darashti et-hashem ve'anani; umikkal-megurotai, hitzilani
I sought the LORD, and He answered me, and delivered me from all my fears.

הִבִּיטוּ אֵלָיו וְנָהָרוּ; וּפְנֵיהֶם, אַל-יֶחְפָּרוּ
hibbitu elav venaharu; ufeneihem, al-yechparu
They looked unto Him, and were radiant; and their faces shall never be abashed.

תְּהִלִּים

בִּדְבַר יְהוָה, שָׁמַיִם נַעֲשׂוּ; וּבְרוּחַ פִּיו, כָּל-צְבָאָם
bidvar hashem shamayim na'asu; uveruach piv, kol-tzeva'am
By the word of the LORD were the heavens made; and all the host of them by the breath of His mouth.

כֹּנֵס כַּנֵּד, מֵי הַיָּם; נֹתֵן בְּאוֹצָרוֹת תְּהוֹמוֹת
kones kanned mei hayam; noten be'otzarot tehomot
He gathereth the waters of the sea together as a heap; He layeth up the deeps in storehouses.

יִירְאוּ מֵיְהוָה, כָּל-הָאָרֶץ; מִמֶּנּוּ יָגוּרוּ, כָּל-יֹשְׁבֵי תֵבֵל
yire'u mehashem kol-ha'aretz; mimmennu yaguru, kol-yoshevei tevel
Let all the earth fear the LORD; let all the inhabitants of the world stand in awe of Him.

כִּי הוּא אָמַר וַיֶּהִי; הוּא-צִוָּה, וַיַּעֲמֹד
ki hu amar vayehi; hu-tzivvah, vaya'amod
For He spoke, and it was; He commanded, and it stood.

יְהוָה, הֵפִיר עֲצַת-גּוֹיִם; הֵנִיא, מַחְשְׁבוֹת עַמִּים
hashem hefir atzat-goyim; heni, machshevot ammim
The LORD bringeth the counsel of the nations to nought; He maketh the thoughts of the peoples to be of no effect.

עֲצַת יְהוָה, לְעוֹלָם תַּעֲמֹד; מַחְשְׁבוֹת לִבּוֹ, לְדֹר וָדֹר
'atzat hashem le'olam ta'amod; machshevot libbo, ledor vador
The counsel of the LORD standeth for ever, the thoughts of His heart to all generations.

אַשְׁרֵי הַגּוֹי, אֲשֶׁר-יְהוָה אֱלֹהָיו; הָעָם, בָּחַר לְנַחֲלָה לוֹ
'ashrei haggoy asher-hashem elohav; ha'am bachar lenachalah lo
Happy is the nation whose God is the LORD; the people whom He hath chosen for His own inheritance.

מִשָּׁמַיִם, הִבִּיט יְהוָה; רָאָה, אֶת-כָּל-בְּנֵי הָאָדָם
mishamayim hibbit hashem ra'ah, et-kol-benei ha'adam
The LORD looketh from heaven; He beholdeth all the sons of men;

מִמְּכוֹן-שִׁבְתּוֹ הִשְׁגִּיחַ-- אֶל כָּל-יֹשְׁבֵי הָאָרֶץ
mimmechon-shivto hishgiach; el kol-yoshevei ha'aretz
From the place of His habitation He looketh intently upon all the inhabitants of the earth;

הַיֹּצֵר יַחַד לִבָּם; הַמֵּבִין, אֶל-כָּל-מַעֲשֵׂיהֶם
hayotzer yachad libbam; hammevin, el-kol-ma'aseihem
He that fashioneth the hearts of them all, that considereth all their doings.

אֵין-הַמֶּלֶךְ, נוֹשָׁע בְּרָב-חָיִל; גִּבּוֹר, לֹא-יִנָּצֵל בְּרָב-כֹּחַ
'ein-hammelech nosha berav-chayil; gibbor, lo-yinnatzel berav-koach
A king is not saved by the multitude of a host; a mighty man is not delivered by great strength.

שֶׁקֶר הַסּוּס, לִתְשׁוּעָה; וּבְרֹב חֵילוֹ, לֹא יְמַלֵּט
sheker hassus litshu'ah; uverov cheilo, lo yemallet
A horse is a vain thing for safety; neither doth it afford escape by its great strength.

תְּהִלִּים

רָנֵּי פַלֵּט; תְּסוֹבְבֵנִי סֶלָה

rannei fallet; tesoveveni selah
with songs of deliverance Thou wilt compass me about. Selah

אַשְׂכִּילְךָ, וְאוֹרְךָ--בְּדֶרֶךְ-זוּ תֵלֵךְ; אִיעֲצָה עָלֶיךָ עֵינִי

'askilecha ve'orecha, bederech-zu telech; i'atzah aleicha eini
'I will instruct thee and teach thee in the way which thou shalt go; I will give counsel, Mine eye being upon thee.'

אַל-תִּהְיוּ, כְּסוּס כְּפֶרֶד--אֵין הָבִין

'al-tihyu kesus kefered ein havin
Be ye not as the horse, or as the mule, which have no understanding;

בְּמֶתֶג-וָרֶסֶן עֶדְיוֹ לִבְלוֹם; בַּל, קְרֹב אֵלֶיךָ

bemeteg-varesen edyo livlom; bal, kerov eleicha
whose mouth must be held in with bit and bridle, that they come not near unto thee.

רַבִּים מַכְאוֹבִים, לָרָשָׁע: וְהַבּוֹטֵחַ בַּיהוָה--חֶסֶד, יְסוֹבְבֶנּוּ

rabbim mach'ovim, larasha vehabboteach bahashem; chesed, yesovevennu
Many are the sorrows of the wicked; but he that trusteth in the LORD, mercy compasseth him about.

שִׂמְחוּ בַיהוָה וְגִילוּ, צַדִּיקִים; וְהַרְנִינוּ, כָּל-יִשְׁרֵי-לֵב

simchu vahashem vegilu tzaddikim; veharninu, kol-yishrei-lev
Be glad in the LORD, and rejoice, ye righteous; and shout for joy, all ye that are upright in heart.

לג

רַנְּנוּ צַדִּיקִים, בַּיהוָה; לַיְשָׁרִים, נָאוָה תְהִלָּה

Rannenu tzaddikim bahashem; layesharim, navah tehillah
Rejoice in the LORD, O ye righteous, praise is comely for the upright.

הוֹדוּ לַיהוָה בְּכִנּוֹר; בְּנֵבֶל עָשׂוֹר, זַמְּרוּ-לוֹ

hodu lahashem bechinnor; benevel asor, zammeru-lo
Give thanks unto the LORD with harp, sing praises unto Him with the psaltery of ten strings.

שִׁירוּ-לוֹ, שִׁיר חָדָשׁ; הֵיטִיבוּ נַגֵּן, בִּתְרוּעָה

shiru-lo shir chadash; heitivu naggen, bitru'ah
Sing unto Him a new song; play skilfully amid shouts of joy.

כִּי-יָשָׁר דְּבַר-יְהוָה; וְכָל-מַעֲשֵׂהוּ, בֶּאֱמוּנָה

ki-yashar devar-hashem vechol-ma'asehu, be'emunah
For the word of the LORD is upright; and all His work is done in faithfulness.

אֹהֵב, צְדָקָה וּמִשְׁפָּט; חֶסֶד יְהוָה, מָלְאָה הָאָרֶץ

'ohev tzedakah umishpat; chesed hashem male'ah ha'aretz
He loveth righteousness and justice; the earth is full of the lovingkindness of the LORD.

תְּהִלִּים

חִזְקוּ, וְיַאֲמֵץ לְבַבְכֶם--כָּל-הַמְיַחֲלִים, לַיהוָה
chizku veya'ametz levavchem; kol-hamyachalim, lahashem
Be strong, and let your heart take courage, all ye that wait for the LORD.

לב

לְדָוִד, מַשְׂכִּיל: אַשְׁרֵי נְשׂוּי-פֶּשַׁע; כְּסוּי חֲטָאָה
Ledavid, maskil ashrei nesui-pesha', kesui chata'ah
[A Psalm] of David. Maschil. Happy is he whose transgression is forgiven, whose sin is pardoned.

אַשְׁרֵי אָדָם--לֹא יַחְשֹׁב יְהוָה לוֹ עָוֺן; וְאֵין בְּרוּחוֹ רְמִיָּה
'ashrei adam, lo yachshov hashem lo avon; ve'ein berucho remiyah
Happy is the man unto whom the LORD counteth not iniquity, and in whose spirit there is no guile.

כִּי-הֶחֱרַשְׁתִּי, בָּלוּ עֲצָמָי--בְּשַׁאֲגָתִי, כָּל-הַיּוֹם
ki-hecherashti balu atzamai; besha'agati, kol-hayom
When I kept silence, my bones wore away through my groaning all the day long.

כִּי, יוֹמָם וָלַיְלָה--תִּכְבַּד עָלַי, יָדֶךָ: נֶהְפַּךְ לְשַׁדִּי--בְּחַרְבֹנֵי קַיִץ סֶלָה
ki yomam valaylah tichbad alai, yadecha nehpach leshaddi; becharvonei kayitz selah
For day and night Thy hand was heavy upon me; my sap was turned as in the droughts of summer. Selah

חַטָּאתִי אוֹדִיעֲךָ, וַעֲוֺנִי לֹא-כִסִּיתִי--אָמַרְתִּי,
chattati odi'acha va'avoni lo-chissiti, amarti,
I acknowledged my sin unto Thee, and mine iniquity have I not hid; I said:

אוֹדֶה עֲלֵי פְשָׁעַי לַיהוָה
odeh alei fesha'ai lahashem
'I will make confession concerning my transgressions unto the LORD'--

וְאַתָּה נָשָׂאתָ עֲוֺן חַטָּאתִי סֶלָה
ve'attah nasata avon chattati selah
and Thou, Thou forgavest the iniquity of my sin. Selah

עַל-זֹאת, יִתְפַּלֵּל כָּל-חָסִיד אֵלֶיךָ--לְעֵת מְצֹא
'al-zot yitpallel kol-chasid eleicha le'et metzo
For this let every one that is godly pray unto Thee in a time when Thou mayest be found;

רַק, לְשֵׁטֶף מַיִם רַבִּים--אֵלָיו, לֹא יַגִּיעוּ
rak, leshetef mayim rabbim; elav, lo yaggi'u
surely, when the great waters overflow, they will not reach unto him.

אַתָּה, סֵתֶר לִי--מִצַּר תִּצְּרֵנִי
'attah seter li mitzar titzereni
Thou art my hiding-place; Thou wilt preserve me from the adversary;

תְּהִלִּים

יְהוָה--אַל-אֵבוֹשָׁה, כִּי קְרָאתִיךָ
hashem al-'evoshah ki keraticha
O LORD, let me not be ashamed, for I have called upon Thee;

יֵבֹשׁוּ רְשָׁעִים, יִדְּמוּ לִשְׁאוֹל
yevoshu resha'im, yiddemu lish'ol
let the wicked be ashamed, let them be put to silence in the nether-world.

תֵּאָלַמְנָה, שִׂפְתֵי-שָׁקֶר: הַדֹּבְרוֹת עַל-צַדִּיק עָתָק--בְּגַאֲוָה וָבוּז
te'alamnah, siftei shaker haddoverot al-tzaddik atak, bega'avah vavuz
Let the lying lips be dumb, which speak arrogantly against the righteous, with pride and contempt.

מָה רַב-טוּבְךָ, אֲשֶׁר-צָפַנְתָּ לִּירֵאֶיךָ
mah rav-tuvecha asher-tzafanta liyre'eicha
Oh how abundant is Thy goodness, which Thou hast laid up for them that fear Thee;

פָּעַלְתָּ, לַחֹסִים בָּךְ; נֶגֶד, בְּנֵי אָדָם
pa'alta lachosim bach; neged, benei adam
which Thou hast wrought for them that take their refuge in Thee, in the sight of the sons of men!

תַּסְתִּירֵם, בְּסֵתֶר פָּנֶיךָ--מֵרֻכְסֵי-אִישׁ:
tastirem beseter paneicha meruchesei ish
Thou hidest them in the covert of Thy presence from the plottings of man;

תִּצְפְּנֵם בְּסֻכָּה; מֵרִיב לְשֹׁנוֹת
titzpenem besukkah, meriv leshonot
Thou concealest them in a pavilion from the strife of tongues.

בָּרוּךְ יְהוָה: כִּי הִפְלִיא חַסְדּוֹ לִי, בְּעִיר מָצוֹר
baruch hashem ki hifli chasdo li, be'ir matzor
Blessed be the LORD; for He hath shown me His wondrous lovingkindness in an entrenched city.

וַאֲנִי, אָמַרְתִּי בְחָפְזִי--נִגְרַזְתִּי, מִנֶּגֶד עֵינֶיךָ
va'ani amarti vechafezi, nigrazti minneged eineicha
As for me, I said in my haste: 'I am cut off from before Thine eyes';

אָכֵן--שָׁמַעְתָּ, קוֹל תַּחֲנוּנַי; בְּשַׁוְּעִי אֵלֶיךָ
achen, shama'ta kol tachanunai, beshavve'i eleicha
nevertheless Thou heardest the voice of my supplications when I cried unto Thee.

אֶהֱבוּ אֶת-יְהוָה, כָּל-חֲסִידָיו: אֱמוּנִים, נֹצֵר יְהוָה
'ehevu et-hashem kol-chasidav emunim notzer hashem
O love the LORD, all ye His godly ones; the LORD preserveth the faithful,

וּמְשַׁלֵּם עַל-יֶתֶר, עֹשֵׂה גַאֲוָה
umeshallem al-yeter, oseh ga'avah
and plentifully repayeth him that acteth haughtily.

תְּהִלִּים

וְלֹא הִסְגַּרְתַּנִי, בְּיַד-אוֹיֵב; הֶעֱמַדְתָּ בַמֶּרְחָב רַגְלָי
velo hisgartani beyad-'oyev; he'emadta vammerchav raglai
And Thou hast not given me over into the hand of the enemy; Thou hast set my feet in a broad place.

חָנֵּנִי יְהוָה, כִּי צַר-לִי: עָשְׁשָׁה בְכַעַס עֵינִי; נַפְשִׁי וּבִטְנִי
chonneni hashem ki tzar-li asheshah vecha'as eini, nafshi uvitni
Be gracious unto me, O LORD, for I am in distress; mine eye wasteth away with vexation, yea, my soul and my body.

כִּי כָלוּ בְיָגוֹן, חַיַּי--וּשְׁנוֹתַי בַּאֲנָחָה:
ki chalu veyagon chayai ushenotai ba'anachah
For my life is spent in sorrow, and my years in sighing;

כָּשַׁל בַּעֲוֺנִי כֹחִי; וַעֲצָמַי עָשֵׁשׁוּ
kashal ba'avoni chochi; va'atzamai asheshu
my strength faileth because of mine iniquity, and my bones are wasted away.

מִכָּל-צֹרְרַי הָיִיתִי חֶרְפָּה, וְלִשְׁכֵנַי מְאֹד
mikkol-tzorerai hayiti cherpah velishachenai me'od
Because of all mine adversaries I am become a reproach, yea, unto my neighbours exceedingly,

וּפַחַד לִמְיֻדָּעָי: רֹאַי בַּחוּץ--נָדְדוּ מִמֶּנִּי
ufachad limyudda'ai ro'ai bachutz; nadedu mimmenni
and a dread to mine acquaintance; they that see me without flee from me.

נִשְׁכַּחְתִּי, כְּמֵת מִלֵּב; הָיִיתִי, כִּכְלִי אֹבֵד
nishkachti kemet millev; hayiti, kichli oved
I am forgotten as a dead man out of mind; I am like a useless vessel.

כִּי שָׁמַעְתִּי, דִּבַּת רַבִּים--מָגוֹר מִסָּבִיב
ki shama'ti dibbat rabbim magor missaviv
For I have heard the whispering of many, terror on every side;

בְּהִוָּסְדָם יַחַד עָלַי; לָקַחַת נַפְשִׁי זָמָמוּ
behivvasedam yachad alai; lakachat nafshi zamamu
while they took counsel together against me, they devised to take away my life.

וַאֲנִי, עָלֶיךָ בָטַחְתִּי יְהוָה; אָמַרְתִּי, אֱלֹהַי אָתָּה
va'ani aleicha vatachti hashem amarti, elohai attah
But as for me, I have trusted in Thee, O LORD; I have said: 'Thou art my God.'

בְּיָדְךָ עִתֹּתָי; הַצִּילֵנִי מִיַּד-אוֹיְבַי, וּמֵרֹדְפָי
beyadecha ittotai; hatzileni miyad-'oyevai, umerodefai
My times are in Thy hand; deliver me from the hand of mine enemies, and from them that persecute me.

הָאִירָה פָנֶיךָ, עַל-עַבְדֶּךָ; הוֹשִׁיעֵנִי בְחַסְדֶּךָ
ha'irah faneicha al-'avdecha; hoshi'eni vechasdecha
Make Thy face to shine upon Thy servant; save me in Thy lovingkindness.

תְּהִלִּים

הָפַכְתָּ מִסְפְּדִי, לְמָחוֹל לִי: פִּתַּחְתָּ שַׂקִּי; וַתְּאַזְּרֵנִי שִׂמְחָה
hafachta mispedi lemachol li pittachta sakki; vatte'azzereni simchah
Thou didst turn for me my mourning into dancing; Thou didst loose my sackcloth, and gird me with gladness;

לְמַעַן, יְזַמֶּרְךָ כָבוֹד--וְלֹא יִדֹּם: יְהוָה אֱלֹהַי, לְעוֹלָם אוֹדֶךָּ
lema'an yezammercha chavod velo yiddom; hashem elohai, le'olam odeka
So that my glory may sing praise to Thee, and not be silent; O LORD my God, I will give thanks unto Thee for ever.

לא

לַמְנַצֵּחַ, מִזְמוֹר לְדָוִד
Lamnatzeach, mizmor ledavid
For the Leader. A Psalm of David.

בְּךָ-יְהוָה חָסִיתִי, אַל-אֵבוֹשָׁה לְעוֹלָם; בְּצִדְקָתְךָ פַלְּטֵנִי
becha hashem chasiti al-'evoshah le'olam; betzidkatecha falleteni
In thee, O LORD, have I taken refuge; let me never be ashamed; deliver me in Thy righteousness.

הַטֵּה אֵלַי, אָזְנְךָ--מְהֵרָה הַצִּילֵנִי: הֱיֵה לִי, לְצוּר-מָעוֹז--לְבֵית מְצוּדוֹת; לְהוֹשִׁיעֵנִי
hatteh elai azenecha meherah hatzileni heyeh li letzur-ma'oz leveit metzudot, lehoshi'eni
Incline Thine ear unto me, deliver me speedily; be Thou to me a rock of refuge, even a fortress of defence, to save me.

כִּי-סַלְעִי וּמְצוּדָתִי אָתָּה; וּלְמַעַן שִׁמְךָ, תַּנְחֵנִי וּתְנַהֲלֵנִי
ki-sal'i umetzudati attah; ulema'an shimcha, tancheni utenahaleni
For Thou art my rock and my fortress; therefore for Thy name's sake lead me and guide me.

תּוֹצִיאֵנִי--מֵרֶשֶׁת זוּ, טָמְנוּ לִי: כִּי-אַתָּה, מָעוּזִּי
totzi'eni, mereshet zu tamenu li; ki-'attah ma'uzzi
Bring me forth out of the net that they have hidden for me; for Thou art my stronghold.

בְּיָדְךָ, אַפְקִיד רוּחִי: פָּדִיתָ אוֹתִי יְהוָה--אֵל אֱמֶת
beyadecha afkid ruchi paditah oti hashem el emet
Into Thy hand I commit my spirit; Thou hast redeemed me, O LORD, Thou God of truth.

שָׂנֵאתִי, הַשֹּׁמְרִים הַבְלֵי-שָׁוְא; וַאֲנִי, אֶל-יְהוָה בָּטָחְתִּי
saneti, hashomerim havlei-shav; va'ani, el-hashem batachti
I hate them that regard lying vanities; but I trust in the LORD.

אָגִילָה וְאֶשְׂמְחָה, בְּחַסְדֶּךָ: אֲשֶׁר רָאִיתָ, אֶת-עָנְיִי
'agilah ve'esmechah, bechasdecha asher ra'ita et-'oneyi
I will be glad and rejoice in Thy lovingkindness; for Thou hast seen mine affliction,

יָדַעְתָּ, בְּצָרוֹת נַפְשִׁי
yada'ta, betzarot nafshi
Thou hast taken cognizance of the troubles of my soul,

תְּהִלִּים

אֲרוֹמִמְךָ יְהוָה, כִּי דִלִּיתָנִי; וְלֹא-שִׂמַּחְתָּ אֹיְבַי לִי
'aromimcha hashem ki dillitani; velo-simmachta oyevai li
I will extol thee, O LORD, for Thou hast raised me up, and hast not suffered mine enemies to rejoice over me.

יְהוָה אֱלֹהָי-- שִׁוַּעְתִּי אֵלֶיךָ, וַתִּרְפָּאֵנִי
hashem elohai; shivva'ti eleicha, vattirpa'eni
O LORD my God, I cried unto Thee, and Thou didst heal me;

יְהוָה--הֶעֱלִיתָ מִן-שְׁאוֹל נַפְשִׁי; חִיִּיתַנִי
hashem he'elita min-she'ol nafshi; chiyitani,
O LORD, Thou broughtest up my soul from the nether-world; Thou didst keep me alive,

מִיָּרְדִי-בוֹר
miyaredi-vor
that I should not go down to the pit.

זַמְּרוּ לַיהוָה חֲסִידָיו; וְהוֹדוּ, לְזֵכֶר קָדְשׁוֹ
zammeru lahashem chasidav; vehodu, lezecher kodsho
Sing praise unto the LORD, O ye His godly ones, and give thanks to His holy name.

כִּי רֶגַע, בְּאַפּוֹ--חַיִּים בִּרְצוֹנוֹ
ki rega be'appo chayim birtzono
For His anger is but for a moment, His favour is for a life-time;

בָּעֶרֶב, יָלִין בֶּכִי; וְלַבֹּקֶר רִנָּה
ba'erev yalin bechi, velabboker rinnah
weeping may tarry for the night, but joy cometh in the morning.

וַאֲנִי, אָמַרְתִּי בְשַׁלְוִי-- בַּל-אֶמּוֹט לְעוֹלָם
va'ani amarti veshalvi; bal-'emmot le'olam
Now I had said in my security: 'I shall never be moved.'

יְהוָה-- בִּרְצוֹנְךָ, הֶעֱמַדְתָּה לְהַרְרִי-עֹז: הִסְתַּרְתָּ פָנֶיךָ; הָיִיתִי נִבְהָל
hashem birtzonecha he'emadtah lehareri oz histarta faneicha, hayiti nivhal
Thou hadst established, O LORD, in Thy favour my mountain as a stronghold--Thou didst hide Thy face; I was affrighted.

אֵלֶיךָ יְהוָה אֶקְרָא; וְאֶל-אֲדֹנָי, אֶתְחַנָּן
'eleicha hashem ekra; ve'el-'adonai, etchannan
Unto Thee, O LORD, did I call, and unto the LORD I made supplication:

מַה-בֶּצַע בְּדָמִי, בְּרִדְתִּי אֶל-שָׁחַת: הֲיוֹדְךָ עָפָר; הֲיַגִּיד אֲמִתֶּךָ
mah-betza bedami beridti el-shachat hayodecha afar; hayaggid amittecha
'What profit is there in my blood, when I go down to the pit? Shall the dust praise Thee? shall it declare Thy truth?

שְׁמַע-יְהוָה וְחָנֵּנִי; יְהוָה, הֱיֵה-עֹזֵר לִי
shema'-hashem vechonneni hashem heyeh-'ozer li
Hear, O LORD, and be gracious unto me; LORD, be Thou my helper.'

תְּהִלִּים

הָבוּ לַיהוָה, כְּבוֹד שְׁמוֹ; הִשְׁתַּחֲווּ לַיהוָה, בְּהַדְרַת-קֹדֶשׁ.
havu lahashem kevod shemo; hishtachavu lahashem behadrat-kodesh
Ascribe unto the LORD the glory due unto His name; worship the LORD in the beauty of holiness.

קוֹל יְהוָה, עַל-הַמָּיִם: אֵל-הַכָּבוֹד הִרְעִים; יְהוָה, עַל-מַיִם רַבִּים.
kol hashem al-hammayim el-hakkavod hir'im; hashem al-mayim rabbim
The voice of the LORD is upon the waters; the God of glory thundereth, even the LORD upon many waters.

קוֹל-יְהוָה בַּכֹּחַ; קוֹל יְהוָה, בֶּהָדָר
kol-hashem bakkoach; kol hashem behadar
The voice of the LORD is powerful; the voice of the LORD is full of majesty.

קוֹל יְהוָה, שֹׁבֵר אֲרָזִים; וַיְשַׁבֵּר יְהוָה, אֶת-אַרְזֵי הַלְּבָנוֹן
kol hashem shover arazim; vayshabber hashem et-'arzei hallevanon
The voice of the LORD breaketh the cedars; yea, the LORD breaketh in pieces the cedars of Lebanon.

וַיַּרְקִידֵם כְּמוֹ-עֵגֶל; לְבָנוֹן וְשִׂרְיֹן, כְּמוֹ בֶן-רְאֵמִים
vayarkidem kemo-'egel; levanon vesiryon, kemo ven-re'emim
He maketh them also to skip like a calf; Lebanon and Sirion like a young wild-ox.

קוֹל-יְהוָה חֹצֵב; לַהֲבוֹת אֵשׁ
kol-hashem chotzev, lahavot esh
The voice of the LORD heweth out flames of fire.

קוֹל יְהוָה, יָחִיל מִדְבָּר; יָחִיל יְהוָה, מִדְבַּר קָדֵשׁ
kol hashem yachil midbar; yachil hashem midbar kadesh
The voice of the LORD shaketh the wilderness; the LORD shaketh the wilderness of Kadesh.

קוֹל יְהוָה, יְחוֹלֵל אַיָּלוֹת--וַיֶּחֱשֹׂף יְעָרוֹת: וּבְהֵיכָלוֹ--כֻּלּוֹ, אֹמֵר כָּבוֹד
kol hashem yecholel ayalot vayechesof ye'arot uveheichalo; kullo, omer kavod
The voice of the LORD maketh the hinds to calve, and strippeth the forests bare; and in His temple all say: 'Glory.'

יְהוָה, לַמַּבּוּל יָשָׁב; וַיֵּשֶׁב יְהוָה, מֶלֶךְ לְעוֹלָם
hashem lammabbul yashav; vayeshev hashem melech le'olam
The LORD sat enthroned at the flood; yea, the LORD sitteth as King for ever.

יְהוָה--עֹז, לְעַמּוֹ יִתֵּן; יְהוָה, יְבָרֵךְ אֶת-עַמּוֹ בַשָּׁלוֹם
hashem oz le'ammo yitten; hashem yevarech et-'ammo vashalom
The LORD will give strength unto His people; the LORD will bless his people with peace.

ל

מִזְמוֹר: שִׁיר-חֲנֻכַּת הַבַּיִת לְדָוִד
Mizmor shir-chanukkat habbayit ledavid
A Psalm; a Song at the Dedication of the House; of David.

תְּהִלִּים

דֹּבְרֵי שָׁלוֹם, עִם-רֵעֵיהֶם; וְרָעָה, בִּלְבָבָם
doverei shalom im-re'eihem; vera'ah, bilvavam
who speak peace with their neighbours, but evil is in their hearts.

תֶּן-לָהֶם כְּפָעֳלָם, וּכְרֹעַ מַעַלְלֵיהֶם
ten-lahem kefo'olam ucheroa ma'aleleihem
Give them according to their deeds, and according to the evil of their endeavours;

כְּמַעֲשֵׂה יְדֵיהֶם, תֵּן לָהֶם; הָשֵׁב גְּמוּלָם לָהֶם
kema'aseh yedeihem ten lahem; hashev gemulam lahem
give them after the work of their hands; render to them their desert.

כִּי לֹא יָבִינוּ, אֶל-פְּעֻלֹּת יְהוָה--וְאֶל-מַעֲשֵׂה יָדָיו
ki lo yavinu el-pe'ullot hashem ve'el-ma'aseh yadav
Because they give no heed to the works of the LORD, nor to the operation of His hands;

יֶהֶרְסֵם, וְלֹא יִבְנֵם
yehersem, velo yivnem
He will break them down and not build them up.

בָּרוּךְ יְהוָה: כִּי-שָׁמַע, קוֹל תַּחֲנוּנָי
baruch hashem ki-shama kol tachanunai
Blessed be the LORD, because He hath heard the voice of my supplications.

יְהוָה, עֻזִּי וּמָגִנִּי--בּוֹ בָטַח לִבִּי, וְנֶעֱזָרְתִּי
hashem uzzi umaginni bo vatach libbi, vene'ezareti
The LORD is my strength and my shield, in Him hath my heart trusted, and I am helped;

וַיַּעֲלֹז לִבִּי; וּמִשִּׁירִי אֲהוֹדֶנּוּ
vaya'aloz libbi; umishiri ahodennu
therefore my heart greatly rejoiceth, and with my song will I praise Him.

יְהוָה עֹז-לָמוֹ; וּמָעוֹז יְשׁוּעוֹת מְשִׁיחוֹ הוּא
hashem oz-lamo; uma'oz yeshu'ot meshicho hu
The LORD is a strength unto them; and He is a stronghold of salvation to His anointed.

הוֹשִׁיעָה, אֶת-עַמֶּךָ--וּבָרֵךְ אֶת-נַחֲלָתֶךָ; וּרְעֵם וְנַשְּׂאֵם, עַד-הָעוֹלָם
hoshi'ah et-'ammecha, uvarech et-nachalatecha; ure'em venasse'em, ad-ha'olam
Save Thy people, and bless Thine inheritance; and tend them, and carry them for ever.

כט

מִזְמוֹר, לְדָוִד: הָבוּ לַיהוָה, בְּנֵי אֵלִים; הָבוּ לַיהוָה, כָּבוֹד וָעֹז
Mizmor, ledavid havu lahashem benei elim; havu lahashem kavod va'oz
A Psalm of David. Ascribe unto the LORD, O ye sons of might, ascribe unto the LORD glory and strength.

תְּהִלִים

עֶזְרָתִי הָיִיתָ; אַל-תִּטְּשֵׁנִי וְאַל-תַּעַזְבֵנִי, אֱלֹהֵי יִשְׁעִי

ezrati hayita; al-tittesheni ve'al-ta'azveni, elohei yish'i
Thou hast been my help; cast me not off, neither forsake me, O God of my salvation.

כִּי-אָבִי וְאִמִּי עֲזָבוּנִי; וַיהוָה יַאַסְפֵנִי

ki-'avi ve'immi azavuni; vahashem ya'asfeni
For though my father and my mother have forsaken me, the LORD will take me up.

הוֹרֵנִי יְהוָה, דַּרְכֶּךָ: וּנְחֵנִי, בְּאֹרַח מִישׁוֹר--לְמַעַן, שׁוֹרְרָי

horeni hashem darkecha unecheni be'orach mishor; lema'an, shorerai
Teach me Thy way, O LORD; and lead me in an even path, because of them that lie in wait for me.

אַל-תִּתְּנֵנִי, בְּנֶפֶשׁ צָרָי

'al-titteneni benefesh tzarai
Deliver me not over unto the will of mine adversaries;

כִּי קָמוּ-בִי עֵדֵי-שֶׁקֶר, וִיפֵחַ חָמָס

ki kamu-vi edei-sheker, vifeach chamas
for false witnesses are risen up against me, and such as breathe out violence.

לוּלֵא--הֶאֱמַנְתִּי, לִרְאוֹת בְּטוּב-יְהוָה: בְּאֶרֶץ חַיִּים

lule, he'emanti lir'ot betuv-hashem be'eretz chayim
If I had not believed to look upon the goodness of the LORD in the land of the living!--

קַוֵּה, אֶל-יְהוָה: חֲזַק, וְיַאֲמֵץ לִבֶּךָ; וְקַוֵּה, אֶל-יְהוָה

kavveh, el-hashem chazak veya'ametz libbecha; vekavveh, el-hashem
Wait on the LORD; be strong, and let thy heart take courage; yea, wait thou for the LORD.

כח

לְדָוִד, אֵלֶיךָ יְהוָה אֶקְרָא--צוּרִי, אַל-תֶּחֱרַשׁ מִמֶּנִּי

Ledavid eleicha hashem ekra, tzuri al-techerash mimmenni
[A Psalm] of David. Unto thee, O LORD, do I call; my Rock, be not Thou deaf unto me;

פֶּן-תֶּחֱשֶׁה מִמֶּנִּי; וְנִמְשַׁלְתִּי, עִם-יוֹרְדֵי בוֹר

pen-techesheh mimmenni; venimshalti, im-yoredei vor
lest, if Thou be silent unto me, I become like them that go down into the pit.

שְׁמַע קוֹל תַּחֲנוּנַי, בְּשַׁוְּעִי אֵלֶיךָ; בְּנָשְׂאִי יָדַי, אֶל-דְּבִיר קָדְשֶׁךָ

shema kol tachanunai beshavve'i eleicha; benase'i yadai, el-devir kodshecha
Hear the voice of my supplications, when I cry unto Thee, when I lift up my hands toward Thy holy Sanctuary.

אַל-תִּמְשְׁכֵנִי עִם-רְשָׁעִים, וְעִם-פֹּעֲלֵי-אָוֶן

'al-timshecheni im-resha'im ve'im-po'alei aven
Draw me not away with the wicked, and with the workers of iniquity;

תְּהִלִּים

אִם-תַּחֲנֶה עָלַי, מַחֲנֶה--לֹא-יִירָא לִבִּי
'im-tachaneh alai machaneh lo-yira libbi
Though a host should encamp against me, my heart shall not fear;

אִם-תָּקוּם עָלַי, מִלְחָמָה--בְּזֹאת, אֲנִי בוֹטֵחַ
im-takum alai milchamah; bezot, ani voteach
though war should rise up against me, even then will I be confident.

אַחַת, שָׁאַלְתִּי מֵאֵת-יְהוָה--אוֹתָהּ אֲבַקֵּשׁ
'achat sha'alti me'et-hashem otah avakkesh
One thing have I asked of the LORD, that will I seek after:

שִׁבְתִּי בְּבֵית-יְהוָה, כָּל-יְמֵי חַיַּי
shivti beveit-hashem kol-yemei chayai
that I may dwell in the house of the LORD all the days of my life,

לַחֲזוֹת בְּנֹעַם-יְהוָה, וּלְבַקֵּר בְּהֵיכָלוֹ
lachazot beno'am-hashem ulevakker beheichalo
to behold the graciousness of the LORD, and to visit early in His temple.

כִּי יִצְפְּנֵנִי, בְּסֻכֹּה--בְּיוֹם רָעָה
ki yitzpeneni besukkoh beyom ra'ah
For He concealeth me in His pavilion in the day of evil;

יַסְתִּרֵנִי, בְּסֵתֶר אָהֳלוֹ; בְּצוּר, יְרוֹמְמֵנִי
yastireni beseter aholo; betzur, yeromemeni
He hideth me in the covert of His tent; He lifteth me up upon a rock.

וְעַתָּה יָרוּם רֹאשִׁי, עַל אֹיְבַי סְבִיבוֹתַי
ve'attah yarum roshi al oyevai sevivotai
And now shall my head be lifted up above mine enemies round about me;

וְאֶזְבְּחָה בְאָהֳלוֹ, זִבְחֵי תְרוּעָה; אָשִׁירָה וַאֲזַמְּרָה, לַיהוָה
ve'ezbechah ve'aholo zivchei teru'ah; ashirah va'azammerah, lahashem
and I will offer in His tabernacle sacrifices with trumpet-sound; I will sing, yea, I will sing praises unto the LORD.

שְׁמַע-יְהוָה קוֹלִי אֶקְרָא; וְחָנֵּנִי וַעֲנֵנִי
shema'-hashem koli ekra, vechonneni va'aneni
Hear, O LORD, when I call with my voice, and be gracious unto me, and answer me.

לְךָ, אָמַר לִבִּי--בַּקְּשׁוּ פָנָי; אֶת-פָּנֶיךָ יְהוָה אֲבַקֵּשׁ
lecha amar libbi bakkeshu fanai; et-paneicha hashem avakkesh
In Thy behalf my heart hath said: 'Seek ye My face'; Thy face, LORD, will I seek.

אַל-תַּסְתֵּר פָּנֶיךָ, מִמֶּנִּי--אַל תַּט-בְּאַף, עַבְדֶּךָ
'al-taster paneicha mimmenni al-tat-be'af, avdecha
Hide not Thy face from me; put not Thy servant away in anger;

תְּהִלִּים

שָׂנֵאתִי, קְהַל מְרֵעִים; וְעִם-רְשָׁעִים, לֹא אֵשֵׁב
saneti kehal mere'im; ve'im-resha'im, lo eshev
I hate the gathering of evil doers, and will not sit with the wicked.

אֶרְחַץ בְּנִקָּיוֹן כַּפָּי; וַאֲסֹבְבָה אֶת-מִזְבַּחֲךָ יְהוָה
'erchatz benikkayon kappai; va'asovevah et-mizbachacha hashem
I will wash my hands in innocency; so will I compass Thine altar, O LORD,

לַשְׁמִעַ, בְּקוֹל תּוֹדָה; וּלְסַפֵּר, כָּל-נִפְלְאוֹתֶיךָ
lashmia bekol todah; ulesapper, kol-nifle'oteicha
That I may make the voice of thanksgiving to be heard, and tell of all Thy wondrous works.

יְהוָה--אָהַבְתִּי, מְעוֹן בֵּיתֶךָ; וּמְקוֹם, מִשְׁכַּן כְּבוֹדֶךָ
hashem ahavti me'on beitecha; umekom, mishkan kevodecha
LORD, I love the habitation of Thy house, and the place where Thy glory dwelleth.

אַל-תֶּאֱסֹף עִם-חַטָּאִים נַפְשִׁי; וְעִם-אַנְשֵׁי דָמִים חַיָּי
'al-te'esof im-chatta'im nafshi; ve'im-'anshei damim chayai
Gather not my soul with sinners, nor my life with men of blood;

אֲשֶׁר-בִּידֵיהֶם זִמָּה; וִימִינָם, מָלְאָה שֹּׁחַד
'asher-biydeihem zimmah; viyminam, male'ah shochad
In whose hands is craftiness, and their right hand is full of bribes.

וַאֲנִי, בְּתֻמִּי אֵלֵךְ; פְּדֵנִי וְחָנֵּנִי
va'ani betummi elech, pedeni vechonneni
But as for me, I will walk in mine integrity; redeem me, and be gracious unto me.

רַגְלִי, עָמְדָה בְמִישׁוֹר; בְּמַקְהֵלִים, אֲבָרֵךְ יְהוָה
ragli amedah vemishor; bemak'helim, avarech hashem
My foot standeth in an even place; in the congregations will I bless the LORD.

כז

לְדָוִד: יְהוָה, אוֹרִי וְיִשְׁעִי--מִמִּי אִירָא
Ledavid hashem ori veyish'i mimmi ira
[A Psalm] of David. The LORD is my light and my salvation; whom shall I fear?

יְהוָה מָעוֹז-חַיַּי, מִמִּי אֶפְחָד
hashem ma'oz-chayai, mimmi efchad
The LORD is the stronghold of my life; of whom shall I be afraid?

בִּקְרֹב עָלַי, מְרֵעִים--לֶאֱכֹל אֶת-בְּשָׂרִי: צָרַי וְאֹיְבַי לִי; הֵמָּה כָשְׁלוּ וְנָפָלוּ
bikrov alai mere'im le'echol et-besari tzarai ve'oyevai li; hemmah chashelu venafalu
When evil-doers came upon me to eat up my flesh, even mine adversaries and my foes, they stumbled and fell.

תְּהִלִּים

צָרוֹת לְבָבִי הִרְחִיבוּ; מִמְּצוּקוֹתַי, הוֹצִיאֵנִי
tzarot levavi hirchivu; mimmetzukotai, hotzi'eni
The troubles of my heart are enlarged; O bring Thou me out of my distresses.

רְאֵה עָנְיִי, וַעֲמָלִי; וְשָׂא, לְכָל-חַטֹּאותָי
re'eh aneyi va'amali; vesa, lechol-chattotai
See mine affliction and my travail; and forgive all my sins.

רְאֵה-אוֹיְבַי כִּי-רָבּוּ; וְשִׂנְאַת חָמָס שְׂנֵאוּנִי
re'eh-'oyevai ki-rabbu; vesin'at chamas sene'uni
Consider how many are mine enemies, and the cruel hatred wherewith they hate me.

שָׁמְרָה נַפְשִׁי, וְהַצִּילֵנִי; אַל-אֵבוֹשׁ, כִּי-חָסִיתִי בָךְ
shamerah nafshi vehatzileni; al-'evosh, ki-chasiti vach
O keep my soul, and deliver me; let me not be ashamed, for I have taken refuge in Thee.

תֹּם-וָיֹשֶׁר יִצְּרוּנִי: כִּי, קִוִּיתִיךָ
tom-vayosher yitzeruni; ki, kivviticha
Let integrity and uprightness preserve me, because I wait for Thee.

פְּדֵה אֱלֹהִים, אֶת-יִשְׂרָאֵל--מִכֹּל, צָרוֹתָיו
pedeh elohim et-yisra'el; mikkol tzarotav
Redeem Israel, O God, out of all his troubles.

כו

לְדָוִד: שָׁפְטֵנִי יְהוָה
Ledavid shafeteni hashem
[A Psalm] of David. Judge me, O LORD,

כִּי-אֲנִי, בְּתֻמִּי הָלַכְתִּי; וּבַיהוָה בָּטַחְתִּי, לֹא אֶמְעָד
ki-'ani betummi halachti; uvahashem batachti, lo em'ad
for I have walked in mine integrity, and I have trusted in the LORD without wavering.

בְּחָנֵנִי יְהוָה וְנַסֵּנִי; צָרְפָה כִלְיוֹתַי וְלִבִּי
bechaneni hashem venasseni; tzarefah chilyotai velibbi
Examine me, O LORD, and try me; test my reins and my heart.

כִּי-חַסְדְּךָ, לְנֶגֶד עֵינָי; וְהִתְהַלַּכְתִּי, בַּאֲמִתֶּךָ
ki-chasdecha leneged einai; vehit'hallachti, ba'amittecha
For Thy mercy is before mine eyes; and I have walked in Thy truth.

לֹא-יָשַׁבְתִּי, עִם-מְתֵי-שָׁוְא; וְעִם נַעֲלָמִים, לֹא אָבוֹא
lo-yashavti im-metei-shav; ve'im na'alamim, lo avo
I have not sat with men of falsehood; neither will I go in with dissemblers.

תְּהִלִּים

זְכֹר-רַחֲמֶיךָ יְהוָה, וַחֲסָדֶיךָ: כִּי מֵעוֹלָם הֵמָּה
zechor-rachameicha hashem vachasadeicha; ki me'olam hemmah
Remember, O LORD, Thy compassions and Thy mercies; for they have been from of old.

חַטֹּאות נְעוּרַי, וּפְשָׁעַי--אַל-תִּזְכֹּר
chattovt ne'urai ufesha'ai, al-tizkor
Remember not the sins of my youth, nor my transgressions;

כְּחַסְדְּךָ זְכָר-לִי-אַתָּה--לְמַעַן טוּבְךָ יְהוָה
kechasdecha zechar-li-'attah; lema'an tuvecha hashem
according to Thy mercy remember Thou me, for Thy goodness' sake, O LORD.

טוֹב-וְיָשָׁר יְהוָה; עַל-כֵּן יוֹרֶה חַטָּאִים בַּדָּרֶךְ
tov-veyashar hashem al-ken yoreh chatta'im baddarech
Good and upright is the LORD; therefore doth He instruct sinners in the way.

יַדְרֵךְ עֲנָוִים, בַּמִּשְׁפָּט; וִילַמֵּד עֲנָוִים דַּרְכּוֹ
yadrech anavim bammishpat; vilammed anavim darko
He guideth the humble in justice; and He teacheth the humble His way.

כָּל-אָרְחוֹת יְהוָה, חֶסֶד וֶאֱמֶת--לְנֹצְרֵי בְרִיתוֹ, וְעֵדֹתָיו
kol-'orechot hashem chesed ve'emet; lenotzerei verito, ve'edotav
All the paths of the LORD are mercy and truth unto such as keep His covenant and His testimonies.

לְמַעַן-שִׁמְךָ יְהוָה; וְסָלַחְתָּ לַעֲוֹנִי, כִּי רַב-הוּא
lema'an-shimcha hashem vesalachta la'avoni, ki rav-hu
For Thy name's sake, O LORD, pardon mine iniquity, for it is great.

מִי-זֶה הָאִישׁ, יְרֵא יְהוָה--יוֹרֶנּוּ, בְּדֶרֶךְ יִבְחָר
mi-zeh ha'ish yerei hashem yorennu, bederech yivchar
What man is he that feareth the LORD? Him will He instruct in the way that he should choose.

נַפְשׁוֹ, בְּטוֹב תָּלִין; וְזַרְעוֹ, יִירַשׁ אָרֶץ
nafsho betov talin; vezar'o, yirash aretz
His soul shall abide in prosperity; and his seed shall inherit the land.

סוֹד יְהוָה, לִירֵאָיו; וּבְרִיתוֹ, לְהוֹדִיעָם
sod hashem liyre'av; uverito, lehodi'am
The counsel of the LORD is with them that fear Him; and His covenant, to make them know it.

עֵינַי תָּמִיד, אֶל-יְהוָה: כִּי הוּא-יוֹצִיא מֵרֶשֶׁת רַגְלָי
'einai tamid el-hashem ki hu-yotzi mereshet raglai
Mine eyes are ever toward the LORD; for He will bring forth my feet out of the net.

פְּנֵה-אֵלַי וְחָנֵּנִי: כִּי-יָחִיד וְעָנִי אָנִי
peneh-'elai vechonneni ki-yachid ve'ani ani
Turn Thee unto me, and be gracious unto me; for I am solitary and afflicted.

תְּהִלִּים

זֶה, דּוֹר דֹּרְשָׁו; מְבַקְשֵׁי פָנֶיךָ יַעֲקֹב סֶלָה
zeh dor doreshav; mevakshei faneicha ya'akov selah
Such is the generation of them that seek after Him, that seek Thy face, even Jacob. Selah

שְׂאוּ שְׁעָרִים, רָאשֵׁיכֶם, וְהִנָּשְׂאוּ, פִּתְחֵי עוֹלָם; וְיָבוֹא, מֶלֶךְ הַכָּבוֹד
se'u she'arim rasheichem, vehinnase'u pitchei olam; veyavo, melech hakkavod
Lift up your heads, O ye gates, and be ye lifted up, ye everlasting doors; that the King of glory may come in.

מִי זֶה, מֶלֶךְ הַכָּבוֹד: יְהוָה, עִזּוּז וְגִבּוֹר; יְהוָה, גִּבּוֹר מִלְחָמָה
mi zeh melech hakkavod hashem izzuz vegibbor; hashem gibbor milchamah
'Who is the King of glory?' 'The LORD strong and mighty, the LORD mighty in battle.'

שְׂאוּ שְׁעָרִים, רָאשֵׁיכֶם, וּשְׂאוּ, פִּתְחֵי עוֹלָם
se'u she'arim rasheichem, use'u pitchei olam
Lift up your heads, O ye gates, yea, lift them up, ye everlasting doors;

וְיָבֹא, מֶלֶךְ הַכָּבוֹד
veyavo melech hakkavod
that the King of glory may come in.

מִי הוּא זֶה, מֶלֶךְ הַכָּבוֹד: יְהוָה צְבָאוֹת--הוּא מֶלֶךְ הַכָּבוֹד סֶלָה
mi hu zeh melech hakkavod hashem tzeva'ot; hu melech hakkavod selah
'Who then is the King of glory?' 'The LORD of hosts; He is the King of glory.' Selah

כה

לְדָוִד: אֵלֶיךָ יְהוָה, נַפְשִׁי אֶשָּׂא
Ledavid eleicha hashem nafshi essa
[A Psalm] of David. Unto Thee, O LORD, do I lift up my soul.

אֱלֹהַי--בְּךָ בָטַחְתִּי, אַל-אֵבוֹשָׁה; אַל-יַעַלְצוּ אֹיְבַי לִי
'elohai, becha vatachti al-'evoshah; al-ya'altzu oyevai li
O my God, in Thee have I trusted, let me not be ashamed; let not mine enemies triumph over me.

גַּם כָּל-קֹוֶיךָ, לֹא יֵבֹשׁוּ; יֵבֹשׁוּ, הַבּוֹגְדִים רֵיקָם
gam kol-koycha lo yevoshu; yevoshu, habbogedim reikam
Yea, none that wait for Thee shall be ashamed; they shall be ashamed that deal treacherously without cause.

דְּרָכֶיךָ יְהוָה, הוֹדִיעֵנִי; אֹרְחוֹתֶיךָ לַמְּדֵנִי
deracheicha hashem hodi'eni; orechoteicha lammedeni
Show me Thy ways, O LORD; teach me Thy paths.

הַדְרִיכֵנִי בַאֲמִתֶּךָ, וְלַמְּדֵנִי-- כִּי-אַתָּה, אֱלֹהֵי יִשְׁעִי; אוֹתְךָ קִוִּיתִי, כָּל-הַיּוֹם
hadricheni va'amittecha velammedeni, ki-'attah elohei yish'i; otecha kivviti, kol-hayom
Guide me in Thy truth, and teach me; for Thou art the God of my salvation; for Thee do I wait all the day.

תְּהִלִּים

נַפְשִׁי יְשׁוֹבֵב; יַנְחֵנִי בְמַעְגְּלֵי-צֶדֶק, לְמַעַן שְׁמוֹ
nafshi yeshovev; yancheni vema'gelei-tzedek, lema'an shemo
He restoreth my soul; He guideth me in straight paths for His name's sake.

גַּם כִּי-אֵלֵךְ בְּגֵיא צַלְמָוֶת, לֹא-אִירָא רָע
gam ki-'elech begei tzalmavet lo-'ira ra'
Yea, though I walk through the valley of the shadow of death, I will fear no evil,

כִּי-אַתָּה עִמָּדִי; שִׁבְטְךָ וּמִשְׁעַנְתֶּךָ, הֵמָּה יְנַחֲמֻנִי
ki-'attah immadi; shivtecha umish'antecha, hemmah yenachamuni
for Thou art with me; Thy rod and Thy staff, they comfort me.

תַּעֲרֹךְ לְפָנַי, שֻׁלְחָן--נֶגֶד צֹרְרָי
ta'aroch lefanai shulchan, neged tzorerai
Thou preparest a table before me in the presence of mine enemies;

דִּשַּׁנְתָּ בַשֶּׁמֶן רֹאשִׁי, כּוֹסִי רְוָיָה
dishanta vashemen roshi, kosi revayah
Thou hast anointed my head with oil; my cup runneth over.

אַךְ, טוֹב וָחֶסֶד יִרְדְּפוּנִי--כָּל-יְמֵי חַיָּי; וְשַׁבְתִּי בְּבֵית-יְהוָה, לְאֹרֶךְ יָמִים
'ach tov vachesed yirdefuni kol-yemei chayai; veshavti beveit-hashem le'orech yamim
Surely goodness and mercy shall follow me all the days of my life; and I shall dwell in the house of the LORD for ever.

כד

לְדָוִד, מִזְמוֹר: לַיהוָה, הָאָרֶץ וּמְלוֹאָהּ; תֵּבֵל, וְיֹשְׁבֵי בָהּ
Ledavid, mizmor. Lahashem ha'aretz umelo'ah; tevel, veyoshevei vah
A Psalm of David. The earth is the LORD'S, and the fulness thereof; the world, and they that dwell therein.

כִּי-הוּא, עַל-יַמִּים יְסָדָהּ; וְעַל-נְהָרוֹת, יְכוֹנְנֶהָ
ki-hu al-yammim yesadah; ve'al-neharot, yechoneneha
For He hath founded it upon the seas, and established it upon the floods.

מִי-יַעֲלֶה בְהַר-יְהוָה; וּמִי-יָקוּם, בִּמְקוֹם קָדְשׁוֹ
mi-ya'aleh vehar-hashem umi-yakum bimkom kodsho
Who shall ascend into the mountain of the LORD? and who shall stand in His holy place?

נְקִי כַפַּיִם, וּבַר-לֵבָב: אֲשֶׁר לֹא-נָשָׂא לַשָּׁוְא נַפְשִׁי; וְלֹא נִשְׁבַּע לְמִרְמָה
neki chappayim, uvar-levav asher lo-nasa lashav nafshi; velo nishba lemirmah
He that hath clean hands, and a pure heart; who hath not taken My name in vain, and hath not sworn deceitfully.

יִשָּׂא בְרָכָה, מֵאֵת יְהוָה; וּצְדָקָה, מֵאֱלֹהֵי יִשְׁעוֹ
yissa verachah me'et hashem utzedakah, me'elohei yish'o
He shall receive a blessing from the LORD, and righteousness from the God of his salvation.

תְּהִלִּים

יֹאכְלוּ עֲנָוִים, וְיִשְׂבָּעוּ
yochelu anavim veyisba'u
Let the humble eat and be satisfied;

יְהַלְלוּ יְהוָה, דֹּרְשָׁיו; יְחִי לְבַבְכֶם לָעַד
yehalelu hashem doreshav; yechi levavchem la'ad
let them praise the LORD that seek after Him; may your heart be quickened for ever!

יִזְכְּרוּ, וְיָשֻׁבוּ אֶל-יְהוָה-- כָּל-אַפְסֵי-אָרֶץ
yizkeru veyashuvu el-hashem kol-'afsei-'aretz
All the ends of the earth shall remember and turn unto the LORD;

וְיִשְׁתַּחֲווּ לְפָנֶיךָ, כָּל-מִשְׁפְּחוֹת גּוֹיִם
veyishtachavu lefaneicha, kol-mishpechot goyim
and all the kindreds of the nations shall worship before Thee.

כִּי לַיהוָה, הַמְּלוּכָה; וּמֹשֵׁל, בַּגּוֹיִם
ki lahashem hammeluchah; umoshel, baggoyim
For the kingdom is the LORD'S; and He is the ruler over the nations.

אָכְלוּ וַיִּשְׁתַּחֲווּ, כָּל-דִּשְׁנֵי-אֶרֶץ
'achelu vayishtachavvu kol-dishnei-'eretz
All the fat ones of the earth shall eat and worship;

לְפָנָיו יִכְרְעוּ, כָּל-יוֹרְדֵי עָפָר; וְנַפְשׁוֹ, לֹא חִיָּה
lefanav yichre'u kol-yoredei afar; venafsho, lo chiyah
all they that go down to the dust shall kneel before Him, even he that cannot keep his soul alive.

זֶרַע יַעַבְדֶנּוּ; יְסֻפַּר לַאדֹנָי לַדּוֹר
zera ya'avdennu; yesuppar la'adonai laddor
A seed shall serve him; it shall be told of the Lord unto the next generation.

יָבֹאוּ, וְיַגִּידוּ צִדְקָתוֹ: לְעַם נוֹלָד, כִּי עָשָׂה
yavo'u veyaggidu tzidkato; le'am nolad, ki asah
They shall come and shall declare His righteousness unto a people that shall be born, that He hath done it.

כג

מִזְמוֹר לְדָוִד: יְהוָה רֹעִי, לֹא אֶחְסָר
Mizmor ledavid; hashem ro'i, lo echsar
A Psalm of David. The LORD is my shepherd; I shall not want.

בִּנְאוֹת דֶּשֶׁא, יַרְבִּיצֵנִי; עַל-מֵי מְנֻחוֹת יְנַהֲלֵנִי
bin'ot deshei yarbitzeni; al-mei menuchot yenahaleni
He maketh me to lie down in green pastures; He leadeth me beside the still waters.

תְּהִלִּים

כָּאֲרִי, יָדַי וְרַגְלָי
ka'ari, yadai veraglai
like a lion, they are at my hands and my feet.

אֲסַפֵּר כָּל-עַצְמוֹתָי; הֵמָּה יַבִּיטוּ, יִרְאוּ-בִי
'asapper kol-'atzmotai; hemmah yabbitu, yir'u-vi
I may count all my bones; they look and gloat over me.

יְחַלְּקוּ בְגָדַי לָהֶם; וְעַל-לְבוּשִׁי, יַפִּילוּ גוֹרָל
yechalleku vegadai lahem; ve'al-levushi, yappilu goral
They part my garments among them, and for my vesture do they cast lots.

וְאַתָּה יְהוָה, אַל-תִּרְחָק; אֱיָלוּתִי, לְעֶזְרָתִי חוּשָׁה
ve'attah hashem al-tirchak; eyaluti, le'ezrati chushah
But Thou, O LORD, be not far off; O Thou my strength, hasten to help me.

הַצִּילָה מֵחֶרֶב נַפְשִׁי; מִיַּד-כֶּלֶב, יְחִידָתִי
hatzilah mecherev nafshi; miyad-kelev, yechidati
Deliver my soul from the sword; mine only one from the power of the dog.

הוֹשִׁיעֵנִי, מִפִּי אַרְיֵה; וּמִקַּרְנֵי רֵמִים עֲנִיתָנִי
hoshi'eni mippi aryeh; umikkarnei remim anitani
Save me from the lion's mouth; yea, from the horns of the wild-oxen do Thou answer me.

אֲסַפְּרָה שִׁמְךָ לְאֶחָי; בְּתוֹךְ קָהָל אֲהַלְלֶךָּ
'asapperah shimcha le'echai; betoch kahal ahaleleka
I will declare Thy name unto my brethren; in the midst of the congregation will I praise Thee.

יִרְאֵי יְהוָה, הַלְלוּהוּ--כָּל-זֶרַע יַעֲקֹב
yir'ei hashem haleluhu, kol-zera ya'akov
'Ye that fear the LORD, praise Him; all ye the seed of Jacob,

כַּבְּדוּהוּ; וְגוּרוּ מִמֶּנּוּ, כָּל-זֶרַע יִשְׂרָאֵל
kabbeduhu; veguru mimmennu, kol-zera yisra'el
glorify Him; and stand in awe of Him, all ye the seed of Israel.

כִּי לֹא-בָזָה וְלֹא שִׁקַּץ, עֱנוּת עָנִי
ki lo-vazah velo shikkatz enut ani
For He hath not despised nor abhorred the lowliness of the poor;

וְלֹא-הִסְתִּיר פָּנָיו מִמֶּנּוּ; וּבְשַׁוְּעוֹ אֵלָיו שָׁמֵעַ
velo-histir panav mimmennu; uveshavve'o elav shamea
neither hath He hid His face from him; but when he cried unto Him, He heard.'

מֵאִתְּךָ, תְּהִלָּתִי: בְּקָהָל רָב--נְדָרַי אֲשַׁלֵּם, נֶגֶד יְרֵאָיו
me'ittecha, tehillati bekahal rav; nedarai ashallem, neged yere'av
From Thee cometh my praise in the great congregation; I will pay my vows before them that fear Him.

תְּהִלִּים

וְאָנֹכִי תוֹלַעַת וְלֹא-אִישׁ; חֶרְפַּת אָדָם, וּבְזוּי עָם
ve'anochi tola'at velo-'ish; cherpat adam, uvezui am
But I am a worm, and no man; a reproach of men, and despised of the people.

כָּל-רֹאַי, יַלְעִגוּ לִי; יַפְטִירוּ בְשָׂפָה, יָנִיעוּ רֹאשׁ
kol-ro'ai yal'igu li; yaftiru vesafah, yani'u rosh
All they that see me laugh me to scorn; they shoot out the lip, they shake the head:

גֹּל אֶל-יְהוָה יְפַלְּטֵהוּ; יַצִּילֵהוּ, כִּי חָפֵץ בּוֹ
gol el-hashem yefalletehu; yatzilehu, ki chafetz bo
'Let him commit himself unto the LORD! let Him rescue him; let Him deliver him, seeing He delighteth in him.'

כִּי-אַתָּה גֹחִי מִבָּטֶן; מַבְטִיחִי, עַל-שְׁדֵי אִמִּי
ki-'attah gochi mibbaten; mavtichi, al-shedei immi
For Thou art He that took me out of the womb; Thou madest me trust when I was upon my mother's breasts.

עָלֶיךָ, הָשְׁלַכְתִּי מֵרָחֶם; מִבֶּטֶן אִמִּי, אֵלִי אָתָּה
'aleicha hashelachti merachem; mibbeten immi, eli attah
Upon Thee I have been cast from my birth; Thou art my God from my mother's womb.

אַל-תִּרְחַק מִמֶּנִּי, כִּי-צָרָה קְרוֹבָה: כִּי-אֵין עוֹזֵר
'al-tirchak mimmenni ki-tzarah kerovah; ki-'ein ozer
Be not far from me; for trouble is near; for there is none to help.

סְבָבוּנִי, פָּרִים רַבִּים; אַבִּירֵי בָשָׁן כִּתְּרוּנִי
sevavuni parim rabbim; abbirei vashan kitteruni
Many bulls have encompassed me; strong bulls of Bashan have beset me round.

פָּצוּ עָלַי פִּיהֶם; אַרְיֵה, טֹרֵף וְשֹׁאֵג
patzu alai pihem; aryeh, toref vesho'eg
They open wide their mouth against me, as a ravening and a roaring lion.

כַּמַּיִם נִשְׁפַּכְתִּי--וְהִתְפָּרְדוּ, כָּל-עַצְמוֹתָי: הָיָה לִבִּי, כַּדּוֹנָג
kammayim nishpachti vehitparedu, kol-'atzmotai hayah libbi kaddonag
I am poured out like water, and all my bones are out of joint; my heart is become like wax;

נָמֵס, בְּתוֹךְ מֵעָי
names, betoch me'ai
it is melted in mine inmost parts.

יָבֵשׁ כַּחֶרֶשׂ, כֹּחִי, וּלְשׁוֹנִי, מֻדְבָּק מַלְקוֹחָי; וְלַעֲפַר-מָוֶת תִּשְׁפְּתֵנִי
yavesh kacheres kochi, uleshoni mudbak malkochai; vela'afar-mavet tishpeteni
My strength is dried up like a potsherd; and my tongue cleaveth to my throat; and Thou layest me in the dust of death.

כִּי סְבָבוּנִי, כְּלָבִים: עֲדַת מְרֵעִים, הִקִּיפוּנִי
ki sevavuni, kelavim adat mere'im hikkifuni
For dogs have encompassed me; a company of evil-doers have inclosed me;

תְּהִלִים

יְהוָה, בְּאַפּוֹ יְבַלְּעֵם; וְתֹאכְלֵם אֵשׁ
hashem be'appo yevalle'em; vetochelem esh
the LORD shall swallow them up in His wrath, and the fire shall devour them.

פִּרְיָמוֹ, מֵאֶרֶץ תְּאַבֵּד; וְזַרְעָם, מִבְּנֵי אָדָם
piryamo me'eretz te'abbed; vezar'am, mibbenei adam
Their fruit shalt thou destroy from the earth, and their seed from among the children of men.

כִּי-נָטוּ עָלֶיךָ רָעָה; חָשְׁבוּ מְזִמָּה, בַּל-יוּכָלוּ
ki-natu aleicha ra'ah; chashevu mezimmah, bal-yuchalu
For they intended evil against thee, they imagined a device, wherewith they shall not prevail.

כִּי, תְּשִׁיתֵמוֹ שֶׁכֶם; בְּמֵיתָרֶיךָ, תְּכוֹנֵן עַל-פְּנֵיהֶם
ki teshitemo shechem; bemeitareicha, techonen al-peneihem
For thou shalt make them turn their back, thou shalt make ready with thy bowstrings against the face of them.

רוּמָה יְהוָה בְעֻזֶּךָ; נָשִׁירָה וּנְזַמְּרָה, גְּבוּרָתֶךָ
rumah hashem be'uzzecha; nashirah unezammerah gevuratecha
Be Thou exalted, O LORD, in Thy strength; so will we sing and praise Thy power.

כב

לַמְנַצֵּחַ, עַל-אַיֶּלֶת הַשַּׁחַר; מִזְמוֹר לְדָוִד
Lamnatzeach al-'ayelet hashachar, mizmor ledavid
For the Leader; upon Aijeleth ha-Shahar. A Psalm of David.

אֵלִי אֵלִי, לָמָה עֲזַבְתָּנִי; רָחוֹק מִישׁוּעָתִי, דִּבְרֵי שַׁאֲגָתִי
'eli eli lamah azavtani; rachok mishu'ati, divrei sha'agati
My God, my God, why hast Thou forsaken me, and art far from my help at the words of my cry?

אֱלֹהַי--אֶקְרָא יוֹמָם, וְלֹא תַעֲנֶה; וְלַיְלָה, וְלֹא-דֻמִיָּה לִי
'elohai, ekra yomom velo ta'aneh; velaylah, velo-dumiyah li
O my God, I call by day, but Thou answerest not; and at night, and there is no surcease for me.

וְאַתָּה קָדוֹשׁ--יוֹשֵׁב, תְּהִלּוֹת יִשְׂרָאֵל
ve'attah kadosh; yoshev, tehillot yisra'el
Yet Thou art holy, O Thou that art enthroned upon the praises of Israel.

בְּךָ, בָּטְחוּ אֲבֹתֵינוּ; בָּטְחוּ, וַתְּפַלְּטֵמוֹ
becha batechu avoteinu; batechu, vattefalletemo
In Thee did our fathers trust; they trusted, and Thou didst deliver them.

אֵלֶיךָ זָעֲקוּ וְנִמְלָטוּ; בְּךָ בָטְחוּ וְלֹא-בוֹשׁוּ
'eleicha za'aku venimlatu; becha vatechu velo-voshu
Unto Thee they cried, and escaped; in Thee did they trust, and were not ashamed.

תְּהִלִּים

יְהוָה הוֹשִׁיעָה: הַמֶּלֶךְ, יַעֲנֵנוּ בְיוֹם-קָרְאֵנוּ
hashem hoshi'ah; hammelech, ya'anenu veyom-kare'enu
Save, LORD; let the King answer us in the day that we call.

כא

לַמְנַצֵּחַ, מִזְמוֹר לְדָוִד
Lamnatzeach, mizmor ledavid
For the Leader. A Psalm of David.

יְהוָה, בְּעָזְּךָ יִשְׂמַח-מֶלֶךְ; וּבִישׁוּעָתְךָ, מַה-יָּגֶל מְאֹד
Hashem be'ozzecha yismach-melech; uvishu'atecha, mah-yageil me'od
O LORD, in Thy strength the king rejoiceth; and in Thy salvation how greatly doth he exult!

תַּאֲוַת לִבּוֹ, נָתַתָּה לּוֹ; וַאֲרֶשֶׁת שְׂפָתָיו, בַּל-מָנַעְתָּ סֶּלָה
ta'avat libbo natattah lo; va'areshet sefatav, bal-mana'ta selah
Thou hast given him his heart's desire, and the request of his lips Thou hast not withholden. Selah

כִּי-תְקַדְּמֶנּוּ, בִּרְכוֹת טוֹב; תָּשִׁית לְרֹאשׁוֹ, עֲטֶרֶת פָּז
ki-tekaddemennu birchot tov; tashit lerosho, ateret paz
For Thou meetest him with choicest blessings; Thou settest a crown of fine gold on his head.

חַיִּים, שָׁאַל מִמְּךָ--נָתַתָּה לּוֹ; אֹרֶךְ יָמִים, עוֹלָם וָעֶד
chayim sha'al mimmecha natattah lo; orech yamim, olam va'ed
He asked life of Thee, Thou gavest it him; even length of days for ever and ever.

גָּדוֹל כְּבוֹדוֹ, בִּישׁוּעָתֶךָ; הוֹד וְהָדָר, תְּשַׁוֶּה עָלָיו
gadol kevodo bishu'atecha; hod vehadar teshavveh alav
His glory is great through Thy salvation; honour and majesty dost Thou lay upon him.

כִּי-תְשִׁיתֵהוּ בְרָכוֹת לָעַד; תְּחַדֵּהוּ בְשִׂמְחָה, אֶת-פָּנֶיךָ
ki-teshitehu verachot la'ad; techaddehu vesimchah, et-paneicha
For Thou makest him most blessed for ever; Thou makest him glad with joy in Thy presence.

כִּי-הַמֶּלֶךְ, בֹּטֵחַ בַּיהוָה; וּבְחֶסֶד עֶלְיוֹן, בַּל-יִמּוֹט
ki-hammelech boteach bahashem; uvechesed elyon, bal-yimmot
For the king trusteth in the LORD, yea, in the mercy of the Most High; he shall not be moved.

תִּמְצָא יָדְךָ, לְכָל-אֹיְבֶיךָ; יְמִינְךָ, תִּמְצָא שֹׂנְאֶיךָ
timtza yadecha lechol-'oyeveicha; yeminecha timtza sone'eicha
Thy hand shall be equal to all thine enemies; thy right hand shall overtake those that hate thee.

תְּשִׁיתֵמוֹ, כְּתַנּוּר אֵשׁ--לְעֵת פָּנֶיךָ
teshitemo ketannur esh le'et paneicha
Thou shalt make them as a fiery furnace in the time of thine anger;

תְּהִלִים

כ

לַמְנַצֵּחַ, מִזְמוֹר לְדָוִד
Lamnatzeach, mizmor ledavid
For the Leader. A Psalm of David.

יַעַנְךָ יְהוָה, בְּיוֹם צָרָה; יְשַׂגֶּבְךָ, שֵׁם אֱלֹהֵי יַעֲקֹב
ya'ancha hashem beyom tzarah; yesaggevcha, shem elohei ya'akov
The LORD answer thee in the day of trouble; the name of the God of Jacob set thee up on high;

יִשְׁלַח-עֶזְרְךָ מִקֹּדֶשׁ; וּמִצִּיּוֹן, יִסְעָדֶךָּ
yishlach-'ezrecha mikkodesh; umitziyon, yis'adeka
Send forth thy help from the sanctuary, and support thee out of Zion;

יִזְכֹּר כָּל-מִנְחֹתֶךָ; וְעוֹלָתְךָ יְדַשְּׁנֶה סֶלָה
yizkor kol-minchotecha; ve'olatecha yedasheneh selah
Receive the memorial of all thy meal-offerings, and accept the fat of thy burnt-sacrifice; Selah

יִתֶּן-לְךָ כִלְבָבֶךָ; וְכָל-עֲצָתְךָ יְמַלֵּא
yitten-lecha chilvavecha; vechol-'atzatecha yemalle
Grant thee according to thine own heart, and fulfil all thy counsel.

נְרַנְּנָה, בִּישׁוּעָתֶךָ--וּבְשֵׁם-אֱלֹהֵינוּ נִדְגֹּל
nerannenah bishu'atecha, uveshem-'eloheinu nidgol
We will shout for joy in thy victory, and in the name of our God we will set up our standards;

יְמַלֵּא יְהוָה, כָּל-מִשְׁאֲלוֹתֶיךָ
yemallei hashem kol-mish'aloteicha
the LORD fulfil all thy petitions.

עַתָּה יָדַעְתִּי--כִּי הוֹשִׁיעַ יְהוָה, מְשִׁיחוֹ
'attah yada'ti, ki hoshia hashem meshicho
Now know I that the LORD saveth His anointed;

יַעֲנֵהוּ, מִשְּׁמֵי קָדְשׁוֹ--בִּגְבֻרוֹת, יֵשַׁע יְמִינוֹ
ya'anehu mishemei kodsho bigvurot, yesha yemino
He will answer him from His holy heaven with the mighty acts of His saving right hand.

אֵלֶּה בָרֶכֶב, וְאֵלֶּה בַסּוּסִים; וַאֲנַחְנוּ, בְּשֵׁם-יְהוָה אֱלֹהֵינוּ נַזְכִּיר
'elleh varechev ve'elleh vassusim; va'anachnu beshem-hashem eloheinu nazkir
Some trust in chariots, and some in horses; but we will make mention of the name of the LORD our God.

הֵמָּה, כָּרְעוּ וְנָפָלוּ; וַאֲנַחְנוּ קַּמְנוּ, וַנִּתְעוֹדָד
hemmah kare'u venafalu; va'anachnu kamnu, vannit'odad
They are bowed down and fallen; but we are risen, and stand upright.

תְּהִלִּים

פִּקּוּדֵי יְהוָה יְשָׁרִים, מְשַׂמְּחֵי-לֵב
pikkudei hashem yesharim mesammechei-lev
The precepts of the LORD are right, rejoicing the heart;

מִצְוַת יְהוָה בָּרָה, מְאִירַת עֵינָיִם
mitzvat hashem barah, me'irat einayim
the commandment of the LORD is pure, enlightening the eyes.

יִרְאַת יְהוָה, טְהוֹרָה--עוֹמֶדֶת לָעַד
yir'at hashem tehorah omedet la'ad
The fear of the LORD is clean, enduring for ever;

מִשְׁפְּטֵי-יְהוָה אֱמֶת; צָדְקוּ יַחְדָּו
mishpetei-hashem emet; tzadeku yachdav
the ordinances of the LORD are true, they are righteous altogether;

הַנֶּחֱמָדִים--מִזָּהָב, וּמִפַּז רָב; וּמְתוּקִים מִדְּבַשׁ, וְנֹפֶת צוּפִים
hannechemadim, mizzahov umippaz rav; umetukim middevash, venofet tzufim
More to be desired are they than gold, yea, than much fine gold; sweeter also than honey and the honeycomb.

גַּם-עַבְדְּךָ, נִזְהָר בָּהֶם; בְּשָׁמְרָם, עֵקֶב רָב
gam-'avdecha nizhar bahem; beshomeram, ekev rav
Moreover by them is Thy servant warned; in keeping of them there is great reward.

שְׁגִיאוֹת מִי-יָבִין; מִנִּסְתָּרוֹת נַקֵּנִי
shegi'ot mi-yavin; minnistarot nakkeni
Who can discern his errors? Clear Thou me from hidden faults.

גַּם מִזֵּדִים, חֲשֹׂךְ עַבְדֶּךָ--אַל-יִמְשְׁלוּ-בִי אָז אֵיתָם
gam mizzedim chasoch avdecha, al-yimshelu-vi az eitam
Keep back Thy servant also from presumptuous sins, that they may not have dominion over me;

וְנִקֵּיתִי, מִפֶּשַׁע רָב
venikkeiti, mippesha rav
then shall I be faultless, and I shall be clear from great transgression.

יִהְיוּ לְרָצוֹן אִמְרֵי-פִי, וְהֶגְיוֹן לִבִּי לְפָנֶיךָ
yihyu leratzon imrei-fi vehegyon libbi lefaneicha
Let the words of my mouth and the meditation of my heart be acceptable before Thee,

יְהוָה, צוּרִי וְגֹאֲלִי
hashem tzuri vego'ali
O LORD, my Rock, and my Redeemer.

תְּהִלִּים

עַל-כֵּן, אוֹדְךָ בַגּוֹיִם יְהוָה; וּלְשִׁמְךָ אֲזַמֵּרָה
'al-ken odecha vaggoyim hashem uleshimcha azammerah
Therefore I will give thanks unto Thee, O LORD, among the nations, and will sing praises unto Thy name.

מִגְדֹּל, יְשׁוּעוֹת מַלְכּוֹ: וְעֹשֶׂה חֶסֶד, לִמְשִׁיחוֹ--לְדָוִד וּלְזַרְעוֹ; עַד-עוֹלָם
magdil magdil yeshu'ot malko ve'oseh chesed limshicho, ledavid ulezar'o, ad-'olam
Great salvation giveth He to His king; and showeth mercy to His anointed, to David and to his seed, for evermore.

יט

לַמְנַצֵּחַ, מִזְמוֹר לְדָוִד
Lamnatzeach, mizmor ledavid
For the Leader. A Psalm of David.

הַשָּׁמַיִם, מְסַפְּרִים כְּבוֹד-אֵל; וּמַעֲשֵׂה יָדָיו, מַגִּיד הָרָקִיעַ
hashamayim, mesapperim kevod-'el; uma'aseh yadav, maggid harakia
The heavens declare the glory of God, and the firmament showeth His handiwork;

יוֹם לְיוֹם, יַבִּיעַ אֹמֶר; וְלַיְלָה לְּלַיְלָה, יְחַוֶּה-דָּעַת
yom leyom yabbia omer; velaylah lelaylah, yechavveh-da'at
Day unto day uttereth speech, and night unto night revealeth knowledge;

אֵין-אֹמֶר, וְאֵין דְּבָרִים: בְּלִי, נִשְׁמָע קוֹלָם
'ein-'omer ve'ein devarim; beli, nishma kolam
There is no speech, there are no words, neither is their voice heard.

בְּכָל-הָאָרֶץ, יָצָא קַוָּם, וּבִקְצֵה תֵבֵל, מִלֵּיהֶם; לַשֶּׁמֶשׁ, שָׂם-אֹהֶל בָּהֶם
bechol-ha'aretz yatza kavvam, uviktzeh tevel milleihem; lashemesh, sam-'ohel bahem
Their line is gone out through all the earth, and their words to the end of the world. In them hath He set a tent for the sun,

וְהוּא--כְּחָתָן, יֹצֵא מֵחֻפָּתוֹ; יָשִׂישׂ כְּגִבּוֹר, לָרוּץ אֹרַח
vehu, kechatan yotzei mechuppato; yasis kegibbor, larutz orach
Which is as a bridegroom coming out of his chamber, and rejoiceth as a strong man to run his course.

מִקְצֵה הַשָּׁמַיִם, מוֹצָאוֹ--וּתְקוּפָתוֹ עַל-קְצוֹתָם
miktzeh hashamayim motza'o, utekufato al-ketzotam
His going forth is from the end of the heaven, and his circuit unto the ends of it;

וְאֵין נִסְתָּר, מֵחַמָּתוֹ
ve'ein nistar, mechammato
and there is nothing hid from the heat thereof.

תּוֹרַת יְהוָה תְּמִימָה, מְשִׁיבַת נָפֶשׁ; עֵדוּת יְהוָה נֶאֱמָנָה, מַחְכִּימַת פֶּתִי
torat hashem temimah meshivat nafesh; edut hashem ne'emanah, machkimat peti
The law of the LORD is perfect, restoring the soul; the testimony of the LORD is sure, making wise the simple.

תְּהִלִּים

וַתְּאַזְּרֵנִי חַיִל, לַמִּלְחָמָה; תַּכְרִיעַ קָמַי תַּחְתָּי
vatte'azzereni chayil lammilchamah; tachria kamai tachtai
For Thou hast girded me with strength unto the battle; Thou hast subdued under me those that rose up against me.

וְאֹיְבַי, נָתַתָּה לִּי עֹרֶף; וּמְשַׂנְאַי, אַצְמִיתֵם
ve'oyevai, natattah li oref; umesan'ai, atzmitem
Thou hast also made mine enemies turn their backs unto me, and I did cut off them that hate me.

יְשַׁוְּעוּ וְאֵין-מוֹשִׁיעַ; עַל-יְהוָה, וְלֹא עָנָם.
yeshavve'u ve'ein-moshia'; al-hashem velo anam
They cried, but there was none to save; even unto the LORD, but He answered them not.

וְאֶשְׁחָקֵם, כְּעָפָר עַל-פְּנֵי-רוּחַ; כְּטִיט חוּצוֹת אֲרִיקֵם
ve'eshchakem, ke'afar al-penei-ruach; ketit chutzot arikem
Then did I beat them small as the dust before the wind; I did cast them out as the mire of the streets.

תְּפַלְּטֵנִי, מֵרִיבֵי-עָם: תְּשִׂימֵנִי, לְרֹאשׁ גּוֹיִם
tefalleteni merivei am tesimeni lerosh goyim
Thou hast delivered me from the contentions of the people; Thou hast made me the head of the nations;

עַם לֹא-יָדַעְתִּי יַעַבְדוּנִי
am lo-yada'ti ya'avduni
a people whom I have not known serve me.

לְשֵׁמַע אֹזֶן, יִשָּׁמְעוּ לִי; בְּנֵי-נֵכָר, יְכַחֲשׁוּ-לִי
leshema ozen yishame'u li; benei-nechar, yechachashu-li
As soon as they hear of me, they obey me; the sons of the stranger dwindle away before me.

בְּנֵי-נֵכָר יִבֹּלוּ; וְיַחְרְגוּ, מִמִּסְגְּרוֹתֵיהֶם
benei-nechar yibbolu; veyachregu, mimmisgeroteihem
The sons of the stranger fade away, and come trembling out of their close places.

חַי-יְהוָה, וּבָרוּךְ צוּרִי; וְיָרוּם, אֱלוֹהֵי יִשְׁעִי
chai-hashem uvaruch tzuri; veyarum, elohei yish'i
The LORD liveth, and blessed be my Rock; and exalted be the God of my salvation;

הָאֵל--הַנּוֹתֵן נְקָמוֹת לִי; וַיַּדְבֵּר עַמִּים תַּחְתָּי
ha'el, hannoten nekamot li; vayadber ammim tachtai
Even the God that executeth vengeance for me, and subdueth peoples under me.

מְפַלְּטִי, מֵאֹיְבָי: אַף מִן-קָמַי, תְּרוֹמְמֵנִי
mefalleti, me'oyevai af min-kamai teromemeni
He delivereth me from mine enemies; yea, Thou liftest me up above them that rise up against me;

מֵאִישׁ חָמָס, תַּצִּילֵנִי
me'ish chamas, tatzileni
Thou deliverest me from the violent man.

תְּהִלִּים

כִּי-אַתָּה, תָּאִיר נֵרִי; יְהוָה אֱלֹהַי, יַגִּיהַּ חָשְׁכִּי
ki-'attah ta'ir neri; hashem elohai, yaggiah choshki
For Thou dost light my lamp; the LORD my God doth lighten my darkness.

כִּי-בְךָ, אָרֻץ גְּדוּד; וּבֵאלֹהַי, אֲדַלֶּג-שׁוּר
ki-vecha arutz gedud; uvelohai, adalleg-shur
For by Thee I run upon a troop; and by my God do I scale a wall.

הָאֵל, תָּמִים דַּרְכּוֹ: אִמְרַת-יְהוָה צְרוּפָה; מָגֵן הוּא, לְכֹל הַחֹסִים בּוֹ
ha'el tamim darko imrat-hashem tzerufah; magen hu, lechol hachosim bo
As for God, His way is perfect; the word of the LORD is tried; He is a shield unto all them that take refuge in Him.

כִּי מִי אֱלוֹהַּ, מִבַּלְעֲדֵי יְהוָה; וּמִי צוּר, זוּלָתִי אֱלֹהֵינוּ
ki mi eloah mibbal'adei hashem umi tzur, zulati eloheinu
For who is God, save the LORD? And who is a Rock, except our God?

הָאֵל, הַמְאַזְּרֵנִי חָיִל; וַיִּתֵּן תָּמִים דַּרְכִּי
ha'el ham'azzereni chayil; vayitten tamim darki
The God that girdeth me with strength, and maketh my way straight;

מְשַׁוֶּה רַגְלַי, כָּאַיָּלוֹת; וְעַל בָּמֹתַי, יַעֲמִידֵנִי
meshavveh raglai ka'ayalot; ve'al bamotai, ya'amideni
Who maketh my feet like hinds', and setteth me upon my high places;

מְלַמֵּד יָדַי, לַמִּלְחָמָה; וְנִחֲתָה קֶשֶׁת-נְחוּשָׁה, זְרוֹעֹתָי
melammed yadai lammilchamah; venichatah keshet-nechushah, zero'otai
Who traineth my hands for war, so that mine arms do bend a bow of brass.

וַתִּתֶּן-לִי, מָגֵן יִשְׁעֶךָ: וִימִינְךָ תִסְעָדֵנִי
vattitten-li magen yish'echa viminecha tis'adeni
Thou hast also given me Thy shield of salvation, and Thy right hand hath holden me up;

וְעַנְוַתְךָ תַרְבֵּנִי
ve'anvatcha tarbeni
and Thy condescension hath made me great.

תַּרְחִיב צַעֲדִי תַחְתָּי; וְלֹא מָעֲדוּ, קַרְסֻלָּי
tarchiv tza'adi tachtai; velo ma'adu, karsullai
Thou hast enlarged my steps under me, and my feet have not slipped.

אֶרְדּוֹף אוֹיְבַי, וְאַשִּׂיגֵם; וְלֹא-אָשׁוּב, עַד-כַּלּוֹתָם
'erdof oyevai ve'assigem; velo-'ashuv ad-kallotam
I have pursued mine enemies, and overtaken them; neither did I turn back till they were consumed.

אֶמְחָצֵם, וְלֹא-יֻכְלוּ קוּם; יִפְּלוּ, תַּחַת רַגְלָי
'emchatzem velo-yuchlu kum; yippelu, tachat raglai
I have smitten them through, so that they are not able to rise; they are fallen under my feet.

תְּהִלִּים

יַצִּילֵנִי, מֵאֹיְבִי עָז; וּמִשֹּׂנְאַי, כִּי-אָמְצוּ מִמֶּנִּי
yatzileni, me'oyevi az; umissone'ai, ki-'ametzu mimmenni
He delivered me from mine enemy most strong, and from them that hated me, for they were too mighty for me.

יְקַדְּמוּנִי בְיוֹם-אֵידִי; וַיְהִי-יְהוָה לְמִשְׁעָן לִי
yekaddemuni veyom-'eidi; vayhi-hashem lemish'an li
They confronted me in the day of my calamity; but the LORD was a stay unto me.

וַיּוֹצִיאֵנִי לַמֶּרְחָב; יְחַלְּצֵנִי, כִּי חָפֵץ בִּי
vayotzi'eni lammerchav; yechalletzeni, ki chafetz bi
He brought me forth also into a large place; He delivered me, because He delighted in me.

יִגְמְלֵנִי יְהוָה כְּצִדְקִי; כְּבֹר יָדַי, יָשִׁיב לִי
yigmeleni hashem ketzidki; kevor yadai, yashiv li
The LORD rewarded me according to my righteousness; according to the cleanness of my hands hath He recompensed me.

כִּי-שָׁמַרְתִּי, דַּרְכֵי יְהוָה; וְלֹא-רָשַׁעְתִּי, מֵאֱלֹהָי
ki-shamarti darchei hashem velo-rasha'ti, me'elohai
For I have kept the ways of the LORD, and have not wickedly departed from my God.

כִּי כָל-מִשְׁפָּטָיו לְנֶגְדִּי; וְחֻקֹּתָיו, לֹא-אָסִיר מֶנִּי
ki chol-mishpatav lenegdi; vechukkotav, lo-'asir menni
For all His ordinances were before me, and I put not away His statutes from me.

וָאֱהִי תָמִים עִמּוֹ; וָאֶשְׁתַּמֵּר, מֵעֲוֹנִי
va'ehi tamim immo; va'eshtammer, me'avoni
And I was single-hearted with Him, and I kept myself from mine iniquity.

וַיָּשֶׁב-יְהוָה לִי כְצִדְקִי
vayashev-hashem li chetzidki
Therefore hath the LORD recompensed me according to my righteousness,

כְּבֹר יָדַי, לְנֶגֶד עֵינָיו
kevor yadai, leneged einav
according to the cleanness of my hands in His eyes.

עִם-חָסִיד תִּתְחַסָּד; עִם-גְּבַר תָּמִים, תִּתַּמָּם
'im-chasid titchassad; im-gevar tamim, tittammam
With the merciful Thou dost show Thyself merciful, with the upright man Thou dost show Thyself upright;

עִם-נָבָר תִּתְבָּרָר; וְעִם-עִקֵּשׁ, תִּתְפַּתָּל
'im-navar titbarar; ve'im-'ikkesh, titpattal
With the pure Thou dost show Thyself pure; and with the crooked Thou dost show Thyself subtle.

כִּי-אַתָּה, עַם-עָנִי תוֹשִׁיעַ; וְעֵינַיִם רָמוֹת תַּשְׁפִּיל
ki-'attah am-'ani toshia'; ve'einayim ramot tashpil
For Thou dost save the afflicted people; but the haughty eyes Thou dost humble.

תְּהִלִים

וַיִּתְגָּעֲשׁוּ, כִּי-חָרָה לוֹ
vayitga'ashu, ki-charah lo
they were shaken, because He was wroth.

עָלָה עָשָׁן, בְּאַפּוֹ--וְאֵשׁ-מִפִּיו תֹּאכֵל
'alah ashan be'appo, ve'esh-mippiv tochel
Smoke arose up in His nostrils, and fire out of His mouth did devour;

גֶּחָלִים, בָּעֲרוּ מִמֶּנּוּ
gechalim, ba'aru mimmennu
coals flamed forth from Him.

וַיֵּט שָׁמַיִם, וַיֵּרַד; וַעֲרָפֶל, תַּחַת רַגְלָיו
vayet shamayim vayerad; va'arafel, tachat raglav
He bowed the heavens also, and came down; and thick darkness was under His feet.

וַיִּרְכַּב עַל-כְּרוּב, וַיָּעֹף; וַיֵּדֶא, עַל-כַּנְפֵי-רוּחַ
vayirkav al-keruv vaya'of; vayede, al-kanfei-ruach
And He rode upon a cherub, and did fly; yea, He did swoop down upon the wings of the wind.

יָשֶׁת חֹשֶׁךְ, סִתְרוֹ--סְבִיבוֹתָיו סֻכָּתוֹ; חֶשְׁכַת-מַיִם, עָבֵי שְׁחָקִים
yashet choshech sitro, sevivotav sukkato; cheshchat-mayim, avei shechakim
He made darkness His hiding-place, His pavilion round about Him; darkness of waters, thick clouds of the skies.

מִנֹּגַהּ, נֶגְדּוֹ: עָבָיו עָבְרוּ--בָּרָד, וְגַחֲלֵי-אֵשׁ
minnogah, negdo avav averu; barad, vegachalei-'esh
At the brightness before Him, there passed through His thick clouds hailstones and coals of fire.

וַיַּרְעֵם בַּשָּׁמַיִם, יְהוָה--וְעֶלְיוֹן, יִתֵּן קֹלוֹ; בָּרָד, וְגַחֲלֵי-אֵשׁ
vayar'em bashamayim hashem ve'elyon yitten kolo; barad, vegachalei-'esh
The LORD also thundered in the heavens, and the Most High gave forth His voice; hailstones and coals of fire.

וַיִּשְׁלַח חִצָּיו, וַיְפִיצֵם; וּבְרָקִים רָב, וַיְהֻמֵּם
vayishlach chitzav vayfitzem; uverakim rav vayhummem
And He sent out His arrows, and scattered them; and He shot forth lightnings, and discomfited them.

וַיֵּרָאוּ, אֲפִיקֵי מַיִם
vayera'u afikei mayim
And the channels of waters appeared,

וַיִּגָּלוּ, מוֹסְדוֹת תֵּבֵל: מִגַּעֲרָתְךָ יְהוָה--מִנִּשְׁמַת, רוּחַ אַפֶּךָ
vayiggalu mosedot tevel migga'aratecha hashem minnishmat, ruach appecha
and the foundations of the world were laid bare, at Thy rebuke, O LORD, at the blast of the breath of Thy nostrils.

יִשְׁלַח מִמָּרוֹם, יִקָּחֵנִי; יַמְשֵׁנִי, מִמַּיִם רַבִּים
yishlach mimmarom yikkacheni; yamsheni, mimmayim rabbim
He sent from on high, He took me; He drew me out of many waters.

תְּהִלִּים

יח

לַמְנַצֵּחַ, לְעֶבֶד יְהוָה--לְדָוִד: אֲשֶׁר דִּבֶּר, לַיהוָה, אֶת-דִּבְרֵי, הַשִּׁירָה הַזֹּאת
Lamnatzeach le'eved hashem ledavid asher dibber lahashem et-divrei hashirah hazzot
For the Leader. [A Psalm] of David the servant of the LORD, who spoke unto the LORD the words of this song

בְּיוֹם הִצִּיל-יְהוָה אוֹתוֹ מִכַּף כָּל-אֹיְבָיו, וּמִיַּד שָׁאוּל
beyom hitzil-hashem oto mikkaf kol-'oyevav, umiyad sha'ul
in the day that the LORD delivered him from the hand of all his enemies, and from the hand of Saul;

וַיֹּאמַר--אֶרְחָמְךָ יְהוָה חִזְקִי
vayomar erchamcha hashem chizki
And he said: I love thee, O LORD, my strength.

יְהוָה, סַלְעִי וּמְצוּדָתִי--וּמְפַלְטִי: אֵלִי צוּרִי
hashem sal'i umetzudati, umefalti eli tzuri
The LORD is my rock, and my fortress, and my deliverer; my God, my rock,

אֶחֱסֶה-בּוֹ; מָגִנִּי וְקֶרֶן-יִשְׁעִי, מִשְׂגַּבִּי
echeseh-bo; maginni vekeren-yish'i, misgabbi
in Him I take refuge; my shield, and my horn of salvation, my high tower.

מְהֻלָּל, אֶקְרָא יְהוָה; וּמִן-אֹיְבַי, אִוָּשֵׁעַ
mehullol ekra hashem umin-'oyevai, ivvashea
Praised, I cry, is the LORD, and I am saved from mine enemies.

אֲפָפוּנִי חֶבְלֵי-מָוֶת; וְנַחֲלֵי בְלִיַּעַל יְבַעֲתוּנִי
'afafuni chevlei-mavet; venachalei veliya'al yeva'atuni
The cords of Death compassed me, and the floods of Belial assailed me.

חֶבְלֵי שְׁאוֹל סְבָבוּנִי; קִדְּמוּנִי, מוֹקְשֵׁי מָוֶת
chevlei she'ol sevavuni; kiddemuni, mokeshei mavet
The cords of Sheol surrounded me; the snares of Death confronted me.

בַּצַּר-לִי, אֶקְרָא יְהוָה--וְאֶל-אֱלֹהַי אֲשַׁוֵּעַ
batzar-li ekra hashem ve'el-'elohai ashavvea
In my distress I called upon the LORD, and cried unto my God;

יִשְׁמַע מֵהֵיכָלוֹ קוֹלִי; וְשַׁוְעָתִי, לְפָנָיו תָּבוֹא בְאָזְנָיו
yishma meheichalo koli; veshav'ati, lefanav tavo ve'ozenav
out of His temple He heard my voice, and my cry came before Him unto His ears.

וַתִּגְעַשׁ וַתִּרְעַשׁ, הָאָרֶץ--וּמוֹסְדֵי הָרִים יִרְגָּזוּ
vattig'ash vattir'ash ha'aretz, umosedei harim yirgazu
Then the earth did shake and quake, the foundations also of the mountains did tremble;

תְּהִלִּים

תָּמֹךְ אֲשֻׁרַי, בְּמַעְגְּלוֹתֶיךָ; בַּל-נָמוֹטּוּ פְעָמָי
tamoch ashurai bema'geloteicha; bal-namottu fe'amai
My steps have held fast to Thy paths, my feet have not slipped.

אֲנִי-קְרָאתִיךָ כִי-תַעֲנֵנִי אֵל; הַט-אָזְנְךָ לִי, שְׁמַע אִמְרָתִי
'ani-keraticha chi-ta'aneni el; hat-'ozenecha li, shema imrati
As for me, I call upon Thee, for Thou wilt answer me, O God; incline Thine ear unto me, hear my speech.

הַפְלֵה חֲסָדֶיךָ, מוֹשִׁיעַ חוֹסִים--מִמִּתְקוֹמְמִים, בִּימִינֶךָ
hafleh chasadeicha moshia chosim; mimmitkomemim, biyminecha
Make passing great Thy mercies, O Thou that savest by Thy right hand from assailants them that take refuge in Thee.

שָׁמְרֵנִי, כְּאִישׁוֹן בַּת-עָיִן; בְּצֵל כְּנָפֶיךָ, תַּסְתִּירֵנִי
shamereni ke'ishon bat-'ayin; betzel kenafeicha, tastireni
Keep me as the apple of the eye, hide me in the shadow of Thy wings,

מִפְּנֵי רְשָׁעִים, זוּ שַׁדּוּנִי; אֹיְבַי בְּנֶפֶשׁ, יַקִּיפוּ עָלָי
mippenei resha'im zu shadduni; oyevai benefesh, yakkifu alai
From the wicked that oppress, my deadly enemies, that compass me about.

חֶלְבָּמוֹ סָגְרוּ; פִּימוֹ, דִּבְּרוּ בְגֵאוּת
chelbamo sageru; pimo, dibberu vege'ut
Their gross heart they have shut tight, with their mouth they speak proudly.

אַשֻּׁרֵינוּ, עַתָּה סְבָבוּנוּ; עֵינֵיהֶם יָשִׁיתוּ, לִנְטוֹת בָּאָרֶץ
'ashureinu attah sevavunu; eineihem yashitu, lintot ba'aretz
At our every step they have now encompassed us; they set their eyes to cast us down to the earth.

דִּמְיֹנוֹ--כְּאַרְיֵה, יִכְסוֹף לִטְרוֹף; וְכִכְפִיר, יֹשֵׁב בְּמִסְתָּרִים
dimyono, ke'aryeh yichsof litrof; vechichfir, yoshev bemistarim
He is like a lion that is eager to tear in pieces, and like a young lion lurking in secret places.

קוּמָה יְהוָה--קַדְּמָה פָנָיו, הַכְרִיעֵהוּ; פַּלְּטָה נַפְשִׁי, מֵרָשָׁע חַרְבֶּךָ
kumah hashem kaddemah fanav hachri'ehu; palletah nafshi, merasha charbecha
Arise, O LORD, confront him, cast him down; deliver my soul from the wicked, by Thy sword;

מִמְתִים יָדְךָ יְהוָה, מִמְתִים מֵחֶלֶד--חֶלְקָם בַּחַיִּים
mimetim yadecha hashem mimetim mecheled, chelkam bachayim
From men, by Thy hand, O LORD, from men of the world, whose portion is in this life,

וּצְפוּנְךָ תְּמַלֵּא בִטְנָם: יִשְׂבְּעוּ בָנִים--וְהִנִּיחוּ יִתְרָם, לְעוֹלְלֵיהֶם
utzefunecha temallei vitnam yisbe'u vanim; vehinnichu yitram, le'oleleihem
and whose belly Thou fillest with Thy treasure; who have children in plenty, and leave their abundance to their babes.

אֲנִי--בְּצֶדֶק, אֶחֱזֶה פָנֶיךָ; אֶשְׂבְּעָה בְהָקִיץ, תְּמוּנָתֶךָ
'ani, betzedek echezeh faneicha; esbe'ah vehakitz, temunatecha
As for me, I shall behold Thy face in righteousness; I shall be satisfied, when I awake, with Thy likeness.

תְּהִלִים

שִׁוִּיתִי יְהוָה לְנֶגְדִּי תָמִיד: כִּי מִימִינִי, בַּל-אֶמּוֹט
shivviti hashem lenegdi tamid; ki miymini, bal-'emmot
I have set the LORD always before me; surely He is at my right hand, I shall not be moved.

לָכֵן, שָׂמַח לִבִּי--וַיָּגֶל כְּבוֹדִי; אַף-בְּשָׂרִי, יִשְׁכֹּן לָבֶטַח
lachen samach libbi vayagel kevodi; af-besari, yishkon lavetach
Therefore my heart is glad, and my glory rejoiceth; my flesh also dwelleth in safety;

כִּי, לֹא-תַעֲזֹב נַפְשִׁי לִשְׁאוֹל
ki lo-ta'azov nafshi lish'ol
For Thou wilt not abandon my soul to the nether-world;

לֹא-תִתֵּן חֲסִידְךָ, לִרְאוֹת שָׁחַת
lo-titten chasidecha, lir'ot shachat
neither wilt Thou suffer Thy godly one to see the pit.

תּוֹדִיעֵנִי, אֹרַח חַיִּים
todi'eni orach chayim
Thou makest me to know the path of life;

שֹׂבַע שְׂמָחוֹת, אֶת-פָּנֶיךָ; נְעִמוֹת בִּימִינְךָ נֶצַח
sova semachot et-paneicha; ne'imot biymincha netzach
in Thy presence is fulness of joy, in Thy right hand bliss for evermore.

יז

תְּפִלָּה, לְדָוִד: שִׁמְעָה יְהוָה, צֶדֶק--הַקְשִׁיבָה רִנָּתִי, הַאֲזִינָה תְפִלָּתִי; בְּלֹא, שִׂפְתֵי מִרְמָה
Tefillah, ledavid. Shim'ah hashem tzedek, hakshivah rinnati, ha'azinah tefillati; belo, siftei mirmah
A Prayer of David. Hear the right, O LORD, attend unto my cry; give ear unto my prayer from lips without deceit.

מִלְּפָנֶיךָ, מִשְׁפָּטִי יֵצֵא; עֵינֶיךָ, תֶּחֱזֶינָה מֵישָׁרִים
millefaneicha mishpati yetze; eineicha, techezeinah meisharim
Let my judgment come forth from Thy presence; let Thine eyes behold equity.

בָּחַנְתָּ לִבִּי, פָּקַדְתָּ לַּיְלָה
bachanta libbi pakadta laylah
Thou hast tried my heart, Thou hast visited it in the night;

צְרַפְתַּנִי בַל-תִּמְצָא; זַמֹּתִי, בַּל-יַעֲבָר-פִּי
tzeraftani val-timtza; zammoti, bal-ya'avor-pi
Thou hast tested me, and Thou findest not that I had a thought which should not pass my mouth.

לִפְעֻלּוֹת אָדָם, בִּדְבַר שְׂפָתֶיךָ--אֲנִי שָׁמַרְתִּי, אָרְחוֹת פָּרִיץ
lif'ullot adom bidvar sefateicha; ani shamarti, orechot paritz
As for the doings of men, by the word of Thy lips I have kept me from the ways of the violent.

תְּהִלִים

נִשְׁבַּע לְהָרַע, וְלֹא יָמִר
nishba lehara', velo yamir
he that sweareth to his own hurt, and changeth not;

כַּסְפּוֹ, לֹא-נָתַן בְּנֶשֶׁךְ--וְשֹׁחַד עַל-נָקִי, לֹא לָקָח
kaspo lo-natan beneshech veshochad al-naki lo lakach
He that putteth not out his money on interest, nor taketh a bribe against the innocent.

עֹשֵׂה-אֵלֶּה--לֹא יִמּוֹט לְעוֹלָם
oseh-'elleh; lo yimmot le'olam
He that doeth these things shall never be moved.

טז

מִכְתָּם לְדָוִד: שָׁמְרֵנִי אֵל, כִּי-חָסִיתִי בָךְ
Michtam ledavid; shamereni el, ki-chasiti vach
Michtam of David. Keep me, O God; for I have taken refuge in Thee.

אָמַרְתְּ לַיהוָה, אֲדֹנָי אָתָּה; טוֹבָתִי, בַּל-עָלֶיךָ
'amart lahashem adonai attah; tovati, bal-'aleicha
I have said unto the LORD: 'Thou art my Lord; I have no good but in Thee';

לִקְדוֹשִׁים, אֲשֶׁר-בָּאָרֶץ הֵמָּה; וְאַדִּירֵי, כָּל-חֶפְצִי-בָם
likdoshim asher-ba'aretz hemmah; ve'addirei, kol-cheftzi-vam
As for the holy that are in the earth, they are the excellent in whom is all my delight.

יִרְבּוּ עַצְּבוֹתָם, אַחֵר מָהָרוּ
yirbu atzevotam acher maharu
Let the idols of them be multiplied that make suit unto another;

בַּל-אַסִּיךְ נִסְכֵּיהֶם מִדָּם; וּבַל-אֶשָּׂא אֶת-שְׁמוֹתָם, עַל-שְׂפָתָי
bal-'assich niskeihem middam; uval-'essa et-shemotam, al-sefatai
their drink-offerings of blood will I not offer, nor take their names upon my lips.

יְהוָה, מְנָת-חֶלְקִי וְכוֹסִי--אַתָּה, תּוֹמִיךְ גּוֹרָלִי
hashem menat-chelki vechosi; attah, tomich gorali
O LORD, the portion of mine inheritance and of my cup, Thou maintainest my lot.

חֲבָלִים נָפְלוּ-לִי, בַּנְּעִמִים; אַף-נַחֲלָת, שָׁפְרָה עָלָי
chavalim nafelu-li banne'imim; af-nachalat, shaferah alai
The lines are fallen unto me in pleasant places; yea, I have a goodly heritage.

אֲבָרֵךְ--אֶת-יְהוָה, אֲשֶׁר יְעָצָנִי; אַף-לֵילוֹת, יִסְּרוּנִי כִלְיוֹתָי
'avarech, et-hashem asher ye'atzani; af-leilot, yisseruni chilyotai
I will bless the LORD, who hath given me counsel; yea, in the night seasons my reins instruct me.

תְּהִלִּים

לִרְאוֹת, הֲיֵשׁ מַשְׂכִּיל--דֹּרֵשׁ, אֶת-אֱלֹהִים
lir'ot hayesh maskil; doresh et-'elohim
to see if there were any man of understanding, that did seek after God.

הַכֹּל סָר, יַחְדָּו נֶאֱלָחוּ: אֵין עֹשֵׂה-טוֹב--אֵין, גַּם-אֶחָד
hakkol sar yachdav ne'elachu ein oseh-tov; ein, gam-'echad
They are all corrupt, they are together become impure; there is none that doeth good, no, not one.

הֲלֹא יָדְעוּ, כָּל-פֹּעֲלֵי-אָוֶן: אֹכְלֵי עַמִּי, אָכְלוּ לֶחֶם; יְהוָה, לֹא קָרָאוּ
halo yade'u kol-po'alei aven ochelei ammi achelu lechem; hashem lo kara'u
'Shall not all the workers of iniquity know it, who eat up My people as they eat bread, and call not upon the LORD?'

שָׁם, פָּחֲדוּ פָחַד: כִּי-אֱלֹהִים, בְּדוֹר צַדִּיק
sham pachadu fachad; ki-'elohim, bedor tzaddik
There are they in great fear; for God is with the righteous generation.

עֲצַת-עָנִי תָבִישׁוּ: כִּי יְהוָה מַחְסֵהוּ
'atzat-'ani tavishu; ki hashem machsehu
Ye would put to shame the counsel of the poor, but the LORD is his refuge.

מִי יִתֵּן מִצִּיּוֹן, יְשׁוּעַת יִשְׂרָאֵל: בְּשׁוּב יְהוָה, שְׁבוּת עַמּוֹ
mi yitten mitziyon yeshu'at yisra'el beshuv hashem shevut ammo
Oh that the salvation of Israel were come out of Zion! When the LORD turneth the captivity of His people,

יָגֵל יַעֲקֹב, יִשְׂמַח יִשְׂרָאֵל
yagel ya'akov, yismach yisra'el
let Jacob rejoice, let Israel be glad.

טו

מִזְמוֹר, לְדָוִד: יְהוָה, מִי-יָגוּר בְּאָהֳלֶךָ; מִי-יִשְׁכֹּן, בְּהַר קָדְשֶׁךָ
Mizmor, ledavid hashem mi-yagur be'aholecha; mi-yishkon, behar kodshecha
A Psalm of David. LORD, who shall sojourn in Thy tabernacle? Who shall dwell upon Thy holy mountain?

הוֹלֵךְ תָּמִים, וּפֹעֵל צֶדֶק; וְדֹבֵר אֱמֶת, בִּלְבָבוֹ
holech tamim ufo'el tzedek; vedover emet, bilvavo
He that walketh uprightly, and worketh righteousness, and speaketh truth in his heart;

לֹא-רָגַל, עַל-לְשֹׁנוֹ--לֹא-עָשָׂה לְרֵעֵהוּ רָעָה; וְחֶרְפָּה, לֹא-נָשָׂא עַל-קְרֹבוֹ
lo-ragal al-leshono, lo-'asah lere'ehu ra'ah; vecherpah, lo-nasa al-kerovo
That hath no slander upon his tongue, nor doeth evil to his fellow, nor taketh up a reproach against his neighbour;

נִבְזֶה, בְּעֵינָיו נִמְאָס--וְאֶת-יִרְאֵי יְהוָה יְכַבֵּד
nivzeh be'einav nim'as, ve'et-yir'ei hashem yechabbed
In whose eyes a vile person is despised, but he honoureth them that fear the LORD;

תְּהִלִּים

יג

לַמְנַצֵּחַ, מִזְמוֹר לְדָוִד
Lamnatzeach, mizmor ledavid
For the Leader. A Psalm of David.

עַד-אָנָה יְהוָה, תִּשְׁכָּחֵנִי נֶצַח; עַד-אָנָה, תַּסְתִּיר אֶת-פָּנֶיךָ מִמֶּנִּי
'ad-'anah hashem tishkacheni netzach; ad-'anah tastir et-paneicha mimmenni
How long, O LORD, wilt Thou forget me for ever? How long wilt Thou hide Thy face from me?

עַד-אָנָה אָשִׁית עֵצוֹת, בְּנַפְשִׁי--יָגוֹן בִּלְבָבִי יוֹמָם
'ad-'anah ashit etzot benafshi, yagon bilvavi yomam
How long shall I take counsel in my soul, having sorrow in my heart by day?

עַד-אָנָה, יָרוּם אֹיְבִי עָלָי
ad-'anah yarum oyevi alai
How long shall mine enemy be exalted over me?

הַבִּיטָה עֲנֵנִי, יְהוָה אֱלֹהָי; הָאִירָה עֵינַי, פֶּן-אִישַׁן הַמָּוֶת
habbitah aneni hashem elohai; ha'irah einai, pen-'ishan hammavet
Behold Thou, and answer me, O LORD my God; lighten mine eyes, lest I sleep the sleep of death;

פֶּן-יֹאמַר אֹיְבִי יְכָלְתִּיו; צָרַי יָגִילוּ, כִּי אֶמּוֹט
pen-yomar oyevi yechaletiv; tzarai yagilu, ki emmot
Lest mine enemy say: 'I have prevailed against him'; lest mine adversaries rejoice when I am moved.

וַאֲנִי, בְּחַסְדְּךָ בָטַחְתִּי--יָגֵל לִבִּי, בִּישׁוּעָתֶךָ
va'ani bechasdecha vatachti yagel libbi, biyshu'atecha
But as for me, in Thy mercy do I trust; my heart shall rejoice in Thy salvation.

אָשִׁירָה לַיהוָה, כִּי גָמַל עָלָי
ashirah lahashem ki gamal alai
I will sing unto the LORD, because He hath dealt bountifully with me.

יד

לַמְנַצֵּחַ, לְדָוִד: אָמַר נָבָל בְּלִבּוֹ, אֵין אֱלֹהִים
Lamnatzeach, ledavid amar naval belibbo ein elohim
For the Leader. [A Psalm] of David. The fool hath said in his heart: 'There is no God';

הִשְׁחִיתוּ, הִתְעִיבוּ עֲלִילָה--אֵין עֹשֵׂה-טוֹב
hishchitu, hit'ivu alilah, ein oseh-tov
they have dealt corruptly, they have done abominably; there is none that doeth good.

יְהוָה--מִשָּׁמַיִם, הִשְׁקִיף עַל-בְּנֵי-אָדָם
hashem mishamayim hishkif al-benei-'adam
The LORD looked forth from heaven upon the children of men,

תְּהִלִּים

כִּי-צַדִּיק יְהוָה, צְדָקוֹת אָהֵב; יָשָׁר, יֶחֱזוּ פָנֵימוֹ
ki-tzaddik hashem tzedakot ahev; yashar, yechezu faneimo
For the LORD is righteous, He loveth righteousness; the upright shall behold His face.

יב

לַמְנַצֵּחַ עַל-הַשְּׁמִינִית, מִזְמוֹר לְדָוִד
Lamnatzeach al-hasheminit, mizmor ledavid
For the Leader; on the Sheminith. A Psalm of David.

הוֹשִׁיעָה יְהוָה, כִּי-גָמַר חָסִיד: כִּי-פַסּוּ אֱמוּנִים, מִבְּנֵי אָדָם
hoshi'ah hashem ki-gamar chasid; ki-fassu emunim, mibbenei adam
Help, LORD; for the godly man ceaseth; for the faithful fail from among the children of men.

שָׁוְא, יְדַבְּרוּ--אִישׁ אֶת-רֵעֵהוּ: שְׂפַת חֲלָקוֹת--בְּלֵב וָלֵב יְדַבֵּרוּ
shav yedabberu ish et-re'ehu sefat chalakot; belev valev yedabberu
They speak falsehood every one with his neighbour; with flattering lip, and with a double heart, do they speak.

יַכְרֵת יְהוָה, כָּל-שִׂפְתֵי חֲלָקוֹת--לָשׁוֹן, מְדַבֶּרֶת גְּדֹלוֹת
yachret hashem kol-siftei chalakot; lashon, medabberet gedolot
May the LORD cut off all flattering lips, the tongue that speaketh proud things!

אֲשֶׁר אָמְרוּ, לִלְשֹׁנֵנוּ נַגְבִּיר--שְׂפָתֵינוּ אִתָּנוּ: מִי אָדוֹן לָנוּ
'asher ameru lilshonenu nagbir sefateinu ittanu; mi adon lanu
Who have said: 'Our tongue will we make mighty; our lips are with us: who is lord over us?'

מִשֹּׁד עֲנִיִּים, מֵאֶנְקַת אֶבְיוֹנִים: עַתָּה אָקוּם, יֹאמַר יְהוָה
mishod aniyim me'enkat evyonim attah akum yomar hashem
'For the oppression of the poor, for the sighing of the needy, now will I arise', saith the LORD;

אָשִׁית בְּיֵשַׁע, יָפִיחַ לוֹ
ashit beyesha', yafiach lo
'I will set him in safety at whom they puff.'

אִמְרוֹת יְהוָה, אֲמָרוֹת טְהֹרוֹת: כֶּסֶף צָרוּף, בַּעֲלִיל לָאָרֶץ; מְזֻקָּק, שִׁבְעָתָיִם
'imarot hashem amarot tehorot kesef tzaruf ba'alil la'aretz; mezukkak, shiv'atayim
The words of the LORD are pure words, as silver tried in a crucible on the earth, refined seven times.

אַתָּה-יְהוָה תִּשְׁמְרֵם; תִּצְּרֶנּוּ, מִן-הַדּוֹר זוּ לְעוֹלָם
'attah-hashem tishmerem; titzerennu min-haddor zu le'olam
Thou wilt keep them, O LORD; Thou wilt preserve us from this generation for ever.

סָבִיב, רְשָׁעִים יִתְהַלָּכוּן; כְּרֻם זֻלּוּת, לִבְנֵי אָדָם
saviv, resha'im yit'hallachun; kerum zullut, livnei adam
The wicked walk on every side, when vileness is exalted among the sons of men.

תְּהִלִּים

תַּאֲוַת עֲנָוִים שָׁמַעְתָּ יְהוָה; תָּכִין לִבָּם, תַּקְשִׁיב אָזְנֶךָ
ta'avat anavim shama'ta hashem tachin libbam, takshiv azenecha
LORD, Thou hast heard the desire of the humble: Thou wilt direct their heart, Thou wilt cause Thine ear to attend;

לִשְׁפֹּט יָתוֹם, וָדָךְ: בַּל-יוֹסִיף עוֹד--לַעֲרֹץ אֱנוֹשׁ, מִן-הָאָרֶץ
lishpot yatom, vadach bal-yosif od; la'arotz enosh, min-ha'aretz
To right the fatherless and the oppressed, that man who is of the earth may be terrible no more.

יא

לַמְנַצֵּחַ, לְדָוִד: בַּיהוָה, חָסִיתִי
Lamnatzeach, ledavid bahashem chasiti
For the Leader. [A Psalm] of David. In the LORD have I taken refuge;

אֵיךְ, תֹּאמְרוּ לְנַפְשִׁי; נוּדִי, הַרְכֶם צִפּוֹר
eich tomeru lenafshi; nudi, harchem tzippor
how say ye to my soul: 'Flee thou! to your mountain, ye birds'?

כִּי הִנֵּה הָרְשָׁעִים, יִדְרְכוּן קֶשֶׁת, כּוֹנְנוּ חִצָּם עַל-יֶתֶר
ki hinneh haresha'im yidrechun keshet, konenu chitzam al-yeter
For, lo, the wicked bend the bow, they have made ready their arrow upon the string,

לִירוֹת בְּמוֹ-אֹפֶל, לְיִשְׁרֵי-לֵב
lirot bemo-'ofel, leyishrei-lev
that they may shoot in darkness at the upright in heart.

כִּי הַשָּׁתוֹת, יֵהָרֵסוּן--צַדִּיק, מַה-פָּעָל
ki hashatot yeharesun; tzaddik, mah-pa'al
When the foundations are destroyed, what hath the righteous wrought?

יְהוָה, בְּהֵיכַל קָדְשׁוֹ--יְהוָה, בַּשָּׁמַיִם כִּסְאוֹ
hashem beheichal kodsho hashem bashamayim kis'o
The LORD is in His holy temple, the LORD, His throne is in heaven;

עֵינָיו יֶחֱזוּ--עַפְעַפָּיו יִבְחֲנוּ, בְּנֵי אָדָם
einav yechezu; af'appav yivchanu, benei adam
His eyes behold, His eyelids try, the children of men.

יְהוָה, צַדִּיק יִבְחָן: וְרָשָׁע, וְאֹהֵב חָמָס--שָׂנְאָה נַפְשׁוֹ
hashem tzaddik yivchan verasha ve'ohev chamas; sane'ah nafsho
The LORD trieth the righteous; but the wicked and him that loveth violence His soul hateth.

יַמְטֵר עַל-רְשָׁעִים, פַּחִים: אֵשׁ וְגָפְרִית, וְרוּחַ זִלְעָפוֹת--מְנָת כּוֹסָם
yamter al-resha'im, pachim esh vegoferit veruach zil'afot, menat kosam
Upon the wicked He will cause to rain coals; fire and brimstone and burning wind shall be the portion of their cup.

תְּהִלִּים

יֵשֵׁב, בְּמַאְרַב חֲצֵרִים--בַּמִּסְתָּרִים, יַהֲרֹג נָקִי
yeshev bema'rav chatzerim, bammistarim yaharog naki;
He sitteth in the lurking-places of the villages; in secret places doth he slay the innocent;

עֵינָיו, לְחֵלְכָה יִצְפֹּנוּ
einav, lechelechah yitzponu
his eyes are on the watch for the helpless.

יֶאֱרֹב בַּמִּסְתָּר, כְּאַרְיֵה בְסֻכֹּה
ye'erov bammistar ke'aryeh vesukkoh
He lieth in wait in a secret place as a lion in his lair,

יֶאֱרֹב, לַחֲטוֹף עָנִי; יַחְטֹף עָנִי, בְּמָשְׁכוֹ בְרִשְׁתּוֹ
ye'erov lachatof ani; yachtof ani, bemashecho verishto
he lieth in wait to catch the poor; he doth catch the poor, when he draweth him up in his net.

יִדְכֶּה יָשֹׁחַ; וְנָפַל בַּעֲצוּמָיו, חֵל כָּאִים
yidkeh yashoach; venafal ba'atzumav, cheil ka'im
He croucheth, he boweth down, and the helpless fall into his mighty claws.

אָמַר בְּלִבּוֹ, שָׁכַח אֵל; הִסְתִּיר פָּנָיו, בַּל-רָאָה לָנֶצַח
'amar belibbo shachach el; histir panav, bal-ra'ah lanetzach
He hath said in his heart: 'God hath forgotten; He hideth His face; He will never see.'

קוּמָה יְהוָה--אֵל, נְשָׂא יָדֶךָ; אַל-תִּשְׁכַּח עֲנָוִים
kumah hashem el nesa yadecha; al-tishkach anavim
Arise, O LORD; O God, lift up Thy hand; forget not the humble.

עַל-מֶה, נִאֵץ רָשָׁע אֱלֹהִים; אָמַר בְּלִבּוֹ, לֹא תִדְרֹשׁ
'al-meh ni'etz rasha elohim; amar belibbo, lo tidrosh
Wherefore doth the wicked contemn God, and say in his heart: 'Thou wilt not require'?

רָאִתָה, כִּי-אַתָּה עָמָל וָכַעַס תַּבִּיט
ra'itah ki-'attah amal vacha'as tabbit
Thou hast seen; for Thou beholdest trouble and vexation,

לָתֵת בְּיָדֶךָ: עָלֶיךָ, יַעֲזֹב חֵלֵכָה; יָתוֹם, אַתָּה הָיִיתָ עוֹזֵר
latet beyadecha aleicha ya'azov chelechah; yatom, attah hayita ozer
to requite them with Thy hand; unto Thee the helpless committeth himself; Thou hast been the helper of the fatherless.

שְׁבֹר, זְרוֹעַ רָשָׁע; וָרָע, תִּדְרוֹשׁ-רִשְׁעוֹ בַל-תִּמְצָא
shevor zeroa rasha'; vara', tidrosh-rish'o val-timtza
Break Thou the arm of the wicked; and as for the evil man, search out his wickedness, till none be found.

יְהוָה מֶלֶךְ, עוֹלָם וָעֶד; אָבְדוּ גוֹיִם, מֵאַרְצוֹ
hashem melech olam va'ed; avedu goyim, me'artzo
The LORD is King for ever and ever; the nations are perished out of His land.

תְּהִלִּים

יָשׁוּבוּ רְשָׁעִים לִשְׁאוֹלָה: כָּל-גּוֹיִם, שְׁכֵחֵי אֱלֹהִים
yashuvu resha'im lish'olah; kol-goyim, shechechei elohim
The wicked shall return to the nether-world, even all the nations that forget God.

כִּי לֹא לָנֶצַח, יִשָּׁכַח אֶבְיוֹן; תִּקְוַת עֲנִיִּים, תֹּאבַד לָעַד
ki lo lanetzach yishachach evyon; tikvat aniyim, tovad la'ad
For the needy shall not alway be forgotten, nor the expectation of the poor perish for ever.

קוּמָה יְהוָה, אַל-יָעֹז אֱנוֹשׁ; יִשָּׁפְטוּ גוֹיִם, עַל-פָּנֶיךָ
kumah hashem al-ya'oz enosh; yishafetu goyim, al-paneicha
Arise, O LORD, let not man prevail; let the nations be judged in Thy sight.

שִׁיתָה יְהוָה, מוֹרָה--לָהֶם: יֵדְעוּ גוֹיִם--אֱנוֹשׁ הֵמָּה סֶּלָה
shitah hashem morah, lahem yede'u goyim; enosh hemmah selah
Set terror over them, O LORD; let the nations know they are but men. Selah

▮

לָמָה יְהוָה, תַּעֲמֹד בְּרָחוֹק; תַּעְלִים, לְעִתּוֹת בַּצָּרָה
Lamah hashem ta'amod berachok; ta'lim, le'ittot batzarah
Why standest Thou afar off, O LORD? Why hidest Thou Thyself in times of trouble?

בְּגַאֲוַת רָשָׁע, יִדְלַק עָנִי; יִתָּפְשׂוּ, בִּמְזִמּוֹת זוּ חָשָׁבוּ
bega'avat rasho yidlak ani; yittafesu bimzimmot zu chashavu
Through the pride of the wicked the poor is hotly pursued, they are taken in the devices that they have imagined.

כִּי-הִלֵּל רָשָׁע, עַל-תַּאֲוַת נַפְשׁוֹ; וּבֹצֵעַ בֵּרֵךְ, נִאֵץ יְהוָה
ki-hillel rasho al-ta'avat nafsho; uvotzea berech, ni'etz hashem
For the wicked boasteth of his heart's desire, and the covetous vaunteth himself, though he contemn the LORD.

רָשָׁע--כְּגֹבַהּ אַפּוֹ, בַּל-יִדְרֹשׁ; אֵין אֱלֹהִים, כָּל-מְזִמּוֹתָיו
rasha', kegovah appo bal-yidrosh; ein elohim, kol-mezimmotav
The wicked, in the pride of his countenance, [saith]: 'He will not require'; all his thoughts are: 'There is no God.'

יָחִילוּ דְרָכָיו, בְּכָל-עֵת--מָרוֹם מִשְׁפָּטֶיךָ, מִנֶּגְדּוֹ; כָּל-צוֹרְרָיו, יָפִיחַ בָּהֶם
yachilu derachav derachav bechol-'et, marom mishpateicha minnegdo; kol-tzoreav, yafiach bahem
His ways prosper at all times; Thy judgments are far above out of his sight; as for all his adversaries, he puffeth at them.

אָמַר בְּלִבּוֹ, בַּל-אֶמּוֹט; לְדֹר וָדֹר, אֲשֶׁר לֹא-בְרָע
'amar belibbo bal-'emmot; ledor vador, asher lo-vera
He saith in his heart: 'I shall not be moved, I who to all generations shall not be in adversity.'

אָלָה, פִּיהוּ מָלֵא--וּמִרְמוֹת וָתֹךְ; תַּחַת לְשׁוֹנוֹ, עָמָל וָאָוֶן
'alah pihu malei umirmot vatoch; tachat leshono, amal va'aven
His mouth is full of cursing and deceit and oppression; under his tongue is mischief and iniquity.

תְּהִלִּים

וַיהוָה, לְעוֹלָם יֵשֵׁב; כּוֹנֵן לַמִּשְׁפָּט כִּסְאוֹ
vahashem le'olam yeshev; konen lammishpat kis'o
But the LORD is enthroned for ever; He hath established His throne for judgment.

וְהוּא, יִשְׁפֹּט-תֵּבֵל בְּצֶדֶק; יָדִין לְאֻמִּים, בְּמֵישָׁרִים
vehu, yishpot-tevel betzedek; yadin le'ummim, bemeisharim
And He will judge the world in righteousness, He will minister judgment to the peoples with equity.

וִיהִי יְהוָה מִשְׂגָּב לַדָּךְ; מִשְׂגָּב, לְעִתּוֹת בַּצָּרָה
vihi hashem misgav laddach; misgav, le'ittot batzarah
The LORD also will be a high tower for the oppressed, a high tower in times of trouble;

וְיִבְטְחוּ בְךָ, יוֹדְעֵי שְׁמֶךָ: כִּי לֹא-עָזַבְתָּ דֹרְשֶׁיךָ יְהוָה
veyivtechu vecha yode'ei shemecha; ki lo-'azavta doresheicha hashem
And they that know Thy name will put their trust in Thee; for Thou, LORD, hast not forsaken them that seek Thee.

זַמְּרוּ--לַיהוָה, יֹשֵׁב צִיּוֹן; הַגִּידוּ בָעַמִּים, עֲלִילוֹתָיו
zammeru, lahashem yoshev tziyon; haggidu va'ammim, alilotav
Sing praises to the LORD, who dwelleth in Zion; declare among the peoples His doings.

כִּי-דֹרֵשׁ דָּמִים, אוֹתָם זָכָר; לֹא-שָׁכַח, צַעֲקַת עֲנָוִים
ki-doresh damim otam zachar; lo-shachach, tza'akat anavim
For He that avengeth blood hath remembered them; He hath not forgotten the cry of the humble.

חָנְנֵנִי יְהוָה--רְאֵה עָנְיִי, מִשֹּׂנְאָי
chaneneni hashem re'eh aneyi missone'ai
Be gracious unto me, O LORD, behold mine affliction at the hands of them that hate me;

מְרוֹמְמִי, מִשַּׁעֲרֵי מָוֶת
meromemi, misha'arei mavet
Thou that liftest me up from the gates of death;

לְמַעַן אֲסַפְּרָה, כָּל-תְּהִלָּתֶיךָ: בְּשַׁעֲרֵי בַת-צִיּוֹן--אָגִילָה, בִּישׁוּעָתֶךָ
lema'an asapperah, kol-tehillateicha besha'arei vat-tziyon; agilah, bishu'atecha
That I may tell of all Thy praise in the gates of the daughter of Zion, that I may rejoice in Thy salvation.

טָבְעוּ גוֹיִם, בְּשַׁחַת עָשׂוּ; בְּרֶשֶׁת-זוּ טָמָנוּ, נִלְכְּדָה רַגְלָם
tave'u goyim beshachat asu; bereshet-zu tamanu, nilkedah raglam
The nations are sunk down in the pit that they made; in the net which they hid is their own foot taken.

נוֹדַע, יְהוָה--מִשְׁפָּט עָשָׂה
noda hashem mishpat asah
The LORD hath made Himself known, He hath executed judgment,

בְּפֹעַל כַּפָּיו, נוֹקֵשׁ רָשָׁע; הִגָּיוֹן סֶלָה
befo'al kappav nokesh rasha'; higgayon selah
the wicked is snared in the work of his own hands. Higgaion. Selah

תְּהִלִים

צֹנֶה וַאֲלָפִים כֻּלָּם; וְגַם, בַּהֲמוֹת שָׂדָי
tzoneh va'alafim kullam; vegam, bahamot sadai
Sheep and oxen, all of them, yea, and the beasts of the field;

צִפּוֹר שָׁמַיִם, וּדְגֵי הַיָּם; עֹבֵר, אָרְחוֹת יַמִּים
tzippor shamayim udegei hayam; over, orechot yammim
The fowl of the air, and the fish of the sea; whatsoever passeth through the paths of the seas.

יְהוָה אֲדֹנֵינוּ: מָה-אַדִּיר שִׁמְךָ, בְּכָל-הָאָרֶץ
hashem adoneinu; mah-'addir shimcha, bechol-ha'aretz
O LORD, our Lord, how glorious is Thy name in all the earth!

ט

לַמְנַצֵּחַ, עַל-מוּת לַבֵּן; מִזְמוֹר לְדָוִד
Lamnatzeach almut labben, mizmor ledavid
For the Leader; upon Muthlabben. A Psalm of David.

אוֹדֶה יְהוָה, בְּכָל-לִבִּי; אֲסַפְּרָה, כָּל-נִפְלְאוֹתֶיךָ
'odeh hashem bechol-libbi; asapperah, kol-nifle'oteicha
I will give thanks unto the LORD with my whole heart; I will tell of all Thy marvellous works.

אֶשְׂמְחָה וְאֶעֶלְצָה בָךְ; אֲזַמְּרָה שִׁמְךָ עֶלְיוֹן
'esmechah ve'e'eltzah vach; azammerah shimcha elyon
I will be glad and exult in Thee; I will sing praise to Thy name, O Most High:

בְּשׁוּב-אוֹיְבַי אָחוֹר; יִכָּשְׁלוּ וְיֹאבְדוּ, מִפָּנֶיךָ
beshuv-'oyevai achor; yikkashelu veyovedu, mippaneicha
When mine enemies are turned back, they stumble and perish at Thy presence;

כִּי-עָשִׂיתָ, מִשְׁפָּטִי וְדִינִי; יָשַׁבְתָּ לְכִסֵּא, שׁוֹפֵט צֶדֶק
ki-'asita mishpati vedini; yashavta lechisse, shofet tzedek
For Thou hast maintained my right and my cause; Thou sattest upon the throne as the righteous Judge.

גָּעַרְתָּ גוֹיִם, אִבַּדְתָּ רָשָׁע; שְׁמָם מָחִיתָ, לְעוֹלָם וָעֶד
ga'arta goyim ibbadta rasha'; shemam machita, le'olam va'ed
Thou hast rebuked the nations, Thou hast destroyed the wicked, Thou hast blotted out their name for ever and ever.

הָאוֹיֵב, תַּמּוּ חֳרָבוֹת--לָנֶצַח
ha'oyev tammu choravot, lanetzach
O thou enemy, the waste places are come to an end for ever;

וְעָרִים נָתַשְׁתָּ--אָבַד זִכְרָם הֵמָּה
ve'arim natashta; avad zichram hemmah
and the cities which thou didst uproot, their very memorial is perished.

תְּהִלִּים

בּוֹר כָּרָה, וַיַּחְפְּרֵהוּ; וַיִּפֹּל, בְּשַׁחַת יִפְעָל
bor karah vayachperehu; vayippol, beshachat yif'al
He hath digged a pit, and hollowed it, and is fallen into the ditch which he made.

יָשׁוּב עֲמָלוֹ בְרֹאשׁוֹ; וְעַל קָדְקֳדוֹ, חֲמָסוֹ יֵרֵד
yashuv amalo verosho; ve'al kadekodo, chamaso yered
His mischief shall return upon his own head, and his violence shall come down upon his own pate.

אוֹדֶה יְהוָה כְּצִדְקוֹ; וַאֲזַמְּרָה, שֵׁם-יְהוָה עֶלְיוֹן
'odeh hashem ketzidko; va'azammerah, shem-hashem elyon
I will give thanks unto the LORD according to His righteousness; and will sing praise to the name of the LORD Most High.

ח

לַמְנַצֵּחַ עַל-הַגִּתִּית, מִזְמוֹר לְדָוִד
Lamnatzeach al-haggittit, mizmor ledavid
For the Leader; upon the Gittith. A Psalm of David.

יְהוָה אֲדֹנֵינוּ--מָה-אַדִּיר שִׁמְךָ, בְּכָל-הָאָרֶץ; אֲשֶׁר תְּנָה הוֹדְךָ, עַל-הַשָּׁמָיִם
hashem adoneinu, mah-'addir shimcha bechol-ha'aretz; asher tenah hodecha, al-hashamayim
O LORD, our Lord, how glorious is Thy name in all the earth! whose majesty is rehearsed above the heavens.

מִפִּי עוֹלְלִים, וְיֹנְקִים--יִסַּדְתָּ-עֹז
mippi olelim veyonekim yissadta oz
Out of the mouth of babes and sucklings hast Thou founded strength,

לְמַעַן צוֹרְרֶיךָ; לְהַשְׁבִּית אוֹיֵב, וּמִתְנַקֵּם.
lema'an tzorereicha; lehashbit oyev, umitnakkem
because of Thine adversaries; that Thou mightest still the enemy and the avenger.

כִּי-אֶרְאֶה שָׁמֶיךָ, מַעֲשֵׂה אֶצְבְּעֹתֶיךָ--יָרֵחַ וְכוֹכָבִים, אֲשֶׁר כּוֹנָנְתָּה
ki-'er'eh shameicha ma'asei etzbe'oteicha; yareach vechochavim, asher konanetah
When I behold Thy heavens, the work of Thy fingers, the moon and the stars, which Thou hast established;

מָה-אֱנוֹשׁ כִּי-תִזְכְּרֶנּוּ; וּבֶן-אָדָם, כִּי תִפְקְדֶנּוּ
mah-'enosh ki-tizkerennu; uven-'adam, ki tifkedennu
What is man, that Thou art mindful of him? and the son of man, that Thou thinkest of him?

וַתְּחַסְּרֵהוּ מְּעַט, מֵאֱלֹהִים; וְכָבוֹד וְהָדָר תְּעַטְּרֵהוּ
vattechasserehu me'at me'elohim; vechavod vehadar te'atterehu
Yet Thou hast made him but little lower than the angels, and hast crowned him with glory and honour.

תַּמְשִׁילֵהוּ, בְּמַעֲשֵׂי יָדֶיךָ; כֹּל, שַׁתָּה תַחַת-רַגְלָיו
tamshilehu bema'asei yadeicha; kol shattah tachat-raglav
Thou hast made him to have dominion over the works of Thy hands; Thou hast put all things under his feet:

תְּהִלִּים

קוּמָה יְהוָה, בְּאַפֶּךָ--הִנָּשֵׂא, בְּעַבְרוֹת צוֹרְרָי
kumah hashem be'appecha, hinnasei be'avrot tzorerai
Arise, O LORD, in Thine anger, lift up Thyself in indignation against mine adversaries;

וְעוּרָה אֵלַי, מִשְׁפָּט צִוִּיתָ
ve'urah elai, mishpat tzivvita
yea, awake for me at the judgment which Thou hast commanded.

וַעֲדַת לְאֻמִּים, תְּסוֹבְבֶךָּ; וְעָלֶיהָ, לַמָּרוֹם שׁוּבָה
va'adat le'ummim tesoveveka; ve'aleiha, lammarom shuvah
And let the congregation of the peoples compass Thee about, and over them return Thou on high.

יְהוָה, יָדִין עַמִּים: שָׁפְטֵנִי יְהוָה
hashem yadin ammim shafeteni hashem
O LORD, who ministerest judgment to the peoples, judge me, O LORD,

כְּצִדְקִי וּכְתֻמִּי עָלָי
ketzidki uchetummi alai
according to my righteousness, and according to mine integrity that is in me.

יִגְמָר נָא רַע, רְשָׁעִים
yigmar-na ra resha'im
Oh that a full measure of evil might come upon the wicked,

וּתְכוֹנֵן צַדִּיק; וּבֹחֵן לִבּוֹת, וּכְלָיוֹת--אֱלֹהִים צַדִּיק
utechonen tzaddik uvochen libbot, uchelayot, elohim tzaddik
and that Thou wouldest establish the righteous; for the righteous God trieth the heart and reins.

מָגִנִּי עַל-אֱלֹהִים; מוֹשִׁיעַ, יִשְׁרֵי-לֵב
maginni al-'elohim; moshia', yishrei-lev
My shield is with God, who saveth the upright in heart.

אֱלֹהִים, שׁוֹפֵט צַדִּיק; וְאֵל, זֹעֵם בְּכָל-יוֹם
'elohim shofet tzaddik; ve'el, zo'em bechol-yom
God is a righteous judge, yea, a God that hath indignation every day:

אִם-לֹא יָשׁוּב, חַרְבּוֹ יִלְטוֹשׁ; קַשְׁתּוֹ דָרַךְ, וַיְכוֹנְנֶהָ
'im-lo yashuv charbo yiltosh; kashto darach, vaychoneneha
If a man turn not, He will whet His sword, He hath bent His bow, and made it ready;

וְלוֹ, הֵכִין כְּלֵי מָוֶת; חִצָּיו, לְדֹלְקִים יִפְעָל
velo hechin kelei-mavet; chitzav, ledolekim yif'al
He hath also prepared for him the weapons of death, yea, His arrows which He made sharp.

הִנֵּה יְחַבֶּל-אָוֶן; וְהָרָה עָמָל, וְיָלַד שָׁקֶר
hinneh yechabbel-'aven; veharah amal, veyalad shaker
Behold, he travaileth with iniquity; yea, he conceiveth mischief, and bringeth forth falsehood.

תְּהִלִים

עָשְׁשָׁה מִכַּעַס עֵינִי; עָתְקָה, בְּכָל-צוֹרְרָי
'asheshah mikka'as eini; atekah, bechol-tzorerai
Mine eye is dimmed because of vexation; it waxeth old because of all mine adversaries.

סוּרוּ מִמֶּנִּי, כָּל-פֹּעֲלֵי אָוֶן: כִּי-שָׁמַע יְהוָה, קוֹל בִּכְיִי
suru mimmenni kol-po'alei aven; ki-shama hashem kol bichyi
Depart from me, all ye workers of iniquity; for the LORD hath heard the voice of my weeping.

שָׁמַע יְהוָה, תְּחִנָּתִי; יְהוָה, תְּפִלָּתִי יִקָּח
shama hashem techinnati; hashem tefillati yikkach
The LORD hath heard my supplication; the LORD receiveth my prayer.

יֵבֹשׁוּ, וְיִבָּהֲלוּ מְאֹד--כָּל-אֹיְבָי; יָשֻׁבוּ, יֵבֹשׁוּ רָגַע
yevoshu veyibbahalu me'od kol-'oyevai; yashuvu, yevoshu raga
All mine enemies shall be ashamed and sore affrighted; they shall turn back, they shall be ashamed suddenly.

ז

שִׁגָּיוֹן, לְדָוִד: אֲשֶׁר-שָׁר לַיהוָה--עַל-דִּבְרֵי-כוּשׁ, בֶּן-יְמִינִי
Shiggayon, ledavid asher-shar lahashem al-divrei-chush, ben-yemini
Shiggaion of David, which he sang unto the LORD, concerning Cush a Benjamite.

יְהוָה אֱלֹהַי, בְּךָ חָסִיתִי; הוֹשִׁיעֵנִי מִכָּל-רֹדְפַי, וְהַצִּילֵנִי
hashem elohai becha chasiti; hoshi'eni mikkol-rodefai, vehatzileni
O LORD my God, in Thee have I taken refuge; save me from all them that pursue me, and deliver me;

פֶּן-יִטְרֹף כְּאַרְיֵה נַפְשִׁי; פֹּרֵק, וְאֵין מַצִּיל
pen-yitrof ke'aryeh nafshi; porek, ve'ein matzil
Lest he tear my soul like a lion, rending it in pieces, while there is none to deliver.

יְהוָה אֱלֹהַי, אִם-עָשִׂיתִי זֹאת; אִם-יֶשׁ-עָוֶל בְּכַפָּי
hashem elohai im-'asiti zot; im-yesh-'avel bechappai
O LORD my God, if I have done this; if there be iniquity in my hands;

אִם-גָּמַלְתִּי, שׁוֹלְמִי רָע; וָאֲחַלְּצָה צוֹרְרִי רֵיקָם
'im-gamalti sholemi ra'; va'achalletzah tzoreri reikam
If I have requited him that did evil unto me, or spoiled mine adversary unto emptiness;

יִרַדֹּף אוֹיֵב נַפְשִׁי וְיַשֵּׂג, וְיִרְמֹס לָאָרֶץ חַיָּי
yiraddof oyev nafshi veyasseg, veyirmos la'aretz chayai
Let the enemy pursue my soul, and overtake it, and tread my life down to the earth;

וּכְבוֹדִי, לֶעָפָר יַשְׁכֵּן סֶלָה
uchevodi le'afar yashken selah
yea, let him lay my glory in the dust. Selah

תְּהִלִים

בְּרֹב פְּשְׁעֵיהֶם, הַדִּיחֵמוֹ--כִּי-מָרוּ בָךְ

berov pish'eihem haddichemo; ki-maru vach

cast them down in the multitude of their transgressions; for they have rebelled against Thee.

וְיִשְׂמְחוּ כָל-חוֹסֵי בָךְ, לְעוֹלָם יְרַנֵּנוּ--וְתָסֵךְ עָלֵימוֹ

veyismechu chol-chosei vach le'olam yerannenu vetasech aleimo

So shall all those that take refuge in Thee rejoice, they shall ever shout for joy, and Thou shalt shelter them;

וְיַעְלְצוּ בְךָ, אֹהֲבֵי שְׁמֶךָ

veya'letzu vecha, ohavei shemecha

let them also that love Thy name exult in Thee.

כִּי-אַתָּה, תְּבָרֵךְ צַדִּיק: יְהוָה--כַּצִּנָּה, רָצוֹן תַּעְטְרֶנּוּ

ki-'attah tevarech tzaddik hashem katzinnah, ratzon ta'terennu

For Thou dost bless the righteous; O LORD, Thou dost encompass him with favour as with a shield.

I

לַמְנַצֵּחַ בִּנְגִינוֹת, עַל-הַשְּׁמִינִית; מִזְמוֹר לְדָוִד

Lamnatzeach binginot al-hasheminit, mizmor ledavid

For the Leader; with string-music; on the Sheminith. A Psalm of David.

יְהוָה, אַל-בְּאַפְּךָ תוֹכִיחֵנִי; וְאַל-בַּחֲמָתְךָ תְיַסְּרֵנִי

hashem al-be'appecha tochicheni; ve'al-bachamatecha teyassereni

O LORD, rebuke me not in Thine anger, neither chasten me in Thy wrath.

חָנֵּנִי יְהוָה, כִּי אֻמְלַל-אָנִי: רְפָאֵנִי יְהוָה--כִּי נִבְהֲלוּ עֲצָמָי

chonneni hashem ki umlal ani refa'eni hashem ki nivhalu atzamai

Be gracious unto me, O LORD, for I languish away; heal me, O LORD, for my bones are affrighted.

וְנַפְשִׁי, נִבְהֲלָה מְאֹד; וְאַתָּה יְהוָה, עַד-מָתָי

venafshi nivhalah me'od; ve'attah hashem ad-matai

My soul also is sore affrighted; and Thou, O LORD, how long?

שׁוּבָה יְהוָה, חַלְּצָה נַפְשִׁי; הוֹשִׁיעֵנִי, לְמַעַן חַסְדֶּךָ

shuvah hashem challetzah nafshi; hoshi'eni, lema'an chasdecha

Return, O LORD, deliver my soul; save me for Thy mercy's sake.

כִּי אֵין בַּמָּוֶת זִכְרֶךָ; בִּשְׁאוֹל, מִי יוֹדֶה-לָּךְ

ki ein bammavet zichrecha; bish'ol, mi yodeh-lach

For in death there is no remembrance of Thee; in the nether-world who will give Thee thanks?

יָגַעְתִּי, בְּאַנְחָתִי--אַשְׂחֶה בְכָל-לַיְלָה, מִטָּתִי; בְּדִמְעָתִי, עַרְשִׂי אַמְסֶה

yaga'ti be'anchati, ascheh vechol-laylah mittati; bedim'ati, arsi amseh

I am weary with my groaning; every night make I my bed to swim; I melt away my couch with my tears.

תְּהִלִים

הַקְשִׁיבָה, לְקוֹל שַׁוְעִי--מַלְכִּי וֵאלֹהָי: כִּי-אֵלֶיךָ, אֶתְפַּלָּל
hakshivah lekol shav'i, malki velohai; ki-'eleicha, etpallal
Hearken unto the voice of my cry, my King, and my God; for unto Thee do I pray.

יְהוָה--בֹּקֶר, תִּשְׁמַע קוֹלִי; בֹּקֶר אֶעֱרָךְ-לְךָ, וַאֲצַפֶּה
hashem boker tishma koli; boker e'eroch-lecha, va'atzappeh
O LORD, in the morning shalt Thou hear my voice; in the morning will I order my prayer unto Thee, and will look forward.

כִּי, לֹא אֵל חָפֵץ רֶשַׁע אָתָּה: לֹא יְגֻרְךָ רָע
ki lo el-chafetz resha attah; lo yegurcha ra
For Thou art not a God that hath pleasure in wickedness; evil shall not sojourn with Thee.

לֹא-יִתְיַצְּבוּ הוֹלְלִים, לְנֶגֶד עֵינֶיךָ; שָׂנֵאתָ, כָּל-פֹּעֲלֵי אָוֶן
lo-yityatzevu holelim leneged eineicha; saneta, kol-po'alei aven
The boasters shall not stand in Thy sight; Thou hatest all workers of iniquity.

תְּאַבֵּד, דֹּבְרֵי כָזָב: אִישׁ-דָּמִים וּמִרְמָה, יְתָעֵב יְהוָה
te'abbed doverei chazav ish-damim umirmah, yeta'ev hashem
Thou destroyest them that speak falsehood; the LORD abhorreth the man of blood and of deceit.

וַאֲנִי--בְּרֹב חַסְדְּךָ, אָבוֹא בֵיתֶךָ
va'ani, berov chasdecha avo veitecha
But as for me, in the abundance of Thy lovingkindness will I come into Thy house;

אֶשְׁתַּחֲוֶה אֶל-הֵיכַל-קָדְשְׁךָ, בְּיִרְאָתֶךָ
eshtachaveh el-heichal-kodshecha beyir'atecha
I will bow down toward Thy holy temple in the fear of Thee.

יְהוָה, נְחֵנִי בְצִדְקָתֶךָ--לְמַעַן שׁוֹרְרָי
hashem necheni vetzidkatecha, lema'an shorerai
O LORD, lead me in Thy righteousness because of them that lie in wait for me;

הַיְשַׁר לְפָנַי דַּרְכֶּךָ
hayshar lefanai darkecha
make Thy way straight before my face.

כִּי אֵין בְּפִיהוּ, נְכוֹנָה--קִרְבָּם הַוּוֹת
ki ein befihu nechonah kirbam havvot
For there is no sincerity in their mouth; their inward part is a yawning gulf,

קֶבֶר-פָּתוּחַ גְּרֹנָם; לְשׁוֹנָם, יַחֲלִיקוּן
kever-patuach geronam; leshonam, yachalikun
their throat is an open sepulchre; they make smooth their tongue.

הַאֲשִׁימֵם, אֱלֹהִים--יִפְּלוּ, מִמֹּעֲצוֹתֵיהֶם
ha'ashimem elohim, yippelu mimmo'atzoteihem
Hold them guilty, O God, let them fall by their own counsels;

תְּהִלִים

בְּקָרְאִי, עֲנֵנִי אֱלֹהֵי צִדְקִי
bekare'i aneni elohei tzidki
Answer me when I call, O God of my righteousness,

בַּצָּר, הִרְחַבְתָּ לִּי; חָנֵּנִי, וּשְׁמַע תְּפִלָּתִי
batzar hirchavta li; chonneni ushema tefillati
Thou who didst set me free when I was in distress; be gracious unto me, and hear my prayer.

בְּנֵי אִישׁ, עַד-מֶה כְבוֹדִי לִכְלִמָּה--תֶּאֱהָבוּן רִיק; תְּבַקְשׁוּ כָזָב סֶלָה
benei ish ad-meh chevodi lichlimmah te'ehavun rik; tevakshu chazav selah
O ye sons of men, how long shall my glory be put to shame, in that ye love vanity, and seek after falsehood? Selah

וּדְעוּ--כִּי-הִפְלָה יְהוָה, חָסִיד לוֹ; יְהוָה יִשְׁמַע, בְּקָרְאִי אֵלָיו
ude'u, ki-hiflah hashem chasid lo; hashem yishma', bekare'i elav
But know that the LORD hath set apart the godly man as His own; the LORD will hear when I call unto Him.

רִגְזוּ, וְאַל-תֶּחֱטָאוּ: אִמְרוּ בִלְבַבְכֶם, עַל-מִשְׁכַּבְכֶם; וְדֹמּוּ סֶלָה
rigzu, ve'al-techeta'u imru vilvavchem al-mishkavchem, vedommu selah
Tremble, and sin not; commune with your own heart upon your bed, and be still. Selah

זִבְחוּ זִבְחֵי-צֶדֶק; וּבִטְחוּ, אֶל-יְהוָה
zivchu zivchei-tzedek; uvitchu, el-hashem
Offer the sacrifices of righteousness, and put your trust in the LORD.

רַבִּים אֹמְרִים, מִי-יַרְאֵנוּ-טוֹב: נְסָה עָלֵינוּ, אוֹר פָּנֶיךָ יְהוָה
rabbim omerim mi-yar'enu tov nesah-'aleinu or paneicha hashem
Many there are that say: 'Oh that we could see some good!' LORD, lift Thou up the light of Thy countenance upon us.

נָתַתָּה שִׂמְחָה בְלִבִּי; מֵעֵת דְּגָנָם וְתִירוֹשָׁם רָבּוּ
natattah simchah velibbi; me'et deganam vetirosham rabbu
Thou hast put gladness in my heart, more than when their corn and their wine increase.

בְּשָׁלוֹם יַחְדָּו, אֶשְׁכְּבָה וְאִישָׁן: כִּי-אַתָּה יְהוָה לְבָדָד; לָבֶטַח, תּוֹשִׁיבֵנִי
beshalom yachdav eshkevah ve'ishan ki-'attah hashem levadad; lavetach, toshiveni
In peace will I both lay me down and sleep; for Thou, LORD, makest me dwell alone in safety.

ה

לַמְנַצֵּחַ אֶל-הַנְּחִילוֹת, מִזְמוֹר לְדָוִד
Lamnatzeach el-hannechilot, mizmor ledavid
For the Leader; upon the Nehiloth. A Psalm of David.

אֲמָרַי הַאֲזִינָה יְהוָה; בִּינָה הֲגִיגִי
'amarai ha'azinah hashem binah hagigi
Give ear to my words, O LORD, consider my meditation.

תְּהִלִּים

ג

מִזְמוֹר לְדָוִד: בְּבָרְחוֹ, מִפְּנֵי אַבְשָׁלוֹם בְּנוֹ
Mizmor ledavid; bevorecho, mippenei avshalom beno
A Psalm of David, when he fled from Absalom his son.

יְהוָה, מָה-רַבּוּ צָרָי; רַבִּים, קָמִים עָלָי
hashem mah-rabbu tzarai; rabbim, kamim alai
LORD, how many are mine adversaries become! Many are they that rise up against me.

רַבִּים, אֹמְרִים לְנַפְשִׁי: אֵין יְשׁוּעָתָה לּוֹ בֵאלֹהִים סֶלָה
rabbim omerim lenafshi ein yeshu'atah lo ve'elohim selah
Many there are that say of my soul: 'There is no salvation for him in God.' Selah

וְאַתָּה יְהוָה, מָגֵן בַּעֲדִי; כְּבוֹדִי, וּמֵרִים רֹאשִׁי
ve'attah hashem magen ba'adi; kevodi, umerim roshi
But thou, O LORD, art a shield about me; my glory, and the lifter up of my head.

קוֹלִי, אֶל-יְהוָה אֶקְרָא; וַיַּעֲנֵנִי מֵהַר קָדְשׁוֹ סֶלָה
koli el-hashem ekra; vaya'aneni mehar kodsho selah
With my voice I call unto the LORD, and He answereth me out of His holy mountain. Selah

אֲנִי שָׁכַבְתִּי, וָאִישָׁנָה; הֱקִיצוֹתִי--כִּי יְהוָה יִסְמְכֵנִי
'ani shachavti, va'ishanah hekitzoti; ki hashem yismecheni
I lay me down, and I sleep; I awake, for the LORD sustaineth me.

לֹא-אִירָא, מֵרִבְבוֹת עָם--אֲשֶׁר סָבִיב, שָׁתוּ עָלָי
lo-'ira merivevot am; asher saviv, shatu alai
I am not afraid of ten thousands of people, that have set themselves against me round about.

קוּמָה יְהוָה, הוֹשִׁיעֵנִי אֱלֹהַי--כִּי-הִכִּיתָ אֶת-כָּל-אֹיְבַי לֶחִי
kumah hashem hoshi'eni elohai, ki-hikkita et-kol-'oyevai lechi
Arise, O LORD; save me, O my God; for Thou hast smitten all mine enemies upon the cheek,

שִׁנֵּי רְשָׁעִים שִׁבַּרְתָּ
shinnei resha'im shibbarta
Thou hast broken the teeth of the wicked.

לַיהוָה הַיְשׁוּעָה; עַל-עַמְּךָ בִרְכָתֶךָ סֶּלָה
lahashem hayshu'ah; al-'ammecha virchatecha selah
Salvation belongeth unto the LORD; Thy blessing be upon Thy people. Selah

ד

לַמְנַצֵּחַ בִּנְגִינוֹת, מִזְמוֹר לְדָוִד
Lamnatzeach binginot, mizmor ledavid
For the Leader; with string-music. A Psalm of David.

תְּהִלִּים

נְנַתְּקָה, אֶת-מוֹסְרוֹתֵימוֹ; וְנַשְׁלִיכָה מִמֶּנּוּ עֲבֹתֵימוֹ
nenattekah, et-moseroteimo; venashlichah mimmennu avoteimo
'Let us break their bands asunder, and cast away their cords from us.'

יוֹשֵׁב בַּשָּׁמַיִם יִשְׂחָק: אֲדֹנָי, יִלְעַג-לָמוֹ
yoshev bashamayim yischak. Adonai, yil'ag-lamo
He that sitteth in heaven laugheth, the Lord hath them in derision.

אָז יְדַבֵּר אֵלֵימוֹ בְאַפּוֹ; וּבַחֲרוֹנוֹ יְבַהֲלֵמוֹ
'az yedabber eleimo ve'appo; uvacharono yevahalemo
Then will He speak unto them in His wrath, and affright them in His sore displeasure:

וַאֲנִי, נָסַכְתִּי מַלְכִּי: עַל-צִיּוֹן, הַר-קָדְשִׁי
va'ani, nasachti malki. Al-tziyon, har-kodshi
'Truly it is I that have established My king upon Zion, My holy mountain.'

אֲסַפְּרָה, אֶל-חֹק: יְהוָה, אָמַר אֵלַי בְּנִי אַתָּה--אֲנִי, הַיּוֹם יְלִדְתִּיךָ
'asapperah, el-chok. Hashem, amar elai beni attah--'ani, hayom yelidticha
I will tell of the decree: the LORD said unto me: 'Thou art My son, this day have I begotten thee.

שְׁאַל מִמֶּנִּי--וְאֶתְּנָה גוֹיִם, נַחֲלָתֶךָ; וַאֲחֻזָּתְךָ, אַפְסֵי-אָרֶץ
she'al mimmenni--ve'ettenah goyim, nachalateca; va'achuzzatecha, afsei-'aretz
Ask of Me, and I will give the nations for thine inheritance, and the ends of the earth for thy possession.

תְּרֹעֵם, בְּשֵׁבֶט בַּרְזֶל: כִּכְלִי יוֹצֵר תְּנַפְּצֵם
tero'em, beshevet barzel. Kichli yotzer tenappetzem
Thou shalt break them with a rod of iron; thou shalt dash them in pieces like a potter's vessel.'

וְעַתָּה, מְלָכִים הַשְׂכִּילוּ; הִוָּסְרוּ, שֹׁפְטֵי אָרֶץ
ve'attah, melachim haskilu; hivvaseru, shofetei aretz
Now therefore, O ye kings, be wise; be admonished, ye judges of the earth.

עִבְדוּ אֶת-יְהוָה בְּיִרְאָה; וְגִילוּ, בִּרְעָדָה
'ivdu et-hashem beyir'ah; vegilu, bir'adah
Serve the LORD with fear, and rejoice with trembling.

נַשְּׁקוּ-בַר, פֶּן-יֶאֱנַף וְתֹאבְדוּ דֶרֶךְ--כִּי-יִבְעַר כִּמְעַט אַפּוֹ:
nasheku-var, pen-ye'enaf vetovedu derech--ki-yiv'ar kim'at appo
Do homage in purity, lest He be angry, and ye perish in the way, when suddenly His wrath is kindled.

אַשְׁרֵי, כָּל-חוֹסֵי בוֹ
Ashrei, kol-chosei vo
Happy are all they that take refuge in Him.

תְּהִלִּים

*Remember: Hebrew is Read from Right to Left
תְּהִלִּים א

אַשְׁרֵי הָאִישׁ--אֲשֶׁר לֹא הָלַךְ, בַּעֲצַת רְשָׁעִים
Ashrei-ha'ish, asher lo halach ba'atzat resha'im
Happy is the man that hath not walked in the counsel of the wicked,

וּבְדֶרֶךְ חַטָּאִים, לֹא עָמָד; וּבְמוֹשַׁב לֵצִים, לֹא יָשָׁב
uvederech chatta'im lo amad; uvemoshav letzim, lo yashav
nor stood in the way of sinners, nor sat in the seat of the scornful.

כִּי אִם בְּתוֹרַת יְהוָה, חֶפְצוֹ; וּבְתוֹרָתוֹ יֶהְגֶּה, יוֹמָם וָלָיְלָה
ki im betorat hashem cheftzo uvetorato yehgeh, yomam valayelah
But his delight is in the law of the LORD; and in His law doth he meditate day and night.

וְהָיָה--כְּעֵץ, שָׁתוּל עַל-פַּלְגֵי-מָיִם: אֲשֶׁר פִּרְיוֹ, יִתֵּן בְּעִתּוֹ
vehayah, ke'etz shatul al-palgei mayim asher piryo yitten be'itto
And he shall be like a tree planted by streams of water, that bringeth forth its fruit in its season,

וְעָלֵהוּ לֹא-יִבּוֹל; וְכֹל אֲשֶׁר-יַעֲשֶׂה יַצְלִיחַ
ve'alehu lo-yibbol; vechol asher-ya'aseh yatzliach
and whose leaf doth not wither; and in whatsoever he doeth he shall prosper.

לֹא-כֵן הָרְשָׁעִים: כִּי אִם-כַּמֹּץ, אֲשֶׁר-תִּדְּפֶנּוּ רוּחַ
lo-chen haresha'im; ki im-kammotz, asher-tiddefennu ruach
Not so the wicked; but they are like the chaff which the wind driveth away.

עַל-כֵּן, לֹא-יָקֻמוּ רְשָׁעִים--בַּמִּשְׁפָּט; וְחַטָּאִים, בַּעֲדַת צַדִּיקִים
'al-ken lo-yakumu resha'im bammishpat; vechatta'im, ba'adat tzaddikim
Therefore the wicked shall not stand in the judgment, nor sinners in the congregation of the righteous.

כִּי-יוֹדֵעַ יְהוָה, דֶּרֶךְ צַדִּיקִים; וְדֶרֶךְ רְשָׁעִים תֹּאבֵד
ki-yodea hashem derech tzaddikim; vederech resha'im toved
For the LORD regardeth the way of the righteous; but the way of the wicked shall perish.

ב

לָמָּה, רָגְשׁוּ גוֹיִם; וּלְאֻמִּים, יֶהְגּוּ-רִיק
Lammah, rageshu goyim; ule'ummim, yehgu-rik
Why are the nations in an uproar? And why do the peoples mutter in vain?

יִתְיַצְּבוּ, מַלְכֵי-אֶרֶץ--וְרוֹזְנִים נוֹסְדוּ-יָחַד: עַל-יְהוָה, וְעַל-מְשִׁיחוֹ
yityatzevu, malchei-'eretz--verozenim nosedu-yachad: 'al-hashem, ve'al-meshicho
The kings of the earth stand up, and the rulers take counsel together, against the LORD, and against His anointed:

תְּהִלִּים

TO FOLLOW ALONG WITH THE HEBREW AUDIO, VISIT:

hebrewaudiobible.com

תְּהִלִּים-Tehillim-Psalms

מִשְׁלֵי-Mishlei-Proverbs

אִיּוֹב-Iyov-Job

א	A			א	1
ב	V			ב	2
בּ	B			ג	3
ג	G			ד	4
ד	D			ה	5
ה	H			ו	6
ו	V	אָ	ah	ז	7
ז	Z	אַ	ah	ח	8
ח	KH	אֲ	ah	ט	9
ט	T	אָה	ah		
י	Y	אֵ	ei	י	10
כ	KH	אֶ	e	יא	11
כּ	K	אֱ	e	יב	12
ל	L	אֵי	ei	יג	13
מ	M	אִ	ee	יד	14
ם	M	אִי	ee	טו	15
נ	N	אֹ	oh	טז	16
ן	N	אֳ	oh	יז	17
ס	S	אָ	oh	יח	18
ע	A	אוֹ	oh	יט	19
פ	F	אֻ	oo	כ	20
פּ	P	אוּ	oo	ל	30
צ	TS	אְ	e	מ	40
ק	K			נ	50
ר	R			ס	60
שׁ	SH			ע	70
שׂ	S			פ	80
ת	T			צ	90
				ק	100

כתובים
Ketuvim
Writings

Made in the USA
Las Vegas, NV
19 May 2022

JEWS, JUDAISM, AND CATHOLIC EDUCATION

DOCUMENTARY SURVEY REPORT

OF

CATHOLIC INSTITUTIONS' IMPLEMENTATION

OF

1965 CONCILIAR STATEMENT ON THE JEWS
1974 ROMAN CATHOLIC GUIDELINES/SUGGESTIONS
1975 U.S. BISHOPS' STATEMENT ON THE JEWS

Prepared for the Twentieth Anniversary

of the 1965

Promulgation of Vatican II Document

NOSTRA AETATE

by

Rose Thering, O.P., Ph.D.

Professor of Education

Seton Hall University

South Orange, New Jersey 07079

Preface

Even before the Second Vatican Council issued its historic 1965 declaration on Jews and Judaism, Nostra Aetate #4, a group of dedicated American Catholic leaders, clergy and lay, had already completed significant work in building positive relations between the two religious communities. Sister Rose Thering was one of the pioneers in the effort to overcome "the teaching of contempt," a 1900-year-old tradition that was widespread in Christian churches.

Her doctoral thesis in 1965 was a systematic examination of Catholic teaching materials vis-a-vis Jews and Judaism. Five years later, she conducted a survey to determine how Nostra Aetate was being implemented in religious education.

In 1985, to commemorate the 20th anniversary of Vatican II, Sister Rose Thering undertook another study of the Roman Catholic education system. The results of this study are both promising and encouraging. Jews and Judaism are no longer esoteric studies in Catholic schools. Indeed, there is a growing interest in Judaism on the part of both students and faculty. But much still remains to be done.

Crucial issues remain, but as Sister Rose's survey indicates, these issues are now being faced and addressed by a growing number of Catholic educators and institutions. For all this and for much more, we commend Sister Rose Thering and others who have committed themselves to building a new and constructive relationship between Jews and Catholics -- a relationship of mutual respect and understanding.

Rabbi A. James Rudin
National Interreligious Affairs
 Director
The American Jewish Committee

Rabbi Leon Klenicki
Director, Department
 of Interfaith Affairs of
 the Anti-Defamation League
 of B'nai B'rith

ACKNOWLEDGEMENT

The researcher and writer of this documentary research survey report is deeply grateful to the Executive Director and the Advisory Committee members of the U.S. Bishops' Secretariat for Catholic-Jewish Relations for their support, encouragement and advice in preparing this report. She is especially grateful to the Anti-Defamation League of B'nai B'rith and to the American Jewish Committee for their financial assistance, thus making possible the documentary survey.

In addition, this writer wishes to acknowledge the support and cooperation of the Institute of Judaeo-Christian Studies, Seton Hall University, and the National Catholic Education Association and the contributions of Seton Hall University.

In particular, the writer expresses her gratitude to Dr. Eugene Fisher, Executive Director of The National Conference of Catholic Bishops' Secretariat for Catholic Jewish Relations, Theodore Freedman, Director, National Intergroup Relations Division of the Anti-Defamation League of B'nai B'rith, Rabbi Leon Klenicki, Director, Interfaith Affairs Department of the Anti-Defamation League of B'nai B'rith, Rabbi James Rudin, National Director, Interreligious Affairs of the American Jewish Committee,

Msgr. John M. Oesterreicher, Director, Institute of Judaeo-Christian Studies, Seton Hall University, Msgr. William L. Baumgaertner, Associate Director of the Association of Theological Schools, Rev. Charles Kavanagh, Executive Director of Seminary Department of the National Catholic Education Association and to the College of Education and Human Services, Seton Hall for its contributions.

The researcher wishes to thank all those who took time to answer the questionnaires. Without them, and her research assistant, Mrs. Mae Delabar, her typist, Mrs. Eileen F. Toplansky, and the adviser for computer programming, Dr. Allen Hodes, the report could not have been completed.

TABLE OF CONTENTS

	Page
ACKNOWLEDGEMENT	ii
TABLE OF CONTENTS	iv
LIST OF TABLES	vi

Chapter

    I.   INTRODUCTION......................... 1

          Purpose
          Methodology

    II.   SURVEY REPORT OF COLLEGES and UNIVERSITIES......................... 4

          Data Analysis
          Implications and Recommendations
          Sampling of Responses

    III.   SURVEY REPORT ON SEMINARIES 23

          Data Analysis
          Implications and Recommendations
          Sampling of Responses

    IV.   SURVEY REPORT on DIOCESAN and ARCHDIOCESAN ECUMENICAL COMMISSIONS................... 36

          Data Analysis
          Implications and Recommendations
          Summary

    V.   SURVEY REPORT on HIGH SCHOOLS 49

          Data Analysis
          Implications and Recommendations

    VI.   SURVEY REPORT on SUPERINTENDENTS' OFFICES 60

          Data Analysis
          Implications

Page

Chapter

VII. SUMMARY and CONCLUSIONS
       RECOMMENDATIONS.................... 69

   Restatement of Problem and Procedure
   Results of 1985 study
   Areas Needing special study
       Holocaust
       Pharisees
       Passion Narratives
       The "Land Tradition"
   Conclusion

APPENDIX 82

   Letter which accompanied Questionnaire
   Questionnaire sent to Colleges/
     Universities and Seminaries
   Questionnaire sent to Diocesan and
     Archdiocesan Ecumenical Commissions
   Questionnaire sent to High Schools
   Questionnaire sent to Superintendents

BIBLIOGRAPHY 99

LIST OF TABLES

Table		Page
1.	<u>COLLEGES/UNIVERSITIES'</u> Courses of Study	5
2.	<u>Jewish Studies Offered</u> in Department	6
3.	Evaluation of Courses on Judaism	7
4.	Difficulty in Offering Courses	8
5.	Resources for Teaching Jewish Studies	9
6.	Program Length	10
7.	Joint Sponsorship	11
8.	Self Evaluation of Response to Jewish Studies	12
9.	Difficulties in Sponsoring Institutes	12
10.	Self Evaluation of Special Institutes	13
11.	Visible Rewards: Open ended Question	14
12.	Overall Self Evaluation of Efforts for Conciliar Documents and NCCB Statement of Catholic-Jewish Relations	15
13.	<u>SEMINARIES'</u> Courses of Study	24
14.	Jewish Studies Offered in Department	25
15.	Evaluation of Courses on Judaism	26
16.	Difficulties in Offering Courses	27
17.	Resources for Teaching Jewish Studies	28
18.	Program Length	28
19.	Joint Sponsorship	29
20.	Self Evaluation of Responses to Special Programs of Jewish Studies	30
21.	Difficulties in Offering Special Programs	30
22.	Visible Rewards in Offering Courses on Judaism	31
23.	Visible Rewards in Offering Institutes, Programs, Seminars of Jewish Studies	32
24.	Overall Self Evaluation of Efforts to Implement Conciliar Documents and NCCB Statement on Catholic-Jewish Relations	33
25.	<u>DIOCESAN/ARCHDIOCESAN</u> Commission Concerns	37
26.	Specific Efforts of Implementation	38
27.	Guidelines (Specific)	42
28.	Guidelines - Lectionary Readings	44
29.	Psalm 22 for Good Friday Reproaches	45
30.	Joint Programming	45
31.	Overall Evaluation of Efforts for Implementation of Conciliar Documents and NCCB Statement on Catholic-Jewish Relations	46

Table		Page
32.	<u>CATHOLIC HIGH SCHOOLS'</u> RESULTS of courses offered	50
33.	Faculty Involved in Teaching Courses	52
34.	Preparation of Faculty and Sponsorship of Jewish-Christian Programs	52
35.	Religion Teaching Methods/Textbooks	53
36.	Self Evaluation of Efforts for Implementation of Conciliar Documents and NCCB Statement on Catholic-Jewish Relations	54
37.	Overall Evaluation of Catholic High Schools' Efforts of Implementation	55
38.	Textbooks of Religion-High Schools	55
39.	<u>SUPERINTENDENTS'METHODS</u> in helping elementary teachers implement documents	60
40.	Methods of helping secondary teachers implement the Documents	62
41.	Religion Texts Treatment of Jews/Judaism	64
42.	Religion Texts ADOPTED for use in Elementary Schools	65
43.	Religion Texts Adopted for use in Secondary Schools	66
44.	Number of Schools and Enrollment covered by Superintendents' Offices	67

CHAPTER I

INTRODUCTION

This researcher, in 1970, prepared a five-year survey report of Catholic Institutions' Implementation of Vatican II Statement on the Jews. That study was financially supported by the American Jewish Committee and the Institute of Judaeo-Christian Studies of Seton Hall University. It was prepared for the Theological Convocation held at Seton Hall University, October 25-28, 1970.

This documentary research is a follow-up of the 1970 study. However, this 1985 study includes the institutions' implementation of not only the 1965 Conciliar Statement on Catholics' Relationship to Jews and Judaism but also the 1974 Roman Catholic Guidelines and Suggestions for Implementation of the 1965 Vatican II Document and the 1975 U.S. Bishops' Statement on the Jews.

The 1985 research seeks to determine what effect, if any, these three important documents may have had on the curricula, teaching methods and materials, ecumenical programs and faculties. It is within these areas that the teachings about Jews and Judaism can be incorporated and disseminated.

To discover these answers, questionnaires were designed and sent to Catholic institutions. The study is not a full coverage but a representative sample survey of the work done in: Catholic Colleges/Universities (209), Seminaries (123), a sampling of high schools (300), offices of Superintendents (180), and Archdiocesan/Diocesan Ecumenical Commissions (213).

No investigation of the elementary schools was done except that which was covered by the Superintendents' offices.

Of the 209 questionnaires sent to higher institutions of learning, 128 or 61.2% responded. Of the 123 questionnaires sent to the Seminaries, responses numbered 40 or 32.5%. A sampling of 300 high schools received the instrument. There was a response of 114 or 38.0%. Of 180 questionnaires sent to offices of superintendents, 43 or 23.9% responded.

The 1985 survey included Ecumenical offices which were not surveyed in 1970. Of the 213 questionnaires sent to Archdiocesan/Diocesan Ecumenical Commissions and Interreligious Affairs, 75 responded or 35.2%.

---

[1] A copy of each of the questionnaires appears in the Appendix.

The percentage of responses at the time of the 1970 study are about the same as the 1985 survey.

CHAPTER II

SURVEY REPORT

OF

COLLEGES/UNIVERSITIES

The questionnaire was distributed to 209 colleges and universities. The responses numbered 128 or 61.2%. The following table reports the findings regarding the "Courses of Study" related either directly or indirectly to the Conciliar and/or U.S. Bishops' documents. These courses of study indicate various approaches to teaching about Jews and Judaism.

Even though, as recorded in Table 1, the study revealed that 91.4% of the colleges/universities do not have a special Department of Jewish Studies, 51% do offer courses in Judaism. Three-fourths or 75% treat Judaism in Comparative or World Religions course, while 49.2% treat Jews and Judaism in a special course. A high percentage (69%) noted that the courses taught in Religious Studies do show a positive relationship between Christianity and Judaism while 20% offer courses covering the Intertestamental Period.

COLLEGES/UNIVERSITIES' RESULTS IN PERCENTAGE

TABLE 1

Courses of Study	Yes	No	No Response
Department of Jewish Studies	3.1	91.4	5.5
Courses in Jewish Studies	51.6	43.8	4.7
Judaism:Comparative/World Religion	75.0	18.8	6.3
Course: Relationship of J/C	68.8	25.0	6.3
Special Course in Judaism	49.2	46.1	4.7
Course: Noting Judaism's Enduring Covenant	59.4	29.7	10.9
Course: Intertestamental	19.5	72.7	7.3
Course: Jewish History after Emergence of Christianity	48.4	45.3	6.3
Holocaust	26.6	68.0	5.5
History of State of Israel	5.5	86.7	7.8
History of Middle East	38.3	53.9	7.8
Items Above Treated Other Courses	51.6	19.5	28.9
Jewish Studies - Undergraduate	41.4	5.5	30.5
Jewish Studies - Graduate	3.1	10.5	32.0
Both	10.9	10.9	32.0

The researcher asked a number of questions not requested in the 1970 survey. One question asked if courses "present Judaism as an enduring covenant which continues to the present time". The institutions' response was an affirmative 59.4%

It would seem that more colleges and universities treat the topic of the Holocaust now than in 1970 when only 1% of those surveyed bothered to teach this painful period of our 20th century history. The 1985 survey revealed that 26.6% offer a special course on the Holocaust; 5.5% teach a separate course on the State of Israel; 38.3% teach a course on the Middle East which could possibly include a study of the History of Israel.

TABLE 2

Jewish Studies Offered in Department* of	%
Theology (Religious Studies)	86.7
History	46.9
Sociology	10.9
Education	4.7
Language (Hebrew)	11.7
English	10.2
Other	10.9

*(Checked more than one)

As one would expect, the Theology and/or Religious Studies Department (87% of the colleges) offer courses in Jewish Studies. Other departments are also involved, namely, History (46.9%), Sociology (10.9%), Education (2.3%), Language (11.7%), English (10.2%), and other (10.9%). Some universities offer courses in Holocaust literature within the Department of English. In the Language Department, there were courses in Hebrew.

The following Table #3 gives an evaluation of the courses on Judaism which are offered.

TABLE 3

Evaluation of Courses on Judaism	%
Excellent	20.3
Good	42.2
Poor	10.2
No Response	27.3

Of the 61.2% of the institutions of higher learning, 42.2% rated the course responses as "Good"; 20.3% indicated an "Excellent" response; 10.2% noted that the student response to the courses was "Poor".

Faculty indicated the reasons for difficulty in offering courses on Jews and Judaism. Their responses are found in Table 4.

TABLE 4

Difficulty* in offering Courses Related to Judaism	%
Lack of time	24.2
Lack of Student Interest	39.9
Lack of Funds	33.6
Lack of Qualified Personnel	27.4
Lack of Leadership	12.1
Other	16.3

*Rated 1-6.

It would seem that the greatest difficulty encountered in offering courses in Jewish Studies was the lack of student interest (39.9%). Lack of funds ran a close second - 33.6%. Other reasons noted were: lack of qualified personnel (27.4%), lack of time (24.2%); lack of leadership (12.1%).

Resources for Teaching Courses Related to Jewish Studies

The questionnaire sought information regarding faculty, library materials and institutes or programs of Jewish Studies. Table 5 gives this basic information.

TABLE 5

Resources for Teaching Courses Related to Jews/Judaism
Faculty - Library - Institutes/Programs   (%)

	Yes	No	N/A	No response
Christian Faculty	37.5	6.3	0.8	55.5
Jewish Faculty	53.9	36.7	-	9.4
Jewish Organization/ Sponsored faculty	44.5	41.4	-	14.1
Library Materials from Jewish Organization	53.9	30.5	-	15.6
Programs (Institutes/ Seminars) of Jewish Studies	39.1	51.6	-	9.4
Jewish/Christian Faculty in Special Programs	35.2	18.8	2.3	43.8
Study Tours to Israel	12.5	74.2	0.8	12.5

In institutions of higher learning, both Jewish and Christian faculty taught courses of Jewish Studies. More Jewish faculty (53.9%) taught the courses in Judaism than did Christian faculty (37.5%). Often Jewish organizations helped institutions obtain a Jewish scholar (44.5%) for teaching the needed courses. These organizations also donated books to the libraries of institutions (53.9%) offering these courses in Jewish-Christian studies. The most frequently involved were the Jewish Chautauqua Society and the Anti-Defamation League of B'nai B'rith.

Programs of Jewish-Christian Studies were offered at the colleges and universities. These often were institutes, seminars (39.1%) or study tours to Israel (12.5%). In such specially designed institutes of 1-3 days, 4-9 days, 10-14 and longer, both Jewish and Christian faculty taught the courses or gave the lectures. Table 6 pictures the length of the programs and the percentage of involvement.

TABLE 6

Length of Special Programs (percentage)	Days				
	1-3	4-9	10-14	N/A	Missing
	32.8	3.1	4.7	3.1	56.2

Another question tried to determine the cooperation of sponsorship of the special institutes/seminars of Jewish-Christian Studies. Table 7, page 11, pictures the responses. About 62.5% co-sponsor programs with other organizations.

The Jewish Chautauqua Society is very much involved (38.8%) and is often a co-sponsor of special programs. The Anti-Defamation League of B'nai B'rith and the National Conference of Christians and Jews (both a 17.2%) also co-sponsor Jewish programs. It was interesting, too, to note the local involvement of the Jewish Councils with an 18.0%.

TABLE 7

Joint Sponsorship of Jewish/Christian Programs of Study	Yes = 62.5% No = 21.9% No Response = 15.6%
WITH:	%
Local Jewish Council*	18.0
American Jewish Committee	6.3
Anti-Defamation League	17.2
Union of American Hebrew Congregations	-
Synagogue Council	0.8
American Jewish Congress	0.8
Jewish Chautauqua Society	38.3
National Conference of Christians/Jews	17.2
Secretariat for Christians/Jews	3.1
Ecumenical Commission	19.5
National Catholic Conference on Interracial Justice	2.3
Other	11.7

*Often this included the local American Jewish Committee. Local ecumenical commissions are also co-sponsors of such Jewish/Christian programs - 19.5%.

The respondents evaluated the general reception to these special programs of Jewish Studies. Table 8, page 12, gives this information.

TABLE 8

Self-Evaluation of Response to Programs of Catholic-Jewish Studies	%
Excellent	17.2
Good	35.9
Poor	3.9
N/A	4.7
No Response	37.5

Again, administrators felt the response to institutes on Jews/Judaism was "Good" (35.9%). Others checked "Excellent" (17.2%); while 3.9% indicated the response was "Poor".

In order to determine reasons for the above response, the researcher asked the respondents to list their difficulties in offering such programs. Table 9 gives the response.

TABLE 9

Difficulties in sponsoring Institutes, Seminars, Programs on Jews and Judaism	%
Lack of: time	36.0
interest	36.7
funds	40.7
personnel	18.0
leadership	14.8
other	14.1

Again, the lack of funds (40.7%), lack of time (36.0%), and lack of interest (36.7%) are the chief obstacles to offering special programs of Jewish Studies.

Visible Rewards

Questions #28 and #29 of the questionnaire asked for a statement of the most visible rewards in offering courses and/or institutes of Judaism and related areas. Each report gives a sampling of the answers given. This researcher, after reading each response, re-read them again and gave each response a judgment classification. Table 10 pictures the responses to question #28.

TABLE 10

Evaluation of Visible Rewards in offering Courses in Judaism and/or related areas	%
Excellent	21.0
Good	53.9
Poor	7.8
Other	13.2
No Response	4.0

Table 10 indicates that of the colleges/universities who responded, about 74.9% were most pleased with the rewards which came from offering courses of Jewish Studies. Ten institutions or 7.8% rated themselves "poor" but also noted that each intended to do more in this area. The reasons when

"Other" was checked were: "we are just beginning", "no time to offer such courses"; or "lack of student interest". However, from the positive responses given, it was most evident that the greatest reward shared by many participants was that they and their students had experienced a deepening of their Christianity by offering courses in Judaism. Respondents felt that they had, indeed, become better Christians.

In an evaluation of the responses given to the open-ended questions, this writer concludes that almost every college engaged in an implementation of the Conciliar Statement, and the 1974 Roman Catholic Guidelines and Suggestions and the U.S. Bishops' Statement, stated, in one way or another, that students, faculty, administrators and the community (both Christian and Jewish) developed a deeper understanding, awareness and appreciation not only of each other but of their own Faith and Tradition.

In Table 11 the reader will note the answers to open-ended question #29.

TABLE 11

Evaluation: Visible rewards in offering institutes, seminars, programs relating to Judaism	%
Excellent	13.2
Good	47.6
Poor	5.4
Other	30.4
No Response	3.1

As indicated above, institutions again pointed out that probing issues such as: "Torah, People and Land" offered the participants a way to become better Christians. Each learned of their relatedness to Judaism; each recognized their prejudices, if these were present, and promised to correct anti-semitism whenever it was encountered. An overwhelming positive response resulted from these institutes/programs - 60.8%.

Table 12 pictures the overall evaluation by each institution of higher learning.

TABLE 12

Overall Self-Evaluation of Efforts for Implementation of Conciliar Documents and U.S. Bishops' Statement	%
Excellent	35.1
Good	41.4
Poor	9.3
Other	10.9
No Response	3.1

Over 76% rated themselves "Good" to "Excellent" for their efforts in implementation of the documents in Christian-Jewish relations. Respondents often remarked that both Testaments of Sacred Scripture became much more meaningful after courses of Jewish Studies. There was a focusing on Jewish roots that had not been done before. A deeper appreciation of Jewish spirituality resulted; a deep interest in Jewish thought was created not only as it related to Christianity and present day situations but a deepened interest and appreciation of the grandeur of Judaism itself resulted.

The institutions of higher learning have made and are making a real effort to implement the Conciliar documents and the U.S. Bishops' Statement.

Implications and Recommendations

The sampling of Catholic Colleges/Universities (61.2% of 209 distributed) shows an overall honest effort to implement the Conciliar Statements (1965 and 1974) and the National Conference of Catholic Bishops' 1975 Statement on Catholic-Jewish Relations. Where programs have not been initiated, plans are now being designed. Many acknowledged that the questionnaire itself was a learning tool bringing faculty to a new awareness.

The 1985 survey indicated that more colleges today are offering courses in Judaism than were offered in 1970. More courses treating the Holocaust (26.6%) are now offered as compared to only one percent (1%) in the 1970 study.

Much still remains to be done. The Rabbinic background of the New Testament and courses on the Intertestamental Period need to be introduced into the curricula. "The Jews, the Bible, and the Land" needs to be presented to students not only to deepen the understanding and appreciation Jews have for the Land but to awaken in Christians a meaningful awareness of the Land and a Christian approach to "The Land of Israel".

Potential teachers are prepared in the liberal arts colleges. They, too, need a preparation in Judaeo-Christian Studies. Above all, future parents, who are the primary teachers need a solid, honest, non-prejudicial presentation of Jews, Judaism and the Holocaust. Hence, Catholic institutions of higher learning, by providing opportunities for taking courses in Jewish Studies will not only offer opportunities for the development of better and liberally educated persons who are the future citizens of this world but will also be implementing the 1965 Conciliar Statement on the Jews, the 1974 Roman Catholic Suggestions and Guidelines and the 1975 National Conference of Catholic Bishops' Statement on Catholic-Jewish Relations. As the 1974 Guidelines state:

> Christians must therefore strive to acquire a better knowledge of the basic components of the religious tradition of Judaism; they must strive to learn by what essential traits Jews define themselves in the light of their own religious experience.

One institution, who was moved by the questionnaire, included a resolution drawn up before the response was returned. It reads:

> Be it resolved: the Board of Trustees of the College of _____ authorizes a program that will focus on Jewish-Christian learning and that a restricted fund, to be specifically designated as "The Program for Jewish-Christian Learning" be established to finance

this program. The purpose of the program will be to increase understanding and knowledge of Christians and Jews between and among themselves. It could include, but not be limited to, academic courses, lectures, symposia, workshops, library books and periodicals, scholarships.

In summary, the colleges and universities are, indeed, aware of their responsibilities and are determined to implement the teachings of the Vatican Council and the U.S. Bishops' Secretariat for Catholic-Jewish Relations.

Sampling of answers to open-ended questions #28, #29, #30.

#28   WHAT HAVE BEEN THE MOST VISIBLE REWARDS IN OFFERING COURSES IN JUDAISM and/or RELATED AREAS?

"Edification and enrichment of Christian students, especially Theology majors;ecumenical exchange, spiritual enrichment for Jewish and Christian students."

"Student satisfaction."

"A reminder to faculty and other participants that the world we live in includes authentic alternate faith traditions."

"High level awareness of important issues, especially regarding the Holocaust."

"Students' awareness and appreciation of Christianity's roots in Judaism; of Judaism as a viable living religion with traditions and insights for humane contemporary living."

"Acceptance of Jewish studies as an integral part of university offerings. Positive responses economically and politically by Jewish community (including annual $25,000 grant)."

"Greater understanding of Judaism and self-knowledge."

"Able to reach our Jewish student population with courses of special interest to them; to broaden the scope of interest and information regarding Judaism, etc., of the Christian and/or non-Jewish student population."

"New ecumenical perspective."

"Breaking through prejudices, affirming links between Christian/Jewish relations."

"Our students arrive at an appreciation and understanding of Judaism and correct some of their erroneous notions, prejudices."

"Increased student awareness plus respect of and rapport with-local Jewish Community."

"Students who have taken Judaism courses are much more responsive and perceptive to issues of Jewish/Christian dynamics, etc., in New Testament courses and other areas of study."

"Students (mainly Christian) increased their knowledge and appreciation of Judaic roots of their faith. Few Jewish students acquired knowledge which was really new since they had no formal religious education."

"Both Jewish and Christian students have better awareness of our common roots and our present challenge to work together to renew the earth; a reduction of prejudices."

"Increased respect for the unique contributions of Judaism to _all_ people; openness to additional learning challenges."

"Student awareness of important western religion and understanding of members of their community."

"Becoming aware of the cooperation and support of the Jewish Community growth in interpersonal understanding and appreciation."

"Deepening of faith and spiritual perceptions of participants, greater social commitment."

#29 WHAT HAVE BEEN THE MOST VISIBLE REWARDS IN OFFERING INSTITUTES, WORKSHOPS AND SPECIAL PROGRAMS RELATED TO JUDAISM?

"A better mutual understanding and a greater sense of brotherhood."

"Better relations with non-Catholic students and local community in general."

"Students were opened to multiple perspectives in religious experience and its expression historically and culturally; their developing of understanding of contemporary socio-political and religious issues is now on a global level."

"Students and faculty who attended were affirmative in their response."

"An appreciation of the Jewish religious perspective; many 'Ecumenical' benefits. A deeper understanding of Christianity and Judaic roots"!

"Collegiality - Scholarship."

"Healing wounds, correcting misconceptions, rising above barriers to face common obstacles together."

"Clearer understanding of Judaism and therefore of Jewish people."

"Student appreciation of the Jewish heritage, of which they tend to have little experience; faculty enrichment and service to extramural community."

"Joint inter-faith, shared experience, traditions."

"Opportunity to introduce students and friends to history of ancient and contemporary Judaism."

#30 GIVE AN OVERALL EVALUATION OF YOUR EFFORTS TO IMPLEMENT DIRECTLY OR INDIRECTLY THE CONCILIAR DOCUMENTS AND THE U.S. BISHOPS' STATEMENT ON CATHOLIC-JEWISH RELATIONS.

Sample responses:

"Good, sincere, continuous effort has been maintained since 1968."

"Have made consistent efforts to implement Vatican II documents, particularly those on Ecumenism. Use all instruments of research and instruction. Climate has changed; most students welcome the knowledge."

"Vatican II Declaration on non-Christian Religions inspired us to offer courses in Judaism and other non-Christian religions. Response to Judaism is best."

"We are familiar with these statements and they have prompted in part the offerings listed."

"Excellent! We have a Seder each year and cannot host all who wish to participate."

"Excellent! Ample opportunity to offer courses in Judaic Studies, especially high interest in Holocaust course."

"Course 'Contemporary Jewish Thought' had high enrollment consistently. Special programs on Judaism caused students to interact with people of Jewish faith in a variety of learning activities. Jewish/Christian relations were discussed and fostered."

"We are in the process of establishing a Center here with donated money and Jewish scholars."

"The offering of an appreciation of our roots in Judaism has been very positive and informative for Christian students."

"Consistent effort to offer course in Judaism each year. One faculty member has been in Israel nine years. She returns to lecture on Jews, Judaism. Another faculty member spent her Sabbatical in Israel."

"We are responding enthusiastically and whole-heartedly."

"My interest stems from a study of the Hebrew Scriptures, traditions and a study of the Holocaust. I received inspiration from Msgr. John M. Oesterreicher, especially his volume of the Bridge - Brothers in Hope."

"University's hiring procedures are truly non-discriminatory. Jewish faculty members often are observant Jews whose Judaism is appreciated rather than 'tolerated.'"

"In the archdiocese of _____, the Inter-faith Commission of which we are a member, designates _____ University as the lead agent in Jewish/Christian studies."

"We have been quite blessed here by a long tradition (pre '65) of Jewish/Christian Dialogue beginning with Father John Kelley, S.M. It has continued to this day in many forms."

"On the level of the Institute of Judaeo-Christian Studies, and the Department that developed out of it, the efforts have been wide-ranging and consistent in an effort to achieve excellence for the long-term needs of the Church and the wider community . . . "

CHAPTER III

SURVEY REPORT ON SEMINARIES

A copy of the same questionnaire which was distributed to Colleges/Universities was mailed to 123 Seminaries. Responses numbered 40. Unfortunately, some of the "seminaries" were either two year, or four year preparatory schools (not seminaries); others were simply returned with a message stating that the seminary had closed. Hence the "No" response and/or "Not applicable" is unusually large.

The response numbered 40 out of 123, hence the percentage of returns from questionnaires sent to seminaries is 32.5%.

Table one (1) gives the data regarding "Courses of Study" related directly or indirectly to the Conciliar and/or U.S. Bishops' documents on Catholic-Jewish Relations.

In an examination of Table 13, the reader will note that of the number of the seminaries responding, there is a treatment of Jews and Judaism in either special courses or in the regular scripture courses. While 32.5% have courses in Judaism, 35.0% consider this topic in a comparative/world religions course and 27.5% have a special course in Judaism. As would be expected, a large percentage,

Seminaries' Results in Percentages

TABLE 13

Course of Study	Yes	No	N/A	No Response
Courses in Jewish Studies	32.5	42.5		25.0
Judaism: Comparative/World Religions	35.0	40.0		25.0
Course: On Relationship of J/C	57.5	20.0		22.5
Special Course in Judaism	27.5	50.0		22.5
Course: Noting Judaism's Enduring Covenant	42.0	30.0		21.5
Course: Intertestamental Period	25.0	52.5		22.5
Course: Jewish History After Emergence of Christianity	25.0	50.0		25.0
Holocaust	10.0	67.5		22.5
History of State of Israel	2.5	75.0		22.5
History of Middle East	15.0	62.5		22.5
Undergraduate	20.0	27.5	15.0	37.5
Graduate	12.5	32.5	15.0	40.0
Both	5.0	40.0	17.5	37.5

57.5% note the relationship between Judaism and Christianity. Another 42.5% specifically note this and present Judaism as an enduring Covenant which continues to the present time. Only 25.0% had a course on "Intertestamental Period;" 25.0% offered a course in Jewish History after the Emergence of Christianity.

The survey of 1970 showed that 6.8% offered a course on the Holocaust; this 1985 study indicates that 10% of the seminaries have a course on the Holocaust. However, some seminaries indicated that this topic is covered in other courses and/or institutes of study. Yom Hashoah (Remembrance Day) was commemorated by a number of the seminaries.

Tables 14, 15, 16 outline the courses related to Jewish Studies.

TABLE 14

Jewish Studies Offered in Department of:	%		
	Yes	No	No Response
Theology (Scripture, Religious Studies)	70.0	2.5	27.5
History	22.5	50.0	27.5
Sociology	2.5	70.0	27.5
Education	-	72.5	27.5
Language	15.0	57.5	27.5
English	2.5	70.0	27.5
Other	2.5	70.0	27.5

Again, as within the colleges, the Theology or Religious Studies Department (70.0%) offers the courses related to Judaism.

Table 15 gives the seminaries' response on "evaluation." Of the responses 32.5% rated themselves "Good" to "Excellent." Once again, the "No response" or missing (42.5%) was due to the fact that some questionnaires were returned because of the closing of the seminary; others were unanswered because the "seminary" was only a two-year institution and/or only preparatory.

TABLE 15

Evaluation of Courses Offered in Judaism	%
Excellent	7.5
Good	25.0
Poor	17.5
Not Applicable	17.5
No Response (Missing)	42.6

When responding to the open-ended questions #28-30, the writer gave reasons for the choices expressed in the above Table 15.

However, in Table 16, one can learn of the difficulties that, at times, hinder the seminary from offering courses related to Jews and Judaism.

TABLE 16

Difficulties in Offering Courses on Jews/Judaism	%
Lack of Time	37.5
Lack of Student Interest	30.0
Lack of Funds	17.5
Lack of Qualified Personnel	22.5
Lack of Leadership	5.0
Other	2.5

Again, it would seem that most seminaries felt that "time" did not allow for the offering of special courses on Judaism.

Tables 17, 18, and 19 picture the Resources and Cooperation with outside agencies/organizations in offering courses of Jewish Studies. See the following pages 28 and 29.

About forty percent (40.0%) of the seminaries co-sponsored programs with other organizations. The American Jewish Committee and the Anti-Defamation League of B'nai B'rith both have been very much involved in a number of seminary programs, each 17.5% respectively. The Jewish Chautauqua Society (12.5%) has also co-sponsored programs of Jewish Studies. The 1985 Survey also noted a relationship with the Secretariat for Catholic-Jewish Relations,

(10.5%), and 12.5% with the Ecumenical Commissions.

TABLE 17

Resources for Teaching Courses of Jewish Studies
Faculty, Library, Institutes

	Yes	No	No Response
Christian Faculty	30.0	2.5	67.5
Jewish Faculty	30.0	42.5	27.5
Faculty-Sponsored by Jewish Organizations	22.5	47.5	30.0
Library Teaching Materials-Sponsored by Jewish Organizations	22.5	40.0	37.5
Programs/Institute of Jewish Studies	37.5	35.0	27.5
Study in Israel	15.0	55.0	30.0
Jewish/Christian Faculty - Institutes	35.0	15.0	47.5

TABLE 18

Length of Special Programs of Jewish Studies	% Days				
	1-3	4-9	10-14	N/A	No Response
	47.5			5.0	47.5

TABLE 19

Cooperation With Jewish or Christian Organizations Such as:*	Yes	% No	No Response
	40.0	30.0	30.0
Local Jewish Community	5.0		
American Jewish Committee	17.5		
Anti-Defamation League B'nai B'rith	17.5		
Union of American Hebrew Congregations	2.5		
Synagogue Council of America	-		
American Jewish Congress	-		
Jewish Chautauqua Society	12.5		
National Conference of Christians and Jews	5.0		
National Catholic Conference on Interracial Justice	-		
Secretariat for Catholic-Jewish Relations	10.0		
Ecumenical Commissions	12.5		
Other	10.0		

*Checked more than one organization

Each of the seminaries was asked to evaluate their own special programs of Jewish Studies. Table 20 gives this picture of Evaluation while Table 21 notes the difficulties seminaries had in offering special programs.

TABLE 20

Evaluation of Responses to Special Programs of Jewish Studies	%
Excellent	12.5
Good	27.5
Poor	2.5
No response	57.5

About 40% rated themselves "Good" to "Excellent." Where there is "no response," the questionnaire was simply returned because of reasons given above on page 26.

TABLE 21

Difficulties in Offering Special Programs of Jewish Studies	%
Lack of time	40.0
Lack of Student Interest	20.0
Lack of Funds	30.0
Lack of Qualified Personnel	7.5
Lack of Leadership	17.5
Other	5.0

Comments coming from the respondents indicated that a crowded curriculum did not allow time for special programs of Jewish Studies (40.0%). However, others indicated that the material was covered in their daily Scripture and/or Religious Studies courses. Table 21 outlines the difficulties some of the seminaries have had in offering special Christian/Jewish programs.

The following Tables 22, 23 and 24 are expressions of the open-ended responses to questions #28, #29, and #30.

TABLE 22

Visible Rewards in Offering Courses on Judaism	%
(Responses Rated by Researcher)	
Excellent	25.0
Good	45.0
Poor	12.5
N/A	17.5

Question #28 asked the respondents: "What have been the most visible rewards in offering courses in Judaism and related areas?"

Seventy (70.0) percent gave responses which this writer could judge to be "excellent" - to - "good." Many indicated that students, community and faculty had a deepened understanding and appreciation of their rootedness in Judaism. Contact with living Faith and Traditions of the Jewish People awakened a respect not entertained before.

Table 23 pictures the respondents' evaluation of special programs, institutes, and/or seminars on Jewish Studies.

TABLE 23

Visible Rewards in Offering Institutes, Programs, Seminars of Jewish Studies	%
Excellent	20.0
Good	22.5
Poor	5.0
Other	32.5
N/A	20.0

Question #29 inquired about rewards in offering special programs which are not a part of the curricula but which relate to it. Table 23 above is this writer's rating of the responses given. About 42% said their efforts were "Excellent" - to - "Good." Since there were many who do not sponsor such programs, 32.5%, we had fewer responses in this category.

Question #30 requested an overall self-evaluation of each respective seminary answering the questionnaire. Table 24 gives this information.

TABLE 24

Overall Self-evaluation of Efforts for Implementation of the Conciliar Documents and U.S. Bishops' Statement on Christian-Jewish Relations	%
Excellent	35.0
Good	32.5
Poor	5.0
Other	10.0
N/A	17.5

Conclusions and Recommendations

It is quite evident that the seminaries who responded to the questionnaire see the great need for implementation of the teaching of the Conciliar 1965 document on Christian-Jewish Relations, the 1974 Roman Catholic Guidelines and Suggestions for carrying out the Vatican II document <u>Nostra Aetate</u>, and the U.S. Bishops' 1975 Statement on Christian-Jewish Relations. Seminary students, above all, are in great need of this area of study. As future priests they will be giving the homilies which are often based on the Scripture readings. Hence, a deepened knowledge of the Rabbinic background of the New Testament, for example, will enrich their sermons and thus help destroy the myths, misinformation, and stereotypes about Jews and Judaism.

A correct understanding of the Passion narratives in the Gospels needs to be presented to the parishioners during Holy Week. Often people leave Holy Week services blaming Jews for the crucifixion of Jesus when, indeed, it was because of the sins of humankind that Jesus suffered and died.

Treatment of the Pharisees must be done as outlined in the recent "Notes on the Correct Way to Present the Jews and Judaism in Preaching and Catechesis in the Roman Catholic Church"[2] from the Vatican Commission for Religious Relations With the Jews, June 24, 1985.

As ever so many seminaries indicated, not only did a deeper understanding of Christianity's rootedness within Judaism result from offering courses on Jewish studies, but also a more profound understanding and a new appreciation of contemporary Judaism was gained.

Samples of Responses to Open-Ended Questions #28-30.

Giving positive responses. (There were no negative responses.)

Sample answers:

> "Respect for other traditions and people."
>
> "Slow but steady progress in challenging old stereotypes and misinformation."
>
> "Great student satisfaction."

---

[2] Vatican Commission on Religious Relations With the Jews, "Notes" June 24, 1985.

"Better understanding and deeper appreciation of both Judaism and Christianity."

"Beautiful contact with living faith of Jewish People."

"Community goodwill and creation of personal friendships."

"Seminary students are enthusiastic in their response in sharing 2 days with Jewish and Protestant students. Our students are pushed to further academic studies in the area as a result."

"A new sensitivity to Christian injustice and lack of awareness."

"Heightened awareness and active care that teaching reflects and promotes a better knowledge of Judaism and esteem of Jewish tradition and of Jewish people themselves."

"We've done well. The Jewish Chautauqua Society established a resident lectureship in Judaism at _____ in 1968. We offer courses each year in Jewish Studies; we have had two very successful study tours to Israel with waiting lists for two years."

"The Professors of Sacred Scripture and Church History make it a point to note wherever they can in their courses the relations between Jews and Christians."

"We have made honest, earnest, and sustained efforts with some modest success. We certainly could do more, and I am sure that we shall."

"Even though we have done many things I would only rate our efforts as 'good,' not 'excellent. Although there is universal faculty support and good student response, the time and schedule factors are inhibiting in a seminary. There are too, too many demands: required heavy course load, field education, placements, formation requirements - the area of Jewish/Christian relation gets all too often lost in the shuffle! Changes will come June 1st; we will have a new Dean!"

CHAPTER IV

SURVEY REPORT ON ARCHDIOCESAN/DIOCESAN
ECUMENICAL COMMISSIONS

The Ecumenical Commissions (213) in the United States each were sent a specially designed questionnaire. Of the 213 mailed, 75 were returned or 35.21%. A number of the Commissions had just been formed; they had no data to report. In other instances, there were very recent appointments to a new chair, turn-over of administration was frequent; hence, the data reflected this. Many questions were left unanswered due to new leadership; hence, the larger numbers of either "No response" or "Not applicable" or "Not known by me." A number of commissions had been formed too recently to respond with valuable data.

The following discussion and tables will give the story of the ecumenical commissions' implementation of the Conciliar Statements and the National Conference of Catholic Bishops'(NCCB) document on Catholic-Jewish Relations.

Thirty-six percent (36.0%) of the Commissions have a sub-committee on Catholic-Jewish concerns;

TABLE 25

Commission Concerns	%		
	Yes	No	None
Sub Committee on Catholic/ Jewish Concerns	36.0	53.0	10.6
Commission as a whole directs Catholic-Jewish concerns	53.0	36.0	10.6
Topic of Catholic-Jewish Concerns: a priority	48.0	42.0	9.3

fifty-three percent (53.0%) of the Commissions, as a whole, direct attention to Catholic-Jewish concerns. In only half of the Commissions is the topic of relations with Jews and Judaism a priority. Some of the respondents claimed that it was not necessary to teach and/or be concerned because of the small Jewish population within their respective jurisdiction.

Another question tried to determine the specific efforts of each commission to implement the teachings of Nostra Aetate concerning Jews and Judaism. Table 26 pictures the various ways the Commissions tried to disseminate knowledge related to Judaism.

TABLE 26

Specific Efforts of Implementation	Yes	% No	No Response
Special Programs	46.66	41.33	16.0
Seminars/Institutes/ Workshop	38.66	44.0	17.3
Publications	16.0	66.66	17.3
Dialogue Groups	50.66	32.0	17.3
Other	43.0		

Special Programs

An interesting and varied number of special programs (46.6%) were held by the different Commissions. Many are celebrating the 20th anniversary of the promulgation of <u>Nostra Aetate</u>, the 1965 Vatican Declaration on the Relations of the Church to the Jewish People. A large number of Commissions hold their own diocesan/archdiocesan Holocaust Remembrance Service. In some dioceses the Bishop has been the leader, addressing groups and/or issuing a Pastoral letter on either "Anti-Semitism" or on "Catholic-Jewish Relations." This was then re-published and distributed by the Commission. Many held joint inter-religious services on Thanksgiving and on Passover held a Seder meal.

Work was done with Religious Educators of the

parishes in the dioceses; for example, a special program on areas related to Jews/Judaism and/or teaching the New Testament was presented by scholars each semester. Dialogue on Passion Narratives was carried out in a number of parishes. When the Heritage Series[3] appeared on television, it was viewed by a number of Commissions. This was followed by discussions using the AJC Study Guides.

The Resource Kit published by the American Jewish Committee, entitled Vatican Council II and Catholic-Jewish Relations[4] (1965-1985) was used by a number of Commissions. Other diocesan commissions indicated that they had just begun and that plans were being designed for implementation.

Seminars/Institutes/Workshops

The Commissions are very much involved in activities relating to teaching about Jews, Judaism and the State of Israel. A number reported on annual programs held in conjuction with the University in the area. Others sponsor workshops with the National Conference of Christians and Jews (NCCJ), World Council of Churches and the diocesan education days with the diocese. One reported that "seminars are held with teachers to sensitize them to the

---

[3] American Jewish Committee. "Heritage: Civilization and the Jews"' An Inter-religious Study Guide, 1984.

[4] American Jewish Committee. Vatican Council II and Catholic-Jewish Relations 1965-1985 (Resource Kit), 1984.

living reality of Judaism, their relationship to the Hebrew Scriptures (the Old Testament) and to the history of modern Israel." A number of institutes have been held for seminarians and/or clergy to examine the Jewish Tradition, thus helping clergy to understand the Jewish background of the New Testament.

Publications

Very few Commissions have entered the field of publishing materials in the area of Catholic-Jewish Relations. Most Commissions try to awaken interest in those publications available from the Secretariat for Catholic-Jewish Relations and from American Jewish Committee, the Anti-Defamation League of B'nai B'rith and Union of American Hebrew Congregations.

Sixteen percent (16%) of the Commissions, however, do have their own publications. These were often in the form of Guidelines for Holy Week Services and/or Good Friday. A number of Commissions have Guidelines for Catholic-Jewish marriages or these are in the planning stage. Another Commission issued "Cautions on Passion Plays" to the parishes. Quite a few indicated that they are in the "planning stage" and "hoped to do more."

Dialogue Groups

About fifty percent (50%) of the Commissions have dialogue groups. The respondents noted that Christian-Jewish Dialogue Groups have been meeting monthly or bi-monthly for over a period of four, five, eight or ten years. A number have regular clergy dialogue groups. Some meet with National Conference of Christians and Jews (NCCJ) dialogue groups at least twice monthly. At least five reported "living room dialogues" or "Facing Issues Together." Another Commission reported on a weekly radio program where a Rabbi, Priest, and Minister held a dialogue regarding issues of concern to each group. Still another Commission holds a dialogue group with Catholics, Jews, and Arab-Americans.

Other

About 43% of the Commissions indicated responses in the category of "Other." There were about four (4) dioceses who are in "planning stages; five (5) noted that their education plans were aided by local Rabbis; six (6) had just begun a "dialogue group"; two (2) indicated much help coming from U.S. Bishops' Secretariat. Some have pulpit exchanges. Another held an art exhibit which was most helpful.

In summary, the Commissions have responded to the Conciliar Documents and are, indeed, trying to carry forth the teachings of the National Conference of Catholic Bishops' (NCCB) Statement on Catholic-Jewish Relations.

Ecumenical Commissions must try to help their constituents "acquire a better knowledge of the basic components of the religious tradition of Judaism,"[5] as outlined by the Vatican Commission For Religious Relations With the Jews.

Table 27 pictures responses to questions (5-10) dealing with specific guideline issues.

TABLE 27

Guidelines	Yes %
Dialogue Groups	21.3
C/J Marriages	25.3
Parish Passion Plays	9.3
For Understanding Passion Narratives	10.6
Treatment of Pharisees	6.6

All of the above issues have been pointed out by the U.S. Bishops' Secretariat as those which may often be a cause of misinformation regarding Jews or Judaism. Guidelines for honest dialogue are necessary and do help those involved to discuss racial, inter-religious, and/or troublesome issues.

About 16 Commissions (21.3%) have their own guidelines for dialogue groups. Others use the

---

[5]Vatican Commission for Religious Relations With the Jews. <u>Guidelines and Suggestions for Implementing the Conciliar Declaration "Nostra Aetate."</u> Rome, December 1, 1974.

National Conference of Christians and Jews' Guidelines.

A number of commissions (19) or 25.3% have guidelines for Catholic-Jewish marriages. Others mentioned that they were "in the planning stage" and not available for publication. Fifteen Commissions (20%) have either suggestions (cautions) for passion plays and/or guides to understanding the passion narratives. Very few Commissions have dealt with the "Treatment of the Pharisees" in the Gospel readings. The "Notes on preaching and teaching about Jews and Judaism"[6] specifically request that treatment of the Pharisees must receive special attention. In fact, the latest Vatican Commission's teachings state that "an exclusively negative picture of the Pharisees is likely to be inaccurate and unjust (cf. Guidelines, Note 1; cf. AAS, loc. cit. p. 76). Preachers and teachers are to point out that "if Jesus shows Himself severe toward the Pharisees, it is because He is closer to them than to other contemporary Jewish groups." (Ibid.).

Question #11 requested information on guidelines for homilists for Sunday Lectionary Readings. Table 28 pictures the responses.

---

[6] Vatican Commission on Religious Relations With Jews. Notes on the Correct Way to Present Jews and Judaism in Preaching and Catechesis in the Roman Catholic Church. June 24, 1985

TABLE 28

Guidelines Lectionary Readings for Sunday Liturgy	
	Yes %
Advent Period	4
Lenten Period	9
Pentecostal Period	3
Ordinary	3

Not many Commissions have issued guidelines for Sunday lectionary readings. It seemed that during the Lenten Period more Commissions (9.0%) prepared either "Comments" or "Suggestions" on the major Sunday readings.[7]

Question #12 asked about the use of Psalm 22 in the Good Friday Liturgy to replace the "Reproaches." See Table 29.

About one-third (36%) of the Commissions who participated in this research have heeded the Bishops' Liturgy Committee of the National Conference of Catholic Bishops and are either using Psalm 22 or other suitable hymns.

---

[7]John M. Oesterreicher. "Comments on the Major Readings for the Sundays of Lent, 1977," presented to Archdiocesan Commission for Ecumenical and Interreligious Affairs for distribution to all Pastors.

TABLE 29

	Yes	No	No Response
Psalm 22/Suitable Hymns in place of The Good Friday Reproaches			
Psalm 22 or Suitable Hymns	36.0	53.3	10.6

About 10% were not aware of this suggestion from the Bishops' Liturgy Committee. Others commented that they were grateful for the reminder and still others indicated that they will do so at the next Good Friday Services.

It was too difficult to determine how many parishes are implementing the above suggestion; hence, this writer did not include a survey of question #13.

Table 30 gives a coverage of responses to question #14 concerning the sponsorship of learning sessions.

TABLE 30

Joint Programming Diocesan Department of Education and/or Office of Religious Education			
	Yes	No	No Response
Department of Education	25.3	65.3	9.4
Office of Religious Education	64.0	36.0	-

Most of the Commissions (64%) jointly sponsor Jewish-Christian study programs with the office of Religious Education. Often these are part of a 2 or 3-day program in the Fall Semester of each academic year.

Each respondent was asked to give a brief self-evaluation to question #15. The writer, after reading the open-ended responses, categorized them into Excellent, Good, Poor, etc. as found in Table 31.

TABLE 31

Overall Evaluation of the Efforts for Implementation of Conciliar Documents and U.S. Bishops' Statement on Jewish/Christian Relations

	%
Excellent	26.6
Good	16.0
Poor	20.0
Other	21.3
No Response	9.3
No Commission	6.6

The responses indicate that 42.6% rated themselves "Good-Excellent." About 20.0% noted that they "could do much more" in this area of Catholic-Jewish Relations. Another 9% gave no response; 6% indicated they had no ecumenical commission or were just beginning.

Conclusions and Summary

The survey of the Diocesan/Archdiocesan Ecumenical and Interreligious Commissions demonstrated that some work was being done in Catholic-Jewish concerns. That much more needs to be done is evident from the responses. However, there are a number of Commissions who are deeply involved in the implementation of the Conciliar Declaration on the Jews and the National Conference of Catholic Bishops Statement. Again, the very reason for the creation of the Commissions is that each might work to implement the Conciliar documents for the 1974 Guidelines[8] specifically state: "the Bishops . . . will create some suitable Commissions or secretariats on a regional level, or appoint some competent person to promote the implementation of the Conciliar directives."[9]

A number of respondents indicated that they did not need to implement the Conciliar statements on the Jews and the National Conference of Catholic Bishops' statement because "not many Jewish people lived in the area." True, this fact may make it difficult to dialogue, co-sponsor and/or invite guest lecturers who are Jewish. Nevertheless, the most recent teaching from the Vatican Commission

---

[8]Vatican Commission on Religious Relations With the Jews. Guidelines and Suggestions, op. cit., p. 7.

[9]Ibid., p. 7.

states:

> Because of the unique relations that exist between Christianity and Judaism - 'linked together at the very level of their identity' (John Paul II, 6th March, 1982), - relations 'founded on the design of the God of the Covenant' (Ibid.), the Jews and Judaism should not occupy an occasional and marginal place in catechesis: their presence there is essential and should be organically integrated.[10]

Hence, whether or not Jews reside within areas adjacent to Catholics, it is absolutely essential that a positive study of Jews and Judaism be a part of our Catholic teachings.

---

[10] "Notes," op. cit., p. 2.

CHAPTER V

SURVEY REPORT ON HIGH SCHOOLS

Each of the questionnaires differed. For the full description of each instrument, please see the appendix.

The high school sample included 300 Catholic High Schools from all areas of the United States. Again, these addresses were supplied by the National Catholic Education Association. There were 114 returns, or 38%.

Special Findings of the Research

Table 32 on page 50 gives the summary responses to questions relating to the curriculum and the faculty.

Only 21.05% offer a special course on Judaism but two-thirds (68.4%) offered a course on Judaism in a World Religions Course. The "Relationship of Christianity to Judaism" seems to be given a great deal of attention since 94.74% indicated a positive response.

The 1985 questionnaire asked the question if the courses on Jews and Judaism "present Judaism as an enduring Covenant to the present time." There were many (82.46%) who responded in the affirmative. Many high school curricula treat the Rabbinic background of the New Testament - 76.32%. Only 37.7% treat "Jewish History since the emergence of Christianity" in a special course.

TABLE 32

Catholic High Schools' results in percentage		
Courses offered or within course:	%Yes	%No
Judaism	21.05	78.9
Comparative/World Religions	68.42	31.58
Relationship of Christianity to Judaism	94.74	5.26
Presenting Judaism as an Enduring Covenant	82.46	17.54
Rabbinic Thought	76.32	23.68
Jewish History since Christianity	37.72	62.28
Lessons on Holocaust	62.28	37.72
Church History including Holocaust	33.33	66.67
Any Course on Holocaust	8.78	91.22
Meaning of State of Israel	30.70	69.30
History of State of Israel	9.65	90.35

There were three questions concerning teachings and/or courses on the Holocaust. In the 1970 study only 13.6% treated the Holocaust; the 1985 research noted that 62.28% teach the "lessons of the Holocaust" while one-third (33.3%) do so in a Church History course. Only 30.0% have a course on the State of Israel noting its meaning; nine percent (9%) offer a course on the History of the State of Israel. Again, in 1970, only 5% bothered to treat the State of Israel; in this study, 35% had teachings on Israel.

Table 33 describes the faculty involved in teaching areas related to Jewish Studies.

TABLE 33

Faculty Involved in Teaching Courses	%	
	Yes	No
Jewish Faculty	2.63	97.36
Local Rabbis/Jewish Adjunct	49.12	50.87
Faculty Participation in programs of Jewish/Christian Studies	44.73	55.26

Often Jewish persons are involved in teaching and/or lecturing on topics related to Judaism - about 51.75%. Faculty also seek to prepare themselves by attending seminars/institutes of Jewish Studies, about 44.7%.

A number of the respondents indicated that they received their enthusiasm for offering courses related to Judaism from participation in Jewish Studies programs, e.g., the Menorah Institute at Seton Hall University, Wheeling College and/or Barat College.

TABLE 34

Preparation of Faculty
Sponsor of Jewish/Christian Programs

	%
Diocese/Archdiocese	14.9
Local Jewish Community	13.15
American Jewish Committee	1.75
Anti-Defamation League	6.14
Union of American Hebrew Congregations	0.9
National Conference of Christians/Jews	6.1
Institute of Judaeo-Christian Studies	3.5
Local Ecumenical Commission	6.1
Other	18.4

It would seem that most faculty received encouragement to teach about Jews and Judaism from their own dioceses (14.9%) About 18.4% indicated "Other" and when spelling this out it happened that individuals participated in programs of Jewish Studies sponsored by colleges/universities. Jewish organizations often co-sponsored these institutes at a number of Catholic universities.

Table 35 on page 53 gives the percentage of responses on religion texts in use at Catholic high schools.

TABLE 35

Religion Teaching Methods
Textbooks/Synagogues

	Yes %
Visited Local Synagogue and/or Temple	21.05
Texts present positive portrayal of Jews	92.98
Texts present Judaism as an Enduring Covenant	70.18

Respondents (21.05%) indicated that their students regularly visited a local synagogue or temple where the Rabbi would lecture to the group of students. A large percentage evaluated their textual materials as being very positive (92.98%) in the treatment of Jews. This positive treatment presented Judaism as an enduring Covenant existing to the present time.

One question asked for a self-evaluation regarding the high school's efforts for implementation of the Conciliar Document of 1965, the Roman Catholic Guidelines and Suggestions of 1974 and the National Conference of Catholic Bishops' Statement on Catholic-Jewish Relations. Table 36 gives this basic information.

TABLE 36

Self-Evaluation of Efforts for Implementation of Conciliar and U.S. Bishops' Documents of Catholic-Jewish Relations	%
Very Satisfactory	15.7
Satisfactory	69.2
Unsatisfactory	14.9

Over two-thirds (69.2%) characterized their efforts as "satisfactory" and 15.7% deemed their efforts were "Very Satisfactory." The respondents gave reasons for their evaluation. At the end of this chapter, the writer has listed a sampling of these responses.

Question #21 asked that respondents summarize their institutions' overall efforts. These open-ended responses were categorized by the writer into "Excellent," "Good," "Poor," and "No Response." See Table 37 on page 55.

The high schools' responses again indicated a very positive approach to teaching about Jews and Judaism. About 75% of those responding evaluated their efforts from "Good" to "Excellent." About 22% felt their efforts were "poor" but each indicated they would try to do more.

Table 38 pictures the religion textbooks most often used by the High Schools. See page 55.

TABLE 37

Overall Evaluation of Catholic High Schools' Efforts of Implementation	%
Excellent	35.9
Good	38.5
Poor	21.9
Other	3.5

TABLE 38

Textbooks, in addition Scriptures Religion (Respondents listed more than one)	%
Wm. C. Brown Co. Series (Wilkin's texts and McCarty's books)	57.01
Ave Maria Press Series	18.42
Sadlier Press Series	18.42
Saint Mary Press Series	15.78
Silver Burdett Company Series	9.64
Benziger Books	9.64
Paulist Press	4.3
Argus	4.3
Pennock	4.3

The most frequently used textbook series, in addition to the Scriptures, was the Wm. C. Brown Company (57.01%). Each high school used a number of various books to teach their students. A number supplemented their teachings with Elie Wiesel's books, especially Night.[11]

Others used Exodus and/or The Diary of Ann Frank. Some used Argus Communications' materials, an excellent series entitled: The Jewish Tradition, synchronized with several filmstrips.

The writer did not request other audio-visual media used for the teaching about Jews and Judaism. There are many films, recordings, filmstrips available for this teaching. The reader may wish to write to the American Jewish Committee for information. From the Anti-Defamation League of B'nai B'rith a wealth of teaching materials is available on Holocaust Studies. The League will be happy to send the reader a catalogue of their materials, books, pamphlets, films, filmstrips, slides and recordings on topics of Jews and Judaism, Holocaust, Israel and other related topics.

The National Conference of Christians and Jews has prepared a booklet entitled: "A Liturgical Interpretation of Our Lord's Passion in Narrative Form" by John T. Townsend.

---

[11] Elie Wiesel. Night. New York: Bantam Books, 1960.

The American Jewish Committee has a special office located in Chicago, Illinois under the auspices of Sister Anna Marie Erst. She directs the National Institute of Catholic-Jewish Relations, helping high school teachers disseminate knowledge about Jews and Judaism. A filmstrip which has proved very helpful is <u>Christians and Jews: A Troubled Brotherhood</u> by Sister Suzanne Noffke, O.P., Ph.D., and published by Alba House Communications, Canfield, Ohio.

Conclusions and Recommendations

In conclusion, this writer recommends that Catholic High Schools' faculty be given more opportunities for furthering their academic qualifications in this field so as to be able to adequately teach courses related to Jews, Judaism, the Holocaust and the State of Israel. A number of States, as has the State of New Jersey, have created "the Governor's Council for Holocaust Studies Within the Public Schools." Special training sessions are held to prepare teachers to teach this period of history. The Council for the State of New Jersey has prepared a Holocaust curricula which is now being used in the schools of New Jersey.[12] This material may be obtained from the National

---

[12] Richard F. Flaim and Edwin Reynolds. <u>The Holocaust and Genocide: A Search for Conscience</u>. New York: The Anti-Defamation League of B'nai B'rith. Revised Edition, 1985.

Office of the Anti-Defamation League of B'nai B'rith.

Again, some institutions indicated that since there were very few Jews in the vicinity of their High School, they had no need to teach or to implement the 1965 Conciliar Declaration on the Jews, the 1974 Guidelines and Suggestions and the 1975 Statement on Catholic-Jewish Relations from the National Catholic Conference of Bishops. To conclude that this has been already accomplished would be to judge wrongly. All Catholics have been given the documents for study and implementation in order to be better Catholics. Christians must recognize and appreciate their rootedenss in Judaism; Christians need this basic knowledge so that each may understand the "good news" of the Gospels and the New Testament writings. With an appreciation of Jews and Judaism, prejudice toward God's Chosen People will be dispelled. Myths and stereotypes will no longer dictate one's actions toward another Faith group- the Jewish People.

In many instances the questionnaire itself was a learning tool. Respondents were grateful for the "reminder" and intended to carry out the Vatican teachings.

In summary, the questionnaire findings indicated that most Catholic institutions have a deep appreciation of their rootedness in Judaism, and for the contributions of the Jewish People; they displayed love and respect for God's People and for contemporary Judaism. Above all, these Christian-Jewish studies increased their own Faith commitment.

Sampling of Responses to Open-Ended Questions #20-#21

"We use the 1965 and 1974 Vatican Documents and the Bishops' Statement on Catholic-Jewish Relations to design courses."

"Faculty is very sensitive to Jewish-Christian issues and traditions."

"Knowledge of Jewish traditions and culture incorporated in Religion and History courses."

"Religion courses emphasize that Christianity has roots, traditions, rituals, beliefs in Judaism."

"Ecumenical attitude prevails. Faculty are familiar with 'To Teach as Jesus Did.' Ideas are implemented in the curriculum, liturgies."

"Faculty and Students are provided with copies of the documents. After reading, discussion follows, then study groups are formed."

"Great effort to present Judaism as enduring Covenant."

"We re-designed courses (Religion, History, etc.) to include Jewish understanding; introduced ecumenical prayer experience; rewrote the school's philosophy to include official Documents."

CHAPTER VI

SURVEY REPORT FROM SUPERINTENDENTS' OFFICES

Of the 180 questionnaires distributed to the offices of superintendents of Catholic schools, 43 or 23.9% responded.

Findings Regarding Elementary Schools

Table 39 pictures responses to question #1.

TABLE 39

Methods of helping teachers implement the Conciliar Statement on the Jews;
the 1974 Guidelines
and U.S. Bishops' 1975 Statement on
Jewish-Christian Relations

	%
Special programs	37.2
Seminars/Institutes	37.2
Unique Teaching Materials	39.5
Other	37.2

Each of the respondents described briefly the various methods used to prepare and motivate their teachers to teach about Jews and Judaism. Some examples were:

"The Seder was explained at a special program."

"Workshop for Educators on 'Teaching the Jewish Experiences in America.'"

"Pulpit exchanges with local Synagogues."

"Discussion: 'Facing History and Ourselves.'"

"Participation in National Conference of Christians and Jews' essay contest and film festival."

"Excellent workshops, working with Jewish community leaders and Diocesan leaders to 'amend' textbooks and prepare guidelines for teachers."

"Worked with _____ university to develop a curriculum to teach Jewish history and the Holocaust."

"Campus Kaleidoscope; Interfaith dialogue; Conference on fighting bigotry and violence; preservation of family heritage."

"Study of Holocaust and Human Behavior."

"We constantly screen texts and resources for their perspective on Jews and Judaism."

"Religion Teachers' Guides, Anti-Defamation League of B'nai B"rith materials."

"We cooperate with Jewish organizations and publish the ready availability of their sources."

"The Holocaust is the core of the curriculum unit, builds concept of conflict and conflict resolution-justice is treated and discussed."

"Rabbis visit our classes; Bar Mitzvah students read the Torah."

"Performed "Echoes of Children" cantata for all students.

"National Catholic Council for Interracial Justice, Chicago Council of Rabbis and B'nai B'rith circulate their 'Justice Library' and filmstrips on Jewish History, the Holocaust, and share Seders.

Findings Regarding Secondary Schools

Table 40, on page 62 gives a picture of the involvement of secondary schools in their methodology for helping faculties gain knowledge of Jews and Judaism.

TABLE 40

Methods of helping teachers (secondary)
implement the Conciliar Statement on the Jews;
the 1974 Guidelines and the U.S. Bishops' 1975 Statement
on Jewish-Christian Relations

	%
Special Programs	39.53
Seminars/Institutes	34.88
Unique teaching materials	41.86
Other	20.93

Things are happening within the diocesan and archdiocesan school systems under the the auspices of the superintendents' offices. Table 40 indicates that 40% of those who responded have programs, seminars, etc. to prepare teachers or to motivate them to carry out the Church's teaching on Jews and Judaism. Examples of their responses describe for the reader just what is going on.

> "We have a series of study sessions on the Holocaust so teachers are prepared to teach this terrible period in our history."

> "We sponsor a tour to Israel, including European travel."

> "Jewish scholars address our teachers on topics relevant to Judaism."

> "We have study sessions on 'State of Israel,' 'Holocaust,' 'Mission to Israel' with Jews and Christians."

"Attend University sessions on 'Teaching on the Holocaust.'"

"Participated in a Jewish Chautauqua program."

"Rabbis supply us with special teaching materials."

"All secondary schools teach Old Testament."

"In World Religions courses, all teachers must be prepared to teach section on Judaism."

"We have institutes on Judaism in the diocese."

Many superintendents responded in like fashion for both elementary and secondary schools. Their programs were similar.

The responses of the superintendents on religion texts and the curricula offered were very positive. About 76.7% are satisfied with the treatment of Jews and Judaism in their texts. The writer is confident that the 13.95% who are dissatisfied will do something about making a change.

Seventy per cent (69.76%) speak of Judaism as "an enduring Covenant to the present day." This, too, is in accord with the teachings of the Vatican documents and, of course, with the teaching of St. Paul in Romans 9:11.[13]

Contemporary Judaism is treated in the Catholic religion textbooks, at least 65.11%. However, the 20.93% that do not mention "Contemporary Judaism" are books which ought not be used or if used must be updated

---

[13]Romans 9:11.

TABLE 41

Questions on Religion Texts and Curricula	Yes	% No	No Response
Religion texts give positive treatment of Jews/Judaism	76.74	13.95	9.3
Religion texts presenting Judaism as an Enduring Covenant	69.76	18.6	11.62
Religion texts treatment of present day Jews and Judaism	65.11	20.93	13.95
Course unit on State of Israel: Elementary	37.2	44.18	18.6
Course unit on State of Israel: Secondary	53.48	32.55	13.95
Course unit on Holocaust: Elementary	44.18	34.88	20.93
Course unit on Holocaust: Secondary	65.11	23.25	11.62
Satisfied with texts' treatment of Jews/Judaism	60.46	16.27	23.25

according to the Conciliar and U.S. Bishop's Statement.

It was, indeed, good to learn that 37.20% of the elementary schools teach a course on the State of Israel while 53.48% do so in secondary schools. However, it was very rewarding to learn that 44.18% have a course on the Holocaust in the elementary school curricula and that 65.11% have one in the secondary school curricula. This was unheard of in the 1970 documentary survey.

About two-thirds or 60.46% were satisfied with the texts' treatment of Jews and Judaism. However, faculties are free to supplement any textual material with other appropriate teaching aids and/or books.

Table 42 lists the series of books most frequently chosen for the elementary schools.

TABLE 42

Religion Textbooks Adopted by Superintendents' Offices for Elementary School Use

Series	%
Sadlier	67.44
Benziger	67.44
Silver Burdett	51.62
Wm. C. Brown	34.88
Loyola	27.90
Winston	23.25
Paulist	11.62
No list of religion texts given	18.60

According to Table 42, elementary schools are using the religion texts (67.44%) from Sadlier and Benziger Brothers (67.44%). The series from Silver Burdett and Wm. C. Brown shows percentages of 51.62% and 34.88% respectively. Other series are not used that often: Loyola (27.90%); Winston (23.25%); and Paulist Press (11.62%).

About 18.6% of the superintendents did not list religion texts for elementary schools. One of these offices had just opened in a new diocese; others did not adopt texts but urged their school systems to make their own selections.

Table 43 gives the data on religion texts adopted for secondary schools. The list coincides very well with the survey report from the high schools themselves.

TABLE 43

Religion Textbooks Adopted by Superintendents' Offices for Secondary School Use	
Series	%
Sadlier	34.88
Wm. C. Brown	30.23
Benziger	23.25
Ave Maria	16.27
Silver Burdett	11.62
Saint Mary Press	9.30
Loyola Press	6.97
Sunday Visitor	6.97
No list of religion texts given	39.53

Even though superintendents may have reported adoptions, almost everyone indicated that high school faculties made their own appropriate choices. See page 55 of the study which indicates the high schools' selection of religion texts.

Question #11 requested an estimate of the number of elementary and secondary schools served by the superintendents' office and the approximate enrollment. Table 44 gives this data.

TABLE 44

Number of Schools and Enrollment covered by Superintendents

Type	Number	Enrollment	No Response
Elementary	2,624	921,589	5
Secondary	414	257,211	4

Implications

It would seem that leaders/officers serving as superintendents from the sample of this study are very eager to carry out the teachings of the 1965 Conciliar Document on Catholics' Relation to Jews and Judaism; the 1974 Vatican Guidelines and Suggestions and the National Conference of Catholic Bishops' (NCCB) Statement on Catholic-Jewish concerns. Through education meetings prior to each school year, programs and/or special conferences could be sponsored on topics such as: "How to teach About Jews and Judaism," or "How to Teach the New Testament in light of Its Jewish Background." This we need to know and appreciate even though no community of Jews resides in the area of the school systems. To gain this knowledge is that by which individuals themselves have an opportunity to become better Christians.

CHAPTER VII

SUMMARY AND CONCLUSIONS

Restatement of the Problem and Procedure

The scope of this research included an analysis of questionnaires distributed to all Catholic Colleges/Universities (209); Seminaries (123), Archdiocesan/Diocesan Ecumenical Commissions (213); a sampling of Catholic High Schools (300); and to all offices of Superintendents (180). The names and addresses were supplied by the National Catholic Education Association Office. The American Jewish Committee and the Anti-Defamation League of B'nai B'rith each supported the research financially. The National Conference of Catholic Bishops' Secretariat for Catholic-Jewish relations and its advisory committee validated the questionnaires and gave their full cooperation. Seton Hall University, especially its College of Education and Human Services endorsed the research survey, and contributed many services to the writer.

The documentary study tried to discover efforts of Catholic Institutions of learning for the implementation of the 1965 Conciliar Statement on the Jews, the 1974 Vatican Guidelines and Suggestions for carrying out the 1965 document and the National Catholic Conference of Bishops' 1975 Statement on Catholic-Jewish Relations. This 1985 documentary research was a follow-up of the 1970 survey completed by this same author.

Results of 1985 Study

The 1985 research indicates an awareness of Catholic-Jewish concerns not noted in the 1970 study. The responses indicated a deep appreciation of Jews and Judaism. Curricula in institutions of higher learning reflected their recognition of Christianity's rootedness in Judaism! Students, because of a knowledgeable faculty and administrators have the opportunity today, not only to be aware of this common rootedness between Christians and Jews, but also to learn of the persecutions, pogroms, expulsions, forced conversions and a whole range of horrible injustices which have all too frequently come from the Christian side and have characterized their "relationship."

As Archbishop Gerety pointed out in his pastoral letter on Catholic-Jewish Relations:

> The duty of love towards our Jewish brothers and sisters has taken on a special urgency during this twentieth century. Never in all the preceding centuries has there been such awful evidence of the evil of anti-semitism as during our time. The Holocaust took place during the years of the Second World War. Six million Jews, men, women and children, old and young, were put to death in a program directed to the extermination of a whole people.

He goes on to tell the reader:

It is true that thousands of others died alongside the

Jews in that terrible slaughter of innocent people. However, the attack on the Jews had about it a particular generalized virulence never before seen in the whole history of humankind.

Archbishop Gerety reminded the readers of a possible source of this attack on Jews. He writes:

Surely the Nazis who directed the slaughter were not Christian. Nevertheless, that the Holocaust took place in the so-called Christian West should never be forgotten. *The seeds of anti-semitism long present among Christians undoubtedly prepared the way for such bitter fruit. This, we most sorrowfully acknowledge. (Italics are those of this author).* [14]

Holocaust Studies

It is evident that the Colleges/Universities and High Schools who responded in this research are definitely aware of the "teaching of contempt"[15] that was partially responsible for the Holocaust. These institutions today have corrected this negative teaching and are offering courses in Judaism, noting its enduring Covenant to the present time. These institutions teach in a positive way about Jews and Judaism. Contemporary Judaism, very seldom treated in textual material after the emergence of Christianity, is now given its rightful place in the curricula.

Courses on the Holocaust have become a part of the

---

[14] Archbishop Peter L. Gerety. "Catholic-Jewish Relations," A Pastoral Letter, published in The Advocate, November 13, 1975, and republished by Archdiocese of Newark's Office of Information Services and Public Affairs.

[15] Jules Isaac. The Teaching of Contempt. New York: Holt, Rinehart, Winston, 1962.

required courses in high schools, some elementary schools and in almost all the colleges and universities. Many institutions observe <u>Yom Hashoah</u> (Remembrance Day) and have special services to remember the atrocities committed against Jews during World War II.

Archbishop Gerety, in his pastoral letter, has this message:

> There must be a determination to cast from our midst any traces of this great evil. The Holocaust must never be permitted to fade from our memory. Anti-Semitism can never be squared with the Gospel imperative given to us by our Lord Himself. 'You shall love your neighbor as yourself.' 16

Even if no Jewish community is living in the area of a particular diocese or archdiocese, institutions of learning have a duty to teach courses, units, topics relating to Jews and Judaism. To do so gives students the opportunity to enhance their own Christian commitment. The entire New Testament, with its Jewish background, takes on new meaning for its readers.

Treatment of Pharisees

Implementation of the Vatican documents means that teaching on the Pharisees will no longer be given in a negative manner as was discovered by this writer in her

---

[16] Archbishop Gerety. <u>Op. cit.</u> p. 2. Also cf. <u>Origins</u>, Oct. 27, 1983 to note Cardinal Roger Etchegaray's message to the Synod of Bishops "The Jewish Root Which Remains Holy," p. 348-349. Cardinal Etchegaray has a strong message for all Catholic Educators, namely, in part: "So long as Judaism remains exterior to our history of salvation, we shall be at the mercy of anti-Semitic reflections."

St. Louis religion textbook research,[17] and verified again by the Fisher research.[18] The 1975 Vatican Guidelines on Catholic-Jewish Relations specifically mentioned the image of the Pharisees as an aspect of Judaism that requires much correction in Christian education teaching and preaching. The responses in this survey did not indicate any corrections of the traditional negative presentations of the Pharisaic movement. However, only one of the questionnaires asked this question. This appeared in the instrument distributed to Archdiocesan and Diocesan Ecumenical Commissions. Six and six-tenths (6.6%) of the Commissions who responded indicated that they have issued guidelines for the treatment of the Pharisees in the New Testament.

The French episcopal commission on relations with Jews issued this admonition:

> Contrary to established ways of thinking, it must be emphasized that Pharisaic doctrine is not opposed to that of Christianity. The Pharisees sought to make the law come alive in every Jew, by interpreting its commandments in such a way as to adapt them to the various spheres of life. Contemporary research has shown that the Pharisees were no more strangers to the innermost meaning

---

[17] Rose Thering, *The Self-Concept Potential in Religion Texts*. St. Louis University: St. Louis, 1961.

[18] Eugene Fisher. *Faith Without Prejudice*. New York: Paulist Press, 1977.

of the law than were the masters of the Talmud.[19]

The "Notes on the Correct Way to Present Jews and Judaism" issued June 24, 1985 urged educators to present a positive picture of the Pharisees. Preachers and teachers who give a negative interpretation would be teaching "inaccurately and unjustly."[20]

It is impossible to give a method of teaching about the Pharisaic Movement within the confines of this research study. The writer urges the readers to consult materials which are readily available to the readers.[21]

Passion Narratives

Another area of omission in the implementation of the Vatican documents and the National Conference of Catholic Bishops' Statement on Catholic-Jewish Relations is the lack of emphasis given to guidelines in the proper understanding of the passion of Jesus and the events surrounding it.[22]

---

[19] Helga Croner. *Stepping Stones To Further Jewish-Christian Relations*. London: Stimulus Books, 1977, p. 62.

[20] Vatican Commission on Religious Relations With the Jews, "Notes," *Op. cit.*

[21] John Pawlikowski. *What Are They Saying About Christian-Jewish Relations*. New York: Paulist Press, 1980. (The books he has listed are excellent resources on the Pharisees). Cf. also:

[22] Harvey Falk. *Jesus The Pharisee*. A New Look at the Jewishness of Jesus. New York/Mahwah: Paulist Press, 1985.

Popular preaching and teaching including Passion Plays have often used Catholic devotion to Christ crucified as an occasion for anti-Jewish statements. The Conciliar Statement on the Jews stated that this is clearly not in harmony with either the truth or the spirit of the Gospel.

In his pastoral letter, Archbishop Gerety stated:

> In the pulpit and classroom, we must guard against cliches and generalizations that would pit "the Jews" or "the Pharisees" against Jesus or the infant Church. The Jewish people of the Second Temple period harbored many spiritual, intellectual and political movements. Although Jesus did not belong to any of these groups, He stood closest to the Pharisees, and this is precisely the reason for the intense debates with some of them. In the majority of passages of the Fourth Gospel using the phrase "the Jews" St. John designates the Jewish authorities, especially in the context of the Passion and Resurrection narratives. The congregation should be made aware of this fact in the Good Friday liturgy and on other occasions when this Gospel is read. I urge our priests to make this clear to our people. 23

If pastors received the proper encouragement from the persons assigned to help others carry out these Vatican and/or Diocesan injunctions, proper instructions, especially during the Holy Week and Good Friday, would be given to the faithful on these days of commemoration and prayer. The Liturgy of the Word on Good Friday would then be such that it would lead the congregants to know their own weaknesses and develop into better persons.

---

[23] Archbishop Gerety's Pastoral Letter, op. cit. p. 13.

Truly, then Christians will see themselves as heirs of the privileges of Israel. Christians have been adopted into the family of Abraham and Sarah; like a wild shoot, Gentiles have been grafted onto the olive tree of Israel, supported by its root and sharing in the riches of its divinely given life.[24] During Lent and Holy Week Christians recall the events relating to the passion and death of Jesus. There is no greater opportunity for Christians to delve into the very heart of their faith. Nor is there a better occasion to appreciate their relationship to the descendants of Abraham and Sarah.[25]

The "Land Tradition"

Lastly, this writer recommends that Catholic institutions of learning rethink the admonition given them in the 1974 Guidelines and Suggestions for carrying out the teachings of the Vatican Councils' Statement on the Jews. The Vatican Commission for Religious Relations With the Jews specifically asked:

> Christians must strive to acquire a better knowledge of the basic components of the religious tradition of Judaism; they must strive to learn by what essential traits the Jews define themselves in the light of their own religious experience. 26

---

[24] Romans 11:16-24.

[25] Archbishop Gerety's Pastoral Letter, op. cit. p. 14.

[26] Vatican Commission for Religious Relations With The Jews, Guidelines and Suggestions, 1974, op. cit.

To this writer and to her colleagues working in the area of Christian-Jewish encounters this means that Christians must come to an understanding of Torah, People, and Land, three very important components of Judaism.

The National conference of Catholic Bishops have asked that:

> In dialogue with Christians, Jews have explained that they do not consider themselves as a church, a sect, or a denomination, as is the case among Christian communities, but rather as a peoplehood that is not solely racial, ethnic or religious, but in a sense a composite of all these. It is for such reasons that an overwhelming majority of Jews see themselves bound in one way or another to the land of Israel. Most Jews see this tie to the land as essential to their Jewishness. Whatever difficulties Christians may experience in sharing this view they should strive to understand this link between land and people which Jews have expressed in their writings and worship throughout two millenia as a longing for the homeland, holy Zion. Appreciation of this link is not to give assent to any particular religious interpretation of this bond. Nor is this affirmation meant to deny the legitimate rights of other parties in the region, or to adopt any political stance in the controversies over the Middle East, which lie beyond the purview of this statement. [27]

Institutions of learning in the Catholic community and diocesan ecumenical commissions must, indeed, come to a basic understanding of Land as Jews see and understand "Land." To omit this important issue is to overlook a vital issue of the dialogue. Books and articles have been written on the topic of "The Jews, The Bible

---

[27] National Conference of Catholic Bishops, 1975.

and the Land." Christians, too, need to develop their own approach to the "Land" tradition. W.D. Davies[28] and Walter Brueggeman[29] have a wealth of information for religious educators.

One needs to ponder what Msgr. John M. Oesterreicher has written in Brothers in Hope[30] and more recently in an article entitled, "The Flight Into Publicity" on the topic of 'Land.'

> For a Christian, the State of Israel can never be the 'beginning of redemption' as it is for Jews. Still it has religious meaning. In giving the Jewish people an opportunity for an independent existence and a rejuvenation of its spirit, it is evidence God has not terminated His Covenant with the people, indeed that He is their faithful Lord.[31]

---

[28]W.D. Davies. The Gospel and the Land. California: University of California Press, 1974.

W.D. Davis. The Territorial Dimension of Judaism. California: University of California Press, 1982.

[29]Walter Brueggeman. The Land. Philadelphia: Fortress Press, 1977.

[30]John M. Oesterreicher (ed.) Brothers in Hope. The Bridge. Vol. 5. New York: Herder & Herder, 1970. cf. "The Theologian and the Land of Israel," pp. 231-243.

[31]John M. Oesterreicher. "The Flight Into Publicity," The Advocate. July 13, 1985, p. 7.

John M. Oesterreicher. The Rediscovery of Judaism. Seton Hall University Institute of Judaeo-Christian Studies, 1971. (See also) James A. Rudin, Israel For Christians. Philadelphia: Fortress Press, 1983. Of course, this writer refers the reader to the Scriptures for the foundational ideas of the relationship of the Jewish People to the Land. (See bibliography).

Rev. Robert A. Everett in his article, "Zionism, Israel and Christian Hope" has claimed:

> Christian resistance to the Jewish State [the Land of Israel] will continue as long as Christians are unable to overcome the theological prejudice which says Jews are to be victims. Until we do overcome, until we are able to support and defend the Jewish State [the Jewish Homeland], we Christians will remain tied to a theological tradition which justifies our playing a role in victimizing the Jewish people. [32]

Rev. Everett reminded his readers:

> But history has now transformed our faith. It is ironic that those considered victims for so long should now be a source of Christian redemption. [33]

This researcher recommends that "the Theological Significance of the Land" be probed in our institutions of learning. What is its "redemptive quality for Christians since the Jewish People have returned to the Land which they never really abandoned?" [34]

Lastly, the 1985 document from the Vatican Commission, "Notes," states

> that the history of Israel did not end in 70 A.D. It continued . . . which allowed Israel to carry to the whole world a witness, often heroic of its fidelity to the one God . . . while preserving

---

[32] Robert E. Everett, "Zionism, Israel and Christian Hope," *Reflection*. Vol. 82, No. 3. New Haven: Yale Divinity School, April 1985, pp. 13-17.

[33] *Ibid.* p. 16.

[34] *Ibid.* p. 16.

> the memory of the Land of their forefathers at
> the heart of their hope. 35

Christians must understand this attachment to the Land.

The "Notes" stated, too, that "the State of Israel should be envisaged not in a perspective which is in itself religious, but in . . . reference to the common principles of international law,"^36 and the document reiterated its invitation to Christians

> to understand the religious attachment which Jews
> have expressed in their writings and worship
> throughout two millenia as a longing for the home-
> land, holy Zion. 37

In conclusion, this writer urges the reader to examine the "Notes" published June 24, 1985 reminding all educators:

> The question is not merely to uproot from among the
> faithful the remains of anti-Semitism still to be
> found here and there, but much rather to arouse
> in them, through educational work an exact
> knowledge of the wholly unique bond which joins us
> as a Church to Jews and to Judaism. 38

---

[35] Vatican Commission for Religious Relations With the Jews, "Notes," op. cit.

[36] "Notes," op. cit.

[37] NCCB Statement on Catholic-Jewish Relations, 1975, op. cit.

[38] "Notes," op. cit.

Indeed, to understand one's own Faith, the Christian needs a knowledge of Jews, Judaism and a deep appreciation and understanding of the basic components of Judaism: Torah, People and Land. [39]

---

[39] cf. Eugene Fisher. *Seminary Education and Catholic-Jewish Relations*, 1983 and Fisher, E. and Rabbi Leon Klenicki. *Understanding the Jewish Experience*, 1980.

APPENDIX

Letter to Constituencies

Questionnaire to Colleges,
    Universities and Seminaries

Questionnaire to Archdiocesan
    Ecumenical Commissions

Questionnaire to High Schools

Questionnaire to Superintendents of Schools

Seton Hall University

South Orange, New Jersey 07079

February 18, 1985

Dear Colleague,

In honor of the Twentieth Anniversary of the promulgation of the Conciliar Statement on the Jews which was issued October 28, 1965, I am conducting a research to determine the implementation of the 1965 Vatican Document, the 1975 Vatican Guidelines and Suggestions for Catholic-Jewish Relations, and the 1975 U.S. Bishops' Statement on Catholic-Jewish Relations, by institutions of learning within the Catholic community. In 1970, in celebration of the Fifth Anniversary, the Institute of Judaeo-Christian Studies of Seton Hall University did a five-year documentary research to note the implementation of the Conciliar Statement on the Jews; hence this research is a follow-up of the 1965-1970 study.

May I request your assistance in this important research? Kindly complete the questionnaire and return it to me as soon as possible. Please use the enclosed self-addressed stamped envelope. Thank you.

I am pleased the U.S. Bishops' Secretariat for Catholic Jewish Relations, the Institute of Judaeo-Christian Studies, Seton Hall University and the National Catholic Educational Association endorse this research project and will be using the findings in the Twentieth Anniversary Celebration in October, 1985.

I await your response.

Shalom!

Sincerely yours,

Rose Thering, O.P.

Rose Thering, O.P., Ph.D.

Enclosure

SETON HALL UNIVERSITY
COLLEGE OF EDUCATION AND HUMAN SERVICES
SOUTH ORANGE, N.J. 07079

SURVEY OF CATHOLIC COLLEGES AND UNIVERSITIES AND SEMINARIES' IMPLEMENTATION OF VATICAN II STATEMENT ON THE JEWS (1965), THE VATICAN GUIDELINES (1975); THE U.S. BISHOPS STATEMENT ON JEWISH/CATHOLIC RELATIONS, 1975

Please Respond by April 15, 1985

Yes	No	
/__/	/__/	1. Does your college or university have a Department of Jewish Studies?
/__/	/__/	2. Do you offer courses in Jewish Studies?
/__/	/__/	3. Is Judaism treated in a course on Comparative/World Religions?
/__/	/__/	4. Do you offer Scripture courses which specifically note the relationship of Christianity to Judaism, such as "Paul to the Romans" or "Rabbinic Background to the New Testament"?
/__/	/__/	5. Do you offer a special course in "Judaism" or the "Theology of Judaism"?
/__/	/__/	6. Do you offer any courses which present Judaism as an enduring Covenant which continues to the present time?
/__/	/__/	7. Do you offer a course on the Intertestamental Period?
/__/	/__/	8. Do you offer courses which treat Jewish history afer the emergence of Christianity?
/__/	/__/	9. Do you offer a course on the Holocaust?
/__/	/__/	10. Do you offer a course on the "History of the State of Israel"?
/__/	/__/	11. Do you offer a course on the "History of the Middle East"?
/__/	/__/	12. Are items 7-9 treated in other courses? If yes, please specify.
/__/	/__/	13. If you offer courses in Jewish Studies, are they in the undergraduate program only?
/__/	/__/	In the graduate program only?
/__/	/__/	In both?

Survey - Implementation continued

-2-

14. Check the Departments which offer courses in Jewish Studies (or related courses).

    _____Theology (Scripture, Religion, etc.)

    _____History

    _____Sociology of Human Relations

    _____Education

    _____Language (e.g., Hebrew)

    _____English ("Literature on the Holocaust")

    _____Other (please specify)

15. What has been the registration in courses in Judaism which you may have offered at your institution?

    _____Excellent

    _____Good

    _____Poor

16. In your estimation, what is the difficulty in offering courses in Studies of Judaism and Christianity? (Please rank order your responses 1-6).

    _____Lack of time

    _____Lack of student interest

    _____Lack of funds

    _____Lack of qualified personnel

    _____Lack of leadership

    _____Other (please explain). _____

    _____

Survey - Implementation continued

-3-

Yes	No		
/__/	/__/	17.	Do you have any Jewish faculty teaching courses of Jewish Studies? If so, please name them.

_____

_____

18. If Christian faculty teach such courses, would you list their names here?

_____

_____

Yes	No		
/__/	/__/	19.	Have you worked with a Jewish organization to obtain a Jewish scholar for your faculty?
/__/	/__/	20.	Have you received library books from Jewish organizations? If so, which Organization(s)?

_____

_____

Yes	No		
/__/	/__/	21.	Do you sponsor institutes, seminars, or special programs relating to studies of Judaism and Christianity?
/__/	/__/	22.	Check the lengths of such institutes, etc.

_____ 1-3 days

_____ 4-9 days

_____ 10-14 days or longer

Yes	No		
/__/	/__/	23.	Have both Christian and Jewish faculty served as faculty for such programs?
/__/	/__/	24.	Do you sponsor an annual study-tour to Israel?

Survey –Implementation continued

-4-

Yes No

/__/ /__/   25. Have you jointly sponsored special programs with any of these Jewish or Christian organizations? Please check.

_____Local Jewish Council

_____American Jewish Committee

_____Anti-Defamation League of B'nai B'rith

_____Union of American Hebrew Congregations

_____Synagogue Council of America

_____American Jewish Congress

_____Jewish Chautauqua Society

_____National Conference of Christians and Jews

_____National Catholic Conference for Interracial Justice

_____Secretariat for Catholic/Jewish Relations

_____Ecumenical Commissions (local)

_____Other. Please name. _____

_____

26. What has been the response to institutes, seminars, or special programs? Please check

_____Excellent

_____Good

_____Poor

27. In your estimation, what is the difficulty in offering institutes, seminars, or special programs? Please rank order your responses. (1-6)

_____Lack of time   _____Lack of qualified personnel

_____Lack of interest

_____Lack of funds   _____Lack of leadership

                                       _____Other. Please specify

                                       _____

87

Survey - Implementation continued

-5-

28. What have been the most visible rewards in offering courses in Judaism and related areas?

_____

_____

_____

29. What have been the most visible rewards in offering institutes, seminars, or special programs relating to Judaism?

_____

_____

_____

30. Would you give an evaluation of the efforts of your institution to implement, directly or indirectly, Vatican II's Statement on the Jews (October 1965). 1975 Vatican Guidelines; U.S. Bishops 1975 Statement on Jewish/Christian Relations. Please use reverse side if you need more space.

_____

_____

_____

_____

_____

_____

_____

Survey - Implementation continued

Thank you for taking time to complete this questionnaire. Please check below if you would like a summary of the study made available to you.

Yes   No

/__/ /__/   I would like a summary of the study

Name of Institution _____

Address_____
             Street   City   State   Zip

Person completing questionnaire _____
                                          Name

                                _____
                                          Title

MAIL TO: Rose Thering, O.P., Ph.D.
           College of Education and Human Services
           Seton Hall University
           South Orange, N.J. 07079

Please return the questionnaire by April 15, 1985

SETON HALL UNIVERSITY
COLLEGE OF EDUCATION AND HUMAN SERVICES
SOUTH ORANGE, N.J. 07079

Survey of Archdiocesan and Diocesan Ecumenical Commissions and Catholic-Jewish Relations Committees' Implementation Efforts of the Vatican II Statement on the Jews (1965); the Vatican Guidelines and Suggestions for Implementation of the Conciliar Statement (1975); and the 1975 U.S. Bishops Statement on Catholic-Jewish Relations.

(Please respond by April 15, 1985).

Yes   No

/__/   /__/   1. Do you have a sub-committee on Catholic-Jewish Concerns?

/__/   /__/   2. Does the Commission on Ecumenism (as a whole) direct its attention to Catholic/Jewish Concerns?

/__/   /__/   3. Is the subject of Catholic-Jewish Relations a priority in your Diocese/Archdiocese?

/__/   /__/   4. Please summarize the specific efforts you may have undertaken to help your constituencies implement the Vatican and the U.S. Bishops statements on C/J Relations.

SPECIAL PROGRAMS:

Seminars/Institutes/Workshops:

Publications:

Dialogue Groups:

Other:

Yes	No	
/__/	/__/	5. Do you have specific guidelines for Dialogue? If so, please include a copy.
/__/	/__/	6. Do you have specific guidelines for Catholic-Jewish marriages? If so, please include a copy.
/__/	/__/	7. Do you have guidelines for parish passion plays? If so, include a copy.
/____/		8. Within your diocese, please give an estimate number for the passion plays given each year.
/__/	/__/	9. Has your commission issued materials which might assist religious educators and/or homilists in preparing the faithful for proper understanding of the passion narratives? If so, please include a copy.
/__/	/__/	10. Has the commission given religious educators and/or homilists suggestions for positive treatment of the Pharisees? If so, please include a copy.

11. Has the Commission issued guidelines for homilists for understanding the Jewish-Christian implications of the Sunday Lectionary Readings for:

Yes	No	
/__/	/__/	Advent Period
/__/	/__/	Lenten Period
/__/	/__/	Pentecostal
/__/	/__/	Ordinary

12. The Bishops Liturgy Committee of NCCB has recommended using Psalm 22 or other suitable hymns in place of Good Friday Reproaches. What has your commission recommended to the parishes in your diocese?

/____/ 13. Please give an estimate of the number of parishes in your diocese implementing the NCCB Liturgy Committee recommendations. (See above).

Yes   No

/__/ /__/   14. Does your Commission have joint-programming on topics of Jewish-Christian Relations with the Diocesan Department of Education and the Religious Education Department of your diocese?

15. Would you give an evaluation of the efforts of your commission to implement the Vatican Documents and the U.S. Bishops Statement on Catholic-Jewish Relations?

16. Kindly enclose guidelines, publications, literature which your commission has issued to guide the faithful in your diocese to a deeper understanding and appreciation of Jews, Judaism, and the State of Israel.

Thank you for taking time to complete this questionnaire. Please check below if you would like a summary of the research made available to you.

Yes   No

/__/ /__/   I would like to receive a summary of the study.

Name of Institution _____

Address _____
 Street   City   State   Zip

Person completing questionnaire _____
                                            Name

                                _____
                                            Title

MAIL TO:

Rose Thering, O.P., Ph.D.
College of Education and Human Services
Seton Hall University
South Orange, N.J. 07079

Please return the questionnaire by April 15, 1985

SETON HALL UNIVERSITY
COLLEGE OF EDUCATION AND HUMAN SERVICES
SOUTH ORANGE, N.J. 07079

SURVEY OF CATHOLIC HIGH SCHOOLS - IMPLEMENTATION OF VATICAN II STATEMENT On the Jews (1965); the Vatican Guidelines (1975); and the U.S. BISHOPS Statement on Catholic/Jewish Relations (1975).

Please respond by April 15, 1985

Yes No

/__/ /__/ 1. Do you offer any courses in "Judaism" or the "Theology of Judaism"?

/__/ /__/ 2. Is Judaism treated in a course on Comparative/World Religion?

/__/ /__/ 3. Do any of your religion/scripture courses treat specifically the relationship of Christianity to Judaism?

/__/ /__/ 4. Do any of your courses present Judaism an an enduring Covenant which continues to the present time?

/__/ /__/ 5. Do any of your courses treat of rabbinic thought in the time of Jesus as a background to understanding the New Testament?

/__/ /__/ 6. Do any of your courses include a treatment of Jewish History since the emergence of Christianity?

/__/ /__/ 7. Are the "Lessons of the Holocaust" treated in a religion course?

/__/ /__/ 8. Is a study of the Holocaust treated in a church history course?

/__/ /__/ 9. Do you offer any courses on "The Holocaust"? If yes, please specify.

/__/ /__/ 10. Do any of your courses explore the meaning of the State of Israel for Christians and Jews?

/__/ /__/ 11. Is "The History of the State of Israel" offered in the curriculum?

/__/ /__/ 12. Do you have a Jewish faculty member teaching any of the courses in Judaism or related studies?

/__/ /__/ 13. Do you invite a local rabbi or Jewish teacher to address any of your classes when subjects relating to Judaism, Jews, Israel are being covered?

/__/ /__/ 14. Have the faculty members of your high school participated in seminars, institutes, programs of Jewish Studies, or Studies in Judaism and Christianity?

Yes	No
/__/	/__/	15. If so, who sponsored the program(s)? Check one or more, as needed.

      _____Diocese or Archdiocese

      _____Local Jewish Community

      _____American Jewish Committee

      _____Anti-Defamation League of B'nai B'rith

      _____Union of American Hebrew Congregations

      _____National Conference on Christians and Jews

      _____Institute of Judaeo-Christian Studies/Seton Hall University

      _____Local Ecumenical Commission of the Diocese

      _____Other. Please specify and give name of institution

_____

/__/ /__/ 16. Have any of your classes, on a regular basis, visited a Synagogue or Temple or been present for Sabbath Services?

/__/ /__/ 17. Do your religion texts present a positive discussion of Jews and Judaism?

/__/ /__/ 18. Do your religion texts present Judaism as an enduring Covenant which continued to develop after the emergence of Christianity?

/__/ /__/ 19. Please evaluate the results of efforts made by your school to implement the Vatican and U.S. Bishops Documents.

      _____Very Satisfactory

      _____Satisfactory

      _____Unsatisfactory

20. Please give reasons for the above choice.

_____

_____

_____

_____

_____

-3-

21. Please give a brief summary of your school's efforts to implement the Vatican and U.S. Bishops documents. Cover the period 1965-1985. (Please use reverse side if needed).

_____

_____

_____

_____

22. Please list the name (s) of the series of textbooks used to teach religion at your school.

_____

_____

_____

Thank you for taking time to complete this questionnaire. Please check below if you would like a summary of the study made available to you.

_____ Yes, I would like a summary of the study.

Person completing the questionnaire _____
                                                Name

Address _____
         Street   City   State   Zip

MAIL TO: Rose Thering, O.P., Ph.D.
            College of Education and Human Services
            Seton Hall University
            South Orange, N.J. 07079

SETON HALL UNIVERSITY
COLLEGE OF EDUCATION AND HUMAN SERVICES
SOUTH ORANGE, N.J. 07079

SURVEY OF DIOCESAN SUPERINTENDENTS OF SCHOOLS - IMPLEMENTATION OF THE Vatican II Statement on the Jews (1965); the Vatican Guidelines (1975); and the U.S. Bishops Statement on Catholic-Jewish Relations (1975).

PLEASE RESPOND BY APRIL 15, 1985

1. Please summarize the specific efforts you may have undertaken to help your teachers implement the 1965 Vatican Statement on the Jews, the Vatican Guidelines and Suggestions for implementing the Conciliar Statement of 1965, and the U.S. Bishops Statement on Catholic-Jewish Relations of 1975.

ELEMENTARY

Special Programs:

Seminars and Institutes:

Teaching Materials:

Other:

2.

SECONDARY

Special Programs:

Seminars and Institutes:

Teaching Materials:

Other:

Yes	No	
/__/	/__/	2. In the religion textbooks adopted for your school system, is there a positive treatment of Jews and Judaism?
/__/	/__/	3. Do the religion texts adopted for your school system present Judaism as an enduring Covenant which continued to develop after the emergence of Christianity?
/__/	/__/	4. Is there a treatment of present day Jews and Judaism?
/__/	/__/	5. Is the study of the "State of Israel" given a place in the elementary school curriculum?
/__/	/__/	6. Secondary school curriculum?
/__/	/__/	7. Is a treatment of the Holocaust covered in the elementary curriculum?
/__/	/__/	8. Secondary curriculum?
/__/	/__/	9. Are you satisfied with the treatment of Jews and Judaism in the textbooks? What kinds of supplementary materials would be helpful?

_____

_____

3.

10. Give the titles of the main religion texts your schools have adopted. If the schools are allowed a choice, please include the list of the texts from which each may choose.

ELEMENTARY

_____

_____

_____

SECONDARY

_____

_____

_____

11. Please give the number of schools and the enrollment within your area.

No. of elementary schools _____ Enrollment _____

No. of secondary schools _____ Enrollment _____

Thank you for taking time to complete the questionnaire. Please check below if you would like a summary of the study made available to you.

_____ Yes, I would like a summary of the study.

Person completing the questionnaire _____
                                              Name

Diocese or Archdiocese _____
                                    Title

Address _____
        Street   City   State   Zip

PLEASE RETURN THE QUESTIONNAIRE BY APRIL 15, 1985. Thank you.

MAIL TO: Rose Thering, O.P., Ph.D.
             College of Education and Human Services
             Seton Hall University
             South Orange, N.J. 07079

SOURCES CITED IN TEXT

Brashear, Robert L. "Corner-Stone, Stumbling Stone: Christian Problems in Viewing Israel," Union Seminary Quarterly Review, XXXVIII, No. 2, 1983.

Brueggeman, Walter. The Land. Philadelphia: Fortress Press, 1977.

Croner, Helga. (Comp.). Stepping Stones To Further Jewish-Christian Relations. London: Stimulus Books, 1977.

_____ and Leon Klenicki. (ed.). Issues in the Jewish-Christian Dialogue. New York: Paulist Press, 1979.

Davies, W.D. The Gospel and the Land. Los Angeles: University of California Press, 1974.

_____. The Territorial Dimension of Judaism. Los Angeles: University of California Press, 1982.

Dawidowicz, Lucy S. War Against the Jews: 1933-1945. New York: Bantam, 1976.

Etchegaray, Cardinal Roger. "The Jewish Root Which Remains Holy," Statement issued at the 1983 Synod of Bishops. Printed in Origins, Vol. 13, October 27, 1983, pp. 348-49.

Everett, Robert E. "Zionism, Israel and Christian Hope," Reflections, Vol. 82, No. 3. New Haven: Yale Divinity School, April, 1985, pp. 13-17.

Falk, Harvey. Jesus The Pharisee. A New Look at the Jewishness of Jesus. New York/Mahwah, New Jersey: Paulist Press, 1985.

Finkel, Asher and Lawrence Frizzell. Standing Before God. New York: Ktav Publishing House, 1981.

Fisher, Eugene. Faith Without Prejudice. New York: Paulist Press.

_____. Seminary Education and Christian-Jewish Relations. Washington, D.C.: NCEA Seminary Department, 1983.

Fisher, Eugene and Rabbi Leon Klenicki. Understanding The Jewish Experience. Washington: U.S. Catholic Conference, Department of Education, 1982.

Flannery, Edward H. The Anguish of the Jews. New York: MacMillan Press, 1965.

Gerety, Archbishop Peter L. "Pastoral Letter on Catholic-Jewish Relations," *The Advocate*, Nov. 13, 1975. Reprinted by the Office of Information Services and Public Affairs, Archdiocese of Newark, 31 Mulberry Street, Newark, New Jersey 07102.

Heschel, Abraham Joshua. *Israel: Echo of Eternity*. New York: Farrar, Straus and Giroux, 1967.

Isaac, Jules. *Jesus and Israel*. (Edited by Claire Huchet Bishop). New York: Holt, Rinehart and Winston, 1971.

_____. *The Teaching of Contempt*. New York: Holt, Rinehart and Winston, 1962.

Klenicki, Leon and Geoffrey Wigoder. (ed.). *A Dictionary of Jewish-Christian Dialogue*. New York: Paulist Press, 1984.

Morley, John F. *Vatican Diplomacy and the Jews During the Holocaust, 1939-1943*. New York: Ktav Publishing House, 1980.

NCCB. "Statement on Catholic-Jewish Relations," Washington, D.C.: U.S. Catholic Conference, Nov. 20, 1975.

Oesterreicher, John M. (ed.). *Brothers in Hope. The Bridge*. Vol. 5. New York: Herder and Herder, 1970. Cf. "The Theologian and the Land of Israel," pp. 231-43. and "Deicide as a Theological Problem," pp. 190-204.

_____. *The Rediscovery of Judaism*. New Jersey: Seton Hall University's Institute of Judaeo-Christian Studies, 1971. (A Re-examination of the Conciliar Statement on the Jews.).

_____. "Flight Into Publicity," *The Advocate*, July 3, 1985.

Pawlikowski, John T. *What Are They Saying About Christian-Jewish Relations?* New York: Paulist Press, 1980.

Rudin, James A. *Israel for Christians*. Understanding Modern Israel. Philadelphia: Fortress Press, 1983.

Scripture Texts dealing with "the Land":
- Gen. 17:18; 26:3
- Dt. 1:35; 4:40; 6:18, 23; 30:3-5.
- Ex. 6:8; 19:5; 33:1.
- Amos 9:13-15.
- Num. 14:23; 23:11.
- Ps. 148:14; 129:1-4.
- Hosea 1:2; 2:4-10.
- Is. 43: 1-3; 5.
- Jer. 31:7-8; 8-10; 13-14.
- Hebrews 11:9.
- Mt. 5:4.

Thering, Rose. The Self Concept Potential in Religion Texts. St. Louis: Saint Louis University, 1961.

Thering, Rose. "1970 Survey Report of Catholic Institutions' Implementation of Vatican II Statement on the Jews," Unpublished Manuscript, Seton Hall University, October 1970.

Thoma, Clemens. "The Link Between People, Land and Religion in the Old and New Testaments," SIDIC, Vol. VIII, No. 2, 1975.

Vatican Commission for Religious Relations With the Jews. "Guidelines and Suggestions for Implementing the Conciliar Declaration, 'Nostra Aetate', (No. 4), December 1, 1974. Printed in Origins, Vol. 14, Jan. 3, 1975, pp. 463 ff.

_____. "Notes on the Correct Way to Present Jews and Judaism in Preaching and Catechesis in the Roman Catholic Church," June 24, 1985. Document was published in Origins, Vol. 15, No. 7, July 4, 1985.

Vatican Council II. "Declaration on the Relations of the Church to Non-Christian Religions. Nostra Aetate, Oct. 28, 1965.

Wiesel, Elie. Night. New York: Bantam Books, 1960.